RENNYO

NANZAN STUDIES IN ASIAN RELIGIONS

Paul L. Swanson, General Editor

Statue of Rennyo at Kōzen-ji, Hirakata, Osaka

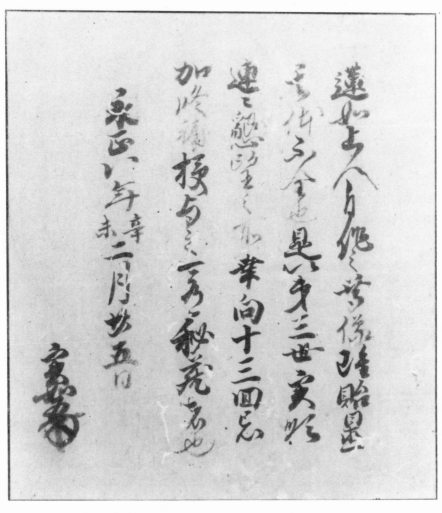

Letter by Jitsunyo, accompanying statue of Rennyo at Kōzen-ji

Rennyo

The Second Founder of Shin Buddhism

With a translation of his letters

Minor and Ann Rogers

ASIAN HUMANITIES PRESS

Berkeley, California

ASIAN HUMANITIES PRESS

Asian Humanities Press offers to the specialist and the general reader alike the best in new translations of major works and significant original contributions to our understanding of Asian religions, cultures, and thought.

Acknowledgments: Map on page xix reprinted from *Medieval Japan: Essays in Institutional History* by John W. Hall and Jeffrey P. Mass, eds., with the permission of the publishers, Stanford University Press. ©1974 by the Board of Trustees of the Leland Stanford Junior University.

Copyright © 1991 by the Nanzan Institute for Religion and Culture

Printed in the United States of America

Library of Congress Cataloging-in-Publication Data

Rogers, Minor, 1930–1991
      Rennyo: the second founder of Shin Buddhism: with a translation of his letters / Minor and Ann Rogers.
        p.   cm. — (Nanzan Studies in Asian Religions; 3)
      Includes bibliographical references and index.
      ISBN 0-89581-929-5 (cloth). — ISBN 0-89581-930-9 (paper)
      1. Rennyo, 1415–1499. 2. Priests, Shin — Japan — Biography.
I. Rogers, Ann, 1938–   . II. Title. III. Series.
BQ8749. R467R64 1992
294.3'976 — dc20   91-43551
  [B]   CIP

To John, Tom, and Elizabeth

Contents

Foreword

ANY STUDIES have been made of Rennyo (1415–1499) by Japanese scholars, but very few by scholars from abroad. Minor Rogers's research marks the beginning of serious studies among the latter, and Ann Rogers's work in translating Rennyo's letters (*Ofumi* 御文 , or *Gobunshō* 御文章)—the primary materials for research on Rennyo—will contribute greatly to future studies.

Rennyo is recognized as the missionary leader who brought about the rapid expansion of the Jōdo Shinshū 浄土真宗 , which considers Shinran (1173–1263) its founder; it was Rennyo who built the Honganji branch of the Shinshū into the largest popular-based religious body in Japan. At present, in respect to its tenets and organization, the Jōdo Shinshū might even be called "Rennyo's sect," with Rennyo understood to be the authoritative interpreter of Shinran's teaching. With a few exceptions, sectarian scholars and historians alike seem to take the continuity of the two as a premise.

Professor Minor Rogers is among the few students of the Jōdo Shinshū who have raised the question as to whether Shinran's "faith" (*shinjin* 信心) and Rennyo's "settled mind" (*anjin* 安心) are the same or not. Until now, that problem has seldom been entertained in serious studies; it relates to the issue of the differences and similarities in the historical nature (the "this-worldliness" or societal character) of Shinran's "faith" and Rennyo's "settled mind." Although historians have noted the differences in Shinran's historical setting and that of Rennyo, no one has seriously investigated how "faith" shapes the forces underlying historical activity and in what way "settled mind" is linked to such activity.

Drawing on Shinran's thought, we find two currents within what we term "Buddhism." Although the first appears on the surface to be Buddhist teaching, its content is certainly not the teaching of the Buddha. The second is properly based on Buddhist tradition. The first involves the pursuit of desires rising from the affirmation of an inherently-existing self; the second shapes a universal subjectivity based on the negation of an inherently-existing self—on "no-self," or "non-self." In general, Japanese Buddhism tends towards self-affirmation and the pursuit of desires; it does not lend itself to the formation of a non-discriminatory ground of consciousness. The true essence (*shinshū* 真宗) of Shinran's Pure Land (*jōdo* 浄土) teaching establishes a non-discriminatory position based on the negation of self; it provides a foundation for human equality and freedom.

Japanese religion is possessed of a structure which, due to a traditional coalescence of state power and religious authority, hinders the establishment of human equality and freedom. Shinran's Buddhist teaching points the way to freedom from such disregard of personality. In providing the foundation for a society in which human beings are equal, Shinran's "faith" plays a vital role in human history.

It is a matter of debate whether or not Shinran's "faith" and its historically-grounded structure, which shoulder universal human problems, have materialized in Shinshū tradition since his time. It is our fervent hope that the Rogers's study of Rennyo will advance research on this issue.

FUTABA Kenkō
Chancellor, Kyoto Women's University
Kyoto, 1990

Acknowledgments

I N RECENT MONTHS, a number of people who have learned about
this study of Rennyo have asked with considerable insistence,
"What is it about Rennyo that has attracted you for so many years"?
Those who ask the question appear to have in mind different sides of
the subject: either Rennyo as an historical figure (*ningen Rennyo*
人間蓮如) or Rennyo as master and saint (*Rennyo Shōnin* 蓮如上人), embodying a teaching from beyond history. In the pages that follow, we
hope to be responsive to both sides of the question – the mundane and
the transcendent.

Beyond the fact of joint authorship, ever more evident over the
past two decades, this study was made possible only with the help of a
series of communities and individuals in Japan and in North America.
In acknowledging our indebtedness to so many different persons and
constituencies, something of the evolution of the project emerges.

In 1965–1966, on leave from my work as an Episcopal missionary
in Japan under the auspices of the Nihon Sei Ko Kai (Episcopal
Church in Japan), it was my good fortune to participate in a seminar
on modern Japanese history taught by Marius B. Jansen, Professor of
Japanese History, at Princeton University. This led to the decision to
pursue a program of graduate studies in the field of comparative religion with a concentration in Japanese Buddhism. At Harvard University, I was introduced to the history of Buddhist thought and to
Rennyo by Masatoshi Nagatomi, Professor of Buddhist Studies. I am
most grateful to him for his patience in guiding me through a dissertation on Rennyo and Jōdo Shinshū piety. Wilfred Cantwell Smith was
Director of the Center for the Study of World Religions during my six
years at Harvard; the extent of my debt to him is only hinted at in the
pages that follow. John B. Carman, Director of the Center, following
Professor Smith, made possible my return as a visiting scholar, 1984–
1985; he has always proved a wise source of counsel. Robert N. Bellah,
my teacher while he was a member of the Harvard faculty, has continued through his writings to be a major influence on my thinking.

The other community essential for this study of Rennyo is Ryūkoku University in Kyoto. Futaba Kenkō, formerly Professor of Japanese Buddhist History and President of the University, has been an unfailing source of encouragement from the time of our first discussions on Rennyo and Shinran in his study in 1970; he graciously agreed to write the foreword for this book. The members of the Ryūkoku University Translation Center exemplify the commitment necessary for translating Buddhist texts into English. They have provided friendship and helped in many ways while I was a research fellow at the University's Institute of Buddhist Cultural Studies in 1979–1980 and again in 1989–1990. Among the members of the Center, I would like to thank in particular Yamada Meiji, Director, Kiyomoto Hidenori, who guided my reading of materials on Rennyo during the first period of research, Hayashi Myōkō, Irisawa Takashi, and Nomura Nobuo. The staff of the University's library at the Ōmiya campus has unfailingly met our requests for help.

In Kyoto, Dennis Hirota, Head Translator of the Shin Buddhism Translation Series, Inagaki Hisao, Professor of Buddhist Studies, Ryūkoku University, and Tokunaga Michio, Professor of Buddhist Studies at Kyoto Women's University, have worked with us over the years and improved our translations immeasurably. Among the other scholars in Japan who have contributed to this study since its inception are Kitanishi Hiromu, formerly Professor of Japanese Buddhist History and President of Ōtani University, who on numerous occasions has shared his intimate knowledge of Rennyo and the Hokuriku, and Professors Bandō Shōjun, Ishida Mitsuyuki, Nakamura Kōjiro, Nakamura Kyōko, Shigaraki Takamaro, and Yashiro Takashi.

In the Shin Buddhist community in North America, I am indebted to Seigen Yamaoka, Bishop of the Buddhist Churches of America; Kenryu Tsuji, the former presiding officer; and Alfred Bloom, Dean of the Institute of Buddhist Studies, Berkeley, California. Each has given me the privilege of addressing members of their community outside of Japan.

I am grateful to The Japan Foundation for a professional fellowship for research in Kyoto, 1979–1980, and to The Japan-United States Educational Commission (Fulbright Program) for a faculty research grant, 1989–1990, funded by the Dainippon and Chemicals Inc., which allowed us to complete this study in Kyoto. Research for and preliminary drafts of chapters five and seven were prepared under the auspices of grants from The National Endowment for the Humanities, the one a group research grant, "Buddhism in Japanese Civilization: Humanistic Inquiries" and the other a summer seminar,

"Scripture: Its Nature and Evolving Role," under the direction of Wilfred Cantwell Smith. Washington and Lee University, through its Glenn Grant and Mellon Grant programs for summer faculty research, has provided support on numerous occasions.

Paul S. Groner, Professor of Buddhist Studies at the University of Virginia, provided guidance and helpful criticism in directing Ann Rogers's M.A. thesis on Rennyo's letters. Among other members of the academic community in the United States who have assisted us with comments on parts of the manuscript are Professors Harlan R. Beckley, John Ross Carter, Edwin D. Craun, James C. Dobbins, Roger B. Jeans, Joseph M. Kitagawa, Whalen Lai, James H. Sanford, W. Lad Sessions, and I. Michael Solomon. We wish also to acknowledge the encouragement of colleagues on the faculty at Washington and Lee University in our respective departments, as well as that of John W. Elrod, Dean of the College, and Mrs. Dale Lyle, who has made countless drafts of the manuscript.

In preparing our manuscript for publication, we were most fortunate in working with the staff of Nanzan University's Institute for Religion and Culture in Nagoya, Japan. The warm support of Jan Van Bragt, Director of the Institute; the helpful questions and comments of James W. Heisig and other fellows of the Institute; the editorial assistance of Edmund R. Skrzypczak; and the careful supervision of Paul L. Swanson, general editor of this new series, "Nanzan Studies in Asian Religions," added greatly to the pleasure of seeing this work through to completion.

In slightly different form, chapter five of this book appears in *The Pacific World: Journal of the Institute of Buddhist Studies*, n.s., 7 (1991), and chapter seven in *Japanese Journal of Religious Studies* 17/1 (1990). Our translation of eighty of Rennyo's letters in five fascicles, *The Letters*, will be published in the Bukkyō Dendō Kyōkai project to make available in English a series of texts from the Chinese Buddhist Canon, *Taishō Shinshū Daizōkyō*. We are most grateful to the Bukkyō Dendō Kyōkai for giving us permission to publish fascicle one of *The Letters* in *The Pure Land: Journal of Pure Land Buddhism*, n.s., 5 (1988), and fascicle five in *The Eastern Buddhist*, n.s., 21/2 (1988), as well as to include the entire translation as part two of this study.

The illustrations for this volume were assembled with the assistance of Asaeda Zenshō, Professor of Buddhist Studies, Ryūkoku University, and officials of the Shinshū Ōtani-ha Nanba Betsu-in, Osaka; the Jōdo Shinshū Honganji-ha Shūmusho and Shuppansha, Kyoto;

Dōbōsha Shuppan, Kyoto; and the Ryūkoku University Library at the Ōmiya campus. We are grateful to them, as well as to representatives of the following Shinshū temples: Kōzen-ji, Hirakata, Osaka; Honpuku-ji, Katada, Shiga; Honganji-ha Yoshizaki Betsu-in, Yoshizaki, Fukui; Zenshō-ji, Kanazawa, Ishikawa; Gyōtoku-ji, Akao, Toyama; Zenshō-ji, Buzen, Fukuoka; and Jōsen-ji, Ichigi, Shimane.

In closing, we would like to thank Zenshō and Hiroko Asaeda and Yoko and Hiroshige Okaichi, whose encouragement and support have heartened us through the years, in Japan and in the United States.

Our sense of indebtedness to the many participants in the Jōdo Shinshū for sharing their faith further heightens our awareness that the shortcomings of this work are entirely our own responsibility.

M.L.R., with A.T.R.
Kyoto, 1990

Illustrations

1. [Cover] Rennyo's Letter "On Realizing Faith"

The tenth letter in fascicle five. From a woodblock printing of a selection of Rennyo's letters under the written seal of Jakunyo (1651–1725), the fourteenth head priest in the Jōdo Shinshū Honganji-ha (Nishi Honganji) lineage. During Jakunyo's tenure, the letters were first referred to as *Gobunshō* 御文章 . From a collection of service books used at Jōsen-ji, Ichigi, Shimane prefecture.

2. [Frontispiece] Statue of Rennyo (Rennyo Shōnin *mokuzō* 蓮如上人木像)

Property of Kōzen-ji, Hirakata, Osaka.

3. [Frontispiece] Letter by Jitsunyo, accompanying (2)

Jitsunyo (1458–1525), Rennyo's successor as leader of the Honganji, attests to repairs made on the image on the thirteenth anniversary of Rennyo's death. Property of Kōzen-ji, Hirakata, Osaka.

4. [p. 51] Preface to the "Chapter on Faith," *Kyōgyōshinshō*

Copied by Rennyo. Property of the Jōdo Shinshū Honganji-ha, Kyoto.

5. [p. 59] Dual seated portrait of Shinran and Rennyo (*nison renzazō* 二尊蓮座像)

Presented by Rennyo to Hōjū and Katada congregation, Ōmi province (present-day Shiga prefecture) in 1461. Property of Honpuku-ji, Katada, Shiga prefecture.

6. [p. 60] The Name in ten characters (*kōmyō jūji myōgō* 光明十字名号)

In Rennyo's hand. Presented by Rennyo to Hōjū of Katada in 1460. Property of Honpuku-ji, Katada, Shiga prefecture.

7. [p. 70] Map of Yoshizaki

Property of Jōdo Shinshū Honganji-ha Yoshizaki Betsu-in, Yoshizaki, Fukui prefecture.

8. [p. 78] Statue of Rennyo, Yoshizaki

A bronze image by Takamura Kōun, completed in 1934. Located at the site of the temple-complex built by Rennyo at Yoshizaki, Echizen province (present-day Fukui prefecture).

9. [p. 104] The Name in six characters (*rokuji myōgō* 六字名号)

One of many written by Rennyo to be given to his followers. Property of the Jōdo Shinshū Honganji-ha, Kyoto.

10. [p. 243] Rennyo's Letter "On the eighty thousand teachings"

In Rennyo's hand. The letter is the second in fascicle five. Property of Zenshō-ji, Kanazawa, Ishikawa prefecture.

11. [p. 279] *Ryōgemon* 領解文

A statement of confession, with written seal of Hōnyo (1707–1789), seventeenth head priest in the Jōdo Shinshū Honganji-ha (Nishi Honganji) lineage. Property of Ryūkoku University, Kyoto.

12. [p. 290] Dōshū of Akao (*Akao Dōshū hōon no zō* 赤尾道宗報恩の像)

Woodblock print by Munakata Shikō. Property of Gyōtoku-ji, Akao, Toyama prefecture.

13. [pp. 320–21] Kōnyo's "Testament" (*Kōnyo Shōnin goikun goshōsoku* 広如上人御遺訓御消息)

A final message by Kōnyo (1798–1871), twentieth head priest in the Jōdo Shinshū Honganji-ha (Nishi Honganji) lineage, to members of his community. In the hand of his son and successor, Myōnyo (1850–1903). Property of Zenshō-ji, Buzen, Fukuoka prefecture.

14. [p. 345] Rennyo's Letter "On White Bones"

The sixteenth letter in fascicle five. A woodblock printing under the written seal of Jūnyo (1673–1739), fifteenth head priest in the Jōdo Shinshū Honganji-ha (Nishi Honganji) lineage. Jōsen-ji collection, Ichigi, Shimane prefecture.

15. [p. 355] Monument to Rennyo (*Rennyo Shōnin myōgō ishibumi* 蓮如上人名号碑)

Inscribed with the Name in six characters. Osaka Castle Park.

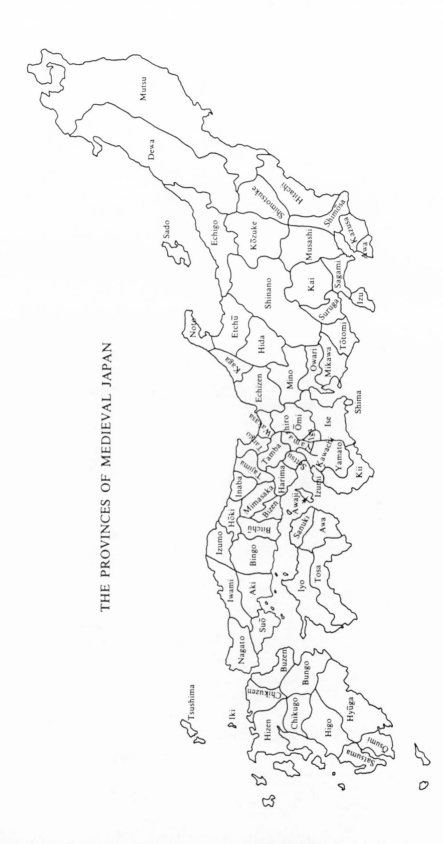

THE PROVINCES OF MEDIEVAL JAPAN

Abbreviations

BGDJ	Nakamura Hajime, ed. *Bukkyōgo daijiten: Shuku-satsuban*
Essentials	Yoshifumi Ueda, gen. ed. *Notes on 'Essentials of Faith Alone': A Translation of Shinran's Yuishinshō-mon'i*
HN	Honganji Shiryō Kenkyūjo, ed. *Honganji nenpyō*
HS	Honganji Shiryō Kenkyūjo, ed. *Honganjishi*. 3 vols.
Inscriptions	Yoshifumi Ueda, gen. ed. *Notes on the Inscriptions on Sacred Scrolls: A Translation of Shinran's Songō shinzō meimon*
Jōdo Wasan	Ryūkoku Translation Center, trans. *The Jōdo Wasan: The Hymns on the Pure Land*
KEJ	Itasaka, Gen, ed. in chief. *Kodansha Encyclopedia of Japan*. 9 vols.
Kōsō Wasan	Ryūkoku Translation Center, trans. *The Kōsō Wasan: The Hymns on the Patriarchs*
Kyō Gyō Shin Shō	Ryūkoku Translation Center, trans. *The Kyō Gyō Shin Shō: The Teaching, Practice, Faith, and Enlightenment*
Letters	Yoshifumi Ueda, ed. *Letters of Shinran: A Translation of Mattōshō*
Once-calling	Yoshifumi Ueda, gen. ed. *Notes on Once-calling and Many-calling: A Translation of Shinran's Ichinen-tanen mon'i*
Passages	Yoshifumi Ueda, gen. ed. *Passages on the Pure Land Way: A Translation of Shinran's Jōdo monrui jushō*
RSG	Inaba Masamaru, ed. *Rennyo Shōnin gyōjitsu*
RSI	Inaba Masamaru, ed. *Rennyo Shōnin ibun*
SDJ	Okamura Shūsatsu, ed. *Shinshū daijiten*. 3 vols.

Shōshin Ge	Ryūkoku Translation Center, trans. *The Shōshin Ge: The Gāthā of True Faith in the Nembutsu*
Shōzōmatsu Wasan	Ryūkoku Translation Center, trans. *Shōzōmatsu Wasan: Shinran's Hymns on the Last Age*
SSG	Akamatsu Toshihide and Kasahara Kazuo, eds. *Shinshūshi gaisetsu*
SSJ	Shinshū Shinjiten Hensankai, ed. *Shinshū shinjiten*
SSS	Kashiwabara Yūsen et al., gen. eds. *Shinshū shiryō shūsei*. 13 vols.
SSZ	Shinshū Shōgyō Zensho Hensanjo, ed. *Shinshū shōgyō zensho*. 5 vols.
T	Takakusu Junjirō et al., eds. and comps. *Taishō shinshū daizōkyō*. 85 vols.
Tanni Shō	Ryūkoku Translation Center, trans. *The Tanni Shō: Notes Lamenting Differences*
Teaching	Yoshifumi Ueda, gen. ed. *The True Teaching, Practice and Realization of the Pure Land Way: A Translation of Shinran's Kyōgyōshinshō*. 4 vols.

INTRODUCTION

Chapter 1

Introduction

WHO IS RENNYO? Medieval Japanese Buddhist priest, charismatic religious leader, shrewd political strategist, igniter of literary imagination, friend for turbulent times, representative figure for Japanese spirituality—these are but a few of the images that abound in the sources available for a study such as this. The images suggest something of the multi-faceted quality of Rennyo's life and thought, a quality that has invited response from participants in his tradition, from sectarian and non-sectarian Buddhist scholars, from students of medieval Japanese social and economic history, from writers in Japan's contemporary literary world, and, in recent years, from students of Japanese civilization in the West.[1]

---

[1] Among those in the West who have undertaken studies relating to Rennyo and his tradition, drawing largely on postwar publications of Japanese scholars— Akamatsu Toshihide, Kasahara Kazuo, Inoue Toshio, Shigematsu Akihisa, Futaba Kenkō, Kitanishi Hiromu, and others—are the following: Ira Michael Solomon, "Rennyo and the Rise of Honganji in Muromachi Japan," Ph.D. dissertation, Columbia University, 1972, "Kinship and the Transmission of Religious Charisma: The Case of Honganji," in *The Journal of Asian Studies* 33/3 (1974): 403–13, and "The Dilemma of Religious Power: Honganji and Hosokawa Masamoto," in *Monumenta Nipponica* 33/1 (1978): 51–65; Minor L. Rogers, "Rennyo Shōnin 1415–1499: A Transformation in Shin Buddhist Piety," Ph.D. dissertation, Harvard University, 1972, "Rennyo and Jōdo Shinshū Piety: The Yoshizaki Years," *Monumenta Nipponica* 36/1 (1981): 21–35, and "The Shin Faith of Rennyo," *The Eastern Buddhist*, n.s., 15/1 (1982): 56–73; Stanley Weinstein, "Rennyo and the Shinshū Revival," in *Japan in the Muromachi Age*, eds. John W. Hall and Toyoda Takeshi (Berkeley: University of California Press, 1977); and James C. Dobbins, "From Inspiration to Institution: The Rise of Sectarian Identity in Jōdo Shinshū," *Monumenta Nipponica* 41/3

Rennyo (1415–1499), eighth head priest in the history of the Honganji branch of the Jōdo Shinshū,[2] occupies a position second only to Shinran (1173–1263),[3] who is revered by sectarian participants as the founder of their tradition. Both Shinran and Rennyo belong to Japan's medieval age—the former to the Kamakura period (1185–1333) and the latter to the Muromachi (1338–1573). The economic, political, and social milieu in which Rennyo lived, however, was strikingly different from that of Shinran.

(1986): 331–43, and *Jōdo Shinshū: Shin Buddhism in Medieval Japan* (Bloomington and Indianapolis: Indiana University Press, 1989).

[2] The translation and interpretation of the Japanese term *jōdo shinshū* 浄土真宗 presents an intriguing challenge in any inquiry about Rennyo. For the empirical observer, the obvious answer is that it identifies a Pure Land Buddhist school, or sect—the Shin (True) Pure Land Sect, or Pure Land Shin Sect—of which Shinran was the founder. One might qualify this by pointing out that Shinran never intended to found a sectarian movement and that participants in the tradition, including Rennyo, are mistaken in claiming Shinran as founder. The matter is not so simple, for we will see presently that Shinshū scholars translating Shinran's writings into English have acknowledged at least two meanings of the term: "the true essence (*shinshū*) of the Pure Land (*jōdo*) teaching" and "the name of their school, with Shinran as the founder" (Yoshifumi Ueda, gen. ed., *Notes on the Inscriptions on Sacred Scrolls: A Translation of Shinran's Songō shinzō meimon*, Shin Buddhism Translation Series [Kyoto: Hongwanji International Center, 1981], 126; hereafter cited as *Inscriptions*).

[3] For the first major studies in English on Shinran, see Alfred Bloom, *Shinran's Gospel of Pure Grace* (Tucson: University of Arizona Press, 1965) and "The Life of Shinran Shōnin: The Journey to Self-Acceptance," *Numen* 15 (1968): 1–62. See also Takamichi Takahatake, *Young Man Shinran: A Reappraisal of Shinran's Life*, SR Supplements, vol. 18 (Waterloo, Ontario: Wilfrid Laurier University Press, 1987). For a detailed historical account of developments in the Shinshū from Shinran to Rennyo, see Dobbins, *Jōdo Shinshū*.

For Shinran's thought, see Yoshifumi Ueda and Dennis Hirota, *Shinran: An Introduction to His Thought* (Kyoto: Hongwanji International Center, 1989). The authors point out that the Mahāyāna structure of Shinran's thought, grounded in the Mādhyamika and the Yogācāra, reflects a reformulation of Pure Land tradition:

> Based on his own experience, [Shinran] asserts that it is possible to enter the activity of Amida's enlightenment while carrying on the samsaric existence of this world, so that our every act, while arising from profound ignorance and self-attachment, is transformed into the Buddha's virtues in the present. Thus, he delineates a path of attainment that fully accords with general Mahāyāna thought, in which each step along the way is nondual with the goal of suchness or true reality (139).

Our study considers the extent to which Rennyo's thought is continuous with Shinran's appropriation of the Mahāyāna.

In numerous presentations of the history of Japanese Buddhism, the medieval age is signaled by the emergence of what is commonly known as the "new Buddhism" (*shin bukkyō* 新仏教) of the Kamakura period, associated with a series of movements founded by charismatic religious leaders: Jōdoshū (Hōnen; 1133–1212), the Zen sects of Rinzai (Eisai; 1141–1215) and Sōtō (Dōgen; 1200–1253), Nichirenshū (Nichiren; 1222–1282), Jishū (Ippen; 1239–1289), as well as Jōdo Shinshū. Recent scholarship, however, has underscored that these leaders and their teachings did not emerge overnight to dominate the religious landscape of medieval Japan simply by replacing the "old Buddhism" (*kyū bukkyō* 旧仏教) of the Nara (710–794) and Heian (794–1185) periods. A mix of esoteric and exoteric teachings and rituals, termed *kenmitsu* 顕密 , was an almost universal feature of Japanese Buddhism from the Heian period on, particularly in the Tendai and Shingon schools. The *kenmitsu* continued as a major constituent of Japanese religious life throughout the medieval period, despite a shift in power from the nobility and the monastery-shrine complexes in Kyoto and Nara to a warrior class in the provinces and Kamakura. The Pure Land movements of Hōnen and Shinran may therefore be seen, in their initial stages, as minor heterodox movements against a background of the orthodoxy of the old Buddhism. It was in this context that Shinran, one of the leaders of this Buddhist "reformation," presented a new teaching responsive to the needs of ordinary men and women in their daily lives.[4]

In the period between Shinran's death and Rennyo's birth a century and a half later, Kakunyo (1270–1351), Shinran's great-grandson, and Zonkaku (1290–1373), Kakunyo's son, played crucial roles in laying the foundation for what was to develop under Rennyo into a widespread and far-reaching movement. Traditional sources are virtually silent in regard to contributions by other head priests in the lineage during this period.

Kakunyo is recognized as the first institutionalizer of the Honganji branch of the Jōdo Shinshū. It was during his tenure as third head priest that Shinran's mausoleum at Ōtani, in the Higashiyama district

---

[4] Kuroda Toshio, "Tenkanki no shidōsha (1)," in *Rennyo*, ed. Minami Midō Shinbun (Osaka: Nanba Betsuin, 1986), 128–31. Also of significance for this study are his *Nihon chūsei no kokka to shūkyō* (Tokyo: Iwanami Shoten, 1975) and *Ōbō to buppō: Chūseishi no kōzu* (Kyoto: Hōzōkan, 1983). For representative figures of the old Buddhism during this period, see Robert E. Morrell, *Early Kamakura Buddhism: A Minority Report* (Berkeley: Asian Humanities Press, 1987); included are studies of Tendai's Jien (1155–1225), Kegon's Myōe (1173–1232), Hossō's Jōkei (1155–1213), and Shingon's Kakukai (1142–1223).

of Kyoto, gained recognition as a temple, Hongan-ji.[5] Kakunyo promoted a view of Shinran as the founder of a new Buddhist sect—Jōdo Shinshū; he contended that the office of custodian (*rusushiki* 留守職) of the mausoleum was to be conferred upon Shinran's direct descendants, legitimizing them as interpreters of the founder's teaching; and he attempted to organize the scattered congregations of Shinran's followers, although with only limited success. In a word, Rennyo's achievement as eighth head priest lay in building the powerful, autonomous religious institution envisioned by Kakunyo and infusing it with the spiritual vitality of Shinran's teaching.

Zonkaku, despite the fact that he never succeeded his father as leader of the Honganji, contributed a number of important writings to the tradition.[6] Among them is *Rokuyōshō*, the first commentary on

---

[5] In this study, "Hongan-ji" 本願寺 designates the head temple of the branch of the Jōdo Shinshū first organized by Kakunyo. Over the succeeding centuries, the temple has been relocated and rebuilt on numerous occasions. Originally established at Ōtani Higashiyama, it was rebuilt at Yamashina, Yamashiro province (present-day Shiga prefecture), by Rennyo and established at Ishiyama (present-day Osaka City) by his son and successor as head priest, Jitsunyo (1458–1525). Under the eleventh head priest, Kennyo (1543–1593), Hongan-ji was reestablished first at Saginomori, Kii province (Wakayama prefecture), and, in succession, at Kaizuka, Izumi province (Osaka prefecture), and Tenma, Settsu province (Osaka City).

In 1591, Toyotomi Hideyoshi ordered Kennyo to reestablish the head temple at a site in the western part of central Kyoto. Kennyo was succeeded by his younger son, Junnyo (1577–1631), having disowned an older son, Kyōnyo (1558–1614), for failing to honor an agreement to surrender the Ishiyama Hongan-ji to Oda Nobunaga. In 1602, however, Kyōnyo received land from Tokugawa Ieyasu for a temple site several hundred yards east of Hongan-ji; here he established a second Hongan-ji. Subsequently, these two temples, each heading a branch of the Honganji, have been popularly known as "Nishi Hongan-ji" and "Higashi Hongan-ji." The formal titles of the two branches in modern times are "Jōdo Shinshū Honganji-ha" and "Shinshū Ōtani-ha," respectively (Shinshū Shinjiten Hensankai, ed., *Shinshū shinjiten*, hereafter cited as SSJ [Kyoto: Hōzōkan, 1984], 455–56). In contrast to "Hongan-ji," we have used "Honganji" to refer to the unified sectarian movement that existed until the split in 1602, and "Nishi Honganji" and "Higashi Honganji" to refer to the two branches that emerged subsequently.

For the establishment of Hongan-ji by Kakunyo, see Akamatsu Toshihide and Kasahara Kazuo, eds., *Shinshūshi gaisetsu*, hereafter cited as SSG (Kyoto: Heirakuji Shoten, 1963), 89–92. Also see Shigematsu Akihisa, *Kakunyo*, Jinbutsu Sōsho, no. 123 (Tokyo: Yoshikawa Kōbunkan, 1966), 80–90.

[6] For an introduction to Kakunyo and Zonkaku, their differences, and their contributions to Shinshū tradition, see Dobbins, *Jōdo Shinshū*, ch. 6.

Shinran's major systematic treatise, *Ken jōdo shinjitsu kyōgyōshō monrui*, commonly known as *Kyōgyōshinshō*. Rennyo and his successors were to draw heavily on Zonkaku's writings, especially in those times when it was necessary to reconcile Shinran's teaching with traditional patterns of Japanese religious thought and practice.

Rennyo's life, spanning much of the fifteenth century, covered a period in which dramatic changes were again taking place in Japanese society. At the very moment that he embarked on the most important and public phase of his work as a religious leader with his move to Yoshizaki in 1471, the social and political order established by the Muromachi government (*bakufu* 幕府) was drawing to a close. With the onset of the Ōnin War (1467–1477), Japan entered the Sengoku (warring states) period, which may be taken to last into the 1560s, when Oda Nobunaga (1534–1582) launched his bid for national hegemony. During this period, the provincial military governors (*shugo* 守護), who had been appointed by the Muromachi shogunate, were displaced by powerful local lords. Despite the turmoil and unrest that accompanied this overturn of power, there was remarkable economic growth as well as a diffusion of culture, formerly limited to the region of the capital, throughout the country. Notable was the role of Zen priests, who taught the Confucian classics, Chinese poetry, and ink-brush painting, as well as the patronage of wealthy merchants on behalf of the traditional arts. While the Sengoku period marked the final stage of medieval Japan, it also heralded the transition to the early modern period—the Tokugawa (1600–1868). It is precisely at this point in Japan's medieval history that Rennyo's gifts as a religious leader were called into play.[7]

The intent of this work is to introduce Rennyo and his contribution

---

[7] Kuroda, in "Tenkanki no shidōsha (1)," 131–32, notes three features of the times confronting Rennyo. First, with the breakdown of the manorial system (*shōensei* 荘園制), a social and economic structure controlled by the nobility, warrior class, and monastery-shrine complexes, the common people organized leagues (*ikki* 一揆) to protect their livelihood and provide themselves with a political power base. Second, with the weakening of the *kenmitsu* ethos, which had shaped the spiritual life of the common people, new religious bodies—Zen, Pure Land, Nichiren, and a systematization of Shinto—came unabashedly into public view. Rennyo struggled at this point to correct distortions of the teaching by adherents of popular religious practices centering on deities associated with happiness, prosperity, and fertility. Third was a shift towards the secularity, diligence, and rationality characteristic of the early-modern and modern periods. It was necessary for Rennyo to respond to these values, so fundamental to the populace that was to be the new bearer of faith (*shinkō* 信仰).

to Jōdo Shinshū history from the perspective of the comparative history of religion. In order to delineate Rennyo's response to Shinran's teaching, we examine the structure of his thought as seen in his writings and trace the implications for the development of Shinshū tradition. To this end, the first part, "Rennyo's Life and Thought," explores what historically went into Rennyo's achievement as restorer of Shinshū tradition in terms of Pure Land thought and Shinran's teaching, in which he was schooled, and in terms of the social and political background of the times to which he responded. A translation of eighty of Rennyo's letters[8] follows in part two, "*The Letters*," placed at the center of the study to make the point that his achievement is best represented by this five-fascicle collection, compiled as scripture after his death. The third and final part, "The Legacy," takes up the other side of Rennyo's identity by exploring something of what has emerged historically from his letters over the past five centuries, in the course of their serving as scripture in form and concept.[9] Here we consider the consequences of Rennyo's definition of orthodox Shinshū piety as gratitude—for ordinary men and women in their daily lives, as well as for the authoritarian and hierarchical aspects of the Honganji as a religious order. The study concludes with an account of some more contemporary images of Rennyo: as the inspirer of a multi-volume medieval historical narrative by the novelist Niwa Fumio (1904–); as the historical subject who comes alive as a friend for a scholar of medieval Japanese Buddhism, Kasahara Kazuo (1917–); and as a repre-

---

[8] *Rennyo Shōnin ofumi* (popularly known as *Gojō ofumi*), Takakusu Junjirō and Watanabe Kaikyoku, eds., *Taishō shinshū daizōkyō* (hereafter cited as T), 85 vols. (Tokyo: Taishō Issaikyō Kankōkai, 1924–32), 83.771–808.

[9] Informative for a study of Rennyo's letters as scripture are two essays by Wilfred Cantwell Smith, "The Study of Religion and the Study of the Bible" and "Scripture as Form and Concept: Their Emergence for the Western World," in *Rethinking Scripture: Essays from a Comparative Perspective*, ed. Miriam Levering (Albany: State University of New York Press, 1989). In the first essay, Smith argues that the Qur'ān as scripture "is significant not primarily because of *what historically went into it* but because of *what historically has come out of it*; what it has done to human lives, and what people have done to it and within it and through it. The Qur'ān is significant because it has shown itself capable of serving a community as a form through which its members have been able (have been enabled) to deal with the problems of their lives, to confront creatively a series of varied contexts" (21; emphasis added). Despite the fact that "scripture" as form and concept has emerged in Western civilization, it may still be useful in explicating the significance of Rennyo's letters in Shinshū history and beyond.

sentative figure of Japanese spirituality for the writer and Buddhist scholar, Suzuki Daisetsu (1870–1966).

These writers and scholars give voice to something that Japanese from many walks of life in modern times have sensed in Rennyo; their responses appear to herald an even wider circle of images. As we approach events commemorating the five-hundredth anniversary of Rennyo's death in 1499, it is not by chance that citizens of Osaka are mindful of him as they recall their city's beginnings five hundred years ago. Rennyo is credited as the first to place the name "Osaka" in the historical record, with a letter dated Meiō 6 (1497).11.25, followed by one written on Meiō 7 (1498).11.21 (the last dated letter in the five-fascicle collection), commonly known as "On building [the temple] at Osaka." Rennyo's special relationship with Osaka has elicited a fresh dimension of responses to his achievement as restorer of the tradition; these responses focus on his genius as organizer, communicator, and even prototypical great industrialist.[10]

There is general agreement among sectarian and non-sectarian scholars that Rennyo was the major figure in the Honganji's transformation into a powerful religious order (*kyōdan* 教団) that came to play a prominent role in a series of popular uprisings, known as the Ikkō

---

[10] Kimura Takeo, a historian of medieval Japan, examines Rennyo's significance for the entrepreneurial ethos of Osaka in his *Rennyo Shōnin ron: Mō hitotsu no Ōsaka Sengokuki* (Tokyo: PHP Kenkyūjo, 1983). In the mid-1980s, the *Minami Midō Shinbun*, the newspaper of the Nanba Betsu-in of the Higashi Honganji branch of the Shinshū in Osaka, ran a series of almost forty articles on Rennyo by scholars including Kasahara Kazuo, Kitanishi Hiromu, Yamaori Tetsuo, Kashiwabara Yūsen, Chiba Jōryū, and writers including Niwa Fumio, Fudeuchi Yukiko, and Matsugi Nobuhiko. In part, the objective was to look again at Rennyo after a lengthy period devoted to exhaustive studies on Shinran, and to offer a fresh evaluation of his achievement from a variety of viewpoints. The articles are collected in Minami Midō Shinbun, ed., *Rennyo*. In 1986, an exhibition of works of art relating to Rennyo and his relationship to Osaka was sponsored by *Minami Midō Shinbun*, Nanba Betsu-in, and the *Asahi Shinbun* in Osaka; see catalogue, Nanba Betsuin and *Asahi Shinbun* Ōsaka Honsha Kikakubu, eds., *Rennyo to Ōsaka* (Osaka: *Asahi Shinbun* Ōsaka Honsha Kikakubu, 1986). In a 1988 study, Kikumura Norihiko, who had written numerous works on Shinran and the Shinshū, points to Rennyo's organizing and communicating skills as the tools enabling him to transform the weak and struggling Honganji into a strong and commanding religious order. See his *Rennyo: Ransei ni ikita oruganaizā* (Tokyo: Suzuki Shuppan, 1988). Finally, Momose Meiji, after a study of traditional sources on Rennyo's life and times, concludes that he is a prototype for the great industrialists and businessmen of modern Japan; see Momose Meiji, *Daijitsugyōka: Rennyo* (Tokyo: Shōdensha, 1988).

[sect] uprisings (*Ikkō ikki* 一向一揆), in late medieval Japan. There is, however, sharp disagreement among these scholars in assessing Rennyo's religious and political significance for Shinshū tradition, the uprisings, and Japan's cultural history as a whole.[11] In general, evaluations of Rennyo have represented two major lines of interpretation: the first is the traditional piety of participants in the Shinshū as reflected in formal doctrinal studies, known as *Shinshūgaku* or Shinshū Studies;[12] the second is the modern critical scholarship (following the Second World War) of historians primarily specializing in the study of medieval Japan.

---

[11] Neil McMullin, in an essay, "Historical and Historiographical Issues in the Study of Pre-Modern Japanese Religions," *Japanese Journal of Religious Studies* 16/1 (1989): 3–40, identifies issues he sees in need of special consideration in studies of premodern Japanese religions. Among these, the relation between Buddhism and Shinto and the relation between religion and politics, pertain directly to this work. As to the latter relationship, he argues that "there was no politics-versus-religion dichotomy in pre-modern Japanese societies: all notions about authority were politico-religious. Indeed, in these societies, religion and politics were so commingled that the very use of the terms 'religion' and 'politics' in reference to them causes an interpretive splitting of them" (15).

In his discussion of historiographical issues, McMullin properly questions the propriety of using the Western concept of "religion" in the Japanese instance (24–25). It was Wilfred Cantwell Smith who, in *The Meaning and End of Religion* (New York: Macmillan, 1962), alerted many in the academic community to the inadequacy of the concept "religion" for the study of the religious life of humankind. Certainly, as Smith has argued, the adjectival forms may be more helpful than the nominal, and this may well hold in the Japanese instance for that reality generally designated by the terms "religion" or "politics." For McMullin's discussion relating to Rennyo, Shinshū, and the Honganji, see his *Buddhism and the State in Sixteenth-Century Japan* (Princeton: Princeton University Press, 1984).

[12] *Shinshūgaku* 真宗学 , also known as Shin Buddhist Studies, is a major constituent of the Faculty of Letters, Ryūkoku University. The Department of Buddhist Studies includes two areas of concentration: Shinshū Studies and Buddhist Studies, the former comparable to Theological Studies in a Western university with a strong religious heritage, as in some Protestant and Roman Catholic institutions in the United States. A Ryūkoku University catalogue (published in English by the Admissions Section, Office of Academic Affairs), undated but in use in the late 1970s, describes Shinshū Studies as follows:

> We expound the True Teaching of Shin Buddhism, which is the culminated form of Mahāyāna Buddhism. Through scientific and objective appreciation of Shinran Shōnin's thought, we aim to realize the structure of the truth embodied in Shin Buddhism. . . . In this materialistic world of today, we require our students to be firmly convinced of the Truth of Amida's Vow and to be able to engage in social activities with an unwavering faith (7).

On the one hand, traditional piety informing Shinshū Studies is predicated on a view of Rennyo as the revered master who restored the Shinshū to the founder's true teaching. Rennyo's image as charismatic religious leader—an image fostered within the Honganji by his writings and his followers' memoirs—is based on the assumption that his teaching, including the structure of his thought, is wholly continuous with that of Shinran; minimal consideration is given to the historical context in which Rennyo's thought developed. On the other hand, students of medieval Japanese society, economics, and politics, as well as Japanese Buddhist history, have been attracted to Rennyo in assessing the dramatic expansion of the Honganji in late medieval Japan; their focus is primarily on the Ikkō uprisings leading into the Honganji's resistance at Ishiyama Hongan-ji to Oda Nobunaga.[13] In certain of these studies, an image emerges of Rennyo as skillful organizer and shrewd political strategist; this is based largely on an historiography—purporting to be empiricist, yet not without its ideological slant—that readily takes for granted the discontinuities in any historical process. These studies, also, fail to probe the structure of Rennyo's religious thought in relation to that of Shinran and its possible implications for the development of Shinshū tradition. For any serious response to the

---

[13] The first of three major studies of the Ikkō uprisings is Kasahara Kazuo's *Ikkō ikki no kenkyū* (Tokyo: Yamakawa Shuppansha, 1962). Kasahara, an historian of medieval Japanese Buddhism at Tokyo University, seeks to understand the social forces at work in the rise of the Honganji to power in late medieval Japan. Next, Inoue Toshio, an historian at Kanazawa University, concerned primarily with economic issues, published the results of his research under the same title, *Ikkō ikki no kenkyū* (Tokyo: Yoshikawa Kōbunkan, 1968). Finally, Kitanishi Hiromu, an historian of Japanese Buddhism at Ōtani University (related to the Higashi Honganji), made an exhaustive study of the topic, again entitled *Ikkō ikki no kenkyū* (Tokyo: Shunjūsha, 1981). Each of these scholars provides rich documentation based on primary sources emphasizing an empirical approach to their subject matter, in contrast to the sectarian emphasis of Shinshū Studies. Kitanishi has argued that the Honganji's participation in the Ikkō uprisings led to the reification and severe distortion of Shinran's teaching, giving rise after Rennyo's death to an authoritarian religious order; see "Watakushi no kenkyū," in Kitanishi Hiromu Hakase Kanreki Kinen Kankōkai, ed., *Rennyo: Gendai to kyōdan* (Kanazawa: Hokuriku Shuppansha, 1985), 23–25. Kitanishi's recent work promises a view of Rennyo that has been overlooked in the interpretations of both traditional piety and modern critical scholarship.

In English, the most extensive discussion of the uprisings is David L. Davis, "*Ikki* in Late Medieval Japan," in *Medieval Japan: Essays in Institutional History*, ed. John W. Hall and Jeffrey P. Mass (New Haven and London: Yale University Press, 1974).

question, "Who is Rennyo?", it is necessary to further clarify two lines of interpretation that have been mutually exclusive—the one, an ahistorical concern with the transcendent or the "religious" side of Rennyo, and the other, an historicist preoccupation with the mundane or the "political" side—and then to present a unified approach that takes account of both from a comparative perspective.

TRADITIONAL PIETY

> If Amida's Primal Vow [*hongan* 本願] is true and real, Śākyamuni's teaching cannot be lies. If the Buddha's teaching is true and real, Shan-tao's commentaries cannot be lies. If Shan-tao's commentaries are true and real, can what Hōnen said be a lie? If what Hōnen said is true and real, then surely my words cannot be empty.
>
> *Tannishō*[14]

A first step for the modern reader seeking to understand Rennyo in terms of traditional piety is to recognize the Mahāyāna Buddhist perspective out of which his predecessor Shinran speaks and writes.[15] Shinran sees himself as standing on the ground of Amida's Vow, which

---

[14] *Tannishō*, in *Shinshū shōgyō zensho*, ed. Shinshū Shōgyō Zensho Hensanjo, 5 vols. (1941; repr. Kyoto: Ōyagi Kōbundō, 1969–70), 2: 774–75; cited hereafter as SSZ. The translation here is by Dennis Hirota, trans., *Tannishō: A Primer* (Kyoto: Ryūkoku University, 1982), 23. In this passage, Shinran refers to two of the seven Pure Land masters: two are Indian, Nāgārjuna (c. 150–250) and Vasubandhu (c. 320–400); three are Chinese, T'an-luan (476–542; Donran), Tao-ch'o (562–645; Dōshaku), and Shan-tao (613–681; Zendō); and two are Japanese, Genshin (942–1017) and Hōnen.

[15] For a focused treatment of Shinran's appropriation of a Mahāyāna philosophical viewpoint, see Ueda and Hirota, *Shinran*, especially ch. 4. Their statement of Shinran's position is engaging, yet its subtlety is difficult to rephrase. Perhaps we can put it this way: Shinran's thought embraces a simultaneity of nonduality and duality—sameness/opposition or oneness/contradiction—underlying dualities such as dharma-body as suchness and dharma-body as compassionate means, Buddha and sentient beings, and timelessness and time; this duality is irresolvable by logical elucidation (169–73); see also n. 88. For Ueda's essay on the structure of Shinran's thought and his other articles, translated by Hirota with additions to and some revision of the Japanese originals, see n. 31. Among those who disagree with Ueda's approach to Shinran's thought is Ryūsei Takeda; see his "Shinran's View of Faith: A Translation Issue of 'Shinjin' and 'Faith'," in Ryūkoku Gakkai, ed., *Ryūkoku daigaku sanbyaku gojūshūnen: Kinen ronbunshū* (Kyoto: Nagata Bunshōdō, 1989), 2–30.

transcends history. Śākyamuni's teaching, Shan-tao's commentaries, and Hōnen's words are perceived not merely as the activity of historical persons, but as manifestations of the mind of Amida's Vow—the transcendent.[16] At the very moment of his realization of faith (*shinjin* 信心), Shinran recognizes the true nature of his own existence within history—the mundane—and the salvific truth of the nenbutsu:

> For a foolish [ordinary] being full of blind passions, in this fleeting world—this burning house—all matters without exception are lies and gibberish, totally without truth and sincerity. The nenbutsu alone is true and real.[17]

Shinran's response to his awakening to faith is to share the teaching, taking his stand on the ground of Amida's Vow, specifically as manifested in the *Larger Sūtra of Immeasurable Life (Daimuryōjukyō)*.[18] He has in mind the *Larger Sūtra* in the opening chapter on "The True Teaching" of his major work, *Kyōgyōshinshō*, when he explains:

> The central purport of this sūtra is that Amida, by establishing his incomparable Vows, has opened wide the dharma-storehouse, and

---

[16] Ueda Yoshifumi, gen. ed., *The True Teaching, Practice and Realization of the Pure Land Way: A Translation of Shinran's Kyōgyōshinshō*, Shin Buddhism Translation Series, 4 vols. (Kyoto: Hongwanji International Center, 1983–90), 1: 41; hereafter cited as *Teaching*. The introduction comments on the above passage from *Tannishō* as follows:

> The view that all of Buddhist tradition has its source in Śākyamuni is essentially the perspective from within history. Shinran, however, views Śākyamuni from a position within the Vow-mind of Amida, which transcends even Śākyamuni; hence, he states: "Amida Buddha, realized in the beginningless past, . . . manifesting himself as Śākyamuni Buddha, accommodated himself and appeared at Gayā castle" (*Jōdo wasan* 88 [SSZ 2: 496]. In the same way, the seven patriarchs are also placed within the flow of Amida's Vow-mind, as instances of the Vow-mind manifesting itself within human history. The flow from Śākyamuni through the seven patriarchs to Shinran may be called a "history of the Vow-mind" (1: 41).

[17] Hirota, *Tannishō*, 44; SSZ 2: 792–93. For the sake of consistency, we have altered quotations in English translations to include diacriticals on terms such as Tathāgata, Śākyamuni, and Hōnen; also, we have standardized the use of "n" (rather than "m") in terms such as "nenbutsu" and "Bunmei."

[18] Commonly referred to as the *Larger Sūtra*; a Sanskrit version, *Sukhāvatī-vyūha sūtra*, and five Chinese translations survive. For Shinran, it is the true teaching and the basis for interpreting two other Pure Land sūtras, the *Sūtra of Contemplation on the Buddha of Immeasurable Life (Kanmuryōjukyō)*, hereafter referred to as the *Contemplation Sūtra*, and the *Amida Sūtra (Amidakyō)*. These three sūtras, known as *sanbukyō* 三部経 have been central to Pure Land tradition in China and Japan. See Ueda and Hirota, *Shinran*, 317–18.

full of compassion for small, foolish beings, he selects and bestows his treasure of virtues. [The sūtra further reveals that] Śākyamuni appeared in this world and expounded the teachings of the way to enlightenment, seeking to save the multitudes of living beings by blessing them with this benefit that is true and real. Thus, to teach the Tathāgata's Primal Vow is the true intent of the sūtra; the Name of the Buddha is its essence.[19]

A second step preliminary to any understanding of Rennyo in terms of traditional piety is to explore the way in which Shinran and his teaching came to be regarded, after his death, as the eternal truth of Amida's Vow-mind manifested within human history. A process of apotheosization is evident in Kakunyo's illustrated biography of Shinran, *Honganji Shōnin Shinran den'e*, the earliest version of which appeared in Einin 3 (1295). The text and illustrations were later separated; the former, in two parts, was entitled *Godenshō*.[20] In the opening section of the first part of the text, Kakunyo gives Shinran's genealogy, tracing his descent from the Fujiwara family and proposing that he was of noble lineage; in the third section, he quotes Shinran naming his own master, Hōnen, as an incarnation of Bodhisattva Mahāsthāmaprāpta (Seishi), and the Prince-regent Shōtoku (573–621) as a manifestation of Bodhisattva Avalokiteśvara (Kannon). In the fourth section, Ren'i, a follower of Shinran, concludes from a dream that Shinran is none other than a manifestation of Amida Tathāgata.[21] The seventh and final section of part two describes a flourishing movement with followers filling every province and district, and devotees — clerical and lay, young and old — flocking to the Founder's Hall every year to express their gratitude for Shinran's teaching.[22] Clearly, the historical data are subordinated here to an idealization of Shinran as the successful founder of a religious institution that is the exclusive vehicle for manifesting Amida's Vow in human history in the last (age of the) dharma (*mappō* 末法).

---

[19] *Teaching*, 1: 63–64; SSZ 2: 2–3.

[20] *Honganji Shōnin Shinran den'e* first appeared as a two-scroll illustrated biography entitled "*Zenshin Shōnin e*." Kakunyo's 1343 expansion of the original, the version on which presently existing copies are based, is now in the possession of the Higashi Honganji. In divided form, the earliest extant copy of *Godenshō* is dated 1349; the illustrations, made into a hanging scroll, are known as *Goeiden*. *Godenshō* and *Goeiden* are both still used at annual thanksgiving services (discussed in this work in chapter four). See *Godenshō*, SSZ 3: 639–54, and SSJ, s.v. "*Godenshō*," 166, and "*Shinran-denne*," 307.

[21] *Godenshō*, SSZ 3: 639–42.

[22] *Godenshō*, SSZ 3: 653–54.

For countless participants in the Honganji branches of the Jōdo Shinshū over the past five centuries, it was Rennyo, Shinran's tenth-generation descendant, who again made it possible for the teaching of Amida's Primal Vow to be heard. Kūzen, an intimate follower of Rennyo, recorded a dream-vision he experienced during a night's vigil before Shinran's image; he concluded:

> One could say that our founder [Shinran] was manifested as Master [Rennyo] and as restorer (*gosaikō* 御再興) of the tradition. . . . And so, since then, I have thought of [Master Rennyo] as a reappearance (*gosaitan* 御再誕) of the founding master and had faith in him.[23]

The *Jitsugo kyūki*, compiled in the late sixteenth century, after the Honganji had become a powerful and tightly-structured religious order, indicates that participants in the Shinshū identified Rennyo as a manifestation of Amida and his words as Amida's:

> There is abundant evidence that Master Rennyo was an incarnation (*gonge no saitan* 権化の再誕) [of Amida Buddha]; this is specifically indicated. Furthermore, he says in one of his poems:
>
> > As a parting gift,
> > I leave behind
> > the Name in six characters —
> > may it be a token of me, too,
> > when I am gone.

---

[23] *Kūzenki*, in *Rennyo Shōnin gyōjitsu*, cited hereafter as RSG, ed. Inaba Masamaru (1928; repr. Kyoto: Hōzōkan, 1948), 25. Kūzen was among those followers and descendants of Rennyo who recorded his sayings and events from his life. The incident mentioned here occurred when Rennyo was eighty, during the week of thanksgiving services (*hōonkō* 報恩講) held annually in memory of Shinran, leading up to the anniversary of his death. Kūzen explains that he had gone at about two in the morning to the Founder's Hall at Yamashina Honganji, where Shinran's image was enshrined, and, as he worshipped, had fallen into a light sleep. His recollection—although he wondered if it were a dream—was that Rennyo had appeared from behind the shrine and that his features had merged with those of Shinran. Puzzled, Kūzen looked inside the shrine, found it empty, and concluded that Shinran had reappeared as Rennyo. See also *Rennyo Shōnin goichidaiki kikigaki*, hereafter cited as *Goichidaiki kikigaki*, SSZ 3:535. Sections from three of the records assembled in RSG—*Kūzenki*, *Jitsugo kyūki*, and *Mukashi monogatariki*—make up *Goichidaiki kikigaki*; for an analysis of sources for this document, see Hosokawa Gyōshin et al., eds., *Kōza: Shinran no shisō*, vol. 9, *Shinran shisō no bunken kaisetsu* (Tokyo: Kyōiku Shinchōsha, 1979), 146–49. For an English translation, see Kosho Yamamoto, trans., *The Words of St. Rennyo* (Tokyo: Karinbunko, 1968), 10–11.

It is clear that he was a manifestation of Amida.[24]

Another passage in the same memoir states:

> It should be understood that the letters are the direct teaching of
> the Tathāgata. When we look at them, [we find] Hōnen; when we
> hear the words, [we realize that] they are the direct teaching of
> Amida.[25]

Rennyo's achievement, from Shinran's Mahāyāna standpoint, might
well be described as manifesting Amida's Vow, the transcendent, with
the transmission of the teaching ensured by the strengthening and
development of the Honganji as an institution. We should note, however, that the perspective of traditional piety, which came to view Rennyo as well as Shinran as manifestations of Amida's Vow, also involved
outright apotheosization. This psychologically-tinted perspective is
not to be equated uncritically with Shinran's view of his own master,
Hōnen; yet, at the same time, it cannot be considered apart from
Shinran's.

The potential for a coalescence of the transcendent and the mundane in the lives of Shinshū adherents may be illustrated by further
examination of the meaning of the Japanese Buddhist term, *jōdo shinshū*, which appears to serve as a major religious symbol.[26] In recent
years, scholars responsible for the Shin Buddhism Translation Series

---

[24] *Jitsugo kyūki*, RSG, 133; SSZ 3: 608.

[25] *Jitsugo kyūki*, RSG, 85; SSZ 3: 563.

[26] It is easy to overlook the dynamic quality of another person's religious
symbols; this is particularly the case when the symbols are those of a tradition
other than one's own. The notion of symbol implicit here is close to that of Wilfred Cantwell Smith in the personalist sense discussed in his essay, "Introduction to Part Eight: Religion as Symbolism," in the "Introduction to Propaedia,"
Encyclopaedia Britannica, 15th ed. (Chicago: Encyclopaedia Britannica, 1974), 1:
498–500. Smith sees as virtually a universal phenomenon people's ability "to
designate some item from within the visible world and to sacralize it in such a
way that it becomes then for them the symbol or locus of the invisible, the transcendent" (498). He notes that different groups choose a great variety of
different things, including concepts, to serve as religious symbols, some of
which are more successful than others.

In his *Towards a World Theology: Faith and the Comparative History of Religion*
(Philadelphia: Westminster Press, 1981), Smith develops his thinking further in
identifying symbols, not only at the first and second levels, but also at zero
level—"higher than the first level, and, indeed, not recognised by the devout
as a 'symbol' at all" (95). Religious symbols such as "Jōdo Shinshū" and
"Honganji," at work in the lives of devout Shinshū adherents, may be examples
of symbols at zero level for some participants in certain contexts.

(which, when completed, will make Shinran's entire literary corpus available in English) have noted two aspects of the term:

> Shinran uses the term *Jōdo-shinshū* to mean the true essence (*shinshū*) of the Pure Land (*jōdo*) teaching of his master, Hōnen. His successors, however, came to use it for the name of their school, with Shinran as the founder, thus distinguishing it from other Pure Land schools that also claimed to succeed in Hōnen's teaching.[27]

At first glance, it might seem that these two usages not only differ, but that they concern entirely unrelated matters. For Shinran, the character 宗 (*shū*) — variously translated into English as "essence," "purport," or "principle" — designates what is at the core of Pure Land teaching as the salvific process of entrusting oneself to the Primal Vow. In *Tannishō*, Yuien records Shinran's statement as to what he was taught: "The late master [Hōnen] said, 'According to the true essence of the Pure Land way [*jōdo shinshū*], one entrusts oneself to the Primal Vow in this life and realizes enlightenment in the Pure Land; this is the teaching I received.'"[28] On the other hand, for Shinran's successors, subsequent to the formation of the Honganji under Kakunyo, *shū* 宗 — translated as "school," "sect," or "teaching" — designates also their religious institution, a matter of historical fact. In one of his letters, Rennyo points out that Shinran did in fact designate the sect (*shū*) as the Jōdo Shinshū.[29]

---

[27] *Inscriptions*, 126. Other volumes in the Shin Buddhism Translation Series under the general editorship of Yoshifumi Ueda include: *Letters of Shinran: A Translation of Mattōshō* (Kyoto: Hongwanji International Center, 1978); *Notes on 'Essentials of Faith Alone': A Translation of Shinran's Yuishinshō-mon'i* (Kyoto: Hongwanji International Center, 1979); *Notes on Once-calling and Many-calling: A Translation of Shinran's Ichinen-tanen mon'i* (Kyoto: Hongwanji International Center, 1980); *Passages on the Pure Land Way: A Translation of Shinran's Jōdo monrui jushō* (Kyoto: Hongwanji International Center, 1982); and *The True Teaching, Practice and Realization of the Pure Land Way: A Translation of Shinran's Kyōgyō-shinshō*, 4 vols. (Kyoto: Hongwanji International Center, 1983–1990).

[28] Hirota, *Tannishō*, 38–39; SSZ 2: 789. Compare Ryūkoku Translation Center, trans., *The Tanni Shō: Notes Lamenting Differences*, 4th ed., Ryūkoku Translation Series, vol. 2 (Kyoto: Ryūkoku University, 1980), 65. Other English translations of Shinran's works in the series are: *The Shōshin Ge: The Gāthā of True Faith in the Nembutsu*, 4th ed., vol. 1 (1966); *The Jōdo Wasan: The Hymns on the Pure Land*, vol. 4 (1965); *The Kyō Gyō Shin Shō (Ken Jōdo Shinjitsu Kyōgyōshō Monrui): The Teaching, Practice, Faith, and Enlightenment* (abridged), vol. 5 (1966); *The Kōsō Wasan: The Hymns on the Patriarchs*, vol. 6 (1974); and *Shōzōmatsu Wasan: Shinran's Hymns on the Last Age*, vol. 7 (1980).

[29] Inaba Masamaru, ed., *Rennyo Shōnin ibun* (1937; repr. Kyoto: Hōzōkan,

The question we might ask, however, is whether a bifurcation of what may be designated as the transcendent and the mundane, exacerbated in English translation, may not be misleading. Translations into English of Buddhist symbols such as *jōdo shinshū* in the writings of Shinran and his successors suggest a degree of reification that may not necessarily be present for participants in the tradition. Rather, the term as used by participants suggests a unity of Shinran's vision of the transcendent, the "true essence of the Pure Land teaching," and, at the same time, his successors' denotation of the mundane, "the name of their school, with Shinran as the founder." Indeed, in the Shin Buddhism Translation Series, the translators of the term *jōdo shinshū* in Shinran's writings appear to have included both meanings for the single character 宗 : "the true *essence* of the Pure Land *way*."[30] This suggests that the translators are informed by a view of reality that appears at the very least ambiguous to those whose vision is not attuned to the unity of the transcendent and the mundane seen by the participant, or more specifically, in the instance of Shinran, to a unity embracing the simultaneity of their sameness and opposition. It is with Shinran's Mahāyāna perspective in mind that the terms "Shinshū" and "Shinshū tradition" are used here in an attempt not to distort traditional piety, to the extent that it is continuous with the structure of Shinran's thought.[31]

1983), 119; hereafter cited as RSI. In Inaba's collection of Rennyo's letters, the letter cited here is number thirty of two hundred and twenty-one considered authentic; its date is the fifth year of Bunmei, the ninth month, the second day (according to the lunar calendar). Citations of Rennyo's letters in this study are dated by year according to the Gregorian and lunar calendars and by month and day according to the lunar. Further, those letters included among the eighty selected in the collected letters in five fascicles (referred to also in this study as *The Letters*) are so indicated. For example, letter thirty in Inaba's collection is also the fifteenth in fascicle one. A full citation hereafter is patterned as follows: RSI, 119 (#30/1:15). In the translation in part two, this same letter is dated Bunmei 5 (1473).9.2.

[30] *Teaching*, 1: 63 (emphasis added; *Kyōgyōshinshō*, SSZ 2: 2). Also see *Inscriptions*, 126.

[31] See the two-part essay by Yoshifumi Ueda, translated by Dennis Hirota with additions to and some revisions of the Japanese original: "The Mahayana Structure of Shinran's Thought," *The Eastern Buddhist*, n.s., 17/1 (1984): 57–78, and 17/2 (1984): 30–54. The unique quality of Shinran's thought is revealed in his two meanings for birth (*ōjō* 往生): birth in the Pure Land at the moment of death is the realization of supreme enlightenment and, simultaneously, birth is the realization of the stage of the truly settled in this present life (73). In Shinran's holding both meanings at once, we see an example of the simultaneity of

Another example of the linking of the transcendent and the mundane may be seen in at least two available meanings of the term "Honganji" as a religious symbol. It is precisely Rennyo's achievement in bringing material prosperity to the Honganji as a religious order that allows Shinran's teaching of Amida's Primal Vow to be heard. For devout participants, the term "Honganji" as a religious symbol may at one and the same time designate their religious institution (including the head temple, Hongan-ji), and, reverberating with the working of the Other Power of Amida's Primal Vow, serve as the locus of a salvific process.[32]

Ōtani Kōshin, the current leader of the Jōdo Shinshū in the Nishi Honganji lineage and twenty-fourth in direct succession to Shinran, spoke out of this same Mahāyāna Buddhist perspective in introducing his tradition to a largely Western audience at a symposium, "Shin Buddhism and Christianity: Textual and Contextual Translation," held at Harvard Divinity School in April 1984:

> The core of Shin Buddhism is the Primal Vow [*hongan*] of Amida Buddha, who, as a bodhisattva, resolved that he would bring all sentient beings to the supreme enlightenment or not attain Buddhahood himself. The Primal Vow is a manifestation of the great compassion . . . that is active at the heart of reality. The way of Shin Buddhism manifests its true significance with the awakening of deep insight into our world, which is incessantly threatened by conflict, and into our condition as human beings. We live in times far distant from Śākyamuni Buddha. Only through Amida Buddha's Primal Vow can a person trapped in the darkness of his own passions and ignorance—who lacks any seed that can lead to enlightenment—attain Buddhahood. . . .
>
> Through the Primal Vow of Amida Buddha, a person is brought to the realization of *shinjin* [faith]. . . . *Shinjin* is the mind of Amida that is given to beings through the Primal Vow. Upon realizing *shinjin*, we enter the life of the nenbutsu—the life of saying the Name of Amida Buddha—and without any contrivance or self-will,

---

sameness and opposition that characterizes the structure of his thought; see n. 15. Also see Ueda's other writings translated by Hirota: "How is *Shinjin* to be Realized?" *The Pacific World: Journal of the Institute of Buddhist Studies*, n.s., 1 (1985): 17–24; "Reflections on the Study of Buddhism," *The Eastern Buddhist*, n.s., 18/2 (1985): 114–30; "Freedom and Necessity in Shinran's Concept of Karma," *The Eastern Buddhist*, n.s., 19/1 (1986): 76–100; and "On the Emergence of Mahāyāna Buddhism," *The Pacific World: Journal of the Institute of Buddhist Studies*, n.s., 2 (1986): 3–10.

[32] For the notion of religious symbol, see n. 26.

we are brought naturally to attainment of supreme Buddhahood in
the Pure Land when life ends.[33]

These passages underscore the centrality of the Primal Vow as a
religious symbol for participants in Shinshū tradition, perhaps especially for members of the Honganji (Primal Vow Temple) branches.
Rennyo's achievement, in making it possible for them to hear the
teaching by restoring the tradition — the mundane, is inseparable from
the realization of *shinjin* — the transcendent.[34] In short, the story of the
Honganji may be told as the unfolding of Amida's Primal Vow in history.

Rennyo's image as restorer of the tradition is based in part on accounts
of his tireless efforts in combating heresies that were sapping the vitality of the Honganji. The institution was depicted as being in a state of
decline from Kakunyo's tenure on; by the time Rennyo was born, the
temple precincts were said to be deserted of visitors and in sad dis-
repair.[35] A memoir recorded by one of Rennyo's disciples suggests a

---

[33] Ōtani Kōshin, Monshu (abbot) of the Jōdo Shinshū Honganji-ha, "Opening Address," in *Amerika no shūkyō o tazunete/Shin Buddhism Meets American Religions*, ed. Hābādo daigaku shinpojiumu to Beikoku tōbu kenshū ryokōdan
(Kyoto: Nishi Honganji Naijibunai "Amerika no shūkyō o tazunete" Henshūgakari, 1986), 240–41; Japanese text, 17–18. The title *monshu* was adopted in the
Nishi Honganji in 1886 to designate the head of the order. For a report on the
symposium, see Minor L. Rogers, "Textual Translation and Contextual Renewal: Reflections on the Shin Buddhism and Christianity Symposium," *Bulletin*, Center for the Study of World Religions, Harvard University (1984): 2–23;
reprinted in *Amerika no shūkyō o tazunete*, 207–23, with Japanese translation, 37–
57.

[34] For an example of a contemporary response illustrating this point, see the
account in chapter eight of a letter received by Niwa Fumio following a lecture
he delivered on Rennyo in Kanazawa.

[35] Chiba Jōryū, ed., *Honpukuji yuraiki*, 324–25, and *Honpukuji atogaki*, 358, in
Honpukuji kyūki (Kyoto: Dōbōsha, 1980); this work includes facsimiles and tran-
scriptions of the original texts. See also Kashiwabara Yūsen, Chiba Jōryū, Hiramatsu Reizō, and Mori Ryūkichi, gen. eds., *Shinshū shiryō shūsei* (hereafter
abbreviated as SSS), 13 vols. (Kyoto: Dōbōsha, 1974–83); for this reference, see
vol. 11, *Rennyo to sono kyōdan* (Kyoto: Dōbōsha, 1977), *Honpukuji atogaki*, 631;
Honpukuji yuraiki, 661–62. The same documents appear in Kasahara Kazuo,
Shinshū ni okeru itan no keifu (Tokyo: Tōkyō Daigaku Shuppankai, 1962).
These materials are frequently cited to characterize the Honganji's condition during Rennyo's early years; see Sakurai Yoshirō and Fukuma Kōchō, eds.,
Ikkyū/Rennyo, Nihon Meisō Ronshū, no. 10 (Tokyo: Yoshikawa Kōbunkan,
1983), 277. Kasahara Kazuo, in emphasizing the decline of the Honganji as pre-
lude to a grand restoration, speaks metaphorically of the "death" of Shinran

reason for the Honganji's condition during the generations of Shinran's (or, more accurately, Kakunyo's) successors as head priest and identifies Rennyo's special contribution as clarifying the salvific process:

> In Master [Shinran]'s tradition, the essential point is the one thought-moment of entrusting. Consequently, generation after generation [of his successors] taught "entrusting," but we did not know precisely how to entrust ourselves. That being the case, the resident priest [Rennyo] preceding the last wrote letters during his tenure and clearly informed us that we should give up the sundry practices and single-mindedly entrust ourselves to Amida for deliverance in [regard to] the afterlife. For this reason, he is recognized as the master who was the restorer (Gosaikō no Shōnin 御再興の 上人) [of the tradition].[36]

The content of this passage forms part of the fabric of Shinshū piety in identifying, as it does, Rennyo's unique place within the Honganji branch of the tradition. Setting aside for the moment his formulation of the process of entrusting, we again note the term *saikō* 再興 , prefixed here by the personal honorific *go* 御 . For participants in the tradition, the epithet "Gosaikō no Shōnin," by which Rennyo soon came to be known, singles him out as the one whose achievement makes it possible again for each of them to hear Amida's summons through the Name, Namu-amida-butsu. Over the centuries, with greater distance and perspective on his achievement, Rennyo has come to be most commonly known as "Chūkō Shōnin 中興上人 ," literally, "the Master who restored [the tradition] in mid-course."[37]

---

and the Honganji in the Muromachi period ("Ima koso Rennyo ni manabu toki," in *Rennyo*, ed. Minami Midō Shinbun, 1–2). For a balanced historical assessment of the Honganji's status at the time of Zonnyo's death in 1457, see Dobbins, *Jōdo Shinshū*, 128–31.

[36] *Goichidaiki kikigaki*, SSZ 3: 577, refers formally to Rennyo's letters as "*Ofumi*," suggesting that a collection was available to Jitsugo (1492–1584), Rennyo's tenth son. The text in *Jitsugo kyūki*, RSG, 100, which we have followed here, uses the term *ofumi* in a general sense.

[37] The first instance of the use of this epithet to come to our notice is in a Shinshū document dated Kansei 11 (1799).11.25, written by Honnyo (1778–1826), the nineteenth head priest in the Nishi Honganji lineage; see SSZ 5: 766–67. This document is also included in Kasahara Kazuo, *Shinran kenkyū nōto* (Tokyo: Tosho Shinbunsha, 1965), 197–98. Subsequently, the term has been used repeatedly within the tradition to refer to Rennyo. Kosho Yamamoto, who translated Rennyo's memoirs into English, concludes his laudatory assessment of Rennyo's deeds in *The Words of St. Rennyo*, 163, as follows:

Memoirs such as these are an essential source for any study of
Rennyo's life and thought, whether by sectarian or non-sectarian
scholars. They include records of Rennyo's sayings, episodes from his
life, and recollections of his disciples and family members—all found
in a wide variety of collections. *Goichidaiki kikigaki*, the best-known of
these collections, is included in full or in part in various editions of the
Shinshū scriptures (*Shinshū seiten*).[38] A Higashi Honganji version,
based on *Shinshū kanashōgō*, contains three hundred and sixteen
items;[39] that of the Nishi, based on *Shinshū hōyō*, contains three hundred and fourteen in two parts.

The major source for a study of Rennyo and his thought must be
his own writings, primarily the letters in their entirety. Rennyo's
grandson, Ennyo (1491–1521), under the direction of his father
Jitsunyo, ninth head priest, assembled over two hundred letters; he
selected eighty for a five-fascicle compilation that came to be known
as *Ofumi* or *Jōnai ofumi*. In Nishi Honganji usage, however, from the
time of Jakunyo (1651–1725), the fourteenth head priest in the lineage, the compilation has been referred to as *Gobunshō* or *Jōnai
gobunshō*. Since the content of both documents is identical, in this study
we refer to the five-fascicle compilation as *The Letters*. Ennyo selected
four other letters for a separate collection known as *Natsu ofumi* in the
Higashi Honganji and *Ge no gobunshō* in the Nishi; these letters, written by Rennyo during the summer before his death, are referred to in
this study as *Summer Letters*. A final letter, designated as *Gozokushō*,
offers a brief account of Shinran's lineage, his life and teaching, and
the significance of the thanksgiving services held annually on the anniversary of his death. Over the last century, these eighty-five letters
have been included in various editions of the Shinshū scriptures, published under the auspices of the Higashi and the Nishi Honganji respectively for use in services, private devotions, and instruction.[40]

It is no wonder that Rennyo is often reverently referred to as "Chūkō-no-Shōnin,"
i.e. the "Venerable One who had Restored the State of Things," which will
amount to say[ing] he is the "Second Founder of Shinshū."

[38] The reasons for translating the term *seiten* as "scripture(s)" are discussed
in chapter five.

[39] For Higashi Honganji version with index, see Ōtani Chōjun, ed., *Rennyo
Shōnin zenshū: Genkōben* (Tokyo: Kawade Shobō Shinsha, 1989).

[40] For a Higashi Honganji compilation, including *Ofumi*, see Kashiwabara
Yūsen, ed., *Shinshū seiten* (1935; repr. Kyoto: Hōzōkan, 1969), 785–865 (also
Gozokushō, 865–67; *Natsu ofumi*, 867–72); for a Nishi compilation, including
Gobunshō, see Ōe Junjō and Ōhara Shōjitsu, eds., *Shinshū seiten* (1956; repr.

Rennyo's letters, written in colloquial Japanese, were his chief instrument in his effort to translate and convey the subtlety of Shinran's
teaching in language familiar to ordinary men and women in late medieval Japan. Following his death, the five-fascicle compilation, *The
Letters*, assumed canonical status; during the Tokugawa period, it increasingly served as a source of authority for sectarian scholars' doctrinal formulations and disputes in defining orthodoxy, particularly
within the Nishi Honganji branch of the Shinshū.[41] Following the
Meiji Restoration in 1868, *The Letters* provided doctrinal support for
legitimizing a sectarian adaptation of the Mahāyāna concept of the
two truths (*shinzoku nitai* 真俗二諦), which came to define the Nishi
Honganji's relationship as a religious institution to the modern nation-
state.[42] This instance, as will be discussed later, presses the question of
whether the structure of Rennyo's thought is wholly continuous with
that of Shinran. In any event, it appears that, within the Nishi Honganji over the past five centuries, both at the institutional and popular
levels, Shinran's teaching has been presented and understood largely
in terms of *The Letters* as the orthodox translation and interpretation
of his writings and the Pure Land textual tradition.

A third source important for any study of Rennyo includes sectarian commentaries on his writings, biographies, sermons, and histories
of the Honganji, all of which expand upon and celebrate his contributions as eighth head priest.[43] In these materials, the possibility of any
discontinuity between Rennyo's thought and that of Shinran is never
entertained, despite their sharply contrasting life histories and the

---

Kyoto: Nagata Bunshōdō, 1969), 660–802 (also *Ge no gobunshō*, 803–11; *Gozokushō*, 812–13). In a recent Nishi Honganji volume of Shinshū scriptures, Shinshū
Seiten Hensan Iinkai, ed., *Jōdo Shinshū seiten: Chūshakuban* (Kyoto: Honganji
Shuppansha, 1988), *Ge no gobunshō* consists of five letters, following an edition
by Hōnyo (1707–1789), the seventeenth head priest, who divided the fourth
letter into two parts (1210–18).

[41] See chapter five for a consideration of the scripturalization of Rennyo's
letters, culminating with the proclamation of Honnyo's *Gosaidan gosho* and
Gosaidan shinmeisho in 1806. Both documents are included in Shinshū Seiten
Hensan Iinkai, ed., *Jōdo Shinshū seiten*, 1411–22.

[42] See chapter six for a discussion of the Nishi Honganji's theory of the two
truths and chapter seven for a discussion of Kōnyo's "Testament" (*Kōnyo Shōnin
goikun goshōsoku*), in which the concept *shinzoku nitai* is formally introduced as
the tradition's dharma-principle.

[43] An explanation of documents relating to compilations of Rennyo's letters
and his memoirs is available in Hosokawa Gyōshin et al., eds., *Shinran shisō no
bunken kaisetsu*, 131–52.

differences in the political and social contexts in which they lived. Drawing on these documents, but primarily on *The Letters* and the memoirs, sectarian studies have consistently nurtured a pattern of piety that we have characterized as traditional. It is not surprising, then, that the image of Rennyo as restorer of the tradition—indeed, as the "reappearance of the founding master"—has endowed him with an authority no less than that of Shinran himself.

MODERN SCHOLARSHIP

> We might say that what was involved was Rennyo's sharpness of insight, his cunning, and his judgment as a politician rather than as a religious leader. [Behind] the methods revealed in his letters, [methods] we could term skillful but crude—propaganda so blatant as to be embarrassing, tearful persuasion, bluffing, cynicism, banter, lies, deception— behind his every expression lurks a far-reaching political strategist, crafty to the point of begging comparison with the ostentatious [Tokugawa] Ieyasu.
>
> Hattori Shisō (1901–1956)[44]

Following the Second World War, works by Japanese scholars including Hattori Shisō, Ienaga Saburō, Akamatsu Toshihide, Kasahara Kazuo, Inoue Toshio, and Kitanishi Hiromu in the fields of intellectual history, Japanese Buddhist history, and medieval economic and social history, drew on the full range of sources used in Shinshū Studies, including the writings of Shinran and Rennyo.[45] The historians, for the most part, found themselves in general agreement with sectarian scholars on the point that Rennyo played a major role in the expansion of the Honganji into a powerful religious order in the course of the Ikkō uprisings in late medieval Japan. They found little common ground with those engaged in Shinshū Studies, however, in evaluating Rennyo's religious and political significance for the uprisings, or in clarifying Rennyo's place within the mainstream of Japan's cultural history. For the most part, their respective lines of interpretation reflected fundamentally different orientations to the subject matter.

---

[44] Hattori Shisō, *Rennyo* (1948; repr. Tokyo: Fukumura Shuppan, 1970), 244–45.

[45] The most complete listing of sources including doctrinal and historical studies relating to Rennyo in Japanese is found in Kimura Takeo, ed., *Rennyo Shōnin no kyōgaku to rekishi* (Osaka: Tōhō Shuppan, 1984), 31–65.

As noted already, neither group has been disposed to assess Rennyo's thought in relation to that of Shinran and the implications that possible differences in their thought may hold for the history of the Jōdo Shinshū.

For the purposes of this study of Rennyo's life and thought and its importance for Shinshū tradition, we turn to the writings of Futaba Kenkō, a specialist in ancient Japanese Buddhist history. In reviewing postwar scholarship, Futaba notes a dramatic change in Japanese historical studies in general, which he links to a discussion of pertinent works in Japanese Buddhist history.[46] By way of establishing a benchmark for earlier studies, he quotes from a work published during the Second World War:

> Over the course of fourteen hundred years, from its initial acceptance until the present, Japanese Buddhism has always taken "protection of the state" (*chingo kokka* 鎮護国家) as its slogan; it has furthered the development of the respective sects by espousing peace for the state and happiness for the populace.[47]

Although Futaba finds the identification of Japanese Buddhist tradition with state Buddhism representative of earlier studies, he claims that such an unequivocal view is entirely unreasonable.[48] He reminds his readers that sectarian officials in the years before the Second World War attempted to censor the text of Shinran's major treatise, *Kyō-gyōshinshō*, by erasing the passage, "The emperor (*shujō* 主上) and his ministers (*shinka* 臣下), opposing the dharma (*hō* 法) and violating [principles of] justice (*gi* 義)."[49] He then points out the contradiction posed by a statement in the wartime study cited above:

> They [Shinran and Hōnen] emphasized individual attainment of buddhahood, available universally, and the "state-protective" banner that has been in evidence since the founding of Japanese

---

[46] Futaba Kenkō, *Shinran no kenkyū: Shinran ni okeru shin to rekishi* (1962; repr. Kyoto: Hyakkaen, 1989), 366–76.

[47] Futaba, *Shinran no kenkyū*, 366; here he quotes Hanayama Shinshō (Nobukatsu), *Nihon bukkyō* (Tokyo: Sanseidō, 1944), 92.

[48] Futaba, *Shinran no kenkyū*, 366–67; Hanayama, *Nihon bukkyō*, 92.

[49] Futaba, *Shinran no kenkyū*, 367; see *Kyōgyōshinshō*, SSZ 2: 201. A legacy of this prohibition carried over into postwar printings of *Shinshū shōgyō zensho*. In a 1967 printing, SSZ 2: 201, there are two blank spaces for the characters 主上 (*shujō*); in a 1977 printing, the characters are back in place. For an English translation that renders the four controversial characters "lords and vassals," see *Kyō Gyō Shin Shō*, 206. For a translation of the entire passage, see chapter seven of this work; see also *Teaching*, 4: 613–14.

Buddhism seemed, to all appearances, to have disappeared for a
time; . . . [but], underneath the surface, they built a correct Japanese
Buddhism, protective of the state in the true sense.[50]

Futaba goes on to discuss the results of postwar Japanese Buddhist
scholarship freed from a narrow nationalistic reading of Buddhist
tradition colored by State Shinto ideology. He concludes that a new
methodology is needed in religious historical studies.[51]

A watershed in historical studies for both sectarian and non-
sectarian scholars was the 1948 publication of two works, *Shinran nōto*
and *Rennyo*, by Hattori Shisō, a Marxist historian.[52] Born in Shimane
prefecture into a Shinshū temple household, Hattori was expected, as
the eldest son, to succeed his father as head priest. He left the temple,
however, to study at Tokyo Imperial University; there he joined the
Shinjinkai, a progressive, Marxist-oriented study group espousing political and social reform.[53] He was also an important contributor to a
series of works by Marxist scholars on the history of the development
of capitalism in Japan, with implications for the overthrow of the emperor system itself. Hattori's publications ceased during the late 1930s,
with the growing suppression of radical thought. After the war ended
in 1945, he resumed his scholarly contributions with publication of the
studies on Shinran and Rennyo.[54]

In the preface to *Shinran nōto*, Hattori explains his work as an attempt to take Shinran out of the temple setting that he himself had left
behind as a young man, and out of a philosophical frame — "a Western-
style temple" — represented by thinkers such as Hegel (1770–1831),
Miki Kiyoshi (1897–1945), and others, and to set him free among the
peasants where he had really lived.[55] He describes his writing as a spiritual journey home; in returning to Shinran and to [Amida] Tathāgata
by way of Shinran, he feels that he has finally realized his father's legacy to him.[56] In the preface to the 1950 publication of a new edition

---

[50] Futaba, *Shinran no kenkyū*, 367. For the context of Futaba's citations, see
Hanayama, *Nihon bukkyō*, 150–51.

[51] Futaba, *Shinran no kenkyū*, 376.

[52] Hattori Shisō, *Shinran nōto* (1948; repr. Tokyo: Fukumura Shuppan, 1967).

[53] Gen Itasaka, ed. in chief, *Kodansha Encyclopedia of Japan* (cited hereafter
as KEJ), 9 vols. (Tokyo and New York: Kodansha, 1983), s.v. "Hattori Shisō
(1901–1956)." In 1928, Hattori published his history of the Meiji Restoration,
Meiji ishinshi, "considered at the time a groundbreaking study . . . from a dialec-
tical-materialist viewpoint" (KEJ, 3: 114).

[54] KEJ, s.v. "Hattori Shisō," 3: 114.

[55] Hattori, *Shinran nōto*, 9–10.

[56] Hattori, *Shinran nōto*, 10.

of his work, Hattori quotes at length from Ienaga Saburō's supportive response to the earlier edition of the essays.[57] An intellectual historian, Ienaga viewed Shinran as one of the epochal figures in premodern Japanese history. For Ienaga, Shinran was, along with the Prince-regent Shōtoku, an exemplar of the "logic of negation" (*hitei no ronri* 否定の論理), which Ienaga uses as a major category for historical interpretation. Implicit in Ienaga's position is a radical critique of much of Japanese Buddhist history from its very beginnings for its state-protective role.[58]

Following the Second World War, Hattori's insistence that Shinran's position was free of utilitarian motifs, including state-protective thought, presented a radical challenge, not only for critical modern scholarship on Japanese thought and Buddhist history, but also for sectarian scholars within Shinshū tradition. Futaba responded to the challenge: he shared with Hattori and Ienaga a concern for critical historical method; as a participant in the Shinshū and committed to Shinran's teaching, he was also concerned with issues of ultimate meaning—how is the transcendent to be expressed materially in history? He pressed these issues in an essay advancing a hypothesis on the relationship of history and Pure Land faith (*ōjō shinkō* 往生信仰); he points to differences in the religious thought of Shinran and Rennyo, drawing out the implications of the latter's interpretation of the teaching for the history of the Honganji.[59]

In Futaba's view, Rennyo, as eighth head priest of the Honganji, did not merely offer a mid-course correction to the tradition; as restorer, he was responsible also for defining and firmly charting the Honganji's course institutionally and doctrinally over the succeeding centuries up until the present. Finally, Futaba maintains that the Honganji as a contemporary religious institution is virtually discontinuous with the founder's vision; in effect, he seconds Ienaga's assessment of Rennyo's Honganji:

The fact that we pay particular attention to Shinran is not because

---

[57] Hattori, *Shinran nōto*, 1–8.

[58] For a detailed treatment of Ienaga's intellectual and spiritual biography, see Robert N. Bellah, "Ienaga Saburō and the Search for Meaning in Modern Japan," in *Changing Japanese Attitudes Toward Modernization*, ed. Marius B. Jansen (Princeton: Princeton University Press, 1965), 369–423.

[59] Futaba Kenkō, "Shinshū ni okeru ōjō shinkō to rekishi to no kankei ni tsuite no kasetsu," in *Shinshūshi no kenkyū*, ed. Miyazaki Enjun Hakase Kanreki Kinenkai (Kyoto: Nagata Bunshōdō, 1966), 507–29; also in *Shinshūgaku kenkyū*, ed. Dendōin Kenkyūbu (1971; repr. Kyoto: Nagata Bunshōdō, 1980), 1: 45–68.

he was the founder of the Honganji order. Both the thought and the activity of the Honganji are of a completely different character than that of Shinran himself. And, to understand the Honganji, studies of Shinran are probably of little use.[60]

Before developing Futaba's position further, we turn to Hattori's *Rennyo*, published in 1948, the same year as his *Shinran nōto*. In the introduction, "Rennyo and Shinran," Hattori sharply contrasts these two dominant figures in Shinshū history. His sense is that intellectuals have been attracted to Shinran because he was not "priestly" or condescending in his teaching; he notes that Shinran is not mentioned in the writings of two of his most outstanding contemporaries, that he had no intention of starting a religious sect, and that he built no temple of his own.[61] In contrast, Hattori holds, Rennyo appealed to few intellectuals outside his own tradition; he was born into a professional priesthood. Hattori's judgment is that his "priestliness" may explain why "no one would voluntarily feature him in a novel or drama," despite the value and appeal of his letters as historical documents and human records. Unlike Shinran, Rennyo was bound to his role as priest—a circumstance which, in Hattori's opinion, limited his appeal.[62]

The year 1948 also saw the publication of *Rennyo Shōnin kenkyū*, a volume of essays by a score of Shinshū scholars, in commemoration of the 450th anniversary of Rennyo's death.[63] Although the essays gave evidence of critical scholarship, they were, for the most part, a reworking of traditional themes in Rennyo's life and thought. The volume provoked Hattori to include in the 1955 republication of his *Rennyo* an additional essay, "On the Occasion of the 450th Anniversary," in which he makes a sustained critique of several of the articles.[64]

Hattori raises two questions in his essay. First: how was Rennyo able to build the Honganji from a state of poverty and weakness into late medieval Japan's most powerful religious order? This question leads to the second: what was the source of the Honganji's power, which peaked in the 1570s with a decade of warfare at Ishiyama

---

[60] Ienaga Saburō, *Chūsei bukkyō shisōshi kenkyū* (1947; repr. Kyoto: Hōzōkan, 1966), 202.

[61] Hattori, *Rennyo*, 11. The contemporaries Hattori mentions are Nichiren and Gyōnen (1240–1321).

[62] Hattori, *Rennyo*, 12.

[63] Ryūkoku Daigaku, ed., *Rennyo Shōnin kenkyū* (Kyoto: Onki Hōyō Jimusho, 1948).

[64] Hattori, *Rennyo*, 207–55.

Hongan-ji in opposition to Oda Nobunaga's efforts to unify Japan?[65] Hattori's purpose here is to relate these questions to the Honganji's resistance to reform. He sees little original in Rennyo's thought, in that Rennyo's answers to the problems of heresy were the same as those formulated by Kakunyo and Zonkaku; in short, there had been no new heresies to which Rennyo was called to respond. Neither does he find Rennyo's letters particularly striking in style or content. Hattori credits the tradition's restoration and the Honganji's expansion, not to Rennyo's innovative thinking or egalitarian views, but to the energy of the peasants who entered its ranks. What fueled the Ikkō uprisings was the energy of low-ranking farmers, rather than a religious awakening catalyzed by Rennyo's teachings and leadership.

Hattori argues that, in Rennyo's time, in contrast to Shinran's two centuries earlier, the peasants were already rising up through their own strength; he asserts that Rennyo was well aware—more than the peasants were themselves—of their power to shake the foundations of the existing political and social structures.[66] Hattori's conclusion, then, is that "what was involved was Rennyo's sharpness of insight, his cunning, and his judgment as a politician rather than as a religious leader."[67]

Since the publication of the commemorative volume in 1948, there has been little in the way of fresh evaluation of Rennyo's thought on the part of sectarian scholars.[68] Those engaged in Shinshū Studies have continued to reflect the position of traditional piety in viewing Rennyo's role as master and restorer of the tradition. It is Futaba Kenkō, a historian, who has sought to incorporate some of the insights of Hattori and Ienaga into his overall view of Japanese Buddhist history as a struggle between a particularist state-centered Japanese religiosity, legitimized by worship of the kami, and a universalist egalitarian vision of the Buddha-dharma, reaching back to Śākyamuni Buddha himself.[69]

---

[65] Hattori, *Rennyo*, 210. See also George Elison, "Ishiyama Honganji," KEJ, 3: 346–47, and McMullin, *Buddhism and the State in Sixteenth-Century Japan*.

[66] Hattori, *Rennyo*, 210.

[67] Hattori, *Rennyo*, 244.

[68] Noteworthy studies, however, are Ishida Mitsuyuki, *Rennyo* (Kyoto: Jinrinsha, 1949) and Mori Ryūkichi, *Rennyo*, Kōdansha Gendai Shinsho, no. 550 (Tokyo: Kōdansha, 1979). Also see Kimura Takeo, ed., *Rennyo Shōnin no kyōgaku to rekishi*, a collection of doctrinal and historical studies of Rennyo—the first since the publication of *Rennyo Shōnin kenkyū* in 1948.

[69] In his major study of ancient Japanese Buddhism, *Kodai bukkyō shisōshi kenkyū: Nihon kodai ni okeru ritsuryō bukkyō oyobi han-ritsuryō bukkyō no kenkyū*

Futaba has advanced a four- or five-stage typology of the development of the Shinshū and the Honganji as a religious order. The first stage centers on Shinran's work of personal conversion and the efforts of those who gathered around him to bring about spiritual transformation within the individual. He sees the values of participants in the nascent Shinshū community standing in opposition to those of traditional religious groups, Buddhist and Shinto, in bondage to established political power legitimized by worship of the kami: Shinran emphatically rejects worship of the kami. The second stage is that of Kakunyo and Zonkaku, with the apotheosization of Shinran as founder and increasing emphasis on institutional power. The third stage, continuous with the second, is that of Rennyo, who, in large measure, realized Kakunyo's institutional goals for the Honganji through his innovative approach to missionary work and teaching. In stages two and three, there is increasing accommodation to the native cult of the kami, which symbolizes the authority of traditional Japanese religious and political institutions. In the fourth stage, corresponding to the early modern period, there is, with the apotheosization of Rennyo, increasing institutionalization of the Honganji as a religious order; the interests and demands of the group suppress any concern for the needs of the individual. In the final stage, that of the modern period from 1868 to the present, all that remains of Shinran's teaching is an institutional shell, powerless to share the salvific truth that he had expressed so compellingly.

(Kyoto: Nagata Bunshōdō, 1962), Futaba utilizes the categories *ritsuryō* and anti-*ritsuryō* to specify two main currents running throughout the history of Japanese Buddhism. *Ritsuryō* are the laws instituted by imperial rescript to govern the state; as such, they are legitimized by indigenous religious entities, the kami standing in opposition to Buddha-dharma. Futaba's position is summarized in English in Asaeda Zenshō, *Heian shoki bukkyōshi kenkyū* (Kyoto: Nagata Bunshōdō, 1980), 8:

> *Ritsuryō* Buddhism, taking into account the native cults and their traditions, fails to stress the independence of the human personality at the psychological and sociological levels. [Thus] it stands in opposition to the universality of legitimate Buddhism, which is realized only through individual conversion and a transformation of the personality. Anti-*ritsuryō* Buddhism, in contrast, represents the adoption of true Buddhism both psychologically and sociologically expressing itself in a universal pattern of thought. In sum, it is the confrontation and interaction of these two types of Buddhism that have shaped the development of the history of Japanese religion, society, and thought.

See also the English summary included in Futaba, *Kodai bukkyō shisōshi kenkyū*, 1–16.

Futaba's thesis is that, since the first stage, the time of Shinran's community of faith, there has been a pattern of excessive accommodation on the part of the Honganji, with political authority legitimized by worship of native deities, the kami.[70] One of the most dramatic instances is seen in the Honganji's response to an imperial state in modern times.

It seems appropriate at this point to note once again Hattori's challenge to the position of traditional piety posed by his works on Shinran and Rennyo. Despite the fact that Hattori was simply mistaken in dismissing Rennyo as "a politician rather than a religious leader," historians of medieval Japanese Buddhism were unable to overlook his critique of Buddhist historical studies. Futaba has noted Hattori's exchange with Akamatsu Toshihide, a professor of Buddhist history at Kyoto University, regarding the nature of Shinran's thought in relation to the state.

In reply to Akamatsu's claim that Shinran's letters indicate concern for the prosperity of the state, Futaba maintains that Shinran's expression of concern for the emperor (*chōka* 朝家) and the nation (*kokumin* 国民) emerges specifically in the context of criticizing his own disciples and calling upon them to change their behavior; this does not mean that Shinran was an advocate of the Buddha-dharma as protective of the state.[71] Further, Futaba notes that Kasahara Kazuo, in his

---

[70] Futaba Kenkō, "Shinshū kindai dendō no mondaiten," in Futaba Kenkō and Satō Michio, eds., *Shinshū kyōgaku kenkyū* (Kyoto: Nagata Bunshōdō, 1980), 3: 27–32. This interpretation of Professor Futaba's typology was developed further in the course of conversations with him in July 1970, and again in July 1977, at Ryūkoku University. Kitanishi Hiromu, drawing on social science theory, has taken issue with Futaba's approach to the relationship of history to Shinran's "faith" and that of Rennyo. For example, see Kitanishi Hiromu, "Shinshū kyōdan ni okeru 'chishiki' to dendō: Jūroku seiki no henbōki o chūshin to shite," in *Nihon shūkyōshi kenkyū*, ed. Nihon Shūkyōshi Kenkyūkai, vol. 1, *Soshiki to dendō* (Kyoto: Hōzōkan, 1967), 139–58, esp. 147–49. For a critique of the exchange between Futaba and Kitanishi regarding faith and history, see Fukuma Kōchō, "Kinsei hōken shakai ni okeru bukkyō: Toku ni Rennyo no shisō to jissen o chūshin ni," *Ryūkoku daigaku ronshū*, 395 (1971): 111–15. The institutionalization of Shinran's religious vision lends itself to a sociological analysis. Especially suggestive in this regard is the work of Thomas F. O'Dea, drawing on Max Weber's social theory; see Thomas F. O'Dea, "Sociological Dilemmas: Five Paradoxes of Institutionalization," in *Sociological Theory, Values and Sociocultural Change: Essays in Honor of Pitirim A. Sorokin*, ed. Edmund A. Tiryakian (New York: Harper and Row, 1967), 71–89.

[71] Futaba cites a passage from *Shinran Shōnin goshōsokushū*, SSZ 2: 697, in his *Shinran no kenkyū*, 368.

study of Shinran and farmers in eastern Japan, acknowledges that Shinran's state-protecting thought functions as an expedient rather than as a fundamental tenet.[72]

There has been general agreement among those engaged in traditional sectarian studies and modern critical scholarship that Rennyo made important contributions to the Honganji's emergence as the most powerful religious body in late medieval Japan. While his significance for the Ikkō uprisings should not be overlooked, he was by no means a pivotal figure; indeed, he was careful to formally distance himself from those followers who were actively engaged in the uprisings. Studies of the Ikkō uprisings differ sharply as to the relevance of Rennyo's teachings and activities for those seeking to overturn the established social order.[73]

Before concluding this discussion of modern critical scholarship, we again draw attention to the writings of Kuroda Toshio, whose field is medieval Japanese history.[74] His position challenges scholarship reflecting traditional sectarian piety as well as that of his colleagues in medieval Japanese historical studies who have focused their attention solely on the new Buddhism heralded by the "reformers" of the Kamakura period. It follows from Kuroda's emphasis on the continuity and tenacity of the influence of the *kenmitsu* ethos into the medieval period that institutions and rituals are to be seen as more important than doctrines in pre-modern Japanese history.[75] In this effort, he offers a corrective to sectarian studies to the extent that they have been preoccupied with doctrinal issues, as well as to the modern critical scholarship generated partially in reaction to the sectarian scholarship. On the other hand, however, against the background of

---

[72] Futaba, *Shinran no kenkyū*, 368; for an evaluation of the influence of Hattori's thesis on Kasahara's earlier work in the context of postwar studies of the Ikkō uprisings, see Inoue, *Ikkō ikki no kenkyū*, 8.

[73] Kitanishi Hiromu points out dramatic interpretive shifts in postwar studies on the Ikkō uprisings. They have been seen as religious movements protecting the Buddha-dharma as well as revolutionary movements opposing those in political authority. He finds these interpretations unsatisfying in that, although claiming to be empiricist, they neglect textual studies, including a careful reading of Rennyo's letters as a whole (Kitanishi, *Rennyo: Gendai to kyōdan*, 23).

[74] See nn. 4, 7.

[75] McMullin, in his essay, "Historical and Historiographical Issues in the Study of Pre-modern Japanese Religions," draws heavily on Kuroda's work in his critique of the study of premodern Japanese religions, both in Japan and the West; see n. 11.

Kuroda's historical perspective, the major religious symbols for a tradition such as the Shinshū, which emphasizes its founder's teaching and, in turn, the importance of doctrinal orthodoxy, are in danger of being relegated to the historian's footnote.

A COMPARATIVE PERSPECTIVE

In an attempt to apprehend what has been unfolding in the history of the religious life of Jōdo Shinshū participants, we have turned to the work of a comparative historian of religion, Wilfred Cantwell Smith. Striking is the degree to which the major categories he uses in approaching religious studies in general are immediately applicable to the most challenging aspects in our study of Rennyo and the Jōdo Shinshū. To borrow a phrase of Smith's, this study approaches Rennyo's life and thought, letters, and legacy as a significant strand in Japanese Buddhists' participation in "a history of religion in the singular." In respect to Rennyo, this means that "the history of [his] religious life, and especially of [his] faith, lived always in a specific context, is intrinsically the locus of both the mundane and the transcendent, unbifurcated."[76] Therefore, in attempting to answer the question "Who is Rennyo?" we are simultaneously concerned with the mundane and with the transcendent. Further, if we are to answer the question with Shinran's Mahāyāna perspective in mind, the mundane and the transcendent stand, as we have suggested, in a relationship of simultaneous sameness and opposition.

This work is then, first of all, inductive, drawing on the broadest possible range of sources available on Rennyo, including both traditional Shinshū Studies and modern critical scholarship. Despite a general failure by sectarian scholarship to raise the issue of possible

---

[76] See Smith's *Towards a World Theology*, ch. 1, "A History of Religion in the Singular," in which he argues that the unity of humankind's religious history is both a historical fact and a matter of theological truth: "The vision to be set forth in this presentation is of the unity or coherence of humankind's religious history. At one level, this unity is a matter of empirical observation. It is an historical fact. At another level, it is a matter of theological truth. . . . The history of religion, by which I understand the history of men and women's religious life, and especially of their faith, lived always in a specific context, is intrinsically the locus of both the mundane and the transcendent, unbifurcated" (3). In this study, we are attempting to find language apposite both to the Mahāyāna structure of Shinran's thought and to the history of religion understood as "the history of men and women's religious life, and especially of their faith."

discontinuities in interpretations of Shinran's teaching within Shinshū history, the power of traditional images of Rennyo is understandable. On the other hand, claims such as Ienaga's—that there is little relationship between Shinran's religious vision and the history of Rennyo's Honganji—cannot be wholly discounted. In taking an inductive approach, we contend that contrasting images are to be taken seriously, in that each has been a constituent of a single historical process that must provide the foundation for any evaluation of Rennyo's contribution to Shinshū tradition.

Second, this work takes seriously that salvific truth—in the Shinshū instance, that birth in the Pure Land is given through the Other Power of Amida's Vow—has been and continues to be an integral part of historical process. In terms of the approaches of Japanese scholars, it is perhaps closest to the position of Futaba Kenkō, whose life's work has been to rethink his own tradition in the larger context of Buddhist history in relation to Japan's cultural tradition.[77] Futaba shares with sectarian scholars in the field of Shinshū Studies a concern with the transcendent, yet the focus of that concern is with the transcendent meaning of mundane facts mined by historians. His orientation— history as the locus of both the mundane and the transcendent—is grounded, I believe, in Shinran's interpretation of the coordinate concepts, ōsō ekō 往相廻向 and gensō ekō 還相廻向 , introduced in the opening verses of the first chapter of Kyōgyōshinshō:

> Reverently contemplating the true essence of the Pure Land way [jōdo shinshū], I see that Amida's directing of virtue [ekō] to sentient beings has two aspects: the aspect for our going forth to the Pure Land [ōsō] and the aspect for our return to this world [gensō]. In the aspect for going forth, there is the true teaching, practice, shinjin, and realization [kyōgyōshinshō].[78]

Futaba sees a unity of these aspects in Shinran's life and thought; they are separate, yet one. In particular, Futaba calls attention to the gensō ekō —"our return to this world"—aspect, whereby one's own assurance of the saving power of Amida's Primal Vow (the transcendent) is ever at work in the affairs of this world (the mundane) on behalf of all sentient beings. In his opinion, the Honganji as a religious order has consistently violated that unity in being disproportionately concerned

---

[77] For glimpses into Futaba's own spiritual pilgrimage, see Futaba Kenkō, *Shinran no hiraita chihei* (Kyoto: Hyakkaen, 1975), especially selections under *Zuisō* (Random thoughts), 187–218.

[78] *Teaching*, 1: 63; SSZ 2: 2.

with the ōsō ekō — "going forth to the Pure Land" — aspect, a concern primarily with salvation in the afterlife at the expense of the social implications of Shinran's thought.[79]

Futaba's approach suggests an affinity with that of Wilfred Cantwell Smith: born in the same year, 1916, both are historians as well as active participants in their respective Buddhist and Christian traditions. Both vigorously resist tendencies in modern scholarship toward reductionist approaches to the study of human affairs that would rule out the transcendent. Both, on occasion, have evoked criticism from their colleagues for moving beyond the traditionally accepted boundaries of the historian's domain.

Apparent differences in the approaches of Smith and Futaba are not to be discounted: Futaba appears to see Buddhist history itself as *Heilsgeschichte* or "salvation-history." He draws a sharp line between a history of the Buddha-dharma in terms reflecting Shinran's vision of a community of companions and fellow practicers (*dōbō dōgyō* 同朋 同行) and the Japanese state-centered cultural tradition, which he claims has failed to acknowledge the fundamentals of human dignity and equality. In his view, the Buddha-dharma has been, from its very inception in Japan's cultural history, inherently in conflict with state-centered religiosity legitimized by worship of the kami. In introducing a series of studies on the relationship of the state and Buddhist tradition from ancient to modern times, Futaba wrote:

> From now on, it is essential that historical studies of Buddhism be conducted with continuous attention to two aspects of its development: the aspect that is accepted into a traditional religious society, and the aspect accepted after surmounting the tradition. Here the relationship between what we term "the State and Buddhism" comes to play a vital role. Specifically, Japan's national development involves a traditional religious structure; on the basis of the tradition, the nation sanctifies political authority and exercises control over the populace. When Buddhism is taken into such a structure, its fundamental universality is altogether lost. On further inquiry, we find that when Buddhism is truly accepted, it will inevitably challenge a nation's religious and political stance. If we consider

---

[79] Futaba, "Shinshū ni okeru ōjō shinkō to rekishi to no kankei ni tsuite no kasetsu," 516–29. Gadjin Nagao underscores the balance necessary to these two aspects in Pure Land thought in his essay, "Ascent and Descent: Two-Directional Activity in Buddhist Thought," *The Journal of the International Association of Buddhist Studies* 7/1 (1984): 176–84. Without citing Shinran's thought specifically, Nagao sets Pure Land Buddhism firmly in the mainstream of the Mahāyāna.

Japanese Buddhist history in this context, we will surely find that if Buddhism had clarified its position as a universal religion, it could not have avoided confrontation with the body politic. From here on, we must carry out an overall analysis of what this has meant in the context of Japanese culture and history.[80]

While Futaba's concern as an historian is with the relationship of Buddha-dharma (the transcendent) and Japan's cultural tradition (the mundane), Smith makes explicit in his writings as a comparative historian of religion that he does not single out the history of any religious tradition, including his own, in exclusivist terms: "All human history is *Heilsgeschichte.*"[81] Given his notion of faith as a universal human potentiality, salvific truth is not limited to any tradition — whether religious or, in his terms, "secular rationalist."[82] It appears, however, that what Futaba Kenkō and Wilfred Cantwell Smith share in common is of even greater significance than their possible differences — their orientation as historians in seeing that religious life, in particular, is the locus of the mundane and the transcendent, with inescapable implications for the quality of moral life in human community.[83]

---

[80] Futaba Kenkō, ed., *Kokka to bukkyō*, Nihon Bukkyōshi Kenkyū, vol. 1 (Kyoto: Nagata Bunshōdō, 1979), 2–3. Other volumes in the series edited by Futaba are: *Kokka to bukkyō: Kinsei/kindaihen*, vol. 2 (1980); *Zoku kokka to bukkyō: Kodai chūseihen*, vol. 3 (1981); and *Zoku kokka to bukkyō: Kinsei/kindaihen*, vol. 4 (1981).

[81] Smith, *Towards a World Theology*, 172.

[82] Smith, *Towards a World Theology*, 145–50. In a chapter entitled "Muslim? Hindu? Jewish? Buddhist? A Theology of Comparative Religion with Special Reference to Communities other than the Christian," Smith includes a representative voice for the "Western rationalist-humanist tradition" as one whose position merits inclusion in a theology of comparative religion. For a discussion of Smith's approach to "faith" and the comparative history of religion in relation to Rennyo, see Rogers, "The Shin Faith of Rennyo," 68–73; in Japanese, see Rogers, "'Shinjin' to 'anjin': Jōdo Shinshū shisōshi ni okeru Faith ni tsuite no ichi kōsatsu," *Shinshūgaku* 63 (1981): 26–43.

[83] See Futaba's writings in English translation: (1) "Shinran and Human Dignity: Opening An Historic Horizon," trans. Kenryu T. Tsuji, *The Pacific World: Journal of the Institute of Buddhist Studies*, n.s., 4 (1988): 51–59 (this article is a translation of Futaba's "Shinran no hiraita rekishiteki chihei," in Futaba Kenkō, ed., *Shinran no subete* [Tokyo: Shinjinbutsu Juraisha, 1984], 7–26) and (2) "Future Challenge for Shinshū Followers in America," trans. Shojo Oi, *The Pacific World: Journal of the Institute of Buddhist Studies*, n.s., 1 (1985): 7–10. For an introduction to Smith's thought concerning the moral challenge of religious pluralism in relation to the intellectual and theological, see *The Faith of Other Men* (New York: Harper and Row, 1972), part two.

There is a final point, especially in relation to the translation of Rennyo's letters, which follows in part two of this study. In recent years, a sensitive issue among Shinshū scholars themselves, as well as in their conversations with Western scholars, has been the question of the translatability of Shinran's core religious symbol, "*shinjin*," into English or other languages.[84]

Until recently, translators of Shinran's writings, including Suzuki Daisetsu, have rendered *shinjin* into English as "faith"; translators in the Ryūkoku Translation Center in Kyoto continue to do so, clarifying their choices of these and other terms with rich annotation.[85] In general, previous translations of Rennyo's *Letters*,[86] taking *anjin* 安心 , another of his core religious symbols, to be indistinguishable from *shinjin*, have rendered both terms as "faith." On the other hand, we have noted the precedent set by the translators of the Shin Buddhism

---

[84] See glossary entry *shinjin* in *Letters*, 83–84. See also Thomas P. Kasulis's review, "Letters of Shinran: A Translation of Mattōshō," in *Philosophy: East and West* 31 (1981): 246–48; and Yoshifumi Ueda, "Response to Thomas P. Kasulis' review of *Letters of Shinran*," in *Philosophy: East and West* 31 (1981): 507–11. For a further exchange relating to this issue, see Luis O. Gómez's review article, "Shinran's Faith and the Sacred Name of Amida," *Monumenta Nipponica* 38 (1983): 73–84; a reply to Gómez by Ueda and Dennis Hirota in "Correspondence," *Monumenta Nipponica* 38: 413–17; and Gómez's reply in the same issue, 418–27. Also see n. 15.

[85] See chapter three on "True Faith," RTS, *Kyō Gyō Shin Shō*, 83–135.

[86] Existing English translations of Rennyo's letters, listed according to publication date:

Troup, James, trans. Fascicle five (entire) in "The Gobunsho or Ofumi, of Rennyo Shōnin." *Transactions of the Asiatic Society of Japan* 17/1 (1889): 101–43.

Yokogawa, Kensho, trans. Rennyo's letters 2:4 and 5:12, in "Shin Buddhism as the Religion of Hearing." *The Eastern Buddhist* 7 (1939): 336–39.

Sugihira, Shizutoshi, trans. Letters 1:3, 2:4, 5:1, 5:2, 5:5, 5:9, 5:10, 5:12, 5:16, and 5:22 in "Rennyo Shōnin, Great Teacher of Shin Buddhism." *The Eastern Buddhist* 8 (1949): 5–35.

Yamamoto, Kosho, trans. Letters 2:7, 3:4, 4:4, 4:13, 4:15, 5:1, 5:2, 5:5, 5:10, 5:11, 5:13, and 5:16 in "The Gobunsho," *The Shinshu Seiten: The Holy Scripture of Shinshu*, 287–98. Honolulu: The Honpa Hongwanji Mission of Hawaii, 1955.

Suzuki, Daisetz Teitaro. "Rennyo's Letters [5:5]," in *Mysticism: Christian and Buddhist*, 126–31. New York: Harper and Row Brothers, 1957.

Tri-State Buddhist Temples, comp. "The Epistles (Gobun Sho)," in *Shinshū Seiten: Jōdo Shin Buddhist Teaching*, 269–90. San Francisco: Buddhist Churches of America, 1978.

Translation Series. In their task of translating the entire corpus of Shinran's works, they have chosen to introduce the unitalicized term "shinjin" into the English text; they argue eloquently that most of the possible connotations of the English word "faith" are entirely inappropriate within their tradition and cannot convey the nuances of *shinjin* free of misleading preconceptions. While they have not translated any of Rennyo's writings, it is possible that Rennyo's concept *anjin* might be treated similarly and introduced unitalicized, with the prospect of both terms becoming part of our English vocabulary. Their approach has much to commend it and will continue to contribute an essential perspective to the ongoing translation of Shinran's Mahāyāna Buddhist sense of the simultaneity of sameness and opposition in the relationship of the sentient being's heart and mind and that of the Buddha.[87]

In this study, however, we have found that Rennyo's use of the concept *anjin* in interpreting, popularizing, and even attempting to define Shinran's concept *shinjin*, raises fresh difficulties in transliterating *shinjin* into English if one assumes continuity with Shinran's use of the term. Further, we see significant differences in the structure of their thought.[88] For these reasons, in this study, we have chosen to

---

Rogers, Ann T. and Minor L. Rogers, translation and introduction. "Rennyo's Letters (*Rennyo Shōnin Ofumi*) Fascicle Five." *The Eastern Buddhist*, n.s., 21/2 (1988): 95–123.

――――, translation and annotation. "Letters of Rennyo (*Ofumi*, Fascicle One)," in *The Pure Land: Journal of Pure Land Buddhism*, n.s., 5 (1988), 74–112.

[87] For an introduction to the meaning of time in Shinran's thought, see the discussion of *shinjin* in chapter four, "The Structure of Shinran's Thought," in Ueda and Hirota, *Shinran*, 167–82. Also see Nishitani Keiji, "The Problem of Time in Shinran," *The Eastern Buddhist*, n.s., 11/1 (1975): 13–26, translated by Hirota.

[88] That difference might be put most cogently in terms of their respective views of birth (*ōjō* 往生); see nn. 15, 31. In contrast to Shinran's holding of two meanings of birth simultaneously as discussed in Ueda's two-part essay "The Mahāyāna Structure of Shinran's Thought," Rennyo emphasizes birth in the Pure Land in the afterlife as the most important matter (*goshō ichidaiji* 後生 一大事) for this life. Ueda puts the issue as follows:

The concept of birth which Shinran had brought to such a high level of development seems to have re-acquired a focus on the moment of death by the time of his descendant Zonkaku. . . . Zonkaku states concerning "immediately attain birth" in the *Larger Sūtra*: "*Attain birth* means that it is settled that one will be born" (*Jōdo shinyōshō*). Here birth is interpreted as having only one meaning (birth in the Pure Land at the moment of death). As we have seen, in Shinran two meanings of birth are established simultaneously, but it appears that the self-translate *shinjin* as "faith" and *anjin* as "settled mind" or "faith," depending on context. To clarify what Japanese term other than *shinjin* is being translated as "faith," we have inserted the Japanese term into the textual passages following each occurrence of the nouns *shin*, *fushin* 不信 , *fushinjin* 不信心 , *anjin*, *mianjin* 未安心 , or *shingyō* 信楽 . While the Shin Buddhism Translation Series approach preserves what is unique to the Mahāyāna structure of Shinran's thought and to Shinshū tradition, we have found that the particular meaning of the terms *shinjin* and *anjin* in the tradition does in fact draw out and underscore the deepest meaning of "faith" and "settled mind" as general religious terms. In this study of Rennyo, we find that *shinjin* as a concept is consistently translated less ambiguously by the word "faith" — a faith that is salvific truth, empowered and given by that which is entirely beyond human effort and calculative thinking. Granted that the term "faith" tends to focus on the mind of the person to be saved, what other English term could at the same time hint at the other pole, in this instance, the salvific mind of the Buddha Amida?

Anjin, "settled mind," suggests the mind in which "the peace that passes all understanding" is settled once and for all, beyond all shadow of doubt. Since *anjin* is translated literally as "easily-[attained] mind" or "serene mind" (*yasuki kokoro* やすきこころ ; letter 2:7), it might seem that "serenity," rather than the compound "settled mind," would be the choice more closely parallel to "faith." "Serenity," however, fails to catch the paradox implicit in *anjin*, in that it emphasizes the quality of mind of the person saved at the expense of the underlying decisiveness — the diamondlike quality — of the mind of Amida. This is evident in translating the term *anjin ketsujō* 安心決定 : it seems quite possible to speak of a person in whom "the settled mind is established" (letter 1:3), but somewhat awkward to refer to one in whom "serenity is established." Since it is the fact of definite establishment that leads to serenity,

---

contradictory character of this concept. . . has prevented its implications from being well understood. Most commentators after Zonkaku [including Rennyo] follow his interpretation, and it remains the dominant understanding among Shin scholars even today (part 2, 54, n. 39).

The structure of Shinran's thought, implicit here, dictates that in the relationship of sentient beings and Amida Buddha there is simultaneity of sameness and opposition that is irresolvable in this life; Rennyo's nenbutsu thought regarding that same relationship suggests that sentient beings merge with Amida Buddha through the absoluteness of Other Power, thereby resolving the paradox of oneness and separateness. As discussed in chapter three of this study, Rennyo's nenbutsu thought is based on the concept *ki-hō ittai* 機法一体 , found in *Anjin ketsujōshō*, a text unavailable to Shinran.

"settled mind," despite the lack of parallelism, may be a workable choice. To reiterate: throughout this study, whenever the terms "faith" and "settled mind" appear, they are intended to refer to the Japanese terms *shinjin* and *anjin* respectively, with any exceptions being indicated by the insertion of the Japanese term in question.

For the importance of linguistic and cultural translation for Shinshū tradition, we may note Ōtani Kōshin's further remarks at the "Shin Buddhism and Christianity" symposium:

> Pure Land Buddhism traditionally emphasizes the way of life in each era. That is to say, the teaching of Amida Buddha's Primal Vow must be translated into the emerging context of each new age. We see this process in the writings of Shinran Shōnin, for he based his teaching on the Pure Land tradition of the Seven Patriarchs: Nāgārjuna and Vasubandhu in India, T'an-luan, Tao-ch'o, and Shan-tao in China, and Genshin and Hōnen in Japan. Shinran's successors [such as Rennyo] have also striven to interpret the teachings for their times. These later interpretations, however, are often subject to criticism as being temporalized or arbitrary. It is difficult to determine what should and should not be translated in each era. . . .
>
> Even in Japan at present, the concrete expressions of Buddhist truth, such as Primal Vow, Pure Land, and shinjin, need to be translated and adapted to the contemporary context. I feel confident that this Symposium will provide us with valuable suggestions not only on intercultural translation, but also on our internal problems of translation and interpretation as well.[89]

This study of Rennyo, most immediately the translation of *The Letters* in part two, is offered as a contribution to the ongoing process of translation in both of these senses. It appears that the question "Who is Rennyo?" leads finally to a further question, "How is Shinran's teaching on faith to be translated as 'the locus of both the mundane and the transcendent, unbifurcated' for this new age?"

---

[89] Ōtani Kōshin, "Opening Address," 236; for Japanese text, 22.

Rennyo's
Life and Thought

Rennyo's Life and Thought

> I have done everything I meant to do. I have restored Master [Shinran]'s tradition, built the Main Hall and the Founder's Hall [at Yamashina], passed on the position of head priest, and built the temple at Osaka; now I have retired. And so it may be said of me, "Fulfilling one's obligations, making a name for oneself, and going into retirement: such is the way of heaven."
>
> Rennyo[1]

R ENNYO IS REFLECTING here on a long and eventful life; he is ill and may well sense that his days are nearly spent. All he intended to do has been realized: Shinran's tradition restored, Hongan-ji rebuilt at Yamashina, and the tradition's continuity assured with his fifth son, Jitsunyo, in office as custodian of the Founder's Hall. He seems at peace with his life, equating its passage with "the way of heaven."

In evaluating these sentences, a contemporary sectarian writer finds beneath their self-congratulatory tone the honest reflection of a man who, ill and worn at the close of his life, has known a full measure of suffering as well as heroic achievement.[2] As a life summary, the passage should be taken in the context of episodes from other memoirs attesting to the adversities Rennyo faced from childhood on: the poverty of his early years in a declining tradition, the loss of his centuries-old temple-home, the painful questioning of his legitimacy to succeed as head priest, criticism and attack by representatives of other religious groups, and, in his final years, moments of despondency over how few members of the Shinshū community were established in faith.[3]

---

[1] From *Jitsugo kyūki*, a memoir by Jitsugo (1492–1584), Rennyo's tenth son. RSG, 94; SSZ 3: 571. The quotation concluding the passage is based on *Lao-tzu* (*Rōshi*), ch. 9.

[2] Umehara Shinryū, *Rennyo Shōnin kikigaki shinshaku* (Kyoto: Nishi Honganji Shuppansha, 1982), 213–15.

[3] Secondary source biographical data are drawn from the following works: Honganji Shiryō Kenkyūjo, ed., *Honganjishi*, vol. 1, hereafter cited as HS (Kyoto:

The theme of heroic achievement in the face of adversity underlies the memoirs' apotheosization of Rennyo as restorer of the tradition. This is not to deny the obvious fact that Shinran is the focal point for Shinshū piety: Shinran's image, enshrined successively in the several different locations of the Founder's Hall, has always been the center of devotion for the Shinshū community. His virtues are celebrated in works such as Kakunyo's *Hōonkō shiki*;[4] his life, in the text and illustrations of *Honganji Shōnin Shinran den'e*.

Granted Shinran's centrality as the focus of piety, it is Rennyo's letters — largely a work of translation of Shinran's teaching into terms readily available to unlettered men and women — that have provided much of the content and meaning for that piety. For example, *Gozokushō*, notes on the founder in colloquial Japanese, provided a readily comprehensible alternative to the *Hōonkō shiki*, written in classical Chinese. In large measure, it is Rennyo's words that have defined orthodox Shinshū piety as gratitude over the past five centuries. We can observe this process of definition at work by following his life and the development of his thought through three stages: his initiation into Shinshū tradition at Ōtani Hongan-ji, his response to the dilemma of the Honganji's religious power during his years at Yoshizaki, and his restoration of the tradition and retirement at Yamashina Hongan-ji.

Before telling this story, one further point: there are those who, from the perspective of Buddhist tradition, might take Rennyo to task for the tone of his life summary cited above. One scholar criticizes him for drifting into a sentimentality inconsistent with the self-denial (*jiko hitei* 自己否定) that might be expected in his declining years;[5] others might point to an absence of the quality of self-negation (*jiga hitei* 自我否定) that lies at the core of what it means to live as a Buddhist.[6]

Jōdo Shinshū Honganjiha, 1961); Sasaki Hōyū, *Rennyo Shōnin den no kenkyū* (Kyoto: Dōbōsha, 1926); Kasahara Kazuo, *Rennyo*, Jinbutsu Sōsho, no. 109 (Tokyo: Yoshikawa Kōbunkan, 1969) and *Ransei o ikiru: Rennyo no shōgai* (Tokyo: Kyōikusha, 1981); and Ōhara Shōjitsu, *Rennyo goroku ni kiku* (Tokyo: Kyōiku Shinchōsha, 1964). These works are based primarily on memoirs and collections of Rennyo's sayings, particularly those found in RSG and SSZ.

[4] The *Hōonkō shiki* (SSZ 3: 655–60) is a service of thanksgiving written in Einin 2 (1294) for the thirty-third anniversary of Shinran's death (see chapter four of this study for further discussion; see also SSJ, 440).

[5] Yamaori Tetsuo, *Ningen Rennyo* (Tokyo: Shunjūsha, 1970), 162–63.

[6] For references to *jiga hitei* in relation to Shinran, see Futaba, *Shinran no kenkyū*, 97, 216, 261, and 333. For a comparison of Shinran's thought with Rennyo's, see Futaba, "Shinshū ni okeru ōjō shinkō to rekishi to no kankei ni tsuite no kasetsu," 516–22.

While such voices are critical of Rennyo's piety as compared to Shinran's in this respect, they also alert us to the multi-faceted quality of a quite remarkable human being.

What kind of person is Rennyo? Is he humble or proud, self-sacrificing or authoritarian, selfless or egotistical? Could there be a single image—the "apolitical sage" of traditional piety, or the "priestly politician" of modern critical scholarship—that would suffice? These are some of the questions we will bear in mind in examining Rennyo's life and thought in part one of this study.

Chapter 2

Initiation: Ōtani Hongan-ji

R ENNYO WAS BORN at Ōtani Hongan-ji, in the Higashiyama district of Kyoto, on Ōei 22 (1415).2.25, during the shogunate of
Ashikaga Yoshimochi (1386–1428). The site held rich associations for participants in Shinshū tradition, for it was here that
Shinran's ashes were reinterred during the winter of Bun'ei 9 (1272)
by his daughter, Kakushinni (1224–1283). A hexagonal chapel, protecting the gravestone and enshrining a wooden statue and portrait of
Shinran, was built on the site; eventually, the chapel and grounds
came to be known as the Ōtani Mausoleum (*Ōtani byōdō*).[1] Under
Kakunyo, the mausoleum gained recognition as a temple and, by
1321, it had been designated "Hongan-ji."[2] Destroyed by fire in 1336
during warfare between the forces of Ashikaga Takauji (1305–1358)
and Emperor Godaigo (r. 1318–1339), Hongan-ji was rebuilt within
a few years as a conventional temple to hold the founder's image.[3]

---

[1] HS 1: 130–32. Kakushinni was financially supported in this effort by numbers of Shinran's followers, many of whom had probably travelled considerable
distances to Ōtani to visit the original, quite simple, grave. Beginning in 1277,
two years after her husband's death, she wrote three letters bequeathing the
property to Shinran's followers "in the countryside" as a permanent memorial
to him; the official deed, however, was left to her descendants, as was custodianship of the mausoleum (HS 1: 136–44); Chiba Jōryū, *Honganji monogatari*
(Kyoto: Dōbōsha, 1984), 13–25.

[2] The first reference to the name "Hongan-ji" appears in a document written by Kakunyo, dated Genkū 1 (1321). See HS 1: 180–83, for circumstances involved in the choice.

[3] In rebuilding, Kakunyo made use of an old temple bought in Ryakuō 1
(1338).11 and moved to the site, a fact which may partly explain the change in
design (HS 1: 183–85).

During the tenure of Rennyo's father, Zonnyo (1396–1457), a second hall was built to enshrine an image of the Buddha Amida.[4]

EARLY YEARS

At the time of Rennyo's birth, his grandfather, Gyōnyo (1376–1440), an eighth-generation descendant of Shinran, held the office of custodian of the Founder's Hall and served as the sixth head priest in the Honganji lineage of the Shinshū. Rennyo's father assisted at the temple, preparing to succeed to the same position; his mother is said to have been a servant to Zonnyo's mother, who was no longer living.[5]

When Rennyo (known in childhood as Hoteimaru) was six, Nyoen of the Ebina family became his father's legal wife. At that point, Rennyo's mother, whose name was to remain unrecorded, slipped away from Ōtani Hongan-ji, never to return. The only memento she took with her was a portrait of her young son;[6] what she left with him, we are told, was an earnest request that he restore Shinran's tradition during his lifetime.[7]

---

[4] Although there seems to be no firm evidence as to when the Amida Hall was built, documents indicate that construction may have occurred relatively early in Rennyo's life, possibly in Eikyō 10 (1438), two years after Gyōnyo transferred leadership of the Honganji to Zonnyo (HS 1: 286–93). Miyazaki Enjun, however, finds a later date more plausible (*Shoki Shinshū no kenkyū* [Kyoto: Nagata Bunshōdō, 1971], 208).

[5] HS 1: 294–95; Kasahara, *Rennyo*, 5–6.

[6] *Jitsugoki*, RSG, 144–45.

[7] *Rennyo Shōnin itokuki*, SSZ 3: 870. The absence of factual information on Rennyo's mother offers wide scope for legendary accounts. From early on, among Rennyo's children and followers, she was believed to be an incarnation of the bodhisattva Kannon of Ishiyama-dera (a Shingon temple, founded in the eighth century on the west bank of the Setagawa, to the south of Ōtsu) or of Rokkakudō (Chōjō-ji, a Tendai temple in Kyoto, dedicated to Kannon, where Shinran was inspired during a period of seclusion to visit Hōnen, who became his teacher in the Pure Land path). In later life, Rennyo evidently sought news of his mother's whereabouts and established the twenty-eighth of the month, the day of her departure, as her memorial day (HS 1: 294–95; see also *Kūzenki*, RSG, 38). For legendary accounts of mother and son, see Satake Chio, comp., *Chūkō Rennyo Shōnin goden'e shō* (1898; repr. Kyoto: Kōkyōshoin, 1940), 1–27; appended material, 10–13. For a contemporary account, see Hirai Shōryū's novel, *Rennyo to sono haha* (Kyoto: Nagata Bunshōdō, 1983). Ishiyama-dera itself is rich in associations with Rennyo and his mother: there is a hall named for Rennyo, and the main hall (where Murasaki Shikibu is said to have written parts of *Genji monogatari*) houses relics reportedly brought by Rennyo's mother

Within two years of his own mother's departure, Rennyo's first stepsister was born, followed soon after by two more. A stepbrother, Ōgen (1433–1503), was born when Rennyo was nineteen. This meant that Rennyo grew up in a household headed by his paternal grandfather, with a father only twenty years his senior and a stepmother concerned with the welfare of her own children, primarily Ōgen, whom she was to put forward as Zonnyo's successor.

A memoir reports that, at fifteen, consistent with his mother's wish, Rennyo vowed to restore Shinran's dharma-teaching and make it known throughout Japan.[8] At seventeen, in the summer of 1431, he was tonsured at Shōren-in (Seiren-in), a Tendai temple immediately adjacent to Ōtani Hongan-ji, and given the name Kenju.[9] In 1440, the year of his grandfather's death and his father's succession as the seventh leader of the Honganji, Rennyo was twenty-six; he was to remain as a member of his father's household until the latter's death in 1457.

During Zonnyo's tenure as head priest, Rennyo accompanied him on preaching and teaching tours in the Kantō (eastern provinces) and in the Hokuriku (northern region) facing the Japan sea,[10] to the northeast of Kyoto. These were regions that, from the time of Shinran's exile in the Hokuriku and lengthy stay in the Kantō, had been active centers for the Shinshū and, since Shinran's death, had provided much of the support for Ōtani Hongan-ji and the maintenance of the Founder's Hall. After Zonnyo's death, a painful succession dispute involving Ōgen was resolved in Rennyo's favor; at age forty-three, he became custodian of the Founder's Hall and eighth head priest of the Honganji.

The memoirs, compiled after Rennyo's death, cite him as the master (*shōnin* 上人) who, through single-minded determination that the teaching flourish, was responsible for the restoration of the Shinshū to a former splendor. Some later sources refer to him and to the previous custodians of the Founder's Hall as *hosshu* 法主 (lit., dharma-lord), an epithet traditionally used for the Buddha.[11]

---

after her sudden departure from Ōtani Hongan-ji. A poem ascribed to her supports the legend that she was an incarnation of the temple's Kannon.

[8] *Rennyo Shōnin itokuki*, SSZ 3: 871.

[9] *Rennyo Shōnin itokuki*, SSZ 3: 871.

[10] Hokuriku, commonly an abbreviation for Hokuriku-dō, is one of eight geographical circuits in medieval Japan. The circuit encompassed seven provinces: Echizen and Wakasa (present-day Fukui prefecture), Kaga and Noto (Ishikawa prefecture), Etchū (Toyama prefecture), and Echigo and Sado (Niigata prefecture).

[11] Kasahara, *Rennyo*, 94. See Kōno Hōun and Kumoyama Ryūju, *Shinshū*

In contrast to what is known of Rennyo's extraordinary accomplishment in restoring the tradition, various records underscore Ōtani Hongan-ji's poverty early in his life.[12] Specific reference is made to the absence of visitors and loneliness of the temple precincts before his birth—a time when pilgrims were flocking "like clouds" to the neighboring Bukkō-ji.[13] In identifying the Honganji as the legitimate vehicle for Shinran's teaching, both memoirs and historical records imply that there had been a sharp decline in the tradition's fortunes, setting the stage for a dramatic revival and restoration under Rennyo. However, as we have said earlier, there is no evidence that the Honganji ever experienced a period of sizeable growth in comparison with other branches of the Shinshū.[14]

The most representative memoir, *Goichidaiki kikigaki*, stresses that the widespread increase in devotion to Buddha-dharma during Rennyo's tenure as head priest was entirely due to the strength of his aspiration to expand the influence of Shinran's teaching, and that his success was directly related to the hardships he had endured earlier in life.[15] Jitsugo describes some of these difficulties: unable to afford lamp oil, Rennyo read the tradition's texts by the light of carefully-rationed firewood or, at times, by moonlight; he generally bathed his feet in cold water and sometimes went without meals for two or three days.[16] His first child, Junnyo (1442–1483), was born to Nyoryō (d.1455), his first wife, when he was twenty-eight; by the time of the death of his father, Zonnyo, there were six more children to be cared for.[17] As there

---

jiten (Kyoto: Hōzōkan, 1968), 688; the term is also read *hossu*. It became customary to designate a particular head priest numerically in order of succession, beginning with Shinran. In referring to Rennyo as the eighth head priest, or to Kakunyo as the third, the implication is that Shinran is the first.

[12] See, for example: *Jitsugo kyūki*, RSG 89–90; SSZ 3: 566–68; HS 1: 296; and Sasaki, *Rennyo Shōnin den no kenkyū*, 11.

[13] Chiba Jōryū, ed., *Honpukuji atogaki*, 358 (and *Honpukuji yuraiki*, 324–25) in *Honpukuji kyūki*. For further references, see introduction, n. 35.

[14] For an account of the Honganji's fortunes under the four head priests following Kakunyo—Zennyo (1333–1389), Shakunyo (1350–1393), Gyōnyo, and Zonnyo—see Dobbins, *Jōdo Shinshū*, 128–31. In short, their efforts to preserve the Honganji's lineage of teaching and to undertake new missionary activities were by no means inconsequential for Rennyo's subsequent achievement.

[15] *Goichidaiki kikigaki*, SSZ 3: 566; see also *Jitsugo kyūki*, RSG, 88.

[16] *Jitsugo kyūki*, RSG, 89; SSZ 3: 567.

[17] Rennyo had twenty-seven children in all; he married five times. His wives—Nyoryō, Renyū (d. 1470), Nyoshō (1448–1478), Shūnyo (d. 1486), and Rennō (1465–1518)—have been the subjects of a two-volume work by Fudeuchi Yukiko, *Rennyo Shōnin to sono gonin no tsumatachi* (Kanazawa: Hokkoku Shuppansha,

were no servants, there were occasions when he washed the babies' clothing himself.[18] Renjun (1464–1550), Rennyo's sixth son, reports that, because of the family's poverty, only Junnyo was raised at home.[19]

On the basis of passages such as these, it is possible to piece together some aspects of Rennyo's early years and to posit some of the factors at work in his life. These include the early separation from his mother, the lengthy period of dependency, first under his grandfather as head of the household and then under his father, and the complexity of his relationship with his stepmother, reflected in the problem of succession. Rennyo had to come to terms with each of these factors, in a setting marked by considerable poverty and invidious comparison with other branches of the Shinshū and branches of the Jōdoshū tracing their lineages directly to Hōnen.[20] This mix was in no sense determinative in shaping the course of his life, yet it is suggestive for a clearer understanding of some of the striking contradictions that have remained unresolved in treatments of Rennyo's life and thought.

A SECTARIAN EDUCATION

Ōtani Hongan-ji, the setting for Rennyo's early years, is reported to have consisted of an Amida Hall roughly eighteen feet square, a Founder's Hall thirty feet square, and a very small priest's dwelling

---

1985). As the mothers of Rennyo's thirteen sons and fourteen daughters, they provided the future leaders of the Honganji. See HS 1: 366–71; Kasahara, *Rennyo*, 9–12, 303–5; and the table at the conclusion of this work, listing Rennyo's wives and children.

[18] *Jitsugo kyūki*, RSG, 89; SSZ 3: 567.

[19] *Renjunki*, RSG, 62; HS 1: 366–71; Kasahara, *Rennyo*, 15–16. According to Renjun's record, Renjō (1446–1504), the second son, was sent into service at Nanzen-ji; Renkō (1450–1531), the third son, became a priest at Kekai-in, with Rensei (1455–1521), the fourth son, also serving there; Rengo (1468–1543), the seventh son, and Yūshin (1463–1490), the seventh daughter, were raised in Tanba prefecture; and Kengyoku (1448–1472) and Juson (1454–1516), the second and third daughters, became nuns at Shōju-an in Yoshida.

[20] The most important branches of the Shinshū at this time were the Bukkō-ji, the Kinshokuji, the Takada, and the Sanmonto (see Dobbins, *Jōdo Shinshū*, 112–31). The most significant of the branches of the Jōdoshū tracing their lineages directly to Hōnen were the Chinzei and the Seizan; in addition, there were the Jishū and the Ikkōshū, acknowledging Ippen and Ikkō Shunjō (1239–1287) respectively as their founders (see Dobbins, *Jōdo Shinshū*, 102–11). For a translation of Ippen's writings and an introduction to his thought, see Dennis Hirota's *No Abode: The Record of Ippen* (Kyoto: Ryūkoku University, 1986).

顯淨土真實信文類序

ソレオモンミレハ　信樂ヲ獲得スルコトハ

如來選擇ノ願心ヨリ發起ス　真心ヲ開闡セリ

スルコトハ　大聖矜哀ノ善巧ヨリ顯彰セリ

シカルニ　末代ノ道俗　近世ノ宗師　自性

4. Preface to the "Chapter on Faith," Kyōgyōshinshō, copied by Rennyo

with a servant's room in the rear, although there was no sign of a servant.[21] In effect, Hongan-ji might well have gone unnoticed, standing as it did in the shadow of more impressive temples in the Ōtani Higashiyama section of Kyoto. Within several hundred yards stood Shōren-in, under whose auspices Shinran's ordination had taken place two hundred and fifty years before Rennyo's.[22] Not far away was Chion-in, a Jōdoshū-related temple that burned down in 1431 but was rebuilt immediately through the good offices of the sixth shogun, Ashikaga Yoshinori (1394–1441).[23]

Following his ordination, Rennyo is said to have pursued doctrinal studies under his father's cousin, Keikaku, abbot of Daijō-in, Kōfuku-ji, Nara, and head of the Hossō sect.[24] Though traditional sources underscore the poverty of Rennyo's early years, they attempt at the same time to identify him with established sects that had connections with families at court. When misfortune later struck Ōtani Hongan-ji, however, no benefactor responded as Ashikaga Yoshinori had for Chion-in.

A passage from a memoir by Renjun suggests both the scope and intensity of Rennyo's studies during his long years of tutelage under his grandfather and father:

> [Rennyo] pored over the scriptures, reading *Kyōgyōshinshō* and *Rokuyōshō* continually and *Anjin ketsujōshō* to such an extent that he wore out three copies. He also questioned Master Zonnyo in detail about the tradition's fundamental teachings.[25]

Shinran's six-chapter *Kyōgyōshinshō*,[26] written in classical Chinese, is a major systematic treatise that serves as the foundational text for Shinshū tradition. In it, Shinran presents a radical reinterpretation of Pure Land teaching, locating it in the mainstream of Mahāyāna thought. Drawing on passages from the commentaries of the seven Pure Land masters, he establishes an authentic line of transmission for "the true essence of the Pure Land way." It is Rennyo's engagement with this text that, more than anything else, takes him to the heart of Shinran's thought.

---

[21] *Jitsugoki*, RSG, 143–44; Kasahara, *Rennyo*, 4.

[22] Shinran was ordained in 1181 under its third head priest, Jien. See SSJ, 287–88.

[23] Coates, Harper Havelock and Ryugaku Ishizuka, trans., *Honen the Buddhist Saint: His Life and Teaching*, compiled by Imperial Order (Kyoto: Chion-in, 1925), 647.

[24] SSG, 123; HS 1: 297–99.

[25] *Renjunki*, RSG, 64; HS 1: 297.

[26] *Kyōgyōshinshō*, SSZ 2: 1–203.

Zonkaku's ten-chapter *Rokuyōshō*,[27] also in classical Chinese, is the first written commentary on *Kyōgyōshinshō*. In its explanation of terms and clarification of doctrine, it came to be regarded as authoritative for the Honganji branch of the Shinshū. Rennyo's own interpretation and popularization of Shinran's teaching owes much to Zonkaku's commentary and his other writings.

The third work listed by Renjun is the two-part *Anjin ketsujōshō*.[28] Two positions have generally been taken as to its origin: Nishi Honganji scholars have stressed sectarian authorship, possibly that of Kakunyo or Zonkaku, and included it with Kakunyo's works in the *Shinshū hōyō*;[29] Higashi scholars have held that the author was connected with the Seizan branch of the Jōdoshū, which traces its lineage through Shōkū (1177–1247)[30] directly to Hōnen, omitting Shinran and his successors in the Shinshū. The fact remains that Rennyo's devotion to this text is crucial for understanding the distinctive quality of his interpretation and popularization of Shinran's teaching.[31]

In his use of the term "scriptures" (*shōgyō* 聖教) in the passage above, Renjun refers explicitly to the works listed but implicitly to the texts on which they are based — the three Pure Land sūtras and the commentaries written by the seven Pure Land masters.[32] It should be pointed out that, while Shinran worked through these texts exhaustively in writing and revising *Kyōgyōshinshō* and in compiling separate collections of important passages such as *Jōdo monrui jushō*, Rennyo read the texts largely through Shinran's eyes; further, he approached *Kyōgyōshinshō* in the light of Zonkaku's commentary, *Rokuyōshō*.

Renjun's concluding remark in this passage is that Rennyo insistently questioned his father, Zonnyo, about the teaching. It seems fair to surmise that his questions may have been stimulated by works that Zonnyo copied on request or for presentation to those who might affiliate with the Honganji. When Rennyo was nine, Zonnyo copied part one of *Anjin ketsujōshō* and presented it to Shōjun, priest of Jōkō-ji,

---

[27] *Rokuyōshō*, SSZ 2: 205–442.

[28] *Anjin ketsujōshō*, SSZ 3: 615–38.

[29] A collection of Shinshū texts in thirty-one volumes, compiled between 1759 and 1765.

[30] For a comparison of Shōkū's thought with that of Shinran, see Dennis Hirota, "Religious Transformation in Shinran and Shōku," *The Pure Land: Journal of Pure Land Buddhism*, n.s., 4 (1987): 57–69.

[31] A discussion of Rennyo's use of *Anjin ketsujōshō* in his formulation of the nenbutsu follows in chapter three.

[32] Chapter five discusses Shinran's use of the term *shōgyō* and its expanding meaning in Shinshū tradition.

in Shinano, Echigo province; in the eighth month of the following year, Ōei 32 (1425), he copied the second part and presented it to Shōjun, together with copies of instructional texts—*Kyōkeshū*, Kakunyo's *Shinran den'e*, and three texts by Zonkaku: *Jimyōshō*, *Jōdo shinyōshō*, and *Shojin hongaishū*. Earlier in the year, he had given Shōjun two other copies of works by Zonkaku, *Ketchishō* and *Jōdo kenmonshū*.[33]

The inclusion of *Anjin ketsujōshō* and *Shojin hongaishū* among the texts presented to Shōjun suggests the breadth of the textual tradition to which Rennyo was exposed in his early years. *Shojin hongaishū* accommodates Shinran's teaching to popular religious attitudes based on the theory of *honji suijaku* 本地垂迹 ; this theory maintains that the various kami are local manifestations (*suijaku*) of particular buddhas and bodhisattvas—representatives of an underlying reality (*honji*) expressed in Buddhist symbols. An additional text of the same genre, copied by Zonnyo and available to Rennyo, was *Shinran Shōnin goin'en hidenshō*, of uncertain authorship. This work, centering on the teaching of salvation through the nenbutsu for those in lay life, gives an account of Shinran's experience in terms responsive to the religious consciousness of common people.[34]

Shinran's own writings were, however, central to the tradition to which Rennyo was introduced; when he was twelve, his grandfather, Gyōnyo, copied *Kyōgyōshinshō*—again for presentation to Jōkō-ji.[35] The preservation of documents copied by both Gyōnyo and Zonnyo supports Renjun's testimony that from his earliest years Rennyo was exposed not only to the formal texts of Shinshū tradition, but also to popular interpretations of Pure Land teachings.[36]

A crucial part of Zonnyo's guidance of Rennyo was the example he provided during preaching and instructional tours, particularly in Ōmi province and the Hokuriku. In Ōmi, the focus of activities was at Honpuku-ji, Katada, on the western shore of Lake Biwa, and at Kane-

---

[33] During Rennyo's early years, his grandfather and father copied other texts for presentations. Gyōnyo copied Kakunyo's *Kudenshō* in 1427, and *Shūjishō* and *Gaijashō* in 1430; Zonnyo copied Zonkaku's *Shojin hongaishū* in 1438 and *Shinran Shōnin goin'en hidenshō* in 1450. In 1437, he presented a copy of Shinran's *Sanjō wasan* to Senkō-ji in Kaga province, and in 1439, copies of *Jimyōshō* and *Kyōkeshū*. For data on texts and dates, see Honganji Shiryō Kenkyūjo, ed., *Honganji nenpyō* (hereafter cited as HN; Kyoto: Jōdo Shinshū Honganjiha, 1981), 55–60. See also SSG, 121–22; HS 1: 299–301 offers additional information.

[34] See SSG, 121–29.

[35] HN, 56.

[36] For a list of texts presented by Gyōnyo and Zonnyo, see HS 1: 275–78; for texts copied by Zonnyo, see HS 1: 279–81.

gamori on the eastern shore. In the Hokuriku, Zonnyo built on the foundations laid by the missionary efforts of Kakunyo and Zonkaku in their tour of Echizen province in 1311 and of Shakunyo in the same area during his tenure as head of the Honganji.[37] In Echizen province, at Ishida, Zonnyo founded Saikō-ji; in Kaga province, he instructed groups at Ogio and Fukuda and donated chapters of Shinran's illustrated biography, *Shinran den'e*, and other texts to Senshō-ji, Senkō-ji, and Kōtoku-ji.[38]

Even before 1440, when Zonnyo became head of the Honganji, father and son had the opportunity to copy texts side by side and to discuss them as they traveled together.[39] One of the earliest extant texts copied by Rennyo is Shinran's *Jōdo monrui jushō*, a work in Japanese abstracting the core of the teaching found in *Kyōgyōshinshō*; he copied the text in 1434, the same year that Zonnyo gave permission for Shinran's *Gutokushō* to be copied by the priest at Jōkō-ji.[40] For more than three decades, until Zonnyo's death in 1457, Rennyo worked closely with his father to present Shinran's teaching in popular terms and to broaden the institutional base of the Honganji, especially in Ōmi province and the Hokuriku.

As might be expected, among the forty extant texts identified as having been copied by Rennyo are many by Shinran, Kakunyo, and Zonkaku.[41] Of Shinran's works, there are five copies of *Sanjō wasan*, the first and last being given to Kyōjun of Kinhō-ji, Kyoto, in 1436 and 1458 respectively; *Gutokushō*, copied in 1446, *Mattōshō* in 1447, and *Kyōgyōshinshō* with his father in 1451. Among Kakunyo's writings are copies of *Kudenshō*, given to the priest at Fukuda-ji, Ōmi province in 1438, and to Hōen, Kyūhō-ji, Kawachi province in 1467; *Shinran den'e* in 1449, *Saiyōshō* in 1457, and *Hōonkō shiki* in 1468. Following his father's example, Rennyo copied a number of Zonkaku's writings, including *Jōdo shinyōshō* in 1438 and again in 1441; *Nyonin ōjō kikigaki* in 1449, *Rokuyōshō* in 1458, *Tandokumon* in 1461, and *Jōdo kenmonshū* in 1477. Of special significance among the works whose authors have not

---

[37] For example, Shakunyo had founded Zuisen-ji in Inami, Etchū province, in the first year of Meitoku (1390).

[38] SSG, 122–23.

[39] For a discussion of the father-son relationship, see Ishida Yoshihito, "Rennyo to sono chichi Zonnyo," in *Rennyo*, ed. Minami Midō Shinbun (Osaka: Nanba Betsuin, 1986), 147–59.

[40] HN, 57.

[41] For a list of texts copied by Rennyo between his twentieth and eighty-second years, see Murakami Sokusui et al., eds., *Kōza: Shinran no shisō*, vol. 8, *Shinran shisō no shūyaku to tenkai* (Tokyo: Kyōiku Shinchōsha, 1978), 90.

been established is *Anjin ketsujōshō*, which Rennyo copied in 1447.[42] Much of the material attributed to Zonkaku, together with a number of other works of uncertain authorship such as *Gose monogatari*, copied in 1439, belong to a literary genre known as sermon handbooks (*dangibon* 談義本), prepared for instructing those whose religious orientation was primarily informed by Japanese folk tradition.[43]

The number and diversity of texts copied by Rennyo is remarkable for a person who, in addition to teaching and preaching, bore extensive administrative and family responsibilities. His devotion to copying the scriptures laid a firm foundation for his own writings, which began to appear in the late 1450s and continued until 1498, the year before he died. Further, the existence of these hand-copied texts supports the memoir writers' view that Rennyo was a man of prodigious energy and extraordinary diligence. While he was never formally trained as a scholar, he was well-grounded in both the traditional and popular writings of the Pure Land textual corpus. At the time of Zonnyo's death, Rennyo assumed full responsibility as the leader of the Honganji for intensifying a program of expansion; it is a tribute to the quality of the many years of tutelage by his father and his grandfather that he was more than ready for the task.

This account of Rennyo's sectarian education, based largely on the memoirs, invites comparison with what we know of Shinran's early life. Both the writers of Rennyo's memoirs and Kakunyo, Shinran's first biographer in *Godenshō*, subordinate the historical data to an idealization of their subjects' achievements.[44] Not to be discounted, however, are the striking differences in their respective familial, social, and political settings, so critical for the development of their thought.

Shinran entered a monastic community at Mt. Hiei at age nine, following the death of his parents; Rennyo was born into a family that had provided priests for generations in an unbroken lineage. Shinran as a young boy had little choice but to make a place for himself in one of the many temples scattered over Mt. Hiei; Rennyo's household was Ōtani Hongan-ji, the family dwelling for more than a hundred and fifty years. At twenty-nine, Shinran discovered Hōnen and his nenbutsu teaching, abandoning a twenty-year search on Mt. Hiei for a satisfactory religious practice; Rennyo grew up nurtured on a well-defined body of Shinshū and Pure Land texts and participating in a

---

[42] Where we have found discrepancies in the dating of the texts between the listing in Murakami Sokusui et al., eds., *Kōza: Shinran no shisō*, vol. 8: 90, and HN, we have followed the latter. Also see HS 1: 281–84.

[43] For a discussion of the *dangibon*, see SSG, 114–17.

[44] *Godenshō*, SSZ 3: 639–54.

firmly-established pattern of religious activities. Shinran, born in a lay household, became a monk — only to declare later that he was neither a monk nor one in worldly life; Rennyo's position as a priest was anticipated from the moment of his birth and continued until his death at eighty-five. Finally, Shinran vigorously resisted any tendency among his followers to idealize his role as a religious leader or to institutionalize his teaching as a new departure.[45] Texts such as Yuien's *Tannishō* reveal the quality of his personal piety — a piety grounded in absolute trust in Amida's Vow and in confidence that his faith was one with that of his master, Hōnen. On the other hand, both Rennyo and the writers of his memoirs take for granted Kakunyo's emphasis on the unique quality of Shinran's teaching and never question the historical basis for Kakunyo's contention that Shinran was founder of the Jōdo Shinshū as a sectarian movement.

In light of our earlier discussion of traditional piety, we might ask to what extent Rennyo's sectarian education introduced him to Shinshū tradition as a pattern of religious life that is "the locus of both the mundane and the transcendent, unbifurcated." In what sense did Rennyo stand beside Shinran on the ground of Amida's Vow-mind in the historical flow of that Vow's manifestation in Śākyamuni's teaching, in the commentaries of the seven Pure Land masters, and in the words of Hōnen? In responding to this question, we will need to bear in mind the consequences of Kakunyo's apotheosization of Shinran as founder of a sectarian tradition emphasizing hereditary transmission of the teaching as a mark of legitimacy. Rennyo's perception of the relationship of the transcendent and the mundane will differ from that of Shinran, in that the sectarian tradition — the Honganji, as bearer of the teaching, is now reified as the manifestation of Amida's Vow-mind.

SUCCESSION AS HEAD PRIEST

Primogeniture had never been an established practice for the Honganji; rather, it was customary for the head priest, as custodian of the Founder's Hall, to designate his successor by written deed from among Shinran's male hereditary descendants. Although other deeds of transfer have been preserved, no copy of Zonnyo's deed is available; it is unknown whether one was ever drafted.[46]

At the time of Zonnyo's death in the first year of Chōroku (1457),

---

[45] *Tannishō*, SSZ 2: 773–74.
[46] HS 1: 304.

Rennyo was forty-three; his stepbrother Ōgen was twenty-five. Nyoen, Rennyo's stepmother, ambitious for her own son to succeed Zonnyo, arranged for Ōgen to officiate at his father's funeral. She elicited support for Ōgen's candidacy among Shinran's descendants, priests in leading temples, and members of the immediate family, including Kūkaku, a younger brother of Zonnyo.[47] The sole opposition to Nyoen's plan came from Nyojō (Senyū; 1412–1460), youngest brother of Zonnyo, uncle of both Rennyo and Ōgen, and an influential leader of the Honganji in the Hokuriku.[48] Nyojō argued that Zonnyo had always treated Rennyo, his only son for nineteen years, as his prospective heir and that Rennyo had frequently represented his father in copying and making presentations of texts. Nyojō, only three years senior to Rennyo, had grown up with him at Ōtani Hongan-ji and was adamant that he was qualified in every respect to succeed Zonnyo.[49]

Nyojō's arguments prevailed, and Rennyo assumed the office of custodian and eighth head priest with the backing of Honganji-related congregations as a whole. He owed much to Nyojō for his unwavering support and, from then on, showed special concern for the welfare of Honsen-ji. After Nyojō's death in 1460, Rennyo appointed Renjō, his second son, to be priest in charge.[50] As a result, Rennyo's ties with congregations in the Hokuriku were greatly strengthened. It was in this same region that Rennyo was to spend the most fruitful period of his life, 1471–1475, in formulating an interpretation of Shinran's teaching that would play a major role in the dramatic growth of the Honganji.

In 1458, the year after his succession, Rennyo presented copies of *Sanjō wasan* and *Rokuyōshō* to temples in Kyoto and Kaga respectively, consolidating relationships that had been established earlier. The center for his missionary activities, however, was Ōmi province. In 1460, he made presentations of hanging scrolls inscribed with Amida's Name (*myōgō* 名号) in ten characters 帰命尽十方無碍光如来 (*ki-myō-jin-jip-pō-mu-ge-kō-nyo-rai*)[51] to a number of congregations (*dōjō* 道場) and temples

---

[47] *Jitsugoki*, RSG, 145–46; HS 1: 303–5.

[48] Nyojō established Honsen-ji at Futamata, Kaga province, in 1442; he was also in charge of Zuisen-ji in Etchū province.

[49] Kitanishi Hiromu, stressing the apolitical aspect of Rennyo's piety, cites evidence that he offered to withdraw his candidacy and thus avoid confrontation with his stepmother over the issue of succession; see "Rennyo Shōnin to Honganji kyōdan," *Shūkyō* 329/7 (1989): 6–11.

[50] Subsequently, Rennyo's seventh and tenth sons, Rengo and Jitsugo, were associated with Honsen-ji; see *Jitsugoki*, RSG, 146–47; HS 1: 303–5.

[51] The Name, "[I] take refuge in the Tathāgata of unhindered light filling the ten directions," was written in gold letters against a dark blue background.

5. Dual seated portrait of Shinran and Rennyo

6. The Name in ten characters (kōmyō jūji myōgō) in Rennyo's hand

in Ōmi province. In this, he was following a precedent set by Kakunyo, who had enshrined a similar inscription in the mausoleum at Ōtani Hongan-ji and explained in *Gaijashō* that this was the main image (*honzon* 本尊) in the Shinshū.[52]

In 1460, among those receiving the Name in ten characters was Hōjū (1397–1479) of Honpuku-ji at Katada, Ōmi; he had first come to Ōtani Hongan-ji on pilgrimage in 1413, found it virtually deserted, and continued on to Bukkō-ji. Later, under Zonnyo's guidance, Hōjū became a devoted member of the Honganji. Rennyo made every effort to deepen his ties with Hōjū; in 1461, he presented the congregation at Katada with a portrait of Shinran that included his own portrait added below (*renzazō* 連座像 ; see illustration 5).[53] Three years later, in 1464, Rennyo gave Hōjū a copy of *Shinran den'e*. Rennyo's care in nurturing his relationship with Hōjū, an influential figure in Ōmi province, and with his followers at Katada was to prove fortuitous for the Honganji in its subsequent trials.

In this period, Rennyo's missionary activity extended also to the eastern shore of Lake Biwa, Ōmi province. In 1460, he wrote *Shōshinge taii*, an explanatory outline in Japanese of Shinran's *Shōshinge*, at the request of Dōsai (1399–1488) at Kanegamori.[54] Dōsai, who had served Ōtani Hongan-ji during the period of Zonnyo's leadership, met frequently with Rennyo and helped consolidate support in Ōmi.[55] At the same time, the Honganji's influence was spreading in Mikawa and Settsu provinces. Within ten years, there were over a hundred congregations in Mikawa, Owari, and Ise provinces. There is evidence that, in Settsu in 1463, members of the Bukkōji were responding to Rennyo's teachings and transferring their allegiance to the Honganji.[56]

In the years immediately following his succession, Rennyo intensified activities begun by his father to expand the influence of the Honganji. His presentation of inscriptions of Amida's Name (see illustration 6), portraits of Shinran, and serial portraits of head priests of the Honganji provided an effective instrument for strengthening

---

[52] HS 1: 312–13. A discussion of the main image follows in chapter three.

[53] Also known as *nisonzō* 二尊像 ; see Chiba Jōryū, ed., *Honpukujishi* (Kyoto: Dōbōsha, 1980), 299. For an illustration of dual portraits of Shinran and Rennyo, see Miyazaki Enjun, Okada Yuzuru, and Horie Tomohiko, *Nishi Honganji: Sono bijutsu to rekishi* (Kyoto: Tankō Shinsha, 1961), 216. Also see reproductions of four serial portraits including Rennyo in Shinkō no Zōkeiteki Hyōgen Kenkyū Iinkai, ed., *Shinshū jūhō shuei*, vol. 9 (Kyoto: Dōbōsha, 1988), 22–29.

[54] HS 1: 309–10.

[55] HS 1: 307.

[56] HS 1: 307–9.

ties with influential leaders such as Hōjū and Dōsai. Nevertheless, it is Rennyo's writings, particularly his letters, that mark his major contribution to the tradition, carrying him far beyond anything achieved by his predecessors.

Rennyo's selection of Shinran's *Shōshinge* for identifying and commenting on the essential points of the teaching in his longest prose work, *Shōshinge taii*, underscores the firm grounding he had received under the tutelage of his grandfather and father. *Shōshinge*, in classical Chinese, is a work of one hundred and twenty lines in quatrains, concluding the chapter on practice (*gyō* 行) in *Kyōgyōshinshō* and serving as a transition to the chapter on faith (*shin* 信). An outline of Pure Land teaching, it sums up the essentials of both the *Larger Sūtra* and the commentaries of the seven Pure Land masters. Although *Shōshinge taii* is not of major literary or doctrinal consequence, it is significant as the first work to be attributed to a leader of the Honganji since the writings of Kakunyo over a century earlier. The sectarian tradition fails to credit Zennyo and Shakunyo, the fourth and fifth head priests, with any significant creative role in the Honganji's intellectual or institutional history, seconding the critical attitude Rennyo is said to have taken toward them.[57]

Rennyo's first extant letter, written in the third month of Kanshō 2 (1461) and addressed to Dōsai, translates the fundamental tenets of Shinran's teaching into colloquial terms. This letter provides a benchmark for tracing the subsequent development of Rennyo's thought as reflected in his interpretation of Shinran's teaching. The text reads:

> The single way of faith taught by our tradition's master [Shinran] is that lay people should not concern themselves with the weight of their evil karma or with the unending delusions and attachments of their minds; rather, they should steadfastly discard their mistaken attachment to the sundry practices and disciplines and simply take refuge in the compassionate vow of Amida Tathāgata; and with the awakening of the one thought-moment in which they entrust themselves single-heartedly and without doubt, Amida Tathāgata immediately sends forth his light and embraces them. This means that we are saved by the Buddha; it also signifies that faith is given by the Tathāgata.
>
> Therefore, once [this is understood], if [people] say the Name, they should not think, "Buddha, please save me" (*butsu tasuke tamae* 仏たすけたまえ). They should simply realize that they are readily

---

[57] *Jitsugo kyūki*, RSG, 111–12; SSZ 3: 587–88. See also RSI, 333 (#112/4:5); SSZ 3: 481–82; and Shigematsu Akihisa, "Hokuriku ni okeru Rennyo no katsudō," in *Chūsei Shinshū shisō no kenkyū* (Tokyo: Yoshikawa Kōbunkan, 1986), 396–97.

saved with the one thought-moment of faith in which they entrust themselves to Amida, and that the nenbutsu is an expression of overwhelming gratitude to Amida Tathāgata for his benevolence in having saved them. This is [the understanding] of a true practicer of the exclusive practice [of the nenbutsu] and single-mindedness; it is also what is meant by "completing the cause [of birth] in ordinary life, with the awakening of the one thought-moment" (*ichinen hokki heizei gōjō* 一念発起平生業成).[58]

The first half of the letter attempts to explain the process whereby faith is realized; the mention of Amida's light might suggest the ten-character inscription of the Name that Rennyo distributed during this period. The second half of the letter defines true practicers as those who take refuge in Amida and recognize the nenbutsu as an expression of gratitude, not of supplication. Since birth in the Pure Land is assured at the moment of entrusting, petitionary nenbutsu recitation, as practiced by nenbutsu devotees in branches of the Jōdoshū and in the Jishū, becomes meaningless. Relating birth in the Pure Land to a person's own efforts — even in a single utterance of the nenbutsu — was antithetical to Shinran's teaching of the salvific quality of Amida's Primal Vow through Other Power. In subsequent letters, however, Rennyo incorporates the phrase *tasuke tamae* into Shinshū teaching and piety as an expedient for instructing those followers for whom it was already a meaningful religious symbol.[59]

The content of Rennyo's first letter reveals both continuity and change in relation to Shinran's expressions of religious thought. Given that the social and institutional context of this letter was significantly different from that of Shinran's works some two hundred years earlier, it is not surprising to find that the meaning of gratitude, for example, was open to new interpretation. In the context of Rennyo's Honganji, the issue may be pressed as to what extent the recipient of benevolence responded to Amida Tathāgata, and to what extent to Amida's repre-

---

58 RSI, 47 (#1).

59 *Ichigon hōdan*, a collection of sayings that guided the lives of recluses and wandering monks — holy men (*hijiri* 聖) — in medieval Japan, includes six instances of the use of the phrase "*butsu* (or *hotoke*) *tasuke tamae*" (#38, #57, #107) or "*tasuke tamae Amida butsu*" (#113, #116, #120). The latter instances occur in sayings attributed to Hōnen, Shōkō (Benchō; 1162–1238), and Nen'a (Ryōchū; 1199–1287) representing the Chinzei branch of the Jōdoshū. There are no sayings specifically attributed to Shōku, founder of the Seizan, or to others in that strand of Pure Land tradition. See translation of *Ichigon hōdan* by Dennis Hirota, *Plain Words on the Pure Land Way: Sayings of the Wandering Monks of Medieval Japan* (Kyoto: Ryūkoku University, 1989).

sentative, Rennyo, the leader of the Honganji.[60] As we have seen, memoirs compiled in the late sixteenth century, after the Honganji had become a powerful and tightly structured religious order, indicate that participants in the Shinshū identified Rennyo with Amida and his words with Amida's teaching.[61]

A similar pattern of apotheosization is found in Kakunyo's biography of Shinran, portraying him as the founder of a religious movement. There is, however, a major difference in how Shinran and Rennyo perceived themselves as participants in Pure Land tradition: whereas Shinran saw himself simply as a follower of the true Pure Land way taught by Hōnen, Rennyo held himself responsible for restoring Shinran's teaching, entrusted to the Honganji.

ŌTANI HONGAN-JI DESTROYED

The climactic event in Rennyo's middle years was the destruction of his ancestral home and temple at Ōtani Hongan-ji in 1465. This event was to prove pivotal for his shaping of Shinran's teaching and Kakunyo's vision into a powerful religious order during the most important phase of his life, beginning in the third year of Bunmei (1471) with his move to Yoshizaki in the Hokuriku.

The letter Rennyo addressed to Dōsai in 1461 signaled a new phase in his efforts to revive and restore the fortunes of the Honganji. By enlisting the support of local leaders in Ōmi province – Dōsai and, in particular, Hōjū of Honpuku-ji, leader of the Katada congregations – Rennyo substantially broadened the economic base of the Honganji. Hōjū, for example, had a strong following among fishermen, weavers, merchants, and farmers on the western shore of Lake Biwa – people who were unusually prosperous as a result of their strategic location on the lake and their ability to control the transportation and trade routes across it. In addition, Katada was a base for itinerant merchants who traveled throughout Japan. Rennyo's demonstrated ability to communicate with people of diverse backgrounds throughout his years of leadership may well derive from his experiences in Katada.[62]

While Rennyo's activities served to unify the congregations at Tahara, Kanegamori, Akanoi, and Katada, scattered around Lake

---

[60] For an extended discussion of this issue, see chapter six.

[61] See *Jitsugo kyūki*, RSG, 85, 133; SSZ 3: 563, 608.

[62] Both *Honpukuji yuraiki* and *Honpukuji atogaki* in Chiba, ed., *Honpukuji kyūki*, give detailed accounts of the Katada congregations during this period.

Biwa at the center of Ōmi province, the monks at Enryaku-ji[63] on Mt. Hiei, overlooking the lake at its southwest corner, construed the Honganji's growing strength as a threat to their interests. Since the days of Kakunyo, they had exercised control over Ōtani Hongan-ji in various ways and exacted tribute from it as a branch temple. Until this time, their prerogatives had not been seriously challenged, and the Honganji had been obliged to accept a weak economic base.[64]

As the sect began to prosper under Rennyo's leadership, demands from Enryaku-ji may have increased; perhaps the Honganji's response was still insufficient, or perhaps all of Enryaku-ji's terms could not be met.[65] In any event, on Kanshō 6 (1465).1.8, the monks seized upon Rennyo's missionary activities as an occasion to draw up a resolution to take action against the Honganji; the reasons they stipulated were doctrinal rather than economic:

> In particular, they have adopted the name "Unhindered Light" (*mugekō* 無碍光) and are steadily building up the sect and preaching to ignorant men and women. Because they address the lowly, young and old, they are forming groups and organizing factions everywhere in the villages and countryside. Furthermore, they burn Buddha images and sūtras and belittle the kami as "[buddhas and bodhisattvas] appearing in diminished light" (*shinmei wakō* 神明和光). Their perverse behavior darkens our sight, and [reports of] their reckless evildoing fill our ears. On the one hand, they are enemies of the Buddha and, on the other, enemies of the kami; for the sake of the right dharma and of the nation, they must be suppressed.[66]

---

[63] The head temple of the Tendai sect, dating from 785, when Saichō (767–822) built a hut on Mt. Hiei for study and practice. Three years later, it became a temple, Hieizan-ji; in 823 it received its current name by imperial order.

[64] Shigematsu Akihisa, "Rennyo no Yoshizaki shinshutsu no keii," in *Shinshūshi no kenkyū*, ed. Miyazaki Enjun Hakase Kanreki Kinenkai (Kyoto: Nagata Bunshōdō, 1966), 287. Shigematsu summarizes the Honganji's predicament at the time of its destruction by locating and describing the Shinshū congregations: within the Kyoto area, the Bukkōji was the most prosperous; within the area from Ōmi province to Yamato, the Kinshokuji was the strongest; and from the Kantō to the Hokuriku, the Senjuji at Takada, under the leadership of Shin'e (1434–1512), was the most expansive. There seemed to be barely enough area for the Honganji to wedge itself in. The fact that Rennyo had, albeit reluctantly, reached the point of resisting the forces on Mt. Hiei was probably unavoidable, given the Honganji's economic situation (287–88).

[65] HS 1: 311.

[66] HS 1: 311. See also Chiba, *Honganji monogatari*, 174–75, and Kitanishi Hiromu, "Honganji kyōdan no seiritsu to sono tenkai: Shūkyōsei sōshitsu no ichidan'men," in *Honganji kyōdan: Shinran wa gendai ni yomigaeru ka*, eds. Uehara Senroku and Matsugi Nobuhiko (Tokyo: Gakugei Shorin, 1971), 87.

The monks' label for the Honganji, "Unhindered Light," probably derived from the fact that the ten-character inscription of Amida's Name—which Rennyo presented to individuals and congregations in the region—was used as the main image. Ten such inscriptions presented in Ōmi province during the five-year period preceding Ōtani Hongan-ji's destruction have been preserved.[67]

On the day after the resolution was issued, a group of about a hundred and fifty monks from Saitō-in on Mt. Hiei attacked and destroyed much of Ōtani Hongan-ji. Although there had been rumors of the impending attack, it came more swiftly than expected. Notice had gone out to followers in the surrounding areas, but only ten guards were present when the monks from Mt. Hiei arrived. They found the gate unbarred, the guards napping, and Rennyo watching a cooper at work. The cooper, reacting swiftly, pretended that he was one of the attackers, seized Rennyo, and led him out, thus enabling him to take shelter at Jōhō-ji, a nearby Tendai temple. Plunder and destruction followed before the attackers were finally routed by a force of about two hundred, led by eighty armored men from Katada.[68]

When followers from the outlying provinces arrived in Katada, a lengthy debate ensued as to whether to respond to Mt. Hiei on points of doctrine or with a monetary offering. Rennyo opposed the latter until Nyokō of Sasaki, Mikawa province, convinced him that he could settle the matter quickly by raising the money himself.[69] On the appointed day, Hōjū and Nyokō climbed Mt. Hiei with a number of others and paid an indemnity through the mediation of Jōhō-ji; in addition, the Honganji accepted status as a branch of Saitō-in and agreed to the payment of a yearly fee.[70] The matter did not end there, however, for on the twenty-first day of the third month, forces from Mt. Hiei attacked again, devastating whatever had been left from the first assault.[71]

With the destruction of Ōtani Hongan-ji, Rennyo lost his birthplace and home of over fifty years. On a public level, the burning of Hongan-ji violated a pilgrimage center that had come to have deep meaning for the scattered Shinshū congregations. Thus Rennyo suffered

---

[67] HS 1: 312–14. More detailed information is available in HN, 63–65.

[68] *Honpukuji yuraiki*, 329–30, and *Honpukuji atogaki*, 364, in Chiba, ed., *Honpukuji kyūki*, 329–30; HS 1: 310, 314.

[69] *Honpukuji yuraiki*, 330–31, and *Honpukuji atogaki*, 367, in Chiba, ed., *Honpukuji kyūki*.

[70] HS 1: 314–15; *Honpukuji atogaki*, 367, in Chiba, ed., *Honpukuji kyūki*; Kitanishi, "Honganji kyōdan no seiritsu to sono tenkai," 87.

[71] HS 1: 315.

the double loss of his own ancestral home and his community's spiritual base. Yet, just as Shinran's exile had been the occasion for the maturation of his faith and the opening of new areas in the Hokuriku and the Kantō for teaching and preaching, so the destruction of the buildings at Ōtani released Rennyo to take a major step in fulfilling his mission to revive and restore the tradition.

Rennyo's own writings never refer to the destruction of Ōtani Hongan-ji. The only extant letter from this period was written during the following year, Bunshō 1 (1466); it appears to be a memorandum for preaching and teaching, including a passage on faith from the *Contemplation Sūtra* and quotations from Nāgārjuna, T'an-luan, Shan-tao, and Shinran.[72] This letter and the record of his other activities suggest his steadiness of purpose in the face of adversity. For example, in the same year, he copied *Kyōgyōshinshō* and, on the twenty-first day of the eleventh month, observed the annual thanksgiving services at Kanegamori, Ōmi province.[73] Records such as this belie the judgment of scholars who see Rennyo's activities primarily in terms of political strategy.

After a series of moves, Rennyo settled in Katada early in the second month of Ōnin 1 (1467); the Ōnin War (1467–1477), named for the era in which it began, had erupted full force in Kyoto the month before. In Katada, Rennyo was evidently able to enjoy a brief period of relative quiet with his family; he celebrated the thanksgiving services there on the twenty-first of the eleventh month and rejoiced in being able to teach and visit followers' homes freely.[74]

The next year, the monks of Mt. Hiei threatened to attack the Katada congregations, alleging acts of piracy on Lake Biwa. Alarmed for the safety of the founder's image, Rennyo moved on Ōnin 2 (1468).3.12 to lodgings in Ōtsu provided by Dōkaku, a member of the Honpuku-ji congregation;[75] here, he was under the protection of Mii-dera through Dōkaku's relationship with its branch temple, Mantoku-in.[76] His move

---

[72] RSI, 48–50 (#2).

[73] HN, 65.

[74] HS 1: 317; Chiba, *Honganji monogatari*, 184–85.

[75] *Honpukuji atogaki*, in Chiba, ed., *Honpukuji kyūki*, 368; Chiba, *Honganji monogatari*, 187. HS 1: 320, cites Bunmei 1 (1469).2.13 as the date for the move, as does HN, 66 (following *Honpukuji yuraiki*).

[76] *Honganji monogatari*, 187. Mii-dera, formally named Onjō-ji, is the head temple of the Jimon branch of the Tendai sect. First built in 674, the temple was established as a branch temple of Enryaku-ji in 858 by Enchin (814–891). In the years that followed, the two temples were frequently in conflict; Mii-dera was burned down several times by monks from Enryaku-ji. At this point, however, the two temples evidently exercised a policy of mutual restraint (Chiba, *Honganji monogatari*, 187).

was none too soon, for within the month, the Mt. Hiei monks successfully attacked the Katada holdings, reducing homes to ashes and eventually forcing payment of a large indemnity.[77] In the first year of Bunmei (1469), in yet another move, Rennyo built a temple in the village of Chikamatsu,[78] where he was as before under the protection of Mii-dera. The founder's image was to remain here until after Rennyo's completion of the Founder's Hall at Yamashina Hongan-ji in 1480.[79]

Records of Rennyo's activities in the years following the destruction of Ōtani Hongan-ji focus on his frequent moves to ensure the safety of the founder's image. The thread of continuity in these moves is his dependence on the direct and indirect support of Hōjū and the Katada congregations. Yet the problems he faced were by no means unusual during the Ōnin War, when all institutions were caught up in the shifting political fortunes of those seeking power with the decline of the Ashikaga shogunate.

Amidst such turmoil, Rennyo did not allow himself to be diverted from working out an independent and aggressive course of action. On Ōnin 2 (1468).3.28, he revised an earlier deed of succession and designated his fifth son, Jitsunyo, as custodian of the Founder's Hall at Ōtani Hongan-ji.[80] This may appear to be a curious decision in that the temple had been physically destroyed, but Rennyo must have been fully confident that it would eventually be replaced. He was perhaps more fearful that there would be a repetition of the kind of succession dispute that he himself had experienced in competition with Ōgen. In an earlier draft of the deed dated Bunshō 1 (1466), he had named his eldest son, Junnyo, to the position; Junnyo, however, declined on the grounds that he was insufficiently prepared. Since Jitsunyo, Rennyo's second choice, was only eleven in 1468, Junnyo was charged with the responsibility of protecting the founder's image.[81] Meanwhile, at the site of the ruins at Ōtani Higashiyama, Inoue Ganchi, formerly of Arai in Echizen province, built a small hall from which he guarded Shinran's grave, a duty reportedly passed on to his descendants.[82]

Rennyo's disposition of the problem of succession and his concern to find a suitable place for the safekeeping of the founder's image anticipated his momentous decision to shift the focus of his preaching

[77] *Honpukuji atogaki*, in Chiba, ed., *Honpukuji kyūki*, 368–69.

[78] The Chikamatsu *bōsha* 坊舎 , later known as Kenshō-ji, stood on the site of the present Chikamatsu Betsu-in.

[79] HS 1: 320; 340–43.

[80] RSI, 509 (#214).

[81] HN, 65. For further discussion, see HS 1: 317–8; Kasahara, *Rennyo*, 117.

[82] HS 1: 320–21.

and missionary activities to the Hokuriku. Many factors may have influenced this decision; both sectarian scholars and historians have offered a variety of explanations for his move to Yoshizaki, located in Echizen province and bordering on Kaga, in the Hokuriku.[83]

As with any decisive change, it was a movement both away from something familiar and established and toward new opportunities. At the time Rennyo left the Kinai region[84] in the fifth month of Bunmei 3 (1471), the Ōnin war had ravaged the area for almost five years. In addition, the opposition of the established Buddhist sects centered at Kyoto and Nara appeared to threaten any significant opportunity for the Honganji's expansion. Rennyo must have realized by the late 1460s that the possibilities for growth in the Kinai had peaked, at least for the time being. The Hokuriku, on the other hand, presented an obvious and attractive alternative. Although the precise point at which Rennyo made his decision to leave for the Hokuriku is unclear, the decision itself was the culmination of a process that was intensified with the destruction of Ōtani Hongan-ji. Some of the positive reasons for his decision are better understood given the strong foundation of nenbutsu thought and practice in the Hokuriku, a factor that was to contribute significantly to the Honganji's rapid expansion.[85]

Until this period of his life, Rennyo's activities had focused largely on the Kinai, with Ōtani Hongan-ji at the center. At the age of fifty-seven, he had already surpassed the achievements of his immediate predecessors in presenting Shinran's teaching with the fervor that characterized his studies, preaching, and first writings. Given the image of Rennyo presented in the memoirs, it would have been inconsistent for him to have elected to simply retire and transfer responsibility for leading the Honganji in troubled times to the heir of his choice.[86] In 1471, he embarked on what was to be the most decisive and fruitful period of his life in an entirely different region of Japan.

---

[83] Shigematsu, "Rennyo no Yoshizaki shinshutsu no keii," 289–306.

[84] In a strict sense, the Kinai consisted of the five provinces in the region of the capital at Kyoto: Yamashiro (part of present-day Kyoto prefecture), Kawachi and Izumi (Osaka prefecture), Yamato (Nara prefecture), and Settsu (part of Hyōgo prefecture). In reference to Rennyo's activities, this would include Ōmi province (Shiga prefecture).

[85] For a discussion of the foundation in the Hokuriku for Rennyo's missionary undertaking at Yoshizaki, see Shigematsu, "Rennyo no Yoshizaki shinshutsu no keii," 306–14.

[86] In regard to Rennyo's move to Yoshizaki, Kitanishi Hiromu discusses personal reasons relating to the family background of Rennyo's third wife, Nyoshō; see "Rennyo Shōnin to Honganji kyōdan," 8–10.

7. *Map of Yoshizaki*

Chapter 3

Crisis: Yoshizaki

RENNYO'S ACTIVITIES were centered at Yoshizaki, in Echizen province near the Kaga border, from the seventh month of Bunmei 3 (1471) to the eighth month of Bunmei 7 (1475), roughly four years. A letter he wrote from Yoshizaki in the ninth month of Bunmei 5 (1473) offers an account of his departure some two years earlier from the precincts of Mii-dera, at Ōtsu in Ōmi province, and his arrival at Yoshizaki several months later:

> Around the beginning of the fourth month of the third year of Bunmei, I just slipped away, without any settled plan, from a place near Mii-dera's southern branch temple at Ōtsu, in the Shiga district of Ōmi province, and travelled through various parts of Echizen and Kaga. Then, as this site — Yoshizaki, in the Hosorogi district of [Echizen] province — was particularly appealing, we made a clearing on the mountain, which for many years had been the habitat of wild beasts. Beginning on the twenty-seventh day of the seventh month, we put up a building that might be called a temple. With the passage of time from yesterday to today and so on, three years have elapsed with the seasonal changes.[1]

Rennyo's account is disarming. With the Ōnin War continuing into its fifth year in Kyoto and unremitting pressure from Mt. Hiei, it was imperative that he find a new center from which to disseminate Shinran's teaching. Nor can considerations for his personal safety be overlooked. Significant elements in Yoshizaki's appeal must have been its strategic location on the Japan sea, providing ready access, and the fortresslike features of the terrain, affording natural defense. Indeed, at the time he wrote this letter, Rennyo had been building fortifications to defend

---

[1] RSI, 108, (#26/1:8); SSZ 3:413.

the community against possible attack by factions in the battle for control of Kaga province.[2] Hence this letter cannot be considered apart from the struggle that erupted in Kaga with the outbreak of warfare in the capital in 1467.

POLITICAL TURMOIL

The Ōnin War signaled the end of a balance of power established in the late fourteenth century between the Muromachi shogunate and its provincial military governors. The two principal governing offices were those of shogun, held in succession by the heads of the Ashikaga family, and deputy (*kanrei* 管領), selected from one of three major families, the Hosokawa, Shiba, and Hatakeyama. By the middle of the fourteenth century there was a decline in the fortunes of the shogunate, and the Shiba and Hatakeyama families were facing internal succession disputes. With the weakening of central authority, the local military governors, including those in the Hokuriku, were also weakened. The stage was set for the outbreak of warfare, which began with a clash between the forces of Hosokawa Katsumoto (1430–1473) and Yamana Sōzen (1404–1473) over the issue of succession in the Ashikaga shogunate. Katsumoto, leader of the eastern forces, and Sōzen, leader of the western,[3] both became ill and died in 1473, and in the same year, the issue of Ashikaga succession was quietly settled with the appointment of Ashikaga Yoshihisa (1465–1489).[4] The outcome mattered little, for effective governance by the Muromachi shogunate had ended, and the country was plunged into a century of turmoil that was

---

[2] RSI, 128–30 (#36), dated Bunmei 5 (1473).10.3.

[3] The eastern and western forces were so designated because of the alignment of the camps they established in the capital, Kyoto.

[4] Katsumoto occupied the office of shogunal deputy for three terms, the last being from 1468–1473. Sōzen, known as Mochitoyo before he became a monk, held high offices in the shogunate. In the shogunal succession dispute of 1465, Sōzen backed Ashikaga Yoshihisa, infant son of the shogun Ashikaga Yoshimasa (1436–1490) and Hino Tomiko, while Katsumoto backed Yoshimasa's younger brother, Ashikaga Yoshimi (KEJ, s.v. "Hosokawa Katsumoto [1430–1473]," 3: 236; s.v. "Yamana Sōzen [1404–1473]," 8: 301). Ashikaga Yoshimasa, after abdicating in favor of Yoshihisa, built the villa that later became the temple Ginkaku-ji. The fact that he was a dedicated patron of the arts—poetry, calligraphy, painting, tea ceremony, and Nō drama—is a reminder of the cultural activity coincident with bitter warfare (KEJ, s.v. "Ashikaga Yoshimasa [1436–1490]," 1: 101).

to last until Oda Nobunaga's bid for a new military hegemony in the 1560s.[5]

In Kaga province, the Togashi family had provided the provincial military governors from the latter part of the Kamakura period. At the beginning of the Ōnin War, however, Kaga was divided into northern and southern factions, with Akamatsu Masanori controlling the north, and Togashi Masachika (d. 1488) the south. Both were aligned with Katsumoto, leader of the eastern forces. Togashi Yukichiyo,[6] Masachika's younger brother, driven out of northern Kaga by Akamatsu, turned to Sōzen, leader of the western forces. When Akamatsu gained control of his home province of Harima, he left northern Kaga, which was then reclaimed by Yukichiyo. Thus the Togashi family was divided into two camps, and fighting ensued between Masachika and Yukichiyo for control of the province as a whole.[7]

Early in the Ōnin War in Kaga, the advantage was with Yukichiyo, who had four powerful supporters: Echizen's military governor, Shiba Yoshikado, and deputy governor, Kai Yashiro; the military general Asakura Toshikage (1428–1481); and Noto prefecture's military governor, Hatakeyama Yoshitsuna. However, in Bunmei 3 (1471), the year of Rennyo's arrival in Yoshizaki, Asakura shifted his support from the Yamana to the eastern forces of the Hosokawa, receiving the military governorship of Echizen and reversing the balance of power in neighboring Kaga. Masachika, who had been fighting in Kyoto in support of the eastern forces, swiftly returned to Kaga in hopes of regaining control of the province.[8]

In Bunmei 4 (1472).8, Asakura defeated the Kai forces in Echizen and established control over the entire province; the Kai dispersed to Kyoto, Ōmi, and Kaga. Those in Kaga aligned themselves with Yukichiyo and, determined to regain control of their former territory, repeatedly made raids on Echizen. On Bunmei 5 (1473).7.9, they successfully attacked Masachika, forcing him to retreat to Echizen; Honganji adherents appear to have been a significant factor in his defeat.[9] The following day, Kai forces raided the Hosorogi district, near

---

[5] See H. Paul Varley, "Ōnin War," in KEJ 6: 106–7. A detailed treatment of the war and its historical background is given in Varley's *The Ōnin War* (New York: Columbia University Press, 1977).

[6] Alternately read as "Togashi Kōchiyo."

[7] Kasahara Kazuo, *Ikkō ikki: Sono kōdō to shisō* (Tokyo: Hyōronsha, 1970), 74.

[8] Kasahara, *Ikkō ikki*, 74; Inoue, *Ikkō ikki no kenkyū*, 335.

[9] Kasahara, *Ikkō ikki*, 74; Inoue, *Ikkō ikki no kenkyū*, 335–36. Shigematsu (who dates the Kai defeat as Bunmei 3.8 and the attack on Masachika as Bunmei 4.9) understands the attacking coalition to have included Honganji adherents who

Yoshizaki; in a major battle on the eighth day of the eighth month, they defeated Asakura (to whom Masachika had appealed for help), pursuing his forces into Kaga.[10]

In the following year, Bunmei 6 (1474).6, a temporary truce was mediated between the Asakura and Kai forces by the military governor of Mino province; Yukichiyo thus lost a powerful ally. On the twenty-sixth day of the seventh month, Masachika attacked Yukichiyo with the support of the Ikkōshū faction, identified with the Honganji;[11] among Yukichiyo's forces were Senjuji adherents of the Shinshū, increasingly alarmed by the Honganji's growth under Rennyo.[12] A series of battles followed; on the first day of the eleventh month, Masachika won a conclusive victory, with the Ikkōshū playing a prominent role and paying a heavy cost.[13]

---

had conspired with Masachika's uncle, Togashi Yasutaka (see quotation and discussion of the *Oyamoto nikki* entry for Bunmei 5 (1473).7.23, in "Hokuriku ni okeru Rennyo no katsudō," 407–8).

[10] *Daijōin jisha zōjiki*, entry for Bunmei 5 (1473).8.15, quoted in Shigematsu, "Hokuriku ni okeru Rennyo no katsudō," 408. Shigematsu makes the point that, although Honganji adherents from Kaga may have supported Kai on this occasion, adherents in Echizen seem not to have been directly involved in the Kai-Asakura conflict, maintaining at least a surface neutrality throughout Rennyo's stay in Yoshizaki. He therefore interprets Rennyo's fortification of Yoshizaki in Bunmei 5 as an attempt (a) to avoid being used by the Kai faction and drawn into the Kai-Asakura hostilities and (b) to prepare for a possible attack by Asakura.

[11] Kasahara, *Ikkō ikki*, 75–76. An underlying question in regard to Honganji adherents' support of Masachika is to what extent Rennyo may have been involved; the answer is somewhat unclear. *Jitsugoki shūi* reports that when Masachika fled to Echizen, Rennyo, who was then at Yoshizaki, assisted him in various ways; Masachika promised that if he regained power in Kaga, he would not overlook Honganji followers who supported him (passage quoted and discussed in Inoue, *Ikkō ikki no kenkyū*, 336–37). Kasahara gives a somewhat different view of Rennyo's role in stating that, prior to Masachika's battle with Yukichiyo, "discussions between Masachika and influential priests and warrior adherents of the Honganji proceeded, effectively bypassing Rennyo" (*Ikkō ikki*, 75).

[12] It is important to note that Rennyo recognized the problems engendered by the sect's growth and the gap between the ideal and the reality of the Honganji; his particular anxiety was its political aims. He said on one occasion, "Our sect's flourishing is not a matter of people gathering in great numbers or of its having great power. Its well-being rests in the realization of faith for even a single person" (Kitanishi, "Rennyo Shōnin to Honganji kyōdan," 8, RSG, 84).

[13] Kasahara, *Ikkō ikki*, 76; Inoue, *Ikkō ikki no kenkyū*, 343–45. Inoue quotes an entry in *Daijōin jisha zōjiki*: "On the first day of the eleventh month, peasants of the Ikkōshū [i.e. the Honganji], calling themselves the 'Sect of Unhindered

From the time of his victory, however, Masachika found himself hard-pressed to control those who had supported him; emboldened by their newly-realized power, they raided estates, resisted the payment of taxes, and attempted by every means to establish their own authority. Breaking his alliance with them, Masachika launched a campaign of suppression that resulted in a confrontation between the two sides in the third month of Bunmei 7 (1475). Underestimating Masachika's power, the peasants and others who participated in the insurrection were defeated; many of their leaders fled to Zuisen-ji in Inami, Etchū.[14]

Hoping for a compromise with Masachika, representatives came to Yoshizaki to request that Rennyo act as an intermediary. Rennyo's intimate disciple and advisor, Aki Rensō, is said to have considered their request but rejected it, advocating a resumption of hostilities rather than reconciliation.[15] Rennyo continued to argue for neutrality

---

Light,' fought against [Yukichiyo's] warrior forces and expelled all of them from the province. Because the deputy governor, Kosugi, sided with the warriors, he was killed. The Ikkōshū lost two thousand men, and the province was ravaged by fires" (344–45). The point here is that, on the surface, it appeared that Ikkōshū adherents had simply risen up against the established order and overthrown the military governor. Subsequently, the event was categorized as the Kaga Ikkō uprising and understood as a militant uprising identified with Honganji adherents in Kaga. Significantly, in a letter dated the second day of the latter part of the ninth month, Bunmei 5 (1473), Rennyo resists the identification of the Honganji with the Ikkōshū (RSI, 118–21 [#30/1:15]).

[14] Kasahara, *Ikkō ikki*, 76–78; Shigematsu, "Hokuriku ni okeru Rennyo no katsudō," 409. In the seventh month, Rennyo also found himself at Zuisen-ji. Having set out for the eastern provinces, perhaps to retrace a trip made by Shinran some hundred and fifty years earlier, he arrived at Zuisen-ji on the sixteenth; he went no further, however, for he attracted such crowds that between five and ten people were crushed to death each day. After moving to a place some distance from the town and drawing even larger crowds, he was forced to give up the trip and return to Yoshizaki, slipping away from Zuisen-ji under cover of night (*Jitsugoki*, RSG, 150, and Chiba, *Honganji monogatari*, 200–1, which give the date as 1473; HN, 71, however, gives 1475.7).

[15] HS 1: 332. Aki Rensō (also known as Shimotsuma Rensō), a native of Asōzu, Asami, Echizen, is a puzzling figure; many of the details of his relationship with Rennyo remain unclear. In a letter dated Bunmei 3 (1471).9.18, Rennyo tells of Rensō's having heard the teaching from a priest of Honkaku-ji (in Wada, Echizen) and joined the Honganji the previous year (RSI, 70–71 [#11]), thus allowing for the possibility that he, together with followers at Honkaku-ji, encouraged Rennyo's move to Yoshizaki. In a preface written two years later (Bunmei 5 [1473].9.27) to accompany a collection of his letters, Rennyo indirectly establishes Rensō as the first person to have made such a collection (see p. 275 below for a translation of the preface). On Bunmei 7 (1475).8.8, Rennyo

and a defensive posture on the part of the Honganji. "As priests, how can we attack an enemy fortress?" he reportedly asked. "Self-defense by fortification is the usual practice."[16]

At this point, however, Rennyo's approach to the problem appears to have been in jeopardy. His deepening concern over the situation is reflected in a letter dated Bunmei 7 (1475).5.7, referring to difficulties with warriors in Kaga and pressing for the observance of ten regulations; a six-item letter followed on the fifteenth day of the seventh month, insisting on payment of taxes.[17] A little over a month later, Rennyo's earlier inclination to leave Yoshizaki reemerged in a clear decision; perhaps he felt that the mounting potential for open conflict might be mitigated if he, as the leader of the community, left the region. In any case, on the twenty-first day of the eighth month, under cover of night, he boarded a skiff belonging to his son Junnyo and sailed to Obama, Wakasa province. Passing through Tanba and Settsu provinces, he arrived in the village of Deguchi, Kawachi province, which, for a little over two years, served as the center for his activities.[18]

During Rennyo's four years in Yoshizaki, the series of losses marking his life intensified. Having suffered the death of his first wife, Nyoryō, in 1455 and the destruction of Ōtani Hongan-ji in 1465, he lost his second wife, Renyū, in 1470, the year before his move to Yoshizaki. His first and fifth daughters, Nyokei (b. 1446) and Myōi (b. 1460), died in 1471; his second and eighth daughters, Kengyoku and Ryōnin (b. 1466), in 1472.[19] In the third month of Bunmei 6 (1474), a

---

gave Rensō a portrait of Shinran and four fascicles of *Honganji Shōnin Shinran den'e*, a gift indicative of the closeness of their relationship. The reasons for Rennyo's leaving Yoshizaki are not entirely clear, however, and according to one explanation, the move was prompted by Rensō's issuing false orders in Rennyo's name for an insurrection in Kaga against Masachika. It is also possible that Rensō's closeness to Rennyo provoked the jealousy of Rennyo's sons, Rensei, Renkō, and Junnyo, who are said to have brought word of a betrayal. Whatever the case, Rennyo evidently did excommunicate Rensō and withhold pardon until Meiō 8 (1499).3.20, five days before his own death on the twenty-fifth. Rensō died three days later, on the twenty-eighth of the month. See Shigematsu, "Hokuriku ni okeru Rennyo no katsudō," 412–14, and HS 1: 330–35; *Jitsugo kyūki*, RSG, 117, gives an account of the pardon.

[16] Tokuryō sode nikki, quoted in Shigematsu, "Hokuriku ni okeru Rennyo no katsudō," 409.

[17] RSI, 236–40 (#79); RSI, 246–50 (#83/3:10).

[18] RSI, 293–94 (#99), dated Bunmei 9 (1477).12.29; HN, 71–73.

[19] Kitanishi, *Ikkō ikki no kenkyū*, 39. In a letter dated Bunmei 5 (1473).8.22 (RSI, 82–86 [#16]), Rennyo writes of Kengyoku's last days and conversion from the Jōdoshū to the Shinshū, of the sense of impermanence that her death

significant number of the buildings at Yoshizaki were destroyed by fire.[20] For Rennyo in late medieval Japan, the metaphor of the world as a "burning house" applied quite literally;[21] this was the world he shared with the throngs of Shinshū adherents, nenbutsu devotees, and warriors who were attracted to Yoshizaki soon after his arrival. The four years at Yoshizaki may be summarized in terms of his efforts, principally through his letters,[22] to resolve two interrelated issues, one internal to the Honganji and the other external, both touched by the turbulence of the age.

---

evoked in him and those who cared for her, and of his certainty that she had attained birth in the Pure Land. Others, thinking of her as a good teacher, could find guidance in her example. Of the extant letters, this and the sixteenth in fascicle five (RSI, 482–83 [#184]; SSZ 3: 513–14) speak most clearly of Rennyo's sense of impermanence (*mujō* 無常). This sensibility also underlies the political turmoil of the day: if the humble were impermanent on the earth, so were the mighty, whose passage might be hastened by those willing to risk their own lives in political uprisings. Partly from his recognition of the hazards of such a response to the fact of transiency, Rennyo stresses with even greater fervor the saving power of Amida Buddha and faith as settled mind (*anjin*); with this, the nuance of the teaching undergoes a subtle shift away from Shinran's this-worldly orientation.

[20] In a letter dated Bunmei 6 (1474).4.8, Rennyo describes how the fire broke out at lodgings at the South Gate and, fanned by a south wind, quickly spread to the temple (*gobō* 御坊) and to the North Gate, destroying the temple and nine lodgings (RSI, 188 [#58]). Fortunately, with Asakura's assistance, reconstruction was soon completed (Chiba, *Honganji monogatari*, 197). One of the more familiar legends of Rennyo and his followers tells of Ryōken (Honkōbō), who, during the fire, gave his life to save Rennyo's copy of the "Chapter on Realization" from the *Kyōgyōshinshō*, treasured because it was in Shinran's hand. Hearing Rennyo's distress at having left it behind when he fled from the flames, Ryōken is said to have reentered the burning building and found the scroll; realizing that he could not get outside again, he cut open his abdomen, thrust the scroll inside, and thus protected it even in death (Chiba, *Honganji monogatari*, 198; *Shinshū jiten*, 772. For a gentler but more detailed account, see Satake, comp., *Chūkō Rennyo Shōnin goden'e shō*, 191–97).

[21] Shinran uses the metaphor in *Shōzōmatsu wasan*, SSZ 2: 517, in reference to transmigration. It also appears in *Tannishō*, SSZ 2: 792–93. In *Kyōgyōshinshō*, it appears on six occasions, always in the context of quotations including Shantao's "Parable of the Two Rivers" (SSZ 2: 56).

[22] To mention only the letters found in the five-fascicle collection: in Bunmei 3 (1471), Rennyo wrote letters one to three in fascicle one; in Bunmei 4 (1472), letter 1:4; in Bunmei 5 (1473), letters 1:5–15, 2:1–2; in Bunmei 6 (1474), letters 2:3–15, 3:1–6, and 5:11; and in Bunmei 7 (1475), letters 3:7–10. In addition to these forty-one letters (out of the total of eighty in *The Letters*), thirty-five others written during this period, including an eleven-article set of prohibitions (RSI, 131–33 [#38], translated later in this chapter) are listed in HN, 67–71.

8. Statue of Rennyo, Yoshizaki

THE DILEMMA OF RELIGIOUS POWER[23]

The first of the issues facing Rennyo at Yoshizaki was internal to his community: if Shinran's teaching was to be heard and the Honganji revived, it was necessary to establish a uniform interpretation of the teaching. The second was external: it was necessary to find a means of accommodating the teaching, presented in the name of the Honganji as an autonomous religious body, to the patterns of religious practice of the shrines and older Buddhist sects allied with those in power in the Hokuriku. Rennyo's dilemma was that the very measures he pursued to resolve the internal issue of the teaching tended to exacerbate the external, politically-related issue, and vice versa. The subtleties of the crisis come into clearer focus through a review of some of the letters he wrote while he was based in the Hokuriku, during the overlapping periods of 1471–1473 and 1473–1475.

Early in the first period, Rennyo recognized that it was imperative to engender in his followers in the rapidly-growing community at Yoshizaki a heightened sense of identification with and loyalty to the Honganji. In order to define the quality and content of piety that was to characterize Shinshū practicers of faith, he began writing letters challenging interpretations of Shinran's teaching deemed heretical within the tradition.[24] Just as Shinran had translated the Pure Land

---

[23] This phrase, the title of Solomon's essay, "The Dilemma of Religious Power," 51–65, captures the irony in the relationship between the Honganji, emerging as a powerful religious order, and Hosokawa Masamoto (1466–1507), a major political figure, in late fifteenth-century Japan. To see and feel the irony presupposes modern Western categories of religion and politics that, we have noted, appear to have been far less reified in premodern Japanese consciousness. Solomon notes that Masamoto became a devoted patron of the Honganji after developing a close relationship — based largely on mutual self-interest — with Rennyo in the 1480s when he was a frequent visitor at Yamashina Honganji. Our use of the phrase "the dilemma of religious power" denotes Rennyo's dilemma at Yoshizaki; his community, in terms of numbers and of commitment to a common ideal, emerged as a potent force in the struggle for control of the province. It was in this period that Rennyo's response to the issue of the Honganji's power as a religious order established a pattern of institutional response that has persisted until the present in the history of the Honganji.

[24] Kitanishi Hiromu has pointed out that, of twenty-five letters addressing heresies, twenty were written from Yoshizaki, beginning in Bunmei 3 (1471). The heresies with which Rennyo was concerned during this period were: reciting [Amida Buddha's] Name without faith (*mushin shōmyō* 無信称名), eight letters;

sūtras and commentaries from Chinese into Japanese patterns of thought, Rennyo sought to translate the teaching into language that could be grasped by ordinary men and women with varied backgrounds in Pure Land thought and practice, including those of rival branches of the Shinshū. Complementing this emphasis on doctrinal purity, he paired Shinran's *Shōshinge* and *Sanjō wasan* for liturgical use, making up a four-fascicle text, *Shōshinge wasan*, printed in Bunmei 5 (1473).3. Notable as the first woodblock printing of Shinshū scripture, the text was eventually disseminated throughout the Honganji.[25]

Rennyo arrived in the Hokuriku well aware of some of the difficulties he would face. A letter written from Honsen-ji, Futamata, Kaga province, just before he took up residence at Yoshizaki, gives a third-person account of a dialogue on faith between a priest of high position (*daibōzu* 大坊主) and a layman (*zokujin* 俗人).[26] Through this dramatic form, he seeks to engage the attention of his listeners; he proceeds, then, to differentiate "authentic" Shinshū teaching from erroneous interpretations held by leaders of Honganji-related congregations in the region.[27] A similar letter, probably written about the same time, goes

---

[the practice of] taking refuge in a teacher [rather than in Amida Buddha] (*chishiki kimyō* 知識帰命), two letters; the secret teaching that worship is unnecessary (*fuhai hiji* 不拝秘事), one letter; the teaching that there is one blessing (*ichiyaku bōmon* 一益法門), one letter; the secret teaching [of the actualization of birth in the Pure Land] ten kalpas ago (*jikkō hiji* 十劫秘事), three letters; and the practice of giving gifts to a teacher as a meritorious act (*semotsu danomi* 施物 だのみ), five letters. Bunmei 6 (1474) was the peak year for Rennyo's letters (ten) on heresy; twenty letters from that same year were to be included in the five-fascicle collection ("Dangibon kenkyū josetsu," *Bukkyō shigaku* 11/3–4 [1964]: 34, 36). See also Shigematsu, "Hokuriku ni okeru Rennyo no katsudō," 388–90, and Rogers, "Rennyo Shōnin 1415–1499," 127–38.

[25] Rennyo's use of the *Shōshinge* and *Sanjō wasan* at morning and evening services replaced the *rokuji raisan*, hymns in praise of Amida, selected for chanting at six fixed times in a twenty-four-hour period (these were originally included in Shan-tao's *Ōjō raisange* and popularized under Hōnen). See *Honganji sahō no shidai*, RSG, 194; HS 1: 325–26.

[26] This letter, dated Bunmei 3 (1471).7.16 (RSI, 64–68 [#9]), is preserved today at Honsen-ji, at Futamata. The temple was founded by Rennyo's uncle, Nyōjō, who had been instrumental in insuring his succession as head priest. Rennyo may have stopped here en route to Yoshizaki; he is said to have laid out the temple garden in memory of his uncle, who died in 1460. Credited with creating several other gardens, Rennyo makes specific reference to one he designed in 1479 at Yamashina (HN, 73; see RSI, 307 [#104] and 317 [#107]).

[27] For other letters written as a third-person narration of a dialogue between a priest and layman, see RSI, 105–7 (#25/1:7); 57–61 (#7); 100–3 (#23); and

to the heart of a number of issues in relating a conversation between a high-ranking priest and a "tall, dark man," clearly Rennyo's spokesman, on a hot day in the Kato district of Kaga in Bunmei 3 (1471).[28] When the layman inquires about Honganji priests' instruction of their followers, he discovers that this particular priest is completely ignorant of the tradition's teaching; he can only say that followers should show respect for the priest of the temple to which they belong, take him gifts, and say the nenbutsu. The layman learns, too, that the priest has no scriptures; his understanding of faith is that people should take refuge in the power of Amida's Vow and say the nenbutsu morning and evening, and that if they simply ask the Buddha to save them, they will surely attain birth in the Pure Land after death. "If this is wrong," says the priest to the layman, "instruct me; I should hear the teaching." Seeing that the priest has no idea of faith according to the tradition, the layman assumes the priest's role—with a gentle reminder that "all in this world are brothers"—and responds:

> What is taught by Master [Shinran] and in his school is that faith is fundamental. For when we cast away the sundry practices (zōgyō 雑行) and single-heartedly take refuge in Amida, birth [in the Pure Land] is assured by the Buddha through the inconceivable working of the Vow. [Attaining] this state is also described as "entering, with the awakening of the one thought-moment [of entrusting], the company of those [whose birth in the Pure Land is] truly settled." The nenbutsu, saying the Name of the Buddha—walking, standing, sitting, or lying down—should then be understood as the nenbutsu of grateful return for Amida's benevolence, through which the Tathāgata has established our birth.[29]

The layman emphasizes that a person in accord with this understanding is one in whom faith is decisively settled (shinjin ketsujō 信心 決定); if the priest understands this himself and teaches it to others, Buddha-dharma will flourish and both he and his followers will surely attain birth. On hearing this, the priest rejoices and repents and, concluding that he should commend his few followers to the layman, asks

290–93 (#98). For letters written with Rennyo as one party in the dialogue and an explanation added, see RSI, 62–64 (#8/1:1); 118–21 (#30/1:15); and 190–92 (#59/2:10). See Inaba's explanatory notes, RSI, 685.

[28] RSI, 57–61 (#7); the letter includes a postscript dated Bunmei 7 (1475).3.2, which was probably added some twenty months later.

[29] RSI, 60–61 (#7). With only minor differences, this section of letter seven in RSI is the same as letter ten in fascicle five; SSZ 3: 507.

for his continued guidance. From now on, he, too, will go frequently to listen to and discuss the teaching.

The layman's statement on faith stands on its own, with only slight variations, as one of the best known and most frequently read of all of Rennyo's letters. It appears to be consistent with Shinran's teaching that absolute trust in Amida Buddha's Other Power is the only path available to the person of karmic evil (*akugō* 悪業)in the last dharma-age. Faith here is a state of mind expressed in the sole "practice" of saying the Name in thanksgiving; it stands in clear contrast to all practices (including nenbutsu recitation) undertaken to effect salvation from the practicer's side.

In emphasizing the importance of the statement on faith, we cannot disregard the content of the letter as a whole and its historical context. Confronting the problem of heterodox teachings, Rennyo must have felt it essential to translate Shinran's concept of *shinjin*, worked out in painstaking detail in the chapter on faith in *Kyōgyōshinshō*, into simpler terms. It was perhaps inevitable that, in the process, something of the original subtlety and complexity was lost. Note, too, that Rennyo's use of terms such as "sundry practices" occurs in a context that differed from that of his predecessor, Shinran; for Rennyo, the term refers to heretical nenbutsu interpretations never encountered by Shinran, but held by participants in branches of the Jōdoshū,[30] in the Jishū, and in the Takada and Sanmonto[31] branches of the Shinshū itself. To answer this challenge, he found it necessary to cast the teaching in fresh terms.

Rennyo's initial task was to establish the Honganji line as authoritative and to educate Shinshū priests in the fundamentals of the teaching. Well before a firm foundation had been laid, however, the mountain retreat at Yoshizaki developed into a thriving temple-town.

---

[30] In his letters, Rennyo cites various branches of the Jōdoshū that look to Hōnen as their founder: Seizan, Chinzei, Kubon, and Chōrakuji; see RSI, 203 (#66/2:15; SSZ 3: 447), 372 (#123), 377 (#126), and 403 (#136). In identifying Shinran's teaching of "the true essence of the Pure Land way" with that of Hōnen, Rennyo notes the major points at which these four branches have departed from the teaching. The Seizan and the Chinzei were the most significant for him. See Dobbins' discussion of these two branches: *Jōdo Shinshū*, 104–7.

[31] Although the Takada and Sanmonto branches of the Shinshū were founded by direct disciples of Shinran, they were not in the hereditary line (*kechimyaku* 血脈) of transmission. These rival groups had grown much stronger than the Honganji, which claimed both hereditary and dharma lineages (*hōmyaku* 法脈). Rennyo's position, similar to that of Kakunyo, was that the lineages validated one another.

In a letter dated Bunmei 5 (1473).8.2, two years after his arrival, Rennyo reports—more in alarm than satisfaction—that Yoshizaki was being described at local shrines and by priests of the older Buddhist sects as a mountain fortress teeming with pilgrims—men and women, priests and laity.[32]

The first hint of serious threat to the Yoshizaki community is signaled in a letter written in the ninth month of Bunmei 5 (1473), in which Rennyo prohibits people assembling at Yoshizaki. His stated reason for the ban is that many come in search of "reputation and personal gain" rather than "enlightenment in the afterlife."[33] Indicative of his distress over the situation is the fact that he leaves Yoshizaki that same month, intending to return to the capital at Kyoto. After getting only as far as Chōshō-ji at Fujishima in Echizen, he returns to the community in the tenth month at the urging of the resident priests.[34]

To the extent that Rennyo was successful in bringing about greater uniformity in the interpretation of Shinran's teaching, he fostered the growth of the Honganji as an autonomous religious institution. In the process, his community became all the more visible as a potentially important constituency in the power struggle for control of Kaga province. Undeniably, it was in the interest of many of those attracted to the community to identify themselves with a closely-knit, distinctive body providing them with a power base to further their own purposes.

Rennyo's return from Fujishima and recommitment to the Yoshizaki community in the fall of 1473 marks the transition to the second period of his sojourn in the Hokuriku, which continues until his sudden departure for the Kinai in the eighth month of Bunmei 7 (1475). During this period, the active participation of Shinshū adherents in the Ikkō uprisings brings to the fore the dilemma of the Honganji's religious power.[35] Rennyo's challenge is to reconcile the Shinshū's involvement in political affairs with the largely apolitical yet community-oriented teaching characteristic of Shinran. In a letter dated Bunmei 5 (1473).10.3, Rennyo refers to the necessity, since the first of the year, of constructing fortifications at Yoshizaki for protection against "attack by warrior bands" (*rōnin shutchō* 牢人出帳).[36] A document written in the

---

[32] RSI, 104 (#24).

[33] RSI, 109 (#26/1:8); SSZ 3: 413.

[34] HS 1: 329–30; see RSI, 129–30 (#36) and 164 (#48).

[35] Shigematsu, "Hokuriku ni okeru Rennyo no katsudō," 398–416.

[36] RSI, 129 (#36). The bands appear to have been elements of the Kai forces opposing Asakura Toshikage, the military governor of Echizen province. See n. 9 above.

same month, in classical Chinese rather than in the colloquial Japanese of the letters, presents a subtle rationalization for the fortifications and is signed "priests in residence [at Yoshizaki]".[37] It suggests that Rennyo was aware of the inherent dangers in allying with either of the competing forces and that he actively sought to preserve Yoshizaki's political neutrality. To this end, he built up fortifications and worked to unify the resident priests in a decision not to submit passively to occupation or to attack, but if necessary, to meet force with force. At the same time, he was careful to disassociate himself from any movement to seize territory in the name of the Honganji and was consistently critical of Shinshū adherents with territorial ambitions.[38] His most pressing concern was to protect his religious community, which he saw as the legitimate guardian of Buddha-dharma in the last age.

This was not the first occasion on which participants in Shinshū tradition found themselves in conflict with other religious bodies and with officials holding political power. In 1207, Shinran himself, together with Hōnen, had been exiled from Kyoto as a result of a petition to the court by the monks of Kōfuku-ji;[39] in 1465, Rennyo had been forced to flee when Ōtani Hongan-ji was attacked and burned by warrior-monks from Mt. Hiei. In 1473, however, at a critical point in the development of the Honganji, when people were attracted to the Yoshizaki community in large numbers, he must have felt that all might be lost if he were to be directly involved in a struggle for political power at that time. It is within the context of the Honganji's institutional crisis — the dilemma of religious power — that his innovative presentation of the teaching can be best understood.

---

[37] RSI, 130–31 (#37). The question of authorship of this document is yet to receive a definitive answer. Some scholars argue that it was written by Rennyo and provides evidence of his positive support for the uprising; others have maintained that it was written in direct opposition to his views. The position taken here is that it reflects a compromise between Rennyo and the clerical representatives.

[38] In RSI, 108–9 (#26/1:8), as noted above, Rennyo speaks in general terms, prohibiting those who are concerned with "reputation and personal gain" from assembling at Yoshizaki; later, on Bunmei 18 (1486).1.4, still facing similar problems, he addresses a letter to four groups in Nomi district, Kaga, specifically instructing them to be diligent and humble in dealing with the provincial governor and land stewards (i.e. to pay their taxes) and forbidding the seizure of land belonging to temples and shrines and estate properties (RSI, 364 [#120]; see also Inoue, *Ikkō ikki no kenkyū*, 364).

[39] *Kyōgyōshinshō*, SSZ 2: 201–2.

DOCTRINAL INNOVATION

Rennyo shared Shinran's religious genius in his ability to formulate expressions of piety that could be appropriated by people of widely diverse social and occupational backgrounds. Unlike Shinran, he took for granted that some form of clearly defined, structured religious institution was essential for the life of faith. For this reason, he addressed himself to questions never seriously considered by Shinran, whose teaching may be seen fundamentally as a response to the working of the Other Power of Amida's Vow in his own life.

Rennyo's dilemma as the leader of an institution increasingly vulnerable to politically-motivated nenbutsu devotees comes into sharper focus. On the one hand, he sought to be faithful to Shinran's teaching, for the most part apolitical, and on the other, to be responsive to the legitimate aspirations of his followers for spiritual nurture and some degree of security amidst political and social instability. The very same historical conditions that had encouraged the rapid expansion of a religious community at Yoshizaki now ironically, but not unexpectedly, threatened to sweep it away. Rennyo's challenge was to preserve the impressive beginning made toward realizing Kakunyo's vision of the Honganji as the right and proper vehicle for Shinran's teaching.

Significant doctrinal innovation emerges in Rennyo's writings during his residence at Yoshizaki, as he addresses the internal and external issues facing the Honganji. At a moment of institutional crisis in the eleventh month of Bunmei 5 (1473), Rennyo put into writing a series of strict controls on the behavior of the members of the community. The term "rules of conduct" or "regulations" (*okite* 掟), heading the document, was introduced at this point into Shinshū literature. Such regulations would, at first, appear to be quite alien to Shinran's piety; there is precedent, however, to be found in lists of prohibitions (*seikin* 制禁) governing the behavior of members of Shinshū congregations drawn up as early as 1285.[40] The eleven articles in Rennyo's document, written in classical Chinese, are as follows:

---

[40] The entire thrust of Shinran's Other-Power thought was to live without calculation, which meant giving up the illusion that obedience to precepts was in any way efficacious for one's religious awakening. There is no shred of evidence to suggest that Shinran ever formulated guidelines in order to attempt to regulate the conduct of members of the first Shinshū congregations; he left only his personal example. Partly for this reason, antinomian behavior was a major problem within the Shinshū community from its inception. Shortly after

Item: There must be no denigration of the various kami and buddhas and the bodhisattvas.

Item: There must be no slander of other teachings and other sects.

Item: There must be no criticism of other sects in [terms of] our sect's practices.

Item: Although taboos are meaningless in relation to Buddha-dharma, they must be strictly observed in the presence of [those of] other sects and in public.

Item: It is impermissible, in the presence of others, to praise Buddha-dharma arbitrarily, in terms not transmitted within this sect.

Item: As people of the nenbutsu, you must be fully obedient to the provincial military governors and local land stewards and not slight them.

Item: Those who are uninformed must not blatantly extol our sect's teaching, trusting to their own interpretations, in the presence of [those of] other sects.

Item: Those who are not yet of settled mind (*anjin*) are not to praise the way of faith (*shinjin*) on hearsay.[41]

Item: There must be no consumption of fish or fowl at nenbutsu meetings.

Item: One loses oneself in drink; there must be no drinking on days on which there are nenbutsu gatherings.

Item: In the nenbutsu community, heedless gambling must stop.

Those who disobey these eleven articles are to be strictly excluded from the community.[42]

Shinran's death, Shinshū congregations developed lists of regulations for their members as a matter of practical necessity. For a list of seventeen items dated Kōan 8 (1285).8.13, to be observed on pain of expulsion from the community, see Chiba Jōryū, *Shinshū kyōdan no soshiki to seido* (Kyoto: Dōbōsha, 1978), 7–9; for an English translation, see Dobbins, *Jōdo Shinshū*, 67.

[41] This item is noteworthy in that Rennyo chooses to link the concept *anjin* with Shinran's concept *shinjin* in his first formal list of regulations. Shinran uses the former term on only three occasions (twice in *Kyōgyōshinshō*, SSZ 2: 51 [T 83.602a] and 2: 117 [T 83.620a] and once in *Gutokushō*, SSZ 2: 464 [T 83.650a]), in quoting from Pure Land commentaries by T'an-luan and Shan-tao. Rennyo first uses the phrases *tōryū anjin ketsujō* (settled faith according to our tradition) and *tōryū no anjin* (RSI, 70–71 [#11]) in a letter dated Bunmei 3 (1471).9.18. The immediate precedent in the tradition for Rennyo's use of the concept *anjin* is Kakunyo's *Gaijashō*; see Rennyo's letter, more properly a list of quotations from *Gaijashō*, dated Bunmei 4 (1472).2.8, which picks up passages from Kakunyo's treatment of the three minds based on Shan-tao (RSI, 76–78 [#14]). Even more significant for Rennyo's appropriation of *anjin* as a core concept, which he identifies with Shinran's *shinjin*, is his attraction to *Anjin ketsujōshō* as a model text for apprehending Other Power.

[42] RSI, 131–33 (#38). For the first mention of regulations, see RSI, 109

The authoritative tone of a leader addressing his followers is obvious, albeit the regulations were drawn up to protect a community that Rennyo saw as the guardian of Buddha-dharma; at the same time, there is little resonance with Shinran's reasoning that it would be preposterous "to call a person 'my disciple' when he says the Name solely through the working of Amida."[43]

With these regulations — a wide-ranging mixture of religious, ethical, and political concerns — Rennyo issued a warning to his more politically-oriented followers, restless under an oppressive social order. His primary objective in this situation was to ensure that those who gathered at Yoshizaki assumed an inoffensive posture towards members of other religious bodies and those holding political power.[44] In this document, for the first time, he explicitly enjoins his followers not to disobey or to ignore the provincial military governors and local land stewards.

The list succinctly sets forth rules of conduct for Shinshū adherents, to be obeyed under threat of expulsion from the Yoshizaki community. Yet it was a much more difficult task for Rennyo to motivate his followers to temper their political inclinations or change ingrained patterns of religious thought and practice. To achieve such a fundamental reorientation, more than a list of prohibitions would be necessary; increasingly, Rennyo maintained that the requisite change in heart and mind would be possible only as each member became firmly established in Other-Power faith. In brief, such a reorientation could never be merely a matter of response to a mandate.

The first article illustrates the difficulty of Rennyo's task. On the

---

(#27/1:9), dated Bunmei 5 (1473).9. Further occurrences in letters from Rennyo's Yoshizaki years are in RSI, 141–43 (#41/2:2), dated Bunmei 5 (1473).12.12; RSI, 199–201 (#64/2:13), dated Bunmei 6 (1474).7.3; and RSI, 236–40 (#79), dated Bunmei 7 (1475).5.7.

[43] Hirota, *Tannishō*, 25; SSZ 2: 776. Rennyo's colophon to the copy he made of *Tannishō* (the earliest extant manuscript) notes the importance of the text for the Shinshū; he cautions that it should not be shown indiscriminately to those lacking good from the past (*shukuzen* 宿善 ; SSZ 2: 795). Among the passages he may have found problematic for general dissemination is Shinran's challenge to conventional morality:

> Moreover, to consider our good and evil thoughts and deeds as an aid or hindrance to attainment of birth, interposing our own judgments and designs, is to strive to do acts that will result in birth according to our own intents and to make the nenbutsu we utter our own practice, without entrusting to the inconceivable working of the Vow (Hirota, *Tannishō*, 29; SSZ 2: 779).

[44] HS 1: 328.

one hand, the need for good relations with shrine leaders, priests in the older Buddhist sects, and those in political authority dictated an open posture toward diverse religious entities. On the other, the need to establish a community firmly grounded on Shinran's teaching pressed for a closed or particularist stance.

A shift in Rennyo's stated position towards the kami and buddhas other than Amida is evident in his writings during these months of acute institutional crisis. In a letter addressing the false "ten kalpas" teaching, written two months prior to his first listing of regulations, Rennyo's attitude to religious entities other than Amida sounds a particularist note consistent with that of Shinran:

> What, then, do we mean by "faith"?
>
> First of all, when we set aside all sundry practices and steadfastly rely on Amida Tathāgata and, giving no thought to any of the kami or to other buddhas, take refuge with singleness of heart exclusively in Amida, the Tathāgata embraces [us] with his light and never abandons us. This is precisely how the one thought-moment of faith is decisively settled.[45]

Clearly, Rennyo is taking to task those members of the community who were deviating from the fundamental teaching of total reliance on Amida. First, he underscores the sharp distinction between Shinran's teaching of Other-Power faith and the sundry practices of those following the Pure Land teachings of Hōnen's other disciples. The problem here, as we have said earlier, is that in addressing adherents deviating from Shinran's position, he was in danger of offending those who follow the Path of Sages. Second, he underscores that exclusive submission to Amida does not permit turning to "any of the kami or to other buddhas." A potential problem in this case was that members of his community, particularly those with a background in the Jishū, maintained a positive attitude toward the kami, indeed identifying them with Amida. Further, any denigration of the kami and the buddhas would clearly offend members of other religious bodies in the Hokuriku. The challenge facing Rennyo called for innovative thought, sensitive to issues of political authority and power, as well as for religious inclusiveness.

Rennyo's response to the dilemma is to stress in his letters that the person of faith is, at the same time, a person of discretion who observes the rules of conduct; he defines this as "keeping firmly to ourselves the teaching transmitted in our tradition and not giving any outward sign

---

45 RSI, 123–24 (#32/1:13), dated Bunmei 5 (1473), the latter part of the ninth month; SSZ 3: 420.

of it."[46] Lamenting that some of his followers antagonize members of other religious bodies by boasting and speaking too freely of their faith, he concludes that his own tradition's bad reputation is "not at all the fault of others, but . . . of our own people."[47] Rennyo's exhortations to the members of his community to exercise a very subtle form of self-control were not to prove effective. In the twelfth month of Bunmei 5 (1473), he moves away from his particularist position on religious entities to one of accommodation through a qualified acceptance of the other buddhas and the kami: "If we rely on Amida Buddha alone, we rely at the same time on each and every one of the buddhas and the kami. Consequently, if we rely on Amida Buddha alone, all the kami and buddhas will rejoice and protect us."[48]

Finally, in a letter dated Bunmei 6 (1474).1.11, he offers a detailed apologetic, carefully explaining how Shinshū adherents are to regard the kami:

By kami manifestations, we mean that [buddhas and bodhisattvas] appear provisionally as kami to save sentient beings in whatever way possible; they lament that those who lack faith (shin) in the Buddha-dharma fall helplessly into hell. Relying on even the slightest of [related past] conditions, they appear provisionally as kami through the compassionate means to lead [sentient beings] at last into the Buddha-dharma.

Therefore, sentient beings of the present time [should realize that] if they rely on Amida and, undergoing a decisive settling of faith, repeat the nenbutsu and are to be born in the land of utmost bliss, then all the kami [in their various] manifestations, recognizing this as [the fulfillment of] their own fundamental purpose, will rejoice and protect nenbutsu practicers. Consequently, even if we do not worship the kami in particular, since all are encompassed when we rely solely on one Buddha, Amida, we give credence [to them] even though we do not rely on them in particular.[49]

Between the ninth month of Bunmei 5 (1473) and the first month of Bunmei 6 (1474), there is an obvious refinement in Rennyo's stated position: he moves from "giving no thought to any of the kami and other buddhas" to a qualified acceptance, in that all such entities are encompassed by Amida Buddha. It must be underscored that these few months were precisely the period in which the Yoshizaki community

[46] RSI, 109 (#27/1:9), dated Bunmei 5 (1473).9; SSZ 3: 414.

[47] RSI, 110 (#27/1:9); SSZ 3: 414.

[48] RSI, 152–53 (#43), dated Bunmei 5 (1473).12.13.

[49] RSI, 167–68 (#50/2:3); SSZ 3: 429–30.

faced the greatest danger, both from internal exploitation by members with an affirmative view of the kami and other buddhas and from external attack by forces that enjoyed the ideological support of the shrines and the older Buddhist sects. The theoretical basis for the change in Rennyo's position was the core Buddhist concept of *honji suijaku*, whereby, as early as the Heian period, the indigenous kami were interpreted as manifestations of buddhas or bodhisattvas, the original entities. For Rennyo, of course, Amida is the original entity; he came to interpret the other buddhas and the kami as manifestations.

It is not intended to suggest that *honji suijaku* thought was entirely alien to Shinshū tradition prior to Rennyo. There is evidence that Shinran neither rejected nor trusted in the kami and other religious entities, but recognized, as he stated in some of his hymns, that these entities pay homage to and protect people who recite the nenbutsu out of true piety.[50] Zonkaku, in an effort to respond to the religious aspirations of ordinary people, provided in his writings a doctrinal framework for accommodation with the kami, drawing on *honji suijaku* thought.[51] Rennyo's appropriation of a similar pattern of thought, entirely congenial to the mainstream of Japanese religiousness, is striking in its timing: precisely at that moment, he is beset with the dilemma of the Honganji's religious power. As the leader of a community under extreme social and political threat, he adopts a position that appears to involve a significant modification of Shinran's thought. Further, he is led to affirm that there is no opposition or contradiction

---

[50] See Shinran's hymns on benefits in the present life (*Genze riyaku wasan*) in *Jōdo wasan*, SSZ 2: 497–99; for a presentation suggesting the subtlety of Shinran's position, see Wakaki Yoshihiko, "Shinran Shōnin no jingikan," *Shinshū kenkyū* 17 (1972): 111–27. In our view, Shinran's thought presents a radical departure from Japan's tradition of religious syncretism. Shinran's sharp criticism of Buddhists—clerical and lay—who outwardly uphold Buddhist forms and rituals, but at heart are no different from those who follow non-Buddhist teachings (*gedō* 外道), is found in his hymns of lamentation and confession (*Gutoku hitan jukkai*) in *Shōzōmatsu wasan*, SSZ 2: 528 (#100, #101, #103, #104). In *Kyōgyōshinshō*, Shinran quotes the *Nirvāṇa Sūtra*: "If one has taken refuge in the Buddha, one must not then take refuge in various gods (*tenjin* 天神)," SSZ 2: 175. The distinctive quality of Shinran's thought, including his critical attitude to the kami and folk tradition, is underscored in the writings of historians of Japanese Buddhism, such as Futaba Kenkō (see introduction to this study), as well as some scholars in Shinshū Studies (see Shigaraki Takamaro, *Gendai Shinshū kyōgaku* [Kyoto: Nagata Bunshōdō, 1979], 107–66).

[51] See Zonkaku's *Shojin hongaishū*, SSS 1: 697–712. For a discussion of Zonkaku's interpretation of Shinshū thought, see Shigaraki, *Gendai Shinshū kyōgaku*, 130–34. In English, see Dobbins, *Jōdo Shinshū*, 86–93.

in setting devotion to Buddha-dharma (*buppō* 仏法) side by side with honoring social obligations based on laws of the state (*ōbō* 王法).[52] The term *ōbō*, used by both Kakunyo and Zonkaku, is introduced into his own writings in a letter dated Bunmei 6 (1474).2.17, immediately following his public appropriation of a more traditional Japanese definition of the relationship between the kami and buddhas.[53] A few months later, in a letter dated Bunmei 6 (1474).5.13, he develops this thought further:

> Again, there is still another point to be understood. You must never slight the provincial military governors and local land stewards, saying that you are a person who reveres the Buddha-dharma and has attained faith. Without fail, meet your public obligations in full.
>
> People who comply with the above exemplify the conduct of nenbutsu practicers in whom faith has been awakened and who aspire to [birth in the Pure Land in] the afterlife. They are, in other words, ones who faithfully abide by the Buddha-dharma and the laws of the state.[54]

It would appear that, at this point, a subtle yet distinct shift in meaning emerges between Shinran's and Rennyo's positions regarding the relation of Buddha-dharma and the laws of the state. The former focuses on faith as fundamental, on taking refuge in Amida alone; the latter stresses a duality of faith and adherence to the laws of the state, with submission to political authority balanced by devotion to Buddha-dharma in the framework of an interpretation of *honji suijaku* thought closely following that of Zonkaku. This difference cannot be entirely accounted for by noting that the founder and the eighth head priest lived almost two centuries apart in vastly different historical settings, or by theorizing that they simply played complementary roles in the institutionalization of a religious movement.

A more fundamental difference may lie in Shinran's and Rennyo's self-perceptions. Shinran saw himself as a follower of Hōnen, through whom he had been led to discover the truth of the nenbutsu. Rennyo,

---

[52] The term *ōbō* has a rich and varied history in both Buddhist and Japanese thought. For some indication of its changing meaning in Japanese history, see Kuroda, *Ōbō to buppō*, 8–22. Michael Solomon's translation of *ōbō* as "civil obedience" catches something of Rennyo's use of the term in an effort to resolve the dilemma of Honganji's religious power at Yoshizaki (see Solomon's unpublished paper, "Honganji under Rennyo: The Development of Shinshū in Medieval Japan," presented at the annual meeting of the American Academy of Religion, St. Louis, October, 1976).

[53] RSI, 180–81 (#54/2:6); SSZ 3: 434.

[54] RSI, 192 (#59/2:10); SSZ 3: 441.

however, saw himself not only as Shinran's legitimate heir, but also as the trustee of Kakunyo's vision for the Honganji as a powerful, autonomous religious institution. He sought to articulate Shinran's teaching in doctrinal terms capable of accommodating Kakunyo's goal. To achieve this purpose, Rennyo drew finally on the concept *ki-hō ittai* 機法一体 (the oneness [in "namu-amida-butsu"] of the person [to be saved] and dharma [that saves]), made available to him in *Anjin ketsujōshō*, a Pure Land text unknown to Shinran.[55]

A NENBUTSU FORMULATION

Rennyo's most striking doctrinal innovation was his appropriation of the concept *ki-hō ittai* for interpreting the Name in six characters 南無阿弥陀仏 (*na-mu-a-mi-da-butsu*). His distinctive interpretation of Shinran's religious thought, beginning with letters written at Yoshizaki, may be traced to *Anjin ketsujōshō*, a text that holds a unique place in his own spiritual nurture. The memoir *Jitsugo kyūki* records that Rennyo once said, "Although I have read *Anjin ketsujōshō* for more than forty years, I have never tired of it. . . . It is the sort of scripture from which one can dig out gold."[56] On another occasion, he remarked, "What I said the other day is just a small part of what is in *Anjin ketsujōshō*; its teaching is extremely important for our tradition."[57] Among Rennyo's own writings, a letter dated Bunmei 18 (1486).11.26

---

[55] *Anjin ketsujōshō*, SSZ 3: 615–38. Photographic reproductions of some of the earliest manuscripts, including a copy by Rennyo, are available in Fugen Kōju, ed., *Anjin ketsujōshō* (Kyoto: Dōbōsha, 1983); also included are several studies of the text by Shinshū scholars. See also Fugen Kōju, "Anjin ketsujōshō to Shinshū ressō no kyōgaku: Anjin ketsujōshō to Kakunyo/Zonkaku no kyōgaku," *Ryūkoku Daigaku ronshū* 415 (1979), 81–107, and "Anjin ketsujōshō to Rennyo kyōgaku," *Shinshūgaku* 62 (1980): 1–29. For further discussion of the significance of *Anjin ketsujōshō* for Rennyo, see Rogers, "Rennyo Shōnin 1415–1499," 234–51, 325–38.

English translations are available in (1) Yamamoto, trans., *The Words of St. Rennyo*, 111–58, and (2) Eizo Tanaka, trans., "Anjin Ketsujo Sho: On the Attainment of True Faith," *The Pure Land: Journal of European Shin Buddhism*, 2/2 (1980): 26–33, 3/1 (1981): 21–25, 3/2 (1981): 24–27, 4/1 (1982): 17–21, 4/2 (1982): 34–36, 5/1 (1983): 35–39, 5/2 (1983): 40–44. For a study from a non-sectarian perspective, see Winston L. King, "An Interpretation of the *Anjin Ketsujōshō*," *Japanese Journal of Religious Studies* 13/4 (1986): 277–98.

[56] *Jitsugo kyūki*, RSG, 119; SSZ 3: 595.

[57] *Jitsugo kyūki*, RSG, 120; SSZ 3: 595.

states, "For the meaning of faith in our tradition, read *Anjin ketsujōshō* very carefully."[58]

As noted earlier, diverse opinions have been held in regard to the origin and authorship of *Anjin ketsujōshō*, with Nishi Honganji scholars generally attributing it to Kakunyo, and Higashi scholars attributing it to the Seizan branch of the Jōdoshū. The doctrinal tenor of *Anjin ketsujōshō* is predicated on *ki-hō ittai*, a concept of radical non-differentiation, which Rennyo introduces in a letter dated Bunmei 7 (1475).2.23. This is a major step in his restatement of Shinran's core concept, *shinjin*, in terms of *anjin*, in the context of Shan-tao's exposition of the Name in six characters:

> Faith (*shinjin*) is [a matter of] clearly discerning the significance of Amida Buddha's Primal Vow and single-heartedly taking refuge in Amida; this we call decisive settlement of Other-Power faith (*anjin*). Therefore, full realization of the significance of the six characters "na-mu-a-mi-da-butsu" is the substance of decisively settled faith. That is, the two characters "na-mu" indicate the receptive attitude of the sentient beings who entrust themselves to Amida Buddha. Next, the four characters "a-mi-da-butsu" signify the dharma through which Amida Tathāgata saves sentient beings. This is expressed as "the oneness [*ittai* 一体] in 'namu-amida-butsu' of the person [*ki* 機] [to be saved] and dharma [*hō* 法] [that saves]." Thus the three acts[59] of sentient beings and the three acts of Amida become one. Referring to this, Master Shan-tao wrote in his commentary, "The three acts of the Buddha and of sentient beings are inseparable."[60]

Rennyo's concern to instruct Shinshū adherents in Shinran's teaching led him to an Other-Power reading and interpretation of *Anjin ketsujōshō* in defining *shinjin* in terms of *anjin*. The *Anjin ketsujōshō* itself sets the realization of settled mind in the context of a form of nenbutsu recitation, *nenbutsu zanmai* 念仏三昧 , inducing a meditative state in which all opposition and contradiction are overcome as the person to be saved (*ki*) merges into oneness (*ittai*) with the saving dharma (*hō*), or Amida Buddha. As we consider Rennyo's interpreta-

---

[58] RSI, 363 (#119).

[59] *sangō* 三業 ; literally, the three [kinds of] acts, bodily, verbal, and mental. In the Nishi Honganji, a bitter controversy raged around this issue in the eighteenth and early nineteenth centuries, reaching its height between 1797 and 1806; see chapter five for a discussion of the debate and its resolution.

[60] RSI, 229–30 (#76/3:7); SSZ 3: 461. Five subsequent letters written in the years 1481, 1485, 1496, and 1498 (2) cite the concept *ki-hō ittai* in interpreting the Name in six characters.

tion of this aspect of *Anjin ketsujōshō*, we are reminded that it was Rennyo who promoted the observance of formal devotional services, including saying the nenbutsu, as a corporate ritual activity for his community. He also emphasized the need for adherents to assemble regularly and speak frankly about their understanding of faith.

Virtually without exception, sectarian scholars have argued that Shinran's concept for faith, *shinjin*, is identical with Rennyo's use of the concept *anjin*.[61] The establishment of *anjin* has been given doctrinal consistency with Other-Power orthodoxy by drawing on a *ki-hō ittai* interpretation of the nenbutsu. Being established in *anjin* became the norm for Shinshū piety and has continued as such up to the present, with major consequences for the tradition, as we shall see in considering Rennyo's legacy.

In sum, it is our position that Rennyo's doctrinal innovations in presenting Shinran's teaching may be seen as allowing for, or even effecting, a subtle transformation in interpretations of the Mahāyāna structure of Shinran's thought (which we have characterized in terms of his experience of the simultaneity of sameness and opposition between Amida Buddha and himself). Further, Rennyo's interpretation of the nenbutsu encourages a loss of individual identity on the part of the practicer of faith, through merging into oneness with Amida. Finally, this transformation in Shinshū piety is consequential sociologically and psychologically in supporting a participant's uncritical identification with the Honganji as a religious institution.[62]

---

[61] Even if the concepts *shinjin* and *anjin* are taken as identical in meaning, each as a religious symbol has the capacity to operate quite differently in the life of a participant in the tradition. Shinran's concept *shinjin* unambiguously points to the true mind of Amida Buddha as the source of salvific truth. Rennyo's concept *anjin* may function in the same way as *shinjin*, with the mind of the devotee being "at rest" or "settled" on Amida Buddha alone. However, with *anjin* as a religious symbol, there is greater risk of psychological and sociological interpretations whereby the mind of the devotee may be "at rest" or "settled" on entities other than Amida Buddha — for instance, on a priest or on an institution. For a discussion of Rennyo's notion of *anjin* in relation to Shinran's *shinjin*, see Rogers, "The Shin Faith of Rennyo," 56–73, and " 'Shinjin' to 'anjin'," 26–43.

[62] In chapter six, we discuss Rennyo's legacy in terms of defining Shinshū piety as gratitude, with its dual aspects of living without calculation and honoring social obligation. The maturation of Rennyo's thought is demonstrated in letters written for the annual thanksgiving services held on the anniversary of Shinran's death after the completion of the new Founder's Hall at Yamashina Hongan-ji in 1480. See RSI, 747, for a listing of letters prepared for these occasions.

In a letter dating from the latter part of the fifth month of Meiō 7 (1498), less than a year before his death, Rennyo cites three passages from *Anjin ketsujōshō* in explication of faith (*anjin*).[63] On this occasion, he quotes the passages without the emendations he had made in an earlier letter dated Bunmei 13 (1481).11.14.[64] In his final days, it appears that he accepted *Anjin ketsujōshō*'s perspective as his own, without qualification. Further, it appears that, in his quest to understand the reality of Amida Buddha in the context of late medieval Japan, he was led to appropriate a religious symbol that lent itself to a fresh formulation of Shinran's teaching. It appears that an interpretation of the nenbutsu not inconsistent with the Tendai concept of primordial enlightenment (*hongaku* 本覚), which Shinran had rejected when he left Mt. Hiei to follow Hōnen's nenbutsu path, moved into the mainstream of Shinshū tradition.[65]

THE MAIN IMAGE

Rennyo's appropriation of the six-character Name as the major symbol for the formulation of Shinran's teaching found visual expression as the main image (*honzon* 本尊) for the Honganji. A memoir attributes the following statement to Rennyo:

> In other traditions, preference is given to painted images of the Buddha over [a scroll bearing] the Name, to wooden images over painted images; in our tradition, preference is given to painted images over wooden images, to the Name over painted images.[66]

Rennyo's summary of the Shinshū position has its roots in Shinran's apparent preference for the hanging scroll. Shinran's teaching that religious awakening takes place during the course of ordinary life through the working of Amida's Vow-mind presented a sharp contrast with the earlier Pure Land teaching of Genshin and Hōnen that Amida comes to meet the devotee at the moment of death (*rinjū raikō* 臨終来迎). The practice evolving from this understanding was to

---

[63] RSI, 427–29 (#147).

[64] RSI, 328–31 (#110).

[65] For the significance of *hongaku* thought for the new Buddhism of the Kamakura period, see Tamura Yoshirō, *Kamakura shinbukkyō shisō no kenkyū* (Kyoto: Heirakuji Shoten, 1965).

[66] SSZ 3: 549; *Inscriptions*, 12.

enshrine a portrait or statue depicting Amida's positive activity in the salvific process.[67]

In his *Songō shinzō meimon*, Shinran provides a set of notes in Japanese explaining Chinese textual passages inscribed on scrolls used as the main image in the first Shinshū congregations.[68] The scrolls contained either the sacred Name (*songō* 尊号) of Amida, written in Chinese characters, or portraits (*shinzō* 真像), primarily of the Pure Land masters. Separately-written inscriptions (*meimon* 名文) relating to the Name or to the portrait were affixed to the scrolls. Exemplary of Shinran's expression of Pure Land thought was his use of the written Name, accompanied by inscriptions, on these scrolls.[69]

Shinran used different forms of the Name: in six characters, *na-mu-a-mi-da-butsu*; in eight, *na-mu-fu-ka-shi-gi-kō-butsu* 南無不可思議光仏 (I take refuge in the Buddha of inconceivable light); in nine, *na-mu-fu-ka-shi-gi-kō-nyo-rai* 南無不可思議光如来 (I take refuge in the Tathāgata of inconceivable light); and in ten, *ki-myō-jin-jip-pō-mu-ge-kō-nyo-rai* 帰命尽十方無碍光如来 (I take refuge in the Tathāgata of unhindered light filling the ten directions). The scrolls depicted a lotus-flower pedestal for the vertically-written Name, suggesting that it was adopted in preference to a painting or sculpture of the Buddha.[70]

Shinran's preference for the written Name as the main image may be explained in terms of its suitability for expressing the core of the teaching:

> The written characters . . . are particularly suited to manifesting a reality that is said to have name and form, Amida Buddha, but which is essentially beyond relative name and form, being identical with the nameless and formless dharmakaya. The Name of Amida is not simply a designation by which we identify the Buddha; it is that by which the Buddha makes himself known to beings. In its transcendence of objectified form, then, the written Name is capable of expressing with greater immediacy the dynamic working of true compassion in the practicer.[71]

Shinran appears to have favored the Name in ten characters over other forms, in that it most effectively symbolized Amida's command

---

[67] Chiba Jōryū, "Rennyo no hongan," in *Rennyo*, ed. Minami Midō Shinbun, 203–4.

[68] The two surviving manuscripts, both written by Shinran, are dated Kenchō 7 (1255).6.2 and Shōka 2 (1258).6.8. See *Inscriptions*, 83.

[69] *Inscriptions*, 11–12.

[70] *Inscriptions*, 13.

[71] *Inscriptions*, 14.

to sentient beings to take refuge in the Primal Vow. Kakunyo, in his *Gaijashō*, states:

> The founding master [Shinran] purposely did not place in his altar the ten-*jō* eight-*shaku* high image based on the eighth of the thirteen contemplative exercises — the contemplation of the image of Buddha — taught in the *Contemplation Sūtra*. Instead, he adopted for the altars of Shin Buddhists the words expressing the gate of worship from Vasubandhu's *Jōdoron*, "I take refuge in the Tathāgata of unhindered light filling the ten directions" [*ki-myō jin-jip-pō mu-ge-kō nyo-rai*].[72]

It was this form of the Name that Rennyo inherited and used so effectively in his missionary work in the period 1460–1466. Taking into account the fact that monks from Mt. Hiei had made the Honganji's use of the word "unhindered" (*muge*) an excuse for their attack on Ōtani Hongan-ji in 1465, Rennyo largely discontinued the distribution of the Name in ten characters. Late in his life, as he turned increasingly to the *Anjin ketsujōshō* and its interpretation of the Name, he appears to have settled on the six-character Name to serve as the main image.

Shinran made innovative use not only of Amida's Name, but also of scroll inscriptions. In this, he drew on a Japanese tradition of scroll inscriptions and a Chinese practice of including legendary inscriptions with portraits. For example, on a scroll with the ten-character Name, he added an upper inscription of three passages from the *Larger Sūtra*, including the Eighteenth Vow, and a lower one of two passages from Vasubandhu's hymn. He wrote the inscriptions; the Name was written by a professional calligrapher. Indicative of the variety of scroll inscriptions for which he prepared notes in two different versions of *Songō shinzō meimon* are those on inscriptions for portraits of each of the seven Pure Land masters; Seikaku (1166–1235), a disciple of Hōnen; Mahāsthāmaprāpta, the bodhisattva of wisdom; Prince-regent Shōtoku; and himself.[73]

Shinran's approach to the main image gave visual expression to the special quality of his thought. Instead of a painted or sculpted portrait of Amida, we find a calligraphic form of Amida's Name. But the Name does not appear alone, mantra-like, as in an esotericized tradition; for Shinran, the Name cannot be apprehended apart from the teaching, which is presented most effectively in passages from the

---

[72] *Inscriptions*, 15 (slightly altered); SSZ 3: 66–67.
[73] See *Inscriptions*, 16–19. Shinran's practice of adding inscriptions to the scrolls was not to be sustained so vigorously by his successors.

sūtras and commentaries. In this respect, his position on the main image reflects the pedagogical approach he took in explicating the teaching in *Kyōgyōshinshō*.

On the basis of Shinran's teaching and example alone, it is difficult to determine his evaluation of the religious significance of a scroll bearing Amida's Name or portrait with an inscription in contrast to a portrait of one of the Pure Land masters or of himself with an inscription. In both instances, he judged it essential to complement the Name or portrait with inscriptions drawn from the Pure Land textual tradition. There is evidence that, late in his life, he may have preferred the use of the Name; six scrolls bearing the Name in his own hand with added inscriptions survive from this period—four with ten characters and one each with six and eight. The scrolls intended for presentation to his disciples were executed on silk by a professional artist.[74] In addition, he had portraits made of himself at the request of his followers.[75]

Rennyo was the heir to Kakunyo's interpretation of Shinran's teaching regarding the main image. It is clear, however, that practices relating to the use of scrolls varied widely among other branches of the Shinshū. For example, Ryōgen (1295–1336), who received instruction from Zonkaku and later founded the Bukkōji branch, made effective use of portrait lineages (*ekeizu* 絵系図) and salvation registers (*myōchō* 名帳) in building up the Bukkōji.[76] In his *Gaijashō*, Kakunyo cites these practices in a list of twenty that he considered to be deviations from Shinran's teaching.[77] Rennyo, as the new leader of the Honganji, was determined to correct such distortions of the teaching. Although he symbolized his ties to Honganji-related temples and homes through the presentation of a wide variety of scrolls, these images, unlike the portrait lineages and salvation registers, contained no promise of salvation for particular members.

Prominent among the images Rennyo prepared—apparently with

---

[74] *Inscriptions*, 28–29.

[75] For example, Shinran gave the portrait known as *Anjō no goei*, dated Kenchō 7 (1255) and attributed to a professional artist, Hōgen Chōen, to his disciple Senkai of Anjō, Mikawa province; Shinran wrote the inscriptions, taking three passages from the *Larger Sūtra*, two from Vasubandhu's *Jōdoron*, and one from his own *Shōshinge* (*Inscriptions*, 7–8). One of the three extant portraits made during his lifetime, it was repaired by Rennyo in Kanshō 2 (1461).10 and again in Bunmei 12 (1480).10 (HN, 63, 73).

[76] For a discussion of the Bukkōji's use of these images, see Dobbins, *Jōdo Shinshū*, 112–17.

[77] Dobbins, *Jōdo Shinshū*, 93–95.

great sensitivity to the religious orientation and aesthetic sensibility of the particular recipient—were those of the Name framed by forty-eight rays of light representing Amida's Vows (*kōmyō myōgō* 光明名号), pictorial images (*ezō* 絵像) of Amida or of Shinran, and dual seated portraits (*nison renzazō* 二尊連座像) of Shinran and himself. Of particular interest is a combination of the latter two, the Name in ten characters emitting rays of light, with Shinran seated to the right of the lotus pedestal and himself to the left.[78] As we noted earlier, his first presentation of a dual portrait of Shinran and himself had been to Hōjū's congregation at Katada, Ōmi, in 1461. On the back of the scroll, he wrote, "A portrait of Master Shinran of Ōtani Hongan-ji," making no mention of the addition of his own portrait.[79] Subsequently, he, too, made presentations of portraits of himself at the request of his followers.

How are we to interpret Rennyo's use of images, including the enshrinement of Shinran's portrait (*goei* 御影) in the Founder's Hall, in a tradition that places primary emphasis on Amida?

First, we need to keep in mind Shinran's own example, especially his reverence for a textual tradition—the Pure Land sūtras and the commentaries of the seven Pure Land masters—as a manifestation of Amida's Vow-mind that enabled him to hear the teaching through Hōnen's words. Inscriptions from the sūtras and commentaries literally frame the Name and portraits of the masters on the scrolls he prepared. It was out of this same perspective that he made presentations of scrolls with his own portrait, similarly framed by inscriptions, at the request of his followers. For Shinran, veneration for a teacher derived entirely from reverence for the teaching itself; Rennyo inherited that tradition.[80]

Second, in regard to serial portraits, Rennyo followed the example of Kakunyo, who had a scroll prepared of the standing figures of Shantao, Hōnen, and Shinran, as well as one of the seated figures of

---

[78] Chiba, "Rennyo no honzon," 218–20.

[79] Chiba, "Rennyo no honzon," 218.

[80] From this perspective, we can better interpret Rennyo's concern following the destruction of Ōtani Hongan-ji for the safety of the founder's image (*goei*). Only after entrusting the image to the care of Mii-dera did he depart for the Hokuriku in 1471. In reflecting on his foremost accomplishments, according to Jitsugo's memoir, he recalls building the Main Hall and the Founder's Hall at Yamashina Hongan-ji. One of the most expressive passages in all of his letters recalls the night of the first thanksgiving service in the new hall: "Realizing that my longing was fulfilled, I was so happy and thankful that my eyes did not close until dawn" (RSI, 317 [#107]).

Shinran, Nyoshin (1235–1300), and himself.[81] Kakunyo's practice may be taken as visually authenticating his reception of the teaching passed down by Shan-tao, Hōnen, Shinran, and Nyoshin. We are reminded yet again that for traditional piety, the Honganji's story is none other than the unfolding of Amida's Primal Vow in history.

Thus for Rennyo, serial portraits on scrolls and wooden images, including his own, are simply expressions of the teaching that faith is bestowed by Amida; his own faith is consequently identical with Shinran's. It is the Name in six characters, however, that is for him the religious symbol par excellence. His single-hearted commitment to enabling others to attain faith through the Name is precisely how he has been remembered. A memoir recalls his writing the Name late at night by candlelight, at Sakai. "I am old," he said. "My hand trembles and my eyes are dim, but I am doing this because the others say they are leaving for Etchū tomorrow. I don't mind hardship. . . . I simply want to enable people to realize faith without causing them trouble." The writer comments that Rennyo "threw himself away" for the sake of his followers.[82]

The extent of Rennyo's devotion to copying the six-character Name is seen in other memoirs. Jitsugo tells of a woman dreaming after Rennyo's death that innumerable copies were hanging in the Osaka temple. When she told Rennō, Rennyo's widow, about the dream, Rennō affirmed it as true — the temple was built with offerings received in return for copies of the Name.[83] Kūzen reports that Rennyo once said, "There's no one in Japan who has written the Name as many times as I have." His disciple Kyōmonbō replied, "It would be hard to find such a person even in the three countries [of India, China, and Japan]!" "That's probably so," agreed Rennyo.[84] Finally, there is a report that Rennyo wrote as many as three hundred copies of the Name before the annual thanksgiving services.[85]

---

[81] Shinkō no Zōkeiteki Hyōgen Kenkyū Iinkai, ed., *Shinshū jūhō shūei*, 213–15. Nyoshin, Zenran's son, is acknowledged as the immediate successor to Shinran and second head priest in the Honganji lineage.

[82] SSZ 3: 589–90.

[83] *Shūjinki*, SSS 11: 607. Cited in Chiba, "Rennyo no honzon," 201–2. See also Miyazaki Enjun, "Honzon to shite no rokuji songō," in *Nihon Jōdokyōshi no kenkyū*, ed. Fujishima Tatsurō and Miyazaki Enjun (Kyoto: Heirakuji Shoten, 1969), 323–32.

[84] *Daihasso onmonogatari Kūzen kikigaki*, SSS 11: 423. Cited in Chiba, "Rennyo no honzon," 202.

[85] *Honganji sahō no shidai*, SSS 11: 568. Cited in Chiba, "Rennyo no honzon," 202.

Rennyo never mistook copies of the Name for a guarantee of salvation. While he was at Yoshizaki, he is said to have given Dōjō of Katada a copy with the reminder, "Even if you wrap yourself in seven or eight layers of these, you won't become a buddha if you don't have faith!"[86] Thus he is remembered within the tradition for an unwavering commitment to bringing others to faith. It appears that his vision of truth is grounded in *Anjin ketsujōshō*'s interpretation of the nenbutsu in terms of the concept *ki-hō ittai* and expressed visually in the six-character Name, distributed far and wide to members of the Honganji.

One expression of Rennyo's response to the dilemma of Honganji's religious power in a period of political turmoil was in doctrinal innovation that culminated in a new formulation of the nenbutsu for the Shinshū. It is this symbolic representation of the teaching, fashioned so compellingly by Rennyo in calligraphic form, that, along with his letters, was to provide definition for orthodox Shinshū piety as gratitude. Our suggestion that this definition is both continuous and discontinuous with Shinran's teaching contrasts with the two lines of interpretation noted in the introduction to this study: the position of traditional piety, which assumes continuity, and that of modern critical scholarship, taking discontinuity for granted.

First, the traditional sectarian view is that Rennyo's *anjin* is identical with Shinran's *shinjin*, and that Rennyo's piety as eighth head priest is, for this reason, wholly continuous with Shinran's. Therefore, any suggestion of change — from a focus on an individual's response to the working of Amida's Other Power and sharing what has been received with others, to a piety giving priority to harmonious relationships within the community and submissiveness to authority — is seen as a threat to the integrity of the tradition. Such a view fails to take account of Rennyo's rich legacy for Shinshū tradition.

Expressive of Rennyo's legacy today is a report of a ceremony in 1977, celebrating the installation of the twenty-fourth head priest of the Nishi Honganji; the writer stresses that participants "could not help but feel the presence of Master Shinran."[87] The feeling is evoked within an institutional setting of a "towering hall with its massive wooden columns," in the context of chanting *Shōshinge* in unison before Shinran's image. The externals of the ceremony are, of course,

---

[86] *Eigenki*, RSG, 259; see also Chiba, "Rennyo no honzon," 220.

[87] Kenryu T. Tsuji, "Hoto Keisho Shiki — Transmission of the Light of Dharma," an article in a monthly publication of the Buddhist Churches of America, *Wheel of Dharma* 4/5 (1977): 1.

drawn from diverse sources. The practice of enshrining Shinran's image was established during the lifetime of his daughter, Kakushinni, following her father's death; the designation of Hongan-ji as the head temple of a religious institution is the work of Kakunyo; and the ritual chanting of Shinran's *Shōshinge* is the legacy of Rennyo. However, it is the emphasis on a collective sense of oneness and gratitude within an institutional setting that marks Rennyo's genius as decisive for defining orthodox Shinshū piety:

> . . . an endless recitation of the Nenbutsu filled the sacred hall like the sound of the wind and the waves on the beach. Unconsciously, we too put our hands together in *gasshō* 合掌 and recited the Nenbutsu, completely immersed in the Buddha's compassionate call.[88]

Orthodox Shinshū piety appears to be characterized by Rennyo's concept of faith (*anjin*), grounded in a *ki-hō ittai* interpretation of the nenbutsu, in contrast to what might be termed the more individualist and dynamic quality of Shinran's concept of faith.[89] It seems that traditional piety has at times taken its own religious symbols too seriously, reifying and accepting them uncritically. Unity and continuity have been sought through a particular interpretation of the nenbutsu as the final, exclusive truth; it follows that interpretations of similar religious symbols within other branches of Pure Land tradition have been seen as temporary and partial.

The second line of interpretation, that of modern critical scholarship, maintains that any change in piety may be readily explained on the basis of social, economic, or political factors, or in terms of psychological and sociological theory applied to Shinran's and Rennyo's roles at different stages of an institution's development. This understanding fails to take religious symbols seriously enough; it also fails to take account of Rennyo's contributions to his tradition.

The suggestion put forward in this study is that Rennyo's discovery in *Anjin ketsujōshō* of an interpretation of the nenbutsu as a religious symbol was dictated neither by political nor by any other stratagems. Rather, he responded to and internalized the *ki-hō ittai* formulation as the way to translate an experience of wholeness symbolized by Shinran's *shinjin*, experienced on an individual and personal

---

[88] Tsuji, "Hoto Keisho Shiki—Transmission of the Light of Dharma," 1.

[89] For a discussion of the contextual meaning of person in Japan's cultural tradition suggestive for comparisons with the concept of individual in Western thought, see Thomas P. Kasulis, *Zen Action/Zen Person* (Honolulu: University of Hawaii Press, 1981), 3–15.

level, into wholeness for an entire community suffering severe political threat. Nevertheless, it is also part of the historical record that Rennyo responded to a religious symbol in a Pure Land text unavailable to Shinran, a symbol conceived and formulated within a rival strand of Pure Land tradition. In certain respects, Rennyo's thought as reflected in his letters differs from that of Shinran, even as sectarian scholars have recognized that Shinran's message is both continuous and discontinuous with that of his Pure Land master, Hōnen.

For five centuries, as participants in the Shinshū have heard, read, copied, or memorized Rennyo's words, they have been nurtured, renewed, and sustained by faith given as Amida's mind through the working of the Other Power of the Primal Vow. The strength, vitality, and naturalness evident in their lives witnesses to continuity with what Shinran discovered. Indeed, a case can be made for a similarity between Shinran's capacity to lead life spontaneously and free of calculative self-effort and what Rennyo, in his mature years, meant by "settled mind."

As we shall see in the following chapters, however, there is also evidence of institutional excess and abuse at the expense of the welfare of individual participants in the tradition. This may be traced in part to Rennyo's zealous efforts to preserve his community at a moment of severe institutional crisis: a pattern of accommodation with those in political authority, perhaps appropriate as compassionate means at that particular time and place, subsequently, in the hands of officials of the Honganji, came to undermine the critical thrust of Shinran's thought. In any event, the letters Rennyo wrote during his Yoshizaki years provided a scriptural basis for an orthodoxy divorced from an awareness of the historical setting in which it was shaped. These same letters have defined Shinshū piety as gratitude until the present. Before turning to the letters themselves in the second part of this study, we will consider Rennyo's final years, in which he rebuilds Hongan-ji at Yamashina and moves into retirement, celebrated as the restorer of the tradition.

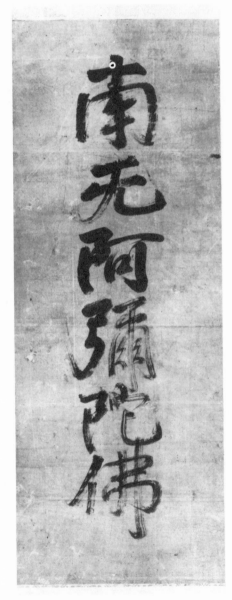

9. The Name in six characters (rokuji myōgō)

Chapter 4

Restoration:
Yamashina Hongan-ji

> Even during the many years when I was moving [from place to place] in the capital and the countryside, what I longed to do was to see the Founder's Hall built during my lifetime and then, with my mind at peace, be born [in the Pure Land]. On the night [of the installation of the founder's portrait], realizing that my longing was fulfilled, I was so happy and thankful that my eyes did not close until dawn.
>
> Rennyo[1]

R ENNYO'S JOY and gratitude in realizing his deeply-felt wish to re-build a Founder's Hall in which to enshrine Shinran's image find fervent expression in this passage, part of a letter written in the eleventh month of Bunmei 12 (1480). In its entirety, the letter reviews the construction of the new Founder's Hall, the temporary installation of Shinran's portrait, and the culminating accomplishment of moving Shinran's image from Ōtsu to Yamashina for permanent installation in the Founder's Hall. The week-long memorial services, which would conclude on the twenty-eighth with the anniversary of Shinran's death, had begun in a new and impressive setting: in large measure, Kakunyo's vision for Hongan-ji as the center of the Shinshū, unified in devotion to Shinran, had been realized.

Following his departure from the Hokuriku in 1475, Rennyo had worked to consolidate the Honganji's position as one of the major

---

[1] RSI, 317 [#107].

religious movements of the day. Important to this undertaking were the letters he wrote during the Yoshizaki years, giving decisive expression to his interpretation of the teaching; they defined for members of the Honganji right belief and conduct for "practicers of faith."[2] For Rennyo, doctrinal innovation had not been a self-conscious, calculative process — he never entertained the possibility that his interpretation of the teaching was anything other than Shinran's. With the rebuilding of Hongan-ji at Yamashina, he must have felt that the issue of religious power had been satisfactorily resolved, at least for the moment. For the first time in its history, the Honganji was a vigorous and highly visible order capable of forging alliances with those in power in the capital. The Yamashina letters tell of the building of the new Hongan-ji and of its splendors; other sources provide evidence of the strengthening of Honganji's ties with the imperial court.

After leaving Yoshizaki, Rennyo found a temporary base in Deguchi, on the south bank of the Yodogawa River in Kawachi province; from here he worked to strengthen the Honganji not only in Kawachi, but also in Settsu and Izumi provinces.[3] He continued his propagation of Shinran's teaching through letters and through gifts of portraits and copies of the Name to be used as a main image; by the end of Bunmei 8 (1476), he had built a temple (Shinshō-in) in Sakai, Izumi, and one in Tonda, Settsu.[4] Rennyo's outward-reaching activities were reciprocated by visits paid to him: Jitsugo records the warm welcome he gave on one occasion to Hōjū (of Katada, Ōmi province), who, intending to make a traditional New Year's visit, arrived late on a bitterly cold and snowy night.[5]

In the first month of Bunmei 10 (1478), Rennyo moved to Yamashina in Yamashiro province, midway between Ōtani Higashiyama,

---

[2] *shinjin no gyōja* 信心の行者 ; see letters 1:3 and 5:18. To place this term in comparativist context, see Wilfred Cantwell Smith's *Towards a World Theology*, chapter two, "Religious Life as Participation in Process."

[3] Kawachi and Izumi are in present-day Osaka prefecture; Settsu, in Hyōgo prefecture.

[4] HS 1: 338–39; HN, 71–2.

[5] Hōjū evidently encountered a snow storm, lost his way, and sent a message to Rennyo that he had decided to spend the night in a nearby village. Rennyo, remembering Hōjū's advanced age, would not hear of him being stranded and sent a horse to bring him to Deguchi. When Hōjū arrived, he went immediately — still in his travelling clothes — to see Rennyo, and master and disciple greeted each other as old friends, with an exchange of poems (Chiba, ed., *Honpukuji atogaki*, in *Honpukuji kyūki*, 374).

the former site of Hongan-ji, and Ōtsu in Ōmi. Although the facts are not entirely clear, it seems that he may have inspected the site on the recommendation of Dōsai of Kanegamori, Ōmi,[6] and obtained it as a consequence of his ties with the retired shogun Ashikaga Yoshimasa.[7] Within a short time, he had put up a simple dwelling and stable,[8] but, suffering the loss of his third wife, Nyoshō, in the eighth month,[9] he spent the end of the year at the temple in Chikamatsu, where Shinran's image had been in safekeeping for more than a decade.[10] Accounts of the next year (1479) tell of planting pines in the garden, landscaping, moving the temple building (Shinshō-in) from Sakai to Yamashina and building living quarters, and procuring pillars and lumber for the Founder's Hall.[11] The following year was one of remarkable accomplishment. In the first month of Bunmei 12 (1480), a scale model was built of the Founder's Hall, and, on the third day of the second month, construction began. By the twenty-eighth day of the eighth month, the Hall was ready for the temporary installation of Shinran's portrait.[12] On the day after, an incense box arrived as a gift from the imperial court in honor of the occasion; on the fourteenth of the tenth month, Hino Tomiko, wife of the retired shogun, came to see the Hall—an event Rennyo declared to be "something unheard of in

---

[6] SSJ, 494.

[7] Immediately preceding the construction of Yamashina Hongan-ji, Yamashina was evidently in the possession of Sanbō-in, Daigo-ji, whose head was Gikaku, Yoshimasa's son. Although Gikaku, who was only eleven at the time, is not likely to have had a direct connection with the event, Rennyo's close ties with the shogun are evidenced by the fact that his fourth daughter, Myōshū (1459–1537), became an attendant to Yoshimasa in Bunmei 9 (1477) and that Yoshimasa's wife, Tomiko, was a member of the Hino family, into which Shinran had been born. It seems likely that these factors contributed to Rennyo's obtaining the site—although the land within the Yamashina estate on which he was to build is said to have been donated by Jōjū, founder of the present Saishū-ji, Yamashina. Jōjū received a portrait as a main image from Rennyo on Bunmei 13 (1481).10.18 (HS 1: 339–40).

[8] RSI, 304 (#104), dated Bunmei 11 (1479).12.

[9] RSI, 300–2 (#102), dated Bunmei 10 (1478).9.17. Nyoshō died the year after the birth of her only child (a daughter), Myōshō (1477–1500). Rennyo writes movingly of her poor health over the years, her suffering and the sense of helplessness and grief of those who attended her at the end, and her extraordinary devotion to the teaching. He closes his tribute to her by saying, "She was gentle and patient, and the same with everyone she met" (302).

[10] HN, 73.

[11] RSI, 306–7 (#104); and RSI, 315 (#107).

[12] RSI, 316–17 (#107).

former times."[13] In the same month, the Anjō portrait of Shinran was repaired, and on the eighteenth day of the eleventh month, Shinran's image was transferred from Chikamatsu to Yamashina in preparation for the annual thanksgiving services, which began on the twenty-first.[14]

A letter of Bunmei 13 (1481) describes continuing construction at Yamashina, with the raising of ridge poles for the Amida Hall on the twenty-eighth day of the fourth month, and the installment of the main image in a temporary altar (*kaributsudan* 仮仏壇) on the eighth day of the sixth month.[15] The imperial court favored the undertaking by responding at last to Rennyo's repeated requests for the return of an illustrated biography of Kakunyo, *Bokie*, from Yoshimasa's extensive collection of art.[16] The fact that Rennyo was successful in this effort indicates the level of influence to which the Honganji had risen. The order's ties to the shogunate had already been strengthened by the presence of Rennyo's daughter Myōshū in Yoshimasa's household,[17] and its prestige was further enhanced by the frequent visits of Hosokawa Masamoto,[18] son and heir of Katsumoto, who, it will be recalled, had been one of the major protagonists in the Ōnin War.

A letter dated Bunmei 15 (1483).8.28 concludes Rennyo's account of the rebuilding of Yamashina Hongan-ji, an accomplishment that appears to have balanced some of the pain of years of struggle and uncertainty at the hands of religious and political forces representative of the traditional establishment. The letter details the completion of the great gate in the first month of Bunmei 14 (1482), of the altar in the Amida Hall, with the installation of the main image on the fifteenth day of the sixth month, and of a Chinese-style front gate

---

[13] HS 1: 342. For further discussion of the Honganji's connections with the imperial court, see 350–53.

[14] HS 1: 342; HN, 73–74.

[15] RSI, 326–27 (#109); HS 1: 343.

[16] HS 1: 352; all but two of the ten scrolls of this work (by Kakunyo's second son Jūkaku [1295–1360]; illustrated by Fujiwara Takamasa and Fujiwara Takaaki) were returned on Bunmei 13 (1481).12.4. See Chiba Jōryū, "Bokie no omote to ura," *Bokie ekotoba*, Zoku Nihon Ekan Taisei 4, ed. Komatsu Shigemi (Tokyo: Chūō Kōronsha, 1985), 102–3. In Bunmei 14 (1482).11, Rennyo had the missing scrolls, one and seven, replaced by Fujiwara Hisanobu (103; SSJ, 446).

[17] See n. 7 above and HS 1: 340, 352.

[18] Solomon focuses on the relationship between the Honganji and Masamoto as the case study for the central thesis of his article, "The Dilemma of Religious Power."

before the year's end.[19] The temple buildings — which were to become the center of an extensive temple-town acclaimed as a buddha-land (*bukkoku* 仏国) — were finally in place, a tangible statement of the strength of the institution.

After several years of work on Rennyo's part toward the further consolidation of the Honganji's religious power, the stage was set for his retirement in 1489, at the age of seventy-five. With the transfer of custodianship to Jitsunyo, his fifth son,[20] he took up residence in Yamashina's southern quarters (*nanden*, or *minamidono* 南殿).[21]

Retirement did not lead to inactivity. Rennyo continued to instruct followers, write letters to Honganji-related congregations, and make hundreds of copies of the six-character Name for use as the main image in the homes of Shinshū adherents. In 1496, at age eighty-two, he began the construction of a temple at Ikutama (site of present-day Osaka), in Settsu; building was completed the following year.[22] Subsequently, this was the location of Ishiyama Hongan-ji, the temple-town and fortress that was the center for the Honganji's prolonged and bitter resistance to Nobunaga late in the sixteenth century. In Meiō 7

---

[19] RSI, 335–38 (#113). Rennyo also describes a problem with drainage, corrected by the construction of a moat, south to north, with pine trees planted along the sides, and bridges for access. To complete work in the Amida Hall, lacquerers came from Nara to finish the altar; artists decorated the Hall's cryptomeria sliding doors and the area behind the altar with painted lotuses. The final stage, completed in Bunmei 15 (1483), was the laying of the tile roof; under the supervision of a tiler, workers were assembled to collect earth for the tiles, a kiln was built, and by the twenty-second of the eighth month, the task completed. The letters having to do with the construction at Yamashina make clear Rennyo's involvement at all stages: he planned the buildings, found the artisans, located materials, and was continually anticipating the next project.

[20] This certificate of transfer (the second addressed to Jitsunyo), dated Entoku 2 (1490).10.28, signed "Kenju," with a written seal, reads:

> The person named above shall assume his responsibilities as custodian immediately, following the precedent of former generations. If there are points of dispute concerning the teaching, however, the office is to be administered collectively by the brothers, thus maintaining its effectiveness. Next, there are many young children [in the family]. They are to be supported as they have been by me, without fail, all my life. If [the custodian] disobeys what is stated above, he marks himself for eternity as unfilial. With this letter, I make the transfer (RSI, 509–10 [#215]).

[21] HS 1: 354; HN, 77. Jitsunyo, who hesitated over the responsibility as his brother Junnyo had, took up residence in the northern quarters on his succession; thus he was referred to on occasion as *kitadonosama* 北殿様 (*Goichidaiki kikigaki*, SSZ 3: 532).

[22] RSI, 445–46 (#156/4:15); SSZ 3: 498–99. See also HS 1: 356.

(1498), Rennyo's health began to fail;[23] he died at Yamashina in the following year, on the twenty-fifth of the third month, at the age of eighty-five.[24]

COLLECTIVE RELIGIOUS OBSERVANCES

During his years at Yoshizaki, Rennyo recognized that the monthly and annual assemblies of Shinshū followers at the services commemorating Shinran's death were especially fortuitous as opportunities for instruction and conversion.[25] The letters he prepared almost every year for the annual services, beginning with the one for services held in Yoshizaki in the eleventh month of 1472 and continuing until the end of his life, came to define an orthodoxy that has persisted until the present. Crucial to this process of definition was Rennyo's interpretation of Shinran's individualist-oriented concept for faith, *shinjin*, in terms of a more group-oriented concept, *anjin*, in the context of corporate worship.

Memorial or thanksgiving services, *hōonkō*, were part of a pattern of religious observance that has an ancient history in Japanese community life. The literal meaning of the term *hōonkō* is "a group (*kō* 講) gathered for the purpose of returning what is owed (*hōon* 報恩)." While such services were held in other Buddhist sects, they became the major religious observance in the Shinshū for schooling members of the community in the teaching and bringing about its internalization as faith.[26] During Shinran's lifetime, his followers in the Kantō assembled each month on the twenty-fifth, the anniversary of Hōnen's

---

[23] *Goichidaiki kikigaki*, SSZ 3: 544; *Kūzenki*, RSG, 37.

[24] *Kūzenki*, RSG, 49.

[25] This is not to suggest that the annual services were unimportant to Rennyo before his move to Yoshizaki and development of letter writing as the primary vehicle for his teaching. In the years following the destruction of Ōtani Hongan-ji, he conducted thanksgiving services on Bunshō 1 (1466).11.21 at Kanegamori, Ōmi, and on Ōnin 1 (1467).11.21 at Honpuku-ji, Katada. These, however, are the first such services noted in the Honganji chronological tables following services held in the eleventh month of Shōhei 1 (1346), during Kakunyo's tenure as head priest (see HN, 38, 65).

[26] For a discussion of the Honganji's services in relation to Japanese folk beliefs in the Yoshizaki area, see Sakurai Tokutarō, *Nihon minkan shinkōron* (Tokyo: Kōbundō, 1970), 282–86. Sakurai's argument is that the Shinshū, in order to broaden its influence, had to accommodate its teachings to traditional folk beliefs held by participants in the groups (*kō*), which represented the most basic level of religious life in village communities (see summary in English, 2–7).

death, for fellowship and nenbutsu recitation. On these occasions, offerings of money, food, or clothing would be made to cover any local needs, and donations were sent to Shinran in Kyoto. After his death on the twenty-eighth day of the eleventh month of Kōchō 2 (1262),[27] the assembly day was shifted to the twenty-eighth of each month, when donations were made for the maintenance of his mausoleum and the property at Ōtani Higashiyama. This practice was given formal institutional expression under the leadership of Kakunyo, as he sought support among the scattered groups of Shinran's followers for the office of custodian and for the maintenance of the mausoleum after it became a temple, Hongan-ji.

The *Hōonkō shiki*, the first work to be attributed to Kakunyo, is a service of thanksgiving for Shinran's virtues. Written in 1294, in classical Chinese, it was used during Kakunyo's lifetime at annual services honoring Shinran's life and legacy. These services lasted seven days, beginning on the twenty-first day of the eleventh month and concluding on the anniversary date of the twenty-eighth. The three parts of the *Hōonkō shiki* celebrate Shinran's achievement as the founder of the Shinshū, his discovery of the true meaning of Amida's Primal Vow, and the benefits bestowed on his followers after his death.[28] Illustrative of works apotheosizing Shinran, this text culminates with a reference to his having been "praised as a manifestation of Amida and declared an incarnation of Master T'an-luan."[29]

One of the earliest extant manuscripts of the *Hōonkō shiki* is a copy made by Rennyo in the tenth month of Ōnin 2 (1468),[30] less than three years before his move to Yoshizaki. In spite of the fact that the text was read according to grammatical principles used for reading Chinese, its very formality would have made it largely unintelligible to the majority of Shinshū followers. Rennyo, sensitive to the text's significance, prepared a letter known as *Gozokushō* for the annual services in the eleventh month of Bunmei 9 (1477), which expresses its main points in colloquial Japanese. Through this letter and others, Rennyo was able to offer fresh interpretations of his tradition's religious symbols.

---

[27] *Godenshō*, SSZ 3: 653. In a reassessment of the year of Shinran's death according to the Western solar calendar, a case has been made for the year 1263; see Masami Fujitani, "Problems of Calendar in Translation—Year of Shinran Shonin's Demise," *The Pacific World: Journal of the Institute of Buddhist Studies* 1 (1982): 13–14.

[28] SSZ 3: 655–60.

[29] SSZ 3: 659.

[30] HN, 66.

Under his guidance, collective religious observances honoring the memory of the founder were transformed into the foremost ritual activity for binding together, ordering, and giving direction to the life of the community as a whole.[31]

The letters that Rennyo wrote annually in the eleventh month in preparation for the thanksgiving services offer a compendium of his interpretations of Shinran's teaching. A letter written on Bunmei 4 (1472).11.27 at Yoshizaki presents traditional points of doctrine in question-and-answer form. The answers may be summarized as follows: (1) Shinran offers an approach to Buddha-dharma through which it is possible to attain salvation in the course of ordinary life, apart from meditative and disciplinary practices; (2) it is unnecessary to wait for Amida to come to meet one at the moment of death; (3) the state of being settled in faith and attaining nirvana are considered to be two benefits, the first occurring in this world and the second in the Pure Land at death; and (4) the nenbutsu is said solely in grateful return for Amida Buddha's benevolence.[32]

Rennyo's first formal proclamation of regulations in the eleventh month of Bunmei 5 (1473),[33] in the face of severe external threat to his community at Yoshizaki, was issued in the month of Shinran's death anniversary. His desperate efforts to preserve the community seem to have been increasingly informed by a deep awareness of indebtedness to Shinran. In a letter written on Bunmei 5 (1473).12.8, he makes explicit reference to the thanksgiving services held in the previous month, noting that, during the services, wives of priests in charge of the lodgings at Yoshizaki had experienced a decisive settling of faith.[34] It appears that the seven days of intensive religious teaching and devotional services, against the background of political turmoil and danger to the community, had been the occasion for a significant number of conversions.

A letter dated almost a year later, Bunmei 6 (1474).11.25, takes note of services then in progress; four days later, with the services still continuing, Rennyo writes:

---

[31] The annual thanksgiving services continue to hold an important place in the life of the Shinshū. At present, the Jōdo Shinshū Honganji (Nishi Honganji) and Takada (Senjuji) branches of the Shinshū hold services from the ninth to the sixteenth of January; the Shinshū Ōtani (Higashi Honganji), Bukkōji, Kōshōji, and other branches hold services from the twenty-first to the twenty-eighth of November (SSJ, 440).

[32] RSI, 88–91 (#18/1:4); SSZ 3: 406–8.

[33] RSI, 131–33 (#38); for translation, see chapter three.

[34] RSI, 138–41 (#40/2:1); SSZ 3: 424–26.

Among those who make the pilgrimage, bring offerings, and come before the [image of] Master [Shinran] to repay their indebtedness and express their gratitude during this anniversary, there will be those who have realized faith. There will also be those who are lacking in faith (*fushinjin*). This is an extremely serious matter. For unless there is a decisive settling of faith, the birth that is to come in the fulfilled land is uncertain. Therefore, those whose faith is lacking (*fushin*) should in all haste attain the decisive mind.[35]

This opening passage, intended to impress on the assembled followers that assurance of birth in the Pure Land in the afterlife depends on the realization of faith here and now, associates veneration of the founder with the settling of faith. In effect, becoming settled in faith is construed as a means of expressing gratitude for Shinran's virtues.

The theme of one of Rennyo's last letters from Yoshizaki, dated Bunmei 7 (1475).5.28, is the monthly services:

Today being the [monthly] anniversary of Master [Shin]ran's death, there are few people who do not intend by all means to repay their indebtedness and express their gratitude for his benevolence. What everyone must understand, however, is how difficult it will be for people to conform to the intention of our master if (as in the case of practicers who have not attained true and real faith through the power of the Primal Vow and in whom the settled mind is yet to be realized [*mianjin*]) they make the visit perfunctorily, for today only, and think that what is essential in the Shinshū is just filling the members' meeting place. Nevertheless, it is probably good for those who are not concerned about the thanksgiving services to be here, even if they attend reluctantly.[36]

Conformity with Shinran's teaching on the attainment of true and real faith is to be interpreted as realization of the settled mind (*anjin*). Monthly services on the anniversary of Shinran's death — an opportunity for hearing the teaching — may be efficacious even for those who attend reluctantly. To commit oneself to listening to the teaching will lead eventually to the settling of faith. Rennyo takes note of a heightened sense of awareness evoked during the services:

Although more than a hundred years have already passed since the master's death, we gratefully revere the image before our eyes. And although his benevolent voice is distant, separated from us by the wind of impermanence, his words of truth have been directly trans-

---

[35] RSI, 227 (#75/5:11); SSZ 3: 507–8.
[36] RSI, 244–45 (#82/3:9); SSZ 3: 464.

mitted by his descendants; they resound with clarity deep in our ears. Thus it is that our school's faith, grounded in the truth and reality of Other Power, has been transmitted until today without interruption.[37]

The first letter written following Rennyo's departure from Yoshizaki is dated Bunmei 7 (1475).11.21, the first day of the thanksgiving services held in Deguchi, Kawachi province. Following an arduous journey and amidst the demands of settling into a new community, Rennyo prepares a letter focusing on his indebtedness to Shinran as master and founder:

> As the twenty-eighth of this month is the anniversary [of the death] of our founder, Master [Shinran], services [have been held] every year without exception, in recognition of our indebtedness and in grateful response to [his] benevolence. Even the most humble fellow practicers [come at this time] from the various provinces and districts; those who fail to recognize their indebtedness must indeed be like wood and stones!
>
> Although this foolish old man has somehow lived for the past four or five years in the Hokuriku, in a remote corner of the mountains by the sea, it is beyond all expectation that he is still alive and has come to this province and that this year, for the first time, we will celebrate thanksgiving services together [in honor] of the master's anniversary. This is indeed [the result of] inconceivable past conditions; I rejoice over it more and more deeply, time and again.
>
> People who gather from this and other provinces should, therefore, first of all, be fully aware of the significance of the regulations (*on'okite* 御掟) established by the founding master. He said, "Even if you are called a cow thief, do not act in such a way that you are seen as a follower of the Buddha-dharma or as an aspirant for [buddhahood in] the afterlife."[38]

Rennyo's use here of the honorific *on'okite* is striking. As we have noted, he had drawn up his first list of regulations, not entirely without precedent in Shinshū congregational life, in the document written in classical Chinese at Yoshizaki in the eleventh month of 1473.[39] He now explicitly enlists Shinran's authority in presenting the regulations as if they were the words of the founder himself. Having done this, he goes on to list again many of the items he had promulgated in earlier letters written at Yoshizaki. On this occasion, however, additional

---

[37] RSI, 245 (#82/3:9); SSZ 3: 464–65.
[38] RSI, 251 (#84/3:11); SSZ 3: 469.
[39] RSI, 131–33 (#38); for translation, see chapter three.

principles involving societal obligations are stressed in the setting of a corporate religious observance:

> [The founder] also carefully stipulated that we should observe [the principles of] humanity, justice, propriety, wisdom, and sincerity; that we should honor the laws of the state; and that, deep within, we should take Other-Power faith established by the Primal Vow as fundamental.[40]

Rennyo observes in the same letter that, although those who assemble appear to rely on Buddha-dharma, there is no decisive settling of faith. In particular, he criticizes priests who, in advocating secret transmission of the teaching, lead members of the community astray. To counteract their influence, he stresses again their obligation to repay their indebtedness and express their gratitude to Shinran:

> Unless each of these people repents and confesses his evil ways and turns to the right teaching during the seven-day thanksgiving services [commemorating] the anniversary of the master's death on the twenty-eighth of this month[, their coming will be to no purpose]; and if they attend these seven-day thanksgiving services just in imitation of others, though they say that they come to repay their indebtedness and express their gratitude for the [master's] benevolence, [their coming] will amount to nothing at all. Hence it is precisely those people who have attained faith through the working of Amida's Vow who will return the Buddha's benevolence in gratitude and respond gratefully to their teacher's virtue.[41]

Keenly aware of his difficulty at Yoshizaki in controlling the activity of community members drawn into the Kaga uprisings, Rennyo calls for repentance and confession — a turning of the heart and mind.[42] In succeeding years, letters written on the occasion of the annual services emphasize a collective veneration of Shinran as the means for nurturing orthodox Shinshū piety. In this way, the rules of conduct were given greater legitimacy and strong moral sanction for acceptance by individual members of the Honganji.

Two years later, in the eleventh month of Bunmei 9 (1477), Rennyo (still resident in Deguchi) wrote the letter *Gozokushō*, which subsequently became a normative document for the Shinshū community. The text, divided into three sections, begins with an account of

---

[40] RSI, 251 (#84/3:11); SSZ 3: 469.

[41] RSI, 252 (#84/3:11); SSZ 3: 470.

[42] The notion of repentance is found in Kakunyo's *Hōonkō shiki*; see SSZ 3: 656. Shinran cites passages from Shan-tao's *Ōjō raisange* relating to confession in *Kyōgyōshinshō*; see SSZ 2: 151–52.

Shinran's background, which might be interpreted in terms of the mundane and of the transcendent:

> A member of the Fujiwara family, he was the son of Arinori, an official in the service of the dowager empress [Taira no Shigeko]; he was a descendant of Lord Uchimaro, [who was himself] a descendant of [the state minister] Gonagaoka. When we inquire into his true origin, [we find that] he was declared an incarnation of Amida Tathāgata and was also said to be the great teacher Tan-iuan reborn.[43]

The section continues with a description of Shinran's ordination, his training on Mt. Hiei, and meeting with Hōnen, and concludes with a summary of his contribution within Pure Land tradition:

> In the spring of his ninth year, he joined the disciples of Master Jichin [Jien]; he was ordained [as a novice] and took the name of a lesser councilor of state, Han'en. After that, he followed the branch line of teaching of Ryōgon-in, Yokawa, and became a profound scholar of the Tendai sect. Later, at the age of twenty-nine, he first visited the hermitage of Master Hōnen; he became one of his foremost disciples. Drawing out the true essence of [Pure Land] tradition, he established the teaching of the single practice and single-mindedness and clarified the faith by which ordinary beings[44] enter promptly and directly [into Amida's salvation]; instructing ignorant lay people, he taught [the way] of birth in the fulfilled land.[45]

In preparing this letter, Rennyo was fashioning an image of Shinran that was to become normative for succeeding generations. In the second section, he describes the services held "every year without exception" on the anniversary of Shinran's death, stressing their importance as services of thanksgiving:

---

[43] RSI, 282 (#96): SSZ 3: 519.

[44] *bonbu* 凡夫 . The term suggests beings caught in the cycle of birth-and-death, reaping the effects of karma stemming from erroneous views and blind passions; it also includes a dimension of meaning explained by the translators of the Shin Buddhism Translation Series, who, in rendering *bonbu* as "foolish being," note that it points to an awakening in which a person

> comes to realize himself as a foolish being who is forever motivated by blindly self-centered desires, attached to the fascinations of this evanescent world, and unable to resolve the contradictions of human existence thoroughly. In fact, Shinran says that true wisdom is brought forth only from the heart and mind of the person who has awakened to Amida's great compassion, and in the light of that compassion realizes himself to be a foolish being (*Passages*, s.v. "Foolish being," 88).

[45] RSI, 282 (#96); SSZ 3: 519.

The immensity of [Shinran's] benevolence is higher than Mount Sumeru and deeper than the blue sea! How could we fail to repay our indebtedness and express our gratitude? For this reason, we have, as a yearly event, held the traditional seven-day services. . . .[46]

For Rennyo, participation in the annual thanksgiving services is the mark of Shinshū piety, the occasion for members of the community to gather from throughout the provinces. In emphasizing this, he attempts to realize what Kakunyo had been unable to achieve — a Shinshū community unified under the Honganji. He concludes:

Alas, the master's birth [in the Pure Land] and this anniversary are widely separated; more than one hundred years have passed [since his death]. Yet the teaching he left is flourishing more than ever; the Name expounded in *Kyōgyōshinshō* is even now before our eyes and remains on peoples' lips.[47]

. . . Those who listen carefully during the seven days of these thanksgiving services, realize the truth of the Primal Vow of Other Power, and become steadfast practicers of the nenbutsu, the single practice, will indeed be in accord with the original intent of the master's anniversary. These will truly be services in which we repay our indebtedness and express our gratitude.[48]

Listening to these words in praise of Shinran served to deepen a collective religious experience and bind together those who assembled. To express gratitude to Shinran — and, by implication, most immediately to Rennyo — was to be settled in faith. From Rennyo's point of view, to do less was to demonstrate a total lack of feeling.

IN THANKSGIVING TO SHINRAN

The pattern of collective religious observances initiated at Yoshizaki and continued at Deguchi assumed a further stage of development with the completion of the main temple buildings at Yamashina Hongan-ji in 1480. With the enshrinement of Shinran's image in the new Founder's Hall, the annual services took on even deeper meaning for the entire Shinshū community. It became customary for each congregation to make an annual contribution to the Honganji, often pre-

---

[46] RSI, 283 (#96); SSZ 3: 519.

[47] A reference to the six-character Name as the main image and in the saying of the nenbutsu.

[48] RSI, 283–84 (#96); SSZ 3: 520. A revised copy of this letter (RSI, 284–86) is dated Bunmei 11 (1479).11.20.

senting it at that time. For example, in a brief letter written on the eighteenth day of the eleventh month (year omitted), Rennyo thanks the congregation at Hongaku-ji in Wada, Echizen, for offerings for the building of the temple and the annual thanksgiving services and for cloth;[49] in another, he thanks a group in Kaga that met on the sixth day of each month, assuring them that their annual offering had arrived.[50]

The lengthy letters Rennyo wrote each year in the eleventh month from 1482 to 1486 place strong emphasis on rules of conduct; their importance for the Honganji is recognized by the inclusion of those for the years 1482–1485 in fascicle four of *The Letters*.[51] Here Rennyo links his concern over Honganji members' involvement in political activities with an emphasis on proper religious observance, expressed most immediately by gratitude to Shinran. In this period, the major influence on his thought, seen especially in letters dated Bunmei 17 (1485).11.23 and Bunmei 18 (1486).11.26, was the text *Anjin ketsujōshō*.

At the annual services in 1482, Rennyo points out that the notion of good (karma) from the past (*shukuzen*) has not been properly understood within the Shinshū from "the middle period" on, since Kakunyo's tenure as head priest:

> Among those who have carried out the teaching in our tradition from the middle period until the present, some have done so without knowing at all whether [their listeners] have, or lack, good from

---

[49] RSI, 513–14 (#220). It appears that Hongaku-ji was charged with responsibility for the temple at Yoshizaki after Rennyo's departure (HS 1: 333–34).

[50] RSI, 492–93 (#192), written on the eighth day of the seventh month (year omitted). See RSI, 492–506, 513–14 (#192–#210, #220–#221), for twenty-one such letters, all but four of which include a short message on faith.

[51] Letters written for the annual thanksgiving services in 1480 and 1481 are: RSI, 319–21, dated Bunmei 12 (1480).11.21 (#108) and RSI, 332–33, dated Bunmei 13 (1481).11.24 (#111). The letters written in the eleventh month for the years 1482–1485 and included in the five-fascicle collection are: RSI, 333–35, dated Bunmei 14 (1482).11.21 (#112/4:5); RSI, 344–47, dated Bunmei 15 (1483).11.22 (#115/4:6); RSI, 350–53, dated Bunmei 16 (1484).11.21 (#117/4:7); and RSI, 354–59, dated Bunmei 17 (1485).11.23 (#119/4:8). For a letter written in the eleventh month of 1486, see RSI, 360–63 [#119], dated Bunmei 18 (1486).11.26, which is a revised version of one dated Bunmei 17 (1485).11.23 (#119). Subsequent letters written in the eleventh month in the context of the annual services are: RSI, 377–78, dated Meiō 3 (1494).11.21 (#126); RSI, 386–87, Meiō 5 (1496).11.21 (#130); RSI, 398–99, Meiō 6 (1497).11.21 (#134) and RSI, 401–2, 11.25 (#135); and RSI, 443–44, Meiō 7 (1498).11.19 (#155/5:9) and RSI, 444–46, 11.21 (#156/4:15).

the past. Simply put, you must be aware of this from now on. When you read the scriptures, for example, or when you speak [even] briefly about the teaching, you must [first] ascertain this, and then proclaim the dharma as taught within our school; or, again, when people gather in large numbers to listen to the Buddha-dharma and you feel that there may be some among those people who lack good from the past, you should not discuss the meaning of our school's true and real dharma. Recently, however, as I observe how people preach, [it is clear that some] lack this awareness and simply feel that, whichever type of person the listener may be, he will surely be grounded in our tradition's faith (anjin) if they preach well. You should know that this is an error. Carry out the teaching in our tradition with full awareness of what is written above. From the middle period until now, there has been no one at all who has understood this and preached with excellence.[52]

It appears that the notion of good from the past served Rennyo well in his efforts to interpret the current situation of his religious community. The maturation of good karma, accumulated in previous lives, brings about favorable conditions in the present; this may have suggested to Rennyo that the realization of Kakunyo's vision for the Honganji depended on the fruition of good karma stored up within the cumulative tradition of the Honganji's response to Shinran's teaching. To appropriate and convey that teaching, following a period in which the concept of good from the past had been misunderstood, it was necessary to "undertake the preaching in the traditional way."[53]

In stressing the benefit of good from the past, a notion Shinran never used directly in his writings (possibly because it could be misinterpreted as having self-power connotations),[54] Rennyo was raising his followers' awareness of the Honganji's legacy of good karma resulting from Shinran's teachings, despite the deviations of "the middle period." Consequently, those assembled were made aware that they were being incorporated into a religious body with a rich heritage and a promising future, and that in joining the community, they were not merely accepting responsibility for themselves, but a collective responsibility for the community at large.

On the other hand, Rennyo's emphasis on good from the past served as a warning to Shinshū priests not to become carelessly involved in open discussions of the teaching in situations that might lead

---

[52] RSI, 333–34 (#112/4:5), dated Bunmei 14 (1482).11.21; SSZ 3: 481–82.

[53] RSI, 334 (#112/4:5); SSZ 3: 482.

[54] The use of the term *shukuzen* is attributed to Shinran by Yuien in chapter thirteen of *Tannishō*, SSZ 2: 782.

to misunderstandings. By anticipating that those lacking good from the past might be unprepared to hear Shinran's teaching, in principle a message of salvation for all, Rennyo was able to justify circumscribing membership in the community. Further, there were grounds for excommunicating those whose conduct was deemed contrary to the interests of the community at large.

As Rennyo continues the letter written for the annual services in 1482, he expresses alarm over a persistent problem:

> In recent years, [some] have confused people to the extreme by spreading distorted teachings (*higa hōmon* ひが法門) not discussed in our tradition; others, reprimanded by local land stewards and domain holders (who are themselves entrenched in wrong views), have come to view our tradition's true and real faith (*anjin*) as mistaken. Is this not a deplorable situation? It is lamentable; it is dreadful.[55]

Here Rennyo may have had in mind his painful experiences in the Hokuriku, where his authority had been undermined by advocates of secret teachings passed from master to disciple. In terms of his efforts to unify the community at Yamashina Hongan-ji, however, there was a danger of followers merely participating in the services without identifying with the religious core underlying the ritual forms. Rennyo attempted to counteract such behaviour by advising that each member of the community undergo conversion — repentance, a turning of the mind, and confession — as an "offering through which we repay our indebtedness and express our gratitude [to Shinran for his benevolence]":

> During the seven days and nights of the thanksgiving services this month, each person should deeply repent; and, leaving none of his own mistaken thoughts at the bottom of his mind, he should undergo a turning of that mind and confess before the revered image [of the founder] in this temple, telling of this every day and every night so that everyone will hear about it. This, in other words, is in accord with [a passage in Shan-tao's] commentary: "With a turning of the mind, [even] slanderers of the dharma and those who lack the seed of buddhahood will all be born [in the Pure Land]"; it also corresponds to the teaching of "realizing faith (*shin*) oneself and guiding others to faith (*shin*)."
>
> Then, on hearing about this turning of the mind and repentance, attentive people will indeed feel the rightness of it, and in some of them the ordinary "bad" mind may be similarly overturned and changed into the "good" mind. This will truly accomplish the fun-

---

[55] RSI, 334 (#112/4:5); SSZ 3: 482.

damental purpose of the master's anniversary this month. In other words, this is the offering through which we repay our indebtedness and express our gratitude [for his benevolence].[56]

A year later, on Bunmei 15 (1483).11.22, Rennyo prepared another homily to be delivered at the services. Noting that followers had assembled from even the most distant provinces, he again points out that although some come with a sincere desire to give thanks, there are also those who simply imitate the piety of others. He advises — with reference to both priests and laity:

> These people should promptly kneel before the revered image and, through a turning of the mind and repentance, enter into the true purport of the Primal Vow and attain true and real faith with the awakening of the one thought-moment [of entrusting].[57]

He next identifies three specific problems facing the community:

Item: Those who are pillars of the Buddha-dharma and hold the position of priest in accord with the tradition are said to have told others about false teachings that are unknown to us and of obscure origin and, recently, to have actively engaged in this far and wide in order to be considered learned. This is preposterous!

Item: It is a great mistake for people to announce that they are making a pilgrimage to the revered image [of the founder] at Hongan-ji, in Kyoto, and then — regardless of the sort of people who are around, especially on main roads and thoroughfares and at checking stations and ferry crossings — to speak indiscriminately to others about matters concerning the Buddha-dharma.

Item: Should there be a situation in which someone asks what sort of Buddha-dharma you rely on, do not answer outright that you are a nenbutsu person in our tradition. Simply reply that you are a person of no particular sect, who just knows the nenbutsu as something precious. This, in other words, is the bearing of a person who, as our tradition's master taught, will not be seen as a follower of the Buddha-dharma.[58]

Rennyo's concern for conformity in conduct as well as for uniformity in teaching transforms the regulations into "items of praxis" in the sense that they come to define absolute standards for participation in the community:

---

[56] RSI, 334–35 (#112/4:5); SSZ 3: 482–83.
[57] RSI, 345 (#115/4:6); SSZ 3: 484.
[58] RSI, 346–47 (#115/4:6); SSZ 3: 484–85.

You must recognize, therefore, that right understanding in our tradition is knowing these points thoroughly and, outwardly, giving no sign of them. Furthermore, none of the points established by the community during the thanksgiving services over the past two or three years are to be altered. If by chance there are points with which members of this community (*gomonto* 御門徒) are at variance, those who differ can no longer be followers of the founding master.[59]

Using the honorific *gomonto* to refer to his followers, Rennyo now underscores that they are intimately linked to the founder. A further implication is that they are under obligation to internalize and obey the regulations that he, as Shinran's legitimate representative, set forth. Shinran, however, spoke only of nenbutsu devotees and his "companions and fellow practicers." The annual services as collective religious observances may be seen to generate and reinforce a group piety within a hierarchical setting at the expense of Shinran's more individualist and egalitarian vision of community.

A year later, in the message prepared on Bunmei 16 (1484).11.21 for the annual services, Rennyo laments the lack of faith (*fushin*) of those who have assembled. His attempt to account for this concludes in what must have seemed the most logical explanation: "If they are people lacking good from the past, perhaps we must say that it cannot be helped."[60] In a six-item list, he addresses two areas of particular concern and issues four directives. The two concerns are reports of priests' failure to discuss faith and rumors of their anger toward ordinary people who had heard the truth of Other-Power faith. The directives are addressed to nenbutsu followers in general: they should be circumspect in discussing Buddha-dharma in public places while on pilgrimage; they should identify themselves simply as nenbutsu devotees of no particular sect; they should clarify their understanding of Buddha-dharma repeatedly, as opposed to relying on second-hand reports; and, through repeated inquiries, they should come to a decisive realization of faith.[61]

The next year, at the services held in Bunmei 17 (1485), the list of items is expanded to eight and given a strong doctrinal thrust in terms of an Other-Power interpretation of *anjin* or *tōryū no anjin* — "our tradition's *anjin*." Rennyo cautions against indiscreet discussion of the teaching, warns against teachings not encountered in the Shinshū,

[59] RSI, 347 (#115/4:6); SSZ 3: 485.
[60] RSI, 350–51 (#117/4:7); SSZ 3: 486.
[61] RSI, 351–52 (#117/4:7); SSZ 3: 486–88.

and prohibits the use of "strange phrases,"[62] which might be construed as mantras, out of keeping with Shinshū nenbutsu recitation. The realization of faith, he stresses, begins with an attitude of repentance leading to confession, and that when one's mind is not yet settled, one should talk openly and honestly within the community about one's true feelings. Priests and disciples are to abide in the same faith (*ichimi no anjin* 一味の安心). He cautions, as he has before, against priests who drink to excess. His final item states: "It must be understood that the decisive settling of faith in our tradition is expressed by the six characters 南無阿弥陀仏 (*na-mu-a-mi-da-butsu*)."[63] Then follows a lengthy explication of the six-character nenbutsu based on Shan-tao's interpretation; he draws on *Anjin ketsujōshō* for the concept of *ki-hō ittai*:

> When sentient beings take refuge in Amida — "namu," Amida Buddha, fully knowing those sentient beings, bestows on them the virtue of a myriad good deeds and practices, countless as the grains of sand in the river Ganges. This is what is meant by "Amida-butsu is the practice." Those who take refuge ("namu") are therefore one with the saving dharma of Amida Buddha; we speak of "the oneness in 'namu-amida-butsu' of the person [to be saved] and dharma [that saves]," indicating this point. We must bear in mind, therefore, that "namu-amida-butsu" expresses the full realization of perfect enlightenment [that was accomplished] when Amida Buddha vowed long ago (when he was the monk Dharmākara) that unless sentient beings attained buddhahood, he too would not attain perfect enlightenment. This, in other words, is evidence that our birth [in the Pure Land] is settled. Hence it should be concluded that our realization of Other-Power faith is expressed in just these six characters.[64]

Rennyo concludes the letter on a personal note:

> The significance of these eight items is as stated. Meanwhile, it has already been nine years since [we began] the construction of this temple.[65] During the thanksgiving services each year, everyone

---

[62] *omoshiroki myōmoku* おもしろき名目 ; similar to the "strange terms (*myōgen* 名言)" mentioned in letter 1:13, in reference to the "ten kalpas" heresy (see fascicle one, n. 84).

[63] RSI, 358 (#119/4:8); SSZ 3: 490.

[64] RSI, 358 (#119/4:8); SSZ 3: 490–91.

[65] Although Rennyo moved to Yamashina in Bunmei 10 (1478), it seems likely that he inspected the site the year before and began some construction at that time. This would lend consistency to the reference in the next paragraph to his "seven or eight years" of residence there. See Izumoji Osamu, ed., *Ofumi*, Tōyō Bunko, no. 345 (Tokyo: Heibonsha, 1978), 297–98.

feels that he has fully heard and understood [the teaching] and undergone a decisive settling of faith, but as the meaning of that faith
differs even as of yesterday and today, it may amount to nothing at
all. But if those lacking faith (*fushinjin*) do not quickly attain true
and real faith during the thanksgiving services this month—during
this year's thanksgiving services in particular—it seems things will
be the same, even with the passage of many years.

This foolish old man has, however, already passed his seventh decade and finds it difficult to anticipate next year's thanksgiving services. For this reason, if there are people who really and truly attain
decisively settled faith (*shin*), I would consider [their realization] to
be, first, an expression of gratitude to the master this month, and,
next, the fulfillment of a desire an old man has cherished over these
seven or eight years.[66]

For the annual services in the following year, Bunmei 18 (1486),
Rennyo recopied this letter, making one important change. He replaced the seventh item with an injunction that Shinshū followers
should study *Anjin ketsujōshō* to understand faith according to the
norms of the tradition in which they were participating.[67] This brief
statement contains the only explicit reference to *Anjin ketsujōshō*
among Rennyo's extant letters. It appears that, in a final effort to dis-
courage the politically-oriented activities of some of those attending
the services, he publicly acknowledged the text that had influenced his
own piety so deeply and commended *Anjin ketsujōshō* as a definitive
work for interpreting orthodox Shinshū piety. It is significant that, at
a moment of acute personal distress, he turns again to this text of
Seizan origin.

By 1486, social and political conditions in Kaga province were
seriously deteriorating, with Shinshū adherents preparing to move
against the forces of Togashi Masachika, the provincial military governor. Rennyo was keenly aware that his own authority was being undermined, and he cited those advocating secret teachings as the cause of
his difficulties. In the beginning of the year, on Bunmei 18 (1486).1.4,
he had addressed a letter to groups of Shinshū followers in Nomi district, Kaga, urging them to be diligent and humble in their relations
with the provincial governor and land stewards and prohibiting the
takeover of properties belonging to shrines or temples.[68] He then
listed five items, reiterating the regulations promulgated at the
thanksgiving services of the previous year. Indeed, it appears that

---

[66] RSI, 358–59 (#119/4:8); SSZ 3: 491–92.
[67] RSI, 363 (#119).
[68] RSI, 364 (#120).

these regulations, enumerated less than two months previously on Bunmei 17 (1485).11.23,[69] had been specifically elicited by the political activity of this group of adherents. In the hopes of discouraging any further inclination toward political involvement, Rennyo urges them to dedicate themselves exclusively to Amida and religious matters, devoting themselves to nenbutsu recitation consistent with the *Anjin ketsujōshō*'s interpretation.

It appears that the letters written annually in the eleventh month made a decisive contribution to the cumulative tradition of the Shinshū, reflecting Rennyo's sustained efforts to build the Honganji on the foundation of Shinran's teaching.[70] It might seem that, at this point, he had achieved many of his goals: Shinran's expressions of piety had been translated into generic terms familiar to nenbutsu devotees lacking formal education; regulations providing greater stability for the community had been promulgated; and the Founder's Hall had been lavishly rebuilt at a new site at Yamashina. However, Rennyo's struggles were not over, for he was confronted again with a dilemma

---

[69] RSI, 354–59 (#119/4:8); SSZ 3: 488–92.

[70] A preliminary step in documenting how *The Letters* may have shaped Shinshū piety at the popular level would involve determining which letters were frequently used in liturgy and sermons and for instruction. We have examined woodblock print collections of letters—*Gobunshō* (*The Letters*)—issued under the seals of seven of Rennyo's successors in the Nishi Honganji lineage: Jitsunyo (1458–1525), ninth head priest; Shōnyo (1516–1554), the tenth; Kennyo (1543–1592), the eleventh; Ryōnyo (1612–1662), the thirteenth; Jakunyo (1651–1725), the fourteenth; Jūnyo (1673–1739), the fifteenth; and Myōnyo (1850–1903), the twenty-first. The editions vary in content and in number of letters from fifteen in the Jitsunyo printing of fascicle four to twenty-four in Jakunyo's edition. The latter collection, most representative of subsequent editions, is made up of letters 2:6, 4:12, 5:1–12, 4:15, 5:16, 2:1, 4:2–3, 1:7, 2:11, 5:21–22, and 4:7. Beginning with Kennyo's edition, each includes a core of 2:6, 4:12, 5:16, 4:15, and at least nine other letters from fascicle five; with Jakunyo's edition, 5:1–12 become part of that core.

Noteworthy for our discussion here is that the last letter in each collection was written in the eleventh month for the annual thanksgiving services: 4:15 (Jitsunyo), 4:6 (Shōnyo), 4:7 (Kennyo), 4:15 (Ryōnyo), 4:7 (Jakunyo), 4:8 (Jūnyo), and 4:8 (Myōnyo). Letters 4:7 and 4:8 are among the foremost examples of Rennyo's presentation of Shinran's concept *shinjin* in terms of *anjin*, with the latter letter drawing on the concept *ki-hō ittai* in explicating the nenbutsu. (The *Gobunshō* manuscripts with the written seals of Jitsunyo, Shōnyo, Kennyo, and Ryōnyo are in the Ryūkoku University library on the Ōmiya campus [call numbers 021/215/1, 021/216/1, 021/213/1, 021/259/1]; the Jakunyo and Jūnyo manuscripts are from Jōsen-ji, Ichigi, Shimane prefecture.)

of religious power similar to that which had driven him from the Hokuriku in 1475.

RETIREMENT AND FINAL YEARS

In Chōkyō 2 (1488), a large-scale Ikkō uprising broke out in Kaga province despite Rennyo's strenuous efforts to forestall the involvement of Honganji adherents. On the twenty-sixth day of the fifth month, they launched an attack on Togashi Masachika, the military governor; on the ninth day of the sixth month, Masachika was defeated and took his own life.[71]

The shogun Ashikaga Yoshihisa, outraged by the death of his ally, Masachika, who had supported him in a recent campaign, demanded of Rennyo that his followers in Kaga be excommunicated. Rennyo — caught once again between his concern for the welfare of Honganji followers and the political realities of the times — summoned those of his sons who were in Kaga to discuss the matter and reportedly said to them that this order was more painful to him than if his own flesh were to be cut away.[72] The crisis was fortuitously resolved by Hosokawa Masamoto, who interceded with the shogun on the Honganji's behalf.[73] Masamoto's close relationship with the Honganji continued

---

[71] HS 1: 335–37; HN, 76. See Inoue, *Ikkō ikki no kenkyū*, 357–71, for a detailed account, beginning with events in Bunmei 9 (1477).

[72] *Jitsugo kyūki*, 123–24; *Goichidaiki kikigaki*, SSZ 3: 599. See also Solomon, "The Dilemma of Religious Power," 58.

[73] The resolution is noted in *Kūzenki*, RSG, 33. It is the view of some scholars that Rennyo then addressed the following letter of reprimand to adherents of Senkō-ji and Kōtoku-ji, Kaga:

> I have heard that some of our adherents plotted a heinous undertaking. This is outrageous. In brief, those who engage in such activity from now on will be forever expelled from Master [Shinran]'s community. This is a point on which there will be strict judgment (RSI, 511 [#217]).

The letter is dated the fourth day of the seventh month, with the year omitted. The traditional interpretation is that the year was Chōkyō 2 (1488); see HN, 76, and Kasahara, *Rennyo*, 290. Kitanishi Hiromu, however, from his study of stylistic changes occurring in Rennyo's written seal from Eikyō 6 (1434) until the end of his life, proposes that the letter was written, not in Chōkyō 2, but in Bunmei 6 (1474), in response to the uprising of that year (Kitanishi Hiromu, "Rennyo hakkyū bunsho no kenkyū: Kaō no henka o chūshin to shite," in Hiramatsu Reizō Sensei Koki Kinenkai, ed., *Nihon no shūkyō to bunka* (Kyoto: Dōbōsha, 1989), 425–34. These letters are the property of Senkō-ji, presently located in Kanazawa, and Kōtoku-ji, Nanao, Ishikawa prefecture (Ishikawa

even after Rennyo's death, and adherents are said to have revered him, quite understandably, as an incarnation of the wise arbitrator, Prince-regent Shōtoku.[74]

In the year following this deeply disturbing event, Rennyo transferred the office of custodian to his son Jitsunyo and entered into retirement at Yamashina Hongan-ji. It would appear that his decision to retire and his failure to temper the political ambitions of Shinshū adherents in Kaga were closely related. Once again, he had been unable to find a satisfactory solution to the kind of dilemma that had led to his departure from Yoshizaki in 1475. Now, fourteen years later, retirement from the office of custodian—a position that inevitably carried responsibilities impinging directly on political issues—appeared to be the proper course. In relinquishing the leadership of a large and prosperous religious institution to his son, he assumed a more symbolic role, divorced from the direct exercise of authority.[75]

Rennyo's advanced age and acute awareness that there were issues he was unable to resolve satisfactorily—an awareness contradictory to the sanguine tone of some of the memoirs—led him to turn his thoughts inward, away from direct responsibility for institutional affairs. Until retirement, he had written his letters as an authoritative leader, exhorting his followers to become practicers of faith whose conduct would serve primarily to preserve and strengthen the Honganji. The letters written following retirement relate more directly to matters of faith, at times voicing his concern about his own birth in the Pure Land, which he sensed as imminent.

A letter written in the sixth month of Entoku 4 (1492) addresses the issue of death during a severe epidemic.[76] Rennyo offers the explanation that this is not the result of the epidemic, but of karma determined from the moment of birth; the only recourse in such times is to take refuge in Amida Buddha. His own experiences had given sharp focus to the notion of the last dharma-age, and it was perhaps out of

---

Kenritsu Rekishi Hakubutsukan, ed., *Ikkō ikki* [Kanazawa: Hashimoto Kenbundō, 1988], 26).

[74] For a description of Masamoto's privileged position in the Honganji, see Inoue, *Ikkō ikki no kenkyū*, 372–73; for an account of his continuing relationship with Jitsunyo and the crisis occasioned by his demand for military support in 1505, see Solomon, "The Dilemma of Religious Power," 60–62. Kūzen records stories from his childhood as well as Honganji adherents' esteem: *Kūzenki*, RSG, 33.

[75] Yamaori sums up Rennyo's role after retirement: "He reigned, but did not rule" (*Ningen Rennyo*, 160).

[76] RSI, 375–76 (#124/4:9); SSZ 3: 492–93.

128 • *RENNYO*

a sense of the difficulty of influencing present events that his thoughts increasingly turned to birth in the Pure Land.

Rennyo's renewed awareness of the transiency of this life, encompassing a strong emphasis on the afterlife, is seen in the numerous letters written in the years 1496-1498.[77] Many exhibit an intensely emotive quality generally lacking in his earlier writings; they suggest a further internalization of the piety characteristic of the nenbutsu interpretation found in *Anjin ketsujōshō*, with any separate sense of self lost in surrender to Amida Buddha. The direct and simple phrase *tasuke tamae* is replaced by a stylized honorific form, *ontasuke sōrae* 御たすけそうらえ , as in this letter dated Meiō 5 (1496).7.14:

> Those who in a single thought-moment deeply entrust themselves to Amida Buddha to save them (*Amida butsu ontasuke sōrae*), whether ten people or a hundred, will all, each and every one, unfailingly be saved.[78]

This rephrased expression of reliance on Amida's all-embracing compassion suggests the intensity of Rennyo's longing for birth in the Pure Land after death and perhaps, at some level, raises a question about his own sense of salvation. His proclivity for redundancy contrasts with the spontaneity of earlier statements affirming the power of Amida's Vow in the salvific process.[79]

In a letter written the following month, on Meiō 5 (1496).8.7, Rennyo returns to a familiar theme in an explication of the nenbutsu in terms of the concept *ki-hō ittai*, emphasizing the essential oneness of the devotee and Amida. His interpretation of the salvific process emphasizes Amida's deep mind (*hō no jinshin* 法の深心) and its saving power, at the expense of the deep mind of the devotee (*ki no jinshin*

---

[77] There are no extant letters from the three years leading up to Rennyo's retirement in Entoku 1 (1489); although there are two from Entoku 2 (1490), there are none from Entoku 3 (1491). From Meiō 1 (1492), there are two letters, one of which is included in *The Letters*; from Meiō 2 and 3 (1493–1494), there is a single letter each; from Meiō 4 (1495), there are no letters. At age 82, Rennyo suddenly enters a period of writing activity not evidenced since the days of building Yamashina Hongan-ji: from Meiō 5 (1496), there are four letters, including one in *The Letters*; from Meiō 6 (1497), eleven, including five in *The Letters*; from Meiō 7 (1498), eighteen, including seven in *The Letters* (one of these, written for his final thanksgiving service on the twenty-first day of the eleventh month [#156/4:15], is the last of the dated letters in the five-fascicle collection). See HN, 75–81.

[78] RSI, 381 (#128). Also see Yamaori, *Ningen Rennyo*, 158–59.

[79] Yamaori, *Ningen Rennyo*, 159–64.

機の深心) aware of karmic evil and separation from Amida.[80] Something of the dynamic quality characteristic of Shinran's thought—sameness/opposition, or oneness/contradiction—is lost with Rennyo's interpretation of the nenbutsu in a formula that emphasizes the oneness (*ittai*) of *ki* and *hō*.

Despite the conceptual simplicity of the formulation, Rennyo insists on members of the community meeting regularly for discussions of matters of faith; he laments the lack of focus in their meetings in a letter dated Meiō 7 (1498).2.25:

> For what purpose have there come to be meetings twice each month? They are [held] for the sake of realizing one's own faith, which leads to birth in the land of utmost bliss, and for nothing else. Although there have been "meetings" everywhere each month, from the past up until now, there is never anything at all that might be called a discussion of faith. In recent years in particular, when there have been meetings (wherever they have been), everyone has dispersed after nothing more than sake, rice, and tea. This is indeed contrary to the fundamental intent of the Buddha-dharma. Although each of those lacking faith (*fushin*) should by all means raise their doubts and discuss what it is to have faith or be without it, they take their leave without coming to any conclusions. This is not as it should be. You must reflect carefully on this matter. In brief, it is essential that each of those lacking faith (*fushin*) have discussions of faith with one another from now on.[81]

Somewhat later in 1498, Rennyo reflects on his failing health and laments his failure to rejoice over the fact that the moment of birth in the Pure Land is imminent:

> Fall and spring have slipped away, and it is already the middle of early summer in this seventh year of Meiō; I have grown old—I am eighty-four. This particular year, however, I have been seriously beset by illness and, as a result, my whole body has suffered—ears, eyes, hands, and feet; I realize, then, that this in itself is the outcome of past karma and also the harbinger of birth in the land of utmost bliss. Master Hōnen said, pursuant to this, "Practicers who aspire for the Pure Land are filled with joy when they become ill"; these are his very words. And yet, it never occurs to me to rejoice over ill-

---

[80] See Yamaori Tetsuo, "Shinran shisō no taishūka ni nirosen," in *Rennyo*, ed. Minami Midō Shinbun (Osaka: Nanba Betsuin, 1986), 74–80.

[81] RSI, 418 (#142/4:12); SSZ 3: 494–95. This letter is among the core letters included in the *Gobunshō* collections of Kennyo, Ryōnyo, Jakunyo, Jūnyo, and Myōnyo; see n. 70.

ness. I am a shameful person. This is disgraceful; it is deplorable. Nevertheless, according to our sect's teaching of "completing the cause [of birth in the Pure Land] in ordinary life, with the awakening of the one thought-moment [of entrusting]," I am now settled in the single path of faith (*anjin*). [My] saying of the Name in grateful return for Buddha's benevolence is therefore unceasing; walking, standing, sitting, or lying down, I am never forgetful.[82]

In this passage, Rennyo touches on one of the crucial issues confronting the practicer of faith—the sorrow of death and the joy of anticipating birth in the Pure Land. It is noteworthy that his quite poignant response is similar to that of Shinran, who empathized with the statement of a follower, Yuien: "Even though I say the nenbutsu, it is rare for any sense of joy to come to my mind, and I have no thought of wanting to go quickly to the Pure Land."[83]

Some of the letters Rennyo writes during this period reveal the vigor characteristic of his life: he is adamant that everyone be established in faith as quickly as possible. Strengthened by a renewed sense of identification with his master, Shinran, he is also comforted, as he faces death, by the teaching he finds in *Anjin ketsujōshō*. This is seen in a four-letter series, the *Summer Letters*, written during what were to be his last summer months.

In a letter written in the fifth month, Rennyo quotes three passages directly from *Anjin ketsujōshō*, passages that he had slightly emended in a letter written seventeen years earlier, on Bunmei 13 (1481).11.14:[84]

> You have all gathered here, saying that you have come to listen to today's scriptures, [but what must be understood is that] this will be of no use at all unless you hear and are convinced, thoroughly understanding what faith means and holding no unsettled thoughts from today on. I will now tell you about [faith]; give me your attention and listen very carefully.
>
> Faith (*anjin*) means discarding the sundry practices and single-mindedly entrusting ourselves to Amida Tathāgata to save us, [bringing us to buddhahood] in the afterlife; those who do this are called practicers in whom faith (*anjin*) is settled. Once we have realized the significance of this, [the nenbutsu] we say is the nenbutsu

---

[82] RSI, 423–24 (#145/4:13); SSZ 3: 495–96.

[83] *Tannishō*, SSZ 2: 777.

[84] RSI, 328–31 (#110). For a comparison of passages in this letter with passages from *Anjin ketsujōshō*, see Rogers, "Rennyo Shōnin 1415–1499," 325–38.

of gratitude for the Buddha's benevolence. Hence the master says in his hymns:

> One's attaining the nenbutsu of wisdom
> is made possible by the power of Dharmākara's Vow;
> and by entering the wisdom of faith,
> one becomes a person who returns
> the Buddha's benevolence in gratitude.[85]

It is essential to understand what this means.

First of all, [*Anjin ketsujōshō*] states in regard to this:

> "When nenbutsu practicers hear the Name, 'Namu-amida-butsu,' they should realize that their birth [in the Pure Land] is already accomplished. This is because it is the Name resulting from the perfect enlightenment of the bodhisattva Dharmākara, who made the Vow that he would not attain perfect enlightenment should birth [in the Pure Land] for sentient beings in the ten directions fail to be accomplished."[86]

Also:

> "When they hear the name 'land of utmost bliss,' they should know that the place where they are to be born has been realized. This is the land of utmost bliss that has been realized by the monk Dharmākara, who made the Vow that he would not attain perfect enlightenment should birth [in the Pure Land] for sentient beings in the ten directions fail to be accomplished."[87]

Further:

> "It would be unfortunate if [nenbutsu practicers] entrusted themselves to the Primal Vow and said the Name but, thinking of it as Buddha's virtue separate [from their birth], wondered why they might not attain birth if they added merit to the Name [by their own repetitions]. With the arising of firm faith that our birth is accomplished through 'namu-amida-butsu,' the Buddha-body itself becomes the practice for our birth. Therefore, whenever there is a single recitation [of the nenbutsu], birth is settled."[88]

---

[85] SSZ 2: 520. This hymn is a combination of two in Shinran's *Shōzōmatsu wasan*: the first two lines are from hymn #35, and the last two from hymn #34. In a letter written in the same month, Rennyo quotes hymn #35 in the original form. See RSI, 430 (#148).

[86] *Anjin ketsujōshō*, SSZ 3: 619. See Rogers, "Rennyo Shōnin 1415–1499," 333.

[87] *Anjin ketsujōshō*, SSZ 3: 619. See Rogers, "Rennyo Shōnin 1415–1499," 334.

[88] *Anjin ketsujōshō*, SSZ 3: 619–20. See Rogers, "Rennyo Shōnin 1415–1499," 334.

> You should recognize that this is the understanding of those who have realized faith (*anjin*).[89]

In this letter, it appears at first that Rennyo is explicating Shinran's hymn in terms of the three passages from *Anjin ketsujōshō*. In his 1481 citation of the first passage, he emended the text of *Anjin ketsujōshō* to eliminate the implication that birth in the Pure Land was accomplished for all sentient beings at the moment of Dharmākara's enlightenment as Amida Buddha. The passage was altered to conform to the interpretation held in his own tradition, that the assurance of birth is determined here and now in the one thought-moment of entrusting. In this letter, however, Rennyo quotes *Anjin ketsujōshō* directly, without the previous emendations.

In his earlier citation of the second passage, Rennyo eliminated the direct implication that, because the monk Dharmākara had attained enlightenment as Amida Buddha—an enlightenment that depended on the birth of all sentient beings in the Pure Land, the birth of all sentient beings had been accomplished. It appears that he is no longer uneasy with such a notion, although it runs contrary to the emphasis on gratitude to Amida for salvation at the moment in which faith is realized. Even though Shinran accepted the proposition that Dharmākara had prepared the land of utmost bliss for ordinary beings, he held that, in this life, the simultaneity of sameness (*ittai*) and opposition between Amida Buddha (*hō*) and ordinary beings (*ki*) persists.

In his earlier citation of the third passage, Rennyo eliminated the sentence, "Therefore, whenever there is a single recitation [of the nenbutsu], birth is settled," and noted that the "secret" interpretation of the nenbutsu was inconsistent with the main intent of the Eighteenth Vow. In the summer letter written seventeen years later, however, he makes no such change.

At this point, it becomes evident that Rennyo's use of the three passages from *Anjin ketsujōshō* to explicate the lines from *Shōzōmatsu wasan* indicates how deeply he had been influenced by *Anjin ketsujōshō*'s perspective. Rather than explaining Shinran's teaching, he seems to be shaping the teaching into conformity with that of *Anjin ketsujōshō*. The three successive summer letters convey the overriding concern of the first, that members of the community be established in faith as an expression of gratitude to Shinran. The second letter, also written in the fifth month of Meiō 7 (1498), underscores that in the process of the settlement of faith, it is beneficial to hear the scriptures read in the Founder's Hall:

---

[89] RSI, 427–29 (#147); SSZ 3: 522–23.

Those who have come before the image of [the founder] today have surely come to hear the scriptures read. . . . The purpose of our reading the scriptures is to enable [everyone] to realize Other-Power faith.[90]

The third letter, written in the following month, elaborates on Rennyo's efforts to present the teaching through scripture reading and expresses his increasing concern over his followers' failure to respond:

> From early in the summer until now, I have chosen and read selections daily in the customary way, from scriptures that are easy to understand. However, as I look out over the priests and lay people in attendance, men and women, I realize that everyone's attitude is as usual and that there are no further signs [of response]. Briefly, the reason for [my saying] this is that, when not a single person comes forth to say what is impressive or praiseworthy in the daily scripture readings, there has been no effect at all.[91]

The last of the letters, written in the middle of the seventh month, reflects something of the frustration Rennyo must have felt. In spite of daily scripture readings, those who have assembled show an utter lack of faith (*mianjin* 未安心) and come only to keep up appearances, gaining no benefit. Rennyo laments that the effect of the readings is "equivalent to a bee sting on a deer's antler!" and compares these followers to people who "enter a treasure-filled mountain and return empty-handed."[92]

It is reported that Rennyo became ill again during this summer (1498) and, on the seventh day of the fifth month, left Osaka to make what he thought would be a final pilgrimage to Yamashina Hongan-ji.[93] The *Summer Letters* indicate that his condition improved to the point of his being able to spend some of this period writing and reading the scriptures to his followers. By the time of the annual services in the eleventh month, he was again in residence in Osaka. He prepared a letter to be read beginning on the twenty-first, offering a glimpse of his state of mind a few months before his death:

> It is extraordinary that, as of this year, this foolish old man has already lived to the age of eighty-four. And as this [life] may indeed have been in accord with the meaning of dharma in our tradition,

---

[90] RSI, 429 (#148); SSZ 3: 523.

[91] RSI, 431 (#149); SSZ 3: 525.

[92] RSI, 433–34 (#150); SSZ 3: 526–27.

[93] *Goichidaiki kikigaki*, SSZ 3: 544; *Kūzenki*, RSG, 37.

I could know no greater satisfaction. But I have been ill since the summer of this year, and at present there is no sign of recovery. I feel it certain at last that I will not fail to attain my long-cherished desire of birth [in the Pure Land] during the coming winter. All I long for, morning and evening, is that there will be a decisive settling of faith for everyone while I am still alive. Although this does indeed depend on good from the past, there is never a moment when it is not on my mind. Moreover, it might even be considered the consequence of my having spent three years in this place. By all means, then, let there be a decisive settling of faith during this seven-day period of thanksgiving services so that everyone may realize the fundamental intent [of the dharma], birth in the land of utmost bliss.

Respectfully.

This letter is to be read, beginning on the twenty-first day of the eleventh month of Meiō 7 [1498], so that everyone may attain faith (*shin*).[94]

Rennyo returned to Yamashina Hongan-ji on the twentieth of the second month of Meiō 8 (1499). His last days were filled with characteristic activities. On the twenty-first, he paid his respects at the Founder's Hall, expressing gratitude that he was able to do so; the following day, he inspected the dirt embankments and moat around the temple complex.[95] On the first of the third month, he visited Jitsunyo and, in good spirits, consulted with him and others of his sons; the following day, with Kūzen's help, he made an excursion to view cherry blossoms.[96] On the seventh, he paid his final visit to the Founder's Hall and the Amida Hall; on the ninth, he gave a talk on the dharma to some of those closest to him, including his disciples Hōkyō (Junsei; 1421–1510) and Kūzen.[97] Concerned for the welfare of the Honganji and harmony

---

[94] RSI, 445–46 (#156/4:15); SSZ 3: 499. Rennyo's followers appear to have made a serious effort to heed his instructions that the letter be read "so that everyone may attain faith." As we have noted earlier, this letter (together with 2:6, 4:12, 5:16, and at least nine others from fascicle five) has been selected from the eighty in *The Letters* for inclusion in collections under the written seals of head priests of the Nishi Honganji for congregational use from the time of Kennyo until the present; see n. 70. Out of the entire corpus of Rennyo's writings, these letters, the four known as *Summer Letters*, and the biographical letter *Gozokushō* appear to have played an important role in shaping Shinshū piety in local temples. The influence of *Anjin ketsujōshō* on Rennyo's thought in a number of these letters is significant.

[95] *Kūzenki*, RSG, 44; HS 1: 358.

[96] *Kūzenki*, RSG, 45; HS 1: 359.

[97] *Kūzenki*, RSG, 46–47; HS 1: 359.

among his sons after his death, he spoke at length on the ninth to Jitsunyo, Renkō, Rensei, Renjun, and Rengo, giving them detailed final instructions, which they recorded after his death.[98] On the twentieth, he pardoned Aki Rensō, restoring a close relationship that had been broken at the close of the Yoshizaki years.[99] Finally, on the twenty-fifth, life slipped away from him; he died peacefully at noon, "as if he had gone to sleep."[100]

---

[98] HS 1: 359–60. See "Rennyo Shōnin goyuigon," *Kūzenki*, RSG, 52–58; also Ōtani Chōjun, ed. *Rennyo Shōnin zenshū: Genkōben* (Tokyo: Kawade Shobō Shinsha, 1989), 277–84.

[99] Rensō died three days after Rennyo, on the twenty-eighth of the third month.

[100] *Kūzenki*, RSG, 49; HS 1: 360. In keeping with his instructions, Rennyo's body was laid in the Founder's Hall before Shinran's image; innumerable followers are said to have come to pay their last respects on the evening of his death. Although the cremation was announced for the second day of the fourth month, it took place the day after his death, on the twenty-sixth, because of concern over the crowds that might gather at the later date. Rennyo's grave is at Yamashina; his posthumous name is Shinshō-in. In the fifteenth year of Meiji (1882), the emperor awarded him the title Etō Daishi.

THE LETTERS

The Letters

THE TEXT FOR THIS TRANSLATION of the five fascicles of Rennyo's letters is *Rennyo Shōnin ofumi.** Of the five fascicles, the first four are arranged chronologically. Fascicle one contains fifteen letters written between Bunmei 3 (1471).7.15 and 5 (1473).9.22, following Rennyo's arrival in the Hokuriku. The fifteen letters in fascicle two are from Yoshizaki; they were written between Bunmei 5 (1473).12.8 and 6 (1474).7.9. Fascicle three contains thirteen letters written between Bunmei 6 (1474).7.14 and 8 (1476).7.18, ten of which were written from Yoshizaki. The fifteen letters in fascicle four were written between Bunmei 9 (1477).1.8 and Meiō 7 (1498).11.21, the year before Rennyo's death. The twenty-two letters in fascicle five are undated; certain ones, however, are identical to passages in dated letters.

These letters, chosen under Jitsunyo's supervision as representative of the tradition's teaching, contain few explicitly personal or historical references. In this respect, they have contributed to an ahistorical interpretation of Rennyo's legacy, giving rise to difficulties in the development of the Honganji (discussed in part three). At the same time, they have been valued for the timeless description of the process of entrusting that is the focus of many. In addition, they provide an identification and repudiation of heterodox teachings and practices; an interpretation of the nenbutsu patterned on that of

---

* Popularly known as *Gojō ofumi* (*The Letters*, lit. "letters in five fascicles"), T 83.771a–808c; see also *Gobunshō*, SSZ 3: 402–518. Throughout this study and in translating *The Letters*, we have followed the general practice in Western scholarship of transliterating the first two characters 南無 of the six-character Name *na-mu-a-mi-da-butsu* 南無阿弥陀仏 as "namu" (Skt. *namas*). "Namo" is an alternate reading; occurring in the earliest texts of Shinran's and Rennyo's writings, it is used in some translations in the Ryūkoku University Translation Series such as *Kōsō Wasan* and *Shōzōmatsu Wasan*. For the standard Nishi Honganji edition of Shinshū texts, see Shinshū Seiten Hensan Iinkai, ed., *Jōdo Shinshū seiten: Gentenban* (Kyoto: Honganji Shuppanbu, 1985). In notes providing the Japanese for translated terms, we have used the modern form of characters and substituted modern *hiragana* forms for the *katakana* of the Taishō text.

Shan-tao; and an emphatic message that salvation is open to all—that "when . . . Other-Power faith is decisively settled, no distinction at all is made between male and female, old and young" (letter 1:2).

Among the many reference works consulted in the course of translating and annotating *The Letters*, two volumes have always been close at hand: a line-by-line commentary by the late Shinshū scholar, Sugi Shirō, *Gobunshō kōwa* (1933; repr. Kyoto: Nagata Bunshōdō, 1979), and an annotated text and commentary by a specialist in Japanese literature, Izumoji Osamu, ed., *Ofumi*, Tōyō Bunko, no. 345 (Tokyo: Heibonsha, 1978). Although this annotation touches only the surface of their scholarship and that of others in Japan, we hope that readers will find the notes useful in following up their own inquiries. In drawing on traditional sectarian studies and modern literary scholarship, our goal has been to present Rennyo's words clearly and accurately and to find the English equivalents most appropriate for a consistent rendering of technical terms. Readers are encouraged to make use of the glossary entries in the translations of Shinran's works in the volumes in the Shin Buddhism Translation Series, the annotated texts in the Ryūkoku Translation Series, and Hisao Inagaki's *A Dictionary of Japanese Buddhist Terms* (Kyoto: Nagata Bunshōdō, 1984).

Fascicle One

I-1 On followers and disciples[1]

Someone has asked: "In our tradition,[2] are followers[3] necessarily considered disciples of a particular priest, or do we speak of them as disciples of the Tathāgata[4] and of Master [Shinran]? I have no clear understanding of this. Also, there are some who have informal groups of followers in various places and are determined these days to keep this from the priest of the temple [to which they belong]. As people say that this is inappropriate, I am confused about it, too. Please instruct me [on these points]."

In reply: I consider these questions to be of the utmost importance indeed. I will state briefly what I have heard in our tradition. Please listen.

The late master said,

[I], Shinran, do not have even a single disciple. The reason for this is that when I expound the Tathāgata's dharma to sentient beings in the ten directions, I am only speaking as the Tathāgata's representative. [I] . . . do not propagate any new dharma at all; I entrust myself to the Tathāgata's dharma and simply teach that to others. Besides that, what do I teach that I would speak of having disciples?[5]

---

[1] Letter titles do not appear in the Taishō edition; those provided here in brackets are translations of titles (based on first lines of the text) found in Ōe and Ōhara, eds. *Shinshū seiten*, 660–802. Titles also appear, in slightly different form, in Kashiwabara, ed., *Shinshū seiten*, 785–865.

[2] *tōryū* 当流 . The Honganji branch of the Jōdo Shinshū.

[3] *monto* 門徒 are those who pass through a teacher's gate (*mon*), receive his teaching, and become disciples. Here the term refers to lay persons who, as followers of Buddha-dharma, give their allegiance to the Honganji.

[4] *Nyorai* 如来 . The term refers, in this instance, to the Buddhas Amida and Śākyamuni.

[5] The first and second sentences of this quotation are drawn from two successive sentences in the sixth chapter of *Tannishō*, SSZ 2: 776 (T 83.729b); the first is quoted directly and the second restated. Kakunyo's *Kudenshō* also contains a phrase similar to the first sentence (SSZ 3: 9 [T 83.740c]; see page 272 below). The remainder of the passage follows the sense of Kakunyo's quotation of Shinran in *Gaijashō*: "I do not have even a single disciple. For, other than holding to Amida's Primal Vow, what do I teach that I could speak of having disciples? Amida's Primal Vow is given through Other Power, the wisdom of the Buddha. Therefore, we are all fellow practicers. No one is my disciple" (SSZ 3: 68–69).

Thus we are one another's companions and fellow practicers. Because of this, the master spoke respectfully of "companions and fellow practicers."

Recently, however, even priests of high position, ignorant of what our school teaches about the settled mind,[6] severely rebuke those among their disciples who happen to go to places where faith[7] is discussed and listen to the dharma; thus, at times, discord arises. Consequently, since the priests themselves do not clearly hear the reality of faith, and since they deal with their disciples in such a manner, faith is not decisively settled either for them or for the disciples, and their lives then pass in vain. It is truly difficult for them to escape blame for harming themselves and others. This is deplorable, deplorable.

An old poem says:

> Long ago,
> joy
> was wrapped in my sleeves —
> but, tonight,
> it's more than I can contain![8]

"Long ago, joy was wrapped in my sleeves" means that, in the past, we felt certain — without any clear understanding of sundry practices and right practice[9] — that we would be born [in the Pure Land] if we

---

[6] *anjin* 安心 is a term variously translated in Buddhist tradition: "settled heart," "assurance," "mind-at-rest," "faith." Although Shinran uses *anjin* on only three occasions (see chapter three, n. 41), Rennyo, drawing on *Anjin ketsujōshō*, introduces the concept *anjin* for interpreting Shinran's concept for faith, *shinjin*. We have translated *anjin* as "settled mind" or "faith," depending on context; when translated as "faith," the Japanese term is inserted in the text, as in letter 1:10. Also note that *shin* 信 is translated as "faith" in letter 1:2 and as "entrusting" in letter 1:3. See the introduction to this work, 38–40; for further discussion of Rennyo's concept *anjin* in relation to Shinran's *shinjin*, see Rogers, "The Shin Faith of Rennyo," 56–73, and " 'Shinjin' to 'anjin'," 26–43.

[7] *shinjin* 信心. See the introduction to this work, 37–40.

[8] See Nishio Kōichi, ed., *Senjūshō*, Iwanami Bunko, no. 6746–6749 (Tokyo: Iwanami Shoten, 1970), 242, where this poem is presented as the composition of a court official on the occasion of his promotion over a rival to the rank of Dainagon. Although *Senjūshō* has traditionally been attributed to the poet-monk Saigyō (1118–1190), post-Meiji scholarship has largely disproved this assumption (5). Sugi Shirō, who takes the traditional view, notes that the promotion occurred during the reign of the Emperor Uda (r. 887–897) and interprets the poem as an adaptation of the official's joy to express the great joy of faith (*Gobunshō kōwa*, 4–5).

[9] *zōgyō shōgyō* 雑行正行. Rennyo's use of these terms derives from an explanation by Shan-tao of the two types of practice. *Zōgyō*, "sundry practices," are all

just said the nenbutsu. "But, tonight, it's more than I can contain" means that the joy of saying the nenbutsu in grateful return for the Buddha's benevolence (button hōjin 仏恩報尽) is especially great now that, having heard and understood the difference between the right and sundry [practices], we have become steadfast and single-hearted, and have thus undergone a decisive settling of faith. Because of this, we are so overjoyed that we feel like dancing—hence the joy is "more than I can contain."

Respectfully.

Bunmei 3 [1471].7.15.

I-2 On becoming a priest in the aspiration for buddhahood

The fundamental principle of Master Shinran in our tradition is not that one should become a priest in the aspiration for buddhahood or that one should renounce family and separate oneself from worldly attachments; it is simply that when, with [the awakening of] the one thought-moment of taking refuge [in Amida],[10] Other-Power faith

---

good acts apart from *shōgyō*, the "right practices" that lead to birth in the Pure Land. The "right practices" are: (1) reciting the Pure Land sūtras, (2) contemplating Amida and his land, (3) worshipping Amida, (4) saying the nenbutsu, and (5) praising and making offerings to Amida. Of these, saying the nenbutsu is the act by which birth is truly settled, as it accords with the Amida's Vow; the remaining four are auxiliary (*Kangyōsho* [*Sanzengi*], SSZ 1: 537–38; T 37.272ab).

For Shinran, the saying of the nenbutsu is the one "right practice," but this is a saying that is to be considered "not-practice" and "not-good," being "totally Other Power" (*Tannishō*, SSZ 2: 777 [T 83.729b]; Hirota, *Tannishō*, 26). In *Mattōshō*, SSZ 2: 672 (T 83.715c), Shinran further explains that the nenbutsu is inseparable from the one moment of faith, which is "to hear and not doubt that you are saved by only a single pronouncing, which is the fulfillment of practice. ... Nenbutsu [*gyō* 行 ; practice] and shinjin [*shin* 信 ; faith] on our part are themselves the manifestations of the Vow" (*Letters*, 40). Rennyo, emphasizing that the saving practice is accomplished wholly on the part of Amida, repeatedly states that the nenbutsu is to be said solely in thanksgiving.

[10] *ichinen kimyō* 一念帰命 . Although *ichinen* has historically encompassed several meanings ("one thought [-moment]" or "one moment," "one thought of entrusting," "one recitation of the nenbutsu"), it may be interpreted here as "single-hearted faith in Amida." In *Ichinen tanen mon'i*, SSZ 2: 605 (T 83.694b), Shinran links the aspects of time and faith: "One thought-moment [*ichinen*] is time at its ultimate limit, where the realization of shinjin [faith] takes place" (*Once-calling*, 32). In *Kyōgyōshinshō*, SSZ 2: 22 (T 83.594c), Shinran explains *kimyō* as follows:

(*tariki no shinjin* 他力の信心) is decisively settled, no distinction at all is made between male and female, old and young. The [*Larger*] *Sūtra* describes the state of having attained this faith (*shin*) as "immediately attaining birth [in the Pure Land] and dwelling in [a state of] non-retrogression";[11] [T'an-luan] says in a commentary (*shaku* 釈), "With the awakening of the one thought [of entrusting], we enter the company of those [whose birth is] truly settled."[12] This, then, is what is meant by talk of "not [waiting for Amida to] come to meet [us at the moment of death]"[13] and of "completing the cause [of birth] in ordinary life."[14]

> In the term "to take refuge" (*kimyō*), *ki* means "to arrive at." . . . *Myō* means "to act," "to invite," "to command," "to teach," "path," "message," "to devise," "to summon." Thus *kimyō* is the command of the Primal Vow calling to and summoning us (*Teaching*, 1: 111).

On many occasions, Rennyo uses the two terms independently, as in letters 1:3 and 1:13, respectively; for an expanded example of the terms in combination, see letter 4:1:

> With the awakening of the one thought-moment [*ichinen hokki*] in which a practicer for whom past good has unfolded takes refuge in Amida, the Buddha embraces that practicer (who has taken refuge through the one thought-moment) with his compassionate light.

[11] *Larger Sūtra* (*Daimuryōjukyō*, referred to here simply as *kyō* 経), SSZ 1: 24 (T 12.272b). See also Shinran's *Jōdo monrui jushō*, SSZ 2: 452 (T 83.646b). This phrase occurs again in letters 1:4 and 4:1.

[12] *ichinen hokki nyū shōjō shi ju* 一念発起入正定之聚 , a phrase that reoccurs in letter 5:10 and, with a slight variation, in 5:21. For *shōjō shi ju* 正定之聚 , see the *Larger Sūtra*, SSZ 1: 24 (T 12.272b); for *nyū daijō shōjō shi ju* 入大乗正定之聚 , see T'an-luan's *Jōdo ronchū*, SSZ 1: 279 (T 40.826b); for *nyū shōjōju shi ju* 入正定聚之数 , see *Kyōgyōshinshō*, SSZ 2: 33 (T 83.597b).

[13] *furaikō* 不来迎 . Rennyo may have in mind the opening passages of *Mattōshō*, SSZ 2: 656 (T 83.711ab), where Shinran explains:

> The idea of Amida's coming [*raikō* 来迎] at the moment of death is for those who seek to gain birth in the Buddha Land by doing religious practices, for they are practicers of self-power. The moment of death is of central concern for such people, for they have not yet attained true shinjin [faith]. . . . The person who lives true shinjin, however, abides in the stage of the truly settled, for he has already been grasped, never to be abandoned [*sesshu fusha* 摂取不捨]. There is no need to wait in anticipation for the moment of death, no need to rely on Amida's coming (*Letters*, 19).

[14] *heizei gōjō* 平生業成 . A phrase used by Kakunyo in *Gaijashō* (SSZ 3: 64), and also by Zonkaku, who explains in *Jōdo shinyōshō*:

> In Master Shinran's school, we teach "completion of the cause [for birth] in ordinary life" and do not stress the expectation of birth at life's end. We speak in terms of [Amida's] not coming to meet [the practicer at the time of death] and do not adhere to the teaching of his coming. . . . If a person encounters the dharma at the end of his life, then that person is born [in the Pure Land] at life's end. We do

In a hymn, [Shinran] says:

> Those who aspire to [birth in] Amida's fulfilled land,[15]
> though outward conditions may vary,
> should truly accept the Name [as promised in] the Primal Vow[16]
> and, sleeping or waking, never forget it.[17]

---

not speak of "ordinary life" or "life's end"; it is simply that when a person attains faith, he is born, or settled (SSZ 3: 123 [T 83.759b]).

The phrase occurs again in letters 1:4, 2:10, 3:8, 4:1, 4:4, 4:13, and 5:21.

[15] *hōdo* 報土. In the Pure Land teaching of Tao-ch'o in *Anrakushū* and Shantao in *Kangyōsho*, the fulfilled land is equated with Amida's Pure Land. Shinran, however, taught that within Amida's fulfilled land there is the true fulfilled land (*shinjitsu hōdo* 真実報土) where the person of true faith becomes "one with the light that is the heart of Tathāgata" at the end of his life (*Letters*, 44; SSZ 2: 675 [T 83.716c]), and an expedient temporary land (*hōben kedo* 方便化土) of various names and aspects where, in accordance with the Nineteenth and Twentieth Vows, those whose practices are mixed with self-power are born and must remain until they realize faith (*Tanni Shō*, 41, n. 1).

[16] *hongan* 本願. The Eighteenth of the Forty-eight Vows (see the *Larger Sūtra*, SSZ 1: 9 [T 12.268a]) made by Amida Buddha as the monk Dharmākara (Hōzō biku 法蔵比丘).

> If, when I attain buddhahood, sentient beings of the ten directions who with sincere mind entrust themselves, aspire to be born in my land, and say my Name perhaps even ten times should not be born there, may I not attain the supreme enlightenment. Excluded are those who commit the five grave offenses and those who slander the right dharma (*Kyōgyōshinshō*, SSZ 2: 48–49 [T 83.601a]).

Rennyo invokes the clause of exclusion only once in *The Letters*, in an admonition against slander (letter 1:14). His position otherwise — which becomes a central theme — is that the Vow is directed precisely at those declared excluded, as explained, for example, in this letter. In letter 2:15, he writes:

> First of all, being deeply convinced that we are worthless beings burdened with the ten transgressions and the five grave offenses, the five obstacles and the three submissions, we then recognize that it is the inconceivable working of Amida Tathāgata's Primal Vow that, as its primary aim, saves just such wretched persons; and when we deeply entrust ourselves and have not the slightest doubt, Amida embraces [us] without fail.

His position is continuous with that of Shinran who, in his only detailed commentary on the clause of exclusion, wrote:

> *Excluded* means that those who commit the five grave offenses are rejected and reveals how grave the evil of slandering the dharma is. By showing the gravity of these two kinds of wrongdoing, these words make us realize that all the sentient beings throughout the ten quarters, without a single exception, will be born in the Pure Land (*Inscriptions*, 35; SSZ 2: 561 [T 83.688c]).

For an analysis of Shinran's interpretation in the context of Pure Land thought, see Ueda and Hirota, *Shinran*, 192–94.

[17] *Kōsō wasan*, SSZ 2: 512b (T 83.663c).

"Outward conditions [may vary]" means that no distinction is made between lay person and priest or between male and female. Next, "should truly accept the Name [as promised in] the Primal Vow and, sleeping or waking, never forget it" means that—no matter what the external form [of our lives] may be, and even if our evil karma includes the ten transgressions[18] and the five grave offenses[19] or if we are among those who slander the dharma (*hōbō* 法謗) or lack the seed of buddhahood[20] —if we undergo a turning of the mind[21] and repent, and, deep within, truly realize that Amida Tathāgata's saving Primal Vow is for just such wretched people, if we entrust ourselves without any double-mindedness to the Tathāgata and, without forgetting, sleeping or waking, are always mindful of Amida, then we are said to be people of faith who rely on the Primal Vow and have attained the decisive mind.

Then, beyond this, even if we say the Name[22] [constantly]—walking,

---

[18] *jūaku* 十悪 : (1) destroying life, (2) stealing, (3) committing adultery, (4) lying, (5) uttering words that cause enmity, (6) uttering harsh words, (7) engaging in idle talk, (8) greed, (9) anger, and (10) wrong views (SSJ, 232).

[19] *gogyaku* 五逆 . Acts that cause one to fall into *avīci* hell. Although the five acts are variously described, the following list (based on Indian texts) may be considered representative: (1) killing one's mother, (2) killing one's father, (3) killing an arhat, (4) causing blood to flow from the body of a Buddha, and (5) disrupting the harmony of the assembly of monks, causing schism or dissolution (BGDJ, 357).

[20] *sendai* 闡提 (abbr. of *issendai* 一闡提); Skt. *icchantika*.

[21] *eshin* 回心 . A turn from the mind of self-power to that of Other Power; see SSJ, 44, s.v. "*eshin* (3)." In *Yuishinshō mon'i*, Shinran writes:

> Turn about [*eshin*] means to overturn and discard the mind of self-power. Since those people who are to be born in the true fulfilled land are without fail taken into the heart of the Buddha of unhindered light, they realize diamond-like shinjin. Thus, they "abundantly say the Name" (*Essentials*, 39–40).

As expressed in the sixteenth chapter of *Tannishō*, SSZ 2: 788 (T 83.733ab):

> For the person of wholehearted, single practice of the nenbutsu, change of heart and mind [*eshin*] occurs only once. A person who has been ignorant of the true significance of the Other Power of the Primal Vow comes to realize, through receiving Amida's wisdom, that he cannot attain birth by means of the thoughts and feelings he has harbored up to then, so he abandons his former heart and mind and entrusts himself to the Primal Vow. This is 'change of heart' (Hirota, *Tannishō*, 39).

[22] *shōmyō su* 称名す ; "say the Name [of the Buddha]," "say the nenbutsu." In *Kangyōsho*, Shan-tao lists "saying the name of the Buddha" as the fourth of the "right practices" and specifies it as the "act of true settlement" for birth in the Pure Land (T 37.272ab). Hōnen, following Shan-tao's interpretation, writes, "The act of true settlement is saying the Name of the Buddha. Saying the Name

standing, sitting, and lying down[23] — we should think of it as an expression of gratitude for Amida Tathāgata's benevolence. Such a person is called a practicer[24] who has realized true and real faith and whose birth is decisively settled.

Respectfully.
Bunmei 3 [1471].7.18.

---

of the Buddha necessarily brings about birth, for it is based on the Buddha's Primal Vow" (*Senjakushū*, T 83.19a). In *Kyōgyōshinshō*, Shinran expounds, "Saying the Name breaks through all the ignorance of sentient beings and fulfills all their aspirations. Saying the Name is the supreme, true, and excellent right act; the right act is the nenbutsu. The nenbutsu is 'namu-amida-butsu'; 'namu-amida-butsu' is right-mindedness. This you should know" (SSZ 2: 8 [T 83.590c–591a]).

[23] *gyōjūzaga* 行住座臥. In regard to Rennyo's use of this phrase, see *Mattōshō*, where Shinran writes:

> In describing the way in which one entrusts oneself to the nenbutsu of the Primal Vow, [Genshin,] the master of Eshin-in states in *Ōjōyōshū*: "It makes no difference whether we are walking, standing, sitting, or lying down, and there need be no consideration of time, place, or other circumstances" (SSZ 2: 659 [T 83.712a]).

In the Eastern Orthodox Christian tradition, there is a strand of piety that teaches participants to "pray without ceasing"; see R. M. French, trans., *The Way of a Pilgrim and The Pilgrim Continues His Way*, 2d ed. (New York: Harper and Brothers, 1952). The devotee is instructed, "Reject all other thoughts. . . . Whether you are standing or sitting, walking or lying down, constantly repeat 'Lord Jesus Christ, have mercy on me'" (12). While the Christian instance of saying the Name of Jesus is not to be equated with saying the Name of Amida according to Other-Power Shinshū orthodoxy, there are similarities:

> The continuous interior Prayer of Jesus is a constant uninterrupted calling upon the divine Name of Jesus with the lips, in the spirit, in the heart. . . . One who accustoms himself to this appeal experiences as a result so deep a consolation and so great a need to offer the prayer always, that he can no longer live without it, and it will continue to voice itself within him of its own accord (8–9).

[24] *gyōja* 行者. Although this term refers generally to one who has entered the Buddhist path and is engaged in various forms of religious practice and discipline, in Shinshū tradition the practicer is defined as "one who, having awakened to the great compassion embodied in Amida's Name and entrusted himself to it, lives in the working of the Primal Vow, which unfolds the supreme enlightenment in him just as he is. He is, therefore, one who has become free of all calculation and effort to attain enlightenment through his own goodness and wisdom" (*Passages*, s.v. "Practicer," 104).

on this hot day
my flowing sweat
may truly be my tears
and what I've written with my brush —
how strange it looks

I-3 On hunting and fishing

First, [realizing] the settled mind in our tradition (*tōryū no anjin* 当流の安心) does not mean that we put a stop to our mind's evil or to the rising of delusions and attachments.[25] Simply carry on your trade or position of service, hunt, and fish. For when we realize deeply that Amida Tathāgata's Primal Vow promises to save such worthless beings as ourselves, confused morning and evening by evil karma (*zaigō* 罪業) when we single-heartedly (without any double-mindedness) rely on the compassionate Vow[26] of the one Buddha Amida, and when sincere faith (*ichinen no shin* 一念の信) is awakened in us with the realization that Amida saves us — then, without fail, we partake of the Tathāgata's saving work.

Beyond this, when there is a question as to with what understanding we should say the nenbutsu, [the answer is that] we are to say the nenbutsu as long as we live, realizing that it is in gratitude, in return for the gracious benevolence that saves us by giving us the power of entrusting, through which our birth is assured. [Those who do] this are to be called practicers of faith, in whom the settled mind of our tradition is established.

Respectfully.
Bunmei 3 [1471].12.18.

---

[25] *mōnen mōju* 妄念妄執 ; mental activity that serves as a hindrance to enlightenment and occurs because of blind passion, which is intrinsic to the human condition. In *The Letters, mōnen mōju* occurs only in this instance; the related term, *bonnō* (煩悩 ; Skt. *kleśa*), occurs once in letter 3:10, twice in 5:5, and three times in 5:13.

[26] *higan* 悲願 ; the Eighteenth Vow (see SSJ, 415).

I-4 Some questions and answers

I am told that Master Shinran's tradition speaks of "completing the cause [of birth in the Pure Land] in ordinary life"[27] and does not adhere to "[Amida's] coming to meet [us at the moment of death]."[28] What does this mean? I do not know anything about "completing the cause [of birth] in ordinary life" or about the significance of "not [waiting for Amida to] come to meet [us at the moment of death]." I would like to hear about this in detail.

Answer: Indeed, I consider these questions to be of the utmost importance in our tradition. From the beginning, this school has taught that "with the awakening of the one thought-moment [of faith], the cause [of birth] is completed in ordinary life."[29] After we have understood that it is through the unfolding of past good[30] that we hear and realize in ordinary life that Amida Tathāgata's Primal Vow saves us, we understand that it is not by our own power, but through the gift of Other Power, the wisdom of the Buddha, that we become aware of how Amida's Primal Vow came to be. This is the meaning of "completing the cause [of birth] in ordinary life." Thus "completing the cause [of birth] in ordinary life" is a state of mind in which we have heard and fully understood this principle, and are convinced that birth is assured; we refer to it as "with the awakening of the one thought-moment, joining the company of those [whose birth is] truly settled,"[31] "completing the cause [of birth] in ordinary life," and "immediately attaining birth [in the Pure Land] and dwelling in [a state of] non-retrogression."[32]

---

[27] See n. 14 above.

[28] *raikō*. See *Mattōshō*, SSZ 2: 656 (T 83.711ab), and n. 13 above.

[29] *ichinen hokki heizei gōjō* 一念発起平生業成 (also found in letters 2:10 and 4:13); similar in meaning to *ichinen hokki nyū shōjō shi ju* (n. 12 above).

[30] *shukuzen* 宿善. Although this term appears only once in Shinran's literary corpus, in the thirteenth chapter of *Tannishō*, SSZ 2: 782 (T 83.731b), Rennyo uses the term frequently, devoting letters 3:12 and 4:1 to developing its significance for the Shinshū. In a letter dated Bunmei 4 (1472).2.8 (RSI, 79–82 [#15]), he lists passages from Kakunyo's *Gaijashō*, SSZ 3: 72, including one linking those with good from the past (*shukuzen*) with a good teacher (*zenjishiki* 善知識) and one linking those who lack good from the past (*mushukuzen* 無宿善) with an evil teacher (*akuchishiki* 悪知識).

[31] *ichinen hokki jushō jōju* 一念発起住正定聚. Cf. n. 12. This phrasing reoccurs in letter 5:21.

[32] This phrase occurs also in letters 1:2 and 4:1; see n. 11 above.

Question: I fully understand the concept of "birth [in the Pure Land] with the awakening of the one thought-moment." However, I still do not understand the meaning of "not [waiting for Amida to] come to meet [us at the moment of death]." Would you kindly explain this?

Answer: As for the matter of "not [waiting for Amida to] come to meet [us at the moment of death]," when we realize that "with the awakening of the one thought-moment, we join the company of those [whose birth is] truly settled," there is no longer any need to expect [Amida's] coming. The reason is that "waiting for [Amida to] come to meet [us]" is a matter of concern to those who perform various other practices. For practicers of true and real faith, it is understood that there is no longer a wait for [Amida's] coming to meet [us] when we immediately receive, with the awakening of the one thought-moment, the benefit of [being protected by] the light that embraces and never abandons.[33]

Therefore, according to the teaching of the master, "[Amida's] coming to meet [us at the moment of death]" pertains to birth through various other practices; practicers of true and real faith are embraced and never abandoned,[34] and for this reason, they join the company of those [whose birth is] truly settled.[35] Because they join those who are truly settled, they will attain nirvāṇa (*metsudo* 滅度) without fail. Hence there is no waiting for the moment of death and no reliance on

---

[33] *sesshu fusha no kōyaku* 摂取不捨の光益. Based on a passage in the *Contemplation Sūtra*: "The Buddha of Immeasurable life has eighty-four thousand attributes; each attribute has eighty-four thousand accompanying features; and each accompanying feature has eighty-four thousand rays of light. Each ray of light shines throughout the worlds of the ten directions, and sentient beings mindful of the Buddha are embraced, never to be abandoned" (SSZ 1: 57 [T 12.343c]). The last sentence of this passage is quoted in letters 2:4, 2:13, and 5:12.

[34] In *Ichinen tanen mon'i*, SSZ 2: 605 (T 83.694b), Shinran explains *sesshu* as follows:

When one realizes true and real shinjin, one is immediately grasped [*sesshu*] and held within the heart of the Buddha of unhindered light, never to be abandoned. "To grasp" (*sesshu*) means to take in (*setsu*) and to receive and hold (*shu*). When we are grasped by Amida, immediately — without a moment or a day elapsing — we ascend to and become established in the stage of the truly settled; this is the meaning of *attain birth* (*Once-calling*, 33).

[35] *shōjōju* 正定聚 . Shinran explains in *Kyōgyōshinshō*, SSZ 2: 103 (T 83.616a):

When foolish beings possessed of blind passions, the multitudes caught in birth-and-death and defiled by evil karma, realize the mind and practice that Amida directs to them for their going forth [*ōsō ekō*], they immediately join the truly settled [*shōjōju*] of the Mahāyāna. Because they dwell among the truly settled, they necessarily attain nirvāṇa (*Teaching*, 3: 355).

[Amida's] coming to meet [us at that time]. We should bear these words in mind.

Question: Should we understand [the state of] being truly settled and [that of] nirvāṇa as one benefit, or as two?

Answer: The dimension of "the awakening of the one thought-moment" is that of "[joining] the company of those truly settled." This is the benefit [we gain] in the defiled world. Next, it should be understood that nirvāṇa is the benefit to be gained in the Pure Land.[36] Hence we should think of them as two benefits.[37]

Question: Knowing that birth is assured when we have understood as you have explained, how should we understand being told that we must go to the trouble of acquiring faith? I would like to hear about this, too.

Answer: This inquiry is indeed of great importance. That is, the very understanding that conforms to what has been explained above is precisely what we mean by decisively settled faith.

Question: I clearly understand that the state in which faith is decisively settled is described as "completing the cause [of birth] in ordinary life," "not [waiting for Amida to] come to meet [us at the moment of death]," and "[joining] the company of those who are truly settled." However, I do not yet understand whether, after faith is decisively settled, we should say the nenbutsu for the sake of birth in the land of utmost bliss,[38] or in gratitude for [Amida] Buddha's benevolence.

Answer: I consider this question, too, to be of great importance. The point is that we must not think of the nenbutsu said after the awakening of the one thought-moment of faith as an act for the sake of birth; it should be understood to be solely in gratitude for Buddha's

---

[36] *jōdo* 浄土 ; a realm that came into being as a result of the fulfillment of the Forty-eight Vows made by Amida as the monk Dharmākara (see SSJ, 276).

[37] *niyaku* 二益 . Rennyo follows Zonkaku's *Rokuyōshō* (SSZ 2: 321) in framing the question and answering it: joining the company of those truly settled and realizing nirvāṇa at death are two benefits. In identifying the former benefit with this defiled world (*edo* 穢土) and the latter with the Pure Land (*jōdo*), he countered the one-benefit teaching, which equated the awakening of the one thought-moment of faith with enlightenment itself. Overall, there appears to be a dualist dimension in Rennyo's thought; this is lacking for Shinran, whose only use of the term "defiled land" (*edo*), apart from a quotation, is in *Yuishinshō mon'i*, SSZ 2: 624 (T 83.700b): "a person is made to reject the defiled world and come to the true and real fulfilled land" (*Essentials*, 33). As we have noted already, the structure of Shinran's thought embraces a simultaneity of opposition and sameness, or duality and nonduality.

[38] *gokuraku* 極楽 . A synonym for the Pure Land (*jōdo*).

benevolence. Therefore, Master Shan-tao explained it as "spending one's entire life at the upper limit, one thought-moment [of faith] at the lower."[39] It is understood that "one thought-moment at the lower" refers to the settling of faith, and "spending one's entire life at the upper limit" to the nenbutsu said in grateful return for Buddha's benevolence. These are things that should be thoroughly understood.

Respectfully.
Bunmei 4 [1472].11.27.

I-5 On pilgrimage in the snow

From [the beginning of] this year,[40] an unexpectedly large number of priests and lay people — men and women from the three provinces of Kashū, Noto, and Etchū — have flocked in pilgrimage to this mountain at Yoshizaki; I am uneasy as to what the understanding of each of these people may be.

The reason for this, first of all, is that in our tradition, assurance of birth in the land of utmost bliss with this life is grounded in our having attained Other-Power faith. However, within this school, there is no one who has attained firm faith. How can people like this be born readily in the fulfilled land? This is the matter of greatest importance. In what frame of mind have they come here through this snow — fortunately having endured the long journey of five to ten *ri*? I am thoroughly apprehensive about this. But whatever their thinking may have been in the past, I will state in detail what should be borne in mind from now on. Be attentive; listen very carefully.

The point is to keep the matter of Other-Power faith firmly in mind; beyond that, you should just say the nenbutsu — walking, standing, sitting, and lying down — in gratitude for [Amida] Buddha's benevolence. With this understanding, the birth that is to come [in the Pure Land] is assured. In the fullness of this joy, go to the temples of

---

[39] The first half of this quotation appears in Shan-tao, *Ōjō raisange*, SSZ 1: 651 (T 47.439b), and in Shinran, *Ichinen tanen mon'i*, SSZ 2: 614 (T 83.697b). Cited in full in Kakunyo, *Kudenshō*, SSZ 3: 33 (T 83.749b).

[40] An alternate text of this letter cites "from the fourth year of Bunmei" as the date at which pilgrims from three provinces flocked to Yoshizaki (RSI, 95 [#20]). This reading is supported by RSI, 162–64 (#48), in which Rennyo describes untold numbers of people gathering at Yoshizaki and his decision at the beginning of Bunmei 4 (1472) to forbid their assembly.

the priests who are your teachers, and offer some tangible expression of your gratitude. [One who does] this is to be declared a person of faith, who has fully understood the principles of our tradition.

Respectfully.
Bunmei 5 [1473].2.8.

I-6 On drowsiness

I don't know why, but recently (this summer), I have been particularly subject to drowsiness, and when I consider why I would be [so] lethargic, I feel without a doubt that the moment of death leading to birth [in the Pure Land] (*ōjō no shigo* 往生の死期) may be close at hand. This thought makes me sad, and I feel in particular the sorrow of parting. And yet, to this very day I have prepared myself with no lack of care, thinking that the time of birth might be imminent. All I continually long for in regard to this, day and night, is that, after [my death], there will be no regression in those among the visitors to this temple whose faith is decisively settled. As things now stand, there should be no difficulties if I die, but each of you is particularly lax in your thinking in regard to birth. As long as you live, you should be as I have described. I am altogether dissatisfied with what each of you has understood. In this life, even tomorrow is uncertain, and no matter what we say, nothing is to any avail when life ends. If our doubts are not clearly dispelled during this life, we will surely [be filled with] regret. I hope that you will bear this in mind.

Respectfully.

This is entrusted to those [assembled] on the other side of the sliding doors.[41] In the years to come, please take it out and read it.

Written on the twenty-fifth day
of the fourth month, Bunmei 5 [1473].

---

[41] Various theories as to whom this letter was to be entrusted include the possibility that it was addressed to those who cared for Kengyoku, Rennyo's second daughter, before her death on Bunmei 4 (1472).8.14. Sugi notes the problem of the letter being dated a year later, but suggests that the death may actually have occurred in Bunmei 5; see Sugi, *Gobunshō kōwa*, 24.

I-7 A discussion about Yoshizaki:
Bunmei 4 [1472], the middle of the third month

This past year (the fourth year of Bunmei), about the middle of the third month as I recall, a few women of some distinction, accompanied by male attendants, were talking about this mountain. "A temple has recently been built on the summit at Yoshizaki," they said. "What a remarkably interesting place that is! Everyone knows that followers of the sect—priests and lay people, men and women—flock to the mountain in pilgrimage, particularly from the seven provinces of Kaga, Etchū, Noto, Echigo, Shinano, Dewa, and Ōshū. This is extraordinary for the last age,[42] and does not appear to be insignificant. But we would like to hear in detail how the nenbutsu teaching is presented to each of these followers and, above all, what it means when people say that 'faith' is taught as most important. We, too—because we suffer the bodily existence of women wretched with the burden of deep and heavy evil karma[43] —wish to aspire for birth by hearing and understanding this 'faith'."

When this inquiry was made of the man [living] on the mountain,[44] he responded, "Without doing anything in particular, but simply realizing that you are wretched beings burdened with the ten transgressions, the five grave offenses, the five obstacles,[45] and the three

---

[42] *matsudai* 末代 . This term, consistently used by Rennyo, is synonymous with *mappō* 末法 (last [age] of the dharma) which he uses only once in *The Letters* (4:3). The last age is the third of three periods following the Buddha's death, the first two being *shōbōji* 正法時 , the period of true dharma, when the Buddha's teaching was practiced and enlightenment could be attained, and *zōbōji* 像法時 , the period of semblance dharma, when the teaching was practiced, but enlightenment was no longer possible. In their discussion of Yoshizaki, the women suggest that it was surprising that so many could come on pilgrimage in the last age, when, according to a widely-held view, people were thought to be incapable of either understanding the dharma or practicing it. For Shinran's concept of the last age, see *Shōzōmatsu Wasan*, xii–xvi.

[43] Rennyo's references to women reflect the traditional Buddhist view that they are burdened with "deep and heavy evil karma." Amida, as he explains here, is the Buddha who saves precisely such persons. See, for example, letters 1:10, 2:1, 3:5, 4:3, 4:10, 5:3, 5:7, 5:14, 5:17, and 5:20. For a translation of the Vow made especially for women, the Thirty-fifth ("Vow of Transforming [a Female] into a Male"), see n. 64.

[44] i.e. Rennyo.

[45] *goshō* 五障 . The five obstacles said to be inherent in a woman's life are that

submissions,[46] you must deeply understand that Amida Tathāgata is the form for saving such persons. For when the one thought-moment [of faith] arises in which we entrust ourselves to Amida without any double-mindedness and realize that [Amida] saves us,[47] the Tathāgata sends forth eighty-four thousand rays of light,[48] with which he graciously embraces us. This is what is meant by saying that 'Amida Tathāgata embraces practicers of the nenbutsu.' 'Embraces and never abandons' means 'receives and does not discard.' We say that [one whose understanding is in accord with] this is a person who has realized faith.[49] Then, beyond this, we must bear in mind that the

---

she cannot become King of the Brahma Heaven (*Bontennō*), Indra (*Taishaku*), a Māra-King (*Maō*), a Cakravarti-King (*Tenrinnō*), or a buddha (see the *Lotus Sūtra*, T 9.35c). Shinran writes, with reference to the Thirty-fifth Vow (n. 64):

> If she does not rely on Amida's Name-Vow —
> even if a billion kalpas pass —
> if she is not free of the five obstacles (*itsutsu no sawari* いつつのさわり),
> how can a woman's form be changed?
>> (*Kōsō wasan*, SSZ 2: 508c [T 83.662b]; based on a
>> passage from Shan-tao's *Kannen bōmon* [T 47.26a,
>> trans. in *Kōsō Wasan*, 87, n. 1]).

[46] *sanshō* 三従. The three submissions for a woman are: first to her parents, then to her husband, and finally to her sons. For a translation of sūtra passages underlying this teaching, see *Jōdo Wasan*, 160; nn. 32, 33.

[47] *tasuke tamae* たすけたまえ. From the thrust of Rennyo's writings, it is apparent that this phrase should not be literally interpreted as a request to Amida to "please save me." The practice of reciting the nenbutsu as a plea for salvation was common among participants in other strands of Pure Land tradition. Rennyo, in contrast, stated in his earliest extant letter, dated Kanshō 2 (1461).3 (RSI, 47 [#1]), that Shinshū adherents were not even to think "Buddha, please save me" in saying the nenbutsu, but to understand it solely as an expression of gratitude. For this reason, in an attempt to avoid the suggestion of self-power, we have translated the phrase indirectly, with slight variations according to context. For example, letter 3:2 reads " 'Na-mu' means . . . entrusting ourselves without double-mindedness [to Amida] *to save us*, [bringing us to buddhahood] in the afterlife" [emphasis added]. Our position is that Rennyo adopted a phrase familiar to many of those attracted to his leadership of the Honganji, yet he brought to it an Other-Power interpretation that was radically different from the customary understanding in Pure Land tradition as a whole.

[48] *kōmyō* 光明. See n. 33 above.

[49] *shinjin o etaru hito* 信心をえたる人. A phrase found in the opening passage of letter three of Shinran's *Mattōshō*, SSZ 2: 661 (T 83.712c):

> Since the person who has realized shinjin necessarily abides in the stage of the truly settled, he is in the stage equal to the perfect enlightenment. In the *Larger Sūtra of Immeasurable Life* the person who has been grasped, never to be aban-

nenbutsu, 'namu-amida-butsu,' which we say sleeping or waking, standing or sitting down, is that nenbutsu, 'namu-amida-butsu,' said by those saved by Amida as an expression of gratitude for Amida's gracious benevolence."

When he had carefully related this, the women and others [who were with them] replied, "There is indeed no way to express our shame over not having entrusted ourselves until now to Amida Tathāgata's Primal Vow, which is so suited to our innate capacity. From now on, we will steadfastly entrust ourselves to Amida; and, believing single-heartedly that our birth has been accomplished by the saving work of the Tathāgata, we will bear in mind that the nenbutsu is, after this, a saying of the Name in gratitude for the Buddha's benevolence. There is no way at all to express our thankfulness and awe at having been given this opportunity through inconceivable conditions from the past and having heard the incomparable dharma. Now it is time to say fare-well."And with this, their eyes brimming with tears, they took their leave.

Respectfully.
Bunmei 5 [1473].8.12.

I-8 On building at Yoshizaki

Around the beginning of the fourth month of the third year of Bun-mei, I just slipped away, without any settled plan, from a place near Mii-dera's southern branch temple [Kenshō-ji] at Ōtsu, in the Shiga district of Ōmi province, and travelled through various parts of Echizen and Kaga. Then, as this site — Yoshizaki, in the Hosorogi district of [Echizen] province — was particularly appealing, we made a clearing on the mountain, which for many years had been the habitat of wild beasts.[50] Beginning on the twenty-seventh day of the seventh month, we put up a building that might be called a temple. With the passage of time from yesterday to today and so on, three years have elapsed with the seasonal changes.

In the meantime, priests and lay people, men and women, have flocked here, but as this appears to be to no purpose at all, I have pro-

---

doned, is said to be in the stage of the truly settled, and in the *Assembly of the Tathāgata of Immeasurable Life [Muryōju nyorai e]* he is said to equal the perfect enlightenment (*Letters*, 26).

[50] Rennyo's metaphor is "tigers and wolves"; clearly, this had been a wild and deserted area.

hibited their coming and going as of this year. For, to my mind, the fundamental reason for being in this place is that, having received life in the human realm[51] and having already met with the Buddha-dharma, which is difficult to meet, it is indeed shameful that one would fall in vain into hell. Thus I have reached a judgment that people who are unconcerned with the decisive settling of nenbutsu faith and attainment of birth in the land of utmost bliss should not gather at this place. This is solely because what is fundamental for us is not reputation and personal gain, but simply a concern for enlightenment[52] in the afterlife.[53] Therefore, let there be no misinterpretation by those who see this or hear about it.

Respectfully.

Bunmei 5 [1473].9.

I-9 On avoiding certain things

For a long time, people have said uniformly that ours is a ridiculous, degenerate sect. This does indeed point to a certain truth: among those in our tradition, [there are] some who unhesitatingly proclaim our teaching in the presence of those of other schools[54] and other sects.[55] This is a great mistake. Observing our tradition's rules of conduct[56] means keeping firmly to ourselves the teaching transmitted in

---

[51] *ningai* 人界 . One of the ten realms of existence through which beings transmigrate: hell (*jigoku* 地獄), hungry spirits (*gaki* 餓鬼), beasts (*chikushō* 畜生), asuras (warring demi-gods, *ashura* 阿修羅), human beings (*ningen* 人間), heavenly beings (*tenjō* 天上), śrāvakas (hearers, *shōmon* 声聞), pratyekabuddhas (solitary buddhas, *engaku* 緑覚), bodhisattvas (*bosatsu* 菩薩), and buddhas (*butsu* 仏). The first six, which make up the desire-realm (*yokkai* 欲界), are sometimes subdivided into the three evil paths (*sanzu* 三途 or *san'akudō* 三悪道) of hell, hungry spirits, and beasts, and the three good paths (*sanzendō* 三善道) of asuras, humans, and heavenly beings.

[52] *bodai* 菩提 ; Skt. *bodhi*.

[53] *goshō* 後生 , synonymous with *gose* 後世 , *raishō* 来生 , and *raise* 来世 . Rennyo makes frequent reference in his letters to "the most important matter of the afterlife" (*kondo no ichidaiji no goshō* 今度の一大事の後生).

[54] *tamon* 他門 . Branches of the Jōdoshū, such as the Chinzei, Kubon, and Seizan, which acknowledged Hōnen as their founder.

[55] *tashū* 他宗 . Traditional sectarian Buddhist movements, such as Tendai and Shingon, as well as Nichiren and Zen – other than Pure Land.

[56] *okite* おきて ; "rules of conduct" or "regulations." Rennyo introduces the term into the Shinshū textual tradition at a critical juncture for the Honganji's

our tradition and not giving any outward sign of it; those who do this are said to be people of discretion. These days, however, some talk carelessly and without reserve about matters concerning our sect in the presence of those of other schools and other sects; as a result, our tradition is considered shallow. Because there are some with mistaken views, others see our sect as degraded and detestable. We should bear in mind that this is not at all the fault of others, but that it is the fault of our own people.

Next, as for the matter of avoiding things that are impure and inauspicious, it is established that in our tradition, within the Buddha-dharma, we do not regard any particular thing as taboo. But are there not things that we should avoid in regard to other sects and the civil authorities?[57] Of course, in the presence of those of other sects and other schools, there are certainly things to be avoided. Further, we should not criticize what others avoid.

Despite all this, it is clearly seen in many passages of various sūtras that those who follow the practices of the Buddha-dharma — not only people of the nenbutsu — should not be concerned to such an extent with the avoidance of things. First, a passage in the *Nirvāṇa Sūtra* . . . says, "Within the Tathāgata's dharma, there is no choosing of auspicious days and favorable times."[58] Also, a passage in the *Sūtra of the Samādhi of All Buddhas' Presence* states: "Lay women who hear of this samādhi and want to practice it! . . . take refuge in the Buddha; take refuge in the Dharma; take refuge in the Sangha. Do not follow other paths; do not worship heavenly beings; do not enshrine spirits; do not look for auspicious days."[59]

Although there are other passages similar to these in the sūtras, I offer these selections. They teach, in particular, that nenbutsu practicers should not follow such ways. Let this be thoroughly understood.

Respectfully.

Bunmei 5 [1473].9.

---

survival, renewal, and expansion in the Hokuriku (discussed in chapter three of this work). For further examples see letters 2:2, 2:13, 3:11, and 4:1. Precedent for Rennyo's itemizing of specific prohibitions may be found in lists of regulations (*seikin*) drawn up for separate Shinshū congregations or temples. Further, in Kakunyo's writings, a distinction is made between precepts governing one's external behavior in society and inner piety (see *Gaijashō*, SSZ 3: 67).

[57] *kubō* 公方 i.e. officials of the Ashikaga shogunate.

[58] *Nehangyō*, T 12.482b.

[59] *Hanju zanmaikyō*, T 13.901b. One of the oldest Mahāyāna sūtras making reference to Amida; it is considered a forerunner of the Pure Land sūtras.

I-10 On the wives of the priests in charge of lodgings at Yoshizaki

Those who become wives of the priests in charge of lodgings[60] on this mountain at Yoshizaki should be aware that this happens because past conditions in their previous lives are not shallow. This awareness, however, will come about after they have realized that the afterlife is the matter of greatest importance and undergone a decisive settling of faith. Therefore, those who are to be wives [of the priests] should, by all means, firmly attain faith.

First of all, because what is known as settled mind in our tradition differs greatly from and is superior to [the understanding of] the Jōdo schools in general,[61] it is said to be the great faith of Other Power.[62] Therefore, we should realize that those who have attained this faith — ten out of ten, one hundred out of one hundred — are assured of the birth that is to come [in the Pure Land].

[Question:] How should we understand this faith (*anjin*)? We do not know about it in any detail.

Answer: This question is indeed of the utmost importance. This is how to attain the faith of our tradition:

To begin with, being women — hence wretched creatures of deep evil karma, burdened with the five obstacles and the three submissions — you were abandoned long ago by the tathāgatas of the ten directions and also by all the buddhas of the three periods;[63] yet Amida Tathāgata alone graciously vowed to save just such persons [as you] and, long ago, made Forty-eight Vows. Among these Vows, beyond [promising in] the Eighteenth Vow to save all evildoers and women, Amida then made a further Vow, the Thirty-fifth,[64] to save women

---

[60] *taya* 多屋. Lodgings for priests and pilgrims within the temple precincts; part of a temple-town.

[61] *Jōdo ikke* 浄土一家. Branches of the Jōdoshū. See letter 2:15: "In Japan, various branches of the Jōdoshū have been established; it is divided into Seizan, Chinzei, Kubon, Chōrakuji, and many others."

[62] *tariki no daishinjin* 他力の大信心. A phrase found in *Anjin ketsujōshō*, SSZ 3: 627 (T 83.925b).

[63] *sanze* 三世. The three periods of time — past, present, and future.

[64] The Thirty-fifth of the Forty-eight Vows in the *Larger Sūtra*, SSZ 1: 12 (T 12.268c); it reads:

because of the depth of their evil karma and doubts. You should have a deep sense of gratitude for Amida Tathāgata's benevolence in having undergone such painstaking endeavors.

Question: After we have come to realize our thankfulness that Amida Tathāgata made vows time and again in this way to save people like us, then in what frame of mind should we entrust ourselves to Amida? We need to have this explained in detail.

Answer: If you wish to attain faith and entrust yourselves to Amida, first realize that human life lasts only as long as a dream or an illusion and that the afterlife [in the Pure Land] is indeed the blissful result in eternity,[65] that human life means the enjoyment of fifty to a hundred years, and that the afterlife is the matter of greatest importance. Abandoning the inclination toward all sundry practices and discarding the tendency to avoid certain things, entrust yourselves single-heartedly and steadfastly to Amida and, without concerning yourselves with other buddhas, bodhisattvas, and the various kami, take refuge exclusively in Amida, with the assurance that this coming birth is a certainty. Then, in an outpouring of thankfulness, you should say the nenbutsu and respond in gratitude for Amida Tathāgata's benevolence in saving you. This is the frame of mind of resident priests' wives who have attained faith.

Respectfully.

Bunmei 5 [1473].9.11.

I-11 On lightning and morning dew

On deep contemplation, we realize that the pleasures of human life last only as long as a flash of lightning or the morning dew, a dream or an illusion. Even if we enjoy a life of pomp and glory and can do as we wish, this is only a matter of some fifty to a hundred years. If the wind of impermanence[66] were to come even now and summon us,

---

If, when I attain buddhahood, those women in the innumerable and inconceivable buddha lands of the ten directions who, hearing my Name, rejoice and entrust themselves, awaken the aspiration for enlightenment, and despise their female bodies should after death again take female form, may I not attain the supreme enlightenment.

[65] *yōshō no rakuka* 永生の楽果 . A phrase found in Shan-tao's *Kangyōsho* (*Gengibun*), T 37.246a, and in Zonkaku's *Kenmyōshō*, SSZ 3: 351, and *Hōonki*, SSZ 3: 280.

[66] *mujō no kaze* 無常のかぜ . All phenomena are characterized by four aspects —

would we not suffer illness of one kind or another and die? And indeed, at the time of death, no part of either the family or wealth on which we have depended for so long can accompany us. Thus, all alone, we must cross the great river of three currents,[67] at the end of the mountain path that we take after death.[68] Let us realize, then, that what we should earnestly aspire to is [birth in the Pure Land in] the afterlife, that the one we should rely upon is Amida Tathāgata, and that the place to which we go, faith having been decisively settled, is the Pure Land of serene sustenance (*anyō no jōdo* 安養の浄土).

These days, however, the priests in this region who are practicers of nenbutsu are seriously at variance with the Buddha-dharma. That is, they call followers from whom they receive donations "good disciples" and speak of them as "people of faith." This is a serious error. Also, the disciples think that if they just bring an abundance of things to the priests, they will be saved by the priests' power, even if their own power is insufficient. This, too, is an error. And so between the priests and their followers, there is not a modicum of understanding of our tradition's faith. This is indeed deplorable. Without a doubt, neither priests nor disciples will be born in the land of utmost bliss; they will fall in vain into hell.

Even though we lament this, we cannot lament deeply enough; though we grieve, we should grieve more deeply. From now on, therefore, [the priests] should seek out those who fully know the details of the great faith of Other Power, let their faith be decisively settled, and then teach the essentials of that faith to their disciples; together, they will surely attain the birth that is to come [in the Pure Land], the most important matter.

Respectfully.

Bunmei 5 [1473],

the middle of the ninth month.

---

birth (or coming into existence), staying, changing, and perishing; this is "impermanence" (*mujō*).

[67] *sanzu no daiga* 三途の大河 . A river in the realm of the dead. The river has three currents or ways of crossing. One is shallow, for those whose sins are shallow; one has a jewelled bridge of gold and silver for the passage of the good; and one has strong, deep rapids where those who have committed evil suffer attack by serpents, crushing blows from a huge rock, and other torments (Izumoji, *Ofumi*, 92–93).

[68] *shide no yamaji* 死出の山路 . A path leading to the palace of Enma, lord of the realm of the dead, who passes judgment on the dead.

I-12 Chōshō-ji's past

For years, the followers at Chōshō-ji[69] have been seriously at variance with the Buddha-dharma. My reason for saying this, first of all, has to do with the leader of the assembly. He thinks that to occupy the place of honor and drink before everyone else and to court the admiration of those seated around him, as well as that of others, is really the most important aspect of the Buddha-dharma. This is certainly of no use for birth in the land of utmost bliss; it appears to be just for worldly reputation.

Now, what is the purpose of monthly meetings in our sect?

Lay people, lacking wisdom, spend their days and nights in vain; their lives pass by meaninglessly, and, at the end, they fall into the three evil paths.[70] The meetings are occasions when, even if only once a month, just those who practice the nenbutsu should at least gather in the meeting place[71] and discuss their own faith and the faith of others. Recently, however, because matters of faith are never discussed in terms of right and wrong, the situation is deplorable beyond words.

In conclusion, there must definitely be discussions of faith from now on among those at the meetings. For this is how we are to attain birth in the true and real land of utmost bliss.

Respectfully.

Bunmei 5 [1473],

the latter part of the ninth month.

I-13 On the false "ten kalpas" teaching in this region

Recently, some of the nenbutsu people in this region have been using strange terms, insisting that they express the attainment of faith; furthermore, they hold to this as if they knew all about our tradition's faith. In their words, "Faith is not forgetting the benevolence of

---

[69] A Honganji-related temple in Fujishima, Fukui, Echizen province, founded by Ton'en (1387–1447; second son of Shakunyo, fifth head priest of the Honganji).

[70] *sanzu* 三塗 . The three realms of retribution for evil deeds; the lowest of the ten realms of existence. See n. 51.

[71] *dōjō* 道場 ; often a private dwelling.

Amida, who settled our birth [in the Pure Land] from the time of his perfect enlightenment ten kalpas ago!"[72] This is a serious error. For even if they know all about Amida Tathāgata's perfect enlightenment, this is useless without knowing the significance of Other-Power faith, by which we are to attain birth.

Therefore, from now on, they should first of all know the true and real faith of our tradition very thoroughly. That faith is expounded in the *Larger Sūtra* as "threefold entrusting";[73] in the *Contemplation Sūtra*,

---

[72] *jikkō shōgaku* 十劫正覚. In both the *Larger Sūtra*, SSZ 1: 15 (T 12.270a) and the *Amida Sūtra*, SSZ 1: 67–68 (T 12.347a), Śākyamuni Buddha teaches his disciples that Amida Buddha attained enlightenment ten kalpas (*jikkō*) ago. Shinran restates this in his *Jōdo wasan*. The first of forty-eight hymns based on T'an-luan's *San Amida butsuge* begins:

> From the time Amida became a Buddha until the present,
> ten kalpas have passed (SSZ 2: 486b [T 83.655c]).

A hymn in the series of twenty-two based on the *Larger Sūtra* reads:

> Although [the sūtras] teach that ten kalpas have passed
> since Amida became a Buddha,
> he seems to be a Buddha
> older than an infinitesimal number of kalpas (*jinden kuongō* 塵点久遠劫).
> SSZ 2: 492b (T 83.657c)

At Yoshizaki, Rennyo was confronted with an interpretation of this teaching considered heretical from a Shinshū perspective. The doctrine of *jikkō shōgaku* attributed to the Seizan branch of the Jōdoshū maintained that what was necessary on the part of aspirants was a single utterance of the Name, provided they had apprehended "the nonduality of Amida's enlightenment aeons ago and the settlement of our birth in Amida's Pure Land" (Hirota, *No Abode*, 28).

[73] *sanshin* 三信. Shinran's interpretation of the Eighteenth Vow (n. 16 above) is that the "three minds" (*sanshin* 三心)—sincere mind (*shishin* 至心), entrusting (*shingyō* 信楽), and aspiring to be born (*yokushō* 欲生)—together comprise "threefold entrusting," three aspects of faith. In *Songō shinzō meimon*, he explicates "threefold entrusting" in terms of the "three minds":

> *With sincere mind entrusting themselves: Sincere* means true and real. "True and real" refers to the Vow of the Tathāgata being true and real; this is what *sincere mind* means.... *Entrusting* is to be free of doubt, believing deeply and without any double-mindedness that the Tathāgata's Primal Vow is true and real. This *entrusting with sincere mind*, then, is that arising from the Vow in which Amida urges every being throughout the ten quarters, "Entrust yourself to my Vow, which is true and real"; it does not arise from the hearts and minds of foolish beings of self-power. *Aspiring to be born in my land*: "Out of the entrusting with sincere mind that is Other Power, aspire to be born in the Pure Land of happiness!" (*Inscriptions*, 33–34; SSZ 2: 560 [T 83.679ab]).

In letter 4:1, Rennyo explains in simpler terms:

> The "Other-Power threefold entrusting" (*tariki no sanshin* 他力の三信) taught in

it is called "three minds";[74] and in the *Amida Sūtra*, it is expressed as "one mind."[75] Although the terms differ in all three sūtras, they are simply meant to express the one mind given to us by Other Power.[76]

What, then, do we mean by "faith"?

First of all, when we set aside all sundry practices and steadfastly rely on Amida Tathāgata and, giving no thought to any of the kami or to other buddhas, take refuge with singleness of heart exclusively in Amida, the Tathāgata embraces [us] with his light and never abandons us. This is precisely how the one thought-moment of faith is decisively settled.

After we have understood this, we must bear in mind that the

---

our tradition is described in the Eighteenth Vow as "with sincere mind, entrusting and aspiring to be born in my land." Although we call this "threefold entrusting," it is simply the one mind [of faith] in which a practicer takes refuge, relying on Amida.

[74] *sanjin* 三心 . Rennyo reads this term, occurring only once in *The Letters*, as *sanjin*. The concept of "three minds," drawn here from the *Contemplation Sūtra*, SSZ 1: 60 (T 12.344c), includes: sincere mind (*shijōshin* 至誠心); deep mind (*jinshin* 深心); and mind aspiring to birth in the Pure Land by the transfer of merit (*ekō hotsuganshin* 回向発願心). In *Kyōgyōshinshō*, SSZ 2: 51–57 (T 83.601c–603c), Shinran quotes a lengthy passage from *Kangyōsho* (*Sanzengi*), in which Shan-tao expounds the "three minds" in the *Contemplation Sūtra*. Shinran finds the meaning of the "three minds" (*sanshin* 三心) to be implicit in the "threefold entrusting" (*sanshin* 三信) of the Eighteenth Vow as stated in the *Larger Sūtra*.

[75] *isshin* 一心 . In the sixth chapter of *Kyōgyōshinshō*, SSZ 2: 156–67 (T 83.630ab), Shinran discusses the explicit and implicit aspects of the three sūtras; in particular, he addresses the question of differences between the "one mind" (*isshin*) in the *Amida Sūtra* and the "three minds" in the *Larger Sūtra* and *Contemplation Sūtra*. Shinran reads the characters 三心 as *sanshin* for both the *Larger Sūtra* and the *Contemplation Sūtra* (see, however, SSJ, 189, for entries on *sanshin* 三心 in relation to the *Larger Sūtra* and *sanjin* 三心 in relation to the *Contemplation Sūtra*). He maintains that, in its explicit aspect, the *Amida Sūtra* encourages nenbutsu practice with the "one mind" of self-power; in its implicit aspect, it reveals the true dharma leading sentient beings to great faith (*daishinjin* 大信心). For Shinran, the implicit aspect of the *Amida Sūtra* is to be seen in a passage drawing on the terms "hold" (*shūji* 執持) and "one mind" (*isshin* 一心 ; SSZ 1: 69 [T 12.347b]). He asserts that, although each of the three sūtras has both explicit and implicit aspects, each aims at clarifying that faith is the cause for attaining nirvāṇa. For an annotated translation of this passage, see *Kyō Gyō Shin Shō*, 185–91.

[76] Here Rennyo draws on Zonkaku's identification of "threefold entrusting" (*sanshin* 三信) in the *Larger Sūtra*, "three minds" (*sanshin* 三心) in the *Contemplation Sūtra*, and "one mind" (*isshin* 一心) in the *Amida Sūtra*; he recognizes all three as expressing "faith" (*shinjin*); see *Jimyōshō*, SSZ 3: 104. Note that Zonkaku, following Shinran, reads the characters 三心 in the *Contemplation Sūtra* as *sanshin*.

nenbutsu expresses our gratitude to Amida Tathāgata for his benevolence in granting us Other-Power faith. With this, we are to be declared nenbutsu practicers in whom faith is decisively settled.

Respectfully.
Written in Bunmei 5 [1473],
the latter part of the ninth month.

I-14 An admonition against slander

Now, among nenbutsu people in our tradition, there must be no slandering of other teachings. First of all, in Etchū and Kaga, this applies to Tateyama, Shirayama,[77] and the other mountain temples; in Echizen, to Heisen-ji, Toyohara-ji,[78] and others. Indeed, we were cautioned specifically about this long ago in the [Larger] Sūtra: "Excluded [from the Eighteenth Vow] are those who commit the five grave offenses and slander the true dharma."[79] Consequently, nenbutsu people especially must not slander other sects. We see, too, that scholars of the various sects of the Path of Sages[80] should never slander people of the nenbutsu. For, although there are many of these passages in the sūtras and commentaries, we have been strictly warned about this, first of all, in the Commentary on the Mahāprajñāpāramitā Sūtra[81] by Bodhisattva Nāgārjuna,[82] the founder of the eight schools.[83] That passage says, "If, out of attachment to the dharma he follows, a person speaks ill of the

---

[77] The two mountains, Tateyama and Shirayama, were sites of Shugendō ascetic practice.

[78] Heisen-ji and Toyohara-ji were Tendai temples related to the avatar (gongen 権現) of Shirayama.

[79] Larger Sūtra, SSZ 1: 9, 24 (T 12.268a, 272b); Kyōgyōshinshō, SSZ 2: 37 (T 83.598b).

[80] shōdō 聖道. In Anrakushū, T 47.13c, Tao-ch'o divides Buddhist tradition into two paths: the Path of Sages (shōdō), formalized religious practices leading to enlightenment, and the Pure Land (jōdo) way leading to birth in the Pure Land. In Rennyo's usage, the term refers to the Tendai, Shingon, and Zen, which were seen as based on self-power practices rather than on Other Power.

[81] Daichidoron.

[82] Nāgārjuna is acknowledged as founder by eight of the main Mahāyāna schools in Buddhist tradition.

[83] The eight schools or sects in Japanese Buddhist tradition are Kusha, Jōjitsu, Ritsu, Hossō, Sanron, Kegon, Tendai, and Shingon.

dharma of others, he will not escape the sufferings of hell, even if he is one who observes the precepts."[84]

Since we have clear testimonials such as this, [we realize that] all are the Buddha's teachings and that we must not mistakenly slander them. As they are all relevant to specific sects, the point is surely that we just do not rely on them; it is outrageous for people in our tradition who have no understanding to criticize other sects. Those who are head priests in each locality must not fail to enforce this strictly.

Respectfully.

Bunmei 5 [1473],
the latter part of the ninth month.

I-15 On the designation of our tradition

Question: How has it come about that there is such a widespread practice of everyone referring to our tradition as the "Ikkōshū"?[85] I am puzzled about this.

Answer: Our tradition's designation as the "Ikkōshū" was certainly not determined by our founder. Generally speaking, the reason everyone says this is because we "steadfastly (ikkō ni 一向に)" rely on Amida Buddha. However, since a passage in the [Larger] Sūtra teaches "steadfast and exclusive mindfulness of the Buddha of Immeasurable Life,"[86] their referring to us as the "Ikkōshū" presents no problem when the implication is "be steadfastly mindful of the Buddha of Immeasurable Life." Our founder, however, did indeed designate this sect as the "Jōdo Shinshū."[87] Hence we know that the term "Ikkōshū" did not come from within our sect. Further, others within the Jōdoshū[88] allow

---

[84] Daichidoron, T 25.63c.

[85] In a letter dated Entoku 2 (1490), Rennyo states that it has been a great mistake for members of the Honganji (as well as others) to refer to their tradition as "Ikkōshū," and that the term "shinshū" was never used by Shinran in a sectarian sense. "Ikkōshū," Rennyo explains, is a designation originating with Ippen and the Jishū (RSI, 372–73 [#123]).

[86] Larger Sūtra, SSZ 1: 24, 25 (T 12.272b).

[87] Rennyo appears to be using the term shū primarily in a sectarian, institutional sense here, contrasting the Jōdo Shinshū with the Jōdoshū and the eight traditional schools or sects in Japanese Buddhism.

[88] Rennyo has in mind the Seizan, Chinzei, Kubon, and Chōrakuji branches (see letter 2:15).

the sundry practices. Our master rejected sundry practices, and it is on this basis that we attain birth in the true and real fulfilled land. For this reason, he specifically inserted the character 真 (*shin* ["true"]).

A further question: I understand clearly that, long ago, [the founder] designated our tradition as the "Jōdo Shinshū." However, I would like to hear in detail how it is, in the teaching of our sect, that—although we are lay people of deep evil karma, burdened with evil acts and grave offenses—we are to be born readily in the land of utmost bliss through reliance on the working of Amida's Vow.

Answer: The import of our tradition is that when faith is decisively settled, we will unfailingly attain birth in the true and real fulfilled land. And so if you ask what this faith is, [the answer is that] it is just [a matter of] relying single-heartedly and without any worry on Amida Tathāgata and, giving no thought to other buddhas and bodhisattvas, entrusting ourselves steadfastly and without any double-mindedness to Amida. This we call "settlement of faith." The two characters 信心 (*shin-jin*) are [literally] read "true mind." We say "true mind" because the practicer is not saved by his mistaken mind of self-power (*jiriki no kokoro* 自力のこころ), but by the right mind of Other Power given by the Tathāgata.

Further, we are not saved simply by repeating the Name without any understanding of it. Hence the [*Larger*] *Sūtra* teaches that we "hear the Name and realize faith and joy."[89] "Hearing the Name" is not hearing the six-character Name 南無阿弥陀仏 (na-mu-a-mi-da-butsu) unreflectively; it means that when we meet a good teacher,[90] receive his teaching, and entrust ourselves ("namu") to the Name ("namu-amida-butsu"), Amida Buddha unfailingly saves us. This is explained in the [*Larger*] *Sūtra* as "realizing faith and joy." Consequently, we should understand that "namu-amida-butsu" shows how he saves us.

After we have come to this realization, we must bear in mind that the Name we say walking, standing, sitting, and lying down is simply an expression of gratitude for Amida Tathāgata's benevolence in saving us. With this, we are to be declared Other-Power nenbutsu

---

[89] *Larger Sūtra*, SSZ 1: 24 (T 12.272b); *Kyōgyōshinshō*, SSZ 2: 49, 62 (T 83.601a). This phrase appears again in letters 3:6 and 5:11. Shinran quotes the phrase in a larger context and explains it in *Ichinen tanen mon'i* (SSZ 2: 604–5 [T 83.594c]; see *Once-calling*, 32).

[90] *zenjishiki*; also read *zenchishiki*. A good teacher or friend who leads one in the Buddhist path.

practicers who have attained faith and will be born in the land of utmost bliss.

Respectfully.

The compilation and writing of this letter was completed between nine and eleven in the morning on the second day of the latter part of the ninth month, Bunmei 5 [1473], at the hot springs at Yamanaka, Kaga province.

Shōnyo, disciple of Śākyamuni.

(written seal)[91]

---

[91] *kaō* 花押 . The written seal is a personalized signature written under an author's name. To prevent its being copied, it was often written as a design, in abbreviated style. Shōnyo's written seal is on the Taishō edition text of *The Letters*, T 83.778a; it was during his tenure as tenth head priest that the text took printed form.

Fascicle Two

II-1 On clearing the channels of faith

I hear that during the past seven days of thanksgiving services,[1] wives of the priests in charge of lodgings and others as well have, for the most part, undergone a decisive settling of faith. This is wonderful, and one could hope for nothing more. And yet, if we just let things be, faith, too, will disappear. It does seem that "time after time, [we must] clear the channels of faith and let the waters of Amida's dharma flow."[2]

In regard to this, [it must be understood that] although women have been abandoned by all the buddhas of the ten directions and the three periods, it is indeed thanks to Amida Tathāgata that they are saved. For to whatever extent women's minds may be true, their inclination to doubt is deep, and their tendency to avoid things [impure and inauspicious] is still more difficult to cast off. Lay women in particular, absorbed in practical matters and in their concern for children and grandchildren, devote themselves only to this life; and while they know the human realm[3] —so patently ephemeral—to be a place of uncertainty for young and old alike, they pass their nights and days to no purpose, giving no thought at all to the fact that they will soon sink into the three evil paths and the eight difficulties.[4] This is the way of ordinary people; it is inexpressibly deplorable.

---

[1] *hōonkō*; annual services lasting for seven days, ending on the anniversary of Shinran's death (the twenty-eighth day of the eleventh month by the lunar calendar, the sixteenth of the first month by the solar).

[2] Sugi offers several possibilities for the source of this quotation. From a Mahāyāna text, the *Ropparamitsukyō*:

For example, when a farmer wants to plant seeds, he first of all clears a channel in order to draw water; . . . in just the same way, bodhisattvas and mahāsattvas dig out channels of wisdom in the midst of birth-and-death, the great field of transmigration, to draw its nectar-waters (T 8.891ab).

From *Ōjōyōshū*:

If we once clear a channel, various waters flow into it naturally; they in turn become a great river and finally join with the sea. Practicers, too, are like this: if they once awaken the aspiration [for buddhahood], the waters of their various roots of goodness flow naturally from then on into the channel of the four bodhisattva vows, and they in turn are born in the land of utmost bliss (SSZ 1: 788 [T 84.50a]). See "Gobunshō yōgikōwa," *Gobunshō kōwa*, 182.

[3] *ningenkai* 人間界 . See *ningai*, fascicle one, n. 51.

[4] *hachinan* 八難 . The eight circumstances that prevent one from seeing a buddha or hearing the dharma: existence in hell; existence in the realm of

They must, therefore, take refuge single-heartedly and steadfastly in the compassionate Vow of the one Buddha Amida and deeply entrust themselves; discarding the inclination to engage in sundry practices, they must also cast off all thought of courting favor with the kami and other buddhas. Then, realizing that Amida Tathāgata made the Primal Vow for the sake of wretched women like themselves and that the Buddha's wisdom is indeed inconceivable, and knowing that they are evil and worthless beings, they should be deeply moved to turn and enter [the mind of] the Tathāgata. Then they will realize that their entrusting [of themselves] and their mindfulness [of Amida] are both brought about through Amida Tathāgata's compassionate means.[5]

People who understand [the teaching] in this way are precisely those who have attained Other-Power faith. Moreover, this state is described as "dwelling in the company of those [whose birth in the Pure Land is] truly settled," "[being certain to] reach nirvāṇa," "reaching the stage equal to perfect enlightenment,"[6] and "[being of] the same

---

hungry spirits; existence in the realm of beasts; existence in the heaven of long life (chōjuten 長寿天), where aspiration to enter the Buddhist path does not arise; existence in a remote land (henji 辺地) — in one of the heavens of the realms of form and formlessness or in Uttan'otsu (Jpn. Hokkuru), one of the four continents in Buddhist cosmology — where sentient beings are absorbed in pleasures and do not seek the dharma; being blind, deaf, or mute (rōmō on'a 聾盲瘖瘂); being knowledgeable about the world and eloquent (sechi bensō 世智弁聡); and living in a period before or after the Buddha's appearance in the world (butsuzen butsugo 仏前仏後). See Nakamura Hajime, ed., Bukkyōgo daijiten: Shukusatsuban (Tokyo: Tōkyō Shoseki, 1987), 1104–5; hereafter cited as BGDJ).

[5] hōben 方便 (Skt. upāya), a term that in the Jōdo Shinshū is generally used in one of two ways: to refer to provisional means (gonke hōben 権仮方便) used to lead beings to the truth and reality of the dharma, or to refer to the compassionate means (zengyō hōben 善巧方便) by which the Buddha saves beings through the manifestation of ultimate truth or reality within the world of form and relativity (SSJ, 444–45). Here, the reference is to the latter, as expressed by Shinran in the Kōsō wasan:

> Śākya and Mida are father and mother of compassion:
> using skillful means in various ways,
> they graciously enable us
> to awaken supreme faith.

SSZ 2: 510a (T 83.662c)

[6] tōshōgaku ni itaru 等正覚にいたる . Shinran explains in Mattōshō:

Since the person who has realized shinjin necessarily abides in the stage of the truly settled [shōjōju], he is in the stage equal to the perfect enlightenment [tōshōgaku]. In the Larger Sūtra of Immeasurable Life the person who has been grasped, never to be abandoned, is said to be in the stage of the truly settled, and [stage] as Maitreya."[7] We also say that these are people whose birth has been settled with the awakening of the one thought-moment [of faith]. Bear in mind that, on the basis of this understanding, the nenbutsu (the saying of the Name) is the nenbutsu of joy, expressing our gratitude for the benevolence of Amida Tathāgata who readily settles our birth.

Respectfully.

First of all, observe our tradition's regulations very carefully in regard to the above. For if [people] fully understand the way of faith as stated here, they will store it deep within themselves and not give any sign of it in the presence of those of other sects and others [not of our tradition]; neither will they talk about faith. As for the kami [and other buddhas], we simply do not rely on them; we must not belittle them. The master also spoke of the person who is "true" as described above — both in matters of faith and of conduct — as a practicer of faith who has discretion. Quite simply, we are to be deeply mindful of the Buddha-dharma.

Respectfully.

I have written this letter on the eighth day of the twelfth month of Bunmei 5 [1473] and am giving it to the wives of the priests in charge of the lodgings on this mountain. If there are other matters still in question, they should inquire again.

With the passage of winter and summer, age 58.

(seal)

---

in the *Assembly of the Tathāgata of Immeasurable Life* [*Muryōju nyorai e*] he is said to equal the perfect enlightenment. Although the names differ, the truly settled and equal to enlightenment have the same meaning and indicate the same stage (*Letters*, 26; SSZ 2: 661 [T 83.712c]).

[7] *Miroku ni hitoshi* 弥勒にひとし. The bodhisattva Maitreya, who resides in the Tuṣita heaven, will appear in this world as its next buddha after 5,670,000,000 years. The person truly settled in faith through the working of Amida is comparable to Maitreya in that both are in the stage immediately preceding buddhahood. In *Mattōshō*, Shinran equates a similar term, *miroku to onajiku* 弥勒とおなじく, with perfect enlightenment (*tōshōgaku*). See *Letters*, 26 (SSZ 2: 661 [T 83.712c]). He also writes in *Shōzōmatsu wasan*:

> Those who reach the stage equal to perfect enlightenment
> by the Vow of birth through the nenbutsu
> are the same as Miroku (*Miroku ni onajikute*)
> and will realize great nirvāṇa.
>
> SSZ 2: 519b (T 83.665c)

I have written this down
as a guide
for future generations —
may these words on the dharma
be my memento.

II-2 On the point of departure

In the school founded by the master, faith is placed before all else. If we ask the purpose of that faith, [the answer is that] it is the point of departure enabling wretched ordinary beings like ourselves, who lack good and do evil, to go readily to Amida's Pure Land. Without attaining faith, we will not be born in the land of utmost bliss but will fall into the hell of incessant pain.[8]

If we then ask how to attain that faith, [the answer is that,] relying deeply on the single Buddha, Amida Tathāgata, we give no thought to any of the various good deeds and myriad practices, and, dismissing the inclination to make petitions to the various buddhas and bodhisattvas just for this life and discarding false, erroneous thoughts such as those of self-power, we entrust (*shingyō shite* 信楽して) ourselves single-heartedly and steadfastly, without double-mindedness, to Amida; without fail, Amida embraces such people with his all-pervading light and will not abandon them. Once we have attained faith (*shin*) in this way, we should bear in mind that the nenbutsu we say at all times, sleeping or waking, expresses our gratitude for the benevolence of Amida who saves us.

Those who understand as explained above are indeed exemplary of what it is to have attained faith correctly, according to our tradition. If there are people who say that there is something else over and above this called "faith," they are greatly mistaken. We can never accept [such a claim].

Respectfully.

What has been set down in this letter is the right meaning of faith, taught by Master Shinran of our tradition. Those who thoroughly understand these points must never discuss anything to do with this faith in

---

[8] *muken jigoku* 無間地獄 ; Skt. *avīci*. The eighth of the eight scorching hells (*hachinetsu jigoku* 八熱地獄 , or eight great hells *hachidai jigoku* 八大地獄). Here, those who have committed the five grave offenses, denied the principle of causality, or slandered the Mahāyāna teaching suffer unceasing pain.

the presence of those of other sects and others [not of our tradition]. Furthermore, we simply do not rely on any of the other buddhas and bodhisattvas or on the various kami; we must never belittle them. We must recognize that each and every one of the various kami is indeed included within the virtue[9] of Amida, the one Buddha. Without exception, do not disparage any of the various teachings. By [adhering to] these points, one will be known as a person who carefully observes our tradition's rules of conduct. Hence the master said, "Even if you are called a 'cow thief,' do not act in such a way that you are seen as an aspirant for [buddhahood in] the afterlife, or as a 'good' person, or as a follower of the Buddha-dharma";[10] these were his very words. We must practice the nenbutsu, keeping these points very carefully in mind.

Written on the evening of the twelfth day,
the twelfth month, of Bunmei 5 [1473].

II-3 On three items, [including] kami manifestations

Within the school of teaching propagated by our tradition's founding master, there have been discrepancies in what everyone has preached. From now on, therefore—from the priests in charge of the lodgings on this mountain on down to those [priests] who read [but] a single volume of the scriptures,[11] each of the people who assemble [here], and each of those who want to be enrolled as followers of this school—[all] must know the provisions of these three items and, henceforth, be governed accordingly.

- Item: Do not slander other teachings and other sects.
- Item: Do not belittle the various kami and buddhas and the bodhisattvas.
- Item: Receive faith and attain birth in the fulfilled land.

Those who do not observe the points in the above three items and

---

[9] *kudoku*. Shinran explains that, without any effort on the part of practicers, all their evil karma is transformed into the highest good, "just as all waters, upon entering the great ocean, immediately become ocean water. We are made to acquire the Tathāgata's virtues through entrusting ourselves to his Vow-power; hence the expression, 'made to become so' " (*Essentials*, 32; SSZ 2: 623 [T 83.700a]).

[10] A quotation differing only slightly from Kakunyo's in *Gaijashō*, SSZ 3: 68. The passage reoccurs in essentially the same form in letters 2:13 and 3:11.

[11] *shōgyō* 聖教 . See the discussion of scripture in chapter five.

take them as fundamental, storing them deep in their hearts, are to be forbidden access to this mountain [community].

I left the capital in mid-summer[12] of the third year of Bunmei and, in the latter part of the seventh month of the same year, occupied a hut in a wind- and wave-lashed place on this mountain. My purpose in staying here over this four-year period has simply been to lead those throughout the Hokuriku who have not undergone a decisive settling of faith according to our tradition into the same faith (*anjin*), [guiding them all] uniformly by what is expressed in these three items. For this reason, I have persevered until now. Therefore, if you honor these [items], knowing their significance, this will indeed accomplish my fundamental intent in staying in this region for these months and years.

- Item: By kami manifestations (*shinmei* 神明), we mean that [buddhas and bodhisattvas] appear provisionally as kami to save sentient beings in whatever way possible; they lament that those who lack faith (*shin*) in the Buddha-dharma fall helplessly into hell. Relying on even the slightest of [related past] conditions, they appear provisionally as kami through the compassionate means to lead [sentient beings] at last into the Buddha-dharma.

  Therefore, sentient beings of the present time [should realize that] if they rely on Amida and, undergoing a decisive settling of faith, repeat the nenbutsu and are to be born in the land of utmost bliss, then all the kami [in their various] manifestations, recognizing this as [the fulfillment of] their own fundamental purpose, will rejoice and protect nenbutsu practicers.[13] Consequently, even if we do not worship the kami in particular, since all are encompassed when we rely solely on one Buddha, Amida, we give credence [to them] even though we do not rely on them in particular.

- Item:[14] Within our tradition, there must be no slandering of other teachings and other sects. As the teachings were all given by Śākya[muni] during his lifetime, they should be fruitful if they are practiced just as they were expounded. In this last age, however, lay people like ourselves are not equal to the teach-

---

[12] *chūka* 仲夏. The fifth month.

[13] This explanation of kami manifestations, beginning in the paragraph above, draws on Zonkaku, *Haja kenshōshō*, SSZ 3: 170–71.

[14] In this paragraph and the two that follow, Rennyo explains the three items listed at the beginning of the letter.

ings of the various sects of the Path of Sages; therefore, we simply do not rely on them or entrust ourselves to them.

• Item: Because the buddhas and bodhisattvas are discrete manifestations (*funjin* 分身) of Amida Tathāgata, [Amida] is the original teacher and the original Buddha (*honshi honbutsu* 本師本仏) for the buddhas of the ten directions. For this reason, when we take refuge in Amida, the one Buddha, we take refuge in all the buddhas and bodhisattvas; hence the buddhas and bodhisattvas are all encompassed within the one body of Amida.

• Item: Amida Tathāgata's true and real Other-Power faith, taught by our founder Master Shinran, is formalized in our entrusting ourselves to the Primal Vow by discarding all the sundry practices and steadfastly and single-heartedly taking refuge in Amida through the single practice [of the nenbutsu] and single-mindedness.[15] Therefore, in accord with what we have heard from our predecessors—bearing in mind continually that Amida Tathāgata's true and real faith is the inconceivable [working] of the Buddha's wisdom that is imparted by Other Power, and having determined that the [awakening of the] one thought-moment [of faith] is the time when birth [in the Pure Land] is assured—[we realize that] it is a matter of course that if one's life continues on after that, there will naturally be many utterances [of the nenbutsu]. Accordingly, we are taught that the many utterances, the [many] callings of the Name, are in grateful return for Buddha's benevolence, birth [in the Pure Land] being assured in ordinary life with [the awakening of] a single thought-moment [of faith].

Therefore, the essential point transmitted by the founding master in our school is but one thing: this faith. Not knowing this [is what distinguishes those of] other schools; knowing it is the mark of [those who participate in] the Shinshū. Further, in the presence of others [not of our tradition], you must never display outwardly what it is to be a person of the nenbutsu according to this tradition. This is the foundation for the conduct of those who have attained the faith of the Shinshū.

[The above] is as stated previously.

Written on the eleventh day
of the first month of Bunmei 6 [1474].

---

[15] *senju sennen* 専修専念. A phrase that, for Rennyo, reflects complete reliance on Other Power. See fascicle one, n. 21.

II-4 On severing crosswise the five evil courses

[Question]: The reason why the Primal Vow of Amida Tathāgata is said to be "all-surpassing" is that it is the supreme Vow made for the sake of ordinary beings like ourselves who, belonging to the defiled world of the last age, commit evil and lack good. Yet we have no clear understanding as to how we should conceive of this, and how we should entrust ourselves to Amida in order to be born in the Pure Land. Please tell us about this in detail.

Answer: Sentient beings [living] at present in the last age should simply entrust themselves exclusively to Amida Tathāgata; even though they do not rely on other buddhas and bodhisattvas as well, the Buddha has vowed with great mercy and great compassion that, however deep their evil karma may be, he will save those who single-heartedly and steadfastly take refuge in one Buddha, Amida. Sending forth the great light [of his compassion], he receives them within that light. Hence the *Contemplation Sūtra* teaches, "[The] light shines throughout the worlds of the ten directions, and sentient beings mindful of the Buddha are embraced, never to be abandoned."[16] Because of this, the way that will surely lead us to the evil courses, the "five paths" or the "six paths,"[17] is closed off through the inconceivable working of Amida Tathāgata's Vow. How this comes about is explained in the *Larger Sūtra*: "One severs crosswise the five evil courses, and the evil courses close off of themselves."[18]

Therefore, however much we may fear that we are going to fall into hell, when we entrust ourselves without a single thought of doubt to the Tathāgata's Vow, those [of us] who are received into Amida Tathāgata's embracing light will not fall into hell through our designing but are certain to go to the land of utmost bliss. When this has become clear to us, since it is we who receive the immeasurable benevolence

---

[16] *Contemplation Sūtra*, SSZ 1: 57 (T 12.343b). Also mentioned in letter 1:4 and quoted in 2:13 and 5:12.

[17] *godō rokudō to ieru akushu* 五道・六道といえる悪趣 . The "evil courses" include the realms of desire and delusion into which sentient beings transmigrate as a result of evil karma. In terms of "five paths," these are the realms of hell, hungry spirits, beasts, human beings, and heavenly beings; there are "six paths" if asuras (found in the realms of hungry spirits, beasts, and heavenly beings) are given a separate category. See fascicle one, n. 51.

[18] *Larger Sūtra*, SSZ 1: 31 (T 12.274b).

of the Tathāgata's great compassion, all we can do—day and night, morning and evening—is to say the nenbutsu in gratitude for the Buddha's benevolence, repeating the Name at all times. This is precisely what it is to have attained true and real faith.

Respectfully.

In the sixth year of Bunmei [1474], the evening of the fifteenth day of the second month, remembering the [day] long ago when the Great Sage, the World-Honored One, passed into nirvāṇa (nyūmetsu 入滅). Beneath the lamp, rubbing my weakening eyes, I have finished the blackening of my brush.

Sixty years of age. (seal)

II-5 On devotional beads

From what I have observed of the ways of nenbutsu people on this mountain over the past three or four years, there is indeed no sign of [anyone] having undergone a decisive settling of the faith (anjin) that is Other Power. The reason for [my saying] this is that there is no one who even carries devotional beads (juzu 珠数). It is as if they grasped the Buddha (hotoke 仏) with bare hands. The master certainly never said that we should venerate the Buddha by discarding the beads. Nevertheless, even if we do not carry them, all that is necessary for birth in the Pure Land is simply Other-Power faith.[19] Given that, there are no obstacles. [Yet] it is well for those of priestly rank to wear robes and carry devotional beads; people who have attained true and real faith unfailingly voice it, and it is evident in their bearing.

At present, then, it seems that those who have properly attained true and real faith are extremely rare. When we ask why this is, we find that, because [priests] do not realize the wonder of Amida Tathāgata's Primal Vow and its suitability for us, they persist in their own thinking in regard to whatever they hear, always pretending that they understand about faith; without really hearing anything, they merely imitate others. In this state, their own birth in the land of utmost bliss seems uncertain. Needless to say, they cannot possibly teach our followers and companions [in the tradition]. In such a frame of mind as this, birth in the fulfilled land in the afterlife is impossible.

---

[19] In Shūjishō, Kakunyo writes: "For birth in the Pure Land, we simply put faith before all else; we do not consider any other [ways]. A matter of such great importance as birth is not one that sentient beings can effect by self-effort; it must be left solely to the Tathāgata" (SSZ 3: 37 [T 83.735c]; quoted in Izumoji, Ofumi, 152).

What a deplorable situation! We must simply calm our minds and reflect on this. Indeed, human life may end at any time, whenever the outgoing breath fails to await the incoming of the next. We must by all means take the Buddha-dharma carefully into our hearts and let faith be decisively settled.

Respectfully.
Written in haste, early in the morning of the sixteenth day of the second month, in the sixth year of Bunmei [1474].

II-6 On rules of conduct

If there are any of you who have heard the meaning of our tradition's Other-Power faith and become decisively settled, you must store the truth of that faith in the bottom of your hearts; do not talk about it with those of other sects or others [not of our tradition]. Furthermore, you must not praise it openly (in the presence of [such] people) on by-ways and main roads and in the villages where you live. Next, do not slight the provincial military governors and local land stewards, claiming that you have attained faith; without fail, meet your public obligations (*kuji* 公事) in full. Further, do not belittle the various kami and buddhas and the bodhisattvas, for they are all encompassed within the six characters 南無阿弥陀仏 (na-mu-a-mi-da-butsu). Besides this, in particular, take the laws of the state as your outer aspect, store Other-Power faith deep in your hearts, and take [the principles of] humanity and justice (*jingi* 仁義) as essential. Bear in mind that these are the rules of conduct that have been established within our tradition.

Respectfully.
Written on the seventeenth day of the second month of Bunmei 6 [1474].

II-7 "Going is easy, yet no one is [born] there"

On quiet consideration, [we realize that] it is indeed due to the efficacy of keeping the five precepts[20] that we receive life in the human realm. This is an extremely rare event. Nevertheless, life in the human realm

---

[20] *gokai* 五戒 . The five precepts for lay people are: not to kill (*fusesshō* 不殺生), not to steal (*fuchūtō* 不偸盗), not to commit adultery (*fujain* 不邪淫), not to lie (*fumōgo* 不妄語), and not to drink intoxicants (*fuonju* 不飲酒).

is but a momentary passage; the afterlife is the blissful result in eternity. And even if we boast of wealth and enjoy overwhelming fame, it is the way of the world that "those who prosper will surely decline, and those who meet are certain to part";[21] hence we cannot hold to such prosperity for long. It will last only fifty to a hundred years. When we hear, too, of the uncertainty of life for old and young alike, [we realize that] there is indeed little upon which we can depend. Accordingly, sentient beings of the present [age] should aspire to birth in the Pure Land through Other-Power faith.

To receive that faith, there is no need at all for wisdom or learning, for wealth and status or for poverty and distress; it does not matter if one is good or evil, male or female. What is fundamental is that we simply discard the sundry practices and take refuge in the right practice. To take refuge in the right practice is just to rely on Amida Tathāgata single-heartedly and steadfastly, without any contriving. Sentient beings everywhere who entrust themselves in this way are embraced within [Amida's] light; he does not abandon them, and when life is spent, he brings them without fail to the Pure Land. It is through this single-minded faith (anjin) alone that we are born in the Pure Land. How readily we attain this settled mind—there is no effort on our part. Hence the two characters 安心 (an-jin) are read "easily-[attained] mind" (yasuki kokoro); they have this meaning.

Through faith alone, single-heartedly and steadfastly relying on the Tathāgata, we will be born without any difficulty at all in the land of utmost bliss. This settled mind—how readily we understand it! And the Pure Land—how easily we go there! Hence the Larger Sūtra teaches: "Going is easy, and yet no one is [born] there."[22] This passage means that when we realize the settled mind and rely steadfastly on Amida, it is easy to go to the Pure Land; but because those who receive faith are rare, although it is easy to go to the Pure Land, no one is [born] there.

Once we have reached this understanding, the Name we say day and night, morning and evening, is solely an expression of gratitude for the benevolence of the universal Vow of great compassion. Deeply mindful of the Buddha-dharma and knowing the significance of faith, which is readily received, we will unfailingly attain the birth that is to come in the fulfilled land, the matter of greatest importance.

---

[21] A common expression of impermanence. In Ōjōyōshū (SSZ 1: 749 [T 84.38c]), Genshin quotes a series of sources on the subject, including a similar passage from the Larger Sūtra.

[22] Larger Sūtra, SSZ 1: 31 (T 12.274b).

Respectfully.
A fair copy, made on the third day
of the third month, Bunmei 6 [1474].

II-8 On the original teacher and the original Buddha

People of evil [karma] who have committed the ten transgressions and the five grave offenses and women, burdened with the five obstacles and the three submissions — all of whom have been excluded from the compassionate vows of all the buddhas of the ten directions and the three periods and helplessly abandoned — these are ordinary beings no different from ourselves. Therefore, since Amida Tathāgata is the original teacher and the original Buddha of all the buddhas of the three periods and the ten directions, it was Amida who (as the Buddha existing from the distant past)[23] made the all-surpassing, great Vow: he himself would save all of us sentient beings equally — women, burdened with the five obstacles and the three submissions, and ordinary beings in the last age like [ourselves] who, lacking good, have been abandoned by all the buddhas. Thus making the supreme Vow, he became Amida Buddha long ago. Apart from relying exclusively on this Tathāgata, there is no way at all for sentient beings in the last age to be born in the land of utmost bliss. Accordingly, those who fully know Other-Power faith, which was taught by Master Shinran, are all certain to be born in the Pure Land, ten persons out of ten.

[Question]: When we think of receiving faith and going to Amida's fulfilled land, what should our attitude be, and what should we understand about the way we receive this faith? I would like to hear about this in detail.

Answer: The meaning of Other-Power faith as taught by Master Shinran in our tradition is that when we simply realize that we are wretched beings of deep evil karma, entrust ourselves single-heartedly

---

[23] *kuon jitsujō no kobutsu* 久遠実成の古仏 . See introduction, n. 16. Given the primacy of the *Larger Sūtra* in his religious experience, Shinran sees Amida as the Buddha existing from the eternal past, manifesting himself in history as Śākyamuni:

> Amida, the Buddha existing from the distant past,
> pitying ordinary beings [in this world] of the five defilements,
> manifested himself as Śākyamuni Buddha
> and appeared at Gayā in correspondence [to their needs].
> *Jōdo wasan*, SSZ 2: 496b (T 83.658c)

and steadfastly to Amida Tathāgata, discard the sundry practices, and devote ourselves to "the single practice and single-mindedness," we will be received without fail within [Amida's] all-pervading light. This is indeed how birth [in the Pure Land] is decisively settled.

Above and beyond this, what we must bear in mind is that, once birth is assured through the one thought-moment of faith in which we single-heartedly and steadfastly take refuge in Amida, the Name that we say walking, standing, sitting, and lying down is the nenbutsu of grateful return for the benevolence of Amida Tathāgata's great compassion in readily settling our birth. This you should know. In other words, this is [the frame of mind of] a person who is decisively settled in our tradition's faith.

Respectfully.

The middle of the third month, Bunmei 6 [1474].

II-9 On "the loyal retainer and the faithful wife"

Why is it that, in relying on Amida Tathāgata, we completely reject the myriad good deeds and practices, designating them as sundry practices? It is [because of] the great Vow, in which Amida Buddha has promised to save sentient beings who rely on him single-heartedly and steadfastly, however deep their evil karma (*tsumi* つみ) may be. Therefore, "single-heartedly and steadfastly" means that we take no other buddha as peer to Amida Buddha. This is the same as the rule in human society that one relies on only one master. Hence, in the words of an outer [non-Buddhist] text (*geden* 外典), "a loyal retainer will not serve two masters; a faithful wife will not take a second husband."[24] Since Amida Tathāgata is the original teacher and master for all the buddhas of the three periods, how can all the buddhas who are his disciples not rejoice when we rely on that Buddha who is the master? You must understand the grounds for this very thoroughly.

Since the substance of practice (*gyōtai* 行体), "namu-amida-butsu," encompasses all the kami, buddhas, and bodhisattvas and, besides these, each and every one of the myriad good deeds and practices, what could be lacking that would necessitate our putting our minds to

---

[24] Izumoji attributes this quotation to the *Shih Chi* (Jpn. *Shiki*; *Records Compiled by the Historian*), compiled by Ssu-ma Ch'ien (Jpn. Shibasen; B.C.E. c.145-86), and notes that it appears in *Genpei jōsuiki* (An account of the Genpei Wars), written in the late Kamakura period (Izumoji, *Ofumi*, 163–64).

the various practices and good deeds? The Name "namu-amida-butsu" completely embodies all the myriad good deeds and practices; hence it is surely trustworthy.

Then, how do we rely on Amida Tathāgata and how do we entrust ourselves and attain birth in the land of utmost bliss?

There is no need of effort on our part; when we just realize deeply that Amida Tathāgata himself graciously made the Vow to save those of us who, as wretched beings burdened with the most deeply-rooted evil, can go only to hell, and when faith is awakened in the one thought-moment of taking refuge, then—surely prompted by the unfolding of past good as well—Other-Power faith is granted through the wisdom of the Buddha. Consequently, the Buddha's mind and the mind of the ordinary being become one;[25] the person who has attained such a state of mind is called a practicer who has attained faith. Beyond this, we must bear in mind that, simply by saying the nenbutsu, sleeping or waking, no matter where or when, we should express our gratitude for the benevolence of the universal Vow of great compassion.

---

[25] *busshin to bonjin to hitotsu ni naru* 仏心と凡心とひとつになる . For Rennyo, *busshin* is Amida's mind; *bonjin* is the mind of the foolish being. In the realization of faith, the two become one. In letter 2:10, written some two months after this one, he elaborates in terms of *busshin to bonjin to ittai ni naru* 仏心と凡心と一体に なる : "When there is not a moment's doubt of the Primal Vow, the Tathāgata, fully knowing that [practicer's] mind, graciously causes the evil mind of the practicer to be entirely the same as the good mind of the Tathāgata." His use of the terms *busshin* and *bonjin* appears to be drawn from the writings of Kakunyo and Zonkaku. See in particular Kakunyo's *Saiyōshō*:

When "faith" (*shinjin* 信心) is read as "true mind" (*makoto no kokoro* まことの こころ), it refers not to the delusory mind of foolish beings (*bonbu no meishin* 凡夫 の迷心), but solely to the mind of the Buddha (*busshin*). When the Buddha graciously gives this mind to foolish beings, it is called "faith" (SSZ 3: 50).

The Shinshū doctrine of *butsu-bon ittai* 仏凡一体 has been compared to *ki-hō ittai* as follows:

Although [the two] are inseparable, both meaning the oneness of Buddha and man, *butsu-bon ittai* indicates the point of realizing shinjin, when Buddha's mind and the mind of sentient beings *become* one, and *ki-hō ittai* characterizes the condition of having realized shinjin, which is none other than the nenbutsu (Appendix: "On Shinjin and 'Faith'," *Inscriptions*, 78).

While there is some basis in Shinran's thought for these doctrines (see *Kōsō wasan*, SSZ 2: 505–6 [T 83.661c]), it is well to recall that he never uses such religious symbols himself. It is our position that Rennyo's pattern of conceptualizing the salvific process in such formulaic expressions simplifies Shinran's teaching in such a way as to invite reification. Thereby, the dynamic structure of Shinran's thought—simultaneity of sameness and opposition—becomes vulnerable to serious misinterpretation.

Respectfully.
Written on the seventeenth day
of the third month, Bunmei 6 [1474].

II-10 On the oneness of the Buddha's mind and the mind of ordinary beings

[Question]: The import of the basic principles taught by Master Shin-ran of our tradition is, first of all, that Other-Power faith is of the utmost importance. It is clearly seen in the sūtras and commentaries that, without fully knowing this Other-Power faith, [realization of] the birth that is to come in the land of utmost bliss — the matter of greatest importance — is indeed not possible. Therefore, when we know what Other-Power faith is all about and aspire to birth in the true and real fulfilled land, what should our attitude be, and what should we do to attain birth in this land of utmost bliss? I do not know about this in any detail. Please let me have your kind instruction. I feel that after hearing this, I will surely attain firm faith.

Answer: The import of Other-Power faith in our tradition is that, without worrying at all about the depth of our evil karma, we simply entrust ourselves single-heartedly and steadfastly to Amida Tathāgata and realize deeply that it is indeed the inconceivable power of the Vow that saves everyone — people of evil [karma], like ourselves, who have committed the ten transgressions and the five grave offenses and even women burdened with the five obstacles and the three submissions; and when there is not a moment's doubt of the Primal Vow, the Tathāgata, fully knowing that [practicer's] mind, graciously causes the evil mind of the practicer to be entirely the same as the good mind of the Tathāgata. This is what is meant by our saying that "the Buddha's mind and the mind of the ordinary being become one."[26] Consequently, we should realize that we have been received within Amida Tathāgata's all-pervading light and that we will dwell within this light for the duration of our lives. Then, when life is spent, [Amida] brings us at once to the true and real fulfilled land.

How, then, do we respond to the gracious, inestimable benevolence of Amida's great compassion?

[The answer is that] by simply repeating the nenbutsu, saying the Name of the Buddha (shōmyō nenbutsu 称名念仏) — day and night,

---

[26] busshin to bonjin to ittai ni naru. See preceding note.

morning and evening—we express our gratitude for Amida Tathāgata's benevolence. Bear in mind that this is what is meant by the teaching of "completing the cause [of birth] in ordinary life, with the awakening of the one thought-moment [of entrusting]," as set forth in our tradition. Therefore, in relying single-heartedly on Amida in this way, there is no need of special effort on our part; and, as it is easy to receive faith, it is easier still to become a buddha—to be born in the land of utmost bliss. How precious Amida's Primal Vow is! How precious Other-Power faith is! There is no doubt at all as to our birth.

Yet, beyond this, there is a further point that should be clearly understood in regard to our conduct. That is, all the kami and buddhas have appeared (as the various kami and buddhas) through the compassionate means to enable us to receive this singular Other-Power faith that we realize now. Therefore, because all the [kami], buddhas, and bodhisattvas are originally discrete manifestations of Amida Tathāgata, all—each and every one—are encompassed within the single thought-moment in which we, entrusting ourselves, say "namu-amida-butsu"; for this reason, we are not to belittle them.

Again, there is still another point to be understood. You must never slight the provincial military governors and local land stewards, saying that you are a person who reveres the Buddha-dharma and has attained faith. Without fail, meet your public obligations in full.

People who comply with the above exemplify the conduct of nen-butsu practicers in whom faith has been awakened and who aspire to [birth in the Pure Land in] the afterlife. They are, in other words, ones who faithfully abide by the Buddha-dharma and the laws of the state.

Respectfully.
Written on the thirteenth day
of the fifth month, Bunmei 6 [1474].

II-11 On the fivefold teaching

In recent years, the import of the teaching of our tradition's Master Shinran has been presented in various ways in the provinces, with a lack of uniformity. This is a most deplorable situation. For, to begin with, although the birth of ordinary beings [in the Pure Land] through Other-Power faith has been of primary importance in our tradition, [some] brush aside the matter of faith and do not consider it. They propose that "faith is not forgetting that Amida Tathāgata has settled our birth from the time of his perfect enlightenment ten kalpas ago."[27] What is completely lacking in this is the element of taking refuge in Amida and realizing Other-Power faith. Therefore, however well they may know that their birth has been settled since the time of [Amida's] perfect enlightenment ten kalpas ago, unless they fully know the significance of Other-Power faith, through which we attain birth, they will not attain birth in the land of utmost bliss. There are also some people who say, "Even if we take refuge in Amida, this is to no avail without a good teacher. Therefore, there is nothing for us to do but rely on a good teacher."[28] These are their words. They, too, are people who have not properly attained our tradition's faith.

The function of a good teacher is just to encourage people to take refuge in Amida single-heartedly and steadfastly. Therefore, a fivefold teaching[29] has been established[, giving the conditions necessary for birth]: first, [the unfolding of] good from the past; second, [meeting] a good teacher; third, [encountering Amida's] light; fourth, [attaining] faith; and, fifth, [saying] the Name [of the Buddha]. Unless this fivefold teaching is realized, it is evident [in the received texts] that birth is impossible. Thus the good teacher is the messenger who tells us to take refuge in Amida Buddha. Without meeting a good teacher through the unfolding of good from the past, birth is impossible. Bear in mind, however, that to abandon Amida, in whom we take refuge, and to take only the good teacher as essential is a serious error.

Respectfully.
Bunmei 6 [1474].5.20.

II-12 On the fifty years of human life

When we consider the fifty years of human life,[30] [we realize that] they

---

[27] This quotation varies only slightly from that in the first part of letter 1:13; see also fascicle one, n. 72.

[28] See fascicle one, nn. 30, 90. The notion of taking refuge in a teacher was not to be easily refuted, as reflected in a letter that Rennyo wrote five years later, in Bunmei 11 (1479).11 (RSI, 303–4 [#103]).

[29] *gojō no gi* 五重の義 . In the outline that follows, Rennyo draws on a passage by Zonkaku in *Jōdo kenmonshū*, SSZ 3: 378.

[30] *ningen no gojūnen*. During Rennyo's time, there were various explanations in regard to the period in which Śākyamuni appeared in the world, but it was widely held to be the ninth period of the kalpa of existence (*jūkō* 住劫), during which the human life-span decreased from 84,000 to 10 years at the rate of one year every hundred years. In *Kyōgyōshinshō*, Shinran states that, as of Gennin 1

correspond to a day and night in the heavens of the four kings.[31] Moreover, fifty years in the heavens of the four kings is but a day and night in the hell of repeated existence.[32] Despite this fact, people take no notice of falling into hell and undergoing suffering; neither do they think deeply of going to the Pure Land and enjoying unsurpassed bliss. Thus they live to no purpose and, passing days and months in vain, pay no attention to the decisive settling of the one mind of their own [faith]. They never look at a single volume of the scriptures, nor do they ever instruct their followers by citing a single passage of the teaching. Morning and evening, they simply watch for spare moments, stretch out with their pillows, and go off to sleep. Surely this is deplorable. Quietly think it over.

From now on, therefore, those who in their negligence fail to uphold the dharma must by all means seek to attain birth in the true and real fulfilled land through the decisive settling of faith; this will indeed bring benefit (*toku* 徳) to them. It should be recognized, moreover, that this is in accord with the principle of benefiting oneself and benefiting others.[33]

(1224), it has been 2,173 years since the Buddha's death (*Teaching*, 4: 79, correcting the figure given in SSZ 2: 168). Therefore, when Rennyo wrote this letter in Bunmei 6 (1474), 2,423 years after the Buddha's death, understood to have occurred when he was eighty, the life-span would have decreased from eighty by twenty-four years, to fifty-six. In letter 4:2, written in Bunmei 9 (1477), 2,426 years after the Buddha's death, Rennyo says specifically, "If we calculate the length of human life, the allotted span at this time is fifty-six years." See Izumoji, *Ofumi*, 253–55.

[31] *shiōden* 四王天 . First of the six heavens of the realm of desire and located immediately above the human realm, this heaven is divided into four realms surrounding Mt. Sumeru. Its four kings, presiding over the four directions, serve Indra (Jpn. Taishaku; originally a Hindu deity) and, like him, protect the Buddhist teaching and its followers. Shinran says of them:

> If we say "Namu-amida-butsu,"
> The great kings in the four-king heaven
> protect us continually, night and day,
> keeping away all evil spirits.
>   *Jōdo wasan*, SSZ 2: 498a (T 83.659b)

[32] *tōkatsu jigoku* 等活地獄 . The first of the eight great hells, reserved for those who kill living beings.

[33] *jigyō keta* 自行化他 . This phrase reflects the bodhisattva ideal of attaining enlightenment, not only for oneself, but also for all sentient beings. Rennyo's understanding, however, draws on Shinran, who equates "true and real faith" with the aspiration for buddhahood, and this aspiration with that of saving all beings (*Jōdo monrui jushō*, SSZ 2: 453 [T 83.646c]): thus the benefiting of self and

Respectfully.

This is written on the second day of the middle period of the sixth month, Bunmei 6 [1474]; I have simply let words flow from the brush in the extreme heat.

II-13 On the reputation of our school

Fully observing the regulations established in our tradition means acting in such a way toward other sects and toward society that we do not draw public attention to our sect; we take this as fundamental. Recently, however, there have been some among the nenbutsu people in our tradition who have deliberately brought to others' notice what our school is all about; they have thought that this would enhance the reputation of our school and, in particular, sought to denigrate other schools. Nothing could be more absurd. Moreover, it deeply contradicts Master [Shinran]'s intention. For he said precisely, long ago, "Even if you are called a 'cow thief,' do not give the appearance of [being a participant in] our tradition."[34] We must keep these words very carefully in mind.

Next, those who seek to know in full what settled mind means in our tradition need no wisdom or learning at all; they do not need to be male or female, noble or humble. For when we simply realize that we are wretched beings of deep evil karma and know that the only Buddha who saves even such persons as this is Amida Tathāgata, and when, without any contriving, but with the thought of holding fast to the sleeve of this Buddha Amida,[35] we entrust ourselves [to him] to

---

others is accomplished through Other Power. See also Kakunyo, *Hōonkō shiki*, SSZ 3: 656 (T 83.755c).

[34] See n. 10 above.

[35] *Amida hotoke no onsode* 阿弥陀ほとけの御袖. A popular image expressed, for example in Fujii Otoo, ed., *Shasekishū* (Tokyo: Bunken Shoin, 1928), 57 (see Robert E. Morrell, trans., *Sand and Pebbles [Shasekishū]: The Tales of Mujū Ichien, A Voice for Pluralism in Kamakura Buddhism* [Albany: State University of New York Press, 1985], 114). The image can, however, be turned:

> Yuirenbō of Tokudai-ji, wanting to know what was meant by "being embraced and never abandoned," prayed at Ungo-ji to Amida. Appearing to him in a dream, Amida caught hold of his sleeve and held onto it firmly, not letting go even when he tried to get away. With this, Yuirenbō realized that "embracing" means catching and holding on to one who may want to escape. Master [Rennyo] referred to this in talking to us (*Goichidaiki kikigaki*, SSZ 3: 582–83 [T 83.824a]; see also *Jitsugo kyūki*, RSG, 106).

save us, [bringing us to buddhahood] in the afterlife,[36] then Amida Tathāgata deeply rejoices and, sending forth from himself eighty-four thousand great rays of light, receives us within that light. This is clearly explained in the [Contemplation] Sūtra: "[The] light shines throughout the worlds of the ten directions, and sentient beings mindful of the Buddha are embraced, never to be abandoned."[37] This you should know.

There is, then, no worry about becoming a buddha. How incomparable is the all-surpassing Primal Vow! And how gracious is Amida Tathāgata's light! Without encountering the [receptive] condition of this light, there can be no cure at all for the fearful sickness of ignorance and karma-hindrance, which has been ours from the beginningless past. Yet now, prompted by the condition of this light, good from the past comes into being, and we assuredly attain Other-Power faith. It is immediately clear, however, that this is faith granted by Amida Tathāgata. Thus we now know beyond question that this is not faith generated by the practicer, but that it is Amida Tathāgata's great Other-Power faith. Accordingly, all those who have once attained Other-Power faith should reflect deeply on how gracious Amida Tathāgata's benevolence is and repeat the nenbutsu, saying the Name of the Buddha always, in gratitude for Buddha's benevolence (button hōsha 仏恩報謝).

Respectfully.
Written on the third day
of the seventh month, Bunmei 6 [1474].

II-14 On "secret teachings"

The "secret teachings"[38] that are widespread in Echizen province are

---

[36] goshō o tasuke tamae to tanomu 後生をたすけたまえとたのむ. See fascicle one, n. 47, for an explanation of the translation of this phrase.

[37] Contemplation Sūtra, SSZ 1: 57 (T 12.343b); this quotation is found in letter 2:4 above and in 5:12.

[38] hiji bōmon 秘事法門 . The term "secret teachings" applies most directly to esoteric traditions (mikkyō 密教) such as the Shingon. In medieval Japan, however, a process of esotericization was common to most Buddhist sects, especially the Tendai on Mt. Hiei, whose teachings Shinran had found unsatisfactory. In Tannishō, Yuien expresses Shinran's view of the utter absurdity of the notion that one attains enlightenment in this existence, filled as it is with blind passions (Tannishō, SSZ 2: 786 [T 83.732c]). Thus he rejects the Shingon esoteric teaching

certainly not the Buddha-dharma; they are deplorable, outer [non-Buddhist] teachings (*gedō no hō* 外道の法). Relying on them is futile; it creates karma through which one sinks for a long time into the hell of incessant pain. You must never, never follow those who are still attached to these secret [teachings] and who, considering them to be of utmost importance, ingratiate themselves with others and deceive them. Separate yourself immediately from those who expound secret [teachings], lose no time in confessing them just as you have received them, and warn everyone about them.

Those who seek to thoroughly know the meaning of our tradition's teaching and be born in the land of utmost bliss must, to begin with, know about Other-Power faith. What is the importance of Other-Power faith?

It is the provision by which wretched ordinary beings like ourselves go readily to the Pure Land.

In what way does Other-Power faith find expression?

We simply entrust ourselves exclusively to Amida Tathāgata, single-heartedly and steadfastly, without any contriving; and with the awakening of the one thought-moment in which we realize that Amida saves us, Amida Tathāgata unfailingly sends forth his embracing light and keeps us safe within this light as long as we are in this world.[39] It is precisely in this state that our birth is assured.

Thus "namu-amida-butsu" expresses the attainment of Other-Power faith. We should bear in mind that this faith expresses the sig-

---

(*hikyō* 秘教) of attainment of buddhahood with one's present body (*sokushin jōbutsu* 即身成仏) through the three kinds of acts—bodily, verbal, and mental. Dobbins, in *Jōdo Shinshū*, has shown that the imparting of secret teachings had been a vexing issue for Shinran in his relationship with his son Zenran in the Kantō (40) and a prevalent practice in the Takada and Sanmonto branches of the Shinshū (124–25, 127–28).

Writing at Yoshizaki on Bunmei 6 (1474).7.5, Rennyo singles out "secret teachings" as creating "karma through which one sinks forever into the hell of incessant pain." After he left Yoshizaki, the problem persisted among the many new adherents drawn to the Honganji from Pure Land movements including other branches of the Shinshū such as the Takada and Sanmonto. Rennyo addresses the problem in letters written at Deguchi in Bunmei 9 (1477).1 (RSI, 269 [#91]) and at Yamashina on Bunmei 12 (1480).6.18 (RSI, 309–11 [#105]) after work has begun on the Founder's Hall: "Those who give secret teachings to people will sink forever into the evil paths" (RSI, 310 [#105]).

[39] *shaba* 娑婆 ; Skt. *sahā*; Jpn. *nindo* 忍土 , *kannindo* 堪忍土 , "land of endurance." The term indicates this present world, in which sentient beings suffer inwardly from their own blind passions and must patiently bear sufferings brought on by external forces.

nificance of "namu-amida-butsu." Then, because we receive this one Other-Power faith, there is no doubt at all that we will be born readily in the land of utmost bliss.

How incomparable is Amida Tathāgata's Other-Power Primal Vow! How are we to respond to this gracious benevolence of Amida? Simply by saying, "Namu-amida-butsu, Namu-amida-butsu," sleeping or waking, we respond to Amida Tathāgata's benevolence. With what mind, then, do we say "Namu-amida-butsu"?

Think of it as the rejoicing mind that realizes with humility and wonder the graciousness of Amida Tathāgata's saving work.

Respectfully.
Bunmei 6 [1474].7.5.

II-15 On Kubon and Chōrakuji

In Japan, various branches of the Jōdoshū have been established; it is divided into Seizan, Chinzei, Kubon, Chōrakuji, and many others. Although the teaching set forth by Master Hōnen is one, when some people who had been followers of the Path of Sages came to the master and listened to Pure Land teaching, they did not properly understand his explanation; because of this, still not having given up the ways of their original sects, they tried instead to bring these into the Jōdoshū. Consequently, there is a lack of uniformity. Nevertheless, we must never slander these [ways]. What is important is simply that we store our sect's faith (*anjin*) deep in our minds and, with our own [faith] decisively settled, exhort others as well.

What is the meaning of faith (*anjin*) within our tradition?

[The answer is that], first of all, being deeply convinced that we are worthless beings burdened with the ten transgressions and the five grave offenses, the five obstacles and the three submissions, we then recognize that it is the inconceivable working of Amida Tathāgata's Primal Vow that, as its primary aim, saves just such wretched persons; and when we deeply entrust ourselves and have not the slightest doubt, Amida embraces [us] without fail. This is precisely what it is to have attained true and real Other-Power faith. In realizing faith in this way, with [the awakening of] the one thought-moment [of entrusting], there is no need of any effort on our part.

This Other-Power faith—how readily we can understand it! And the Name [of the Buddha]—how readily we can practice it! Realizing faith is therefore nothing other than this, and understanding the six characters 南無阿弥陀仏 (na-mu-a-mi-da-butsu) is the substance of Other-Power faith.

What is the meaning of "namu-amida-butsu"?[40]

The two characters " 南無 (na-mu)" mean that, aspiring for birth in the land of utmost bliss, we deeply entrust ourselves to Amida. Then Amida Buddha takes pity on sentient beings who entrust themselves in this way, and although ours is an existence burdened with terrible offenses for myriads of kalpas from the beginningless past, because we encounter the [receptive] condition of Amida Tathāgata's light, all the deep offenses of ignorance and karma-hindrance are immediately extinguished, and we assuredly dwell among those [whose birth is] truly settled; then, discarding the ordinary body (*bonshin* 凡身), we attain the buddha-body (*busshin* 仏身). This is what "Amida Tathāgata" signifies. It is on these grounds that the three characters " 阿弥陀 (a-mi-da)" are read "receives, saves, and delivers" (*osame, tasuke, sukuu* おさめ , たすけ , すくう).

Once faith has been decisively settled in this way, if we then realize the graciousness of Amida Tathāgata's benevolence and simply repeat the nenbutsu, saying the Name of the Buddha, that will truly fulfill the principle of responding in gratitude to Amida Tathāgata's benevolence.

Respectfully.
Written on the ninth day
of the seventh month, Bunmei 6 [1474].
Shōnyo, disciple of Śākyamuni.
(written seal)

---

[40] The passage that follows, explaining the nenbutsu in terms of the complementary parts "namu" and "amida-butsu," is based on a statement by Shan-tao in *Kangyōsho* (*Gengibun*), SSZ 1: 457 (T 37.250ab), expounded by Shinran in *Kyōgyōshinshō*, SSZ 2: 22 (T 83.594c). Its importance for Rennyo is shown by the fact that he raises it again in letters 3:2, 3:4–8, 4:2, 4:8, 4:14, 5:5, 5:8–9, 5:11, and 5:13, quoting Shan-tao in part in letters 3:8, 4:8, and 5:11 and fully in letters 4:14 and 5:13.

Fascicle Three

III-1 On people who are only listed by name

People who are only listed by name in our tradition as well as those
who have been followers for a long time [should realize that] if they
do not fully understand what the settled mind is, they must by all
means, from this day on, carefully inquire of others about the great
faith that is Other Power, so that their birth in the fulfilled land may
be decisively settled. Realizing the settled mind in our tradition is simply [a matter of] relying deeply and exclusively on Amida Tathāgata.
But what sort of buddha is this Amida Buddha, and what sort of person
does he save?

It was Amida Buddha who made the great Vow that he alone
would save us ordinary beings and women, wretched and abandoned
by all the buddhas of the three periods. He meditated for five kalpas
and, undergoing practices for measureless kalpas,[1] vowed to save even
those sentient beings whose evil karma includes the ten transgressions
and the five grave offenses, those who slander the dharma, and those
who lack the seed of buddhahood. Surpassing the compassionate vows
of the various buddhas, he completely fulfilled this Vow and thus became Amida Tathāgata (whom we know also as Amida Buddha).[2]

Then how do we entrust ourselves to this Buddha, and what frame
of mind should we have to be saved?

[The answer is that] we disregard the depth of our evil karma and
simply entrust ourselves to Amida Buddha steadfastly and without
double-mindedness, and when we are completely free of doubt, [he]
will save us without fail.

Amida Tathāgata, then, assuredly delivers all sentient beings by
two means, "embracing" and "light." First of all, when those with good
from the past are illumined by this light, the evil that has accumulated

---

[1] In *Shōshinge taii*, RSI, 26–27 (SSZ 3: 387), Rennyo describes a kalpa as the
time necessary to wear down a stone forty *ri* (2.44 miles) in length and width
if a heavenly being brushed over it once every three years with a feather robe
the weight of three-quarters of a *zeni* (an extremely thin, light coin). In writing
of the Buddha's immeasurably long meditation and practices, he draws on
the *Larger Sūtra* account of Amida who, as the monk Dharmākara, meditated
for five kalpas, established the Forty-eight Vows, and underwent practices for
untold kalpas to fulfill them. See SSZ 1: 7–14 (T 12.267c–269c).

[2] Dharmākara's attainment of buddhahood is described in the *Larger Sūtra*,
SSZ 1: 15 (T 12.270a).

as karma-hindrances is all extinguished. Then, as for "embracing," since all evil hindrances are extinguished when we encounter the [receptive] condition of this light, sentient beings are immediately received within it. Hence these two, "embracing" and "light," are of the utmost importance in Amida Buddha's [saving work]. In saying that faith is settled with [the awakening of] the one thought-moment of taking refuge [in Amida], we mean that it is when we encounter this embracing light that the settling of faith occurs.[3] It is clear at this present time, therefore, that the substance of practice, "namu-amida-butsu," expresses in six characters precisely how it is that we are to be born in the Pure Land. Knowing this, I am more and more thankful and filled with awe.

Then, once faith is decisively settled, we should — sleeping or waking — just say the nenbutsu in gratitude, joyfully remembering that we have received Amida Tathāgata's benevolence beyond measure. That is indeed the practice that truly returns the Buddha's benevolence.

Respectfully.
Written on the fourteenth day
of the seventh month, Bunmei 6 [1474].

III-2 On practicing as prescribed

The teachings of the various sects differ, but since they were all [expounded] during Śākya[muni]'s lifetime, they are indeed the incomparable dharma. For this reason, there is absolutely no doubt that people who practice them as prescribed will attain enlightenment and become buddhas. However, sentient beings of this last age are of the lowest capacity; this is a time when those who practice as prescribed are rare.

Here [we realize that] Amida Tathāgata's Primal Vow of Other Power was made to save sentient beings in such times as these. To this end, [Amida] meditated for five kalpas and, performing practices for measureless kalpas, vowed that he would not attain perfect enlightenment unless sentient beings, who commit evil and lack good, reach buddhahood.[4] Completely fulfilling that Vow, he became the Buddha

---

[3] In *Mattōshō*, Shinran says: "Because true faith is awakened through the working of the two revered ones, Śākya Tathāgata and Amida Tathāgata, the settling of faith occurs when one is embraced" (SSZ 2: 674; T 83.716b).

[4] After his enunciation of the Forty-eight Vows, the monk Dharmākara (Amida)

Amida. Sentient beings of this last age can never become buddhas unless they deeply entrust themselves to Amida, relying on this Buddha's Primal Vow.

How do we entrust ourselves to Amida Tathāgata's Other-Power Primal Vow, and what frame of mind should we have to be saved?

Entrusting to Amida simply means that those who truly know what Other-Power faith is will all be born in the land of utmost bliss, ten people out of ten.

Then what is that Other-Power faith?

It is simply "namu-amida-butsu." Fully knowing the meaning of the six characters " 南無阿弥陀仏 (na-mu-a-mi-da-butsu)" is precisely what Other-Power faith is all about. We must, therefore, thoroughly understand the substance of these six characters.

To begin with, what do the two characters "na-mu" mean?

"Na-mu" means relying on Amida single-heartedly and steadfastly, without any contriving, and entrusting ourselves without doublemindedness [to him] to save us, [bringing us to buddhahood] in the afterlife.

Then, what do the four characters "a-mi-da-butsu" mean?

"A-mi-da-butsu" means that, without fail, Amida sends forth from himself light that illumines sentient beings who rely on him singleheartedly and are free of doubt, as explained above; he receives them within that light, and when their span of life comes to an end, he brings them to the Pure Land of utmost bliss. This is "a-mi-da-butsu."[5]

According to what is commonly said about the nenbutsu, people think they will be saved if they just repeat "Namu-amida-butsu" with their lips. That is uncertain. There are, however, some within the Jōdo school who teach this. Let us not judge it as right or wrong. I simply explain our tradition's way of faith (*anjin*), which was taught by the founder of our sect. Those who have [good] conditions from the past should hear this and promptly attain [assurance of] the birth that is to come in the land of utmost bliss. Those who understand this should say the Name of the Buddha; [remembering] the benevolence of Amida Tathāgata who readily saves us, they should repeat the nenbutsu, saying the Name of the Buddha in grateful return for the Buddha's benevolence, which we receive beyond measure.

---

said: "If these Vows are not fulfilled, may I not realize perfect enlightenment" (*Larger Sūtra*, SSZ 1: 13 [T 12.269b]).

[5] An explanation based on *Kangyōsho* (*Gengibun*), SSZ 1: 457 (T 37.250ab); *Kyōgyōshinshō*, SSZ 2: 22 (T 83.594c). It first appears in *The Letters* in 2:15 and, following this citation, is repeated in this fascicle in letters four through eight.

Respectfully.
Written on the fifth day
of the eighth month, Bunmei 6 [1474].

III-3 On the followers of [the priest] Shōkō

Concerning the followers of [the priest] Shōkō[6] of Kawashiri in this region: I cannot but feel uneasy about their understanding of faith according to the Buddha-dharma. I will now, however, discuss our tradition's basic principles in detail. Each person should listen to this attentively, take it as fundamental, and thus be assured of the birth that is to come in the land of utmost bliss.

What does "Amida Tathāgata's Primal Vow of birth through the nenbutsu"[7] mean?

[The answer is that] if only Other-Power faith alone is decisively settled, lay people lacking wisdom and even those who have committed the ten transgressions and the five grave offenses will all be born in the land of utmost bliss.

How difficult is it, then, to attain that faith?

Those who, without any worry, simply entrust themselves exclusively (with no double-mindedness) to Amida Tathāgata and keep their thoughts from straying in other directions will all become buddhas, ten people out of ten. It is easy to hold to this single mind [of faith]. People who merely repeat the nenbutsu aloud have only a partial understanding; they will not be born in the land of utmost bliss. It is those who fully realize the significance of this nenbutsu who will become buddhas. If only the single thought of fully entrusting ourselves to Amida is settled, we will go readily to the Pure Land.

Besides this, remember that it is outrageous to cite complicated secret [teachings] and not reverence the Buddha.

And so, because Amida Tathāgata's Other-Power Primal Vow is

---

[6] Shōkō, a follower of Rennyo in Echizen, who originally belonged to the Zen sect (Sugi, *Gobunshō kōwa*, 145).

[7] *nenbutsu ōjō no hongan* 念仏往生の本願 ; the Eighteenth Vow. In *Senjakushū* (SSZ 1: 947 [T 83.6c]), Hōnen uses this term, drawing on Shan-tao; Shinran continues the usage, as does Rennyo in this letter and in letter 5:1. Nenbutsu interpretations varied widely among Hōnen's disciples, but for Shinran and Rennyo, both the saying of the Name and birth in the Pure Land occur entirely through Other Power, not through any effort on the part of the practicer. See Sugi, *Gobunshō kōwa*, 145, and Dobbins, *Jōdo Shinshū*, 102–11.

meant to save people of deep evil karma in this last age, it is the Primal Vow of Other Power that is completely suited to lay people like ourselves. How thankful I am for Amida Tathāgata's Vow! And how thankful I am for Śākya[muni] Tathāgata's golden words! Revere them. Entrust yourselves to them. For those who understand as I have explained above truly exemplify the nenbutsu practicer in whom our tradition's faith is decisively settled.

Then, beyond this, remember that the nenbutsu we say throughout our lives expresses our gratitude for the measureless benevolence of Amida Tathāgata who readily saves us.

Respectfully.
Written on the sixth day
of the eighth month, Bunmei 6 [1474].

III-4 On the Great Sage, the World-Honored One

When we carefully consider the ephemeral nature of human life, we realize that the living inevitably face death and that the prosperous eventually decline.[8] And so we only live out our years, spending nights to no purpose and days to no avail. This is indeed inexpressibly sad. What is difficult to escape, then, is impermanence — whether at the highest level, that of the Great Sage, the World-Honored One [Śākyamuni], or at the lowest, that of Devadatta,[9] who committed transgressions and evil offenses. Now, what is extremely difficult to receive is human form; what is difficult to meet is the Buddha-dharma.[10] Even though we may chance to meet the Buddha-dharma, the way

---

[8] A rephrasing of a quotation in *Ōjōyōshū* (SSZ 1: 749; T 84.39a).

[9] Daibadatta, or Daiba, a cousin of Śākyamuni and follower of his teaching, but one who grew jealous of the Buddha's authority. Attempting to seize leadership, he disrupted the sangha by raising followers of his own, incited Prince Ajātaśatru to kill his father and usurp the throne of Magdala, and even attempted to kill the Buddha. Because of the gravity of his offenses, he is said to have fallen into hell alive.

[10] In the chapter on faith in *Kyōgyōshinshō*, Shinran quotes *Muryōju nyorai e*:
It is immensely difficult to receive human existence,
And, again, difficult to encounter a Tathāgata's appearance in the world.
Teaching, 2: 208; SSZ 2: 50 (T 83.601b)
In an earlier passage in the chapter on practice, he quotes a passage in *Ōjōyōshū* describing the Buddha as being as "rare to encounter as the blossoming of the udumbara" (*Teaching*, 1: 133; SSZ 2: 32 [T 83.597a]) — a flower said to bloom only once in three thousand years.

leading to emancipation from birth-and-death by the path of self-power practices is, at the present time in the last age, difficult and beyond our reach. Because of this, our lives will pass by in vain unless we encounter the Primal Vow of Amida Tathāgata.

Now, however, we are able to meet the single teaching of the universal Vow. Therefore, the only thing we should aspire to is [birth in] the Pure Land of utmost bliss, and the only one we should rely upon is Amida Tathāgata; with faith decisively settled, we should say the nenbutsu. But what ordinary people generally have in mind is that if they merely repeat "Namu-amida-butsu" aloud, they will be born in the land of utmost bliss. That is most uncertain.

What, then, is the meaning of the six characters "na-mu-a-mi-da-butsu"?

We must realize that when anyone relies steadfastly on Amida Tathāgata, the Buddha saves him, fully knowing that sentient being. This is what is expressed in the six characters "na-mu-a-mi-da-butsu."

Then, how should we entrust ourselves to Amida Tathāgata in order to be saved in [regard to] the afterlife — the most important matter?

[The answer is that] when we entrust ourselves without any worry or double-mindedness — casting away all sundry practices and miscellaneous good acts [*zōzen* 雑善] and relying on Amida Tathāgata single-heartedly and steadfastly — [Amida] sends forth his light and embraces within it the sentient beings who rely on him. This is called "receiving the benefit of Amida Tathāgata's embracing light."[11] It is also called "[receiving] the benefit of the Vow that never abandons us."[12] Once we have been received in this way within Amida's Tathāgata's light, we will be born immediately into the true and real fulfilled land when life is spent. Let there be no doubt about this.

Besides this, what good would it do to rely on other buddhas or to perform meritorious good deeds (*kudoku zengon* 功徳善根)? How wonderful and gracious Amida Tathāgata is! How can we express our gratitude for this measureless benevolence?

Understand that it is simply by saying aloud "Namu-amida-butsu, Namu-amida-butsu" that we return the [Buddha's] benevolence in profound gratitude.

---

[11] *Mida nyorai no sesshu no kōyaku ni azukaru* 弥陀如来の摂取の光益にあずかる . See fascicle one, n. 33.

[12] *fusha no seiyaku* 不捨の誓益 . In explicating the term *fusha* in *Ichinen tanen mon'i*, Shinran states: "These words tell us that people of faith are embraced and protected within the mind of the Buddha of wisdom-light and that, having come within that mind of light, they are never abandoned" (SSZ 2: 609 [T 83.695c]).

Respectfully.
Bunmei 6 [1474].8.18.

III-5 On the compassionate vows of other buddhas

When we inquire in detail as to why it is that Amida's Primal Vow surpasses the compassionate vows of other buddhas, [we realize that] the
buddhas of the ten directions are unable to save sentient beings with
extremely deep evil karma or women burdened with the five obstacles
and the three submissions. Hence it is said that Amida Buddha's Primal Vow surpasses other buddhas' vows.

What sort of sentient beings does Amida Tathāgata's all-surpassing
great Vow save?

It is the great Vow that, without exception, saves evildoers who
have committed the ten transgressions and the five grave offenses and
even women burdened with the five obstacles and the three submissions. Hence it is [through] the working of the great Vow of Other
Power that [Amida] proclaims that he will unfailingly lead to the land
of utmost bliss [all] sentient beings, ten people out of ten, who single-
heartedly and steadfastly entrust themselves to him.

Then how do wretched ordinary beings like ourselves rely on
Amida Buddha's Primal Vow, and in what frame of mind should we
entrust ourselves to Amida? Please explain in detail. Attaining faith
according to this teaching, we will entrust ourselves to Amida, aspire
to [birth in] the land of utmost bliss, and say the nenbutsu.

Answer: To begin with, what is now widely taught about the nenbutsu makes people think they will be saved if they merely repeat
"Namu-amida-butsu" without any understanding. That is very doubtful. The teaching of the Jōdoshū is divided into various schools in the
capital and the provinces. We do not, however, judge that as right or
wrong. We simply explain our founder's teaching as it has been transmitted within the tradition.

Now, listen carefully, with the ears of one aspiring to emancipation and with your heads lowered in reverence; you may realize the
[one] thought of faith and joy.[13] Lay people and those who have committed evil all through their lives should simply disregard the depth of

---

[13] *shinjin kangi no omoi* 信心歓喜のおもい. A paraphrase of the *Larger Sūtra* passage, "Hear the Name and realize faith and joy," which Rennyo quotes and
explains in letters 1:15, 3:6, and 5:11. See fascicle one, n. 89.

their evil karma and deeply accept Amida Tathāgata's Primal Vow as the inconceivable Vow-power centered on saving just such wretched beings [as themselves]. Relying single-heartedly and steadfastly on Amida, they should solely seek to attain the faith that is Other Power.

What, then, is Other-Power faith?

The six-character Name "na-mu-a-mi-da-butsu" shows how it is that Amida Buddha saves us; we say that a person who has understood this in detail is one who has attained Other-Power faith. The two characters "na-mu" signify sentient beings' entrusting themselves to Amida Buddha single-heartedly and steadfastly, with no other thought than that he will save them; this is called "taking refuge." Next, the four characters "a-mi-da-butsu" signify that, without exception, Amida Buddha saves sentient beings who entrust themselves ("na-mu"). This means, in other words, that he "embraces and never abandons us." "Embraces and never abandons" means that Amida Tathāgata receives nenbutsu practicers within his light and will not forsake them. And so, in regard to the import of "namu-amida-butsu," we know that it is in testimony to Amida Buddha's saving us that the Name is expressed in these six characters, "na-mu-a-mi-da-butsu." When we have understood in this way, we are assured of birth in the land of utmost bliss. How gracious and wonderful this is! And beyond this, since we have been saved by Amida Tathāgata once and for all, the nenbutsu expresses the joy of having been saved. Hence we describe this nenbutsu as "the saying of the Name in gratitude for the Buddha's benevolence" and "the saying of the Name after [the realization of] faith (*shin* 信)."

> Respectfully.
> Written on the sixth day
> of the ninth month, Bunmei 6 [1474].

III-6 On saying the Tathāgata's Name only, at all times

What is the meaning of "namu-amida-butsu"?

To begin with, the two characters "na-mu" have two meanings, "to take refuge" and "to aspire to be born and to direct virtue."[14] Also,

---

[14] *Ekō* 回向 literally means "turn and move toward" or "redirect," i.e. "turn (or transfer) one's merit to another." This concept, central to Mahāyāna teaching, reflects the bodhisattva tradition of undertaking religious practices, not only for one's own benefit, but, out of deep compassion, for the sake of all sentient beings. In the Path of Sages, encompassing teachings other than those of

"namu" is the Vow; "amida-butsu" is the practice. When we cast away the sundry practices and miscellaneous good acts and entrust ourselves to Amida Tathāgata with the single practice and single-mindedness, awakening the one thought-moment of taking refuge in which we realize that he saves us, [Amida] graciously sends forth his all-pervading light and receives us. This is precisely what is meant by the four characters "a-mi-da-butsu" and, also, by "aspiring to be born and directing virtue." We see, then, that the six characters "na-mu-a-mi-da-butsu" comprise the Name that fully expresses the significance of Other-Power faith, through that we are to be born [in the Pure Land].

For this reason, the passage on the fulfillment of the Vow teaches that we "hear the Name and realize faith and joy."[15] The meaning of this passage is that, hearing the Name, we rejoice in faith. "Hearing the Name" is not just hearing it in a general way; it should be understood that, when we have met a good teacher and heard and fully realized the significance of the six characters (na-mu-a-mi-da-butsu), that realization is Other-Power faith, through which we are to be born in the fulfilled land. Hence "realize faith and joy" means that when faith is settled, we rejoice, knowing that birth in the Pure Land is assured.

And so, when we reflect on Amida Tathāgata's painstaking endeavors of five kalpas [of meditation] and innumerable, measureless kalpas [of practice], and when we think of the graciousness and wonder of his saving us so readily, it is hard to express our feelings. [Shinran] refers to this in a hymn:

> The benevolence of "namu-amida-butsu," [Amida's] directing
>   of virtue,
> is vast and inconceivable;
> as the benefit of his directing virtue for our going [to the Pure
>   Land],

the Pure Land, *ekō* was interpreted in terms of a practicer directing merit for the sake of his own and others' attainment of enlightenment; in traditional Pure Land teaching, it came to be understood as a directing of merit toward one's own attainment of birth in the Pure Land, where one would realize enlightenment and then return to this world to work on behalf of all beings. Shinran, however, established an Other-Power interpretation of *ekō* in terms of Amida directing his virtue to practicers. In the first lines of *Kyōgyōshinshō*, he defines two aspects of this activity, *ōsō ekō* and *gensō ekō* (SSZ 2: 2; T 83.589b), explicating the two throughout the *Kyōgyōshinshō*. See SSJ, 42–43, and *Passages*, s.v. "Directing virtue," 79–80.

[15] See n. 13 above.

we are led into his directing [virtue] for our return to this world.[16]

Also, in *The Gāthā of True Faith*,[17] there is [the following passage]:

Saying the Tathāgata's Name only, at all times,
we should respond in gratitude to the universal Vow of great
compassion.[18]

Hence [we realize] all the more that—walking, standing, sitting, and lying down, irrespective of time, place, or other circumstances—we should simply repeat the nenbutsu, saying the Name of the Buddha in grateful return for the Buddha's benevolence.

Respectfully.
Written on the twentieth day
of the tenth month, Bunmei 6 [1474].

III-7 On the three acts of the Buddha and of sentient beings

What Master Shinran emphasized above all else was Other-Power faith, the single path by which lay practicers lacking wisdom in the defiled world of the last age are born promptly and without difficulty in the Pure Land; this he taught as fundamental. Everyone knows very well, then, that Amida Tathāgata unfailingly saves each and every one of the people of utter foolishness who have committed the ten transgressions and the five grave offenses and even women burdened with the five obstacles and the three submissions. But how do we ordinary beings entrust ourselves to Amida Buddha, and in what way do we rely on him now in order to be born in the world of utmost bliss?[19]

[The answer is that] we simply entrust ourselves exclusively to Amida Tathāgata and, casting off all other [practices], steadfastly take refuge in Amida; and when we single-heartedly entrust ourselves to the Primal Vow without double-mindedness in regard to Amida Tathāgata, then, without fail, we will be born in the land of utmost bliss. This is precisely what it is to have attained Other-Power faith.

---

[16] *Shōzōmatsu wasan*, SSZ 2: 522a (T 83.666b).

[17] *Shōshinge*.

[18] *Shōshinge*, SSZ 2: 44 (T 83.600b).

[19] *gokuraku sekai* 極楽世界. A synonym for the Pure Land; a term used by Shinran in *Amida nyorai myōgō toku*, SSZ 2: 734.

Faith is [a matter of] clearly discerning the significance of Amida Buddha's Primal Vow and single-heartedly taking refuge in Amida; this we call decisive settlement of Other-Power faith (*anjin*). Therefore, full realization of the significance of the six characters "na-mu-a-mi-da-butsu" is the substance of decisively settled faith. That is, the two characters "na-mu" indicate the receptive attitude of the sentient beings who entrust themselves to Amida Buddha. Next, the four characters "a-mi-da-butsu" signify the dharma through which Amida Tathāgata saves sentient beings. This is expressed as "the oneness in 'namu-amida-butsu' of the person [to be saved] and dharma [that saves]."[20] Thus the three acts[21] of sentient beings and the three acts of Amida become one. Referring to this, Master Shan-tao wrote in his commentary, "The three acts of the Buddha and of sentient beings are inseparable."[22]

There should be no doubt at all, therefore, that those in whom faith is decisively settled with the one thought-moment of taking refuge will all be born without fail in the fulfilled land. Those who cast off the evil on their side, attachment to self-power, and rely single-heartedly on Amida, deeply entrusting themselves and realizing that this is the inconceivable working of the Vow, will all unfailingly attain birth in the true and real fulfilled land, ten people out of ten. Once

---

[20] *ki-hō ittai no namu-amida-butsu* 機法一体の南無阿弥陀仏. The phrase is also found in letters 4:8, 4:11, and 4:14, and in letter #120, dated Bunmei 18 (1486).1.4 (RSI, 366). For the term *ki-hō ittai*, see also RSI, 328 (#110), dated Bunmei 13 (1481).11.14, and RSI, 448 (#158), dated Meiō 7 (1498).12.15. Rennyo appropriated the concept *ki-hō ittai* directly from *Anjin ketsujōshō*, in which it appears in a variety of phrases. For *ki-hō ittai no namu-amida-butsu no shōgaku* 機法一体の南無阿弥陀仏の正覚, see *Anjin ketsujōshō*, SSZ 3: 615 and 625; for *ki-hō ittai ni shite namu-amida-butsu*, see SSZ 3: 622; for *ki-hō ittai no nenbutsu zanmai* 機法一体の念仏三昧, see SSZ 3: 625; and for *ki-hō ittai no shōgaku*, see SSZ 3: 621, 627, 631, and 633.

It is probable that both Kakunyo and Zonkaku were familiar with *Anjin ketsujōshō*. The term *ki-hō ittai* appears in Kakunyo's *Ganganshō*, SSZ 3: 46, and Zonkaku's *Zonkaku hōgo*, SSZ 3: 366, although without direct application to the nenbutsu. The term is also found in *Kenshōryūgishō* (T 83.843c), a writing by Rennyo's contemporary, Shin'e, head priest of Senju-ji. For a detailed treatment of the influence of *Anjin ketsujōshō* on the thought of Kakunyo and Zonkaku from the viewpoint of Shinshū Studies, see Fugen, "Anjin ketsujōshō to Shinshū resso no kyōgaku," 94–107; see also chapter three of this study, n. 55.

[21] Bodily, verbal, and mental; see chapter five for a discussion of the Sangō Upheaval, a major doctrinal controversy that occurred in the eighteenth and early nineteenth centuries.

[22] *Kangyōshō (Jōzengi)*, SSZ 1: 522 (T 37.268a).

[we have understood] this, we should say the nenbutsu in gratitude at all times, mindful only of Amida Tathāgata's deep benevolence.

Respectfully.
Bunmei 7 [1475].2.23.

III-8 On the false "ten kalpas" teaching in this province and others

In this province and others,[23] [there are many] these days who are sharply at variance with what our tradition teaches about the settled mind. Each person feels that he understands correctly, and few think of making further effort to attain true and real faith by asking others about views that run counter to dharma. This is indeed a deplorable attachment. Unless the birth that is to come in the fulfilled land is decisively settled by their quickly repenting and confessing these views and abiding in our tradition's true and real faith, it is indeed just as if they went to a mountain of treasure and returned empty-handed. They say, in words that are at variance with that faith, "Faith is not forgetting or doubting at present that Amida Tathāgata completely settled our birth from the time of his perfect enlightenment ten kalpas ago."[24] Dwelling in this [mistaken view]—without taking refuge in Amida and having their faith decisively settled—they cannot be born in the fulfilled land. This is, therefore, a deviant and mistaken understanding.

If we are to clarify what the settled mind is in our tradition, we say that to fully understand "namu-amida-butsu" is to have attained Other-Power faith. Hence Shan-tao explains the six characters "na-mu-a-mi-da-butsu" by saying, "'Namu' means 'to take refuge.' It also signifies aspiring to be born and directing virtue."[25]

What does this mean?

[The explanation is that] when Amida Tathāgata, in his causal stage [as the monk Dharmākara],[26] determined the practice through

---

[23] According to one account, Echizen and the neighboring provinces Kaga and Etchū; according to a second, "this province" refers to Kaga (Sugi, *Gobunshō kōwa*, 164).

[24] See letters 1:13 and 2:11 for similar quotations.

[25] *Kangyōsho (Gengibun)*, SSZ 1: 457 (T 37.250a); *Kyōgyōshinshō*, SSZ 2: 21 (T 83.594c).

[26] Shinran, in *Yuishinshō mon'i*, defines Amida's "causal stage" (*inchū* 因中) in terms of his activity as the monk Dharmākara (SSZ 2: 626 [T 83.701a]).

which we ordinary beings are to be born [in the Pure Land], he labored on our behalf because ordinary beings' directing of virtue is based on self-power and is therefore difficult to accomplish. In order to give this virtue to us, he fulfilled [the practice] through which virtue is directed; he gives it to us ordinary beings with the [awakening of the] one thought-moment of our taking refuge — "namu." Consequently, this is not a directing of virtue from the side of ordinary beings, but the Tathāgata's directing of virtue, which we call a non-directing of virtue from the practicer's side. Thus the two characters "na-mu" mean "to take refuge"; they also mean "to aspire for birth and to direct virtue." On these grounds, [Amida] unfailingly embraces and never abandons sentient beings who take refuge ("namu"); for this reason, we say "Namu-amida-butsu."

This is precisely what we mean when we refer to nenbutsu practicers who have attained Other-Power faith through the one thought-moment of taking refuge and who have completed the cause [of birth] in ordinary life. This you should know. People who understand in this way should repeat the nenbutsu, saying the Name of the Buddha [at all times] — walking, standing, sitting, and lying down — truly acknowledging Amida Tathāgata's deep and boundless benevolence. [Shinran] expresses this in the [following] lines:

> The moment we are mindful of Amida's Primal Vow,
> we are naturally brought to enter the stage of the definitely
> settled;
> saying the Tathāgata's Name only, at all times,
> we should respond in gratitude to the universal Vow of great
> compassion.[27]

Respectfully.
Bunmei 7 [1475].2.25.

III-9 On the anniversary of Master Shinran's death

Today being the [monthly] anniversary of Master [Shin]ran's death, there are few people who do not intend by all means to repay their indebtedness and express their gratitude for his benevolence. What everyone must understand, however, is how difficult it will be for people to conform to the intention of our master if (as in the case of practicers

---

[27] *Shōshinge*, SSZ 2: 44 (T 83.600b).

who have not attained true and real faith through the power of the Primal Vow and in whom the settled mind is yet to be realized [*mianjin*]) they make the visit perfunctorily, for today only, and think that what is essential in the Shinshū is just filling the members' meeting place. Nevertheless, it is probably good for those who are not concerned about the thanksgiving services to be here, even if they attend reluctantly.

Those who intend to come without fail on the twenty-eighth of every month [must understand that] people in whom the settled mind is yet to be realized (*mianjin*) and for whom the customary ways of faith are not decisively established should, by all means, quickly attain Other-Power faith based on the truth and reality of the Primal Vow, thereby decisively settling the birth that is to come in the fulfilled land; it is this that will truly accomplish their [own] resolve to repay their indebtedness and express their gratitude for the master's benevolence. This also means that, as a matter of course, their objective of birth in the land of utmost bliss is assured. It is, in other words, entirely consistent with what is expressed in [Shan-tao's] commentary:

> To realize faith oneself and to guide others to faith
> is the most difficult of all difficulties;
> to tell of great compassion and awaken beings everywhere
> is truly to respond in gratitude to the Buddha's benevolence.[28]

Although more than a hundred years have already passed since the master's death,[29] we gratefully revere the image[30] before our eyes. And although his benevolent voice is distant, separated from us by the wind of impermanence, his words of truth have been directly transmitted by his descendants; they resound with clarity deep in our ears. Thus it is that our school's faith, grounded in the truth and reality of Other Power, has been transmitted until today without interruption.

Therefore, given this present occasion, if there are people who have not realized the faith that is the truth and reality of the Primal Vow, we must indeed conclude they have not received the prompting of good from the past. If there were not people for whom good from

---

[28] *Ōjō raisange*, SSZ 1: 661 (T 47.442a).

[29] *nyūmetsu*, lit., "entry into nirvāṇa," a translation inappropriate in a Shin Buddhist context. Shinran died early in 1263.

[30] *shin'ei* 真影 , a statue of Shinran, though not the one that Rennyo left in safekeeping in Chikamatsu in Bunmei 1 (1469) and later moved to Yamashina Hongan-ji (for which, see fascicle four, n. 21). In a letter dated Bunmei 6 (1474).1.20, Rennyo specifically refers to a "main image" [of Amida] and an "image of the founder" at Yoshizaki (RSI, 170 [#51]).

the past had unfolded, all would be in vain and the birth that is to come [in the Pure Land] could not be settled. This would be the one thing to be lamented above all else.

And yet, although it is now difficult to encounter the one way of the Primal Vow, we are, on rare occasions, able to meet this supreme Primal Vow. This is indeed the joy of all joys — what could compare with it? We should revere [the Primal Vow]; we should entrust ourselves to it. People who thus overturn the evil delusions that have persisted in their minds over time and are then and there grounded in Other-Power faith, based on the ultimate truth of the Primal Vow, will truly conform to the master's intention. This in itself will surely fulfill our resolve to repay our indebtedness and express our gratitude for the master's benevolence today.

Respectfully.
Written on the twenty-eighth day
of the fifth month, Bunmei 7 [1475].

III-10 On six items, including "kami manifestations"

Followers of our tradition should be aware of the significance of the provisions of the six items [below] and, inwardly entrusting themselves deeply to the Buddha-dharma, should act in such a way as to give no outward sign of it. Therefore, it is a serious error that, these days, nenbutsu people in our tradition deliberately make known to those of other sects the way things are in our school. To put it briefly: from now on you must follow the Buddha-dharma, observing the intent of these provisions. Those who go against these rules will no longer be counted among the followers [of our tradition].

- Item: Do not make light of shrines.
- Item: Do not make light of the buddhas, bodhisattvas, or temples [enshrining deities].
- Item: Do not slander other sects or other teachings.
- Item: Do not slight the provincial military governors or local land stewards.
- Item: The interpretation of the Buddha-dharma in this province[31] is wrong; therefore, turn to the right teaching.
- Item: Other-Power faith as established in our tradition must be decisively settled deep in our hearts and minds.

---

[31] Echizen.

First, all "kami manifestations" are transformations; in their original state, they are buddhas and bodhisattvas, but when they look
upon the sentient beings of this realm, they realize that it is somewhat
difficult [for those beings] to approach buddhas and bodhisattvas.
Hence they appear provisionally as kami as the compassionate means
to form a bond with sentient beings and to encourage them, through
the strength [of that bond], to enter finally into the Buddha-dharma.
This is the meaning of [the passage] that says, "The first stage in form-
ing a bond is softening the light and mixing with the dust; the final
stage in benefiting beings is [manifesting] the eight aspects and attaining the way."[32] Therefore, sentient beings in the present world [should
realize that] those who entrust themselves to the Buddha-dharma and
say the nenbutsu will surely be recognized by kami [in their various]
manifestations as [the fulfillment of] their original intent. For this reason, although we do not specifically worship kami or entrust ourselves
to them, when we take refuge in the compassionate Vow of the one
Buddha Amida, the thought of similarly entrusting ourselves to [the
kami] is contained in that.

Second, as "buddhas and bodhisattvas" are the original state[33] for
"kami manifestations," when sentient beings of the present time entrust themselves to Amida Tathāgata and say the nenbutsu, the other
buddhas and bodhisattvas feel that this is the fulfillment of their original intent, since they all rely on their original teacher, Amida
Tathāgata. For this reason, although we do not rely specifically on the
other buddhas, when we entrust ourselves to the one Buddha, Amida
Buddha, all the buddhas and bodhisattvas are encompassed — each
and every one.[34] Simply realize that when we take refuge in Amida

---

[32] Based on *Makashikan* (*Mo ho chih kuan*), T 46.80a, a Mahāyāna text by
Chih-i, founder of the T'ien-t'ai school. Zonkaku, too, in *Shōjin hongaishū*, explains that the Tathāgata and bodhisattvas appear temporarily as kami manifestations in order to benefit sentient beings (SSS 1: 697). The term "eight aspects"
refers to a buddha (or bodhisattva) descending from Tuṣita heaven, entering the
mother's womb, being born, renouncing the world, defeating devils, becoming
enlightened, preaching the dharma, and entering nirvana.

[33] *honji* 本地 . In *Shōjin hongaishū*, Zonkaku maintains: "Buddhas are the
original state (*honji*) from which kami are manifested; kami manifestations are
manifestations (*suijaku* 垂迹) of the buddhas" (SSS 1: 697).

[34] In *Shōjin hongaishū*, Zonkaku states: "Although [buddhas and bodhisattvas
in their] original states differ in various ways, they are all encompassed within
the wisdom of Amida, the one Buddha. Therefore, if we take refuge in Amida,
we take refuge in all the buddhas and bodhisattvas. Because of this, even if we
do not specifically serve the kami manifestations, we take refuge in them as a
matter of course" (SSS 1: 702).

Tathāgata single-heartedly and steadfastly, all the other buddhas' wisdom and virtue come to be encompassed within the one body, Amida [and so become ours].

Third, it is a great mistake to slander other sects and other teachings. The reason for this was shown long ago in the triple Pure Land sūtras.[35] Moreover, scholars of other sects should never disparage people of the nenbutsu. In view of the law [of karma], it is clear that neither [followers of] our sect nor [those of] others can escape retribution for this offence.

Fourth (in regard to the provincial military governors and local land stewards), deal carefully with fixed yearly tributes and payments to officials and, besides that, take [the principles of] humanity and justice as fundamental.

Fifth, the interpretation of the Buddha-dharma in this province is not the right teaching of our tradition; it appears to be a wrong view (*jaken* 邪見). In brief: listening from now on to our tradition's right teaching, which is true and real, you must overturn customary evil attachments and move toward a mind that is good.

Sixth, true people of the nenbutsu in our tradition fully know the right teaching established by the founder and, although they commit evil and lack good, they take attainment of birth in the land of utmost bliss to be the fundamental intent of our sect.

The right understanding of our school's settled mind is that, without any striving, we rely single-heartedly and steadfastly on Amida Tathāgata and recognize how inconceivable it is that, although we are wretched beings burdened with evil deeds and blind passion, the working of Amida's Vow—the strong cause [of birth]—is directed toward saving such worthless beings; and when just a single thought free of doubt becomes firm, Amida unfailingly sends forth his unhindered light and embraces us. People who have undergone a decisive settling of faith in this way will all, each and every one, be born in the fulfilled land—ten people out of ten. What this means, in other words, is that these are people in whom Other-Power faith is decisively settled.

Above and beyond this, what we should bear in mind is that it is indeed [through] Amida Tathāgata's gracious and vast benevolence [that birth in the Pure Land is settled]; and with this realization, sleeping or waking, we simply say "Namu-amida-butsu" in gratitude for the Buddha's benevolence. What else, then, do we need besides this for [birth in] the afterlife? Is it not truly deplorable that [some people] confuse others by talking about false teachings (*ese bōmon* えせ法門)

---

[35] The *Larger Sūtra*, the *Contemplation Sūtra*, and the *Amida Sūtra*.

that are of uncertain origin and unknown to us, and — furthermore — that they debase the transmission of the dharma? You must reflect on this very carefully.

Respectfully.

Bunmei 7 [1475].7.15.

III-11 On the services held every year without exception

As the twenty-eighth of this month is the anniversary[36] [of the death] of our founder, Master [Shinran], services [have been held] every year without exception, in recognition of our indebtedness and in grateful response to [his] benevolence. Even the most humble fellow practicers [come at this time] from the various provinces and districts; those who fail to recognize their indebtedness must indeed be like wood and stones!

Although this foolish old man has somehow lived for the past four or five years[37] in the Hokuriku, in a remote corner of the mountains by the sea, it is beyond all expectation that he is still alive and has come to this province[38] and that this year, for the first time, we will celebrate thanksgiving services together [in honor] of the master's anniversary. This is indeed [the result of] inconceivable past conditions; I rejoice over it more and more deeply, time and again.

People who gather from this and other provinces should, therefore, first of all, be fully aware of the significance of the regulations established by the founding master.[39] He said, "Even if you are called a cow

---

[36] *goshōki* 御正忌 . The twenty-eighth day of the eleventh month by the lunar calendar, the sixteenth of the first month by the solar.

[37] Rennyo was in the Hokuriku from early in the sixth month of Bunmei 3 (1471) until the latter part of the eighth month of Bunmei 7 (1475). See RSI, 128–30 (#36), dated Bunmei 5 (1473).10.3, and RSI, 293–96 (#99), dated Bunmei 9 (1477).12.29.

[38] Kawachi. Rennyo had left Yoshizaki three months earlier.

[39] *kaisan Shōnin no sadameokareshi on'okite no mune* 開山聖人のさだめおかれし御掟のむね . There is no evidence to suggest that Shinran ever used the term *okite*. Indeed, he vigorously resisted any implication that in the last age adhering to proper conduct was a possible means for freeing sentient beings from birth-and-death (*Tannishō*, SSZ 2: 775 [T 83.731c]). In his letters, however, he warns members of the nenbutsu community in the Kantō against antinomian behavior and, finally, he felt compelled to disown his own son, Zenran, for distorting the teaching.

thief, do not act in such a way that you are seen as a follower of the Buddha-dharma or as an aspirant for [buddhahood in] the afterlife."[40] Besides this, he also carefully stipulated that we should observe [the principles of] humanity, justice, propriety, wisdom, and sincerity; that we should honor the laws of the state; and that, deep within, we should take Other-Power faith established by the Primal Vow as fundamental.[41]

But recently, although people these days act as if they knew the Buddha-dharma, [it is clear] from what I have observed that, while they give an outward appearance of relying on the Buddha-dharma, there is no decisive settling of faith (anjin), the single path in our tradition. Besides that, on the strength of their own ability, they read texts that are not authenticated in our tradition and then talk about unknown, false teachings. Wandering among the followers of our [sect] and others, they make up lies and, finally, under "orders from the head temple," they deceive people and take things [from them], thereby debasing the fundamental principles of our tradition. Is this not truly deplorable?

Therefore, unless each of these people repents and confesses his evil ways and turns to the right teaching during the seven-day thanksgiving services [commemorating] the anniversary of the master's death on the twenty-eighth of this month[, their coming will be to no purpose]; and if they attend these seven-day thanksgiving services just in imitation of others, though they say that they come to repay their indebtedness and express their gratitude for the [master's] benevolence, [their coming] will amount to nothing at all. Hence it is precisely those people who have attained faith through the working of Amida's Vow who will return the Buddha's benevolence in gratitude and respond gratefully to their teacher's virtue. Those who thoroughly understand this and come to pay homage to the master are the ones who are truly in accord with [Amida's] intention; they, in particular, will be deeply possessed of the resolve to repay their indebtedness and express their gratitude for his benevolence during this month's anniversary.

Respectfully.
Written on the twenty-first day
of the eleventh month, Bunmei 7 [1475].

---

[40] As reported by Kakunyo in Gaijashō, SSZ 3: 68.
[41] Rennyo draws here on Kakunyo's exposition in Gaijashō, SSZ 3: 67.

III-12 On the presence or absence of good from the past

These days, as in the past, it seems that many of those who call themselves followers of the Buddha-dharma and extol and proclaim the
teaching in various places in the provinces are themselves not truly
grounded in the right teaching of our tradition. When we ask the reason for this, [the answer is that], in the first place, although they act as
if they knew the Buddha-dharma in depth, no part of their understanding has been gained from authentic sources. Some have heard
the teaching quite by chance, from the edge of a veranda or from outside a sliding door; their aspiration for the Buddha-dharma is in truth
shallow, and they think there is no one who knows better than they
what the Buddha-dharma is all about. Consequently, when they happen to see people who proclaim our tradition's right teaching in the
correct manner, they cling persistently to their own shallow views. Is
it not, in the first place, arrogant for them to immediately assume that
only they fully know [the teaching]?

In this frame of mind, they wander from place to place among
followers [of our tradition] and read the scriptures – and, in addition
to that, they simply ingratiate themselves with people, make up lies,
and take things [from them], saying that they are sent from the head
temple when they are carrying out personal matters. How can these
people be called good followers of the Buddha-dharma or readers of
scripture? This is utterly deplorable. It is the one thing we should
lament above all else. Those who want to present our tradition's teaching and instruct others must therefore, first of all, be fully aware of the
steps in instruction.

When we consider presenting our tradition's Other-Power faith,
we must first distinguish between the people who have good from the
past and those who lack good from the past.[42] For, however long ago
a person may have listed his name as a participant in this [tradition],
it will be difficult for one who lacks good from the past to attain faith.
Indeed, faith (*shin*) will of itself be decisively settled in the person for
whom past good has unfolded. And so, when we discuss the two [kinds
of] practice – right and sundry – in the presence of people who lack
good from the past, this may lay the foundation for slander, contrary
to what one would expect. To teach extensively in the presence of or-

---

[42] *mushukuzen*. See fascicle one, n. 30.

dinary people without understanding this principle of the presence or absence of good from the past is in total opposition to our tradition's rules of conduct.

Hence the *Larger Sūtra* says, "If a person lacks roots of good, he will not be able to hear this sūtra"[43] and, "To hear this sūtra and to sustain faith (*shingyō*) are the most difficult of all difficulties; nothing surpasses these difficulties."[44] Also, Shan-tao states, "If a person has already practiced this dharma at one time in the past and is able to hear it again now, he will immediately realize joy."[45] In any case, it is clear, according to the sūtras and commentaries, that everything depends on good from the past. Thus we understand that we should watch over people in whom there is good from the past and transmit the dharma of our tradition to them. We must be fully aware of the significance of this and then instruct others.

In particular, first of all, take the laws of the state as fundamental and, giving priority to [the principles of] humanity and justice, follow the generally accepted customs; deep within yourself, maintain the settled mind of our tradition; and, outwardly, conduct yourself in such a way that the transmission of the dharma you have received will not be evident to those of other sects and other schools. This distinguishes the person who fully knows our tradition's right teaching, which is true and real.

Respectfully.

Bunmei 8 [1476].1.27.

Shōnyo, disciple of Śākyamuni. (written seal)

III-13 On followers of our tradition

Followers of our tradition — both those in whom the settled mind is already established and those [whose faith is] yet to be established but who seek to attain the settled mind — must bear in mind the following points:

First of all, outwardly, take the laws of the state as fundamental and do not hold any of the kami, buddhas, or bodhisattvas in contempt; do not slander other sects or other teachings. Do not slight the provincial military governors or local land owners, but meet fixed

---

[43] *Larger Sūtra*, SSZ 1: 27 (T 12.273a); *Kyōgyōshinshō*, SSZ 2: 158 (T 83.630c).

[44] *Larger Sūtra*, SSZ 1: 46 (T 12.279a); *Kyōgyōshinshō*, SSZ 2: 162 (T 83.631c).

[45] *Kangyōsho* (*Jōzengi*), SSZ 1: 507 (T 37.264a).

yearly tributes and payments to officials in full. Besides that, take [the principles of] humanity and justice as essential. Inwardly, rely single-heartedly and steadfastly on Amida Tathāgata for [birth in the Pure Land in] the afterlife and give no thought to any of the sundry practices and miscellaneous good acts; when we entrust ourselves without a single thought of doubt, we will be born without fail in the true and real Pure Land of utmost bliss. With this understanding, one is to be declared a nenbutsu follower who has realized faith through Amida Tathāgata's Other Power.

Having thus attained the faith that is expressed through the nenbutsu, we should then realize that, although we are wretched beings of deep evil karma who commit evil all our lives, when we once awaken faith with the one thought-moment of taking refuge [in Amida], we are readily saved by the working of the Buddha's Vow. Then, deeply recognizing the graciousness of Amida Tathāgata's inconceivable, all-surpassing Primal Vow—the strong cause [of birth]—we simply say the nenbutsu, sleeping or waking, in gratitude for the Buddha's benevolence, and repay our indebtedness to Amida Tathāgata.

Nothing we know beyond this is of any use for the [attainment of birth in the] afterlife, but these days, people talk absurdly—as if something were lacking—about unknown, eccentric teachings that have not been transmitted [within our tradition]; thus they confuse others and debase the unsurpassed transmission of the dharma. This is indeed a deplorable situation. We must think about it very carefully.

Respectfully.
Bunmei 8 [1476].7.18.

Fascicle Four

IV-1 On Shinshū nenbutsu practicers

There are many among the Shinshū nenbutsu practicers who have no understanding of the dharma. Hence I have, for the most part, set down the main points. In brief, practicers of the same mind are to take these words as fundamental from now on.

There are two points in regard to this. First, before all else, one must be settled in the faith (*anjin*) through which one's own birth [in the Pure Land] is accomplished. Second, in teaching others, one must determine the presence or absence of good from the past. We must keep these principles firmly in mind.

As for the first matter of one's own birth, then, store the faith that is awakened in the one thought-moment deeply within yourselves; moreover, persevere in saying the Name in gratitude for [Amida] Buddha's benevolence through Other Power. In addition to this, honor the laws of the state and take [the principles of] humanity and justice as fundamental. Further, do not slight the various [kami and] buddhas and the bodhisattvas or belittle other teachings and other sects; simply follow the customs of ordinary life. Outwardly, do not show your devotion to our tradition to those of other sects and other schools. By this, one is to be declared a Shinshū nenbutsu practicer who observes the regulations of our tradition's Master [Shinran]. In particular, act with extreme caution, as this is a time when people determinedly strain their ears to hear anything that can be distorted and spread in slander.

The "Other-Power threefold entrusting" taught in our tradition is described in the Eighteenth Vow as "with sincere mind, entrusting and aspiring to be born in my land."[1] Although we call this "threefold entrusting," it is simply the one mind [of faith] in which a practicer takes refuge, relying on Amida. That is to say, with the awakening of the one thought-moment in which a practicer for whom past good has unfolded takes refuge in Amida, the Buddha embraces that practicer (who has taken refuge through the one thought-moment) with his compassionate light.[2] Indicating this moment, we speak of "threefold

---

[1] *Larger Sūtra*, SSZ 1: 9 (T 12.268a); *Songō shinzō meimon*, SSZ 2: 577 (T 83.679a). See fascicle one, n. 73.

[2] *shinkō* 心光 ; the light that shines from the Buddha's heart and mind of compassion. Zonkaku, expounding the term in *Rokuyōshō* (SSZ 2: 307), draws on a passage in the *Contemplation Sūtra* that states: "The mind of the buddhas is great

entrusting—with sincere mind, entrusting and aspiring to be born." The passage on the fulfillment of the Vow further explains it as "immediately attaining birth [in the Pure Land] and dwelling in [a state of] non-retrogression."[3] Or again, we may say that [a person in] this state is a person of true and real faith, a practicer with deep past causes, and one who has completed the cause [of birth] in ordinary life. Hence there is nothing, be it taking refuge in Amida or attaining faith, that is not related to good from the past.

We find, therefore, that if people who [seek] birth through the nenbutsu [do not realize faith] through the prompting of past causes, the birth to come in the fulfilled land is impossible. In the words of the master, the point of this is: "If you should realize faith, rejoice in conditions from the distant past."[4] And so, the understanding in our tradition is that efforts to teach others will be useless if we fail to determine the presence or absence of good from the past. For this reason, one should instruct others after having considered their innate capacity [for birth] in light of the existence or non-existence of good from the past.

Recently, the way of followers of the Buddha-dharma in our tradition has been to talk indiscreetly about the teaching, with no clear understanding of what is right and what is wrong; hence we hear that the true meaning of Shin teaching has been utterly lost. It is with detailed knowledge of the above that one is to proclaim our tradition's basic principles.

Respectfully.
Bunmei 9 [1477].1.8.

IV-2 On the allotted span of life

If we calculate the length of human life, the allotted span at this time is fifty-six years.[5] At present, however, it is indeed noteworthy for a person to have lived to fifty-six. Given this, at sixty-three, I am already well into the years of decline. By my count, my life has already been

---

compassion. With this unconditioned compassion, all sentient beings are embraced" SSZ 1: 57 (T 12.343c).

[3] *Larger Sūtra*, SSZ 1: 24 (T 12.272b); *Jōdo monrui jushō*, SSZ 2: 452 (T 83.646b).

[4] *Jōdo monrui jushō*, SSZ 2: 447 (T 83.645a).

[5] See fascicle two, n. 30.

extended by seven years. I feel uneasy on this point as to what sort of illness I may encounter in meeting the conditions leading to death,[6] this being the working effect of karma from the past (*zengō* 前業). This is something that certainly cannot be predicted.

In particular, as I observe the present state of affairs, [it is clear that] because this is a time of instability, human sorrow exceeds all imagination. If this is a world where we can surely die at once if we want to die, why have I lived on until now? Quite simply, the place where I am eager to be born is the Pure Land of utmost bliss, and what I aspire to and long to attain is the undefiled buddha body. But then, for a person who has, through the wisdom of the Buddha, realized the settled mind that is Other Power [with the awakening] of the one thought-moment of taking refuge, what could be lacking that he would hasten the time of death established in a previous life (having reached the point of devoting himself until life's end to the saying of the Name in grateful return for the Buddha's benevolence)? To the contrary, he might be foolishly deluded. Such is the reflection of this foolish old man. Others, too, should be of this mind.

The way of the world is, above all, that we continue on as if unaware of the uncertainty of life for young and old alike. Existence is as ephemeral as a flash of lightning or the morning dew, and the wind of impermanence may come even now. Yet we think only of prolonging this life for as long as possible, without ever aspiring to [birth in the Pure Land in] the afterlife. This is inexpressibly deplorable.

From today, we should quickly entrust ourselves to Amida Tathāgata's Primal Vow of Other Power. Steadfastly taking refuge in the Buddha of Immeasurable Life, we should aspire to birth in the true and real fulfilled land and repeat the nenbutsu, saying the Name of the Buddha.

Respectfully.

When [these thoughts] suddenly came to mind, I wrote them down quickly, finishing before seven in the morning, on the seventeenth day of the ninth month, Bunmei 9 [1477].

Shinshō-in [Rennyo].

Age sixty-three.

---

[6] *shi no en* 死の縁 . In *Shūjishō*, Kakunyo explains: "All sentient beings' circumstances differ, as do their karma-causes from the past. The conditions leading to death are also innumerable. Some people die from illness, some by the sword. Some die from drowning, some from fire. Some die asleep in their rooms, some in a drunken frenzy. These are all causes deriving from the karma of previous lives" (SSZ 3: 42 [T83.737b]).

though written to be left behind,
this is a letter
that simply flowed from the brush —
phrases here and there
may indeed seem strange

IV-3 On the present state of affairs

The present state of affairs is such that no one knows when things will settle down. Consequently, as this is a time when it is difficult even to pass along the roads between the provinces, it is a period of utter confusion for the Buddha-dharma and for mundane law (sehō 世法). As a result, in some instances, no one even visits the temples and shrines of wondrous effects (reibutsu reisha 霊仏霊社).

When we hear, in regard to this, that the human realm is [a place of] uncertainty for young and old alike, [we might feel that] we should quickly cultivate whatever meritorious good deeds may be possible and aspire to whatever enlightenment and nirvāṇa may be attainable. Yet, at this time — though we call the present world "the last dharma-age of defilement and confusion"[7] — Amida Tathāgata's Other-Power Primal Vow is mysteriously thriving all the more.[8] Therefore, lay people [must understand] that unless they rely on this vast, compassionate Vow, realize the one thought-moment of faith, and attain birth in the Pure Land of suchness (eternity and bliss), it is indeed as if they went to a mountain of treasure and returned empty-handed. Quieten your minds and deeply reflect on this.

Thus it is that when we inquire in detail about the vows of all the buddhas, we hear that they were unable to save women burdened with the five obstacles and evildoers who have committed the five grave offenses. We are reminded in regard to this that it was Amida Tathāgata who alone made an unsurpassed, incomparable Vow — the

---

[7] mappō jokuran 末法濁乱 . This is the only occurrence of the term mappō in the five fascicles; it is synonymous with matsudai, used on numerous occasions. See fascicle one, n. 42.

[8] In Shōzōmatsu wasan, Shinran writes:

The world having entered the semblance and last ages of the five defilements,
the teachings left by Śākyamuni are hidden.
[Yet] Amida's compassionate Vow is spreading,
and birth through the nenbutsu is flourishing.
SSZ 2: 518b (T 83.665b)

great Vow that he would save ordinary beings burdened with evils and offenses and women burdened with the five obstacles. How gracious [a Vow]—and how inadequate words are to describe it.

Accordingly, long ago, when Śākyamuni expounded the *Lotus* [*Sūtra*], the wondrous text of the One Vehicle,[9] on Mount Gṛdhrakūṭa, Devadatta provoked Ajātaśatru to acts of treachery; Śākya[muni] then led Vaidehī to aspire for the land of serene sustenance. Because [Śākyamuni] graciously withdrew from the assembly gathered at Mount Gṛdhrakūṭa where he was expounding the *Lotus* [*Sūtra*], descended to the royal palace, and set forth the Pure Land teaching for Vaidehī's sake, Amida's Primal Vow has flourished to this day.[10] This is why we say that the teachings of the *Lotus* and the nenbutsu were given at the same time.

In other words, it is clear that Śākya[muni] used the five grave offenses in which Vaidehī, Devadatta, and Ajātaśatru were involved as compassionate means to cause women and those who have committed the five grave offenses in the last age to aspire for birth in the land of serene sustenance; [he assured us that] even such people would unfailingly attain birth in the land of serene sustenance if they took refuge in the inconceivable Primal Vow. This you should know.

Respectfully.
Written on the twenty-seventh day
of the ninth month, Bunmei 9 [1477].

---

[9] *ichijō* 一乗. The single teaching, given in the *Lotus Sūtra*, by which all sentient beings can attain buddhahood. The Three-Vehicle (*sanjō* 三乗) teaching, in contrast, addresses bodhisattvas, pratyekabuddhas, and śrāvakas separately in correspondence to their nature and ability. Shinran, identifying the teaching of the One Vehicle with that of the Eighteenth Vow, expounds:

> "One Vehicle" refers to the great vehicle (Mahāyāna). The great vehicle is the Buddha vehicle. To realize the One Vehicle is to realize the highest perfect enlightenment. . . . In the great vehicle, there are no "two vehicles" or "three vehicles." The two vehicles and three vehicles lead one to enter the One Vehicle. The One Vehicle is the vehicle of highest truth. There is no One Vehicle other than the One Buddha-Vehicle, the Vow (*Teaching*, 1: 147–48; SSZ 2: 38 [T83.598c]).

[10] These events are recorded in the *Contemplation Sūtra*. Although Rennyo's summary of the events is close to Shinran's in the preface to *Kyōgyōshinshō*, Shinran specifically interprets the actions of Devadatta, Ajātaśatru, and Vaidehī in terms of "selfless love" (*nin* 仁; see *Teaching*, 1: 57; SSZ 2: 1 [T 83.589a]); Rennyo speaks, perhaps more pragmatically, of their offenses being used as compassionate means.

IV-4 On a hymn in three verses

As fall and spring slip away, the months and years go by; yesterday is spent, and today draws to a close. Little did I know that I would grow old before I was aware of it, with the unnoticed passage of the years. Yet, on occasion during that time, I must have known the beauty of flowers and birds, the wind, and the moon; I must also have met with the joy and sorrow of pleasure and pain. But now there is not even a single instance that I remember in particular. How sad it is to have grown gray with age, having done no more than pass nights and days to no purpose. But when I deeply reflect on the apparent soundness of my own existence, not yet having been called away by the relentless wind of impermanence, it seems like a dream, like an illusion. As for now, there is nothing left but to aspire to the one way of getting out of birth-and-death. And so, when I hear that it is Amida Tathāgata's Primal Vow that readily saves sentient beings like ourselves in this evil future age, I feel truly confident and thankful.

When we simply take refuge in this Primal Vow with sincere mind, with the [awakening of the] one thought-moment in which there is no doubt,[11] then, without any anxiety, birth [in the Pure Land] is assured if we die at that time.[12] Or, if life is prolonged, during that time, we should say the nenbutsu in gratitude for Buddha's benevolence and await life's end.[13] As I have indeed heard that this is precisely what is

---

[11] This clause appears to be a restatement of the "three minds" found in the Eighteenth Vow; its presentation is consistent with Shinran's exposition of "the threefold mind as the mind that is single," a mind "untainted by the hindrance of doubt." See fascicle one, n. 73, and *Teaching*, 2: 227–29 (SSZ 2: 59 [T 83.604a]).

[12] Zonkaku states: "If one entrusts oneself at life's end, birth is assured at life's end; if one realizes sincere mind during ordinary life, birth is determined during ordinary life. This has nothing to do with ordinary life or life's end; it is concerned simply with the moment one encounters the Buddha-dharma" (*Jōdo shinyōshō*, SSZ 3: 127 [T 83.761a]).

[13] Kakunyo writes, after citing passages from the *Larger Sūtra*: "As all these passages take impermanence as fundamental, they teach that we establish the [awakening of the] one thought-moment [of faith] as the time when birth is settled, and that if life continues on after that, there will naturally be many utterances of the nenbutsu. Therefore, it is evident that we are in accord with the attesting passages in our many utterances of the nenbutsu in ordinary life, in gratitude for the Buddha's benevolence once birth is settled through the one thought-moment" (*Kudenshō*, SSZ 3: 34 [T 83.749c]).

meant by "completing the cause [of birth] in ordinary life,"[14] this teaching of decisively settled faith continues to sound in the depths of my ears even now. How grateful I am — and how inadequate it is to say only that.

And so, in overwhelming awe and thankfulness for Amida Tathāgata's Primal Vow of Other Power, I will express what is written above as a hymn, [simply] giving way to what rises to my lips:

> The mind
> that even once
> relies on Amida: that mind
> is in accord
> with true dharma.

> When, deeply burdened with evil karma,
> we come to rely profoundly
> on the Tathāgata,
> by the power of dharma,
> we will go to the West.

> When our minds
> are settled in the path
> of hearing the dharma,
> let us simply say,
> "Namu-amida-butsu."

I write this in spite of myself, in response to the incomparable single teaching of the Primal Vow. The meaning of the three verses is as follows:

The first tells what it is for faith to be decisively settled through the one thought-moment of taking refuge. The next verse gives the meaning of "unfailingly attaining nirvāṇa," the benefit of "entering the company of those [whose birth is] truly settled."[15] The intent of the next is to explain what it is to "know Amida's benevolence and express gratitude,"[16] once we have rejoiced in diamond-like faith.

---

[14] *Jōdo shinyōshō*, SSZ 3: 122–23 (T 83.759b). See fascicle one, n. 14.

[15] Shinran writes in *Kyōgyōshinshō*, in the "Chapter on Realization": "When foolish beings . . . realize the mind and practice that Amida directs to them for their going forth [to the Pure Land], they immediately join the truly settled of the Mahāyāna. Because they dwell among the truly settled, they necessarily attain nirvāṇa" (*Teaching*, 3: 355; SSZ 2: 103 [T 83.616a]). In the "Chapter on Faith": "When we realize the diamond-like true mind, we . . . unfailingly gain ten benefits in the present life." The tenth of these is "the benefit of entering the state of the truly settled" (*Teaching*, 2: 257–58; SSZ 2: 72 [T 83.607b]).

[16] *chion hōtoku* 知恩報徳 . Shinran numbers this as the eighth of the benefits

I felt, then, that even such a quiet voicing as this, since it is based on the awakening of Other-Power faith, might at least serve as an act of devotion in grateful return for Amida Buddha's benevolence; I also thought that those who hear, if they have [the necessary] past conditions, might come to the same mind. I am, however, already in my seventh decade and feel it ridiculous, particularly as one who is both foolish and untalented, to speak of the teaching in this inadequate and uninformed way; yet, at the same time—simply filled with awe at the single path of the Primal Vow—I have written down these poor verses, letting them flow from the brush without further reflection. Let those who see them in days to come not speak badly of them. Indeed, they may serve as a condition leading to praise of the Buddha's teaching and as a cause leading to the turning of the dharma wheel. By all means, there should never be any disparagement of them.

Respectfully.

I have written this down in a short time by the fire, in the middle of the twelfth month, the ninth year of Bunmei.

The above letter was picked up in the road and brought back to this temple by [a priest of] Busshō-ji who was out on an errand and walking from Harinokihara to Kukenzaike.[17]

Bunmei 9 [1477].12.2.

IV-5 From the middle period until the present

Among those who have carried out the teaching in our tradition from the middle period[18] until the present, some have done so without knowing at all whether [their listeners] have, or lack, good from the past. Simply put, you must be aware of this from now on. When you

---

realized in this present life (*Teaching*, 2: 258; SSZ 2: 72 [T 83.607b]).

[17] Inaba's editorial note following this letter (#97) in RSI, 290, suggests that the postscript was intended for the next letter, #98, and that the date Bunmei 9.12.2 may be a copyist's error for Bunmei 9.12.12. Izumoji points out a similar postscript in the standard text for letter #98, dated Bunmei 9.12.23; he also notes the inconsistency in letter 4:4 of the five-fascicle collection (translated here) between "the middle of the twelfth month" and the date Bunmei 9.12.2 (Izumoji, *Ofumi*, 274). Whatever the final answer may be in regard to these problems, the priest from Busshō-ji is identified as Kyōkō, a disciple of Rennyo (see also Sugi, *Gobunshō kōwa*, 215–17), and "this temple," as the temple in Deguchi, where Rennyo was at the time (*Ofumi*, 275).

[18] *chūko* 中古 . From the time of Kakunyo (Sugi, *Gobunshō kōwa*, 226).

read the scriptures, for example, or when you speak [even] briefly about the teaching, you must [first] ascertain this, and then proclaim the dharma as taught within our school; or, again, when people gather in large numbers to listen to the Buddha-dharma and you feel that there may be some among those people who lack good from the past, you should not discuss the meaning of our school's true and real dharma. Recently, however, as I observe how people preach, [it is clear that some] lack this awareness and simply feel that, whichever type of person the listener may be, he will surely be grounded in our tradition's faith (*anjin*) if they preach well. You should know that this is an error. Carry out the teaching in our tradition with full awareness of what is written above. From the middle period until now, there has been no one at all who has understood this and preached with excellence. You are to undertake the preaching in the traditional way, fully recognizing these points. As the twenty-eighth of this month marks an annual ceremony, there are many who faithfully anticipate observing nenbutsu services to repay their indebtedness and express their gratitude for the benevolence of our founder, Master [Shinran]. This is because of their clearly knowing the truth of "drawing from the stream to discover the source."[19] It is entirely due to the pervasiveness of the master's teaching.

Meanwhile, in recent years, [some] have confused people to the extreme by spreading distorted teachings (*higa hōmon*) not discussed in our tradition; others, reprimanded by local land stewards and domain holders (who are themselves entrenched in wrong views), have come to view our tradition's true and real faith (*anjin*) as mistaken. Is this not a deplorable situation? It is lamentable; it is dreadful.

In sum, during the seven days and nights of the thanksgiving services this month, each person should deeply repent;[20] and, leaving none of his own mistaken thoughts at the bottom of his mind, he should undergo a turning of that mind and confess before the revered image [of the founder][21] in this temple, telling of this every day and every night so that everyone will hear about it. This, in other words,

---

[19] Based on a sentence in Kakunyo's *Hōonkō shiki*, SSZ 3: 657 (T 83.756a).

[20] This developed into a formal ceremony: see *Honganji sahō no shidai*, RSG, 226–27.

[21] A wooden image of Shinran, which by the time this letter was written, had been in place at Yamashina Hongan-ji for two years. Rennyo refers to the statue as the "central image" (*konpon no goeizō* 根本の御影像) in RSI, 317 (#107), writing of its move to Yamashina on Bunmei 12 (1480).11.18 from the Chikamatsu temple in Ōtsu, where it had been in safekeeping since the first year of Bunmei (1469).

is in accord with [a passage in Shan-tao's] commentary: "With a turning of the mind, [even] slanderers of the dharma and those who lack the seed of buddhahood will all be born [in the Pure Land]";[22] it also corresponds to the teaching of "realizing faith (*shin*) oneself and guiding others to faith (*shin*)."[23] Then, on hearing about this turning of the mind and repentance, attentive people will indeed feel the rightness of it, and in some of them the ordinary "bad" mind may be similarly overturned and changed into the "good" mind. This will truly accomplish the fundamental purpose of the master's anniversary this month. In other words, this is the offering through which we repay our indebtedness and express our gratitude [for his benevolence].

Respectfully.
Bunmei 14 [1482].11.21.

IV-6 On three items

The thanksgiving services this month are held as an annual ceremony of long standing, marking the anniversary of the death of the founder, Master [Shinran]. Consequently, followers of our tradition in provinces far and near are filled with eagerness for the pilgrimage and wish to express the sincerity of their gratitude on this occasion. And so it is that, for seven days and nights every year, they concentrate on and devote themselves to the nenbutsu services. This is precisely why practicers of true and real faith are flourishing. Indeed, we might almost say that the period of firm practice of the nenbutsu has come.[24]

Among those who make pilgrimages during the seven-day period as a result of this, there may indeed be some who come to worship before the revered image [of the founder] only in imitation of others. These people should promptly kneel before the revered image and,

---

[22] *Hōjisan*, SSZ 1: 567 (T 47.426a); *Kyōgyōshinshō*, SSZ 2: 101 (T 83.615c).

[23] *Ōjō raisange*, SSZ 1: 661 (T 47.442a).

[24] *nenbutsu tokukengo no jisetsu* 念仏得堅固の時節. A phrase that, in this context, Rennyo may have drawn from Zonkaku. In *Haja kenshōshō*, Zonkaku quotes sources including *Zōhōketsugikyō* in a discussion of practices undertaken following Śākyamuni's death: "During the five hundred years of the right dharma [age], the precepts will be firmly upheld; during the thousand years of the semblance dharma, the practice of meditation will be firm; and during the ten thousand years of the last dharma, practice of the nenbutsu will be firm (*nenbutsu kengo nari* 念仏堅固なり ; SSZ 3: 166). For further discussion, see Izumoji, *Ofumi*, 283; Sugi, *Gobunshō kōwa*, 232.

through a turning of the mind and repentance, enter into the true purport of the Primal Vow and attain true and real faith with the awakening of the one thought-moment [of entrusting].

We must realize that "namu-amida-butsu" is the essence of the settled mind for nenbutsu practicers. This is because "namu" means "to take refuge." We must know that, for ordinary beings like ourselves who lack good and do evil, "taking refuge" expresses the [entrusting] mind that relies on Amida Buddha. This entrusting mind is none other than the mind of Amida Buddha, who receives sentient beings into his great light of eighty-four thousand rays and grants to sentient beings the two aspects of the Buddha's directing of virtue, outgoing [from birth-and-death] and returning [into birth-and-death].[25] Thus faith has no other meaning than this. Everything is encompassed within "namu-amida-butsu." Recently, some people have been thinking otherwise.

In regard to this, among the followers of our tradition in various provinces, there are many who confuse the meaning of the dharma by propounding obscure teachings not prescribed in the scriptures designated by our founder. This is indeed ridiculous. In brief, people like these should certainly take part in this seven-day period of thanksgiving services, reverse their mistakes, and ground themselves in the right teaching.

- Item: Those who are pillars of the Buddha-dharma and hold the position of priest in accord with the tradition are said to have told others about false teachings that are unknown to us and of obscure origin, and, recently, to have actively engaged in this far and wide in order to be considered learned. This is preposterous!
- Item: It is a great mistake for people to announce that they are making a pilgrimage to the revered image [of the founder] at Hongan-ji, in Kyoto, and then — regardless of the sort of people who are around, especially on main roads and thoroughfares and at checking stations and ferry crossings — to speak indiscriminately to others about matters concerning the Buddha-dharma.
- Item: Should there be a situation in which someone asks what sort of Buddha-dharma you rely on, do not answer outright that you are a nenbutsu person in our tradition. Simply reply that you are a person of no particular sect, who just knows the

---

[25] See fascicle three, n. 14.

nenbutsu as something precious. This, in other words, is the bearing of a person who, as our tradition's master taught, will not be seen as a follower of the Buddha-dharma.

You must recognize, therefore, that right understanding in our tradition is knowing these points thoroughly and, outwardly, giving no sign of them. Furthermore, none of the points established by the community during the thanksgiving services over the past two or three years are to be altered. If by chance there are points with which members of this community are at variance, those who differ can no longer be followers of the founding master.

Respectfully.

Bunmei 15 [1483].11.

IV-7 On six items

As the thanksgiving services this month are an annual ceremony of long standing, there has been no lapse up to now in our seven-day observations of them. On this occasion, therefore, followers from various provinces come with an earnest resolve to repay their indebtedness and express their gratitude; they devote themselves to the fundamental practice of the nenbutsu, saying the Name of the Buddha. This is indeed the virtue of the single practice and single-mindfulness, through which birth [in the Pure Land] is settled.[26]

In regard to those on pilgrimage from the provinces, however, it seems that few dwell in the same faith (*anjin*). The reason for this is that their aspiration is not truly for the Buddha-dharma — and if they are simply imitating others or following social convention, it is indeed a lamentable situation. For when those in whom the settled mind is yet to be realized (*mianjin*) do not even discuss their doubts, they betray the utmost lack of faith (*fushin*). And so, although they endure a journey of thousands of *ri* and undergo great hardship in coming to the capital, it is to no purpose at all. This is utterly deplorable. But if they are people lacking good from the past, perhaps we must say that it cannot be helped.

---

[26] *senju sennen ketsujō ōjō no toku* 専修専念決定往生の徳 . The virtue of faith, given by the Buddha. "Even dull-minded and negligent people who have neither wisdom nor even energy are born [in the Pure Land] if they realize the faith of the single practice and single-mindfulness" (*Songō shinzō meimon*, SSZ 2: 573 [T 83.692c]).

- Item: Although it seems that the Buddha-dharma has been flourishing in recent years, we hear that those who hold the position of priest are indeed the last ones to have any discussion whatsoever of faith. This is a deeply lamentable situation.
- Item: Although there are many ordinary followers who hear the truth of Other-Power faith, it is said that priests have been angry about this. This is preposterous!
- Item: There is a point to be borne in mind by each of those who come on pilgrimage from the countryside: it is inexcusable for them to discuss the Buddha-dharma with no hesitation over being among outsiders or being on main roads and byways, at checking stations and on ferry boats. This must definitely stop.
- Item: If there is a situation in which someone asks a nenbutsu person in our tradition what sect [he belongs to], he should not answer outright that he is a nenbutsu person of this sect. He should simply reply that he is a nenbutsu person of no particular sect. This, in other words, is the conduct [of one] who, as our master taught, will not be seen as a follower of the Buddha-dharma. Be thoroughly aware of this point and, outwardly, give no sign [of being a participant in our tradition]. This indeed is the right understanding in regard to the conduct of nenbutsu people in our tradition.
- Item: Even if you feel that you understand the significance of the Buddha-dharma — having listened through sliding doors or over a hedge — faith will be decisively settled [only] by your repeatedly and carefully asking others about its meaning. If you leave things to your own way of thinking, there will invariably be mistakes. It has been said recently that there are many such instances these days.
- Item: You should ask others, time after time, about what you have understood of faith, until Other-Power faith (*anjin*) is decisively settled. If you listen but once, there will surely be mistakes.

The above six items should be carefully borne in mind. I have noticed recently that, although everyone listens to the Buddha-dharma, there is no one who has undergone a true and real settling of faith by just hearing the teaching in a general way; consequently, [their realization of] the settled mind, too, is not as it should be.

Respectfully.
Bunmei 16 [1484].11.21.

IV-8 On eight items

The thanksgiving services on the twenty-eighth of this month are a tradition handed down from the past. Accordingly, this is the occasion on which followers from provinces far and near come with an earnest resolve to repay their indebtedness and express their gratitude [for the benevolence of Master Shinran]. There has been no lapse these days or in the past in the continual repetition of the nenbutsu, the saying of the Buddha's Name. This is the legacy of the founding master's transmission of the dharma, the peerless teaching that extends to all under heaven and across the four seas.

On this occasion of seven days and nights, therefore, let those persons who oppose the dharma in their lack of faith (*fushin*) attain the faith that leads to birth in the Pure Land. This in itself would serve as a repayment of indebtedness on the master's anniversary this month. It may be that those who fail to do so are lacking in resolve to repay their indebtedness and express their gratitude. For, among those who call themselves Shinshū nenbutsu people, there are some these days who have not truly — from the bottom of their hearts — undergone a decisive settling of our tradition's faith (*anjin*); some give every indication of expressing gratitude for [the sake of] reputation, others perfunctorily. This is a situation that should never be. For it is a lamentable state of affairs that those who come to the capital, having endured a journey of thousands of *ri* and undergone great hardship, should then be uselessly concerned with reputation or blindly follow others. It must be emphasized that this is extremely shallow thinking. But, for those lacking good from the past, this cannot be helped. If they make a full confession, however, and direct themselves toward the right-mindedness of the one mind [of faith],[27] they may yet achieve the master's fundamental intent.

- Item: Among those on pilgrimage from the various provinces, there are some who, regardless of where they are — even on main roads and thoroughfares, at checking stations and on

---

[27] *isshin no shōnen* 一心の正念 . In *Mattōshō*, Shinran writes of the right-mindedness that is Other Power: " 'Right-mindedness' refers to the settling of faith (*shingyō*) [given] through the Primal Vow. . . . This faith is the 'one mind'; the 'one mind' is the diamond-like mind; the diamond-like mind is the mind of great enlightenment" (SSZ 2: 656 [T 83.711a]).

ferry boats—talk to others openly about matters concerning the Buddha-dharma. This should not be.

• Item: In various places, there are many who praise rarely-encountered teachings that we do not discuss at all in our tradition; similarly, they use strange phrases not found in our sect's teachings. This is seriously mistaken thinking. From now on, it must definitely stop.

• Item: During this seven-day period of thanksgiving services, those whose faith is not settled should, without exception, make up their minds to repent and confess without holding back anything in their hearts and thus attain true and real faith.

• Item: There are some people who have not yet undergone any decisive settling of faith (*anjin*) and should for this reason raise their doubts. They keep these things to themselves, however, and do not talk openly about them. When we press and question them, they just try to evade the point, without saying frankly what is on their minds. This is inexcusable. They should speak unreservedly and thus ground themselves in true and real faith.

• Item: In recent years, priests who are pillars of the Buddha-dharma have been seriously lacking in faith while followers [of the tradition]—companions—have, on the contrary, undergone a decisive settling of faith. When they then talk about the priests' lack of faith, [the priests] become very angry. This is absurd. From now on, both priests and disciples must abide in the same faith.

• Item: Recently, there have been rumors of extremely heavy drinking on the part of those in the position of priest. This is outrageous; such a thing should not be. We do not tell those who drink intoxicants that they must stop altogether. [But] when there is heavy drinking, there are sure to be times when there is nothing but drunken confusion in connection with the Buddha-dharma and with followers; thus it is improper. If those in the priest's position stop on such occasions, they will indeed contribute to the prospering of the Buddha-dharma. If they are unable to stop completely, one cup may be permissible. It may follow as a matter of course that they do not stop because their aspiration in regard to the Buddha-dharma is weak. These are points that deserve deep reflection.

• Item: If those in whom faith is decisively settled have frequent discussions of faith with each other when there are meetings for fellow practicers, this will provide the basis on which the Shinshū will flourish.

- Item: It must be understood that the decisive settling of faith in our tradition is expressed by the six characters 南無阿弥陀仏 (na-mu-a-mi-da-butsu). Shan-tao explained long ago in his commentary: " 'Namu' means 'to take refuge.' It also signifies aspiring to be born and directing virtue. 'Amida-butsu' is the practice."[28]

When sentient beings take refuge in Amida—"namu," Amida Buddha, fully knowing those sentient beings, bestows on them the virtue of a myriad good deeds and practices, countless as the grains of sand in the river Ganges. This is what is meant by "Amida-butsu is the practice." Those who take refuge ("namu") are therefore one with the saving dharma of Amida Buddha; we speak of "the oneness in 'namu-amida-butsu' of the person [to be saved] and dharma [that saves]," indicating this point. We must bear in mind, therefore, that "namu-amida-butsu" expresses the full realization of perfect enlightenment [that was accomplished] when Amida Buddha vowed long ago (when he was the monk Dharmākara) that unless sentient beings attained buddhahood, he too would not attain perfect enlightenment. This, in other words, is evidence that our birth [in the Pure Land] is settled. Hence it should be concluded that our realization of Other-Power faith is expressed in just these six characters.

The significance of these eight items is as stated. Meanwhile, it has already been nine years since [we began] the construction of this temple.[29] During the thanksgiving services each year, everyone feels that he has fully heard and understood [the teaching] and undergone a decisive settling of faith, but as the meaning of that faith differs even as of yesterday and today, it may amount to nothing at all. But if those lacking faith (fushinjin) do not quickly attain true and real faith during the thanksgiving services this month—during this year's thanksgiving services in particular—it seems things will be the same, even with the passage of many years.

This foolish old man has, however, already passed his seventh decade and finds it difficult to anticipate next year's thanksgiving services. For this reason, if there are people who really and truly attain decisively settled faith (shin), I would consider [their realization] to be, first, an expression of gratitude to the master this month, and, next,

---

[28] Kangyōsho (Gengibun), SSZ 1: 457 (T 37.250ab); Kyōgyōshinshō, SSZ 2: 21 (T 83.594c). This quotation occurs again in letters 4:14 and 5:11.

[29] See chapter four, n. 65.

the fulfillment of a desire an old man has cherished over these seven or eight years.

Respectfully.
Bunmei 17 [1485].11.23.

IV-9 On an epidemic

Recently, people have been dying in great numbers, reportedly from an epidemic. It is not that they die primarily because of the epidemic. It is [because of] determinate karma that has been settled from the first moment of our birth. We should not be so deeply surprised by this. And yet when people die at this time, everyone thinks it strange. It is really quite reasonable.

Amida Tathāgata has declared that he will unfailingly save those sentient beings who single-heartedly rely on him—ordinary beings in the last age and people like ourselves, burdened with evil karma, however deep the evil may be.[30] At such a time as this, we should entrust ourselves to Amida Buddha all the more deeply and, realizing that we will be born in the land of utmost bliss, relinquish every bit of doubt, steadfastly and single-heartedly acknowledging how gracious Amida is. Once we have understood this, our saying "Namu-amida-butsu, Namu-amida-butsu"—sleeping or waking— is an expression of gratitude conveying our joy and thankfulness [that Amida] readily saves us in this way. This, in other words, is the nenbutsu of gratitude for Buddha's benevolence.

Respectfully.
Entoku 4 [1492].6.

IV-10 On the present age

Let all women living in the present age deeply entrust themselves with singleness of mind to Amida Tathāgata. Apart from that, they must realize, they will never be saved in [regard to] the afterlife, whatever teaching they may rely upon.

How, then, should they entrust themselves to Amida, and how should they aspire to the afterlife?

---

[30] A reference to the Eighteenth Vow. See letter 5:1.

They should have no doubt at all that there will unfailingly be deliverance for those who, without any worry, simply rely single-heartedly on Amida and entrust themselves [to him] to save them, [bringing them to buddhahood] in the afterlife. Once [they have understood] this, they should just say the nenbutsu in gratitude for Buddha's benevolence, recognizing it as [an expression of] thankfulness that there will assuredly be deliverance.

Respectfully.

Age 83.

(seal)

IV-11 On the oneness of the person [to be saved] and dharma [that saves]

What is the meaning of "namu-amida-butsu?" And further, how are we to entrust ourselves to Amida and attain birth in the fulfilled land?

What we must understand, first of all, is that we entrust ourselves to Amida by carefully discerning what the six characters "na-mu-a-mi-da-butsu" are all about. "Namu-amida-butsu" is essentially nothing other than the [entrusting] mind of us sentient beings who rely on Amida to save us, [bringing us to buddhahood] in the afterlife. In other words, Amida Tathāgata, fully knowing the sentient beings who entrust themselves, readily bestows virtue of unsurpassed, great benefit. This is what is meant by saying that he "directs virtue to sentient beings."[31] Therefore, because those who entrust themselves to Amida are inseparable from Amida Buddha's saving dharma, we speak of this as "the oneness in 'namu-amida-butsu' of the person [to be saved] and dharma [that saves]"; it has this meaning. We must bear in mind that this is Other-Power faith, through which our birth [in the Pure Land] is settled.

The writing of this [letter] was completed on the twenty-fifth day of the fifth month, Meiō 6 [1497].

Age 83.

---

[31] In *Jōdo monrui jushō*, Shinran writes, explaining the mind of entrusting: "The Tathāgata directs this joyful trust that is pure, true, and real to all sentient beings" (*Passages*, 51; SSZ 2: 452 [T 83.646a]).

IV-12 On monthly meetings

For what purpose have there come to be meetings twice each month?[32] They are [held] for the sake of realizing one's own faith, which leads to birth in the land of utmost bliss, and for nothing else. Although there have been "meetings" everywhere each month, from the past up until now, there is never anything at all that might be called a discussion of faith. In recent years in particular, when there have been meetings (wherever they have been), everyone has dispersed after nothing more than sake, rice, and tea. This is indeed contrary to the fundamental intent of the Buddha-dharma. Although each of those lacking faith (*fushin*) should by all means raise their doubts and discuss what it is to have faith or be without it, they take their leave without coming to any conclusions. This is not as it should be. You must reflect carefully on this matter. In brief, it is essential that each of those lacking faith (*fushin*) have discussions of faith with one another from now on.

The import of our tradition's settled mind is that, regardless of the depth of our own evil hindrances, there is no doubt whatsoever that [Amida] will save all sentient beings who simply put a stop to their inclination toward the sundry practices, single-heartedly take refuge in Amida Tathāgata, and deeply entrust themselves [to him] to save them in [regard to] the most important matter, [the birth] that is to come in the afterlife. Those who understand thoroughly in this way will indeed be born [in the Pure Land], one hundred out of one hundred.[33] Once [they have understood] this, if they recognize the holding of meetings each month as a repayment of indebtedness and expression of gratitude, they may indeed be named as practicers endowed with true and real faith.

Respectfully.

---

[32] During Rennyo's time, it was customary for Shinshū adherents to meet on Hōnen's and Shinran's death anniversaries. As Hōnen died on Kenryaku 2 (1212).1.25, it is likely that this letter marked the monthly observances for him.

[33] From *Ōjō raisange*, SSZ 1: 652 (T 47.439b), quoted by Shinran: "When . . . people continue utterance on utterance of Amida's Name to the very end of their lives, then if there are ten people, ten will be born; if one hundred, one hundred will be born. This is because there are no obstructing conditions. It is because they realize right-mindedness; because they are in accord with the Buddha's Primal Vow; because they do not deviate from the teaching; because they follow the Buddha's words" (*Teaching* 1:104; *Kyōgyōshinshō*, SSZ 2: 19 [T

Written on the twenty-fifth day of the second month, Meiō 7 [1498].
To the members of the congregations that meet twice each month.

Age 84.

IV-13 Reflections in early summer

Fall and spring have slipped away, and it is already the middle of early summer in this seventh year of Meiō; I have grown old — I am eighty-four. This particular year, however, I have been seriously beset by illness and, as a result, my whole body has suffered — ears, eyes, hands, and feet; I realize, then, that this in itself is the outcome of past karma and also the harbinger of birth in the land of utmost bliss. Master Hōnen said, pursuant to this, "Practicers who aspire for the Pure Land are filled with joy when they become ill";[34] these are his very words. And yet, it never occurs to me to rejoice over illness. I am a shameful person. This is disgraceful; it is deplorable. Nevertheless, according to our sect's teaching of "completing the cause [of birth in the Pure Land] in ordinary life, with the awakening of the one thought-moment [of entrusting]," I am now settled in the single path of faith (anjin). [My] saying of the Name in grateful return for Buddha's benevolence is therefore unceasing; walking, standing, sitting, or lying down, I am never forgetful.

What follows are the reflections of this foolish old man:

Generally speaking, in observing the attitude of followers of this sect in the various places where I have stayed, I have found no indication of faith being clearly and decisively settled. This is most lamentable. For if (in testimony to this old man having already lived some eighty years) there were a flourishing of practicers for whom faith was decisively settled, this might be considered the mark of a long life. But I see no sign at all of [faith] being clearly settled.

What are the grounds [for this lament]? Considering that the human realm is a place of uncertainty for young and old alike, we will surely undergo some sort of illness and die. Everyone must under-

---

83.594a]).

[34] Similar quotations appear in the forty-third fascicle of *Denzūkinyūshō* (Jōdoshū Kaishū Happyakunen Kinen Kyōsan Junbi Kyoku, ed. *Jōdoshū zensho* [Kyoto: Sankibō Busshorin, 1970], 3: 935), completed by Seikei in Ōei 2 (1395), and in the fourth fascicle of *Senjakushū shishūshō*, by Kōe. A source attributable

stand that, given the circumstances in a world like this, it is essential that faith be settled decisively and promptly—indeed, as soon as possible—and that we be assured of the birth to come in the land of utmost bliss. [It is also essential] that we live out our lives after that in conformity with the ordinary circumstances of human life. We must think seriously about this and, deep within, awaken the aspiration to entrust ourselves single-mindedly to Amida.

Respectfully.

Meiō 7 [1498], the first day

of the middle period of early summer.

Written by an old priest, eighty-four years of age.

If ever we are able to hear

the Name of Amida,

let us all entrust ourselves,

"Namu-amida-butsu."

IV-14 On our school's settled mind

Our school's settled mind is expressed by the six characters "na-mu-a-mi-da-butsu." This you should know. Master Shan-tao explains these six characters, saying, "'Namu' means 'to take refuge.' It also signifies aspiring to be born and directing virtue. 'Amida-butsu' is the practice. Because of this, we unfailingly attain birth."[35]

First, the two characters "na-mu" mean "to take refuge." "To take refuge" expresses the [entrusting] mind of sentient beings who rely on Amida Buddha to save them, [bringing them to buddhahood] in the afterlife. Then, "aspiring for birth and directing virtue" expresses the [Buddha's] mind that embraces and saves sentient beings who entrust themselves. This is the precise meaning of the four characters "a-mi-da-butsu."

What attitude should ignorant sentient beings like ourselves take, then, and how should we entrust ourselves to Amida?

When we abandon the sundry practices and steadfastly and single-heartedly rely on Amida to save us in [regard to] the afterlife, there is no doubt at all that we will be born without fail in the land of utmost bliss. Thus the two characters "na-mu" signify the sentient being, the person who relies on Amida. Further, the four characters "a-mi-da-

---

to Hōnen, however, has yet to be found. See Sugi, *Gobunshō kōwa*, 278–79.

butsu" express the dharma that saves sentient beings who entrust themselves. This, then, is precisely what we mean by "the oneness in 'namu-amida-butsu' of the person [to be saved] and dharma [that saves]." Through this teaching, we know that birth [in the Pure Land] for all of us sentient beings is realized in "namu-amida-butsu."

Respectfully.
Meiō 7 [1498].4.

IV-15 On building [the temple] at Osaka

After seeing Osaka (in Ikutama estate, Higashinari district, Settsu province) for the first time, I had a simple temple built promptly in the traditional way, surely through some link to the place from the past. [Building] began in the latter part of autumn in the fifth year of Meiō; as of this year, three years have already sped by.[36] I feel this to be none other than the result of profound conditions from the distant past.

My fundamental reason for being in this place, then, has never been to live out my life in tranquility, to seek wealth and fame, or to enjoy the beauty to be found in flowers and birds, the wind, and the moon; my only longing is that practicers of decisively settled faith may flourish and that fellow practicers who say the nenbutsu may come forth for the sake of the supreme enlightenment. Moreover, if there are any in the world who harbor prejudice [against us] or if any difficult issues arise, I will give up my attachment to this place and immediately withdraw. Therefore, if [everyone] — regardless of whether they are of noble or humble birth, priest or lay — could be brought to a definite settling of faith that is firm and diamondlike, this would truly be in accord with the Primal Vow of Amida Tathāgata and, in particular, in conformity with the fundamental intent of Master [Shinran].

It is extraordinary that, as of this year, this foolish old man has already lived to the age of eighty-four. And as this [life] may indeed have been in accord with the meaning of dharma in our tradition, I could know no greater satisfaction. But I have been ill since the summer of this year, and at present there is no sign of recovery. I feel it certain

---

[35] See n. 28 above.

[36] Rennyo's seventh son, Rengo, writes similarly of Rennyo's choice of this site, adding that the temple was to be the place of his retirement (*Rennyo Shōnin itokuki*, SSZ 3: 880). The building of the temple began in 1496, on the twenty-ninth day of the ninth month, and was finished by the eighth of the tenth

at last that I will not fail to attain my long-cherished desire of birth [in the Pure Land] during the coming winter. All I long for, morning and evening, is that there will be a decisive settling of faith for everyone while I am still alive. Although this does indeed depend on good from the past, there is never a moment when it is not on my mind. Moreover, it might even be considered the consequence of my having spent three years in this place. By all means, then, let there be a decisive settling of faith during this seven-day period of thanksgiving services so that everyone may realize the fundamental intent [of the dharma], birth in the land of utmost bliss.

Respectfully.

This letter is to be read, beginning on the twenty-first day of the eleventh month of Meiō 7 [1498], so that everyone may attain faith (*shin*).[37]

Shōnyo, disciple of Śākyamuni.
(written seal)

---

month (HN, 79).

[37] Rennyo wrote this letter in anticipation of the annual thanksgiving services, which were to be his last. Although this letter is the final one in *The Letters* to which a date can be assigned, two other dated letters follow in RSI: #157, 446–47, dated Meiō 7 (1498).11, and #158, 448–49, dated Meiō 7.12.15.

Fascicle Five

V-1 On lay men and women, lacking wisdom in the last age

Lay men and women, lacking wisdom in the last age, [should realize that] sentient beings who rely deeply and with singleness of mind on Amida Buddha and entrust themselves single-heartedly and stead-fastly (without ever turning their minds in any other direction) to the Buddha to save them are unfailingly saved by Amida Tathāgata, even if their evil karma is deep and heavy. This is the essence of the Eighteenth Vow of birth [in the Pure Land] through the nenbutsu.

Once [faith] has been decisively settled in this way, they should — sleeping or waking — repeat the nenbutsu, saying the Name of the Buddha as long as they live.

Respectfully.

V-2 On the eighty thousand teachings

It has been said that those who do not know [the importance of] the afterlife[1] are foolish, even though they may understand eighty thousand sūtras and teachings; those who know about the afterlife are wise, even though they may be unlettered men and women who have renounced the world while remaining in lay life.[2] The import of our tradition is, therefore, that for those who do not realize the significance

---

[1] *gose* 後世 . See fascicle one, n. 53.

[2] It seems likely that this passage draws on one of several texts included in *Tendai myōmoku shiruiju*, assembled by Jukei of Yokawa (one of the three geographical divisions of Enryaku-ji on Mt. Hiei; first established in 829). As the collection was completed in Kanshō 4 (1463), it would have been available as a source for this letter, which Sugi dates from Bunmei 5–6 (1473–1474; *Gobunshō kōwa*, 306–7). Of the works that make up the collection, three contain passages similar to Rennyo's: *Shōhōgekyō*, *Ruizōshō*, and *Shōhōnenkyō*. Considering the fact that additional texts could be cited as sources, the passage was clearly in common use (Izumoji, *Ofumi*, 321; Sugi, *Gobunshō kōwa*, 307–9). A related passage from *Ichigon hōdan* (Dennis Hirota, trans. *Plain Words on the Pure Land Way: Sayings of the Wandering Monks of Medieval Japan* [Kyoto: Ryūkoku University, 1989]) reads:

> You may become conversant with all eighty-thousand Buddhist teachings, but as one in the condition of human foolishness you will still be given to error. All that is critically important is the thought, "Buddha, save me!" (18).

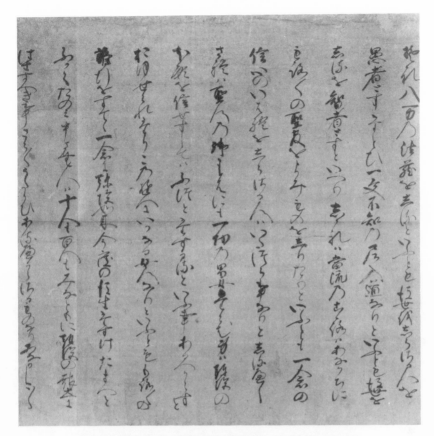

10. Rennyo's Letter "On the eighty thousand teachings"

of the one thought-moment of faith — even though they may diligently read the various scriptures and be widely informed — all is in vain. This you should know.

Therefore, as Master [Shinran] has said, no man or woman will ever be saved without entrusting to Amida's Primal Vow.[3] Hence there should be no doubt at all that those who abandon the sundry practices

---

[3] Shinran wrote:

In this fifth five-hundred-year period of the last age,
if the sentient beings of this world
do not entrust themselves to Amida Tathāgata's compassionate Vow,
there can be no moment of emancipation.

Shōzōmatsu wasan, SSZ 2: 517c (T 83.665a)

For a hymn referring to women and to the Thirty-fifth Vow, see fascicle one, n. 45.

and, with [the awakening of] the one thought-moment, deeply entrust themselves to Amida Tathāgata to save them in [regard to] the afterlife will all be born in Amida's fulfilled land, whether ten persons or one hundred—whatever sort of [men or] women they may be.

Respectfully.

V-3 On women who have renounced the world while remaining in lay life and on ordinary women

Women who have renounced the world while remaining in lay life and ordinary women as well should realize and have absolutely no doubt whatsoever that there is deliverance for all those who simply rely deeply (single-heartedly and steadfastly) on Amida Buddha and entrust themselves to [the Buddha] to save them, [bringing them to buddhahood] in the afterlife. This is the Primal Vow of Other Power, the Vow of Amida Tathāgata. Once [they have realized] this, when they then feel the thankfulness and joy of being saved in [regard to] the afterlife, they should simply repeat "Namu-amida-butsu, Namu-amida-butsu."

Respectfully.

V-4 On men and women

Those of deep evil karma, both men and women, [should realize that] even if they entrust themselves to the compassionate vows of the various buddhas, it is extremely difficult for them [to be saved] by the power of those buddhas since the present period is the evil world of the last age.[4] Therefore, the one we revere as Amida Tathāgata, surpassing all [other] buddhas, made the great Vow that he would save even evildoers who have committed the ten transgressions and the five

---

[4] Buddhas other than Amida have pitied sentient beings but have been unable to save them in their existence as ordinary beings in the last age. Rennyo also refers in *The Letters* to those who were simply omitted from other buddhas' vows—women and those guilty of the ten transgressions and the five grave offenses. In *Shōzōmatsu wasan*, Shinran explains that, although it has been possible to awaken the aspiration for enlightenment under innumerable buddhas who have appeared in the world, sentient beings have been incapable of fulfilling the aspiration (SSZ 2: 518b [T 83.665b]).

grave offenses; [fulfilling the Vow,] he became Amida Buddha. Since it is Amida who vowed that he would not attain enlightenment if he failed to save sentient beings who deeply rely on this Buddha and single-mindedly entrust themselves [to him] to save them, there is no doubt at all that they will be born in the land of utmost bliss.

Hence it is certain that those who, without doubting, deeply (single-heartedly and steadfastly) entrust themselves to Amida Tathāgata to save them, leave their deep evil karma to the Buddha, and undergo a settling of the one thought-moment of faith will all be born in the Pure Land — ten out of ten, one hundred out of one hundred. Once [they have realized] this, then when a sense of awe wells up in their hearts, they should say the nenbutsu, "Namu-amida-butsu, Namu-amida-butsu," whatever the hour, wherever they may be. This, in other words, is the nenbutsu of gratitude for the Buddha's benevolence.

Respectfully.

V-5 On realizing faith

Realizing faith means understanding the Eighteenth Vow. Under-standing this Vow means understanding what "namu-amida-butsu" is. For within the one thought-moment of taking refuge — "namu" — there is aspiration for birth and directing of virtue.[5] This, in other words, is the mind that Amida Tathāgata directs to ordinary beings. In the *Larger Sūtra*, this is explained as "enabling all sentient beings to fulfill their virtue."[6] Thus it is taught that the evil karma and blind passions accumulated from the beginningless past are extinguished (with no traces remaining) by the inconceivable working of the Vow, and that we dwell in the company of those [whose birth in the Pure Land is] truly settled, in the stage of nonretrogression. This, then, is what we mean by "attaining nirvāṇa without severing blind passions."[7] This is a matter presented exclusively in our tradition; there should be no discussion of the above with those of other traditions. Bear this carefully in mind.

Respectfully.

---

[5] See fascicle two, n. 40.

[6] *Larger Sūtra*, SSZ 1: 15 (T 12.269c).

[7] *Kyōgyōshinshō*, SSZ 2: 44 (T 83.600a).

V-6 On the great benefit bestowed with [the awakening of] the one thought-moment [of faith]

In the *Hymns [on the Last Age]*,[8] Master [Shinran] states that virtue of unsurpassed and great benefit is bestowed on practicers who, with [the awakening of] the one thought-moment, entrust themselves to Amida:

> When sentient beings of this evil world of the five defilements[9]
> entrust themselves to the selected Primal Vow,[10]
> indescribable, inexplicable, and inconceivable virtue
> fills the existence of these practicers.[11]

In this hymn, "sentient beings of this evil world of the five defilements" refers to all of us, [including] women and evildoers. Therefore, although we are such wretched beings who commit evil throughout our lives, there is no doubt at all that those who rely single-heartedly and steadfastly on Amida Tathāgata and entrust themselves to [the Buddha] to save them in [regard to] the afterlife will unfailingly be saved. Amida bestows "indescribable, inexplicable, and inconceivable great virtue" on those who entrust themselves in this way.

"Indescribable, inexplicable, and inconceivable virtue" means unlimited great virtue. Because this great virtue is directed to us sentient beings who single-mindedly entrust ourselves to Amida, karma-hindrances of the three periods of the past, future, and present are

---

[8] *Shōzōmatsu wasan.*

[9] *gojoku akuse* 五濁悪世 . The five types of defilements prevalent (and interrelated) in the last dharma-age are, according to one explanation: (1) defilement of the age itself, with an increase of wars, plagues, and famine, all contributing to societal and environmental defilement; (2) defiled views, with the spread of evil views; (3) defiled passion, characterized by an increase of greed, anger, confusion, and corruption; (4) defiled beings, characterized by a deterioration of effects from past acts, dull minds, weak bodies, and an increase of suffering, all resulting in an overall decline in the quality of human life; and (5) defiled life, with the human lifespan becoming progressively shorter, decreasing to ten years at the end of the period (BGDJ, 369).

[10] *senjaku hongan* 選択本願 . The term may refer in general to the Forty-eight Vows chosen by the monk Dharmākara; it has come to refer specifically to the Eighteenth, as it does here, because that Vow singles out the nenbutsu as the cause of birth in the Pure Land.

[11] *Shōzōmatsu wasan*, SSZ 2: 519c (T 83.665c).

instantly extinguished, and we are established in the stage of those who are truly settled, or in the stage equal to perfect enlightenment. Again, this is expressed in the *Hymns [on the Last Age]*:

> Entrust yourselves to the Primal Vow of Amida.
> All those who entrust themselves to the Primal Vow will,
> through the benefit of being embraced and never abandoned,
> reach [the stage] equal to perfect enlightenment.[12]

"Being embraced and never abandoned" also means that sentient beings who single-mindedly entrust themselves to Amida are received within the [Buddha's] light, and since the entrusting mind does not change, they will not be forsaken. Although there are various teachings besides this, there should never be any doubt that sentient beings who entrust themselves solely to Amida in the one thought-moment will, each and every one, be born in the fulfilled land.

Respectfully.

V-7 On the five obstacles and the three submissions

Because the bodily existence of women is defined by the five obstacles and the three submissions, they are burdened with deep evil karma exceeding that of men. For this reason, the buddhas of the ten directions[13] can never, by their own power, bring any woman to buddhahood. Yet Amida Tathāgata, having made the great Vow[14] that he himself would save women, delivers them. Without entrusting herself to this Buddha, a woman is unable to become a buddha.

What attitude should [a woman] have, then, and how should she entrust herself to Amida Buddha and become a buddha?

By just entrusting herself solely to Amida Buddha (with no double-mindedness, with steadfastness, and with the single thought that [Amida] saves her in [regard to] the afterlife), [a woman] will readily

---

[12] This hymn appears to be a combination of the first two lines of *Shōzōmatsu wasan*, hymn #1 (SSZ 2: 516a), and the last two lines of hymn #25 (519a). See also T 83.664bc, 665b.

[13] These are buddhas other than Amida throughout the universe, the ten directions being the four cardinal points, the four intermediate directions, the zenith, and the nadir.

[14] The Thirty-fifth of the Forty-eight Vows in the *Larger Sūtra* SSZ 1: 12 (T 12.268c); see fascicle one, n. 64.

become a buddha. If this mind is free of the slightest doubt, she will unfailingly go to the land of utmost bliss and become a splendid buddha.

Once [she understands] this, what she must then bear in mind is that whenever she says the nenbutsu, she says [it] only to express her joy and thankfulness for the benevolence of Amida Tathāgata who readily saves such a wretched being as herself. Let [this] be understood.

Respectfully.

V-8 On the meditation of five kalpas

Both the Primal Vow following the meditation of five kalpas and the practice of innumerable, measureless kalpas are simply compassionate means to save all of us sentient beings without fail. To this end, Amida Tathāgata underwent painstaking endeavors and made the Primal Vow, "namu-amida-butsu"; he became "namu-amida-butsu," having vowed that he would not attain enlightenment if he failed to save sentient beings (erring beings) who, with [the awakening of] the one thought-moment, entrust themselves to Amida Buddha, abandon the sundry practices, and rely on Amida steadfastly and single-heartedly. We should know that this is precisely why we can be born readily in the land of utmost bliss.

The meaning of the six characters "na-mu-a-mi-da-butsu" is, therefore, that all sentient beings are to be born in the fulfilled land. For when we take refuge—"namu"—Amida Buddha immediately saves us. Hence the two characters "na-mu" express sentient beings' turning to Amida Tathāgata and entrusting themselves [to Amida] to save them, [bringing them to buddhahood] in the afterlife. We must realize that those who entrust themselves to Amida in this way are saved without exception; this itself is the essence of the four characters "a-mi-da-butsu."

Therefore, those who abandon the sundry practices and wholeheartedly entrust themselves [to Amida] to save them in [regard to] the afterlife (even if they are women burdened with the ten transgressions and the five grave offenses, the five obstacles and the three submissions) will be saved without exception—each and every one, whether there are ten persons or one hundred. Those who believe this without doubting will be born in Amida's true and real Pure Land.

Respectfully.

V-9 On all the scriptures

The meaning of settled mind in our tradition is wholly expressed by six characters, "na-mu-a-mi-da-butsu." That is, when we take refuge — "namu" — Amida Buddha immediately saves us. Hence the two characters "na-mu" mean "taking refuge." "Taking refuge" signifies the mind of sentient beings who abandon the sundry practices and steadfastly entrust themselves to Amida Buddha to save them, [bringing them to buddhahood] in the afterlife. [The four characters "a-mi-da-butsu"] express the mind of Amida Tathāgata who, fully knowing sentient beings, saves them without exception.

Accordingly, since Amida Buddha saves sentient beings who entrust themselves — "namu" — we know that the import of the six characters "na-mu-a-mi-da-butsu" is precisely that all of us sentient beings are equally saved. Hence our realization of Other-Power faith is itself expressed by the six characters "na-mu-a-mi-da-butsu." We should recognize, therefore, that all the scriptures have the sole intent of bringing us to entrust ourselves to the six characters "na-mu-a-mi-da-butsu."

Respectfully.

V-10 On faith as fundamental

What is taught by Master [Shinran] and in his school is that faith is fundamental. For when we cast away the sundry practices and single-heartedly take refuge in Amida, birth [in the Pure Land] is assured by the Buddha through the inconceivable working of the Vow. [Attaining] this state is also described as "entering, with the awakening of the one thought-moment [of entrusting], the company of those [whose birth is] truly settled."[15] The nenbutsu, saying the Name of the Buddha, should then be understood as the nenbutsu of grateful return for Amida's benevolence, through which the Tathāgata has established our birth.

Respectfully.

---

[15] See fascicle one, n. 12.

V-11 On the anniversary [of Master Shinran's death]

Among those who make the pilgrimage, bring offerings, and come before the [image of] Master [Shinran] to repay their indebtedness and express their gratitude during this anniversary, there will be those who have realized faith. There will also be those who are lacking in faith (*fushinjin*). This is an extremely serious matter. For unless there is a decisive settling of faith, the birth that is to come in the fulfilled land is uncertain. Therefore, those whose faith is lacking (*fushin*) should in all haste attain the decisive mind.

The human realm is a place of uncertainty. The land of utmost bliss is one of eternity. Hence we should not make our abode in the uncertain human realm, but rather, aspire to [birth in] the eternal land of utmost bliss. In our tradition, therefore, the matter of faith is placed before all else; unless we are fully aware of the reason for this, everything is meaningless. We must promptly undergo a decisive settling of faith (*anjin*) and aspire to birth in the Pure Land.

What is widespread in the world and what everyone has in mind is that if they just say the Name with their lips, without any understanding, they will be born in the land of utmost bliss. That is most uncertain. Receiving Other-Power faith is a matter of fully knowing the import of the six characters "na-mu-a-mi-da-butsu" and, by this, undergoing a settling of faith.

As for the substance of faith, [a passage] in the [*Larger*] *Sūtra* states: "Hear the Name and realize faith and joy."[16] Shan-tao has said: "'Namu' [means] 'to take refuge.' It also signifies aspiring to be born and directing virtue. 'Amida-butsu' is the practice."[17] The meaning of the two characters "na-mu" is that we abandon the sundry practices and, without doubting, entrust ourselves single-heartedly and steadfastly to Amida Buddha. The meaning of the four characters "a-mi-da-butsu" is that, without any effort on our part, [Amida] saves sentient beings who single-heartedly take refuge in him. This is the very essence of the four characters "a-mi-da-butsu." To understand "namu-amida-butsu" in this way is, therefore, to receive faith. This, in other words, is [the understanding of] the nenbutsu practicer who has fully realized Other-Power faith.

Respectfully.

---

[16] See fascicle one, n. 89.
[17] See fascicle four, n. 28.

V-12 On [Amida's] sleeve

Those who wish to know in full what settled mind means in our tradition need no wisdom or learning at all. For when we simply realize that we are wretched beings of deep evil karma and know that the only Buddha who saves even such persons as this is Amida Tathāgata, and when, without any contriving, but with the thought of holding fast to the sleeve of this Buddha Amida, we entrust ourselves [to him] to save us, [bringing us to buddhahood] in the afterlife, then Amida Tathāgata deeply rejoices and, sending forth from himself eighty-four thousand great rays of light, receives us within that light. Hence this is explained in the [Contemplation] Sūtra: "The light shines throughout the worlds of the ten directions, and sentient beings mindful of the Buddha are embraced, never to be abandoned."[18] This you should know.

There is, then, no anxiety over becoming a buddha. How incomparable is the all-surpassing Primal Vow! And how gracious is Amida Tathāgata's light! Without encountering the [receptive] condition of this light,[19] there can be no cure at all for the fearful sickness of ignorance and karma-hindrance, which has been ours from the beginningless past.

Prompted by the condition of this light, and with the ripening of good from the past, we assuredly attain Other-Power faith now. It is immediately clear, however, that this is faith granted by Amida Tathāgata. Hence we know now, beyond question, that this is not faith generated by the practicer, but that it is Amida Tathāgata's great Other-Power faith. Accordingly, all those who have once attained Other-Power faith should reflect gratefully on Amida Tathāgata's benevolence and repeat the nenbutsu, saying the Name of the Buddha always, in gratitude for Buddha's benevolence.

Respectfully.

---

[18] See fascicle two, n. 16.

[19] This metaphor draws on a passage in *Kyōgyōshinshō*, SSZ 2: 33 (T 83.597b), which analyzes the cause and conditions for birth. Shinran's *Mattōshō*, SSZ 2: 694 (T 83.722a), closes with the same metaphor: "The Name fulfilled in the Primal Vow is the active cause of our birth; in other words, it is our father. The radiant light of great compassion is the receptive condition for our birth; it is our mother" (*Letters*, 64).

V-13 On the unsurpassed,
most profound virtues and benefits

Since the phrase "namu-amida-butsu" consists of only six characters, we may not realize that it has such virtue;[20] yet the magnitude of the unsurpassed, most profound virtues and benefits[21] within this Name of six characters is absolutely beyond measure. We should know, therefore, that the realization of faith is contained in these six characters. There is absolutely no faith apart from this, outside of the six characters.

Shan-tao explains the six characters of this "na-mu-a-mi-da-butsu," saying, "'Namu' means 'to take refuge.' It also signifies aspiring to be born and directing virtue. 'Amida-butsu' is the practice. Because of this, we unfailingly attain birth."[22]

How should we understand this explanation?

[The answer is that] if, with [the awakening of] the one thought-moment [of entrusting], a person takes refuge in Amida Buddha — even if [his is] an existence like ours, burdened with evil karma and blind passions — [Amida], knowing that person, will save him without fail. In other words, "taking refuge" means that we entrust ourselves [to Amida] to save us. [Amida's] bestowal of unsurpassed and great benefit on sentient beings who entrust themselves in the one thought-moment is called "aspiring to be born and directing virtue." Because [Amida] bestows on us sentient beings great goodness and great virtue[23] through [his] "aspiring to be born and directing virtue," the evil

---

[20] *kunō* 功能 : literally, "virtuous working" or "virtuous activity."

[21] In *Kyōgyōshinshō*, SSZ 2: 20 (T 83.594a), Shinran quotes Shan-tao's explanation of these virtues and benefits:

> Question: What virtues and benefits in the present life accrue from saying the Name of Amida Buddha and worshipping and contemplating him?

> Answer: If one utters a single voicing of "Amida Buddha," one immediately eradicates the grave karmic evil that will bind one to eighty billion kalpas of birth-and-death.

> *Teaching*, 1: 105–6.

[22] *Kangyōsho* (*Gengibun*), SSZ 1: 457 (T 37.250ab); *Kyōgyōshinshō*, SSZ 2: 21, 22 (T 83.594c). A slight extension of the quotation found in letters 4:8, 4:14, and 5:11.

[23] *daizen daikudoku* 大善大功徳 . A term corresponding to *zengon* 善根 , "roots of good" — good acts producing good results. *Zengon* occurs in letters 3:4 and 4:3.

karma and blind passions accumulated over myriads of kalpas from the beginningless past are instantly extinguished; hence our blind passions and evil karma all disappear, and we dwell even now in the company of those [whose birth in the Pure Land is] truly settled, in the stage of non-retrogression.[24]

We understand more and more clearly, then, that the six characters "na-mu-a-mi-da-butsu" affirm that we are to be born in the land of utmost bliss. Therefore, one who fully understands the meaning of the six characters of the Name—"settled mind," or "faith"—is said to be a person who has realized great faith given by Other Power. Since there is this incomparable teaching, let us deeply entrust ourselves.

Respectfully.

V-14 On [women of] noble and humble birth

We must realize that, unbeknownst to others, all women have deep evil karma;[25] whether of noble or humble birth, they are wretched beings. How, then, should they entrust themselves to Amida?

[The answer is that] women who rely firmly and without any anxiety on Amida Tathāgata and accept that [Amida] saves them in [regard to] the most important matter, the afterlife, will unfailingly be saved. If, leaving the depth of their evil to Amida,[26] they simply rely single-heartedly on Amida Tathāgata to save them in [regard to] the afterlife, there is no doubt that [Amida], fully knowing those beings, will save

---

[24] *futaiten* 不退転 . Originally, the term described a bodhisattva whose enlightenment was assured as the result of a non-dichotomous realization of suchness; in Pure Land thought, it describes those whose birth in the Pure Land enables them, through further practice, to attain enlightenment. For Shinran and Rennyo, those who have realized faith have reached the stage of non-retrogression, having "entered the ocean of Amida's Primal Vow" (*Passages*, s.v. "Non-retrogression," 100).

[25] The traditionally-held contrast is between women's outward appearance and their inner condition. See Sugi, *Gobunshō kōwa*, 376.

[26] To do this is to take the necessary step of abandoning self-power. Shinran clarifies this process in *Yuishinshō mon'i*:

"To abandon the mind of self-power" admonishes the various and diverse kinds of people . . . to abandon the conviction that one is good, to cease relying on the self, to stop reflecting knowingly on one's evil heart, and further to abandon the judging of people as good and bad.

Essentials, 40; SSZ 2: 628 (T 83.701c)

them. Whether there are ten persons or one hundred, they need not have the slightest doubt whatsoever that all — each and every one — will be born in the land of utmost bliss. Women who entrust themselves in this way will be born in the Pure Land. They should entrust themselves ever more deeply to Amida Tathāgata, realizing how shameful it is that until now they have not trusted such an easy way.

Respectfully.

V-15 On the Primal Vow of Amida Tathāgata

What sort of sentient being does the Primal Vow of Amida Tathāgata save? Also, how do we entrust ourselves to Amida, and through what attitude are we saved?

To begin with, in regard to the persons [to be saved], even if they are evildoers who have committed the ten transgressions and the five grave offenses or women burdened with the five obstacles and the three submissions, they should not be concerned about the depth and weight of their evil karma. It is only by great faith alone, Other Power, that we realize birth in the true and real land of utmost bliss.

As for faith, then, what should our attitude be, and how should we entrust ourselves to Amida?

In realizing faith, we simply cast off the sundry practices and disciplines and the evil mind of self-power and, without any doubts, single-heartedly and deeply take refuge in Amida. This we call true and real faith. Amida Tathāgata, fully knowing the sentient beings who single-heartedly and steadfastly entrust themselves in this way, graciously sends forth rays of light, receives these beings within the light, and enables them to be born in the land of utmost bliss. We speak of this as "[Amida's light] embracing sentient beings [who are practicers] of the nenbutsu."[27]

Beyond this, even though we say the nenbutsu throughout our lives, we should understand that it is the nenbutsu of gratitude for the Buddha's benevolence. With this, one is to be declared a nenbutsu practicer who has fully realized our tradition's faith.

Respectfully.

---

[27] See fascicle one, n. 33.

V-16 On white bones

When we deeply consider the transiency of this world, [we realize that] what is altogether fleeting is our own span of life: it is like an illusion from beginning to end. And so we have not yet heard of anyone living ten thousand years. A lifetime passes quickly. Can anyone now live to be a hundred? Will I die first, or will my neighbor? Will it be today or tomorrow? We do not know. Those we leave behind and those who go before us are more numerous than the dewdrops that rest briefly beneath the trees and on their leaftips.[28] Hence we may have radiant faces in the morning, but in the evening be no more than white bones.[29]

With the coming of the wind of impermanence, both eyes are instantly closed, and when a single breath is forever stilled, the radiant face is drained of life, and its vibrant glow is lost. Although family and relatives may gather and grieve broken-heartedly, this is to no avail. As there is nothing else to be done, [the once-familiar form] is taken to an outlying field, and when it has vanished with the midnight smoke, nothing is left but white bones. This is indeed indescribably sad.

And so, because the impermanence of this world creates a condition of uncertainty for young and old alike, we should all immediately take to heart the most important matter, the afterlife, and, deeply entrusting ourselves to Amida Buddha, say the nenbutsu.

Respectfully.

---

[28] This paragraph differs only slightly from a passage found in *Mujō kōshiki*, written by Emperor Gotoba (1180–1239) while in exile. See *Mujō kōshiki*, in Hosokawa Gyōshin, "'Hakkotsu no ofumi' sakugenkō," Hiramatsu Reizō Sensei Koki Kinenkai, ed., *Nihon no shūkyō to bunka* (Kyoto: Dōbōsha, 1989), 420. See also a passage by Zonkaku, which, written in 1356, draws on the Emperor's words: *Zonkaku hōgo*, SSZ 3: 360. The dewdrop imagery provides a metaphor for the uncertainty of human life; for a detailed discussion of this, see Izumoji, *Ofumi*, 349–50.

[29] This sentence is based on a poem in *Wakan rōeishū* (c. 1013), compiled by Fujiwara Kintō (966–1041). See Hosokawa, "'Hakkotsu no ofumi' sakugenkō," 414–15.

V-17 On all women

All women — if they are concerned about the afterlife and have a sense of reverence for the Buddha-dharma — should simply entrust themselves deeply to Amida Tathāgata, cast off the sundry practices, and rely single-heartedly and firmly [on Amida] to save them, [bringing them to buddhahood] in the afterlife. They should have no doubt whatsoever that [such] women will be born without fail in the land of utmost bliss. After they have understood this, then — sleeping or waking — they should just say, "Namu-amida-butsu, Namu-amida-butsu," realizing deeply and wholeheartedly how gracious and wonderful it is that Amida Tathāgata readily receives them within his saving work. We speak of these [women] as people of the nenbutsu who have received faith.

Respectfully.

V-18 On Master [Shinran] of our tradition

[In realizing] the settled mind expounded by Master [Shinran] of our tradition, we first, without any calculating, cast off our wretchedness and the depth of our evil and dismiss any inclination toward the sundry practices and disciplines; and then, with [the awakening of] the one thought-moment, we entrust ourselves single-heartedly and deeply to Amida Tathāgata to save us, [bringing us to buddhahood] in the afterlife. All those who do this will be saved without exception, ten out of ten, or one hundred out of one hundred. There should not be the slightest doubt about this. Those who fully understand in this way are called "practicers of faith."

Once [we have realized] this, when we then think of the joy of being saved in the afterlife, we should — sleeping or waking — say "Namu-amida-butsu, Namu-amida-butsu."

Respectfully.

V-19 On evildoers of the last age

Let all evildoers and women of the last age deeply entrust themselves with singleness of mind to Amida Buddha. Apart from that, whatever dharma they may rely upon, they will never be saved in [regard to] the afterlife.

How, then, should they entrust themselves to Amida Tathāgata and how should they aspire for the afterlife? They should have no doubt at all that there will unfailingly be deliverance for those who simply rely single-heartedly and firmly on Amida Tathāgata and deeply entrust themselves [to Amida] to save them, [bringing them to buddhahood] in the afterlife.

Respectfully.[30]

V-20 On women attaining buddhahood

All women who firmly rely on Amida Tathāgata and entrust themselves [to Amida] to save them in [regard to] the afterlife will unfailingly be delivered. For, concerning women abandoned by all [other] buddhas, Amida Tathāgata himself made the supreme great Vow,[31] thinking, "If I do not save women, which of the other buddhas will save them?"

Resolving to go beyond all [other] buddhas and save women, he meditated for five kalpas; undergoing practices for measureless kalpas, he made the all-surpassing great Vow.[32] Thus it is Amida who originated the incomparable Vow, "Women's Attainment of Buddhahood." For this reason, women who deeply rely on Amida and entrust themselves [to him] to save them in [regard to] the afterlife will all be born in the land of utmost bliss.

Respectfully.

V-21 On passages in the [*Larger*] *Sūtra* and in [T'an-luan's] commentary

[The meaning] of settled mind in our tradition [is that] we abandon

---

[30] This letter is similar to 4:10, in which Rennyo notes that he is 83; the year is Meiō 6 [1497].

[31] The Thirty-fifth Vow. See fascicle one, n. 64.

[32] Sugi points out that, more correctly, after meditating for five kalpas, Amida made the Vow; undergoing practices for measureless kalpas, he brought the Vow to fulfillment (*Gobunshō kōwa*, 402).

the inclination towards the sundry practices and disciplines; whatever our evil karma may be (even though it is deep), we leave that to the Buddha and simply, with [the awakening of] the one thought-moment, entrust ourselves single-heartedly and deeply to Amida Tathāgata. Sentient beings who rely on [Amida] to save them will all be delivered, ten out of ten or one hundred out of one hundred. There should not be the slightest doubt whatsoever about this. We speak of those who entrust themselves in this way as people in whom faith (anjin) is firmly and rightly settled.

Passages in the [Larger] Sūtra and in [T'an-luan's] commentary express this clearly, stating that "with the awakening of the one thought-moment [of entrusting], we dwell in the company of those [whose birth in the Pure Land is] truly settled";[33] this refers to "practicers who have completed the cause [for birth in the Pure Land] in ordinary life." We must, therefore, bear in mind that simply entrusting ourselves deeply to Amida Buddha with [the awakening of] the one thought-moment is of the utmost importance. Other than this, we should say the nenbutsu always — walking or resting, sitting or lying down — realizing the profound benevolence of Amida Tathāgata who readily saves us.

Respectfully.

V-22 On the import of our tradition's teaching

Those who seek to know thoroughly the meaning of our tradition's teaching and be born in the land of utmost bliss must first of all know about Other-Power faith.

What is the essential point of Other-Power faith?

It is the provision by which wretched ordinary beings like ourselves go readily to the Pure Land.

In what way does Other-Power faith find expression? We simply entrust ourselves exclusively to Amida Tathāgata, single-heartedly and steadfastly, and with the awakening of the one thought-moment in which we realize that Amida saves us, Amida Tathāgata unfailingly sends forth his embracing light and keeps us safe within this light as long as we are in this world. It is precisely in this state that our birth is assured.

Thus "namu-amida-butsu" expresses the attaining of Other-Power faith. We must bear in mind that this faith is the source of

---

[33] See fascicle one, n. 12.

"namu-amida-butsu." Then, because we receive this one Other-Power faith, there is no doubt at all that we will be born readily in the land of utmost bliss. How incomparable is Amida Tathāgata's Primal Vow!

How are we to respond to this gracious benevolence of Amida?

Simply by saying, "Namu-amida-butsu," sleeping or waking, we respond to Amida Tathāgata's benevolence.

With what mind, then, do we say "Namu-amida-butsu"?

Think of it as the rejoicing mind that realizes how gracious and wonderful it is that Amida Tathāgata saves us.

Respectfully.

Shōnyo, disciple of Śākyamuni

(written seal)[34]

---

[34] This letter is almost identical to the latter half of 2:14, dated Bunmei 6 (1474).7.5.

THE LEGACY

The Legacy

> Having reflected on the inferior ability of beings of the last age, examined the sūtras and commentaries and the explanations of the masters and their disciples, and grasped the essential point for readily-attainable birth [in the Pure Land] for ignorant, ordinary people, [Rennyo] wrote many important letters, beginning about the first year of the Kanshō era [1460]. They are a clear light for the last age (*matsudai no meitō* 末代の明燈) and the sole guide for this defiled world.
>
> Rengo[1]

RENNYO'S SPOKEN and written words are his greatest legacy – the writers of his memoirs affirm this again and again. Although they recall what he said at length and in detail, their gratitude focuses on his letters and on the teaching conveyed through them. For Rengo, Rennyo's seventh son, these letters are a beacon, the only source of help in the last dharma-age. Jitsugo, the tenth son, writes: "Day after day we hear the golden words of the letters; he has given us jewels."[2] And again, from Jitsugo's record: "It should be understood that the letters are the direct teaching of the Tathāgata. When we look at them, [we find] Hōnen; when we hear the words, [we realize that] they are the direct teaching of Amida."[3]

We begin this third part of our study with a chapter reviewing the process by which random collections of Rennyo's letters were formally compiled into a canonical work, *The Letters*, and came to serve as scripture. Recognized as authoritative for interpreting Shinran's teaching, this text has provided the framework and doctrinal foundation for Shinshū tradition, including a confessional statement and a document issued to settle a divisive controversy within the Nishi Honganji over the meaning of faith.

Given that this compilation of Rennyo's letters is his major legacy,

---

[1] *Rennyo Shōnin itokuki*, SSZ 3: 870.
[2] *Jitsugo kyūki*, RSG, 130; *Goichidaiki kikigaki*, SSZ 3: 605.
[3] *Jitsugo kyūki*, RSG, 85; *Goichidaiki kikigaki*, SSZ 3: 563.

we move in chapter six to an examination of the role it has played in Shinshū history in defining orthodox Shinshū piety as gratitude. This gratitude is marked by two ideal qualities, or aspects: an absence of self-power calculation and unquestioning commitment to honoring social obligations.

The non-calculating aspect emerges in Rennyo's interpretation of the nenbutsu as a spontaneous expression of gratitude coincident with the realization of faith. This is exemplified in the lives of saintly people who came to be known in the Shinshū as *myōkōnin* 妙好人 , for whom a prototype is Dōshū of Akao, one of Rennyo's most loyal disciples.

The second aspect, the honoring of social obligations at all costs, grew out of Rennyo's unrelenting desire to restore the Honganji and to foster its growth at every opportunity. This led, in turn, to a consistent pattern of accommodation with those in positions of political power, as well as to a centralization of authority within the Honganji's institutional hierarchy. A piety allied with power, both within and without, is all too evident in prerogatives assumed by the family council (*ikkeshū* 一家衆), which Rennyo established, and by his successors in the leadership of the Honganji; after his death, the council and the head priest came to wield absolute authority over the lives of Shinshū adherents. The authority to excommunicate members of the Honganji—to judge who was saved and who was not—was, in effect, authority to decide who was to live and who to die, given the harsh social conditions facing those separated from their communities in sixteenth-century Japan.[4]

In chapter seven, the discussion of Rennyo's definition of orthodox Shinshū piety as gratitude leads into an examination of the Nishi Honganji's relationship to the modern nation-state based on the concept *shinzoku nitai*. The study concludes with a chapter presenting several instances of Rennyo's legacy at work through *The Letters* in modern times.

---

[4] On the development of the authority to excommunicate vested in the leadership of the Honganji, see Kasahara, *Shinshū ni okeru itan no keifu*, 181–223. See also Solomon, "Kinship and the Transmission of Religious Charisma," 409–11, for a discussion of the family council and its exercise of authority.

Chapter 5

Scripture: *The Letters*

THE LETTERS OF RENNYO,[1] written in colloquial Japanese, have been compared to Martin Luther's translation of the Bible into German. Both Rennyo and Luther (1483–1584), virtually contemporaries, participated in religious reformation in opposing the established religious institutions of their day, in suffering persecution, and in becoming involved in some way with popular uprisings of farmers.[2] A point to underscore here is that, through translation into the vernacular, each made readily available a scriptural tradition for the general populace in their respective times and places; a second point, a commonplace, is that every translation is an interpretation that adds to, as well as subtracts from, the words originally spoken or written. To the extent the latter holds true for Luther, so much more does it apply for Rennyo, who, in authoring his letters, reformulated and simplified Shinran's teaching in his effort to communicate effectively at a popular level.

We have seen that Rennyo's initiation into the Honganji branch of the Shinshū under the prolonged tutelage of his father and grandfather was, in large measure, an introduction to a Pure Land textual tradition. Through a process of hearing, watching others copy, memorizing and reciting, reading, and doing his own copying, Rennyo was introduced to a diverse body of texts: the three Pure Land sūtras; the

---

[1] Several essays edited by Miriam Levering in *Rethinking Scripture* inform the discussion of *The Letters* as scripture in this chapter. In particular, see Wilfred Cantwell Smith, "The Study of Religion and the Study of the Bible," 18–28, and "Scripture as Form and Concept: Their Emergence for the Western World," 29–57, and William A. Graham, "Scripture as Spoken Word," 129–69.

[2] Kimura, ed., *Rennyo Shōnin ron*, 149.

commentaries of the seven Pure Land masters; the writings of Shinran, Kakunyo, and Zonkaku; Pure Land texts reflecting popular folk religiousness; and, in particular, *Anjin ketsujōshō*. It was primarily through the medium of the written word that Rennyo responded to the major challenges in his life, beginning with the crisis years at Yoshizaki, where he wrote many of his most innovative and enduring letters. Again, the restoration of the Honganji, signaled by the building of the Founder's Hall at Yamashina, was accompanied by a series of letters prepared especially for reading at the annual thanksgiving services. Finally, his retirement years elicited a renewed flow of literary reflection on Shinran's teaching, in language informed largely by his devotion to the text *Anjin ketsujōshō*.

In this chapter we will review the stages through which Rennyo's successors selected certain of his letters to serve as a canonical text,[3] drew on *The Letters* as the primary source for a confessional statement defining orthodox Shinshū piety, and cited it as the final authority in arbitrating a disruptive doctrinal controversy internal to the Nishi Honganji. First, however, it is necessary to set Rennyo's writings in context within a Pure Land Buddhist movement inaugurated by a founder's unique reading, understanding, and translation of received texts.

THE TEACHING

A pamphlet in English, prepared by a former presiding officer of the Buddhist Churches of America, introduces Shinshū tradition as follows:

> The accepted date of the founding of this denomination is 1224, when the first draft of Shinran's most important book "Teaching, Practice, Faith, and Attainment" (Kyo Gyo Shin Sho) was completed.[4]

---

[3] Shizutoshi Sugihira, Shinshū scholar and author of an essay on the occasion of the 450th anniversary of Rennyo's death, uses the term "canonical book": "Eighty pieces of the Ofumi were selected out and compiled into five fasciculi, and this five fasciculi compilation of the Ofumi has attained the position of a canonical book of the sect" ("Rennyo Shōnin, the Great Teacher of Shin Buddhism," 34).

[4] Kenryu Takashi Tsuji, "Brief Introduction to Jodo Shinshu" (San Francisco: Buddhist Churches of America, n.d.), 1. The instance cited here is from a pamphlet in English introducing Shinshū tradition in a Protestant Christian North American setting, where the need for a religious community to have a written text is no doubt strongly felt. Chronologies of Shinran's life include a

Despite conflicting theories for the date of the final revision of *Kyōgyōshinshō*, the point stands that the writing of a text is seen as marking the birth of a radically new Pure Land movement, the Jōdo Shinshū, in Japanese history; Shinran speaks of this movement as "the culmination of the Mahāyāna."[5]

Composed in classical Chinese, *Kyōgyōshinshō* is Shinran's most systematic presentation of his thought. The introduction to a recent translation of the first two chapters renders a judgement with which many would agree: "[It] stands seven hundred years after its composition as a monumental classic of Japanese religious thought, and one of the most seminal and original contributions in the long history of Japanese Buddhism."[6] Without question, *Kyōgyōshinshō* is a major religious symbol for participants in Shinshū tradition; nevertheless, it remains largely unread, except by sectarian scholars and students of religion. For example, only a small section of this important text, the 120-line *Shōshinge*, is included among the selections representing Shinran in a multi-volume series of Japanese literary classics.[7] Together with *Shōshinge*, the texts chosen as representative of Shinran are selections of his original compositions in Japanese: hymns and letters, as well as Yuien's *Tannishō*. It is an indisputable fact, however, that there is no way to come to terms intellectually and aesthetically with the depth, subtlety, and architectonic beauty of Shinran's thought without encountering *Kyōgyōshinshō*'s chapter on faith, known as the *Shinkan* 信巻 .

Shinran's preface to *Kyōgyōshinshō* clarifies the fundamental importance of the written word—the three Pure Land sūtras and discourses of the two Pure Land Indian masters as well as the commentaries of

---

high proportion of entries relating to texts. For example, among a dozen or so entries in the chronology in Ueda and Hirota, *Shinran*, 18, are the following: 1205, his copying of Hōnen's *Senjaku hongan nenbutsushū*; 1224, the earliest date for *Kyōgyōshinshō*; 1247, his granting of permission to others to copy *Kyōgyōshinshō*; 1248, the writing of his first hymns in Japanese; 1251, his letters to followers in the Kantō; and 1258, his letter on *jinen*, frequently translated as naturalness or spontaneity.

[5] *Mattōshō*, SSZ 2: 658.

[6] *Teaching*, 1: 21.

[7] Nabata Ōjun et al., eds. *Shinranshū/Nichirenshū*, Nihon Koten Bungaku Taikei, vol. 82 (Tokyo: Iwanami Shoten, 1964). The text, in Japanese translation with notes, is included in a series on Japanese thought; see Hoshino Genpō, Ishida Mitsuyuki, and Ienaga Saburō, eds., *Shinran*, Nihon Shisō Taikei, vol. 11 (Tokyo: Iwanami Shoten, 1971).

the five masters in China and Japan—for the transmission of the Buddha-dharma and the realization of faith:

> I, Gutoku Shinran, disciple of Śākyamuni—how joyful I am! It is difficult to meet with the scriptures (*seiten* 聖典) from India and the commentaries (*shishaku* 師釈) of the masters of China and Japan, but now I have been able to meet them. It is difficult to hear them, but I have indeed been able to hear. Entrusting myself with reverence to the teaching, practice, and realization that are the true essence of the Pure Land way, I am in particular aware of the profundity of the Tathāgata's benevolence. Here I rejoice over what I have heard and praise what I have received.[8]

In this passage, Shinran uses the term *seiten*, which in contemporary usage has taken on the meaning "scripture" or, perhaps, a meaning analogous to "Bible" for English-speaking participants in Shinshū tradition.[9] However, *seiten*, also read *shōten*, appears in only two other

---

[8] SSZ 2: 1. A concordance makes it possible to trace Shinran's use of virtually any term with reference to the text of *Kyōgyōshinshō*, SSZ 2: 1–203. See Ryūkoku Daigaku Shinshū Gakkai, ed., *Shinran Shōnin chosaku yōgo sakuin: Kyōgyōshinshō no bu* (Kyoto: Ryūkoku Daigaku Shinshū Gakkai, 1977). A second volume, Ryūkoku Daigaku Shinshū Gakkai, ed., *Shinran Shōnin chosaku yōgo sakuin: Wakan senjutsu no bu* (Kyoto: Ryūkoku Daigaku Shinshū Gakkai, 1978) is available for his other writings in Chinese and Japanese.

[9] For many years, Japanese-American participants in the Shinshū—Shin Buddhists—living in Hawaii felt the need for "an English Shinshu Seiten." (The terms "Shin Buddhist" and "Shin Buddhism" were coined by Suzuki Daisetsu as collateral terms to "Zen Buddhist" and "Zen Buddhism." In this study, they are used primarily in the context of participation in Shinshū tradition outside of Japan, where, as in North America, Buddhists constitute a very small minority of the population.) In 1950, a representative of the Honpa Honganji Mission of Hawaii visited Japan to negotiate for the translation and compilation of "a holy scripture in English." Yamamoto Kōshō, a Shinshū priest and professor at Ryūkoku University in Kyoto, agreed to undertake the project. Some five years later, the English Shinshu Seiten Compilation Committee of the mission published an English version of the Shinshū scriptures (see Honpa Hongwanji Mission of Hawaii, comp., *The Shinshu Seiten: The Holy Scripture of Shinshu* [1955; repr. Honolulu: The Honpa Hongwanji Mission of Hawaii, 1961], vii–viii). The preface to the 1961 edition, printed on the occasion of the seven-hundredth anniversary of Shinran's death, begins: "It is now seven hundred years since Shinran Shonin, the founder of Jodoshinshu, passed away in Kyoto. And in Kyoto the Church of Honganji observed this spring, on a nation-wide scale, the seven hundredth anniversary in memory of the Shonin in whose teaching we all live" (v).

In 1978, a new compilation by the Tri-State Buddhist Temples, *Shinshū*

places in Shinran's writings: one, in chapter six of *Kyōgyōshinshō*, in a lengthy quote from *Mappō tōmyōki*, attributed to Saichō; the other, in Shinran's *Jōdo monrui jushō*, in a verse referring to Hōnen:

> Genkū [Hōnen], clearly understanding the scriptures,
> turned compassionately to foolish beings, good and evil;
> establishing in this remote land the teaching and realization
> that are the true essence of the Pure Land way,
> he transmits the selected Primal Vow to the defiled world. . . .[10]

Here again, Shinran's use of the term *seiten* refers specifically to the three major Pure Land sūtras and the discourses by the Indian masters, Nāgārjuna and Vasubandhu. As noted earlier, he is vividly aware of standing on the ground of Amida's Vow-mind, secured by an unbroken line of transmission of spoken and written texts.[11] His entire life, as he says in the preface to *Kyōgyōshinshō*, is a joyful response to the Tathāgata's benevolence in allowing him to encounter the scriptures and the commentaries of the Pure Land masters.

For Shinran, the *Larger Sūtra* is the preeminent text; he uses passages culled from a wide range of other Mahāyāna writings, with minimal commentary of his own, to support what he has discovered through it. On the basis of his punctuation and notations of the Chinese texts for reading in Japanese,[12] he is largely content to have the texts speak for themselves. For example, at the end of the first chapter of *Kyōgyōshinshō*, "A Collection of Passages Revealing the True Teaching of the Pure Land Way," he writes: "These passages give clear testimony that the *Larger Sūtra* reveals the true teaching."[13] Again, in his *Jōdo monrui jushō*: "Assuredly this [*Larger*] *Sūtra* is the true teaching for which the Tathāgata appeared in the world. It is the preeminent scripture [*ten* 典], rare and most excellent."[14]

Seiten: Jōdo Shin Buddhist Teaching, was published by the Buddhist Churches of America. Endorsed by the Honpa Honganji Mission of Hawaii and the Buddhist Churches of Canada, it includes many new translations of the texts by Japanese and Japanese-American scholars. In the same year, the first volume in the Shin Buddhism Translation Series was published; the foreword to *Letters of Shinran* notes that the series "will include all of Shinran's works as well as other basic scriptures." In 1979, the preface to the second volume, *Notes on 'Essentials of Faith Alone,'* announced a twelve-year program "for the translation and publication in English of the basic Canons of Jodo Shinshu."

[10] SSZ 2: 450.
[11] Hirota, *Tannishō*, 23; SSZ 2: 774–75.
[12] See "Notes on Shinran's Readings," *Teaching*, 1: 174–75.
[13] *Teaching*, 1: 67; SSZ 2: 4.
[14] *Passages*, 30; SSZ 2: 443.

It is not surprising that Shinran's unique reading and utilization of these passages has invited criticism; a Buddhist scholar charges that Shinran, rather than quoting the passages, changes their meaning:

"It is difficult to recognize them as quotations; they are basically nothing more than original passages. In order to set forth his own views, he borrowed passages from the sūtras, treatises, and commentaries that suited his own purposes."[15]

Scholars engaged in the translation of Shinran's writings into English respond as follows:

. . . It may be said that Shinran's readings are the most faithful to the original—the source—meaning of the texts. He did not alter the texts ignoring the original meaning as some have charged; quite to the contrary, he read the source meaning of the scriptures more deeply and clearly than the original authors, and in order to bring it out, he changed the traditional readings where he felt that they were inadequate.[16]

Underlying Shinran's translation and interpretation of the passages is his confidence that Amida's call has been conveyed to him through the Chinese texts.

In order to develop Shinran's notion of written text beyond his limited but significant use of the term *seiten* (or *shōten*), we turn to a second term, *shōgyō* 聖教, frequently translated within the sectarian tradition as "sacred writings" or "sacred scriptures." *Shōgyō* occurs in three quotations from Chinese texts included in *Kyōgyōshinshō* and several times in Shinran's Japanese writings, as well as in Yuien's *Tannishō*.

The *Kyōgyōshinshō* includes a quotation from Tao-ch'o's *An li chi* (Jpn. *Anrakushū*), a commentary on the *Contemplation Sūtra*:

It is said that the nenbutsu of those of long practice may often be done in accordance with the above [instructions]. In the nenbutsu practice of beginners, it is permissible to keep count of the number of utterances. This conforms with the sacred scriptures [*shōgyō*].[17]

The *Kyōgyōshinshō* also contains a quotation from the *Sassha nikenshikyō*, a passage describing the second of the five grave offenses applying to bodhisattvas, pratyekabuddhas, and śrāvakas as:

slandering the three-vehicle dharma, saying that it is not scripture

---

[15] This is the position of Mochizuki Shinkō as quoted in *Teaching*, 1: 39.

[16] *Teaching*, 1: 40.

[17] *Teaching*, 1: 141; SSZ 2: 35.

(*shōgyō*), impeding [its spread], damaging [the texts], halting or making [their transmission] difficult, or concealing and obscuring them.[18]

In the postscript to *Tannishō*, Yuien laments the confusion that may arise after his death in regard to Shinran's teaching. He advises:

When you are confused by people who discuss among themselves such views as those noted above, carefully read the sacred writings [*onshōgyō* 御聖教] that accord with the late master's thought and that he himself used to read. In the sacred writings, the true and real and the accommodated and provisional are mixed. That we abandon the accommodated and take up the real, set aside the provisional and adopt the true is Shinran's fundamental meaning. You must under no circumstances misread the sacred writings. I have selected a number of important scriptural passages [*shōmon* 証文] and appended them to this volume as a standard.[19]

Shinran also uses the term *kyōten* 教典 in the traditional sense of "sutra" (the recorded words of the Buddha) in quotations from Shan-tao and from the *Nirvāṇa Sūtra* appearing in *Kyōgyōshinshō*. Of particular interest is the scroll inscription in *Songō shinzō meimon*, quoting a passage from Vasubandhu's *Jōdoron*:

Relying on the sūtras [*shu-ta-ra*] *in which the manifestation of the true and real virtues is taught, I*: With *I*, Vasubandhu, the author of the treatise, declares himself. *Relying on the sūtras*: *Sūtra* is an Indian term for the recorded words [*kyōten*] of the Buddha, including both the Mahāyāna and Hīnayāna teachings. Here, however, "sūtra" indicates the Mahāyāna sūtras, not those of the Hīnayāna. The "three scriptures [*kyōten*]" which we use are Mahāyāna sūtras, and Vasubandhu's phrase means "depending on these three Mahāyāna sūtras." *True and real virtues*: the sacred Name that embodies the Vow. *Manifestation*: form.[20]

As evidenced by his own writings and Yuien's record, Shinran resists any implication that the teaching is something of his own creation. He sees himself as the transmitter of what he has received directly through his master, Hōnen. Convinced that he is incapable of accomplishing any good through his own efforts, Shinran responds in written form to the salvific truth of the Tathāgata's benevolence, received through a textual tradition. Within that tradition, the *Larger*

---

[18] SSZ 2: 102.
[19] Hirota, *Tannishō*, 43; SSZ 2: 791–92.
[20] *Inscriptions*, 46; SSZ 2: 585.

Sūtra bears indisputable witness that Amida's Vow—the transcendent—has been manifested in India in Śākyamuni's teachings—the mundane.

TEXTS AND CONTEXTS

On the occasion of the thirty-third anniversary of Shinran's death, Kakunyo prepared his *Hōonkō shiki*, a celebration of Shinran's virtues. Kakunyo's perception of the core of the textual tradition increasingly focused on the words of Shinran, whom he identifies as a manifestation of Amida Tathāgata:

> That is to say, [Shinran's] widespread teaching (*kyō*) and practice (*gyō*) should most certainly be regarded as Amida's direct teaching— which, by clearly setting forth the pure light of wisdom, dispels the darkness of delusion in this defiled world, and by sprinkling the dharma-rain in its sweetness everywhere, slowly but steadily permeates our dryness, our ignorance and confusion. Realizing that this is its purpose, we should entrust ourselves to it and revere it.[21]

While the content of the Shinshū's textual tradition expands to include the writings of Kakunyo, Zonkaku, and Rennyo, there is increasing emphasis on scripture as a major religious symbol for the tradition.

Kakunyo's *Kudenshō* reports an incident that offers further insight as to how the written word was perceived within the tradition. According to this account, Shinran was in disagreement with his former disciple Shingyō, to whom he had given scriptures and an image of the Buddha. When Shingyō was on the point of returning to his own province, having rejected Shinran's teaching, other disciples went to Shinran, saying that he should demand the return of the image and the texts. Kakunyo reports that Shinran replied:

> It would be highly inappropriate to take back the main image and scriptures (*shōgyō*). The reason for this is that [I], Shinran, do not have even a single disciple. What do I teach that I could speak of having disciples? As we are all disciples of the Tathāgata, we are all fellow practicers. . . .
>
> The image and the scriptures are compassionate means for the benefit of all sentient beings. . . . Therefore, even if scriptures in which my name was written were discarded in the mountains or in a field, . . . many sentient beings in that place might be saved by

---

[21] *Godenshō*, SSZ 3: 647.

those scriptures and each and every one receive benefit from them.[22]

Shinran's single-minded devotion to Amida and gratitude for the teaching manifested in the Pure Land sūtras, the commentaries of the Pure Land masters, and the person of Hōnen is redirected by Kakunyo to focus on the person of Shinran as founder and on his writings as scripture. In due course, the writings of both Kakunyo and Zonkaku, despite disownment of the latter, came to be included also in the Shinshū scriptural corpus.

Rennyo, as we have seen, was initiated into his tradition through a process of copying Pure Land texts and thus internalizing the teaching. In a tradition that rejected any notion of gaining merit through self-effort, copying texts may be understood in terms of spiritual discipline as an act of thanksgiving. In any event, Rennyo takes the Shinshū textual tradition very seriously indeed: in his letters, he deplores those priests who are barely acquainted with the scriptures (shōgyō);[23] he takes to task others who, in neglecting them, disregard the settling of their own faith and fail to instruct their followers.[24] He warns those responsible for presenting the teaching:

When you read the scriptures, for example, or when you speak [even] briefly about the teaching, you must [first] ascertain [whether the listeners have, or lack, good from the past].[25]

Among the followers of our tradition in various provinces, there are many who confuse the meaning of the dharma by propounding obscure teachings not prescribed in the scriptures designated by our founder. This is indeed ridiculous.[26]

The import of our tradition is . . . that for those who do not realize the significance of the one thought-moment of faith — even though they may diligently read the various scriptures and be widely informed — all is in vain.[27]

We should recognize . . . that all the scriptures have the sole intent

---

[22] *Kudenshō*, SSZ 3: 9–10. For a discussion of this and other incidents recorded in *Kudenshō* and a brief evaluation of the text, see Phillip K. Eidmann, "Nyoshin and the Kudensho," *The Pacific World: Journal of the Institute of Buddhist Studies* 1/1 (1982): 16–17.

[23] RSI, 166 (#50/2:3); SSZ 3: 428.

[24] RSI, 195 (#61/2:12); SSZ 3: 443.

[25] RSI, 333 (#112/4:5); SSZ 3: 481.

[26] RSI, 346 (#115/4:6); SSZ 3: 484.

[27] RSI, 471 (#173/5:2); SSZ 3: 500.

of bringing us to entrust ourselves to the six characters "na-mu-a-mi-da-butsu."[28]

Each of Rennyo's *Summer Letters*, written in preparation for what was to be his final celebration of the annual seven-day thanksgiving services in 1498, underscores the significance of scripture in relation to the realization of Other-Power faith. From the first, written during the latter part of the fifth month of Meiō 7 (1498):

> You have all gathered here, saying that you have come to listen to today's scriptures, [but what must be understood is that] this will be of no use at all unless you hear and are convinced, thoroughly understanding what faith means and holding no unsettled thoughts from today on.[29]

From the second, written during the same month:

> The specific purpose of our reading the scriptures is to enable [everyone] to realize Other-Power faith; it is done so that you will hear and understand its significance and correct the shallowness of your own faith. This is the fundamental intent in Buddha-dharma. Therefore, although there is scripture [reading] every day, unless you make an attempt to understand, your coming will amount to nothing at all.[30]

From the third, written during the middle of the sixth month:

> The sole purpose in reading the scriptures is to enable [those who listen] to realize Other-Power faith.[31]

From the fourth, written during the middle of the seventh month:

> Although I have always selected and read important passages of scripture every day, not one person has spoken of what was impressive or what was unclear in the day's scriptures; not a single person has come forth. . . . There are now only thirty days left for the reading of these scriptures. [To listen] unconcernedly, as if [the reading would continue] forever, and without improvement in one's understanding most certainly [reveals] a lack of aspiration. Indeed, it is just as if one went to a mountain of treasure and returned empty-handed.[32]

---

28 RSI, 444 (#155/5:9); SSZ 3: 506–7.

29 RSI, 427 (#147); SSZ 3: 552.

30 RSI, 429 (#148); SSZ 3: 523–24.

31 RSI, 432 (#149); SSZ 3: 525.

32 RSI, 433–34 (#150); SSZ 3: 527.

Through his innovative liturgical use of scripture, Rennyo introduces members of the Shinshū community to an ancient Mahāyāna textual tradition, presenting it as a vehicle for the establishment and nurture of Other-Power faith. During his last summer, those who assemble at Yamashina Hongan-ji hear readings from the three Pure Land sūtras, in particular the *Larger Sūtra*; recite in unison *Shōshinge*, drawn from the heart of the founder's *Kyōgyōshinshō*; and listen to Rennyo read his own letters, which were phrased in terms familiar to them. Rennyo, drawing on a rich heritage of Pure Land texts, attempts to make Shinran's teaching come alive in colloquial language replete with religious symbols through which ordinary men and women might discover the truth and reality of Amida's Primal Vow.

A CANONICAL BOOK

Participants in Shinshū tradition have accepted without question the reverential view of Rennyo's letters presented by the memoir writers, who refer to them by the honorific form, *ofumi* 御文 . In the letters themselves, however, Rennyo uses the plain form, *fumi* 文 , as evidenced in a preface dated Bunmei 5 (1473).9.23, written to accompany a collection of his Yoshizaki letters copied by Aki Rensō:

> The following letters (*fumi*) are ones that I wrote impulsively one after another as they came to mind, from the third year of Bunmei [1471] to the fall of the fifth year [1473]. There will surely be peculiarities in the style, and there may be discontinuity between phrases and so forth. As none of this is appropriate, I have hesitated [over what to do]; but because [Rensō] has already obtained paper for the fascicle and copied it, I can only release it, however it may be. It should certainly not be seen by others [outside the community]. It is to be kept simply for personal use in spare moments.[33]

---

[33] RSI, 127–28 (#35). Rensō's collection consists of seventeen separate items dated Bunmei 3 (1471).7.15 to 5 (1473).11.21; all are to be found in Inaba's *Rennyo Shōnin ibun*: #8 (1:1), #9, #10 (1:2), #11, #12 (1:3), #18 (1:4), #13, #14, #15, #20 (1:5), #21, #19, #25 (1:7), #28 (1:10), #22 (1:6), #29, and #39. For the most part, the letters were copied chronologically, with the final letter added following Rennyo's writing of the preface two months earlier (letter #35 above). We have consulted a reproduction of a manuscript, *Shobunshū* 諸文集 , now in the possession of Nishimura Saiji, on loan once a year to Saikō-ji, Ishikawa prefecture. The Nishimura manuscript, dated Tenshō 15 (1587).4.3, appears to be in Rensō's own hand; it includes the preface in Rennyo's hand and his written seal.

Rennyo's diffidence may reflect in part a hesitance to speak openly at a time when Yoshizaki was subject to severe scrutiny and possible attack. Several months later, however, he refers to another letter as *fumi*,[34] suggesting that he did not use the term in any formal sense.

The underlying tone of *The Letters* is one of authority, yet there is very limited evidence to suggest that, even after his retirement, Rennyo ever consciously sought to establish his words as having special status in a scriptural sense. The transition from *fumi* to *ofumi* was made by members of his immediate family and other memoir writers after his death. This development, promoting Rennyo's letters as a scriptural basis for orthodox Shinshū teaching, is a not insignificant step in the Honganji's consolidation as a tightly structured religious order. The letters came to provide a new locus of authority, substituting, to the degree that was possible, for the force of Rennyo's personal charisma.

Ennyo, commissioned by his father Jitsunyo, selected eighty-five of Rennyo's most important letters from the several hundred that were available: eighty edited as *The Letters*; four comprising the *Summer Letters*; and the letter entitled *Gozokushō*, giving Shinran's genealogy. The fifty-eight letters in the first four of the five-fascicle compilation were arranged in chronological order; the twenty-two in the fifth fascicle are undated.[35] Many of the letters most significant from a historical viewpoint are omitted, and even when such letters are included, the fact that there is no accompanying commentary suggests that historical context was not a point of concern. An underlying theme in this study is that the ahistorical presentation of the teaching by the leaders of the Honganji, as well as sectarian scholars, was to lead to a bifurcation of the transcendent and the mundane, with serious consequences for Shinran's teaching.

The five-fascicle compilation of letters is significant for two reasons:

First, *The Letters* has provided a definitive text for interpreting Shinran's teaching from the time of the ninth head priest, Jitsunyo. An edition of the Shinshū scriptures, published by the Nishi Honganji in 1969, notes that Ennyo's compilation was made in order to edify unlettered laymen on essential points of Shinshū doctrine; that the letters contained in it were revered from the first as exemplifying faith (*anjin*); that under the leadership of the head priests of the Honganji following Rennyo, *The Letters* became the standard for instruction in

---

[34] RSI, 142 (#41/2:2); SSZ 3: 426–28.
[35] See p. 139, the introduction to part two, for information on the dating of the letters.

the Shinshū community; and that it was customary even during Rennyo's lifetime for Shinshū congregations to gather before an image of Amida Buddha and listen to readings from it. Copies of the five-fascicle collection were printed and widely distributed beginning in 1537, during the tenure of Shōnyo as head priest. Granted the repetitiveness of many of the letters, the text is honored in its entirety within both the Nishi and the Higashi Honganji.[36]

For this study, there is a second reason for noting the special significance of this compilation: the intimate relationship that exists between the content of many of the chronologically-dated letters in the first four fascicles and the social and political events of the years in which they were written. No less than forty of the fifty-eight dated letters were written during the fifty-month period that Rennyo was in the Hokuriku, and at least thirty-six of these forty were written during the most critical period of his stay at Yoshizaki while he was struggling to resolve the dilemma of the Honganji's religious power. It appears that his vigorous literary response at that time produced a series of writings that, as the core materials of the canonized text, came to define orthodox Shinshū piety.

As we have seen, the letters written during Rennyo's Yoshizaki years, particularly those included in *The Letters*, reveal remarkable innovation in his interpretation of Shinran's teaching. The central place he gives to a formulation of the nenbutsu using the concepts *anjin* and *ki-hō ittai* from *Anjin ketsujōshō* is new for the Shinshū; he reemphasizes and refines his use of this formula in a period of intense literary activity in his last years, 1496–1498. Notably, out of thirty-nine extant letters attributed to this period, six are included in the five-fascicle collection and four make up the *Summer Letters*.[37] In addition, a number of the undated letters may be assigned to this period.

A CONFESSIONAL STATEMENT

The Letters and the memoirs, perhaps even more than Shinran's writings, came to serve as devotional texts at the popular level for members of the Honganji. Not only were Rennyo and some of his most intimate followers seen as exemplars of orthodox Shinshū piety, Rennyo's writings, as well as his spoken words, became authoritative for the interpretation of Shinran's teaching. In part, for this reason,

[36] Ōe and Ōhara, eds., *Shinshū seiten*, 893–94.
[37] Kitanishi, "Dangibon kenkyū josetsu," 164.

he has been generally credited as author of a brief "Confessional State-ment," known as *Ryōgemon* within the Nishi Honganji and as *Gaikemon* within the Higashi.[38] It is clear that *The Letters* provided the doctrinal framework for the statement, but there is no evidence that it was writ-ten by Rennyo himself in its present form.[39] The first of the four pas-sages reads:

> Casting off the self-power mind of the sundry practices and dis-ciplines, we single-mindedly entrust ourselves to Amida Tathāgata to save us [in regard to] the birth that is to come [in the Pure Land], the most important matter (*kondo no ichidaiji no goshō ontasuke sōrae* 今度の一大事の後生御たすけそうらへ).[40]

This explication of the salvific process — the casting off of the mind of self-power, single-minded trust in Amida, and the phrasing, "the birth that is to come, the most important matter" — is fully consistent with Rennyo's interpretation of Shinran's teaching; the passage could well have been written by Rennyo. The statement continues:

> We know that at the time of the one thought-moment of entrusting (*tanomu ichinen* たのむ一念), birth [in the Pure Land] is assured; it is settled that we are saved. Once [we have realized] this, we say the

---

[38] The *Ryōgemon* appears in a Nishi Honganji edition between Rennyo's *Gozokushō* and the memoir, *Goichidaiki kikigaki* (Ōe and Ōhara, ed., *Shinshū seiten*, 814); also see SSZ 3: 529–30. The statement, in its present form, was published in Tenmei 4 (1784).3, during the tenure of Hōnyo (1707–1789), seventeenth head priest in the Nishi Honganji lineage (HN, 195), with an appended com-mentary by Monnyo (1744–1799), who, in 1789, became the eighteenth. In a Higashi Honganji edition of the Shinshū scriptures, *Gaikemon* is listed under Rennyo's name in the table of contents (Kashiwabara, ed., *Shinshū seiten*, 4).

[39] Four versions of the confessional statement are listed among fourteen items of questionable authenticity attributed to Rennyo; see RSI, 515–18. For a detailed study of the composition of the statement, see Umehara Ryūshō, "Jōdo Shinshū ni okeru shinkō kokuhakumon no seiritsu," in *Shinshūshi no kenkyū*, ed. Miyazaki Enjun Hakase Kanreki Kinenkai (Kyoto: Nagata Bunshōdō, 1966), 83–116.

[40] *Ryōgemon*, SSZ 3: 529. Previous English translations include: Masaharu Anesaki, *History of Japanese Religion, With Special Reference to the Social and Moral Life of the Nation* (1930; repr. Rutland, Vt., and Tokyo: Charles E. Tuttle, 1963), 231, who identifies *Ryōgemon* as one of Rennyo's letters; Charles Eliot, *Japanese Buddhism* (1935; repr. New York: Barnes and Noble, 1969), 377, who refers to the *Ryōgemon* as "a sort of creed"; and Tri-State Buddhist Temples, comp., *The Shinshū Seiten*, 299, which lists "The Ryogemon: The Creed," attributing it to "Rennyo Shonin."

（前略）此雑行雑修自力のこゝろをふりすてゝ一心に

阿弥陀如来我等か今度此一大事の後生御たすけ

候へとたのみまうしてさふらふ（以下略）

一定御たすけ治定と存んこのうへの称名御恩報謝と

存んよろこひまうし候（中略）

さふらふ事

御開山聖人御出世より次第相承の善知識のあさけ

御勧化の御恩ともありかたく（以下略）

御たゝ々々く一向仰の（中略）

本願寺釋法如 （花押）

信證院連如師之定おゝせられ伝也真宗念佛

右領解出言之文ハ

行者已ゝ一念帰命信心發得せゝ領解せゝ快如ゝゝ放ゝ古今一宗ゝ

Name joyfully, in gratitude (*hōsha* 報謝) for [Amida's] graciousness.[41]

The use of the term "entrusting" (*tanomu*) to mean "faith" (*shinjin*), along with saying the Name in gratitude (*shōmyō hōon* 称名報恩), is a hallmark of Rennyo's thought. The third passage reads:

> We gratefully acknowledge that our hearing and understanding these truths is [due to] the benevolence of the founding master in having appeared in this world and to that of the good teachers (*zenchishiki*), his successors in the transmission [of the teaching], whose exhortations were not shallow.[42]

This passage, implying that Shinran's successors in the office of head priest are to be formally designated as good teachers, appears uncharacteristic of Rennyo's thought in *The Letters*.

We recall that Shinran expressed his deep sense of gratitude not only to Amida, but also to Śākyamuni and the seven Pure Land masters.[43] Meeting Hōnen, the good teacher (*yoki hito* よきひと), was the turning point in his life.[44] Rennyo, however, uses the term *zenchishiki* in a more general and less intimate way. For Rennyo, "the function of the good teacher is just to encourage people to take refuge in Amida single-heartedly and steadfastly."[45] He singles out none of his predecessors in the Honganji, including his father, Zonnyo, in the sense that Shinran referred to Hōnen; his extant letters do not explicitly mention Zonnyo or even Kakunyo, although the names of Zonnyo and Zonkaku are to be found in the memoir *Goichidaiki kikigaki*.[46]

It appears, then, that the third passage of the confessional statement reflects a post-Rennyo development: Shinran's successors, the head priests of the Honganji, come to be acknowledged as the good teachers in a sense never envisioned by Rennyo. In a letter dated Bunmei 6 (1474).1.20, he remonstrates with some who, on pilgrimage to Yoshizaki, would have centered their devotion on him; he tells them that it is better for them to worship before a stūpa (*sotoba* 卒都婆).[47]

---

41 *Ryōgemon*, SSZ 3: 529.

42 *Ryōgemon*, SSZ 3: 529.

43 See *Shōshinge*, hymns of praise to Amida, Śākyamuni, and the seven Pure Land masters; SSZ 2: 43–46.

44 For the radical quality of Shinran's sense of indebtedness to Hōnen, see chapter two of *Tannishō*, SSZ 2: 774.

45 RSI, 193–94 (#60/2:11).

46 For Zonnyo, see *Goichidaiki kikigaki*, SSZ 3: 567; for Zonkaku, see SSZ 3: 570 and 610.

47 RSI, 170–71 (#51).

The confessional statement concludes:

> Beyond this, we will observe the established rules of conduct (*on'okite*) throughout our lives.[48]

As noted earlier, the term "rules of conduct" in its honorific form was first used by Rennyo in a letter dated Bunmei 7 (1475).11.21, in the context of the annual thanksgiving services at Deguchi, Kawachi province.[49] At that time, he attempted to give greater authority to the regulations that he had promulgated in response to the crisis at Yoshizaki, seeking to legitimize them by linking them directly to Shinran's teaching. In this final passage of *Ryōgemon*, the rules of conduct are interpreted to include the laws of the state (*ōbō*); Shinshū practicers of faith are duty-bound to obey them, and to be grateful.[50]

The adoption of a formal confessional statement into the liturgical life of the Honganji would appear to represent yet a further stage in the institutionalization and politicization of Shinran's piety. Two centuries after Shinran, Rennyo's enumeration of rules of conduct at the annual thanksgiving services came in response to issues threatening the very life of his community. After his death, however, obedience to such rules became the test of orthodox participation in the Honganji order. Authority was focused in the office of the head priest and family council, the descendants of both "founders," Shinran and Rennyo. Elements of Rennyo's thought, abstracted from *The Letters* without regard to the historical context in which they originated, provided the framework for the statement. It was important that Rennyo, considered the definitive interpreter of Shinran's teaching, be recognized as the author. The statement has continued to serve as a major religious symbol within Shinshū tradition: at times, it has nurtured what is most sublime, as in *myōkōnin* piety; at others, it has bound participants in the tradition to policies defined by a religious order that had resolved the dilemma of power by total accommodation to temporal authority. In Meiji Japan, it came to be seen as authoritative for the dharma-principle of *shinzoku nitai*.[51]

---

[48] *Ryōgemon*, SSZ 3: 529.

[49] RSI, 251 (#84/3:11); SSZ 3: 469–70.

[50] Ōe and Ōhara, eds., *Shinshū seiten*, 814.

[51] For example, Charles Eliot, in his *Japanese Buddhism*, comments that the *Ryōgemon* is "perhaps the simplest and most authoritative statement respecting Shintai and Zokutai" (377). Further, he observes that the phrase *shinzoku nitai* is frequently used to sum up Shinshū teaching:

> [It] describes the two great divisions of religion, faith and morality. Shintai refers

A LETTER OF ADJUDICATION

We have reviewed a process of scripturalization during which a compilation of Rennyo's letters steadily acquired authority in the Honganji branch of the Shinshū. A selection of letters became *The Letters*, a canonical text defining the teaching and extending it to rules of conduct deemed necessary for authentic participation in the tradition. A further stage in this process was signaled by the proclamation of a document known as "A Letter of Adjudication" (*Gosaidan no gosho*), signed by Honnyo (1778–1826), nineteenth head priest in the Nishi Honganji lineage. This letter is dated Bunka 3 (1806).11.6; it was accompanied by an announcement (*Gosaidan shinmeisho*) dated one day earlier.[52]

These two documents render a final judgement on a bitter, tenyear doctrinal controversy known as the Sangō Upheaval (*sangō wakuran* 三業惑乱), which erupted within the Nishi Honganji in Kansei 9 (1797), during the tenure of Honnyo's predecessor, Monnyo.[53] The source of the controversy, the "three acts" teaching, made its first clearly-stated appearance as early as Shōtoku 3 (1713), in a document unassumingly entitled, "Dust Specks on a Jar by a Southern Window" (*Nansōjinko* 南窓塵壺), by Chikū (1634–1718), second head of the Gakurin.[54] In this document, Chikū expounded in question-and-answer form the teaching that "with the awakening of the one thought-moment [of entrusting], the cause [of birth] is completed in ordinary life (*ichinen hokki heizei gojō*)," interpreting it to mean that the moment of taking refuge (entrusting) would involve the "three [kinds of] acts," bodily, verbal, and mental; therefore, aspiration for birth

---

mainly to the next world, the salvation offered by Amida and how to obtain it.Zokutai is a man's duty as a member of society, but duty in the sense of conduct arising from faith (377).

[52] HN, 208. For texts of both documents and brief commentaries, see Shinshū Seiten Hensan Iinkai, ed. *Jōdo Shinshū seiten*, 1411–15; 1417–22.

[53] In Kansei 9 (1797).5, Chidō (1736–1805) became the seventh head of the Gakurin (first known as the Gakuryō), a scholastic movement founded within the Honganji in Kan'ei 15 (1638) by Ryōnyo, the thirteenth head priest. Chidō's six-article statement on faith and his lectures in 1797 and 1798, all of which stressed "taking refuge, [manifesting] the three acts" (*sangō kimyō* 三業帰命), provoked a storm of response (Asaeda Zenshō, "Igi: Sangō wakuran," in *Shinshū denshō no ayumi* [1]," Jōdo Shinshū Gendai Hōwa Taikei, vol. 7 [Kyoto: Dōbōsha, 1987]: 351–52).

[54] HS 2: 359.

would necessarily be accompanied by a physical manifestation of reverence and by saying the nenbutsu.[55]

Declared orthodox by the authoritative scholastic body, the Gakurin, the teaching appeared again with Gikyō (1694–1768), the fifth-generation head, who stressed that it was fully consistent with Rennyo's teaching;[56] by the time of the sixth head, Kōzon (1720–1796), it had become a strong force within the Nishi Honganji. In Hōreki 12 (1762).2, Kōzon wrote a two-fascicle exposition, "On Taking Refuge with [the Awakening of] Aspiration for Birth" (Ganshō kimyō ben 願生帰命弁), representative of and further strengthening the "three acts" position.[57] It was undoubtedly his emphasis on the "three acts" that gave the Sangō Upheaval its name.[58]

The doctrinal issue at stake was no less than the meaning of faith; in the summer of Tenmei 4 (1784), Dairin, a member of the Zaiya, an unofficial scholastic group opposing the Gakurin, authored "A Compilation of Correct and False Views on Faith in the Shinshū" (Shinshū anjin seigihen 真宗安心正偽篇), criticizing Kōzon's position. The Gakurin responded with two documents, prompting a round of debate; the treatise that finally undermined their position was "The Diamond Essence of the Jōdo Shinshū" (Jōdo Shinshū kongōhai 浄土真宗 金剛錍), completed in the tenth month of Kansei 9 (1797) by Daiei (1760–1804).[59] Daiei argued that the three minds of the Primal Vow were unified as the one mind of entrusting (shingyō 信楽), not as the one mind of the aspiration for birth (yokushō 欲生); thus the right cause of birth is entrusting (or faith), not the aspiration for birth. On publication, the document is said to have sold out in three days with two hundred copies; eventually, close to seven hundred copies were distributed throughout the country.[60]

---

[55] Asaeda, "Igi: Sangō wakuran," 345; SSJ, 184, 356.

[56] HS 2: 359.

[57] This work records four lectures given by Kōzon in 1762, on the last day of the second month and the first day of the third, at the branch temple in Fukui, Echizen province; it was published in Meiwa 1 (1764).1 (HS 2: 355–56; Asaeda, "Igi: Sangō wakuran," 346; HN, 183).

[58] Asaeda, "Igi: Sangō wakuran," 347.

[59] This was the earliest of four versions of the treatise; with the addition of two prefaces, it was published as "The Diamond Essence of the Direct Path of Crosswise Transcendence" (ōchō jikidō kongōhai), in the fifth month of Kyōwa 1 (1801). For accounts of the exchanges leading up to this event, see HS 2: 360–64, 374–75; Asaeda, "Igi: Sangō wakuran," 348–51 (giving the publication date as Kansei 12).

[60] Asaeda, "Igi: Sangō wakuran," 348–51. The Gakurin, unable to ignore

In Kansei 9 (1797), when Chidō, a strong supporter of the "three acts" position, became head of the Gakurin, the argument intensified; the level of discord in Mino province prompted intervention by the shogunate;[61] and in Kyōwa 3 (1803), from the fourth to the tenth month, both sides were examined in Kyoto.[62] The investigation then moved to Edo, with Chidō among the representatives for the Gakurin, and Daiei among those for the Zaiya; on Bunka 2 (1805).4.26, the *sangō kimyō* position was declared heretical.[63] On Bunka 3 (1806).7.11, with a judgement by the Commission on Shrines and Temples (*jisha bugyō* 寺社奉行), the Sangō Upheaval was officially concluded.[64] Honnyo's two letters were issued that same year in support of the orthodox position.[65]

Of particular significance for our discussion is Honnyo's interpretation of Shinran's teaching in Rennyo's terms, emphasizing Other-Power faith as the true essence of the Pure Land way transmitted by Shinran. The text of the "Letter of Adjudication" is as follows:

The founding master [Shinran] taught as fundamental that the

---

such a response, declared the document in error and, for a time, successfully opposed its reprinting. They argued that the document refuted the sentence, "Casting off the self-power mind of the sundry practices and disciplines, we single-mindedly entrust ourselves to Amida Tathāgata to save us [in regard to] the birth that is to come [in the Pure Land], the most important matter" (*Moromoro no zōgyō zōshu jiriki no kokoro o furisute, isshin ni Amida Nyorai warera ga kondo no ichidaiji no goshō ontasuke sōrae to tanomitatematsuru* もろもろの雑行雑修自力のこころをふりすて , 一心に阿弥陀如来我等が今度の一大事の後生御たすけ候へとたのみ奉る) as an expression of self-power; in addition, they claimed that it also refuted the *Ryōgemon*, since the sentence at issue was virtually the same as that statement's opening sentence. This was met with a denial that the document refuted either *The Letters* (in which variations of the phrase *goshō tasuke tamae to tanomu* 後生たすけたまへとたのむ appear) or the *Ryōgemon* and a demand to be shown just where this appeared; the Gakurin replied that the entire document interpreted "*goshō tasuke tamae to tanomu*" in such a simplistic way that it thoroughly confused the clearly-transmitted teaching on faith (HS 2: 376). Rennyo's writings were obviously central to the arguments of both sides, a fact that—ironically—underscores his role as the arbiter of orthodoxy.

61 HS 2: 377–79.
62 HS 2: 385–86.
63 HS 2: 386–90.
64 HS 2: 391.
65 HS 2: 393. For a discussion of the concept of heresy and the significance of the Sangō Upheaval, see James C. Dobbins, "The Concept of Heresy in the Jōdo Shinshū," *Transactions of the International Conference of Orientalists in Japan* 25 (1980): 41–44.

essential point transmitted in our school is simply Other-Power faith. The [Larger] Sūtra explains that faith as "hearing the Name and realizing faith and joy, for even a single thought-moment";[66] the [Jōdo]ron interprets it as "single-mindedly taking refuge."[67] Hence the master, explaining the [Jōdo]ron's [use of the] term "single-mindedly," said: " 'Single-mindedly' means being without double-mindedness and without doubt in regard to the words of the master of the teaching, the World-Honored One. This, in other words, is true and real faith."[68] Therefore, from the founder on down, generation after generation [of his successors] have received and transmitted this [teaching]; in particular, Shinshō-in [Rennyo] carefully teaches this single path in the five-fascicle [compilation of his] letters.

The meaning of "faith" is that we simply discard the self-power mind of the sundry practices and disciplines and entrust ourselves single-heartedly and steadfastly to Amida Tathāgata to save us in [regard to] the most important matter, the birth that is to come [in the Pure Land]; and when sincere faith is awakened in us, Amida unfailingly sends forth his all-pervading light, with which he graciously embraces us. This, in other words, is the teaching established in our tradition that "with the awakening of the one thought-moment of entrusting, the cause [of birth] is completed in ordinary life."[69] It must be understood that, once faith is decisively settled, the Name we say day and night, morning and evening, is the nenbutsu of gratitude for [Amida] Buddha's benevolence. Those who understand in this way are indeed exemplary of what it is to have fully realized our tradition's faith.

Recently, however, we hear that [some people] raise the principle of the three acts (sangō 三業) [of the Buddha and of sentient beings], which is not discussed in our tradition, and, prefixing "the necessary [manifestation of]" to "the three acts," debate whether [others] do or do not know the year, month, day, and hour [at which faith was settled]. Some completely misinterpret "the one thought-moment of taking refuge," or, hesitant over "the three acts," reject the word "entrust"; some are confused about other points as well. This is indeed a lamentable situation.

In Master [Shinran]'s teaching, we are specifically admonished, "Thinking that one can be born in the Pure Land by correcting

---

[66] *Larger Sūtra*, SSZ 1: 24 (T 12.272b); *Kyōgyōshinshō*, SSZ 2: 49, 62 (T 83.601a, 605a).

[67] *Jōdoron*, SSZ 1: 269 (T 26.230c).

[68] *Songō shinzō meimon*, SSZ 2: 563–64 (T 83.681c).

[69] *ichinen hokki heizei gōjō*. See letter 1:4 for references to Rennyo's use of the term.

one's confusion over acts, words, and thoughts, and practicing good [acts] is 'self-power'."[70] In brief, regardless of what your understanding was previously, you must from now on overturn your evil delusions and ground yourself in Other-Power faith based on the truth and reality of the Primal Vow; those who do so will truly accord with the master's intention. Beyond that, carefully observe the laws of the land (*ōbō*) and the laws of the provinces (*kokuhō* 国法), honor the [principles of] humanity and justice, and continue properly in the dharma. Hold to and never relinquish the fundamental intent of the items that have been established as stated above.

Bunka 3 [1806].11.6
Honnyo, disciple of Śākyamuni
(written seal)[71]

The "Letter of Adjudication" opens with a discussion of Shinran's emphasis on Other-Power faith, underscoring the master's foundation in Pure Land texts as it explains the realization of that faith. In stressing the continuous transmission of the teaching, it makes a particular point of Rennyo's contribution, a continuing legacy conveyed by the five-fascicle compilation, *The Letters*.

The second paragraph draws powerfully on the familiar style and content of Rennyo's letters to describe the process by which faith is settled and to define the nenbutsu in terms of gratitude. Against this prologue, the third paragraph makes a clear contrast between the "three-act" misinterpretations and the orthodox position, underscoring the depth of the issue with a warning against "self-power" thought and practice.

The conclusion, an admonition that again draws on Rennyo, gives a hint of the disruptive effects of the Sangō Upheaval in reminding its readers of the two dimensions of their lives—the inner, in which they should be grounded in Other-Power faith in accord with Shinran's teaching, and the outer, in which they must carry out their responsibilities as citizens and as members of society. It is significant that, following the Sangō Upheaval, the Nishi Honganji entrusted authority for the determination of heresy to a body of scholar-priests (*Kangakuryō*) in an attempt to avoid further disputes, this one having led to such bitterness and divisiveness within the community.[72]

To sum up the significance of *The Letters* as scripture: for Shinran,

---

[70] *Mattōshō*, SSZ 2: 658.

[71] Shinshū Seiten Hensan Iinkai, ed., *Jōdo Shinshū seiten*, 1413–15.

[72] Dobbins, "The Concept of Heresy in the Jōdo Shinshū," 43.

the truth and reality of Amida's Vow, which transcends history, is manifested in history textually as the *Larger Sūtra*,

> the right exposition for which the Tathāgata appeared in the world, the wondrous scripture [*myōten* 妙典] rare and most excellent, the conclusive and ultimate exposition of the One Vehicle, the precious words disclosing perfect, instantaneous fulfillment, the sincere words praised by all the Buddhas throughout the ten quarters, the true teaching in consummate readiness for the beings of this day.[73]

The commentarial tradition of the seven Pure Land masters is continuous with the *Larger Sūtra* in transmitting the truth and reality of Amida's Primal Vow. This is the teaching received by Shinran and manifested in his writings.

Some two centuries later, Shinran is reported to have reappeared as Rennyo to restore the teaching to its former purity; following Rennyo's death, the five-fascicle compilation of his letters came to be seen as the authoritative statement of that same teaching. With the Honganji's further institutionalization, *The Letters* came to provide, in the Tokugawa period, the doctrinal basis for a confessional statement defining orthodox belief and practice. Again, when the Nishi Honganji was torn by an internal dispute over the proper interpretation of faith, *The Letters* was a major source of authority for adjudicating the issue.

A final note: scripturalization of the teaching continues within the Nishi Honganji in the context of translating Shinshū texts into Western languages in modern times. Contemporary Shinshū scholars writing in English have appropriated the term "scripture(s)" (also "canon") to designate and delimit their ancient textual tradition: Pure Land sūtras of Indian and central Asian origin; commentaries by the seven Pure Land masters; and, in particular, the works of their founder, Shinran, and his successors, Kakunyo, Zonkaku, and Rennyo.

Following Japan's modern encounter with the West and the return of Christian missionaries in the latter part of the nineteenth century, participants in Shinshū tradition, in Japan and later in the West, expressed the need for their own book of scriptures. Similarities as well as differences in the concept of sacred text—whether spoken or written—underlying the Shinshū Scriptures (*Shinshū seiten*), the Hebrew

---

[73] *Teaching*, 1: 67–68; SSZ 2: 4.

Bible, and the Christian Bible are suggestive for further comparative study of scripture as a generic form.[74]

---

[74] The Shinshū's textual tradition initially drawn from India and China appears to have been influenced more recently in subtle ways by Western religious traditions. For example, beginning in the Meiji period, the covers of compilations of Shinshū texts, printed on gilt-edged pages, have folds to protect their contents. Christian missionaries in Japan at the turn of the century used Bibles and prayer books of similar design; it appears that not only the concept but also the form for packaging scripture left its mark on modern Japanese religious consciousness. There has been, and continues to be, experimentation with the form in which to present the Shinshū textual tradition. See, for example:

(1) *Shinshū shōgyō daizen*, 3 vols. (1903; repr. Tokyo: Shinkō Honten, 1906), in traditional folio bindings, is comprehensive in contents;

(2) *Shinshū seiten zensho* (1907; repr. Tokyo: Fusanbō, 1932), in two volumes (one with Chinese texts and the other with Japanese), has leather covers with folds to protect the contents on gilt-edged pages;

(3) *Seiten: Jōdo Shinshū* (Tokyo: Meiji Shoin, 1919), a single volume containing major texts beginning with Shinran's writings, has a leather cover with the inscription, *Seiten*, and folds to protect the contents on gilt-edged pages similar to a small Bible or prayer book;

(4) *Shinshū shōgyō zensho* (1941; repr. Kyoto: Ōyagi Kōbundō, 1969–1970), in five volumes with hard covers, is the most comprehensive in contents;

(5) *Shinshū seiten* (1956; repr. Kyoto: Nagata Bunshōdō, 1969), a single comprehensive volume with a red plastic cover contains texts, liturgies, and hymns; and

(6) *Jōdo Shinshū seiten: Chūshakuban* (Kyoto: Honganji Shuppanbu, 1988), largely similar in contents to the *Shinshū seiten* (item 5 above), includes also brief commentaries on the texts and a glossary of terms.

Chapter 6

Gratitude: Shinshū Piety

A WOODBLOCK PRINT depicts a recumbent figure not unlike those sanctified persons sculpted in stone on tombs in European cathedrals. The figure in the print is Dōshū (d. 1516), a devoted disciple of Rennyo, who lived in the village of Akao in Etchū province. He sleeps on a pallet of forty-eight sticks of split firewood, his nightly reminder of Amida Buddha's eons of bodhisattva activity in fulfilling the forty-eight Vows that assure him of birth in the Pure Land in the afterlife.[1]

---

[1] The woodblock print, by the artist Munakata Shikō, was inspired by a small wood carving of Dōshū known as the "Gratitude Image" (報恩の像 *hōon no zō*), in the collection of Gyōtoku-ji, a temple said to have been founded by Dōshū in Akao, Toyama prefecture. The story behind the carving is told as follows:

Dōshū had many scars that he always tried to hide from other people, and if anyone noticed and asked about them, he got very embarrassed and refused to say anything. In the room where he slept, he had a large stack of split wood where one would ordinarily keep bedding. When a neighbor, overcome with curiosity, peeked in to see what Dōshū was doing at bedtime, he discovered him saying the nenbutsu and arranging the wood, piece by piece. Eventually he lay down on top of the wood, pulled a thin quilt over himself, and went off to sleep. Whether it was because he was unable to get to sleep or because he was uncomfortable, he would say the nenbutsu every time he turned over. It was obvious why there were always scars on his body.

Astonished by what he had seen, the man later went to Dōshū, admitted to what he had done, and said, "You always tell us that we will be saved just by entrusting ourselves to Amida Buddha, but there's more to it, isn't there? Really, we have to do that difficult kind of practice to be saved, don't we?" "Not at all," replied Dōshū. "There's no more to it than what I said. But if a stubborn fellow like me sleeps on top of bedding, he'd sleep the whole night through, completely unaware of the Buddha's benevolence. By making it difficult to sleep,

12. Dōshū of Akao; woodblock print by Munakata Shikō

Roughly-scripted in the upper right-hand area of the print is Dōshū's rule, "As long as life lasts, never forget the most important matter, the afterlife (*goshō no ichidaiji* 後生の一大事)." This is the first of a list of twenty-one drawn up by Dōshū some two years after Rennyo's death.[2] The recurring theme of the rules is implicit in the first. Overall, they provide guidelines for a life of gratitude to Amida and to those who have transmitted the teaching: the seven Pure Land masters, Shinran, and, most immediately, Rennyo. Matters of doctrine are construed as less relevant than the issue of how to conduct one's life as a grateful participant in Shinshū tradition and loyal member of the Honganji.[3]

Apart from Dōshū's set of rules, our knowledge of him is drawn primarily from several passages in the memoir *Goichidaiki kikigaki*, and

---

I'm at least able to think of the Tathāgata's compassion when I wake and say the nenbutsu" (Iwami Mamoru, *Akao no Dōshū* [1956; repr. Kyoto: Nagata Bunshōdō, 1983], 44–46. See also Asaeda Zenshō, *Myōkōnin no kokoro* [Kyoto: Nagata Bunshōdō, 1987]).

[2] The list is dated Bunki 1 (1501).12.24 (Iwami, *Akao no Dōshū*, 97).

[3] Dōshū's list of rules invites comparison with Rennyo's forty-one-item testament, dictated several weeks before his death; see *Kūzenki*, RSG, 52–58. For a comparison of Rennyo's testament with Hideyoshi Toyotomi's twenty-one-item code and an interpretation of the significance of the testament in the context of the Honganji's hereditary lineage, see Yamaori Tetsuo, "Rennyo ni miru 'yuigon' to 'ketsuen'," in *Rennyo*, ed. Minami Midō Shinbun (Osaka: Nanba Betsuin, 1986), 81–87.

from one of Rennyo's letters, dated Meiō 5 (1496).2.28, which refers to Dōshū by his lay name, Yashichi.[4] The memoir records Dōshū's statement:

> Our daily resolve should be to offer the morning service without fail; our monthly resolve, to go to a nearby place where the founder's image is enshrined; and, our yearly resolve, to make a pilgrimage to the head temple.[5]

For Dōshū, this meant daily attendance at the Inami branch temple in Akao, monthly trips to the district temple in Inami (in winter, passing through massive snowdrifts via a dangerous mountain path), and an annual pilgrimage to Yamashina Hongan-ji in Kyoto, where he visited Rennyo. He considered Rennyo to be a manifestation of Amida and once, in a burst of devotion, said that if Rennyo told him to, he would "fill in the lake in Ōmi province," the present-day Lake Biwa.[6]

Dōshū sought at every opportunity to share the teaching with others and on one occasion begged Rennyo to give him a letter for the villagers at Akao. The memoir reports:

> When Dōshū requested a letter from the resident priest [Rennyo] who preceded the last, [Rennyo] said: "A letter may slip from your hands, but if you will just hold faith (shin) in your heart, you won't lose it." The following year, [Rennyo] did write a letter for him.[7]

Dōshū also testified to his own attentiveness in listening to the teaching: "I always hear the same words, but I'm as grateful as if I were hearing them for the first time."[8]

A TWOFOLD LEGACY

The image that emerges from these brief glimpses of Dōshū in the

---

[4] RSI, 379–80 (#127).

[5] The memoir entry notes that, on hearing Dōshū's statement, Ennyo, compiler of *The Letters*, exclaimed "Well said!" (*Mukashi monogatariki*, RSG, 251; *Goichidaiki kikigaki*, SSZ 3: 545). This passage is quoted in Suzuki Daisetsu, *Suzuki Daisetsu zenshū*, vol. 8, *Nihonteki reisei/Nihon no reiseika*, eds. Hisamatsu Shin'ichi et al. (Tokyo: Iwanami Shoten, 1968), 173–74. See also Daisetz Suzuki, *Japanese Spirituality*, comp. Japanese National Commission for Unesco, trans. Norman Waddell (Tokyo: Japan Society for the Promotion of Science, 1972), 169.

[6] *Jitsugo kyūki*, RSG, 101.

[7] *Jitsugo kyūki*, RSG, 128.

[8] *Jitsugo kyūki*, RSG, 86.

memoirs and from the single reference in Rennyo's letters is that of a saintly figure whom Suzuki Daisetsu cites as "heading the list of Myōkōnin," extraordinarily good people who, he feels, provide "fine material for any work concerned with the historical development of Japanese spirituality."[9] What appears to attract Suzuki to persons such as Dōshū is the spontaneity of their living wholly in grateful response to the working of Amida's Vow-mind; he recognizes a quality that we describe as the non-calculative aspect of orthodox Shinshū piety as gratitude.[10] Saying the Name in gratitude is the persistent refrain of Rennyo's letters.

A second aspect of orthodox Shinshū piety, noted only incidently by Suzuki in his portrait of Dōshū, is that of gratitude as social obliga-tion: Suzuki associates Dōshū's devotion with a Confucian ethos, see-ing him as "courageous and resolute in seeking and following the Way."[11] What Suzuki fails to touch upon in his discussion of Japanese spirituality is that this sense of obligation "in seeking the Way" is vulnerable to coercion by the leaders of a religious order enjoining conformity, submissiveness, and obedience. In Dōshū, this second as-pect emerges as an unquestioning acceptance of Rennyo's injunctions to honor social obligations, whether in relation to ecclesiastical or to political authority. In the final item of his twenty-one rules, Dōshū says to himself:

> Oh, you mind, once again, don't go against what I have just said; be strict with me and discreet in everything. Once again, don't let me violate the regulations (on'okite 御おきて) or the laws of the country (hatto はっと); inwardly, let me hold fast to the trustworthiness and sanctity of the one thought-moment and, outwardly, let me act with deep humility.[12]

---

[9] Suzuki, *Japanese Spirituality*, 167; Suzuki, *Suzuki Daisetsu zenshū*, 8: 171–72.

[10] In this study, we use the terms "non-calculative" and "without calcula-tion" to express that aspect of Rennyo's piety resonating most closely with Shin-ran's *jinen* 自然 (frequently translated as "naturalness" or "spontaneity"). Close to a literal translation of Shinran's phrase *hakarai ni arazu* はからいにあらず , "without calculation" seems to avoid the ambiguities of "naturalness" and to offer a precision of meaning for that quality of piety so distinctive of Shinran's life and thought. The phrase *hakarai ni arazu* is used in a number of Shinran's writings: for example, see the discussion of *jinen* in *Shōzōmatsu wasan*, SSZ 2: 530ab; *Ichinen tanen mon'i*, SSZ 2: 611; and *Mattōshō*, SSZ 2: 663–67. As expressed in *Tannishō* in regard to the nenbutsu, "No [self] working is the [true] working" (Hirota, *Tannishō*, 75; SSZ 2: 778).

[11] Suzuki, *Suzuki Daisetsu zenshū*, 8: 174; Suzuki, *Japanese Spirituality*, 169.

[12] Iwami, *Akao no Dōshū*, 152–53.

Thus Dōshū embodies both aspects of Rennyo's twofold legacy: gratitude as living without calculation and as honoring social obligations. For Dōshū, non-calculative piety in relation to the transcendent and fulfillment of obligations in regard to the mundane coalesce in a deeply-held unity. "Heading the list of Myōkōnin" in this respect, he is properly among the most notable exemplars of Shinshū piety, following Shinran and Rennyo, in the history of Japanese spirituality.

Shinran's writings in his final years clearly identify spontaneous, non-calculative gratitude as the quality that should undergird and color all of life. As we have seen, part of Rennyo's contribution to Shinshū tradition was to give ritual expression to Shinran's teaching through corporate acts of thanksgiving, nurturing and shaping a piety normative for the entire Shinshū community.

As with the institutionalization of any founder's vision, there was with Rennyo an inevitable shift in emphasis from spontaneous individual acts to corporate rituals inseparable from constraints of social obligation. With this shift in emphasis, the potential for reification of Shinran's teaching and bifurcation of the transcendent and the mundane was greatly enhanced. This tendency towards reification, in some degree common to all religious traditions, was exacerbated by the challenges facing the Shinshū community during Rennyo's tenure as head priest.[13]

In our earlier discussion of the annual thanksgiving services, we noted the importance of the coordinate concepts of *on* 恩 and *hōon* 報恩, rendered with varying emphases according to context. *On*, frequently translated into English as "benevolence," may be construed as the saving power of Amida's Vow; it elicits a response, *hōon*, expressed through acts of thanksgiving, the only appropriate response to Amida's benevolence in a tradition that eschews any trace of self-power practices.[14] An examination of Shinran's and Rennyo's use of *on*

---

[13] For social theory readily applicable to this process, see O'Dea, "Sociological Dilemmas," 71–89.

[14] While *on* is a concept central to understanding Japanese civilization as a whole, the concept *hōon* has special significance for the Japanese Buddhist tradition, especially for the new Buddhist movements of the Kamakura period. Robert N. Bellah distinguishes two main categories of the divine in his analysis of Japanese religion: (1) a supernatural entity such as Amida, who dispenses nurture, care, and love; and (2) the ground of being, or the inner essence of reality. As to the former, religious action is *hōon* in whatever form it may take: "Action with respect to deity as a benevolent superordinate [Amida] gets us at once into the theory of *on*. Deity in some form dispenses blessings (*on*) and it is the obligation of the recipient to make return for these blessings (*hōon*). Reli-

and *hōon*, their compounds, and their cognates suggests differences in emphasis in their respective interpretations.[15] Shinran's spontaneous expressions of gratitude carry the sense that Amida's benevolence is directed to him personally—"for my sake alone." In Rennyo's case, there is a shift in focus: he enjoins members of his community to express their gratitude and repay their indebtedness to Shinran by attaining faith and by fulfilling their obligations as members of society.

LIVING WITHOUT CALCULATION

Shinran's *Kyōgyōshinshō* begins and ends with expressions of joy for what he has received from Amida Buddha. Having "entered the Sea of the Vow once and for all,"[16] his writings, and indeed his whole life, constitute a grateful response to Amida's benevolence in awakening him to the true essence of the Pure Land way. In the preface, Shinran sets the tone for the entire work:

> Reverently entrusting myself to the teaching, practice, and realization that are the true essence of the Pure Land way, I am especially aware of the profundity of the Tathāgata's benevolence. Here I rejoice in what I have heard and extol what I have attained.[17]

Reflecting in chapter six, "Transformed Buddha-Bodies and Lands,"

---

gious action, then, is the various forms this *hōon* may take" (*Tokugawa Religion: The Values of Pre-Industrial Japan* [Glencoe: The Free Press, 1957], 70).

[15] For Shinran and Rennyo, *button* 仏恩 is "[Amida] Buddha's benevolence"; *chion* 知恩 is "recognizing [Amida's] benevolence;" *ondoku* 恩徳 is "the virtue of [Amida's] benevolence" or, simply, "benevolence"; and *goon* 御恩 is the honorific form used in specific reference to Amida's benevolence. Other Shinshū documents refer to *chōon* 朝恩 "imperial benevolence" and *kōon* 皇恩 "emperor's benevolence." Also, *hō* 報 is found frequently in its verbal form *hōzu* 報ず, "respond [in gratitude]," or "repay [a debt]." Compound forms include *hōtoku* 報徳 "respond [in gratitude] to [Amida's] benevolence" or "repay [Amida's] benevolence," and *hōsha* 報謝 and *hōjin* 報身, "respond in gratitude" or "repay indebtedness." The term *hōon shatoku* 報恩謝徳, used frequently in Rennyo's writings, is rendered in reference to Amida as "repayment of indebtedness and expression of gratitude for [Amida's] virtue," linking gratitude with the return for *on* as social obligation. The *hōonkō* is a thanksgiving service held on the anniversary of Shinran's death as the corporate expression of the community's gratitude for his great virtue as founder.

[16] *Kyōgyōshinshō*, SSZ 2: 166. Also see Bandō Shōjun, "Shinshū to hōon shisō," *Shinshū kyōgaku kenkyū* 5 (1981): 16–25.

[17] *Teaching*, 1: 59; *Kyōgyōshinshō*, SSZ 2: 1.

on the three stages of his conversion (*sangan tennyū* 三願転入), Shin-ran's joy and gratitude abound as he examines the process through which he has come to realize the saving power of Amida's Eighteenth Vow:

> Now that I have entered the sea of the Vow forever, I am deeply aware of the Buddha's benevolence. To express my gratitude for his utmost virtue, I have gathered the essential passages of the true teaching and continually say the [Name], the sea of inconceivable virtue. I rejoice in it more and more, and, above all, I receive it with gratitude.[18]

The postscript resounds with similar expressions of joy and gratitude to the Tathāgata and to the Pure Land masters:

> I am deeply aware of the Tathāgata's compassion and sincerely re-vere the benevolence of the masters' teaching. As my joy increases, my sense of indebtedness grows deeper and deeper. Accordingly, I have collected the essentials of the true teaching and gathered the important Pure Land passages. I simply reflect on the depth of the Buddha's benevolence, and am not shamed by people's abuse.[19]

The inspiration for Shinran's work is his experience of Amida's com-passion and, most immediately, the benevolence of his own master, Hōnen; as his joy increases, his desire to share the teaching deepens.

The three passages cited above are drawn from the rare autobio-graphical sections of *Kyōgyōshinshō*, each introduced by the phrase: "I, Gutoku Shinran, disciple of Śākyamuni. . . ." Granted that this treatise is the most carefully crafted and painstakingly revised of all of his works, his faith bursts forth at moments in lyrical praise and thanks-giving for Amida's saving power. One is reminded of Karl Barth's *Evangelical Theology*, which concludes with the "Gloria Patri."[20]

In *Tannishō*, we glimpse again the deeply personal quality of Shin-ran's gratitude for what Amida's Vow has done in his life:

---

[18] *Kyōgyōshinshō*, SSZ 2: 166.

[19] *Kyōgyōshinshō*, SSZ 2: 203.

[20] Karl Barth, *Evangelical Theology: An Introduction* (Grand Rapids: Eerdmans, 1980), 206: "it is the very purpose of theological work, at any rate, to know about this love [Agape] and, therefore, to join in the praise of God as expressed in the words of that familiar section of the liturgy of the early Church, with which we may now conclude:

> Gloria Patri et Filio et Spiritui sancto
> Sicut erat in principio et (est) nunc et (erit) semper
> et in saecula saeculorum!"

> When I deeply consider Amida's Vow, which arose from five kalpas
> of contemplation, [I feel that] it was entirely for my sake alone. Then
> how grateful I am for the Primal Vow, by which—though I am so
> deeply burdened with karma—Amida resolved to save me.[21]

Shinran's gratitude for the Primal Vow derives from his conviction
that Amida persisted in five kalpas of meditation entirely for his sake.
His joyful awareness of the saving power that resulted from Amida's
bodhisattva activities as Dharmākara is the source of his sense of indebtedness to Hōnen, the good teacher who made available to him the
true essence of the Pure Land way. Shinran repeatedly emphasizes the
continuity of his teaching with that of the Pure Land masters. In the
chapter on faith in *Kyōgyōshinshō*, he lists the ten kinds of benefit
granted to those who "realize the diamond-like true mind."[22] The
eighth, that of "being aware of Amida's benevolence and of responding in gratitude to his virtue," also permeates and overflows his other
writings, particularly the hymns.

Of Shinran's three major collections of hymns, *Jōdo wasan* and
Kōsō wasan were prepared immediately following the completion of
the earliest draft of *Kyōgyōshinshō*, and *Shōzōmatsu wasan* a decade later
in his final years. We are told by Shinran himself that he repeated "the
same things over and over" so that even those who were painfully ignorant could easily understand.[23] It was in the hymns that Shinran
sought to express the most profound tenets of Pure Land teaching in
popular form. We see this in several hymns illuminating the fundamental structure of his thought as expressed in the coordinate concepts—*on* and *hōon*, Amida's benevolence and the gratitude of the
practicer of faith. From *Jōdo wasan*:

> Those who truly realize faith
> and say Amida's Name
> are always mindful of the Buddha
> and of returning his benevolence in gratitude.[24]

In Shinran's thought, faith has two sides. On Amida's side, there
is nonduality: Amida's mind and the mind of sentient beings are identical. On the side of sentient beings, there is duality: Amida's mind and

---

[21] *Tannishō*, SSZ 2: 792.

[22] *Kyōgyōshinshō*, SSZ 2: 72; for a translation of the ten kinds of benefit, see
Teaching, 2: 257–58.

[23] *Yuishinshō mon'i*, SSZ 2: 638; for a translation of the entire passage, see
Essentials, 52.

[24] *Jōdo wasan*, SSZ 2: 485a.

the mind of sentient beings are mutually exclusive. Through the inconceivable activity of the nenbutsu, the two sides of faith are in dynamic interaction.[25] In *Shōzōmatsu wasan*, Shinran explains:

> On entering the vast sea of Amida's wisdom-Vow,
> the waters of foolish beings' minds, good and evil,
> are immediately transformed
> into the mind of great compassion.[26]

As the realization of faith is possible only through the working of Amida's compassion, practicers of faith should return his benevolence in gratitude, recognizing, too, that their praise furthers the spread of the teaching:

> We praise the Buddha's wisdom and virtue
> so that all in the ten directions who have ties [with the teaching]
> may hear.
> Those who have truly realized faith
> should continually express their gratitude for the Buddha's benevolence.[27]

Aware of their inability to cultivate virtue through self-effort, practicers of faith acquire virtue through the working of Amida's Vow. Shinran explains the process of transformation in *Yuishinshō mon'i*:

> "To be made to become so [*jinen*]" means that without the practicer's calculating in any way whatsoever, all his past, present, and future evil karma is transformed into the highest good [i.e. Buddha's virtue]. To be transformed means that evil karma, *without being nullified or eradicated*, is made into the highest good, just as all waters, upon entering the great ocean, immediately become ocean water. We are made to acquire the Tathāgata's virtues through entrusting ourselves to his Vow-power; hence the expression, "made to become so."[28]

Those who engage instead in self-power practices have no awareness of the Buddha's benevolence:

> Practicing the auxiliary [acts] together with the right [act][29]

---

[25] See introduction, n. 15; in an effort to catch the subtlety of Shinran's thought, we characterized it as embracing "a simultaneity of nonduality and duality—sameness/opposition or oneness/contradiction." See also Rogers, "The Shin Faith of Rennyo," 59–63, and " 'Shinjin' to 'anjin'," 26–36.

[26] *Shōzōmatsu wasan*, SSZ 2: 520c.

[27] *Jōdo wasan*, SSZ 2: 491c.

[28] *Essentials*, 32 (emphasis added); *Yuishinshō mon'i*, SSZ 2: 623.

[29] *joshō* 助正 . A contraction of *jogō* 助業 (auxiliary acts) and *shōgō* 正業 (right

is called "[following] sundry disciplines."[30]
Since people [who do this] have not realized the one mind [of
  faith],[31]
they have no thought of returning the Buddha's benevolence
  in gratitude.[32]

Shinran differentiates practicers of faith from those who follow the
Path of Sages (Tendai, Shingon, or Zen monks pursuing traditional
Buddhist practices) and from those who say the nenbutsu with a self-
power understanding (devotees of the Pure Land path—Jōdoshū). In
contrast to practicers of faith, those engaged in mixed practices are unaware of the working of Amida's compassion and therefore lacking in
gratitude.

For practicers of faith, the only means of expressing gratitude is
through the nenbutsu, which arises spontaneously in response to the
working of Amida's Vow. Shinran writes in *Kōsō wasan*:

If we do not receive the power of the universal Vow,
when will we leave this present world?[33]
Deeply realizing the Buddha's benevolence,
we should always say Amida's Name.[34]

For Shinran, saying the nenbutsu is nothing other than Amida's Name
working in him, a foolish being, and awakening faith in his heart and
mind. In *Mattōshō*, he adds:

[The] practice [of nenbutsu] is to say it perhaps once, perhaps ten
times, on hearing and realizing that birth into the Buddha Land is
attained by saying the Name fulfilled in the Primal Vow. . . . there
is no shinjin separate from nenbutsu. . . . there can be no nenbutsu
separate from shinjin.[35]

In Pure Land tradition, Shinran was the first to clarify the identity of
faith and the nenbutsu. It is precisely in the context of faith that saying
the nenbutsu becomes the exclusive act of thanksgiving, an expression
of gratitude for Amida's benevolence. Again from *Kōsō wasan*:

---

act). Taken together, these constitute the five right practices (*goshōgyō* 五正業) as
classified by Shan-tao. See fascicle one, n. 9.

[30] *zasshu* 雑修 . A term in contrast with *senju* 専修 "single practice"; it refers
to mixing the right practice of the nenbutsu with the four auxiliary acts, or to
practicing the nenbutsu for self-serving purposes. See *Once-calling*, 88–89.

[31] See fascicle one, n. 75.

[32] *Kōsō wasan*, SSZ 2: 509a.

[33] See fascicle two, n. 39.

[34] *Kōsō wasan*, SSZ 2: 511b.

[35] *Letters*, 39–40; *Mattōshō*, SSZ 2: 672.

It is by the power of Śākyamuni, the original teacher,
that we cast off the suffering of measureless kalpas in this present
world
and await [birth in] the uncreated [realm]³⁶ of the Pure Land;
we should always express our gratitude for his compassionate
benevolence.³⁷

Each of the verses cited from *Kōsō wasan* is based on one or more passages in Shan-tao's commentaries. While Shan-tao had recognized a subordinate role for mixed, or self-power, practices, the radical quality of Shinran's position lay in his total rejection of such practices and his insistence on the "practice" of faith alone.

The *Shōzōmatsu wasan*, expressing Shinran's thought in its maturity, refocuses attention on the identity of the realization of faith and saying the Name and on the dynamic relationship of the coordinate concepts *hō* and *hōon* — mindfulness of Amida's benevolence and the desire to respond in gratitude:

Through the compassion of Śākyamuni and Amida
one realizes the aspiration for Buddhahood;
and by entering the wisdom of faith,
one becomes a person who returns the Buddha's benevolence
in gratitude.³⁸

In the same collection of hymns, Shinran makes the point in another way:

By doubting the inconceivable working of the Buddha's wisdom
and choosing self-power nenbutsu [practice],
one stops at the borderland, the realm of indolence and pride,³⁹

---

³⁶ *mui* 無為 ; Skt. *asaṃskṛta. Mui* contrasts with the conditioned world; it refers to the eternal, absolute reality beyond birth, death, and change (BGDJ, 1312–13). "Supreme nirvāṇa is the uncreated dharma-body (*mui hosshin* 無為 法身); the uncreated dharma-body is true reality (*jissō* 実相)" (*Kyōgyōshinshō*, SSZ 2: 103).

³⁷ *Kōsō wasan*, SSZ 2: 511b. This hymn is based on three passages from Shan-tao's *Hanjusan*: SSZ 1: 701, 707, 725 (see *Kōsō Wasan*, 112).

³⁸ *Shōzōmatsu wasan*, SSZ 2: 520a. For further examples, see SSZ 2: 519c (#30), translated into English in *Shōzōmatsu Wasan*, 30; SSZ 2: 521c (#49), *Shōzōmatsu Wasan*, 49; SSZ 2: 523a (#59), *Shōzōmatsu Wasan*, 59; SSZ 2: 526b (#87), *Shōzōmatsu Wasan*, 87.

³⁹ *henji keman* 辺地解慢 . Shinran equates these two realms: the borderland (*henji*), Amida Buddha's transformed land, is the place of birth for those who doubt the Buddha's wisdom; the realm of indolence and pride (*kemangai* 解慢界) is the place of birth for those who engage in the sundry practices and disciplines

and there is no thought of returning the Buddha's benevolence in gratitude.[40]

Those who seek birth in the Pure Land through their own efforts cut themselves off from the working of Other Power and therefore feel none of the gratitude that flows from the recognition of the Buddha's benevolence.

Shinran's *Kyōgyōshinshō*, hymns, and other writings make abundantly clear that gratitude for the Buddha's benevolence is fundamental for the life of faith. This gratitude is expressed without calculation in the spontaneous saying of Amida's name. Shinran rejects the notion that saying the Name even out of a sense of filial piety is efficacious in any way; according to *Tannishō*, he attests: "I have never once said the nenbutsu for the sake of my father and mother."[41] Rather, "the [many utterances of the] nenbutsu said throughout one's life should all — each and every one — be considered expressions of gratitude for the benevolence of the Tathāgata's great compassion and of thankfulness for the [Buddha's] virtue."[42]

Practicers of faith are those who live free of calculative self-effort, despite their failure to be rid of blind passions. It is *jinen* that best characterizes the quality of their lives, lived in grateful response to the benevolence of Amida and their teachers: "If one is in accord with the reality of jinen, one will surely awaken to the benevolence of the Buddha and of one's teachers and respond with gratitude."[43] As Shinran's heir, Rennyo properly conveyed the founder's teaching that, in the last dharma-age, the only possible way to live authentically is in saying the Name in gratitude to Amida for the saving power of the Vow. Given the exigencies of the times in which he lived, it is not surprising that there would be a need for a fresh interpretation and translation of the teaching in popular terms.

HONORING SOCIAL OBLIGATIONS

Rennyo's definition of orthodox Shinshū piety as gratitude provides a

---

(other than the five right practices for birth in the Pure Land established by Shan-tao). See BGDJ, 1214; SSJ, s.v. "*kemangai*," 134; and *Shōzōmatsu Wasan*, 61, for notes in English on *henji* and *keman*.

[40] *Shōzōmatsu wasan*, SSZ 2: 523b.

[41] *Tannishō*, SSZ 2: 776.

[42] *Tannishō*, SSZ 2: 785.

[43] Hirota, *Tannishō*, 26; SSZ 2: 777.

twofold legacy of living without calculation and honoring social obligations, as exemplified in the life of his follower Dōshū of Akao. We have noted the similarity of *myōkōnin* piety exemplified by Dōshū with Shinran's in its spontaneous expression of gratitude. This aspect of *myōkōnin* piety, however, is complemented by a second—gratitude as social obligation, expressed in an unquestioning loyalty to the leaders of the Honganji and obedience to the laws of the state. This aspect of piety is not without irony: loyal and obedient participation—largely apolitical, in keeping with piety of the founder—in the context of a highly politicized religious order. To explore this second aspect of Rennyo's legacy, we turn to developments in the Honganji in the years following his death.

Rennyo had set the stage for the further consolidation and expansion of the Honganji with his transfer of authority as custodian of the Founder's Hall to his fifth son, Jitsunyo. The letter of transfer stipulates that Jitsunyo was to administer the office in cooperation with his brothers if there were disputes over the teaching.[44] We have also noted that Rennyo's last testament, in forty-one articles, contains the signatures and written seals of five of his sons, including Jitsunyo. Of these sons who constituted the core of the family council, three headed temples at strategic points in Kaga prefecture in the Hokuriku: Renkō, the third son, at Shōkō-ji, Hasadani; Rensei, the fourth, at Kōgyō-ji, Yamada; and Rengo, the seventh, at Honsen-ji, Futamata. The second son, Renjō, was in charge of Zuisen-ji, at Iwanami, Etchū province, and then of Honsen-ji in Kaga. Jitsugo, the tenth son and author of one of the important memoirs, was to become the head of Gantoku-ji, also in Kaga.[45]

The remaining members of Rennyo's family were in service, whenever feasible, in support of the Honganji's interests. Renjun, the sixth and a signatory of his father's last testament, was first at Kenshō-ji, Chikamatsu, Ōtsu, and then at Ganshō-ji, Nagashima, Ise province. Rengei (1484–1523), Rennyo's eighth son, was to serve at Kyōgyō-ji, Settsu province; Jikken (1490–1523), the ninth, at Shōtoku-ji, Katada, Ōmi province; Jitsujun (1494–1518), the eleventh, at Saishō-ji, Kawachi province; Jikkō (1495–1553), the twelfth, at Honzen-ji, Yamato province; and the last son, Jitsujū (1498–1564), at Junkō-ji in Kyoto. Rennyo's practice of cultivating marriage ties advantageous to

---

[44] For a translation of the letter of transfer (RSI, 509–10 [#215]), see chapter four, n. 20.

[45] For biographical data on members of Rennyo's family, see SSJ entries.

the Honganji on behalf of his many daughters was continued under Jitsunyo's leadership.[46]

During this same period, *The Letters*, assuming authority as a canonical text, fostered a collective piety—loyalty to the Honganji as an expression of gratitude to the founder, Shinran. Thus the stability of an organization in which relationships were cemented by a web of kinship ties was further enhanced. On the other hand, a polity based on religious authority vested in a hierarchical structure of kinship relationships was not without its potential for distorting the teaching. The notion of relying on and submitting to the authority of the head priest as the good teacher (*zenchishiki* 善知識) was deliberately encouraged. This was a delicate issue, in that the practice of taking refuge in one's teacher (*chishiki kimyō*) at the expense of absolute reliance on Amida had been considered heretical since the time of Shinran. Rennyo himself had been highly critical of those who transmitted secret teachings (*hiji bōmon*); in his estimation, such people were "evil teachers" (*akuchishiki* 悪知識).[47] In contrast, memoirs written after Rennyo's death served to enhance the status of the head priest by referring to the holder of the office as "the good teacher." A passage from *Eigenki* notes:

> From generation to generation, the good teacher [head priest] has been the true representative of the founder. After Master Rennyo entered retirement at the Osaka residence, Master Jitsunyo once visited him there. Rennyo said that the relationship between a parent and child is a private affair, but that he thought of this visit as if it were made by the founder. For this reason, the ceremonial exchange of sake cups took a long time.[48]

This passage suggests that, after Rennyo's death, there was a need within the community to invest the charisma of religious leadership in an ecclesiastical office. Rennyo identifies Jitsunyo, the incumbent, as the founder's representative, and his ritualized greeting publicly demonstrates that respect for the office and subservience to its holder take precedence over all other relationships, even that of father and son. Although a satisfactory analysis of the complex issue of Shinshū's

---

[46] For a discussion of the significance of kinship ties and the transmission of the teaching during this period of the Honganji's history, see Solomon, "Kinship and the Transmission of Religious Charisma," 409–13.

[47] Kitanishi, "Dangibon kenkyū josetsu," 158–76. Rennyo links veneration of "evil teachers" with absence of good from the past (RSI, 81 [#15]).

[48] *Eigenki*, RSG, 264–65. Also quoted in Kitanishi, "Honganji kyōdan no seiritsu to sono tenkai," 95.

polity of dual lineages—dharma-transmission (*hōmyaku*) and blood relationship (*kechimyaku*) lies beyond the scope of this study,[49] the above
passage demonstrates that the incumbent head priest, embodying
both lineages, is designated the good teacher who is worthy of the
same reverence as the founder himself.

The move towards consolidation of authority in an ecclesiastical
office culminates under Shōnyo's tenure as head priest with the leaders of the Honganji becoming arbiters in matters of life and death for
its members.[50] In identifying obedience to a regulated pattern of participation in the order with salvation—the assurance of birth in the
Pure Land, the head priest's prerogative of excommunication (*hamon*
破門) became a life-and-death matter, both spiritually and physically.[51]
Expulsion from a village community in this period of social upheaval
frequently meant death through starvation or through attack from
some hostile band. With the emergence of such hierarchical and
authoritarian polity, the Honganji entered what has been termed its
feudalistic stage.[52]

What possible precedent is available in Shinshū tradition for excommunication? The fact that Shinran disowned his own son, Zenran,
immediately comes to mind. The most plausible reason for Shinran's
decision, undoubtedly a painful one, was Zenran's distortion of the
teaching among the first Shinshū congregations in the Kantō.[53] The
question of Shinran's motivation for such an action may be pressed:
was his decision based on a strategy to build up a powerful movement
of nenbutsu followers, or to preserve the purity of the teaching? Any
answer must, finally, take account of a pattern of piety grounded in his

---

[49] Yamaori touches on this issue in his *Ningen Rennyo* and in a short article,
"Rennyo ni miru 'yuigon' to 'ketsuen'," 81–87. The mingling of the two lineages appears to be the Honganji's greatest strength and greatest weakness—a
very mixed blessing; the phenomenon of hereditary lineage in Japan's cultural
history calls for a comparative study that might include, along with the lineages
of the Honganji, those in the arts and in the imperial household. See also Solomon, "Kinship and the Transmission of Religious Charisma," 403–13.

[50] See passages from *Jitsugoki* cited by Kitanishi in "Honganji kyōdan no
seiritsu to sono tenkai," 102. Also see section on the governing organization of
Honganji in SSG, 277–85.

[51] See Solomon, "Kinship and the Transmission of Religious Charisma,"
410–11.

[52] See Kitanishi's writings, especially his essay, "Honganji kyōdan no
seiritsu to sono tenkai," 96–101.

[53] For a discussion of the incident, see Dobbins, *Jōdo Shinshū*, 40–42, and
Takahatake, *Young Man Shinran*, 134–35.

conviction that Amida's Vow was realized precisely for his sake alone as a person of karmic evil (akunin 悪人). There would appear to be no precedent in his life and thought for excommunication in the context of developments in sixteenth-century Japan.

It is more difficult to evaluate Rennyo's position on an issue such as this. The priest Zuirin is quoted as having said to Rennyo that anyone the head priest (hōinsama 法印さま) considered evil was surely deserving of punishment—a statement that reflects the degree to which the head priest had been elevated in popular opinion.[54] In Rennyo's own writings, however, the only possible reference to punishment is tenuous: a letter written in the middle of the twelfth month of Bunmei 5 (1473), reports the observations of a group of lay teachers who, amazed at the community that had developed at Yoshizaki, were sure that anyone who disparaged the sect, including themselves, would immediately be punished.[55] At the time Rennyo wrote this letter, he felt that an attack on Yoshizaki was imminent; only two months earlier, he had, in a letter under the signature of the resident priests (tayashu 多屋衆), declared their joint intention to fight defensively, if necessary, to preserve the community.[56]

Rennyo's decision was based on a conviction that salvation for ordinary people at that time and place, in the last dharma-age, was possible only through participation in the life of his community. For this reason, Yoshizaki was to be defended by force if necessary, and those whose political ambitions threatened the community's safety were to be excluded.[57] As a last resort, expulsion from the community might become necessary, as in the case of Aki Rensō.[58] However, the painfulness of such a step for Rennyo is evidenced in his reaction to the demand

---

[54] The passage reads: "Once the priest Zuirin said to the master [Rennyo], 'Anyone who thinks ill of the Honganji is evil himself. Anyone whom the head priest considers evil is surely deserving of punishment.' With a gesture of surprise, the master said, 'I don't subject anyone to punishment.' Then the priest replied, 'Even if you don't consider [a person] altogether evil, one who says or thinks ill of things having to do with the Honganji is surely evil'" (Daihasso onmonogatari Kūzen kikigaki, SSS 11: 430; quoted in Kitanishi, "Honganji kyōdan no seiritsu to sono tenkai," 96).

[55] RSI, 154 (#44).

[56] RSI, 128–30 (#36), which includes a brief reference to rōnin and to Rennyo's preoccupation with fortifications and construction; RSI, 130–31 (#37) gives a somewhat longer reference, concluding with the decision to fight.

[57] See, for example, letters 1:8 (Bunmei 5 [1473].9), 2:3 (Bunmei 6 [1474]), and RSI, 133 (#38; trans. in full in chapter three of this work).

[58] See chapter three, n. 15.

of the shogun Ashikaga Yoshihisa that Honganji followers participating in the 1474 Ikkō uprisings be excommunicated.[59]

Complementing the prerogative of expulsion was a practice that, in effect, guaranteed [birth in] the afterlife (*goshō gomen* 後生御免), a major issue within the Honganji by the time of Shōnyo. The only evidence of Rennyo assuming such authority is seen in two episodes, both recorded by Jitsugo. One case involved Jōseiji, doctor as well as priest, who was a close friend of Honganji's benefactor, Hosokawa Masamoto. Jōseiji evidently had little confidence in his own realization of faith and is quoted as having said that he left the things of this world to the Ise Grand Shrine, and matters of the next life to Rennyo — a responsibility that Rennyo appears to have accepted.[60]

The other case involved Kasuga-no-tsubone, a woman who had raised Rennyo's daughter Myōshū[61] from childhood in the household of the shogun Yoshimasa. Rennyo was deeply grateful to her, and, concerned over her understanding of faith, said on a number of occasions that he took responsibility for her in regard to the life to come.[62] Although Rennyo may have responded spontaneously in these two situations, the practice of authorizing birth in the afterlife crystallized by the time of Shōnyo to the point of being challenged as contrary to Shinran's teaching.[63]

It appears, then, that certain of Rennyo's recorded statements as well as his letters, written in a particular social and political context, were used by subsequent leaders of the Honganji to legitimize their exercise of authority, whether seen as ecclesiastical or political. In addition, Rennyo provided, albeit unwittingly, a canonical text for the religious order that was to emerge in the middle of the sixteenth century. Under the leadership of his successors, the Honganji was to become the dominant force in the Ikkō uprisings, which culminated with Oda Nobunaga's decade-long siege at Ishiyama Hongan-ji. In the process, the Honganji was transformed into a powerful and militant organization; its militancy ended only after a settlement was negotiated with Nobunaga in 1580 through the intercession of the imperial court. In 1602, with the division of the Honganji into the Higashi and Nishi branches, both organizations were utilized by the Tokugawa

[59] See chapter four, p. 126 above.
[60] *Jitsugoki*, RSG, 170; Kasahara, *Shinshū ni okeru itan no keifu*, 208–9.
[61] See chapter four, n. 7.
[62] *Jitsugoki*, RSG, 169–70; Kasahara, *Shinshū ni okeru itan no keifu*, 209–10.
[63] *Honganji sahō no shidai*, RSG, 230–31; Kasahara, *Shinshū ni okeru itan no keifu*, 213–14.

government as instruments of control over people's lives in communities throughout Japan.

These brief comments on the use of authority in the Honganji's institutional history are in no way intended to discount the efficacy of the tradition's religious symbols at work in the lives of those who continued to hear the teaching as a manifestation of Amida's Vow, the transcendent. That story continued to unfold, despite the all-too-familiar instances of institutional excess found at times in the history of virtually every religious community. As we have noted already in this chapter, Rennyo's shaping of an orthodox Shinshū piety as gratitude—a twofold legacy of an ideal of living without calculation and honoring social obligations—found unified expression throughout the Tokugawa period in the lives of saintly persons known to us through works such as the *Myōkōninden*.[64]

This rich legacy, however, cannot be isolated from the Honganji's propensity for uncritically forging alliances with those holding political power. At the time of the Meiji Restoration, any residual unity of the transcendent and the mundane in Shinshū piety was further bifurcated. The concept *shinzoku nitai*[65] was formally introduced as the dharma-principle defining the Honganji's relationship to the modern nation-state in the parting message of Kōnyo, twentieth head priest of the Nishi Honganji. Interpretations of this principle, purportedly rooted in the Mahāyāna theory of the two truths, have generated reams of sectarian studies as well as vigorous controversy among Shinshū scholars in the modern period.[66] The significance of this

---

[64] In a limited sense, the term *myōkōninden* 妙好人伝 refers to materials assembled by Gōsei (1721–1794), a Shinshū priest, relating to the lives of nenbutsu devotees of exceptional piety. Included are men and women, mostly unlettered, from all walks of life. Gōsei's materials eventually took shape as a work known today as *Myōkōninden*, published in a variety of editions; for example, see Nagata Bunshōdō Henshūbu, ed. *Myōkōninden* (Kyoto: Nagata Bunshōdō, 1987). For a critical discussion of *myōkōnin* literature and the significance of this tradition of piety for Japanese Buddhism, see Leslie S. Kawamura, "The Myōkōnin: Japan's Representation of the Bodhisattva," in *Myōkōninden kenkyū*, ed. Asaeda Zenshō (Kyoto: Nagata Bunshōdō, 1987), 40–55. For an account of the dynamics of faith at work in the life of such a person, see Taira Satō, "The Awakening of Faith in the Myokonin Asahara Saichi," trans. Thomas L. Kirchner, *The Eastern Buddhist*, n.s., 18/1 (1985): 71–89.

[65] Shigaraki Takamaro, "Shinshū ni okeru shinzoku nitairon no kenkyū: Sono ichi," *Ryūkoku daigaku ronshū* 418 (1981): 57–67, and "Shinshū ni okeru shinzoku nitairon no kenkyū: Sono ni," *Shinshūgaku* 65 (1982): 1–13.

[66] Shigaraki, *Gendai Shinshū kyōgaku*, 260–68.

doctrinal formulation for the lives of members of the Honganji has
been far-reaching.

SHINSHŪ'S TWO TRUTHS

The coordinate terms for the two truths in the Mahāyāna Buddhist
tradition—*shintai* 真諦 (Skt. *paramārthasatya*) and *zokutai* (Skt. *saṃvṛti-
satya*)—appear in a variety of sūtras and commentaries. For the Mahāyāna in general, *shintai* is the ultimate and timeless non-discriminatory
truth of the supramundane (*shusse* 出世) or the transcendent; complementing this is *zokutai* 俗諦 , the relative and temporal discriminatory
truth of the mundane (*sezoku* 世俗).[67] From the perspective of ultimate
truth, everything is empty of inherent existence; in that there is no discrimination, everything is identical. From the perspective of relative
truth, everything exists in the conventional sense; in that there is
discrimination, everything is separate.[68]

In Shinshū tradition, the pair of concepts, *shintai* and *zokutai*, has
developed meanings quite different from those traditionally found in
Mahāyāna texts. A widely-used Nishi Honganji manual outlining the
essentials of Shinshū teaching includes in the final section a chapter
on *shinzoku nitai* that treats the practical application of doctrine to daily
life.[69] The claim is made that the Shinshū as a "religion" (*shūkyō* 宗教)
teaches that the ultimate meaning of salvation is birth in the Pure

---

[67] BGDJ, 784–85.

[68] In regard to the two truths in the Mahāyāna, see Gadjin Nagao, *The Foundational Standpoint of Mādhyamika Philosophy*, trans. John P. Keenan (Albany:
State University of New York Press, 1989), in which he presents his view of the
Mahāyāna as grounded in Nāgārjuna's Mādhyamika philosophy. Nagao's thesis
consists of two parallel themes: first is the identification of dependent co-arising
(Skt. *pratītya-samutpāda*; Jpn. *engi* 縁起) with emptiness (Skt. *śūnyatā*; Jpn. *kūshō*
空性); second is that the identity of dependent co-arising and emptiness must
be established in the light of the two truths: ultimate truth and conventional
truth. Relevant to our consideration of Shinshū thought is Nagao's use of Pure
Land themes—ascent/descent (*ōsō ekō/gensō ekō*) and Other Power/self-power
(*tariki/jiriki*). Also see his essay, "Ascent and Descent," 176–84. For a detailed discussion of the development of Mādhyamika philosophy in China beyond the
theory of the two truths, see Paul L. Swanson, *Foundations of T'ien-T'ai Philosophy:
The Flowering of the Two Truths Theory in Chinese Buddhism* (Berkeley: Asian
Humanities Press, 1989).

[69] Ryūkoku Daigaku, ed., *Shinshū yōron* (1953; reprint Kyoto: Hyakkaen,
1978), 169–75. An abridged English translation is available: Tri-State Buddhist
Temples, ed., "Outline of Jōdo Shinshū," *Shinshū Seiten*, 391–489.

Land after death, but that, as a lay movement, it does not ignore the daily needs of ordinary human beings. The relationship between piety (*shinkō*) and ethical action (*dōtoku* 道徳) is clarified on the basis of the following interpretations of the concepts *shintai* and *zokutai*:

> *Shintai* means "to devote oneself to the saying of the Name in gratitude, having heard and entrusted oneself to the Buddha's Name." Since faith and saying the Name are the supramundane dharma (*shussekenbō* 出世間法) that relates to Buddha and transcends the cycle of birth and death, we call this "the transcendent truth (*shintai*)."
>
> *Zokutai* means "to live humanely and obey the law of the land." Since humane behaviour and the law of the land are the mundane dharma (*sekenbō* 世間法) that relates to human beings, we call this "the mundane truth" (*zokutai*).[70]

Our decision to translate *shintai* as "the transcendent truth" and *zokutai* as "the mundane truth" is informed by several considerations. The first is to underscore their correlation with the categories of *shussekenbō*, "the supramundane dharma," and *sekenbō*, "the mundane dharma," used in sectarian explanations of the concept *shinzoku nitai*. An even more important consideration is to emphasize a correlation with the categories of the transcendent and the mundane, at the heart of the comparative perspective adopted in this study. Specifically, this involves the conviction that "the history of [a person's] religious life, and especially of [his or her] faith, lived always in a specific context, is intrinsically the locus of both the mundane and the transcendent, unbifurcated."[71] The cogency of the categories of the transcendent and the mundane is their capacity to elucidate materials representative of quite different religious traditions, including possible comparisons between theist and non-theist; at the same time, they appear to catch the subtleties of a variety of responses within a single tradition such as the Jōdo Shinshū. Therefore, for the purposes of this study, we have translated *shinzoku nitai* as "the transcendent and the mundane as two truths," recognizing the limitations of any single translation, given the richness and complexity of this concept in Mahāyāna Buddhist thought.

A major undertaking for scholars engaged in Shinshū Studies has been to show that modern interpretations of the terms *shintai* and *zokutai* and of the concept *shinzoku nitai* are entirely consistent with a

---

[70] Ryūkoku Daigaku, ed., *Shinshū yōron*, 169–70.
[71] Smith, *Towards a World Theology*, 3; see also p. 33 above, n. 76.

textual tradition including the Pure Land sūtras, but especially with Shinran's teaching as found in *Kyōgyōshinshō*. The argument runs as follows:

> The founder [Shinran], quoting Saichō's *Mappō tōmyōki*, says, "The benevolent king and the dharma-king enhance one another and enlighten sentient beings. Supramundane truth and mundane truth function interdependently to spread the teaching." The benevolent king is the emperor who governs the country; the dharma-king is Buddha who propagates dharma. The mundane truth is the imperial law administered by the emperor; the supramundane truth is the dharma propagated by the Buddha. *Mappō tōmyōki* therefore designates the right relationship between politics and religion as essential to government.[72]

An immediate difficulty posed by this statement is the fact that Shinran never uses the terms *shintai* and *zokutai* directly in his writings to conceptualize his vision of reality. The terms occur on the single occasion noted above, in the sixth chapter of *Kyōgyōshinshō*, as part of a lengthy quotation of the major portion of *Mappō tōmyōki*.[73] For Shinran, however, the *Mappō tōmyōki*'s teaching concerned the last dharma-age: monks under no illusions about the possibility of living according to the precepts were the authentic monks of the times.[74] His purpose in citing this text is apparently to account for the decadence of monks like himself in that age; he is unconcerned with enunciating a doctrinal principle relating the two truths, a theoretical formulation at the core of Tendai thought. His teaching, particularly following the experience of exile and recognition that he was "neither a monk nor one in worldly life," testifies to his insight into the ambiguous quality of every facet of mundane authority.

For Shinran, as we have noted frequently, only the nenbutsu is true and real.[75] The structure of his thought offers little to support the dharma-principle of the two truths in the way in which it was formulated and promoted at the beginning of the Meiji period and used in defining the Honganji's relationship to the state until the present. Despite the rationale advanced in manuals on the essentials of Shinshū

---

[72] Ryūkoku Daigaku, ed., *Shinshū yōron*, 170.

[73] *Kyōgyōshinshō*, SSZ 2: 168–74. For English translation of *Mappō tomyōki*, see *Shōzōmatsu Wasan*, 125–35. Also see Robert F. Rhodes, trans. and intro., "Saichō's *Mappō Tōmyōki*: The Candle of the Latter Dharma," *The Eastern Buddhist*, n.s., 13/1 (1980): 79–103.

[74] See introduction by Rhodes, "Saichō's *Mappō Tōmyōki*," 79–86.

[75] *Tannishō*, SSZ 2: 793.

teaching, it is necessary to look to Shinran's successors for possible sources on which to base such a formulation.

Especially pertinent to the development of the concept *shinzoku nitai* is Kakunyo's statement in *Gaijashō*:

> The teaching passed down to us is that we should observe benevolence, justice, propriety, wisdom, and sincerity (known as "the five precepts [*gokai* 五戒]" in the supramundane dharma [*shusse*] and as "the five virtues [*gojō* 五常]" in the mundane dharma [*seppō* 世法]) and store within our hearts the inconceivable working of Other Power.[76]

Shinshū adherents, relating to the supramundane truth through inner faith, were, in effect, to be guided in mundane affairs by ethical principles derived from Confucian thought. Although Kakunyo's position is consistent with Shinran's in that he sees the five Buddhist precepts as inapplicable in the last dharma-age, he then substitutes an ethical system based on principles that were, in theory, readily identifiable with existing social norms. Thus, as early as Kakunyo, we see the emergence of a structure of thought that was to provide a foundation for the Meiji dharma-principle of *shinzoku nitai*: the transcendent truth refers to inner faith and the mundane truth to external affairs. Shinran's radical position of nenbutsu alone, which went beyond any ethical system—Buddhist or Confucian—was fundamentally restructured. The ethical ideals based on Confucian virtues, rules of conduct that Shinran had rejected as inapplicable in the last dharma-age, were reappropriated by the movement he had inspired.

Zonkaku, in his commentary, *Rokuyōshō*, takes special note of Shinran's lengthy quotation from *Mappō tōmyōki*. He sees in Shinran's single citation of the terms *shintai* and *zokutai* a basis for defining the relationship between Buddha-dharma and imperial law:

> This work [*Mappō tōmyōki*] states the principle underlying the rule of Buddha-dharma and imperial law; that is, it clarifies the mutual dependence of the transcendent truth and the mundane truth. Further, since there is a difference in the three [dharma]-ages (the right, the semblance, and the last), there is a difference in the abilities of persons to be saved. In regard to a single dharma, therefore, there will be both praise and criticism—acceptance and rejection. Points such as these fully clarify the matter.[77]

---

[76] *Gaijashō*, SSZ 3: 67; quoted in Shigaraki, "Shinshū ni okeru shinzoku nitairon no kenkyū: Sono ichi," 46.

[77] *Rokuyōshō*, SSZ 2: 410–11; quoted in Shigaraki, "Shinshū ni okeru shinzoku nitairon no kenkyū: Sono ichi," 47–48.

In *Haja kenshōshō*, Zonkaku elaborates on the mutual dependence of Buddha-dharma and imperial law:

Buddha-dharma and imperial law are a pair of dharmas. They are just like two wings of a bird or two wheels of a cart; it is impermissible that one should be missing. Therefore, we observe imperial law through Buddha-dharma and respect Buddha-dharma through imperial law. . . . The indebtedness we bear to the present emperor is far heavier than what we owed to sovereigns in former generations. We depend on his benevolence and virtue in regard to both the mundane and the supramundane. How could we disregard imperial law? And how much more should followers of the single practice of the nenbutsu everywhere be aware that they are dependent overall on the imperial court in the Kantō and, in particular, on the domain holders and local land stewards for their subsistence.[78]

A pervading theme here is gratitude as social obligation. Dependence for one's very subsistence on those holding political power, whether in the capital or in the provinces, dictated a piety of obedience and submissiveness in the interest of social stability.

Finally, in a work attributed to Zonkaku, *Shōtoku Taishi kōshiki*, the point is pressed even further:

On reflection, [we realize that] we spread Buddha-dharma by imperial law and observe the mundane truth by the transcendent truth. The transcendent and the mundane are interdependent, and these two truths arise together.[79]

Zonkaku's writings go far in providing the major ingredients for the Shinshū's subsequent appropriation of the concept *shinzoku nitai*. In effect, he relativizes the absolute value of Shinran's nenbutsu alone in stressing the interdependence of the two truths. The supramundane dharma (Amida Buddha) is set on equal footing with the mundane dharma (imperial law). We will see in the following chapter that Zonkaku's expression of the absolute parity of the two truths was extended in modern times to apply to the relationship between Amida and the emperor.

Another dimension to Zonkaku's thought is an accommodation of Shinran's teaching to Japanese folk tradition, inseparably bound up with the kami. He draws on the tradition of *honji suijaku* thought in

---

[78] *Haja kenshōshō*, SSZ 3: 173; quoted in Shigaraki, "Shinshū ni okeru shinzoku nitairon no kenkyū: Sono ichi," 48.

[79] *Shōtoku Taishi kōshiki*, SSZ 5: 706; quoted in Shigaraki, "Shinshū ni okeru shinzoku nitairon no kenkyū: Sono ichi," 49.

which the kami are interpreted as manifestations or marks (*ato* 迹) of the buddhas, the underlying reality.[80] In addition to ancestral kami, Zonkaku includes deities related to foxes, snakes, and other entities from popular folk tradition, seeing each as a manifestation of Amida Buddha. Zonkaku's position opens up Shinshū tradition, albeit through Amida Buddha, to the full range of Japanese religious entities.[81] Kōnyo's "Testament," as we will see, draws on Zonkaku's thought without citing him directly; the doctrinal statement in *Shinshū yōron*, however, does quote Zonkaku's "two wings of a bird or two wheels of a cart" metaphor in an effort to identify roots for the concept *shinzoku nitai* in Shinshū tradition.[82]

The final and most crucial step in the Honganji's effort to construct a plausible apologetic for the Shinshū's dharma-principle of the two truths is Rennyo's translation and interpretation of Shinran's teaching for the populace at large. Sectarian scholars turn to *The Letters* as the authoritative text for defining Shinshū orthodoxy. As we have noted, it incorporates the points in Kakunyo's and Zonkaku's writings and in Rennyo's own interpretations of the teaching that are relevant to such a concept as *shinzoku nitai*.

Before taking up the events in modern Japanese history that led to the Nishi Honganji's enunciation of *shinzoku nitai* as a dharma-principle, it is useful to summarize the place of Shinran's teaching in Rennyo's thought. Fundamental to our presentation of Shinshū tradition is an acknowledgement of the continuity of Rennyo's faith with Shinran's faith, even as Shinran's faith is held to be continuous with Hōnen's. In one sense, it cannot be otherwise; by definition, a person's faith (*shinjin* 信心), given by Amida Buddha, is "true, real, and sincere heart and mind" (*makoto no kokoro* まことのこころ).

In *The Letters*, the last of the dated letters, one prepared for the annual thanksgiving services in the eleventh month of Meiō 7 (1498), Rennyo wrote:

> All I long for, morning and evening, is that there will be a decisive settling of faith (*shinjin ketsujō*) for everyone while I am still alive. Although this does indeed depend on good from the past, there is never a moment when it is not on my mind.[83]

This passage, written shortly before Rennyo's death, sums up his lifelong commitment to the settling of faith — the truth of Amida's Vow —

---

[80] Shigaraki, *Gendai Shinshū kyōgaku*, 130–31.
[81] Shigaraki, *Gendai Shinshū kyōgaku*, 132–33.
[82] Ryūkoku Daigaku, ed., *Shinshū yōron*, 170.
[83] RSI, 444–46 (#156/4:15).

in the hearts and minds of all who hear the teaching. To that end, he draws on all the resources he has inherited from Pure Land tradition and beyond.

Other than Shinran's writings, the major influences on Rennyo life and thought from within his tradition are the writings of Kakunyo and Zonkaku. The crisis years at Yoshizaki are decisive in shaping Rennyo's legacy for the Shinshū. In this period, confronted with the dilemma of Honganji's religious power, he appropriates elements of Kakunyo's thought identifying the five Confucian virtues with existing social norms. Herein lies the seed for a duality: inner faith, relating to the transcendent truth, and the honoring of one's obligations in society, relating to the mundane truth. Furthermore, in his uncritical acceptance of Zonkaku's position on *honji suijaku*, Rennyo provides fertile soil for a radical accommodation of the Buddha-dharma to imperial absolutism in modern Japan. *The Letters* emphasize that the kami are a means by which Amida encourages people to follow the Buddha-dharma.[84] Rennyo repeatedly enjoins his followers not to offend priests or worshippers at the shrines and temples and not to speak ill of the kami, buddhas, or bodhisattvas. To the extent that all religious entities are submerged in Amida Buddha, he takes a position not inconsistent with Shinran's single-minded devotion to Amida Buddha; on the other hand, he allows for a significant degree of accommodation with a vital Japanese folk tradition espoused by Zonkaku, which Shinran had rejected.[85]

The tone of Rennyo's letters is very much shaped by his awareness of the transiency of human life — a pervasive consciousness in late medieval Japan. A possible interpretation of his repeated emphasis on the afterlife as the most important matter (*goshō ichidaiji*) is that he sees this life merely as a "waiting room" for birth in the Pure Land. His emphasis on the afterlife — on the aspect of going to the Pure Land for birth (*ōsō ekō*) — weakens the aspect of bodhisattva activity, returning to this defiled world to work for the enlightenment of all sentient beings (*gensō ekō*).[86] It appears that the structure of his thought does allow for a dualistic interpretation — this life and the afterlife, this defiled world and the Pure Land. In contrast, the Mahāyāna structure of Shinran's

---

[84] RSI, 167–68 (#50/2:3); SSZ 3: 428–31.

[85] Shinran is severely critical of popular religious practices for their self-power orientation; see the hymns known as *Gutoku hitan jukkai* (Gutoku [Shinran's] Lamentation and Confession), in *Shōzōmatsu wasan*, SSZ 2: 527–29.

[86] Futaba, "Shinshū ni okeru ōjō shinkō to rekishi to no kankei ni tsuite no kasetsu," 521.

thought posits that the going and the return are two sides of the same coin; the consequence of the interaction of these two — sameness/opposition — is to see this world simultaneously as Amida's world and as the world of suffering in which one is summoned to work on behalf of all sentient beings.

Finally, Rennyo's contribution to a Shinshū apologetic for the dharma-principle of *shinzoku nitai* is summed up in his dictum: "Take the laws of the state as your outer aspect, store Other-Power faith deep in your hearts, and take [the principles of] humanity and justice as essential."[87] Even as Rennyo stressed the primacy of faith, he simultaneously emphasized observance of the laws of the state, equated with the five ethical principles in Confucian thought.

Building on Zonkaku's position of Buddha-dharma and imperial law as mutually supportive, Rennyo underscores the obligation of Shinshū adherents to conform to existing social norms while treasuring faith in the bottom of their hearts; by this, they are assured of birth in the Pure Land. Both Kōnyo in his "Testament" and contemporary Shinshū scholars writing in *Shinshū yōron* depend finally on Rennyo's thought in setting forth their reasoning for *shinzoku nitai* as the dharma-principle.[88] Both the content and the structure of thought of Kōnyo's "Testament," as we shall see, owe much to an orthodoxy constructed on the basis of *The Letters* and the memoirs of Rennyo's followers.

During the Tokugawa period, consistent with Rennyo's twofold legacy, *myōkōnin* piety was held up by the leaders of the Honganji as exemplary of orthodox Shinshū piety as gratitude, both in terms of non-calculative living and of honoring social obligations. At the same time, the Honganji as a religious order served as the loyal, obedient, and efficient servant of the state. Its scholarship, directed toward the clarification of faith, frequently gave evidence of factional struggles, as evidenced by the Sangō Upheaval. Much of the intellectual energy that might have been available for critical thought on larger social issues was channeled into efforts to reconcile Shinran's teaching with the thought of his successors, Kakunyo, Zonkaku, and Rennyo. The question of possible discontinuities in the teaching was never broached within the world of traditional piety. It was against a background of orthodox Shinshū piety as gratitude — including obedience to government officials and service to the state and, in return, the

---

[87] RSI, 181 (#54/2:6); SSZ 3: 434.

[88] Ryūkoku Daigaku, ed., *Shinshū yōron*, 170–71.

enjoyment of special privilege for a priestly hierarchy—that the Honganji was to suffer the trauma of persecution. The anti-Buddhist movement coincided with the first years of the Meiji Restoration.

Chapter 7

Nishi Honganji: Guardian of the State

> On your brow, wear imperial law; within the depths of your heart, treasure Buddha-dharma.
>
> Rennyo[1]

IN 1868, THE LEADERS of the Meiji Restoration revived the Jingikan (Department of Kami Affairs) as part of a move to pattern the government on that of the first (legendary) emperor, Jinmu, and to restore the nation to a polity unifying religious and political affairs (*saisei itchi* 祭政一致).[2] In the same year, a government edict separated "Shinto" affairs from Buddhist (*shinbutsu bunri* 神仏分離). In effect, Buddhism was disestablished in favor of a newly-created State Shinto: Buddhist rituals at Shinto shrines and at official state functions were banned, Buddhist images were burned, temples stood empty, and

---

[1] *Jitsugo kyūki*, RSG, 88; SSZ 3: 566.

[2] For a comprehensive survey of historical developments in Japanese religion in the Meiji period, see Hideo Kishimoto, ed., *Japanese Culture in the Meiji Era: Religion*, trans. John F. Howes, Centenary Cultural Council Series, vol. 2 (Tokyo: The Toyo Bunko, 1969), parts 1 and 2. Also see Tsunetsugu Muraoka, *Studies in Shinto Thought*, trans. Delmer M. Brown and James T. Araki (Tokyo: Ministry of Education, 1964), chaps. 6 and 7. For an analysis of Shinto as religion and ideology in relation to Japan's cultural tradition, see Joseph M. Kitagawa, "Some Remarks on Shintō," *History of Religions* 27/3 (1988): 227–45. Kitagawa traces the meaning of the term *saisei itchi* in the history of Japanese thought in his essay, "*Matsuri* and *Matsuri-goto*: Religion and State in Early Japan," *On Understanding Japanese Religion* (Princeton: Princeton University Press, 1987), 117–26.

perhaps most far-reaching, temple estates were confiscated, resulting in the loss of an economic base. Such a discriminatory policy directed at Buddhists was virtually unprecedented in Japanese history; it ran counter to the ancient tradition of mutual tolerance of religious entities, enunciated theoretically in terms of the local kami as manifestations of an underlying reality expressed in Buddhist symbols (*honji suijaku*).

Compounding the shock to Buddhists in early Meiji was the fact that their institutions had served the state diligently and to great effect throughout the Tokugawa period; far from harboring ill-will towards those who ruled, Buddhist officials had sought vigorously to guard against all external threats, including that of the foreign religion introduced by Europeans in the sixteenth century—Christianity. But now, suddenly, Buddhists found themselves abandoned by the state and subject to severe persecution by a popular and militant but unofficial movement for eradication of the influence of Buddhist institutions (*haibutsu kishaku* 廃仏毀釈). A further threat was the reappearance of Christianity as the spiritual ground for the advanced learning and military power of modern Western nation-states.[3]

The Buddhists' initial response, as might be expected, was to seek at all costs to reestablish firm ties to the state by attesting to their loyalty to the newly-restored imperial system and by underscoring the practical benefits Buddhist thought and practice might provide the nation in meeting the renewed challenges — martial, political, technological, spiritual — from the West. And, secondly, with the lifting of the proscription against Christianity in early Meiji, they set about elaborating an apologetic designed to point up the inadequacies of Christian teachings for a modern Japan. Outstanding in this regard were the philosophical writings of Inoue Enryō (1858–1919) in defense of Buddha-dharma. In due course, vigorous efforts at Buddhist reform were also to unfold: advocacy by Shimaji Mokurai (1838–1911) of a separation of religion and state; approaches by Fukuda Gyōkai (1806–1888), Shaku Unshō (1827–1909), Murakami Senshō (1851–1929), and Kiyozawa Manshi (1863–1903) to the cultivation of a deeper spir-

---

[3] For a detailed historical study of the interactions between Buddhists and Christians in the second half of the nineteenth century and the religious implications, see Notto R. Thelle, *Buddhism and Christianity in Japan: From Conflict to Dialogue, 1854–1899* (Honolulu: University of Hawaii Press, 1987). See also Hideo Kishimoto, ed., *Japanese Culture in the Meiji Era: Religion*, 17–22, and Shigeyoshi Murakami, *Japanese Religion in the Modern Century*, trans. H. Byron Earhart (Tokyo: University of Tokyo Press, 1980), 33–40.

itual life; the social criticism of the "New Buddhism" movement; and extraordinary achievements in the field of Buddhist scholarship. A balanced evaluation of the degree of success of efforts at Buddhist reform is not possible here; Ienaga Saburō has, however, offered a challenging analysis of the difficulty for Buddhist institutions in carrying through deep structural changes in patterns of thought and practice during Japan's modern period.[4]

In creating State Shinto as the spiritual foundation and source of legitimization for imperial rule, leaders of the Meiji Restoration were, in effect, initiating a major effort at the reconceptualization of Japanese religious life. In response to Western concepts of religious freedom and separation of church and state, Buddhism, Christianity, and eventually sectarian Shinto came to be designated as "religions," while State Shinto — not so designated — was intended to become an essential constituent of the government administration of a modern nation-state.

This unique position of State Shinto was to be maintained for some seventy years until 1945, when the end of the Second World War brought the disestablishment of State Shinto and the realization of guarantees of religious freedom under a new constitution.[5] Granted the complexities of interpreting the Western concept of "religion" within the Japanese tradition, the precise relationship between religious institutions and state continues to be an issue of extreme sensitivity in contemporary Japan. The postwar constitution and official government policies do not appear to fully reflect certain deeply-held Japanese notions of what that relationship ought to be.

This chapter examines the Jōdo Shinshū, especially the Nishi Honganji branch, as it sought to define its relationship to the state at two critical moments in modern Japanese history. First, we review the contents of a major Shinshū document, Kōnyo's "Testament" (*Kōnyo Shōnin goikun goshōsoku*) the final message of the twentieth head priest, Kōnyo (1798–1871), to members of the Honganji, as recorded by his son, Myōnyo, the twenty-first head priest. The testament, issued at a

---

[4] Ienaga Saburō, "Nihon no kindaika to bukkyō," in *Kōza: Kindai bukkyō*, vol. 2 (Kyoto: Hōzōkan, 1961), 21. An English translation of Ienaga's essay is available as "Japan's Modernization and Buddhism," *Contemporary Religions in Japan* 6/1 (1965): 1–41.

[5] Kitagawa, in "Some Remarks on Shintō," notes that since State Shinto was not considered a religion, "[it] had great latitude in utilizing the national and local governments, the public educational system, and the army and navy to propagate the Shintō version of ancestor worship, the emperor cult, and patriotic morality" (241).

moment of institutional and national crisis in early Meiji, introduced the concept of the transcendent and the mundane as two truths (*shinzoku nitai*) as the dharma-principle defining the proper relationship of members of the Honganji to the state. Second, in examining an incident in 1940, when significant phrases in the Shinshū scriptures were censored for public use and eventually erased from the texts in question, we consider how the concept *shinzoku nitai* may have served as a religious symbol[6] to sacralize the Honganji's participation as a Buddhist institution in modern Japanese history.

The focus on religious and ideological concepts and on exegesis of key Shinshū documents and texts illuminates a pervasive theme in Japanese civilization—that of the intrinsic difficulty for Japanese society in general and the Shinshū in particular in developing categories for differentiating between the state and religious authority. The concept of the transcendent and the mundane as two truths appears to have served the Honganji in modern times in ways analogous to those in which concepts such as the unity of religious and political affairs and the mutual tolerance of the kami and buddhas have served Japanese civilization since the very formation of a state and the early encounter with the Buddhist tradition.

MEIJI RESTORATION

Kōnyo, head priest of the Nishi Honganji, died on Meiji 4 (1871).8.19, at age seventy-seven. His parting message, referred to here as his "Testament," was officially promulgated in the same year, at the peak of the anti-Buddhist movement noted above. In this document, he attempts to define the proper response of members of his community to the crisis facing them as members of the Honganji and as loyal citizens of a nation seeking to maintain its autonomy in the face of pressures from the Western powers.

The "Testament," in fewer than one thousand characters in Japanese, formally introduced to members of the Nishi Honganji the dharma-principle of the transcendent and the mundane as two truths, a principle held to have antecedents in Mahāyāna Buddhist tradition and special significance for the Shinshū. In explaining and legitimizing this carefully-wrought religious symbol, Kōnyo quotes passages from the *Larger Sūtra*; from a collection of Shinran's letters, *Goshōsokushū*; from *The Letters*; and from the memoir, *Goichidaiki kikigaki*.

---

[6] For notes on religious symbols, see the introduction to this work, n. 26.

13. Kōnyo's "Testament"

The document rings with near-parental concern for the members of his community; it draws on elements of Buddhist and Neo-Confucian thought as well as on Shinshū doctrine in directing them to be loyal and obedient subjects of the emperor, who is recognized as the absolute head of a familial state.

The text reads as follows:

From the spring of Bunsei 10 [1827], when I became custodian of the Ryūkoku temple [Nishi Hongan-ji], until now, I have taught for over forty years, deviating in no way from the dharma-principles inherited by our sect from previous masters, and following the way of teaching of generation after generation of incumbents. Having already passed seventy, I have been unwell since last year and am unable to carry out daily activities as I would like. Morning and evening, I am grieved that, as a matter of course, it will become difficult for me to guide others in the way.

Also, the heat this summer was unusually intense. An old man, I am becoming weaker day by day and think that within the year I will have accomplished my long-cherished desire to be born in the Pure Land. Feeling that, at the least, the well-being of like-minded followers should be the hallmark of my longevity, I have had my successor [Myōnyo] take his brush in hand and write down what I say; you should listen very carefully.

Of all those born in this imperial land, there is no one who has not received the emperor's benevolence. These days especially, he labors from morning to night in his deliberations in administering the just government of the restoration, maintaining order among the many people within [the country], and standing firm against all foreign countries. Is there then anyone, priest or lay, who would not support the imperial reign and enhance its power? Moreover, as the spread of Buddha-dharma is wholly dependent on the patronage of the emperor and his ministers, how can those who trust in Buddha-dharma disregard the decrees of imperial law?

Accordingly, it has been long since established in our sect that one should "take imperial law as fundamental; take humanity and

(Kōnyo Shōnin goikun goshōsoku)

justice as foremost,"[7] revere the kami, and uphold morality. In other words, if, through the [Thirty-third] Vow's benefit of touching beings with light and making them gentle-hearted,[8] a person becomes one who "reveres the virtues, cultivates compassion, and endeavors in courtesy and humility,"[9] then he will surely conform to the [Buddha's] golden words, "There is harmony everywhere, and the sun and moon are pure and bright,"[10] and return a small part of the emperor's benevolence.

Hence our founding master taught that "we should desire peace in the world and the spread of Buddha-dharma."[11] Given that, it is deplorable that [some people] are confused and think that if they just believe in Buddhist teachings, they can let mundane teachings be as they may. [Rennyo], the restorer of the tradition (*chūkō shōnin*) taught in regard to this: "On your brow, wear imperial law (*ōbō*); within the depths of your heart, treasure Buddha-dharma (*buppō*)."[12]

Buddha-dharma is the single truth of the Other Power of the Primal Vow. As you have often heard, we must first of all realize deeply that we are evil, worthless beings and discard the sundry practices and disciplines and the doubting mind of self-power; and in the single thought-moment in which we single-heartedly and steadfastly entrust ourselves to Amida Tathāgata to save us, [bringing us to buddhahood] in the afterlife,[13] Amida unfailingly embraces and will not discard us, and it is settled that we will be born in the Pure Land. In the recollection of this joy, even in hurried moments or in time

---

[7] The substance of this phrase is put in slightly different ways in a number of Rennyo's letters. For example, see RSI, 256 (#86, dated Bunmei 9 [1477].3); RSI, 259 (#86/3:12, dated Bunmei 8 [1476].1.27).

[8] The Thirty-third of the Forty-eight Vows enumerated in the *Larger Sūtra*, SSZ 1: 11.

[9] *Larger Sūtra*, SSZ 1: 41.

[10] *Larger Sūtra*, SSZ 1: 41.

[11] *Shinran Shōnin goshōsokushū*, SSZ 2: 697.

[12] *Jitsugo kyūki*, RSG, 88; SSZ 3: 566.

[13] A phrase that in slightly varied readings occurs frequently in Rennyo's letters; see RSI, 380 (#127); 436 (#151); 455 (#162); 464 (#168).

of danger, rejoice in the Buddha's benevolence; whether walking, standing, sitting, or lying down, say the nenbutsu; and you will truly continue in the dharma-principle.

My hope is that our sect's priests and lay people will firmly grasp the correct meaning of what has been transmitted, as stated above; that they will not err in regard to the dharma-principle of the transcendent and the mundane as two truths; that in this life, they will be loyal subjects of the empire and reciprocate the unlimited imperial benevolence; and that in the life to come, they will attain birth in the [Pure Land in the] West and escape aeons of suffering. If, to this end, one makes harmony fundamental, observes one's own discipline, and guides others, there is finally no better way to be bathed in the founder's dharma-stream.

Again, because the well-being of [our sect's] followers is my long-cherished desire, it is my request that you regard this letter as my legacy and take careful note [of its contents].

With respect.
The fourth year of Meiji [1871],
the end of early autumn.

The preceding letter is the final message of the former head priest; it states the sectarian doctrine, inherited from our founder, of the excellent principle of the transcendent and the mundane as two truths. Those who belong to this sect should take these instructions as fundamental; outwardly, they should carefully follow the government's ordinances and, inwardly, they must bear in mind what is necessary for salvation. This is what is essential.

The fifth year of Meiji [1872], the first month.
Myōnyo, disciple of Śākyamuni,
Ryūkoku Temple Affairs.[14]

This document, following Kōnyo's forty years of service as head priest, is, in effect, his last will and testament. He speaks as the twentieth in descent from Shinran, in terms of both dharma-lineage and blood-lineage. Failing in health, weakened after a summer's heat, and grieving over the crises facing his community, he urges members of the Honganji to be attentive to the dharma-principle relating the transcendent and the mundane.[15]

---

[14] For text, see SSZ 5: 777–78. See also Futaba Kenkō, ed., *Shiryō: Nihon bukkyōshi* (Kyoto: Yamazaki Hōbundō, 1971), 352–54.

[15] This document is similar in style and tone to letters written by Rennyo during his last summer, when he was in failing health. See RSI, 427–35 (#147, #148, #149, and #150).

Kōnyo begins the body of the letter by reminding members of the community that early Meiji Japan is a land under benevolent imperial rule. Implicitly, he endorses the restoration leaders' aim of unifying religious and political affairs, returning to a pattern characteristic of the ancient Japanese state as a means of promoting harmony among the populace in the face of pressures from abroad. He urges a personal response to the emperor's efforts: "He labors from morning to night in his deliberations . . . is there then anyone, priest or lay, who would not support the imperial reign and enhance its power?" Such support is considered tantamount to support of Buddha-dharma, which is itself dependent on the goodwill and patronage of the emperor and his ministers.

Kōnyo turns next to the most pressing issue for Honganji members subject to the anti-Buddhist movement, which enjoyed the unofficial support, or, at the least, the passive acquiescence of the governing administration. That issue concerned the proper relationship of the Honganji to the state in modern Japan.

Drawing on a series of quotations from the Shinshū scriptures, Kōnyo seeks to legitimize and buttress his presentation of the dharma-principle of the transcendent and the mundane as two truths, giving it the patina of inheritance and tradition. In quoting Rennyo's injunction to "take imperial law as fundamental; take humanity and justice as foremost," Kōnyo strengthens his own directive that those who trust in Buddha-dharma are to support the wishes of the emperor and his ministers. Reverence for the kami and respect for morality appear to be identified with taking imperial law as fundamental.

> . . . if, through the [Thirty-third] Vow's benefit of touching beings with light and making them gentle-hearted, a person becomes one who "reveres the virtues, cultivates compassion, and endeavors in courtesy and humility," then he will surely conform to the [Buddha's] golden words, "There is harmony everywhere, and the sun and moon are pure and bright," and return a small part of the emperor's benevolence.

Here, Rennyo's advocacy of imperial law—or, as he understood the matter, the laws of the state—as fundamental and humanity and justice as foremost is, in turn, supported by phrases from the *Larger Sūtra*. In short, those touched by Amida's light will be people of virtue and compassion, both respectful of others and humble themselves—surely loyal and obedient members of the Honganji, responsive to the emperor's benevolence. Gratitude for the blessings of Amida's Primal Vow is translated into gratitude to the emperor. The harmony of such an imperial state reflects the purity and brightness of the natural order.

"We should desire peace in the world and the spread of Buddha-dharma."

This passage, from Shinran's *Goshōsokushū*, appears in a letter to Shōshinbō, a follower living in the Kantō at a time in which the nascent Shinshū community appeared to be in conflict with the governing administration in Kamakura. The citation is a rebuke to those who are "confused" or who espouse antinomian tendencies by disregarding social norms; Kōnyo implies that there should be no conflict or tension between religious community and state authority.

Indeed, Shinran's injunction to say the nenbutsu for the good of the imperial court and for the nation[16] is taken to mean that Honganji members are to assent positively to existing social norms. Kōnyo underscores this crucial point in quoting a sentence attributed to Rennyo:

"On your brow, wear imperial law; within the depths of your heart, treasure Buddha-dharma."

Rennyo's statement serves to define the proper relationship between the two truths. First is the mundane, the outer or public realm affirmative of imperial law and existing social norms. Second is the transcendent, the inwardly-known truth of Buddha-dharma. Kōnyo's interpretation, entirely consistent with that of Zonkaku, is that these two truths are complementary: Honganji members fulfill their obligations to imperial law through loyalty and obedience to the emperor, and to Buddha-dharma through inner piety and devotion to Amida. Outer and inner truths, the mundane and the transcendent, mutually support each other.

. . . In the single thought-moment in which we single-heartedly and steadfastly entrust ourselves to Amida Tathāgata to save us, [bringing us to buddhahood] in the afterlife, Amida unfailingly embraces and will not discard us, and it is settled that we will be born in the Pure Land.

Kōnyo continues by explicating Buddha-dharma in terms of orthodox Shinshū teaching as set forth in *The Letters*, culminating in the saying of Amida's Name. People are recognized as helpless to effect their own salvation; they are absolutely dependent on Amida for escape from suffering and birth in the Pure Land in the afterlife. Given this inca-

---

[16] *Shinran Shōnin goshōsokushū*, SSZ 2: 697.

pacity for good through self-effort, Shinshū adherents are to say the nenbutsu solely in thanksgiving for Amida's benevolence. Secure in the assurance of birth in the Pure Land in the afterlife, it is then their positive duty to be loyal citizens, thus repaying the emperor's benevolence. To inherit the founder's dharma-stream, it is essential that there be no mistake as to the correct meaning of the dharma-principle of the transcendent and the mundane as complementary truths.

In Kōnyo's "Testament," we witness the birth of *shinzoku nitai* as a powerful religious symbol that, in large measure, was to shape the Honganji's responses to the crises of modern Japanese history.[17] *Shinzoku nitai* as dharma-principle touches on the most fundamental issue for religious institutions in modern Japan until the end of the Second World War—the proper relation between those institutions and the state, and, more specifically in the Shinshū, the proper response of Honganji members to Amida in relation to the emperor.

IMPERIAL JAPAN

As noted in the opening section of this chapter, the Jingikan in the Meiji era had sought to create and establish a state-centered Shinto as the source of spiritual and moral authority for an imperial state. It soon became evident that such an exclusivist policy would not work for a modern nation-state; the policy was offensive not only to Japanese Buddhists and to those who held traditional syncretistic attitudes, but also to foreign nations pressing for the opening of Japan. In 1871, the Jingishō (Ministry of Shinto Affairs), which had replaced the Jingikan, was abolished, and the government quickly established the Kyōbushō (Ministry of Religion and Education). In 1872, the new Department

---

[17] Teaching the principle *shinzoku nitai* is cited as the fundamental aim of the Shinshū in a catechism listing one hundred questions and answers, *Shinshū hyakuwa*, published in Meiji 42 (1909). The work, structured in four chapters, is primarily concerned with doctrinal questions relating to *shintai* (nos. 31–71) and *zokutai* (nos. 72–100). Item thirty-three states that the principle is common to all Buddhist sects, but that only in Shinshū teaching are "religious faith (*shintai*)" and "worldly conduct (*zokutai*)" harmonized. In support of the principle, Rennyo's teaching is evidently paraphrased, yet the passage is directly attributed to him as "Chūso Daishi 中祖大師." The content and structure of the catechism suggests the dominance achieved by the concept *shinzoku nitai* in Shinshū thought by the end of the Meiji period. See Nishimoto Ryūgen, *Shinshū hyakuwa* (Tokyo: Morie Shoten, 1909), 49–51; for an English translation of the entire work, see A.K. Reischauer, "A Catechism of the Shin Sect (Buddhism)," *Transactions of the Asiatic Society of Japan* 38/5 (1912): 331–95.

promulgated three guiding principles: respect for the kami and love of country; propagation of heavenly reason and the way of humanity; and reverence for the emperor and obedience to his authority.[18]

We examine now several developments relating to the Nishi Honganji's handling of scripture, culminating in the issuance on April 5, 1940, of a document entitled *Shōgyō no haidoku narabi ni inyō no kokoroe* 聖教の拝読ならびに引用の心得 , giving members detailed instructions on the use of scriptural readings and quotations.

As early as the summer of 1871, Shimaji Mokurai, representing the Nishi Honganji, had petitioned the government to establish a Department of Religion and Education. The Honganji, armed with the dharma-principle of the transcendent and mundane as two truths, was in a most favorable position to forge a partnership with the imperial state in promoting the three guiding principles listed above. At about that time, in an effort to underscore the Honganji's depth of commitment to such a partnership, a Shinshū scholar, Mizuhara Kōen, proposed that four characters whose meaning was judged disrespectful to the emperor and his ministers in Shinran's postscript to *Kyōgyōshinshō* be replaced by asterisks. He recommended that the same apply to a sentence in Shinran's biography, *Godenshō*, which described a commoner's indifference to ceremonial rules and disrespect to the kami as he made his way to the Kumano Shrine.[19]

The postscript to *Kyōgyōshinshō*, in which the four characters appear, is a rare autobiographical statement in which Shinran notes the historical reasons for his exile as Hōnen's disciple. He points out that the emperor and his ministers, opposing the nenbutsu teaching, were responsible for improprieties in their investigation of charges against Hōnen and his disciples; for indiscriminate death sentences for some of them; for the deprivation of priesthood for others, including Shinran; and for their exile under criminal names. The controversial passage reads:

> The emperor (*shujō*) and his ministers (*shinka*), opposing the dharma and violating [principles of] justice, harbored anger and resentment [against the nenbutsu teaching]. Because of this, Master Genkū [Hōnen], the great promulgator of the true teaching, and his followers were, without consideration of their crimes, arbitrarily condemned to death or deprived of their priesthood, given [secular]

---

[18] Shigaraki, "Shinshū ni okeru seiten sakujo mondai," 227. Also see Kishimoto, ed., *Japanese Culture in the Meiji Era*, 69–70.

[19] Shigaraki, "Shinshū ni okeru seiten sakujo mondai," 228. See *Godenshō*, SSZ 3: 652.

names, and sentenced to distant banishment. I am one of those. Hence I am neither a monk nor one in worldly life. For this reason, I took the name Toku 禿 . Master Genkū [Hōnen] and his disciples were banished [separately] to various remote provinces and spent five years in exile.[20]

Shinran's statement is substantiated later in the text by an indication that during the reign of the succeeding emperor, Sado-no-In (Juntoku; r. 1210–1221), Hōnen was pardoned by imperial order.

In 1886, Nishi Honganji promulgated a new set of sectarian principles. The office of Monshu was established as the head of the highly centralized institution. The second principle in the statement, clearly shaped by Rennyo's thought, reads as follows:

> According to the teaching of our sect, "the transcendent truth (*shintai*)" is to hear and entrust ourselves to the Buddha's Name and to say the Name in gratitude for the working of great compassion; "the mundane truth (*zokutai*)" is to live humanely and to obey the imperial law. Therefore, if we are people who dwell in a state of Other-Power faith (*anjin*) and strive to return the benevolence [shown us by society], then we manifest the excellent principle of the mutual support of the two truths.[21]

Threads of a partnership between the Honganji and the imperial state were woven into the very fabric of a religious institution in modern times; the principle of the transcendent and the mundane as two truths was the loom essential to that process.

In June 1933, that continuing partnership was tested by an incident in Osaka. An article entitled "Shinkō ōfuku no sho 信仰往復の書 ," which appeared in a Nishi Honganji-related publication, *Ichimi* 一味 , contained the phrase, "the great compassion of Amida's command (*chokumei* 勅命)." The editor was called before the Osaka special police and ordered to make written apology for the disrespect to the emperor evidenced by the use of the word "command" in relation to Amida. Subsequently, a representative of the Honganji made a request to the Ministry of Education for an explanation of the police action; the government official listened without offering any explanation for such a severe act of censorship.[22]

---

[20] *Kyōgyōshinshō*, SSZ 2: 201–2. See p. 25 above, n. 49. "Distant banishment" was the most severe punishment possible under the *ritsuryō* code.

[21] Quoted in Shigaraki, "Shinshū ni okeru shinzoku nitairon no kenkyū: Sono ichi," 44. This statement is the basis for a theory of *shinzoku nitai* found in Ryūkoku Daigaku, ed., *Shinshū yōron*, 169–70.

[22] Shigaraki, "Shinshū ni okeru seiten sakujo mondai," 228.

By this time, Japan was well along the road towards becoming a totalitarian state: the Manchurian incident had taken place in 1931 and the Shanghai incident in 1932; in 1933, the proletarian novelist Kobayashi Takiji (1903–1933) was beaten to death by secret police in Tokyo, and Takigawa Yukitoki (1891–1962) was forced to give up his academic post at Kyoto Imperial University. In 1936, against a background of increasing repression, the Honganji published a revised version of the scriptures, *Kaitei Shinshū seiten* 改訂真宗聖典 . Among the revisions is the insertion of the genitive particle の (*no*) in that most sensitive phrase, *shujō shinka*, used by Shinran in *Kyōgyōshinshō*. The revised version reads "ministers *of* the emperor (*shujō no shinka* 主上の 臣下)," rather than "the emperor and his ministers."[23]

Censorship in the name of absolutizing the role of the emperor reached a new level of intensity in 1939. The minister of education, Araki Sadao (1877–1966), charged that *Shinshū yōgi* 真宗要義 , a text used in the Department of Shinshū Studies at Ryūkoku University, included materials disrespectful to the imperial office. The terms *chokumei, kyōchoku* 教勅 , and *butchoku* 仏勅 , significant concepts in Shinshū thought, were prohibited for use in such a context. After the appropriate revisions were made, the University was allowed to continue to use the text for instruction.[24]

The above events strengthened even further the partnership between the Honganji and the state. The two existed side by side as separate entities representing the two truths, the former as a religious body symbolic of the transcendent, the latter as a political (in theory at least, not a religious) entity representing the mundane. Working together in harmony as partners, however, they increasingly constituted an organic whole. Thus, in theory, the concept *shinzoku nitai* as a religious symbol allowed for differentiation between the Honganji and the state, despite treating them as complementary truths. Eventually, in practice, the national polity (*kokutai* 国体) was to subsume categories for both the transcendent and the mundane.

On April 5, 1940, officials of the Nishi Honganji issued a document providing comprehensive guidelines for the public use of Shinshū scriptures.[25] This set of instructions called attention to passages in Shinran's *Kyōgyōshinshō, Kōsō wasan, Shōzōmatsu wasan,* and other writings; Kakunyo's *Godenshō*; and *The Letters*. In all, some fifty-three items were identified as ones that might be construed as disrespectful

---

[23] Shigaraki, "Shinshū ni okeru seiten sakujo mondai," 228–29.

[24] Shigaraki, "Shinshū ni okeru seiten sakujo mondai," 229–30.

[25] Shigaraki, "Shinshū ni okeru seiten sakujo mondai," 217.

of the emperor and the imperial state. Detailed instructions were given as to the proper reading of scripture and its quotation or citation in sermons and writings. In addition, a number of phrases were to be deleted from the texts and, in effect, ruled out of the Shinshū canon. A scholar in Shinshū Studies, writing in the 1970s, interprets the Honganji's action as an effort "to express loyalty to the imperial state, recognizing that Shinshū scriptures contradicted the principle of the emperor's divinity (*tennō shinsei* 天皇神聖) and that passages of some texts were incompatible with the Japanese concept of national polity."[26] The charges Shinran had made in his postscript to *Kyōgyōshinshō* against imperial authority in thirteenth-century Japan became an intolerable burden and source of embarrassment for the Honganji amidst the hysteria of thought-control in 1940. Officials of the Nishi Honganji decided to proscribe even more drastically portions of scripture that even hinted at offense to the imperial system. For example, the entire sentence, "The emperor and his ministers, opposing the dharma and violating [principles of] justice, harbored anger and resentment [against the nenbutsu teaching]," could no longer be used in services or in quotation in sermons or writings. Blank spaces were to be left in whatever text was involved.[27] A legacy of this prohibition even carried over into postwar printings of the Shinshū scriptures. As we noted earlier, in the 1967 printing of *Shinshū shōgyō zensho*, there are blank spaces for the two characters 主上 (*shu-jō*); in the 1977 printing, the characters are back in place.[28]

There are further examples of scriptural items seen to be in conflict with the imperial state ideology of 1940:

- In *Kyōgyōshinshō*, when the term *chokumei* appears in the text, as in "to take refuge is the command (*chokumei*) of the Primal Vow, calling to and summoning us,"[29] the reading specified for the term was "*onmei* 恩命 " rather than "*chokumei*." "*Chokumei*" was reserved exclusively for imperial commands symbolic of the emperor's divinity. In another of Shinran's texts, *Jōdo monrui jushō*, the Tathāgata's *kyōchoku* was to be read *kyōmei* 教命 .

- A passage from a Mahāyāna text, *Bosatsukaikyō*, quoted in the sixth chapter of *Kyōgyōshinshō*, was proscribed; the text enjoins

[26] Shigaraki, "Shinshū ni okeru seiten sakujo mondai," 217.

[27] Shigaraki, "Shinshū ni okeru seiten sakujo mondai," 218.

[28] See 1967 and 1977 printings of *Kyōgyōshinshō*, SSZ 2: 201.

[29] Shigaraki, "Shinshū ni okeru seiten sakujo mondai," 218–19; see *Kyōgyōshinshō*, SSZ 2: 22.

monks not to bow before kings or parents.[30] What could possibly be more offensive to State Shinto or Neo-Confucian sensibilities?

• When reference is made to an emperor in *Kyōgyōshinshō* or *Godenshō*, a special honorific was to be used. The reading "Go-Sado-no-In," became "*Goshitatematsuru*-Sado-no-In."[31] In *Kyōgyōshinshō* or *Godenshō*, Shinran's phrase, "without consideration of their crimes," was proscribed.[32]

• The chapters in *Godenshō* relating Shinran's vision in the Rokkaku-dō and sequences portraying the kami of the Hakone and Kumano shrines in anything less than the absolutist terms of State Shinto were proscribed.[33] A passage in *Godenshō*, in which Shōtoku Taishi prostrates himself before Shinran, was deleted.[34]

• Certain of Shinran's hymns were not to be read. Two from his *Kōsō wasan*:

Genkū was manifested as [the bodhisattva] Seishi;
at times, he was revealed to be Amida.
Emperors and many ministers revered him;
people of the capital and of the countryside paid him honor.

A retired emperor during the Jōkyō [era]
took refuge in Master Genkū;
monks and scholars alike
entered equally into the true teaching.[35]

• One from *Shōzōmatsu wasan*:

World-saviour Kannon, the great bodhisattva,
manifested himself as Prince Shōtoku;

---

[30] Shigaraki, "Shinshū ni okeru seiten sakujo mondai," 218; see *Kyōgyō-shinshō*, SSZ 2: 191–92.

[31] Shigaraki, "Shinshū ni okeru seiten sakujo mondai," 218; see *Kyōgyō-shinshō*, SSZ 2: 202, and *Godenshō*, SSZ 3: 648.

[32] Shigaraki, "Shinshū ni okeru seiten sakujo mondai," 218; see *Kyōgyō-shinshō*, SSZ 2: 201, and *Godenshō*, SSZ 3: 648.

[33] Shigaraki, "Shinshū ni okeru seiten sakujo mondai," 219; see *Godenshō*, SSZ 3: 640–41; 650–53.

[34] Shigaraki, "Shinshū ni okeru seiten sakujo mondai," 219; see *Godenshō*, SSZ 3: 641–42.

[35] Shigaraki, "Shinshū ni okeru seiten sakujo mondai," 219; see *Kōsō wasan*, SSZ 2: 513 (#106, #107). Also see English translations and notes in *Kōsō Wasan*, 131–32.

like a father, he never abandons us;
like a mother, he is always with us.[36]

The message was clear: emperors do not pay homage to a sage appearing as a bodhisattva or even as Amida; retired emperors do not go for refuge to a teacher; and even a great bodhisattva does not appear as an imperial prince.

A final clause enjoins those who read the scriptures at public functions or at services to show respect for the imperial household by bowing at each reference. The instructions were distributed to Nishi Honganji temples with a reminder from the Honganji staff director that at the core of Shinran's spiritual vision was belief in imperial law as fundamental and devotion to the notion of an imperial state.[37] Participants in the tradition were informed that, by observing these instructions, they were being true to the founder's spirit as understood both in Japanese history and in Shinshū tradition.

These demands for radical accommodation to an imperial state in the use of the Shinshū scriptures did not emerge in a vacuum. As we have seen, they were the culmination of developments in the medieval and early-modern history of the Honganji; they were also the result of a series of responses by the Nishi Honganji at critical moments in modern Japanese history. To some extent, they were also a response to internal pressures within the Honganji itself.

AMIDA AND EMPEROR

In late 1941, with Japan's direct involvement in the Second World War imminent, the final step was taken in absolutizing the emperor's authority. As partners with the imperial state, both Nishi and Higashi Honganji scholars developed wartime or battleground theologies. Among the many titles published were: *Bukkyō no chūgi tetsugaku* 仏教の忠義哲学 (A Buddhist philosophy of loyalty, 1940); *Kannagara no michi to Jōdo Shinshū* 神ながらの道と浄土真宗 (The way of the kami and Jōdo Shinshū, 1941); and *On ichigenron: Kōdō bukkyō no shinzui* 恩一元論 — 皇道仏教の心髄 (A theory of the oneness of benevolence: The essence of imperial-way Buddhism, 1942).[38]

---

[36] Shigaraki, "Shinshū ni okeru seiten sakujo mondai," 219; *Shōzōmatsu wasan*, SSZ 2: 526c. Also see English translation in *Shōzōmatsu Wasan*, 84.

[37] Shigaraki, "Shinshū ni okeru seiten sakujo mondai," 219–20.

[38] Shigaraki, "Shinshū ni okeru seiten sakujo mondai," 237–38. For documents relating to these works, see "Senji Kyōgaku" Kenkyūkai, ed., *Senjikyōgaku*

On ichigenron, which presents a theory of the oneness of the emperor's and Amida's benevolence, was the work of a sectarian scholar, with a foreword contributed by the president of Ryūkoku University. The author's theory brought into play a logic that had served his tradition repeatedly at moments of crisis over the centuries, enabling the Honganji not only to survive as a religious order, but to prosper. In broader scope, it is a logic that goes back to the founding myths of land and people and the notion of the unity of religious and political affairs, and again to the encounter with an alien religious tradition—the Buddhist—and the theory of the native kami as manifestations of an underlying Buddhist reality. The Shinshū as a Japanese Buddhist tradition appears to have inherited from Shinran's teaching few resources, conceptual or other, to question, much less to resist, the demands of the state. The absolute authority of the emperor's command in prewar Japan may be seen as an extreme instance within this pattern. Shinran's symbols for the transcendent—Amida, Primal Vow, faith, and nenbutsu—are, in theory, differentiated from the mundane and thus hold a capacity for criticism of all temporal authority, including that of the state. Instead, these religious symbols were subsumed by symbols for the national polity and imperial system.

At one point in *On ichigenron*, the author speculates that if the Buddha were to appear at that moment in wartime Japan, there is no question but that he would expound upon the absoluteness of the emperor and clarify the meaning of national polity.[39] Further, the origins and developments of a theory of the oneness of benevolence (*on*), including treatments of the great Kamakura Buddhists, are worked out in detail; a lengthy section discusses the imperial national polity and the Shinshū:

> The Shinshū teaches that, in living as citizens in the mundane world, we are to take imperial law as fundamental and submit absolutely to the [emperor's] command; this is basic to Amida's intent. People who oppose [this] are, consequently, excluded from Amida's salvation. Hence it cannot be true that the Shinshū's dharma-principle is incompatible with the imperial national polity. In other words, we can be good citizens of the empire because we dwell firmly in Amida's saving power; it is the Shinshū that is the very best religion (*shūkyō*) in terms of compatibility with the imperial national polity.[40]

---

to *Shinshū*, vol. 1 (Kyoto: Nagata Bunshōdō, 1988).

[39] Shigaraki, "Shinshū ni okeru seiten sakujo mondai," 238.

[40] Sasaki Kentoku, *On ichigenron: Kōdō bukkyō no shinzui* (Kyoto: Kōkyō

Numerous other examples might be cited from Shinshū writings that illustrate how both the Nishi and the Higashi Honganji supported — virtually demanded — full participation of their members in the war effort, with an elaborately constructed wartime theology. Indeed, Shinran's teaching appears to have been transformed into the handmaiden of imperial absolutism. The identification of Amida's benevolence with that of the emperor made it possible to sacralize every sacrifice as an act of piety, including the giving of one's very life for the imperial state.

For Shinran, nenbutsu alone — faith alone — is true and real.[41] His conviction is that the only path for people in the last dharma-age is to live without calculation through the Other Power of Amida's Primal Vow, free of the delusion that they have any power of their own to effect good for themselves or for others. Shinran's declaration that he is "neither a monk nor one in worldly life" symbolizes his experience of self-negation that brings about, naturally, a realization of the underlying unity of the transcendent and the mundane, unbifurcated — a unity that is dynamic in its simultaneity of sameness and opposition. He never elaborates on concepts such as *shinzoku nitai*, although they were readily available to him in the Mahāyāna texts of the Tendai strand of his Buddhist heritage. For him, reality is the transcendent truth of Amida's Primal Vow, or Buddha-dharma, manifesting itself as the mundane truth in the teachings of Śākyamuni, in the commentaries of Pure Land masters, and in the words of his master, Hōnen. On the basis of his own experience of exile, he knew that there would be times when conflict between the truth of the nenbutsu and the expectations and demands of the social order was to be anticipated.

Kakunyo and Zonkaku, as we have seen, are the two figures following Shinran who contribute decisively to shaping the tradition leading up to Rennyo's tenure as head priest. Living in a social and historical setting quite different from that of Shinran, they interpreted the tradition in ways that led to an elaboration of pairs of concepts such as *shin* and *zoku*, *buppō* and *ōbō*. For Kakunyo, the transcendent relates to birth in the Pure Land after death; the mundane relates to an ethical basis for living this life in the assurance of birth in the Pure Land in the afterlife. Zonkaku also stresses the mundane in his attempt to reconcile Shinshū teaching with Japan's indigenous religious tradition by setting the transcendent and the mundane side by side.

Shoin, 1942), 298; quoted in Shigaraki, "Shinshū ni okeru seiten sakujo mondai," 238.
[41] *Tannishō*, SSZ 2: 793.

For him, the relationship is as closely-balanced as a bird's two wings or a cart's two wheels. A final implication of his position is that Buddha-dharma is to serve imperial law, in that the latter represents the source of subsistence, the provision of food and shelter, in this life.

Rennyo's thought is both continuous and discontinuous with each of his predecessors, Shinran, Kakunyo, and Zonkaku. From Shinran, Rennyo inherited the teaching that Other-Power faith is the *sine qua non* of the Pure Land nenbutsu path; from Kakunyo, a deep commitment to promoting and empowering the Honganji as the exclusive vehicle for guarding the transcendent; and from Zonkaku, *honji suijaku* thought, which provided a theoretical basis for accommodating the transcendent to the mundane by emphasizing the observance of existing social norms. Rennyo's approach, in an entirely different historical context, reflects his perception of the transient quality of the age in which he lived. His position has been described as dualist in that he appears to emphasize the afterlife (the transcendent) as the most important matter (*goshō ichidaiji*) in contrast to this life (the mundane) — the Pure Land in contrast to this defiled world. Certainly, there is a degree of bifurcation here that is not found in Shinran's thought.

During the Tokugawa period, the Honganji, in large measure dedicated to the service of those who governed, politicized and thereby dissipated much of its spiritual energy in a rigorously controlled scholasticism.[42] Kōnyo, who lived virtually all of his life in the Tokugawa period, speaks in his final message as the heir to Shinran, Kakunyo, Zonkaku, and especially Rennyo, at a moment of crisis for the Nishi Honganji in early Meiji. The Honganji's modern history has carried forward much of Kōnyo's pattern of thinking. What is perhaps new in the modern world is a disintegration of the capacity of religious symbols in most traditions to be effective in differentiating between the transcendent and the mundane. In that respect, Japan's imperial absolutism in the 1930s cannot be understood apart from influences derived from the encounter with modern Western secular and religious thought.

In conclusion, we offer several tentative observations on the relevance of the Nishi Honganji's pattern of response to what we have characterized as the dilemma of religious power.

First, a pervasive theme in the materials we have presented is an overriding concern to preserve the Honganji as a religious order. The

---

[42] This statement is not intended to discount the continued vitality and flourishing of the rich tradition of *myōkōnin* piety noted earlier.

point is complex, for the Honganji not only represents a line of dharma-transmission, it is also representative of a familial line of blood kinship (in respect to which significant parallels with Japan's imperial institution might be drawn).[43] The preservation of both dharma and familial lineages appears to have been a guiding impulse for over six hundred years—beginning with Kakunyo's founding of a temple, Hongan-ji, at Shinran's mausoleum in Kyoto, and continuing with Rennyo's dramatic institutional expansion in late medieval Japan, Kōnyo's response to the anti-Buddhist movement in early Meiji, and the writing of wartime theologies in the 1940s. The pattern remains largely unchanged in both branches of the Honganji at present, at the close of the twentieth century.

Second is that a dual standard of attitudes exists—one shared among members of the community and another directed at those deemed to be outsiders. At different points in the history of the Honganji, the outsiders have been taken to be rival Buddhist groups— whether other branches of the Shinshū, branches of the Jōdoshū, or the pre-Kamakura sects—as well as, in the modern period, the Christian missionary enterprise, and then the enemies of imperial Japan. It is important to note that internal controversy, including sharp differences on matters of doctrine, has been tolerated as long as the disputes have not posed a serious threat to the harmony and stability of the community or to the prosperity of the institution. It was even possible as late as 1942, despite the extreme pressures of imperial absolutism, for groups of Shinshū priests to voice sharp opposition to changing a single character in the Shinshū scriptures.[44]

---

[43] Suggestive in this respect are the writings of Kiyoko Takeda; among her relevant publications in English are *The Dual-Image of the Japanese Emperor* (New York: Macmillan, 1988) and "Emperor Hirohito and the Turbulent Shōwa Era," *The Japan Foundation Newsletter* 16/5–6 (1989): 1–5, 8.

[44] Further study of this issue would call for a comparative treatment of wartime responses of several branches of the Shinshū to imperial absolutism. While the present study has considered the Nishi Honganji's institutional response, there is little to suggest that the Higashi's response was significantly different. One would want to consider also branches of the Shinshū for whom Rennyo is not seen as the restorer, such as the Takada and Bukkōji. The Nishi Honganji, in particular, has made a concerted effort to address issues raised by their wartime doctrinal positions and institutional activities; see the first volume edited by a "wartime theology" study group, "Senji Kyōgaku" Kenkyūkai, ed., *Senji kyōgaku to Shinshū*; also see Ikeda Gyōshin, "Senji kyōgaku no riron kōzō," 211–25, and Ōe Osamu, "Honganji kyōdan no minshūka to sensō sekinin," 227–88, in Shigaraki Takamaro, ed., *Kindai Shinshū kyōdanshi kenkyū* (Kyoto: Hōzōkan, 1987). For material on the war years regarding major Buddhist sects—

Third, participants in Shinshū tradition—following Shinran's own example—saw no need to develop categories for sharp differentiation of religion and state. Indeed, at moments of crisis, highly ambiguous religious symbols such as *shinzoku nitai* have emerged, which have the potential to blur distinctions in the interest of preserving unity and solidarity in the community. At an affective level, it would appear that *shinzoku nitai* as a religious symbol has served the Honganji in ways similar to that in which *honji suijaku* theory has served Japanese Buddhists in general over the centuries; it is perhaps also similar to the way the notion of *saisei itchi* has served Japanese tradition as a whole.

A historian of religions, in writing of the "seamlessness" of the early Japanese world of meaning in relation to the lasting imprint of Chinese script and the Buddha's image on Japanese culture and society, discusses the connectedness of government, religion, and art:

> Indeed, the fact that political administration (*matsuri-goto*), religious cults (*matsuri*), and cultural activities, especially art, came to be thought of as interrelated but nonetheless separate dimensions of life indicates the extent to which the seamlessness of the early Japanese world of meaning was transformed under the influence of foreign [Buddhist] perspectives on life and the world. Nevertheless, we also find the persistent impulse of the Japanese to re-homologize and to maintain the connection between various dimensions of life, especially that between political administration and religion, as well as that between religion and art.[45]

In the case of the Shinran's concept of *shinjin*, we have observed the emergence of a Buddhist symbol with potential for differentiating between political administration—the imperial state—and a religious institution—the Honganji. Further, Shinran's thought has the capacity to question a traditional view of the "seamlessness" between religion and art, or between religious value and aesthetic value. The issue is complex in that, for Japan's cultural tradition, the frequently-made generalization does not appear to hold: religious value tends to be related immediately to specific concrete phenomena rather than to a theoretical or abstract absolute. For Shinran, however, might we not interpret his nenbutsu response to Amida's command, or, more specifically, the experience of faith as *shinjin* in its purity, adamantine

---

Nichiren, Zen, Shinshū, and Shingon, see Nakano Kyōtoku, ed., *Senjika no bukkyō*, in *Kōza: Nihon kindai to bukkyō*, no. 6 (Tokyo: Kokusho Kankōkai, 1977).

[45] Joseph M. Kitagawa, "Reality and Illusion: Some Characteristics of the Early Japanese 'World of Meaning,'" *Oriental Society of Australia Journal* 11 (1976): 14.

hardness, absence of doubt, and distrust of form as having aesthetic value? There would appear to be an aesthetic dimension to Shinran's Buddhist experience as set forth in his writings that is something other than simply non-differentiation between religion and art. On the other hand, Rennyo's nenbutsu response, the experience of faith as *anjin*, conceptualized in symbols informed by *Anjin ketsujōshō*, reflects that impulse "to re-homologize and to maintain the connection between various dimensions of life, especially that between political administration and religion, as well as that between religion and art."[46]

In our inquiry into the history of a major Shinshū concept, *shinzoku nitai*, and its relationship to Japanese civilization, we have seen that, while the concept allows for differentiation of the transcendent and the mundane, this pair of entities has been viewed primarily in terms of a merging of separate identities into stasis. A similar pattern may be seen in response to concepts for the oneness of religious and political affairs and for the kami as manifestations of an underlying reality expressed in Buddhist symbols. How are we to understand this pattern of response to religious symbols?

One possible interpretive approach, especially congenial to those primarily familiar with symbols of radical transcendence in Western religious traditions, is to evaluate responses to such symbols using categories of separateness and oneness, dynamism and passivity. From this perspective, the symbols tend to be seen as successful insofar as they elicit dynamic responses. In this case: (1) the oneness of political and religious affairs means that religious symbols are not ruled out as a source of criticism of temporal authority; (2) the kami as manifestations of reality in Buddhist terms means that the universality of Buddhadharma may challenge the particularity of the Japanese kami; and (3) the transcendent and the mundane as two truths means that there may be resistance to merging separate entities into one. On the other hand, these same symbols are seen as unsuccessful insofar as they elicit passive responses. In this instance: (1) the oneness of religious and po-

---

[46] This matter requires considerable clarification, perhaps starting doctrinally with Shinran's view of "dharmakāya as suchness (formlessness)" in relation to "dharmakāya as compassion (form)." It is largely with Rennyo, drawing on Kakunyo's legacy, that more traditional Japanese Buddhist aesthetic sensibilities evidenced in liturgical chanting and in temple furnishings are formally appropriated and begin to be standardized within the Shinshū. In sum, it appears that Shinran's "*shinjin* aesthetic" is of a somewhat different order that Rennyo's "*anjin* aesthetic": Shinran's involves a negation of form, or, at the least, invites a continuing dialectic of form and formlessness; Rennyo's aesthetic offers an uncritical affirmation of form.

litical affairs is interpreted to mean that worship is ancillary to government; (2) the kami as manifestations of Buddhist reality is interpreted to mean that the buddhas passively serve the kami, or vice versa; and (3) the transcendent and the mundane as two truths is interpreted to mean that Amida merges into the figure of the emperor. The eye (mind and heart) of the observer nurtured on religious symbols of radical transcendence is drawn first to the separateness of the pair of entities and to their potential for dynamic interaction and mutual criticism. In stressing the dynamic potential of that separateness, the harmonious passivity of their oneness may be entirely overlooked. In sum, to interpret Japanese religious symbols from such a perspective may be to miss their point entirely. Where are we to turn for clarification?

We look again to Shinran's view of reality as expressed in his writings and, in particular, to Rennyo's extraordinary efforts to institutionalize that vision in history as the Honganji. We note that Shinran avoids the use of concepts (such as *shinzoku nitai*) that we have discussed. As a result of his experience of Tendai's teaching of primordial enlightenment and insight into his own condition as foolish being, he was alert to the danger of pressing for too much oneness too soon; he knew quite simply that what surpasses conceptual understanding—a simultaneity of sameness and opposition—is irreducible to any single concept. However, without such concepts, how could the profundity of his vision be conveyed to successive generations? Kakunyo, Zonkaku, Rennyo, Kōnyo, and modern Shinshū scholars turned to such concepts to serve as religious symbols. Noteworthy is Rennyo's innovative appropriation of the concept of the oneness of the person to be saved and Amida who saves (*ki-hō ittai*) to designate the salvific process at work in saying Amida's Name. What then is the alternative to such symbolization?

The answer is surely that, finally, there is no single satisfactory solution. There is always the risk with religious symbols of missing their point entirely, of failing to recognize the sublimity of a founder's vision of the transcendent truth. This risk was all the greater for the Honganji in modern Japan at a moment when reality for the national community was defined in terms of an empire founded for eternity by imperial ancestors. In such a context, who would have been disposed to hear Amida's command apart from the imperial command to submit passively to the state's authority in the service of the nation? Indeed, there may have been some who discovered, through their engagement with the concept *shinzoku nitai* as a religious symbol, that their submissiveness to the governing authority of their cherished land and people had been sacralized.[47]

There were also, however, those members of the Honganji, including some sectarian scholars, who heard another command. This was the same command that Shinran had heard: Amida's compassionate summons to each of them to participate freely, without calculation, in this world as Amida's world, and not without strong reservations in regard to the uncritical partnership of emperor and Amida.[48] Nevertheless, given the uniqueness of Shinran's teaching for Japan's cultural tradition, the Honganji's claim to be his authentic heir was severely tested in its assumed role as guardian of the state during a crucial period in the nation's history.

---

[47] A case can be made that, at times, the dharma-principle *shinzoku nitai* served as a "lightning-rod" to protect members of the Honganji from government harassment and deflect possible criticism by their fellow citizens outside the tradition, particularly during the war years. The same could be said for wartime doctrinal studies. From this perspective, it is possible to argue that the Honganji's role as guardian of the state in modern Japan served primarily to guard the dharma (*gohō* 護法); following this rationale, enemies of Japan might be construed as enemies of the dharma (*hōteki* 法敵). For a discussion of the significance of *gohō* for Rennyo, see Solomon, "Honganji Under Rennyo," and McMullin, *Buddhism and the State in Sixteenth-Century Japan*, 38–39.

[48] Representative of this position is the work of scholars such as Futaba Kenkō and Shigaraki Takamaro, who argue that the Honganji at times severely compromised what is most true and real in Shinran's teaching. Their witness of critical participation in Shinshū tradition is not to be taken for granted; it suggests something of the unique legacy of Shinran's thought for Japan's religious tradition as a whole.

Chapter 8

The Legacy Today

W
HO IS RENNYO? Who is to say, finally? No single image is entirely satisfactory. As in any humanistic study involving the meaning of symbols, there is always more to be discovered than meets the eye. In exploring the varied responses to Rennyo's life and thought as presented in *The Letters,* we have, however, recognized something of the multi-faceted quality of his legacy.

Although we paint on a broad canvas in this final chapter, we can treat only a few of the many contemporary images of Rennyo in Japanese culture at the popular level, in the lives of specific individuals (both sectarian and non-sectarian) who find in Rennyo a close companion, and finally in the field of comparative studies concerned with the religious history of humankind. As is already apparent, there is no way to isolate Rennyo's legacy from Shinran's or, for that matter, Shinran's from Hōnen's, from the Pure Land masters', and from Śākyamuni's, and so it has gone over the millennia. We have, however, sought to highlight instances where Rennyo is in special focus as subject.

IN JAPANESE CULTURE

When we deeply consider the transiency of this world, [we realize that] what is altogether fleeting is our own span of life: it is like an illusion from beginning to end. . . . We may have radiant faces in the morning, but in the evening be no more than white bones.[1]

These words, known by heart in Japanese to participants in Shinshū tradition and hauntingly familiar to others throughout Japanese

---

[1] RSI, 482–83 (#184/5:16); SSZ 3: 513.

society in times of loss, are recited as part of the liturgy at Shinshū funerals. It is not so well known that they are drawn from one of Rennyo's undated letters, "On white bones," the sixteenth in fascicle five. Through the reading of these verses, the Buddha-dharma has been heard and responded to for over five centuries. The widespread use of this letter provides perhaps the best example of Rennyo's presence in popular Japanese culture today. Several such examples, including a further discussion of the letter, are presented here.

First, an image from a more formal perspective on Japanese cultural history is that of Rennyo as one of Japan's most eminent Buddhist priests. An introduction to his life and thought and selections of his letters are included in major series on important figures in Japanese cultural history.[2] In a ten-volume work on fourteen renowned Japanese Buddhist priests, Rennyo is selected for the volume with Ikkyū (1394–1481).[3] He is the last chronologically in a line beginning in the Nara period with Gyōgi (668–749) and Ganjin (688–763); followed by Saichō, Kūkai (774–835), and Genshin in the Heian; seven priests from the Kamakura: the rebuilder of Tōdai-ji, Chōgen (1121–1206), revivers of the old Nara Ritsu school, Eison (1201–1290) and Ninshō (1217–1303), and then the great Kamakura "reformers" — Hōnen, Shinran, Dōgen, and Nichiren; and, finally, from the Muromachi, Ikkyū and Rennyo. Given the criteria for selection — those priests who were either acknowledged as founders or who have decisively marked the transmission of their respective traditions, no priests from the Tokugawa or modern periods are included.[4] Obviously, not everyone would arrive at precisely the same listing — Hakuin (1685–1768) immediately comes to mind as a candidate from the Tokugawa. In any event, it would be extremely difficult to omit Rennyo, given the stature of his achievement as the restorer of the Jōdo Shinshū.

Two further images reflecting Rennyo's legacy in popular culture are drawn from contemporary Japanese novels in which reference is made to Shinshū piety in the context of daily life, albeit at moments of crisis. The first is found in *Kuroi ame* (1965; Black rain), a documentary

---

[2] For example, see: Kasahara Kazuo, *Rennyo*, Jinbutsu Sōsho, no. 109 (1963; repr. Tokyo: Yoshikawa Kōbunkan, 1969); Kasahara Kazuo and Inoue Toshio, eds., *Rennyo/Ikkō ikki*, Nihon Shisō Taikei, no. 17 (Tokyo: Iwanami Shoten, 1972); Kasahara Kazuo, *Shinran to Rennyo: Sono kōdō to shisō*, Nihonjin no Kōdō to Shisō, no. 40 (Tokyo: Hyōronsha, 1978); and Mori Ryūkichi, *Rennyo*, Kōdansha Gendai Shinsho, no. 550 (Tokyo: Kōdansha, 1979).

[3] Sakurai Yoshirō and Fukuma Kōchō, *Ikkyū/Rennyo*, Nihon Meisō Ronshū, no. 10 (Tokyo: Yoshikawa Kōbunkan, 1983).

[4] Sakurai and Fukuma, "Kankō no kotoba," *Ikkyū/Rennyo*.

novel by Ibuse Masuji (1898–). Through an alternation of narrative passages and diary entries, this work tells of the struggles of survivors of the atomic bomb dropped on Hiroshima on August 7, 1945.[5] One episode is a matter-of-fact report of a company manager and employee facing the problem of the funeral of another worker, killed by the lingering effects of the explosion. The story is told by Shizuma, the employee charged with carrying out the manager's instructions: Shizuma contacts the works section to have a coffin made as quickly as possible, sends notice of the death to the town hall and asks for instructions for the disposal of the body, and dispatches another worker to find a doctor and priest. Word soon comes back that the town hall is virtually closed down, has refused even to accept death notices, and has no advice to give on the disposal of bodies. The doctor is out, the priest too busy to come.[6]

It is decided that the only thing to be done is to cremate the deceased on the river bed, along with countless others from throughout the area. At this point, the manager turns to Shizuma:

> "We can't just simply cremate them. You can't just say, 'why, he's dead!' and whisk him off and burn him and have done with it. It's a bit hard on the deceased, surely, unless he gets at least something more than that. Personally, now, I don't believe in the immortality of the soul, but I do believe one should dispose of the dead with respect. Look, Shizuma — I want you to take the priest's place and read the service whenever there's a death."[7]

Shizuma protests his total inexperience in such matters. The manager, however, insists that he find a temple and make notes on the scriptures read at cremations: "I was also told to take down the texts favored by the Shin sect, since many Hiroshima people belonged to it."[8] He finds a temple where an aged and infirm priest calls for five scriptures to be brought to him: the threefold refuge, the dedication, the hymn in praise of the Buddha, the *Amida Sūtra,* and Rennyo's letter, "On white bones."[9] Shizuma copies them; he finds the first selections difficult to understand, although notations give the proper readings for the Chinese characters. Rennyo's letter, however, was "in

---

[5] Ibuse Masuji, *Kuroi ame*, Shinchō Bunko, no. 400 (Tokyo: Shinchōsha, 1989). In English translation: Masuji Ibuse, *Black Rain*, trans. John Bester (1979; repr. Tokyo and New York: Kodansha International, 1988).

[6] Ibuse, *Black Rain*, 130–31; *Kuroi ame*, 136–37.

[7] Ibuse, *Black Rain*, 131–32; *Kuroi ame*, 138.

[8] Ibuse, *Black Rain*, 132; *Kuroi ame*, 139.

[9] Ibuse, *Kuroi ame*, 140.

gentler, homelier Japanese, in a beautiful language that struck home to the heart."[10] The old priest explains how the texts are to be used, pointing out that while the *Amida Sūtra* is being read, those present offer incense. "Next comes 'On white bones,'" he continues, "and this time, we read facing the congregation, not the Buddha."[11] As we have seen, the letter tells of the transiency of human existence and of Amida as the only refuge:

> Because the impermanence of this world creates a condition of un-certainty for young and old alike, we should all immediately take to heart the most important matter, the afterlife, and, deeply entrusting ourselves to Amida Buddha, say the nenbutsu.[12]

Following the services, Shizuma reports that three office employees asked if they might copy the letter. When he asked why they made the request, one said she liked the language; another said that she wanted to memorize the text.[13]

By the following day, Shizuma found he was being treated just like a priest. As he was reading the service for the funeral of a young girl, he was so moved by Rennyo's letter that his voice finally choked. He hurried from funeral to funeral throughout the day. The final sentence of his diary entry for August 8 reads:

> I remembered the other body awaiting me, and set off back along the embankment, murmuring . . . [Rennyo's letter] to myself as I went. This time, I got through it without so much as a glance at my notes.[14]

In Ibuse's narrative, Rennyo's words resound with immediacy and power to touch and comfort those caught up in the horror of that moment in history. Of the texts recommended to Shizuma, Rennyo's letter alone was readily comprehensible to all who heard it; his further legacy was in the liturgical use of these materials, including the recital of the *Amida Sūtra*.

Another major novelist writing in postwar Japan is Shiroyama Saburō (1927–), who documented the life and death of Hirota Kōki (1878–1948), foreign minister and prime minister of Japan in the years leading up to the war. Following the war, Hirota was arrested,

---

[10] Ibuse, *Black Rain*, 133; *Kuroi ame*, 140–41.

[11] Ibuse, *Kuroi ame*, 141.

[12] RSI, 482–83 (#184/5:16); SSZ 3: 513.

[13] Ibuse, *Black Rain*, 135; *Kuroi ame*, 143.

[14] Ibuse, *Black Rain*, 138; *Kuroi ame*, 146.

charged, tried, convicted, and executed as a war criminal. Shiroyama's account, *Rakujitsu moyu* (1974; Burning sunset) concludes with the events leading up to the execution.[15] The condemned, six former army officers and Hirota, the single civilian, were visited regularly by the Sugamo prison chaplain, Hanayama Shinshō, a Shinshū priest who was also on the faculty of Tokyo University. Shiroyama reports that Hirota appeared unresponsive to the chaplain's words and re-signed to whatever was to come: "When the condemned men assembled in the chapel and joined Hanayama in chanting the nenbutsu, Hirota alone sat reading a sūtra in silence."[16]

Shiroyama draws on Hanayama's own account of an interview with Hirota, in which Hanayama had attempted to break through the condemned man's unresponsiveness:

> "Don't you have any parting poem, say, or any impressions you want to record?"
>
> "The things I've done since I went into government service still stand; I don't think I want to add anything further."
>
> Undeterred by this apparent indifference, Hanayama went on, "Not even any comments on . . .?"
>
> "Nothing. Just to die without fuss [*shizen ni*] . . . He broke off.
>
> "Nothing at all?" Hanayama pressed.
>
> "I've always taken things simply, as they came," Hirota replied in a quiet voice as though talking to himself, "saying what I had to say and doing my job as well as I could, so in fact there's nothing for me to add now. Just to live naturally and to die naturally."
>
> Hanayama, who was a priest of the Shin sect of Buddhism, asked whether Hirota's state of mind derived from Zen, and Hirota replied that it was close to it. The only sign of emotion he showed was when Hanayama told him that five members of his family had come to see him the day before. . . .[17]

---

[15] Shiroyama Saburō, *Rakujitsu moyu*, Shinchō Bunko, no. 440 (Tokyo: Shinchōsha, 1986). In English translation: Saburō Shiroyama, *War Criminal: The Life and Death of Hirota Koki*, trans. John Bester (Tokyo, New York and San Francisco: Kodansha International, 1977).

[16] Shiroyama, *Rakujitsu moyu*, 367; *War Criminal*, 291.

[17] Shiroyama, *War Criminal*, 292; *Rakujitsu moyu*, 367–68. Shiroyama acknowledges the source of the exchange as Hanayama Shinshō, *Heiwa no hakken: Sugamo no sei to shi no kiroku* (Tokyo: Asahi Shinbunsha, 1949), 188–89. Hanayama's work is also in English translation: Shinshō Hanayama, *The Way of Deliverance: Three Years With the Condemned Japanese War Criminals*, trans. Hideo Suzuki et al. (New York: Charles Scribner's, 1950).

キカス一生スキヤスレイ二イタリテ

タレカ百年ノ形躰ヲタモツヘキヤ我ヤ

サキ人ヤサキ ケフトモシラスアストモ

シラスラクレサキタツ人ハモトノシツク

スヱノ露ヨリモシケレトイヘリ サレハ

朝二紅顔アリテタ六白骨トナル

身ナリステ二無常ノ風キタリヌレハ

14. Rennyo's Letter "On White Bones"

The final scene is of Hirota's entry into the execution hall, where the Allied representatives and officers serving as witnesses stood in line:

> The other condemned men muttered to themselves, recited the scriptures, stumbled, but Hirota walked steadily, gazing calmly into each of the alien faces as he passed. He was like a judoist casting his eyes over the opposing team, or a diplomat sizing up a row of guests at a party.[18]

Shiroyama's narrative reflects the commonplace generalization that steadfastness of mind and little display of emotion are associated with Zen piety, while a show of emotion—for example, in reciting the scriptures or saying the nenbutsu—is closer to Shin Buddhist piety. It is difficult to reconcile such a simplified portrayal of Shin Buddhism as a matter of the heart (versus Zen as a matter of the mind) with Shinran's teaching. In particular, Hirota's parting words to Hanayama, "Just to live naturally and die naturally," are strikingly apposite to the piety of naturalness and non-calculative living expressed by Shinran in his later years. At the same time, it may be argued that Hirota's words are exemplary of Japanese Buddhist piety in general, and of a strand of human religiousness that is universal.

This sharp distinction between Shin Buddhist and Zen piety, held by the general reader and scholar alike, was reified (certainly for Western students of Japanese Buddhism) by Suzuki Daisetsu's interpretation of these two major strands of Japanese Buddhist tradition. Among the tributes to Suzuki following his death in 1966 was that of Ōtani Kōshō, head priest of the Tokyo Hongan-ji and heir to the leadership of the Higashi branch of the Shinshū. He wrote of Suzuki's deepening interest in Shinshū in his later years:

> In my observation, the more congenial his attitude became towards Shin Buddhism, the more often he uttered "Thank you." This "Thank you," with his own unique tone, derives from Dr. Suzuki's upbringing in a Shin Buddhist atmosphere in Kanazawa. In other words, Shin Buddhism bloomed in the warmth of his feeling, and Zen manifested itself in the sharpness and resoluteness of his mind; as if the former were his mother and the latter his father, these two elements formed Dr. Daisetz Suzuki.[19]

This evaluation, while entirely congenial to Suzuki's own thought

---

[18] Shiroyama, *War Criminal*, 298; *Rakujitsu moyu*, 377. For Hanayama's evaluation of the episode, see his *The Way of Deliverance*, 273–74.

[19] Kōshō Ōtani, "In Memory of D. T. Suzuki," *The Eastern Buddhist*, n.s., 2/1 (1967): 164–65.

and writings, prompts questions about the underlying assumptions as to what constitutes Shinshū piety. To what extent was Ōtani Kōshō reflecting Suzuki's own typologizing of Shin and Zen? It is quite possible that Suzuki owes more to Rennyo's interpretation of the teaching than to Shinran's teaching itself. Further clarification of this point would call for an examination of the influence of Shinshū tradition on the development of Suzuki's thought during his early years in Kanazawa. What is readily evident, however, is Suzuki's attraction to Rennyo and a number of his letters, which owe much to the text *Anjin ketsujōshō*.[20]

Thus, as we have noted, in Japanese culture at the popular level, Rennyo is recognized as one of the nation's most eminent Buddhist priests and religious leaders. Further, the works of two major contemporary writers—Ibuse Masuji's *Kuroi ame* and Shiroyama Saburō's *Rakujitsu moyu*—present views of Shinshū piety in which Rennyo's legacy appears to be determinative in shaping that piety.

IN INDIVIDUALS' LIVES

> Master Rennyo れん仁よさま is a good person
> he puts treasures in *The Letters* ごぶん正さま
> and kindly shows them to Saichi;
> his benevolence fills me with joy.
> Namu-amida-butsu.
>
> Asahara Saiichi (1850–1932)[21]

Another series of images reflecting Rennyo's presence in contemporary piety is that of persons attracted to him through a variety of personal circumstances: a scholar of Japanese Buddhist history discovers

---

[20] References by Suzuki to *Anjin ketsujōshō* are not infrequent in his writings on Pure Land, the Shinshū, and saintly people such as Saiichi. In his essay, "The Development of the Pure Land Doctrine in Buddhism," *Collected Writings on Shin Buddhism* (Kyoto: Shinshū Ōtaniha, 1973), Suzuki notes that "the author [of *Anjin ketsujōshō*] is not known, but the book is one of the most important of all the Shin writings" (23). In reference to Saiichi's "jottings," he comments, " . . . they read like the *Anjin Ketsujō Shō*. Or we might even compare them with Ippen's *Sayings*" (Suzuki, *Japanese Spirituality*, 197; see also *Suzuki Daisetsu zenshū*, 8: 205).

[21] Suzuki Daisetsu, ed., *Myōkōnin Asahara Saiichi shū* (Tokyo: Shunjūsha, 1967), 79. Although "Saiichi" is the romanized form of the name as written in Chinese characters, Saichi refers to himself simply as さいち "Saichi," as does Suzuki. His unique orthography for major Shinshū symbols is indicated in the translations and discussion below.

Rennyo as a man of enduring wisdom who comes alive as a friend for turbulent times; a contemporary novelist devotes ten years to telling the story of Rennyo as a major religious figure in medieval Japan; a Buddhist scholar and apologist to the West finds his religious ideals embodied by those whose spirituality appears to be shaped in large measure by Rennyo. These images are not simply representative of modern scholarship—they go further in their depth of personal involvement; nor are they those of traditional sectarian piety—they go further in their breadth of historical and comparative perspective. At the same time, these views cannot be understood apart from the traditional and modern images already presented.

First, we turn again to Kasahara Kazuo (1917–), whose early scholarly interest in Rennyo deepened into a lifelong spiritual partnership. In order to gauge Rennyo's place in Kasahara's own pilgrimage, it is helpful to see how Kasahara understands the role of religion in more general terms. Kasahara, who came from a Jōdoshū household in a rural area of Nagano prefecture, was one of twelve Japanese scholars who were asked by the editor of *Fukyō: The Japan Missionary Bulletin,* the journal of the Oriens Institute for Religious Research, for their views on Christianity. When asked what role he would ascribe to Christianity in Japanese society, he questioned whether or not it was performing any role other than being the setting for the tax-free sale of Western culture, adding, "In my opinion, the primary function of religion is the support of people in their troubles. . . ."[22]

In responding to a question about Christianity's slow expansion in Japan, he raised the problem of its being commonly perceived as a foreign importation, comparing it with Japanese Buddhism, which, initially foreign, became indigenized; Buddhism's ability to produce the thought of men such as Hōnen, Shinran, and Nichiren might lie, he suggested, in there being no ties with China.[23] In regard to Christian doctrine, he had this to say:

> A religion's life does not appear in the twilight of an era, but in the vanguard, in taking on human suffering. The founders of Kamakura Buddhism were such people. By the norms of ancient Buddhism, they were heretical (*itan* 異端). So were Christ and Luther. In heresy, too, there is a backward-looking type that emerges in

---

[22] Kasahara Kazuo, "Jibun no ashi de ayume," *Fukyō: The Japan Missionary Bulletin* 21/1 (1967): 42; see also Joseph J. Spae, "Twelve Scholars Comment on Christianity," *Fukyō: The Japan Missionary Bulletin* 22/2 (1968): 131.

[23] Kasahara, "Jibun no ashi de ayume," 43; also see Spae, "Twelve Scholars Comment on Christianity," 131–32.

struggles over power; but . . . history demonstrates that forward-looking heresy has preserved religious life. I think it would be good if there were more such heresy in Christianity; the problem is that this must be sanctioned.[24]

Over the years, Kasahara appears to have discovered in Rennyo the person representative of the spirituality for which he had been searching: one who supports people when times are hard, whose teachings are truly indigenous, and who is heretical in a forward-looking sense, "in taking on human suffering." In 1978, he reflected on his deepening bond with Rennyo in the preface to a work on Shinran and Rennyo.[25] The bond had been forged almost four decades earlier, with his inquiry as a graduate student at Tokyo Imperial University into the social, economic, and religious reasons for the development of the Shinshū in the Hokuriku region during Rennyo's time. A steady stream of publications followed over the next decade, including studies of Rennyo and the Ikkō uprisings. Following this, Kasahara took up a study of Shinran, but, lacking the detailed historical knowledge that he had of Rennyo's Sengoku period, he found Shinran a more remote figure. He likens his long-term devotion to studies of Shinran and Rennyo to climbing Mt. Fuji in that the view is broadened at each stage. Shinran and Rennyo are his teachers and friends: they influence his thinking and his writing; they teach him how to live.[26]

Only three years later, in 1981, in the preface to a volume on Rennyo as a source of wisdom in turbulent times, Kasahara stressed Rennyo's continuing legacy in the fields of personal religion, religious thought, and institutional religion. For Kasahara, the core of that legacy is Rennyo's ability to distinguish the possible from the impossible; this is the quality that validates him as a guide. Finally, Kasahara identified Rennyo's character as teacher and friend as the force that had held him to his studies for forty years; he expects the relationship to continue, as he has yet to reach the summit.[27]

---

[24] Kasahara, "Jibun no ashi de ayume," 43–44; also see Spae, "Twelve Scholars Comment on Christianity," 132.

[25] Kasahara, *Shinran to Rennyo*, 1–4.

[26] Kasahara, *Shinran to Rennyo*, 3.

[27] Kasahara Kazuo, *Ransei o ikiru: Rennyo no shōgai* (Tokyo: Kyōikusha, 1981), 3–6. Among Kasahara's more recent tributes to Rennyo are: "Rennyo ni manabu koto," in *Rennyo to Ōsaka*, ed. Nanba Betsuin/*Asahi Shinbun* Ōsaka Honsha Kikakubu (1986), 9–11; "Ima koso Rennyo ni manabu toki," in *Rennyo*, ed. Minami Midō Shinbun (1986), 1–7; "Rennyo no genkō," in *Rennyo ni deau*, eds. Niwa Fumio et al. (Tokyo: Ōbunsha, 1986), 49–92.

In turning next to a contemporary novelist's image of Rennyo, we might recall Hattori Shisō's judgment that Rennyo lacked the stature to be chosen as a subject for novels or dramas.[28] Less than three decades after Hattori made this comment, Niwa Fumio (1904–) completed a study of Rennyo as the central figure in a medieval religious and historical drama. Niwa's work was serialized over a ten-year period (1971–1981) in 121 installments in the monthly magazine *Chūō kōron,* before being published as an eight-volume novel, *Rennyo* (1982–1983).

The eldest son of a temple family belonging to the Takada branch of the Shinshū,[29] Niwa, in his late twenties, gave up his hereditary duties as priest to enter the literary world and become a writer. A number of his works (for example, *Bodaiju* [1955], translated into English as *The Buddha Tree* [1966]), pick up themes from his early life in the temple precincts. In a later work, a spiritual autobiography, he reflects on the fact that Rennyo was active on behalf of the Honganji at the same time that Shin'e was priest at Senju-ji, the head temple of the Takada branch.[30] Rennyo and Shin'e had competed vigorously in their evangelistic endeavors.[31] While no match, finally, for Rennyo in the scope

---

[28] On 22–24 December 1989, a group of students at Ōtani University, Kyoto, staged a series of performances of a play, *Rennyo.* The drama, written by one of the students, was based on the known historical events of Rennyo's life leading up to his move to Yoshizaki. Its theme was Rennyo's inner conflict: whether to heed the summons to work for the restoration of the impoverished Honganji or to follow a path that would allow him to enjoy the simple pleasures of ordinary family life. The poignancy of the presentation was not unrelated to the fact that a number of the students involved were from temple families; they themselves were participants in a tradition based on a polity of dharma and blood-related lineages. It is this very human side of Rennyo that has made him such a compelling figure in contemporary Japan, especially for those engaged in the literary arts.

[29] See chapter two, nn. 26, 70.

[30] Niwa Fumio, *Hotoke ni hikarete: Waga kokoro no keiseishi* (Tokyo: Yomiuri Shinbunsha, 1971), 15.

[31] At one time, Shin'e enjoyed a close relationship with Rennyo, almost twenty years his senior. As competition between the Takada and Honganji branches intensified, that relationship became strained. With Rennyo's move to Yoshizaki in Bunmei 3 (1471) and his dramatic success in expanding the Honganji's influence, significantly at the expense of the Takada, Shin'e became severely critical of Rennyo's teachings. In the second month of Bunmei 4 (1472), Shin'e drafted *Kenshōryūgishō,* in which he takes to task those followers of Shinran who belittle the saying of the nenbutsu in their preoccupation with matters of faith *(shin)* and denigrate Buddhist images *(Kenshōryūgishō,* T 83.842b, 844c). Chiba Jōryū maintains that Rennyo, vulnerable to both charges, was the immediate object of Shin'e's criticisms. On the first count, Chiba cites a

of his achievement, Shin'e was successful in building up Senju-ji, receiving the epithet "Chūkō Shōnin" himself within the Takada branch of the Shinshū. Niwa speculates that, had it not been for Rennyo, Shin'e might have guided the Takada to the preeminence subsequently enjoyed by the Honganji.[32]

It is against the background of his heritage in the Takada branch that Niwa reflects on Shinshū history. During a four-year period, 1965–1969, his study of Shinran was serialized in a newspaper before being published as a five-volume novel. In 1971, the same year in which his autobiographical work was published, he embarked on a study of Rennyo that was to last a decade. Niwa refers to his Shinran-Rennyo fourteen-year endeavor as his life's work. He claims to be neither a historian nor a religious scholar, yet his bibliographies include virtually every scholarly writing available, including primary sources. He lists all of the relevant writings of scholars such as Tsuji Zennosuke, Hattori, Miki, Akamatsu, Kasahara, Inoue, and Mori, as well as formal sectarian studies of Rennyo.[33]

Niwa's *Rennyo* begins with Kakunyo's establishment of the temple, Hongan-ji, at the site of Shinran's mausoleum, the point at which his work on Shinran had ended. He arrives at Rennyo's birth only in the middle of volume four, concluding in volume eight with the events immediately following Rennyo's death. The narrative is historically grounded, revealing a careful use of sources; he is sensitive to the religious quality of Shinran's writings, as well as those of Kakunyo and Rennyo. Finally, however, we must accept Niwa's statement that his primary concern, as a novelist, is to plumb the depths of Rennyo's character.[34]

---

letter dated Bunmei 3 (1471).7.16, about six months prior to Shin'e's writing of *Kenshōryūgishō*, in which Rennyo ridicules a priest of high rank who says the nenbutsu but seems totally ignorant of Shinran's teaching on faith (RSI, 64–68 [#9]). On the second count, Chiba cites an episode described in *Jitsugo kyūki*: Rennyo is reported to have heated water by burning images revered by his predecessors (RSG, 111–12; SSZ 3: 587). See Chiba Jōryū, "Rennyo no ikonokurasumu," *Chiba Jōryū hakase koki kinen*, ed. Chiba Jōryū Hakase Koki Kinenkai (Kyoto: Nagata Bunshōdō, 1990), 19–29.

[32] Niwa, *Hotoke ni hikarete*, 15.

[33] Niwa Fumio, *Shinran*, 5 vols. (Tokyo: Shinchōsha, 1969), 5: 230–32; Niwa Fumio, *Rennyo*, 8 vols. (Tokyo: Chūō Kōronsha, 1983), 8: 322–24.

[34] For critical comments by a scholar in the field of Japanese religion concerning Niwa's possible motivations in writing his *Rennyo*, see Yamaori Tetsuo, "Chosho *Ningen Rennyo* o megutte," in *Rennyo*, ed. Minami Midō Shinbun (Osaka: Nanba Betsuin, 1986), 67–73.

In the seventh volume, Niwa devotes a chapter to three popular criticisms that have been made of Rennyo: first, that he was the devious instigator of the Ikkō uprisings; second, that, as a cunning political strategist, he led the Honganji in absorbing the temples of other Buddhist sects, in particular, those of other branches of the Shinshū including the Takada; and, third, that, as a Buddhist priest, he married five times and fathered twenty-seven children, the last four of whom were born when he was in his eighties.[35] Niwa attempts to respond to these criticisms as fairly as possible by drawing on all of the available sources. There was no way, however, for him to erase from his consciousness the fact of his own background as a priest in a rival branch of the Shinshū going back fifteen generations, a lineage which but for Rennyo might have prevailed over the Honganji.

In a postscript to the last volume, he tells of an incident following a talk he gave on Rennyo in 1982 in Kanazawa, a city in the heart of the Hokuriku. After the lecture, he received a letter from a woman who had been in the audience and who had, in hearing the lecture, reached a level of understanding beyond his own. Moved by the spontaneity of her account, he substituted her letter in full for the postscript he had planned for the final volume in the *Rennyo* series. It seemed to him to complete his ten years of labor—it was as if someone had written for him precisely what he had hoped to realize himself.[36]

The woman tells first of having read Niwa's *Shinran* with tears of gratitude. Although she had been raised in a pious Buddhist home, she had begun to question her faith as she grew older and had been unable to resolve the issues. In reading Niwa's *Shinran,* however, she felt able to "draw correctly and clearly from the deep well of Shinran's teachings." It seemed to her that Niwa spoke as Shinran himself and that she was accepted, for the first time, with an unwavering certainty. She had hesitated to write to Niwa until she learned that he would be coming to Kanazawa; as we know, her letter eventually followed his visit.[37]

Significant in her experience was that she was the youngest in a family of six children. Her father died at fifty-two, when she was only five. Sensitive to the difficulties she would face after his death, he had lavished affection on her during the brief years they shared together. This experience led her to wonder later in her life how Rennyo had viewed the children born in his last years. Although he had been badly

---

[35] Niwa, *Rennyo,* 7: 191–207.

[36] Niwa, *Rennyo,* 8: 317–18.

[37] Niwa, *Rennyo,* 8: 318.

treated by his own stepmother, he had allowed his children to be raised, one after another, by a succession of stepmothers. Why had he, in his old age, chosen young partners in marriage? Having children of her own, she was amazed at what she perceived as Rennyo's insensitivity and could not imagine acting in such a way herself.[38] In listening to Niwa's lecture, however, she "noticed a very important thing":

> It was possible for me to be raised within this teaching precisely because of Rennyo's meritorious accomplishment in bringing prosperity to the Honganji and the Jōdo Shinshū when they were in an extreme state of decline. Because of what he did, you are here, and I was able to come upon your *Shinran*. When I realized that, I began to wonder to what extent Rennyo's private life was important. I feel that I want to live until I read the last of your *Rennyo*.[39]

After the close of her letter, Niwa concludes:

> Up to this point in the novels, I had presented the facts on the three issues for which Rennyo was criticized and argued against the misconceptions that he was an instigator of the Ikkō uprisings and that the Honganji had adroitly absorbed other sects; I believe I was able to gain a positive hearing. In regard to the five marriages and the twenty-seven children, however, I could not add any new interpretation. It was an elderly lady who by chance came to hear my lecture, who was able, while listening to my talk, to lay aside her preconceptions in regard to Rennyo's personal life in a completely natural way—as she said in her letter, "I noticed a very important thing." That was the thing that I, a novelist, could never come up with, either in my novels or in facing an audience.[40]

Niwa has devoted much of his long career as a writer to topics stemming from the Shinshū background he had sought to reject institutionally in giving up his priestly responsibilities at his family temple. The subject matter he had found so constricting at the level of sectarian participation was compelling when he approached it at a more universal and aesthetic level as a writer and artist. It appears that, in a very personal way, he continues to participate in Shinshū tradition, moving beyond the particularity of the sectarian boundaries of his own branch of the tradition to include Rennyo and even the Honganji.

Another contemporary image of Rennyo is found in the works of

---

[38] Niwa, *Rennyo*, 8: 319–20.
[39] Niwa, *Rennyo*, 8: 320.
[40] Niwa, *Rennyo*, 8: 320–21.

Suzuki Daisetsu, best known to readers of his large corpus of writings in English as Daisetz Suzuki or D. T. Suzuki, the seminal figure in the postwar introduction of Rinzai Zen to the West. Those who have examined his work more closely also know of his writings on Japanese spirituality (*nihonteki reisei* 日本的霊性) and of his comparative study of Christian and Buddhist mysticism. The core of these studies are presentations of materials which, for him, exemplify mature expressions of Japanese religious consciousness and mystical awareness — the personalities and writings of *myōkōnin*.[41] He describes the first of these studies as a preliminary and unsystematic effort to trace that consciousness in the history of Japanese thought, the purest form of which emerges in the Kamakura expressions of Jōdo thought and in Zen, both of which he feels to be intrinsically Japanese.[42] He stresses the necessity to distinguish between Shinshū as a sect and as Shinshū experience, the foundation for the former. It is that Shinshū experience that is "really nothing else than the exercise of Japanese spirituality."[43]

For Suzuki, Shinran was the first person to awaken to a distinctively Japanese religious consciousness, a consciousness that was engendered while he was living among peasant farmers, having been divested of his priesthood and exiled from the capital. After Shinran's death, however, with the Honganji's dramatic rise to power and wealth, this quality of religious consciousness was lost within the tradition. Yet it survived in another setting:

> Although the true nature of Shinran's sect disappeared from the opulent structures of Kyoto, it has continued to live in the humble thatched dwellings of the Myōkōnin, with their worn and leaky

---

[41] Suzuki Daisetsu's first publication on Japanese spirituality was *Nihonteki reisei* (Tokyo: Daitō Shuppansha, 1944). See also Suzuki Daisetsu, *Suzuki Daisetsu zenshū*, vol. 8, *Nihonteki reisei/Nihon no reiseika*. For English translation of *Nihonteki reisei*, see Daisetz Suzuki, *Japanese Spirituality*. Based on Suzuki's own statement (written in October, 1945) in his preface to the second printing, Norman Waddell, the translator, notes that the book was written "between trips to the air-raid shelter during some of the heaviest bombing of the war" (viii). Other works on Japanese spirituality by Suzuki followed: *Reiseiteki Nihon no kensetsu* (1946); *Nihonteki reiseiteki jikaku* (1946); and *Nihon no reiseika* (1947). Complementing these studies in Japanese are his *Myōkōnin* (1948), and his editing of *Myōkōnin Asahara Saiichi shū* (1967). In English is Suzuki's *Mysticism: Christian and Buddhist*, World Perspectives, vol. 12 (New York: Harper and Brothers, 1957; repr. Westport, Conn.: Greenwood Press, 1975).

[42] Suzuki, *Japanese Spirituality*, ix, 17–18; Suzuki, *Suzuki Daisetsu zenshū*, 8: 3, 24–26.

[43] Suzuki, *Japanese Spirituality*, 20; Suzuki, *Suzuki Daisetsu zenshū*, 8: 27–28.

15. Monument to Rennyo, with the Name in six characters; Osaka Castle Park

roofs. Myōkōnin—surely there is no more honored name in the sect of Shinran. The Person [Shinran] always lives in him. The authoritative and learned scholar-priests were not the inheritors of Shinran's faith and belief.[44]

At first glance, it is surprising that Suzuki does not identify the opulence of the sectarian temples in Kyoto with Rennyo's achievement as the builder and consolidator of the Honganji. Unlike Hattori, Ienaga, and others, Suzuki offers no criticism of Rennyo's spirituality. On the contrary, he takes for granted that Rennyo is very much the legitimate heir to Shinran's teaching and piety, as evidenced in his evaluation of Rennyo's disciple, Dōshū. Suzuki's assessment of Rennyo is reflected again in his comparative studies on Christian and Buddhist mysticism, in which he presents Asahara Saiichi as the representative Buddhist mystic comparable to the German Dominican monk, Meister Eckhart (c.1260–1328).[45] Saiichi, until he was fifty, worked as a ship's carpenter; after that, he became a clog-maker. Living with Amida day by day in a state of religious fervor, he continually said the nenbutsu; night after night, he jotted down his thoughts on wood shavings from his workshop floor.[46]

Crucial to the *myōkōnin* expression of religious consciousness is the concept *ki-hō ittai* in explication of the Name, "Namu-amida-butsu." According to Suzuki, when the Name is pronounced, a mystical identification between the worshiper—*namu*, or *ki*—and the worshiped—Amida Buddha, or *hō*—takes place. To illustrate this point, Suzuki offers the following translation of one of Saiichi's poems:

> As I pronounce "Namu-amida-butsu,"
> I feel my thoughts and hindrances are like the spring snows:
> They thaw away as soon as they fall on the ground.[47]

Suzuki's interpretation of Saiichi's religious experience is that

as soon as the "Namu-amida-butsu" is pronounced, he [Saiichi] as "*Namu*" (*ki*) melts into the body of Amida (*hō*) which is "the ground" and "support." He cannot reason it out, but "Here I am!" What has taken place is the identification of Amida (*hō*) and Saichi (*ki*). But the identification is not Saichi's vanishing. Saichi is still conscious of his individuality and addresses himself to Amida Buddha in a rather

---

[44] Suzuki, *Japanese Spirituality*, 86–87; Suzuki, *Suzuki Daisetsu zenshū*, 8: 91.
[45] Suzuki, *Mysticism*, 142–58.
[46] Suzuki, *Japanese Spirituality*, 177; Suzuki, *Suzuki Daisetsu zenshū*, 8: 182–84. See also Satō, "The Awakening of Faith in the Myokonin Asahara Saiichi," 71–89.
[47] Suzuki, *Mysticism*, 147.

familiar fashion saying, "O Nyorai-san!" and congratulating himself on his being able to write about the happy event.[48]

The concept *ki-hō ittai* きほをい太い , written by Saiichi, provides the foundation for the structure of his nenbutsu thought. As we have seen, this concept was introduced into the mainstream of Shinshū tradition through *The Letters,* as a result of Rennyo's appropriation of the thought and piety of *Anjin ketsujōshō.*[49]

In Saiichi's expressions of his religious experience, Rennyo is seen both as revered master and, embodied in the nenbutsu through *The Letters,* as his present companion:

> hey you Saichi
> who'd you hear
> Namu-amida-butsu from   well I
> heard it from Master Rennyo
> oh come now, you,
> there's four or five hundred years between us and Master Rennyo
> that's telling a lie Saichi
> it isn't a lie
> it's in *The Letters*
> those letters are Master Rennyo
> well then what sort of person
> is Master Rennyo
> you Saichi won't you
> tell me   yes Namu-amida-butsu
> is Master Rennyo
> Namu-amida-butsu couldn't be
> Master Rennyo   well
> when Namu-amida-butsu lives and works
> that's Master Rennyo[50]

---

[48] Suzuki, *Mysticism,* 147.

[49] On occasion, Saiichi includes the title of the text, *Anjin ketsujōshō* あんじん けつじよ正 in his verses; see Suzuki, *Myōkōnin Asahara Saiichi shū,* 168. See also Fujihara Toshie, *Asahara Saiichi no uta* (Kyoto: Hōzōkan, 1989), 92–93, for a verse that might be rendered:

> in every way
> Master Rennyo
> follows *Anjin ketsujōshō*
> he is the good teacher
> who enables Saichi to hear it
> Namu-amida-butsu

[50] Suzuki, *Myōkōnin Asahara Saiichi shū,* 79–80.

The honorific forms used here in reference to Master Rennyo, *Rennyosama*, and to the letters, *Gobunshōsama*, are distinctive expressions of Saiichi's piety.[51] In Saiichi's jottings, we also find the term *oyasama* をやさま (used for Amida), the concept *shinzoku nitai* しんぞく仁太い, and even the *sangō wakuran* 三ごをわくらん incident serving as religious symbols.[52]

In respect to the content of *The Letters*, Suzuki sees two major aspects of religious consciousness: ". . . the sense of wickedness and depravity and . . . the feeling of gratitude for being saved from an utterly helpless situation."[53] He appears to find Rennyo exemplary of the piety so deeply embedded in Saiichi's verses. Following his translation of Rennyo's fifth letter in fascicle five, "On realizing faith," Suzuki concludes: "The translation of such documents as Rennyo's letters is full of difficulties as they are so laden with technical terms that defy in many cases replacement by any other languages."[54] From such a gifted translator, this comes as a challenging statement. At the same time, the letters are a major source of symbols capable of spirituality, expressing the content and form of Japanese spirituality as exemplified in Saiichi's piety and verses.[55]

Saiichi's inner-directed piety has been compared with that of Genza (1842–1930), his contemporary and fellow participant in the Nishi Honganji branch of the Shinshū. Yanagi Sōetsu (1889–1961), an art historian and leader of the Japanese folk-craft movement, has noted that Genza consistently sought out people to talk to about the Buddha-dharma. To differentiate between Saiichi's and Genza's piety, Yanagi draws on the two aspects of Amida's directing of virtue to sentient beings, *ōsō ekō* and *gensō ekō*, so fundamental to Shinran's teaching.[56] On the one hand, he sees Saiichi's piety oriented towards the *ōsō*

---

[51] The references in Saiichi's verses to *Rennyosama* and *Gobunshōsama* are frequent. For the former, see Suzuki, *Myōkōnin Asahara Saiichi shū*, 13, 28, 32, 51, 58, 79, 83, 105, 106, 168, 200, 240, 275, 309, 362, 379, 413, 435; for the latter, see 36, 66, 82, 116, 127, 132, 177, 189, 200, 237, 302, 323, 352, 360, 409, 412, 440.

[52] See Suzuki, *Myōkōnin Asahara Saiichi shū:* for *oyasama*, 81; *shinzoku nitai*, 8, 26, 41, 79, 110, 121, 340; *sangō wakuran*, 419.

[53] Suzuki, *Mysticism*, 167.

[54] Suzuki, *Mysticism*, 167–69. For the letter, see RSI, 407–8 (#139/5:5); SSZ 3: 502–3.

[55] Saiichi includes phrases drawn directly from *The Letters;* for example, see Suzuki, *Myōkōnin Asahara Saiichi shū*, 170 and 312 (letter 1:1); 59 and 304 (letter 5:1); 138 (letter 5:8); and 174 (letter 5:10).

[56] Soetsu Yanagi, "Genza, the Myokonin (3)," trans. Dennis Hirota, *The Pure*

ekō aspect (of Amida's directing of virtue for sentient beings' movement from birth-and-death to the Pure Land); on the other hand, he sees Genza as oriented towards the *gensō ekō* aspect (for beings' return from the Pure Land to birth-and-death).[57] Since both activities are manifestations of the working of the Other Power of Amida's Primal Vow on behalf of sentient beings, one cannot be evaluated more highly than the other. As seen in the symbolism of yin and yang, it is imbalance that is less good.

We are reminded here that the argument being made for *The Letters* as a primary source for *myōkōnin* piety must not be pressed too far.[58] Indeed, Saiichi's jottings are replete with references to Shinran

---

Land: Journal of European Shin Buddhism 5/1 (1983): 20–24. Parts one and two of this translation by Hirota are in *The Pure Land* 4/1 (1982): 24–33, and 4/2 (1982): 37–44. An abridged version of the entire translation is reprinted in *Myōkōninden kenkyū*, ed. Asaeda Zenshō (Kyoto: Nagata Bunshōdō, 1987), 56–72. For Shinran's *ōsō/gensō* thought, see *Teaching*, 1: 63; SSZ 2: 2.

[57] Yanagi, "Genza, the Myokonin (3)," 20–22. In section two of his article, Yanagi describes Genza's piety in some detail: "Genza, well-known as an early riser, generally got up around one or two in the morning. Upon arising, he would immediately go to the altar room and perform the morning service. His practice was to chant Shinran's hymn, the *Shōshinge*, and one of Rennyo's *Letters*, which, being illiterate, he recited from memory" (Soetsu Yanagi, "Genza, the Myokonin [2]," 38.

[58] A comparative study of the influence of *The Letters* and of Shinran's writings on the lives of Shinshū *myōkōnin* remains to be undertaken. The *Myōkōninden*, a compilation of biographies of devout nenbutsu adherents, initiated by Gōsei (1721–1794), includes the life of Okaru (1801–1856). The persistent theme in Okaru's poems is gratitude, despite the fact that her life was filled with suffering. Striking is the paucity of formal religious language: Amida is referred to as *oyasama*, *ojihisama* お慈悲様 , or simply by context; there is no explicit mention of Shinran, Rennyo, or the Pure Land. In one instance, however, Okaru responds to hearing selections from *The Letters* read during thanksgiving services for Shinran:

> How thankful I am!
> Living on in this uncertain life,
> how glad I am
> to meet with *The Letters* once again.

Nishimura Shinsen, ed., *Okaru dōgyō*
(Shimonoseki: Rokkōkai, 1988), 28

For an essay on Okaru's life and a translation of her poems, see Hōyū Ishida, "O-karu: Poems of Deep Sorrow and Joy," in *Shinran to Jōdokyō*, ed. Shigaraki Takamaro Kyōju Kanreki Kinen Ronshū Kankōkai (Kyoto: Nagata Bunshōdō, 1986), 25–78.

as founder (*Gokaisansama* ごかい三さま) and phrases culled from Shin-ran's hymns and *Shōshinge,* enduring staples of Shinshū piety at large. Our point is to underscore the apparent convergence of what Suzuki designates as Japanese spirituality, reflected in Saiichi's piety, with the structure of Rennyo's thought. What they hold in common appears to be the *Anjin ketsujōshō*'s formulation of the nenbutsu in terms of the concept *ki-hō ittai.*

As we have noted from time to time, the dynamics of *ki-hō ittai,* working as a religious symbol in the hearts and minds of participants in Shinshū tradition, engender oneness and non-differentiation at the expense of that which would allow for a degree of differentiation be-tween the individual and the group. At their best, symbols such as *ki-hō ittai* are a potential resource for spiritual insight and for inclusiveness and responsible participation in community. At their worst, they lose their capacity, as symbols of the transcendent, to challenge the exclu-siveness of any single group and merely reinforce uncritical accommo-dation to societal norms.

Underlying the many images of Rennyo held by persons of quite diverse backgrounds in modern Japan—Kasahara Kazuo, Niwa Fumio, and Suzuki Daisetsu—are *The Letters,* the foremost legacy of his life and thought.[59] Possibly there is a common thread in their re-sponses to Rennyo. Perhaps they have seen in him something akin to what attracted Dōshū of Akao and numberless others living in a period of political turmoil and social upheaval in late medieval Japan. It ap-pears that *The Letters* continue to provide symbols for the nurture of what Suzuki has identified as Japanese spirituality. At the same time, some may have discovered that, through Rennyo's words, they have been embraced by a truth and reality that transcends even that spirituality.

---

[59] A further instance of those responding to Rennyo today as representative of Japanese spirituality is Fujikawa Yū, a physician and writer, whose *Shinsen myōkōninden* (Tokyo: Daizō Shuppan, 1971) offers a new selection of candidates under the rubric of saintly persons. Among the eight are Rennyo, Myōe (1173–1232), Matsuo Bashō (1644–1694), Ishida Baigan (1685–1744), and Seikurō (1678–1750) of Yamato province, a pious Honganji member who is also the sub-ject of other *myōkōnin* studies.

IN A RELIGIOUSLY PLURAL WORLD

> Pure Land Buddhism traditionally emphasizes the way of
> life in each era. That is to say, the teaching of Amida
> Buddha's Primal Vow must be translated into the emerg-
> ing context of each new age. We see this process in the writ-
> ings of Shinran Shōnin. . . . Shinran's successors have also
> striven to interpret the teachings for their times. . . . Even
> in Japan at present, the concrete expressions of Buddhist
> truth . . . need to be translated and adapted to the contem-
> porary context.
>
> Ōtani Kōshin[60]

If Rennyo is one of the most revered figures in Japan's religious history, he is equally among the most controversial. His genius is
reflected in the fact that, through religious symbols, expressions of his
piety have been amenable to universalization to an extraordinary degree within the context of the Japanese intellectual and religious tradition as a whole. For this reason, the truth of Amida's Vow-mind has
been manifested in history for ordinary men and women seeking to
live authentically in Japanese society over the past five hundred years
and, more recently, in the West.

With Shinran's teaching as inspiration and Kakunyo's vision for
the Honganji as framework, Rennyo was able to construct a clearly
defined, vital religious body. While it is obvious that without Shinran,
Rennyo would not have appeared on the stage of Japanese history, it
is also fair to say that without Rennyo's translation of Shinran's expressions of piety into generic terms, the memory of Shinran might have
faded from Japanese religious consciousness. In this event, Shinran
would have been in the position of other pious nenbutsu devotees of
the early Kamakura period whose names remain unrecorded in the
annals of history. We do well to keep in mind, then, that the contributions of these two religious leaders are, in the final analysis, inseparable, and that polarization of their thought and piety is to be avoided.

Placing emphasis on the fundamental continuity in the thought of
these two "founders" of the Shinshū should not negate the contrasts
between them, an important point in this study. The significance of
the distinction between the individualist, person-centered emphasis in

---

[60] Ōtani Kōshin, "Opening Address," 236; for Japanese text, 22.

Shinran's piety and the collectivist, Honganji-centered emphasis in Rennyo's is not to be discounted. Certainly, Rennyo's legacy involves a fresh translation and interpretation as well as simplification and popularization of Shinran's teaching; following Rennyo's death, there were times when his successors employed manipulative as well as compassionate means in their use of *The Letters* to legitimize interpretations that served a complex mix of political and religious concerns. Therefore we oversimplify if we designate Rennyo either as merely the "restorer" of Shinran's teaching or as an ambitious "institutionalizer" who muddied the spiritual purity of Shinran's thought.

The conclusions of this study may be better interpreted when set in the context of a generalization that has been made about Japan's intellectual and religious history as a whole. Robert N. Bellah, drawing on Ienaga Saburō's studies in Japanese intellectual history, has pointed out that "a long cultural tradition of transcendence in Japan . . . has been a submerged and almost drowned tradition but, nevertheless, has repeatedly had important social consequences."[61] This may be illustrated in the relationship between a universalist Mahāyāna Buddhist tradition and a particularist, state-centered Japanese religious tradition. The former has the intellectual resources, through Mahāyāna thought, to offer a critique of prevailing social norms; it has the sociological resources, through the community of monks, to offer an alternative to and a refuge from society for the individual. The difficulty in the Japanese instance lies in a failure to seek and find conceptual and institutional expression for a tradition of transcendence that would provide an alternative to and a basis for critique of the existing social order.[62]

From this perspective, it becomes apparent that the dilemma of religious power confronting Rennyo at Yoshizaki was resolved in a manner quite traditional for Japanese society: namely, in favor of intense efforts to accommodate and join with those holding political power. As has been observed in this study, there were also other moments when Rennyo retired from the scene of action rather than struggle further with the dilemma. Following the destruction of Ōtani Hongan-ji in 1465, to what extent was his move to the Hokuriku an advance towards new opportunities, and to what extent a retreat from further confrontation? To what degree was his decision to retire in 1489 dictated by

---

[61] Robert N. Bellah, "Values and Social Change in Modern Japan," *Beyond Belief: Essays on Religion in a Post-Traditional World* (New York: Harper and Row, 1970), 117–18.

[62] Bellah, "Values and Social Change in Modern Japan," 114–45.

political considerations occasioned by the outbreak of the Ikkō uprisings in Kaga province? While it is foolhardy to speculate on whether
Shinran would have stood up at such moments as the representative
of a "tradition of transcendence," it is important to reiterate the strong
apolitical and non-institutional tenor of his piety in theory as well as
in fact.

Both Shinran and Rennyo, living under very different historical
conditions, were obliged to respond to the issue of individual identity
in relation to community. We have stressed throughout this study the
significance of the structure of Shinran's thought for persons as individuals, in the sense that he believed that Amida had fulfilled the Vow
"for my sake alone"; it appears, however, that his teaching has persistently been interpreted in a manner consistent with a view traditional
in Japanese culture, that the community is the locus of value.[63]
Rennyo's response to the dilemma of Honganji's religious power re-
inforces such a generalization.

Next, it is instructive to turn to Shinshū tradition as interpreted in
more recent times. In the course of Japan's religious history, participation in the Shinshū has evoked, and continues to evoke, a rich variety
of responses among those who seek salvific truth in Japanese society
through the true Pure Land way. We have noted that one type of response has been that of the saintly persons celebrated by Suzuki
Daisetsu. Their piety and that of Suzuki himself appear to have been
deeply influenced by The Letters, particularly by the ki-hō ittai interpretation of the nenbutsu as found in Anjin ketsujōshō.[64] There are, of
course, many modern intellectuals who have looked to Shinran's

---

[63] See first item in Bellah's presentation of six constituents of the Japanese
value pattern, "Values and Social Change in Modern Japan," 116–17.

[64] It is doubtful that Suzuki ever had reason to reflect on the facts that the
concept ki-hō ittai was never used by Shinran or that the concept anjin does not
appear to have been significant for his thinking. In any event, Suzuki's sustained interest in Rennyo's interpretation of Japanese spirituality found in
Shinshū tradition is evidenced by his concern shortly before he died to find a
proper translation of the term anjin. Ōtani Kōshō, writing in the memorial issue
for Suzuki in The Eastern Buddhist, recalls the following incident:

Last May [1966], when I called on him, he hurled a question at me about anjin, a
term mostly used in Shin Buddhism, for which he was trying to find a translation.
"Anjin, strictly speaking," [he said,] "is neither 'peace of mind' nor security of
mind'."

Their conversation on anjin was to remain uncompleted. See Kōshō Ōtani, "In
Memory of D. T. Suzuki," 164.

expressions of piety, as found most frequently in *Tannishō*, for personal instruction and solace.[65]

Japanese intellectuals in modern times, whether in fact indebted more to *The Letters* or to Yuien's *Tannishō*, appear to be attracted by a non-clerical, non-institutional dimension of Shinshū piety that, for obvious reasons, may be identified most readily with Shinran. Even Suzuki, despite his high evaluation of Rennyo's spirituality, dissociates himself from the group-centered, collectivist piety of the Honganji that intellectuals have categorized from time to time as feudalistic, authoritarian, reified, and inconsistent with pure religion. Are we not offered, here, an insight into the function of what Suzuki has termed "Japanese spirituality"? Namely, it provides an arena for personal refreshment and individual growth and, at the same time, enables participants in a particular tradition to be reconciled to the most severe demands of group life.[66]

In the postwar years, evidence of a yearning to return to Shinran surfaced among participants in both the Nishi and Higashi branches of the Honganji. This attitude is reflected in the title of a 1971 publication containing contributions by scholars from both branches; the title asks whether Shinran is to live again in the present in the Honganji as a religious order.[67] It appears that some of the contributors were motivated partly by a nostalgic longing for an apolitical, purified religion, evoked primarily by Shinran's expressions of personal piety. At the same time, they were hoping to discover, through a return to Shinran, less authoritarian and more egalitarian principles for governing the Honganji. Dissatisfaction with the Honganji's inter-

---

[65] For Maruyama Masao, see his *Thought and Behavior in Modern Japanese Politics*, ed. Ivan Morris (London: Oxford University Press, 1963), 239–40. For evidence of Shinran's spiritual legacy for the modern Japanese religious consciousness, see the five-volume set (which is itself part of a larger series) giving brief biographies and selections from the writings of more than forty modern Japanese, ranging from Saiichi to Nishida: Dōbōsha Shuppan, ed., *Shinran ni deatta hitobito*, 5 vols. (Kyoto: Dōbōsha, 1989).

[66] See item six in Bellah's presentation of the Japanese value pattern in "Values and Social Change in Modern Japan," 117:

In spite of how completely the individual is merged in group life there is one place where he [or she] can be relatively independent: the realm of personal expressiveness, including art, mysticism, recreation, and skill. But this sphere does not legitimize failure to fulfill group expectations. It actually helps reconcile the individual to group demands.

[67] Uehara Senroku and Matsugi Nobuhiko, eds., *Honganji kyōdan: Shinran wa gendai ni yomigaeru ka* (Tokyo: Gakugei Shorin, 1971).

pretation of Shinran's teaching in contemporary Japan has led also to the founding of an independent reform movement, the Jōdo Shinshū Shinrankai.[68]

We should recognize that both the Nishi and Higashi Honganji of today are, in fact, religious institutions with a wealth of resources, given their common heritage in the lives and thought of Shinran and Rennyo, two of Japan's most extraordinary religious figures. For almost five centuries, their respective teachings have served participants in the tradition (although not necessarily at a conscious level) as contrasting and complementary models of piety in a wide variety of social contexts. In the period following Rennyo's death, the apotheosization of his life and writings led to the crystallization of an orthodoxy emphasizing obedience and submission to community-oriented norms — a collectivist piety. In modern Japan, with an exposure to individualistic Western values, Shinran's writings, especially with the rediscovery of *Tannishō*, have been a rich resource for spiritual nurture.[69]

---

[68] The Shinrankai, a reform movement within Shinshū tradition, directs its protests primarily against the Nishi Honganji as the largest branch. It was founded in 1958 by Takamori Kentetsu, a graduate of Ryūkoku University, who grew up in a temple household in Toyama prefecture, formerly Kaga province. Takamori is seen by members of the Shinrankai as the good teacher (*zenchishiki*) within a dharma-lineage beginning with Śākyamuni and continuing through the seven Pure Land masters to Shinran, Kakunyo, and Rennyo. The authority of other head priests in the Honganji hereditary lineage is not recognized. Under Takamori's leadership, the Shinrankai vigorously and persistently summons the Honganji to return to Shinran's true teaching, unsullied by what are perceived to be distortions that developed in the years following Rennyo when the Honganji became a privileged and powerful religious institution. A striking aspect of the Shinrankai is that, in espousing a return to Shinran, there is no effort to downgrade or bypass Rennyo. Indeed, the organization's image of Rennyo is very close to that of traditional sectarian piety, taking for granted that his teaching is wholly continuous with that of the founder. The Shinrankai's liturgical practice regularly includes the reading of one of *The Letters*, either "On realizing faith," *Shōnin ichiryū no shō* (5:5), or "On white bones," *Hakkotsu no shō* (5:16); see Jōdo Shinshū Shinrankai, ed., *Shōshin seiten* (Takaoka: Shinrankai, 1988). Indicative of the movement's aggressive stance is the title of one of its publications, challenging the Honganji to respond to its charges; see Jōdo Shinshū Shinrankai, ed., *Shinrankai kaku kotaeru/ Honganji naze kotaenu* (Takaoka: Shinrankai, 1985), with part one by Takamori. The Shinrankai headquarters are in Takaoka, Toyama, with groups in major cities in Japan as well as with representatives in Brazil and North America.

[69] See Michio Tokunaga's introduction to Hirota, *Tannishō:* "It is remarkable that the merit of *Tannishō*, although so well-known today, began to be widely recognized only from the early 1900s on. Before that, its very existence was

Shinran and Rennyo, in emphasizing the individual and the group respectively, represent models of piety essential for the development of any religious body. Those advocating a return to Shinran, in discounting the contribution made by Rennyo, may be forsaking hard, practical issues for an illusory world of pure religion. In addition, they may fail to take into account deeply-rooted cultural factors exacerbating Rennyo's dilemma, namely the difficulty of differentiating—even minimally—the mix of political and religious aspects of every group, whether overtly political or religious. Indeed, as we have noted earlier, a sharp distinction between the religious and the political in the study of premodern Japanese religions is exceedingly tenuous.

On the other hand, a return-to-Shinran emphasis that takes Rennyo's historical context into account may be better prepared to make a fresh translation and interpretation of the teaching in the years ahead. Such a translation must deal more adequately with the dilemma of religious power, which Rennyo resolved in such a way as to limit the possibilities for conceptualizing and institutionalizing a tradition of transcendence. What for him may be seen as a matter of expediency, if not of compassionate means, came to provide a basis for rationalization and legitimization of radical accommodation to political power in the Tokugawa period and in Meiji and Imperial Japan.

In concluding this study of Rennyo, several thoughts come to mind relative to human religious history as a whole. An attempt has been made to uncover the historical process whereby Rennyo came to be regarded as the authoritative translator and interpreter of Shinran's teaching and *The Letters* to be seen as the definitive text for the tradition in the language of ordinary men and women. Yet, deeply-etched impressions linger as to the difficulty of distinguishing between Rennyo the man and Rennyo the master or saint; they also linger in regard to the extraordinary collective forces that bring about the apotheosization of a religious leader. The life and teachings of a charismatic leader so readily assume a symbolic quality—particularly when the relationship with that leader may have effectively conveyed an experience of "a unity of the transcendent and the mundane, unbifurcated."

Further, despite our efforts to delineate Rennyo's particular contributions to Shinshū tradition, it becomes ever more apparent that his

---

virtually unknown even among Shin Buddhists. . . . For six centuries after it was written, *Tannishō* was a book buried to the world" (16).

continuity with Shinran runs deep in his effort to transmit the true essence of the Pure Land way. In a very real sense, Rennyo's faith is none other than Shinran's, just as Shinran's was one with Hōnen's.[70] Given the subtleties of evaluating where Shinran ends and Rennyo begins, the notion of "two founders" is not as inept as it may appear at first glance. To point up the complementary roles of Shinran and Rennyo, a Buddhist scholar has compared the Honganji in its institutional expression to the translucent shield around a burning flame.[71] The shield protects the flame from a chance breeze that might extinguish it, but at times the shield becomes covered with soot and obscures the light of the flame it is designed to guard. In just such a way, Rennyo's translation and interpretation of the teaching, intended to rekindle and transmit the "flame of faith" ignited by Shinran, led to reification and, at times, to obscuration of what it was intended to protect.

Shinran's life history attests to the fact that he found himself enslaved to self-power practices for the twenty years he spent at Mt. Hiei before he met Hōnen and discovered what he termed "the true essence of the Pure Land way." As part of this process, the nenbutsu came alive for him simultaneously with the realization of faith, and vice versa. Shinran's major insight is of the unity of two meanings of birth: birth here and now and birth in the Pure Land at the moment of death. For him, this discovery was the decisive turning point—the recognition of a life directed by Other Power, a life lived naturally in gratitude for what he had received.

The stages in Rennyo's spiritual development are less clearly defined, less decisive. During his Yoshizaki years, a period in which he was confronted most acutely with the dilemma of Honganji's religious power and with deep personal loss, he responded with innovative and simplified expressions of Shinran's teaching. In particular, his formulation of the six-character Name in terms of ki-hō ittai lent itself to what might be termed a sacramental interpretation: the nenbutsu as the outward and visible manifestation of the inward and spiritual working of Amida's Vow-mind. What Rennyo could not foresee was that au-

---

[70] In the postscript to Tannishō, Yuien relates Shinran's account of an incident in which his master, Hōnen, verified that their faith was one and the same. Hōnen said (referring to himself as Genkū), "My faith was granted by the Tathāgata; Zenshin's [Shinran's] faith, too, has been given by the Tathāgata. Therefore they are one. A person with a different faith will surely not go to the Pure Land to which I will go" (SSZ 2: 790–91).

[71] From a conversation with Masatoshi Nagatomi, Professor of Buddhist Studies, Harvard University, in 1971.

thority for evaluating the authenticity of an individual's faith and nenbutsu experience would come to lie in the hands of religious leaders who failed to recognize that their wielding of power was properly the cause for dilemma and, possibly, a distortion of the fundamental nature of Shinran's teaching. Instead, the dilemma of religious power was taken as settled once and for all in favor of radical accommodation to prevailing societal norms.

What, then, are the prospects for Rennyo's legacy of *The Letters* continuing as the definitive interpretation of Shinran's teaching? We are reminded again of Ōtani Kōshin's challenge, "The teaching of Amida's Primal Vow must be translated into the emerging context of each new age." What is new today is an ever-increasing historical awareness that we live in a religiously plural world in which the boundaries between religious communities are not as fixed as we had once imagined. In a word, we are discovering that there is—and always has been—a history of religion in the singular. An awareness of this fact may appear to be cause for alarm, especially for those who see themselves as participants in an exclusivist religious tradition. Yet, this awareness also holds promise for renewal.

The *sine qua non* for translating and interpreting Shinran's teaching of Amida's Primal Vow in the emerging context of the twenty-first century would appear to lie in a critical awareness of the meaning of Rennyo's life and thought for Shinshū tradition. Such awareness calls for a careful examination of the sources that Rennyo draws on from outside his own tradition, as well as a recognition that what he taught cannot simply be accepted as wholly identical with Shinran's teaching. Indeed, it may well be that the tradition has endured precisely for the reason that what Rennyo taught was in some respects different from what Shinran taught. This is not to deny the oneness of faith to the extent that faith is none other than a manifestation of Amida's Vow-mind—the transcendent. As we have pointed out, however, a significant distinction is to be made between Shinran's *shinjin* and Rennyo's *anjin* at the human conceptual level:

> *Shinjin* and *anjin* may express individual and collective aspects of a person's faith. It would appear that the vitality and richness of Shinshū as a religious tradition rests precisely on the availability of these two distinct yet complementary religious symbols. . . . It is to be expected that, of necessity, at moments *shinjin* and *anjin* will stand in considerable tension. In Shinshū history, the dominant pattern has been to seek to minimize, even to eliminate, that tension by stressing the communal aspect of personal faith at the expense of the individual aspect. In this sense . . . Shinshū as a religious move-

ment becomes vulnerable to being reduced to general patterns of Japanese religiosity both in shaping and in becoming accommodated to the norms of Japanese civilization.[72]

The challenge facing members of the Honganji as they approach the five-hundredth anniversary of Rennyo's death in 1999 and enter the twenty-first century is none other than that facing participants in every major tradition today—living as practicers of faith in a religiously plural world. Among the resources for renewing Shinshū tradition is a rich legacy—the lives, the thought, and the writings of two of the greatest religious figures in the history of Japanese civilization. In working to restore their tradition once again, they will be responding to the same summons heard by Shinran and Rennyo, as well as contributing a new and important chapter to "a history of religion in the singular."[73]

---

[72] Rogers, "The Shin Faith of Rennyo," 73, and " 'Shinjin' to 'anjin'," 41. Suggestive for further comparative study of *shinjin* and *anjin* as religious symbols is Doi Takeo's exploration of the role of the individual in Japanese society (Doi Takeo, *Omote to ura* [Tokyo: Kōbundo, 1985]; in English translation, see *The Anatomy of Self: The Individual Versus Society* [Tokyo: Kodansha International, Ltd., 1986]). In this study, Doi, a psychiatrist, draws on the paired concepts *omote* 表 , meaning *kao* 顔 (face) and *ura* 裏 meaning *kokoro* こころ (heart and mind), in classical Japanese *(The Anatomy of Self*, 24). He sees a parallel between the concepts *omote* (*tatemae* 建て前 ; *soto* 外) and *ura* (*honne* 本音 ; *uchi* 内) and the Western concepts of institution and individual (48–58). Our view is that Shinran's concept for faith presents a notable exception to the dyadic pattern discussed by Doi in that the single concept *shinjin* points simultaneously to Amida's mind and the mind of foolish beings. On the other hand, Rennyo's use of the concept to interpret and popularize Shinran's teaching in an institutional setting formalizes the dyadic pattern within the Shinshū. To the extent that *shinjin* is uncritically equated with *anjin*, Shinran's emphasis on the individual aspect of faith is submerged all too readily in the collective aspect, at the expense of institutionalizing a tradition of transcendence based on Buddhist symbols.

[73] A promising development, in this regard, is the formation of the Rennyo Shōnin Kenkyūkai, in 1989, under the leadership of Kitanishi Hiromu. In anticipation of the five-hundredth anniversary of Rennyo's death in 1999, the study group is to publish a volume of studies on Rennyo in 1995, which "explains in a straightforward way the meaning of faith as the right cause for birth in the Pure Land and of saying Amida's Name as an expression of thanksgiving." The approach of these broadly-based studies is fundamentally Buddhist in its stated commitment not to be caught up in attachments to sect (*shūga* 宗我) or to self *(jiga)*. A new era of Rennyo studies may help prepare the Jōdo Shinshū to make a welcome and much needed contribution to the challenge of living in a religiously plural world. See Kitanishi Hiromu, "Rennyo Shōnin kenkyū no kaname," *Rennyo Shōnin kenkyūkai kaishi* 1 (1989), 1–2.

CHRONOLOGY,
WIVES AND CHILDREN,
BIBLIOGRAPHY,
INDEX

Chronology of Rennyo's Life

This chronology primarily documents Rennyo's literary activity — copying texts and writing the eighty letters in the five-fascicle collection, *The Letters*. For a comprehensive listing of events in his life, including the many presentations of texts and a variety of main images to Honganji-related priests and congregations, see HN, 53-82, which cites sources for each item. Some of the letters are dated according to the beginning, middle, or end of a month, indicated here by B, M, or E.

Date	Rennyo's Age	Events
Ōei 22 (1415)	1	2.25. Born at Ōtani Hongan-ji, Higashiyama, Kyoto; first child of his father, Zonnyo (20); grandson of Gyōnyo (40).
Ōei 27 (1420)	6	12.28. Mother leaves Ōtani Hongan-ji.
Ōei 29 (1422)	8	Stepsister Nyojū born to stepmother Nyoen.
Ōei 31 (1424)	10	10.15. Zonnyo copies part one of *Anjin ketsujōshō*.
Ōei 32 (1425)	11	8. Zonnyo copies *Shinran den'e*, *Jimyōshō*, part two of *Anjin ketsujōshō*, *Shojin hongaishū*, and other texts.
Ōei 34 (1427)	13	9.8. Gyōnyo copies *Kudenshō* and part of *Kyōgyōshinshō*.
Eikyō 1 (1429)	15	Rennyo resolves to restore the Honganji.
Eikyō 3 (1431)	17	Summer. Takes the tonsure at Shōren'in and receives the name Kenju.
Eikyō 5 (1433)	19	Birth of stepbrother, Ōgen.
Eikyō 6 (1434)	20	2.13. Zonnyo copies *Gutokushō*. 5.12. Rennyo copies *Jōdo monrui jushō*.
Eikyō 8 (1436)	22	3.28. Gyōnyo (61) gives custodial deed to Zonnyo (41). 8.M. Rennyo copies *Sanjō wasan*.

Eikyō 10 (1438)	24	8.15. Rennyo copies *Jōdo shinyōshō*; Zonnyo adds postscript.
		10.13. Zonnyo copies *Shojin hongaishū*.
Eikyō 11 (1439)	25	7.29. Rennyo copies *Gose monogatari*.
		7.E. Copies *Tariki shinjin kikigaki*.
Eikyō 12 (1440)	26	10.14. Gyōnyo (65) dies.
Kakitsu 1 (1441)	27	9.7. Rennyo copies *Jōdo shinyōshō*.
Kakitsu 2 (1442)	28	Birth of first child (a son), Junnyo, to first wife, Nyoryō (d. 1455). Uncle, Nyojō (31), builds Honsen-ji at Futamata, Kaga.
Bunnan 3 (1446)	32	1.M. Rennyo copies *Gutokushō*.
		Birth of first daughter, Nyokei, and of second son, Renjō.
Bunnan 4 (1447)	33	1.E. Rennyo copies *Anjin ketsujōshō*.
		2.28. Copies *Rokuyōshō*; on the last day of the month, copies *Mattōshō*.
Bunnan 5 (1448)	34	10.19. Copies *Gensō ekō kikigaki*.
		Birth of second daughter, Kengyoku.
Hōtoku 1 (1449)	35	5.6. Copies chapter four, "Realization," *Kyōgyōshinshō*.
		5.28. Copies *Sanjō wasan*.
		6.3. Copies *Anjin ketsujōshō*.
		7.M. Copies *Nyonin ōjō kikigaki*.
		10.14. Copies *Godenshō*.
		Travels to the Hokuriku with Zonnyo.
Hōtoku 2 (1450)	36	3.4. Zonnyo copies *Shinran Shōnin goin'en hidenshō*. Birth of third son, Renkō.
Hōtoku 3 (1451)	37	7.8. Rennyo continues copying *Kyōgyōshinshō*.
Kyōtoku 2 (1453)	39	11.22. Copies *Sanjō wasan*.
Kyōtoku 3 (1454)	40	4.17. Continues copying *Ōjō yōshū*.
		7.8. Continues copying *Kyōgyōshinshō*.
		Birth of third daughter, Juson.
Kōshō 1 (1455)	41	Birth of fourth son, Rensei.
		7.19. Copies *Bokieshi*.
		11.23. Death of first wife, Nyoryō.
Chōroku 1 (1457)	43	2.20. Copies *Saiyōshō*.
		4.B. Copies *Jimyōshō*.
		6.18. Death of Zonnyo (62).
		Rennyo becomes eighth head priest of the Honganji.
Chōroku 2 (1458)	44	2.4. Copies *Sanjō wasan*.
		8.10. Birth of fifth son, Jitsunyo, to second wife, Renyū (d.1470), younger sister of Nyoryō. Junnyo (16), first son, takes the tonsure.

Chōroku 3 (1459)	45	Birth of fourth daughter, Myōshū.
Kanshō 1 (1460)	46	1.26. Rennyo's uncle, Nyojō, (49) dies. 2.24. Presents a copy of the Name in ten characters to Hōjū of Katada, Ōmi province. 6. Writes *Shōshinge taii* at request of Dōsai of Kanegamori, Ōmi. 10.4. Death of stepmother, Nyoen. Birth of fifth daughter, Myōi.
Kanshō 2 (1461)	47	1.6. Presents a copy of the Name in ten characters to Hōjū and followers at Katada, Ōmi. 3. Writes the first of his letters (RSI #1). 10. Repairs Shinran's portrait (*anjō goei*). 12.8. Copies *Tandokumon*. 12.23. Presents dual seated portrait of Shinran and himself (*nison renzazō*) to Hōjū and followers at Katada.
Kanshō 3 (1462)	48	Birth of sixth daughter, Nyokū.
Kanshō 4 (1463)	49	2.11. Sees firelight performance of Nō drama in Nara with family. Birth of seventh daughter, Yūshin.
Kanshō 5 (1464)	50	Birth of sixth son, Renjun. Observes twenty-fifth anniversary of Gyōnyo's death.
Kanshō 6 (1465)	51	1.9. Ōtani Hongan-ji partially destroyed by monks from Enryaku-ji. 1.M. Rennyo moves the founder's image from Muromachi, Kyoto, to Konhō-ji. 3.21 Ōtani Hongan-ji demolished by Enryaku-ji monks. Enryaku-ji monks attack followers at Akanoi, Ōmi.
Bunshō 1 (1466)	52	7.8. Continues copying *Kyōgyōshinshō*. 11.21. Conducts annual thanksgiving services at Kanegamori, Ōmi province. Birth of eighth daughter, Ryōnin. Turns over care of the temple and site to Junnyo. Writes letter (RSI #2).
Ōnin 1 (1467)	53	1.1 Ōnin war breaks out. 2.B. Transfers founder's image from Annyō-ji, Ōmi province, to Honpuku-ji, Katada, Ōmi. 11.21. Conducts annual thanksgiving services at Honpuku-ji, Katada, Ōmi. Birth of ninth daughter, Ryōnyo.
Ōnin 2 (1468)	54	3.12. Moves founder's image from Honpuku-

		ji to Dōkaku's congregation in Ōtsu. 3.28. Writes deed of transfer designating Jitsunyo as successor. 10.M. Copies *Hōonkō shiki.* Birth of seventh son, Rengo.
Bunmei 1 (1469)	55	Spring. Builds the Chikamatsu priest's dwelling in the southern detached quarters of Miidera, Ōtsu, and names it Kenshō-ji. Birth of tenth daughter, Yūshin.
Bunmei 2 (1470)	56	12.5. Death of second wife, Renyū.
Bunmei 3 (1471)	57	2.6 Death of first daughter, Nyokei. 4.B. Leaves Ōtsu, passing through Kyoto, and proceeds to Yoshizaki, Echizen. 7.15. Writes Letter 1:1 of *The Letters.* 7.18. Letter 1:2. 7.27. Builds priest's dwelling in Yoshizaki. 12.18. Letter 1:3.
Bunmei 4 (1472)	58	1. Prohibits the gathering of followers at Yoshizaki. 4.E. Writes letters (RSI #13, #14, and #15). 8.14. Death of second daughter, Kengyoku. 11.27. Letter 1:4.
Bunmei 5 (1473)	59	1. Moves from Yoshizaki to Fujishima, Echizen province. 2.8. Letter 1.5. 4.25. Letter 1.6. 8.12. Letter 1.7. 9.11. Letter 1.10. 9.M. Letter 1:11. 9.22. Letter 1:15. 9.E. Letters 1:12-14. 9. Letters 1:8-9. 10.3. Returns to Yoshizaki. 12.8. Letter 2:1. 12.12. Letter 2.2.
Bunmei 6 (1474)	60	1.11. Letter 2:3. 2.15. Letter 2:4. 2.16. Letter 2:5. 2.17. Letter 2:6. 3.3. Letter 2:7. 3.17. Letter 2:9. 3.M. Letter 2:8. 3.28. Yoshizaki priest's dwelling burns. 5.13. Letter 2:10. 5.20. Letter 2:11.

6.12. Letter 2:12.
7.3. Letter 2:13.
7.5. Letter 2:14.
7.9. Letter 2:15.
7.14. Letter 3:1.
8.5. Letter 3:2.
8.6. Letter 3:3.
8.18. Letter 3:4.
9.6. Letter 3:5.
10.20. Letter 3:6.
11.1. Ikkō uprising in Kaga
11.25. Letter 5:2 (RSI #75).

Bunmei 7 (1475)   61   2.23. Letter 3:7.
2.25. Letter 3:8.
3.E. Followers in conflict with Togashi Masachika in Kaga.
5.28. Letter 3:9.
7.15. Letter 3:10.
8.21. Leaves Yoshizaki, arrives at Wakasa and, passing through Tanba, Settsu, comes finally to Deguchi.
11.21. Letter 3:11.

Bunmei 8 (1476)   62   1.27. Letter 3:12.
7.18. Letter 3:13.

Bunmei 9 (1477)   63   1.8. Letter 4:1.
9.17. Letter 4:2.
9.27. Letter 4:3.
10.27. Copies *Kyōgyōshinshō taii*.
11.B. Writes *Gozokushō* (RSI #96).
12.2. Letter 4:4.
12.M. Copies *Jōdo kenmonshū*.
Birth of eleventh daughter, Myōshō, to third wife, Nyoshō.

Bunmei 10 (1478)   64   1.29. Begins construction of priest's dwelling at Yamashina, Yamashiro.
8.17. Death of third wife, Nyoshō.

Bunmei 11 (1479)   65   12.30. Renjun takes the tonsure.

Bunmei 12 (1480)   66   1. Builds a small hall at Yamashina.
2.3. Begins construction of Founder's Hall.
8.28. Installs Shinran's portrait in the Founder's Hall.
10.15. Further repairs to Shinran's portrait (*anjō goei*).
11.18. Moves Shinran's image from Chikamatsu, Ōtsu, to Yamashina.

Bunmei 13 (1481)	67	2.4. Begins construction of Amida Hall at Yamashina. 6.8. Installs main image in a temporary altar in the Amida Hall. 6.11. Celebrates twenty-fifth anniversary of Zonnyo's death. 12.4. Return of *Bokie* from the shogunate.
Bunmei 14 (1482)	68	6.15. Installs main image in altar in the Amida Hall. 11.21. Letter 4:5. Birth of twelfth daughter, Renshū, to fourth wife, Shūnyo (d. 1486).
Bunmei 15 (1483)	69	5.29. Death of first son, Junnyo. 11. Letter 4:6.
Bunmei 16 (1484)	70	11.21. Letter 4:7. Birth of eighth son, Rengei.
Bunmei 17 (1485)	71	11.23. Letter 4:8.
Chōkyō 1 (1487)	73	Birth of thirteenth daughter, Myōyū, to fifth wife, Rennō (d.1518).
Chōkyō 2 (1488)	74	6.9. Death of Togashi Masachika.
Entoku 1 (1489)	75	8.28. Transfers office to Jitsunyo; retires to southern hall of Hongan-ji, Yamashina. 10.28. Continues copying *Kyōgyōshinshō*.
Entoku 2 (1490)	76	10.28. Writes a second letter of transfer to Jitsunyo. Death of seventh daughter, Yūshin. Birth of ninth son, Jikken.
Meiō 1 (1492)	78	6. Letter 4:9. Birth of tenth son, Jitsugo. Death of sixth daughter, Nyokū.
Meiō 3 (1494)	80	Birth of eleventh son, Jitsujun.
Meiō 4 (1495)	81	Builds Gangyō-ji and Honzen-ji in Yamato province. Birth of twelfth son, Jikkō.
Meiō 5 (1496)	82	1.11. Copies *Hōnen Shōnin onkotoba*. 9.24. Selects temple site at Ishiyama, Settsu province. 9.29. Breaks ground for priest's dwelling, Ishiyama. 10.8. Erects priest's dwelling.
Meiō 6 (1497)	83	2.16. Letter 5:8 (RSI #131). 5.25. Letter 4:11. 11.E. Priest's dwelling at Ishiyama completed. Conducts annual thanksgiving services at

Osaka and Fukuda.

Letters 4:10, 5:5 (RSI #139), and 5:6 (RSI #140).

Birth of fourteenth daughter, Myōshū.

Meiō 7 (1498)	84	2.25. Letter 4:12.

3. Letter 5:14 (RSI #143).

4.B. Taken ill.

4.11. Letter 4:13.

4. Letter 4:14.

5.7. Pays respects before Shinran's image in a final visit to Yamashina.

5.E. *Summer Letters* (RSI #147, #148).

6.M. *Summer Letters* (RSI #149).

7.M. *Summer Letters* (RSI #150).

11.19. Letter 5:9 (RSI #155).

11.21. Letter 4:15.

Birth of thirteenth son, Jitsujū.

Meiō 8 (1499)	85	2.18. Sets out from Osaka for Hongan-ji, Yamashina.

2.20. Arrives in Yamashina.

2.21. Worships in the Founder's Hall.

3.1. Talks with Jitsunyo and other sons.

3.9. Parting instructions given to Jitsunyo, Renkō, Rensei, Renjun, and Rengo.

3.20. Pardons Aki Rensō.

3.25. Dies at midday.

3.28. Death of Aki Rensō.

4.25. Final instructions to five sons, *Rennyo Shōnin goyuigon*, are set down.

Meiji 15 (1882)	Awarded title, Etō Daishi, by Emperor Meiji.

Rennyo's Wives and Children

Wives	Rennyo's Age	Children
Nyoryō 如了 (d. 1455)	28	Junnyo 順如 , first son (1442–1483)
	32	Nyokei 如慶 , first daughter (1446–1471)
	32	Renjō 蓮乗 , second son (1446–1504)
	34	Kengyoku 見玉 , second daughter, (1448–1472)
	36	Renkō 蓮綱 , third son (1450–1531)
	39	Juson 寿尊 , third daughter (1454–1516)
	41	Rensei 蓮誓 , fourth son (1455–1521)
Renyū 蓮祐 (d. 1470)	44	Jitsunyo 実如 , fifth son (1458–1525)
	45	Myōshū 妙宗 , fourth daughter (1459–1537)
	46	Myōi 妙意 , fifth daughter (1460–1471)
	48	Nyokū 如空 , sixth daughter (1462–1492)
	49	Yūshin 祐心 , seventh daughter (1463–1490)
	50	Renjun 蓮淳 , sixth son (1464–1550)
	52	Ryōnin 了忍 , eighth daughter (1466–1472)
	53	Ryōnyo 了如 , ninth daughter (1467–1541)
	54	Rengo 蓮悟 , seventh son (1468–1543)
	55	Yūshin 祐心 , tenth daughter (1469–1540)
Nyoshō 如勝 (1448–1478)	63	Myōshō 妙勝 , eleventh daughter (1477–1500)
Shūnyo 宗如 (d. 1486)	68	Renshū 蓮周 , twelfth daughter (1482–1503)
	70	Rengei 蓮芸 , eighth son (1484–1523)
Rennō 蓮能 (1465–1518)	73	Myōyū 妙祐 , thirteenth daughter (1487–1512)
	76	Jikken 実賢 , ninth son (1490–1523)
	78	Jitsugo 実悟 , tenth son (1492–1584)
	80	Jitsujun 実順 , eleventh son (1494–1518)
	82	Jikkō 実孝 , twelfth son (1495–1553)
	83	Myōshū 妙宗 , fourteenth daughter (1497–1518)
	84	Jitsujū 実従 , thirteenth son (1498–1564)

Selected Bibliography

PRIMARY SOURCES

Primary source titles, in most instances, follow abbreviated forms in common use in Jōdo Shinshū literature, particularly as found in the table of contents of volumes of *Shinshū shōgyō zensho* (SSZ).

Amidakyō 阿弥陀経 [Amida sūtra; Skt. *Sukhāvatīvyūha sūtra*, Smaller sūtra of immeasurable life]. SSZ 1: 67–72 (T 12.346–348).

Amida Sūtra. See *Amidakyō*.

Anjin ketsujōshō 安心決定鈔 [On establishing the settled mind]. SSZ 3: 615–38 (T 83.921–929).

Anrakushū 安樂集 [Passages on the land of happiness]. SSZ 1: 377–440 (T 47.4–220).

Bokie 慕帰絵 [A pictorial biography in fond memory (of Kakunyo)]. SSS 1: 907–29.

Bosatsu kaikyō 菩薩戒経 [Sūtra of the bodhisattva precepts; Chin. *P'u sa chieh ching*]. T 24.997–1010.

Contemplation Sūtra. See *Kanmuryōjukyō*.

Daichidoron 大智度論 [Commentary on the *Mahāprajñāpāramitā sūtra*]. T 25.57–756.

Daihasso onmonogatari Kūzen kikigaki 第八祖御物語空善聞書 [Matters relating to the eighth Master (of the Honganji) as heard by Kūzen]. SSS 11: 419–38.

Daimuryōjukyō 大無量寿経 [Larger sūtra of immeasurable life; Skt. *Sukhāvatīvyūha sūtra*]. SSZ 1: 1–47 (cited as *Bussetsu muryōjukyō* 仏説無量寿経); T 12.265–279.

Eigenki 栄玄記 [Eigen's record]. RSG, 257–71.

Gaijashō 改邪鈔 [Notes on the correction of heresies]. SSZ 3: 64–89.

Ganganshō 願願鈔 [Notes on the Vows] SSZ 3: 44–49.

Gobunshō 御文章 [The letters (of Rennyo)]. SSZ 3: 402–518.

Godenshō 御伝鈔 [A biography (of Honganji's Master Shinran)]. SSZ 3: 639–54 (T 83.750–755).

Gosaidan gosho 御裁断御書 [A letter of adjudication]. Shinshū Seiten Hensan Iinkai, ed. *Jōdo Shinshū seiten*, 1411–15.

Gosaidan shinmeisho 御裁断申明書 [An announcement of adjudication]. Shinshū Seiten Hensan Iinkai, ed. *Jōdo Shinshū seiten*, 1417–22.

Gose monogatari 後世物語 [Matters related to the afterlife]. SSZ 2: 757–65 (T 83.916–919); cited as *Gose monogatari kikigaki* 後世物語聞書 [What we have heard about matters related to the afterlife].

Gozokushō 御俗姓 [(Shinran's) genealogy]. SSZ 3: 519–21 (T 83.832–833).

Gutokushō 愚禿鈔 [Gutoku's (Shinran's) notes]. SSZ 2: 455–79 (T 83.647–654).

Haja kenshōshō 破邪顕正抄 [A tract refuting the erroneous and revealing the right]. SSZ 3: 155–87.

Hanjusan 般舟讃 [Hymns (on the samādhi) of all buddhas' presence]. SSZ 1: 685–727 (T 47.448–456).

Hanju zanmaikyō 般舟三昧経 [Sūtra of the samādhi of all buddhas' presence]. T 13.897–902.

Hōjisan 法事讃 [Hymns of the nenbutsu liturgy]. SSZ 1: 561–617 (T 47.424–438).

Honganji Shōnin Shinran den'e 本願寺聖人親鸞伝絵 [An illustrated biography of Honganji's Master Shinran]. See *Godenshō*.

Honganji sahō no shidai 本願寺作法之次第 [An outline of rites and practices in the Honganji]. RSG, 175–247; SSS 11: 559–87.

Honpukuji atogaki 本福寺跡書 [Additional notes on Honpuku-ji]. In *Honpukuji kyūki* 本福寺旧記 , ed. Chiba Jōryū; SSS 11: 629–660.

Honpukuji yuraiki 本福寺由来記 [A record of Honpuku-ji's history]. In *Honpukuji kyūki*, ed. Chiba Jōryū; SSS 11: 661–78.

Hōonki 報恩記 [A chronicle of thanksgiving]. SSZ 3: 256–81.

Hōonkō shiki 報恩講式 [A service of thanksgiving (for Shinran's virtues)]. SSZ 3: 655–60 (cited as 報恩講私記); T 83.755–756.

Ichinen tanen mon'i 一念多念文意 [Notes on once-calling and many-calling]. SSZ 2: 604–20 (T 83.694–699).

Jimyōshō 持名鈔 [On holding to the Name (of the Buddha)]. SSZ 3: 91–108.

Jitsugoki 実悟記 [Jitsugo's record]. RSG, 139–73.

Jitsugoki shūi 実悟記拾遺 [Gleanings from *Jitsugo's record*]. *Shidenpen*, vol.

7, *Shinpen Shinshū zensho*, ed. Shinpen Shinshū Zensho Kankōkai, 119–44. Kyoto: Shibunkaku, 1976.

Jitsugo kyūki 実悟旧記 [Jitsugo's old record]. RSG, 69–137.

Jōdo kenmonshū 浄土見聞集 [A collection of information on Pure Land (teaching)]. SSZ 3: 375–83.

Jōdo monrui jushō 浄土文類聚鈔 [Passages on the Pure Land way]. SSZ 2: 443–54 (T 83.644–647).

Jōdoron 浄土論 [Treatise on the Pure Land]. SSZ 1: 269–78 (T 26.230–233).

Jōdo ronchū 浄土論註 [Commentary on the *Treatise on the Pure Land*]. SSZ 1: 279–349 (T 40.826–844). Also *Ōjō ronchū* 往生論註 .

Jōdo shinyōshō 浄土真要鈔 [On the true essentials for (birth in) the Pure Land]. SSZ 3: 119–53 (T 83.758–769).

Jōdo wasan 浄土和讚 [Hymns on the Pure Land]. SSZ 2: 485–500 (T 83.655–660).

Kangyōsho 観経疏 [Commentary on the *Contemplation sūtra*; Chin. *Kuan ching shu*]. SSZ 1: 441–560 (T 37.245–278). *Kangyōsho* is in four parts: *Gengibun* 玄義分 [The essential meaning of the sūtra]; *Jobungi* 序分義 [On the introductory part of the sūtra]; *Jōzengi* 定善義 [On meditative practice]; and *Sanzengi* 散善義 [On non-meditative practice].

Kanmuryōjukyō 観無量寿経 [Sūtra of contemplation on the Buddha of immeasurable life]. SSZ 1: 48–66 (T 12.340–346).

Kannen bōmon 観念法門 [Methods of contemplating (Amida Buddha)]. T 47.22–30.

Kegongyō 華厳経 ; Skt. *Avataṃsaka sūtra* [Garland sūtra]. T 9.395–10.444.

Ken jōdo shinjitsu kyōgyōshō monrui 顕浄土真実教行証文類 [Collection of passages revealing the true teaching, practice, and realization of the Pure Land way]. SSZ 2: 1–203 (T 83.589–643).

Kenmyōshō 顕名鈔 [A tract revealing the (origin of Amida's) Name]. SSZ 3: 325–52.

Kenshōryūgishō 顕正流義鈔 [Tract revealing the tradition's true teaching]. T 83.841–846.

Ketchishō 決智鈔 [A tract establishing wisdom]. SSZ 3: 188–220.

Kōnyo Shōnin goikun goshōsoku 広如上人御遺訓御消息 [Master Kōnyo's "Testament"]. SSZ 5: 777–78.

Kōsō wasan 高僧和讚 [Hymns on the (Pure Land) masters]. SSZ 2: 501–15 (T 83.660–664).

Kudenshō 口伝鈔 [A tract (on Shinran's life) based on oral transmission]. SSZ 3: 1–36 (T 83.738–750).

Kūzenki 空善記 [Kūzen's record]. RSG, 3–58.

Kyōgyōshinshō 教行信証 [The true teaching, practice, and realization of the Pure Land way; abbr. of *Ken jōdo shinjitsu kyōgyōshō monrui*]. SSZ 2: 1–203 (T 83.589–643).

Larger Sūtra. Abbr. of *Larger Sūtra of Immeasurable Life*; see *Daimuryōjukyō*.

Letters, The. See *Gobunshō*.

Lotus Sūtra. See *Myōhō rengekyō*.

Makashikan 摩訶止観 [Treatise on śamatha and vipaśyanā]. T 46.1–140.

Mappō tōmyōki 末法燈明記 [Lamp for the last age]. *Dengyō Daishi zenshū* 1: 415–26.

Mattōshō 末燈鈔 [Letters of Shinran (lit., Lamp for the last age)]. SSZ 2: 656–94 (T 83.711–722).

Mida nyorai myōgō toku 彌陀如來名号徳 [The virtue of Amida Tathāgata's Name]. SSZ 2: 733–38.

Mukashi monogatariki 昔物語記 [A record of incidents and sayings from the past]. RSG, 249–55.

Muryōju nyorai e 無量寿如来会 [Sūtra of the Tathāgata of immeasurable life]. T 11.91–101.

Myōhō rengekyō 妙法蓮華経 . Abbr. as *Hokekyō* 法華経 [Lotus sūtra; Skt. *Saddharma puṇḍarīka–sūtra*]; T 9.1–62.

Natsu ofumi 夏御文 (*Ge no gobunshō* 夏御文章) [(Rennyo's) summer letters]. SSZ 3: 522–28.

Nehangyō 涅槃経 [Nirvāṇa sūtra]; abbr. of *Daihatsu nehangyō* 大般涅槃経 [Skt. *Mahāparinirvāṇa sūtra*]. T 12.365–604.

Nirvāṇa sūtra. See *Nehangyō*.

Nyonin ōjō kikigaki 女人往生聞書 [Women's birth (in the Pure Land) according to oral tradition]. SSZ 3: 109–18.

Ōjō raisange 往生礼讃偈 [Hymns on birth (in the Pure Land)]. SSZ 1: 648–84 (T 47.438–448).

Ōjōyōshū 往生要集 [Essentials for attaining birth (in the Pure Land)]. SSZ 1: 729–927 (T 84.33–90).

Renjunki 蓮淳記 [Renjun's record]. RSG, 61–68.

Rennyo Shōnin goichidaiki kikigaki 蓮如上人御一代記聞書 [A record of Master Rennyo's life, according to oral tradition]. SSZ 3: 531–613 (T 83.809–832).

Rennyo Shōnin itokuki 蓮如上人遺徳記 [A record of the benefits derived from Master Rennyo's virtuous deeds]. SSZ 3: 869–91.

Rennyo Shōnin ofumi 蓮如上人御文 [The letters of Master Rennyo]. T 83.771–808.

Rokuyōshō 六要鈔 [A tract on the essentials of the six (chapters of the *Kyōgyōshinshō*)]. SSZ 2: 205–442.

Ryōgemon 領解文 [A confessional statement]. SSZ 3: 529–30.

Saiyōshō 最要鈔 [On the foremost essentials (in Jōdo Shinshū)]. SSZ 3: 50–53.

San Amida butsuge 讃阿弥陀仏偈 [Hymns to Amida Buddha]. T 47.420–424.

Sanjō wasan 三帖和讃 [Hymns in three fascicles]; a general title encompassing the *Jōdo wasan, Kōsō wasan,* and *Shōzōmatsu wasan.* SSZ 2: 485–531.

Sassha nikenshikyō 薩庶尼乾子経 [Sūtra taught to Nigranthas]. T 9.317–365.

Senjakushū 選択集 [Selected passages]; abbr. of *Senjaku hongan nenbutsushū* 選択本願念仏集 [Passages on the nenbutsu selected in the Primal Vow]. SSZ 1: 929–94 (T 83.1–110).

Shinran Shōnin goin'en hidenshō 親鸞聖人御因縁秘伝鈔 [A selection of hidden notes on circumstances in Master Shinran's (life)]. *Shinranden sōsho,* ed. Sasaki Gesshō, 69–85. Tokyo: Mugasanbō, 1910.

Shinran Shōnin goshōsokushū 親鸞聖人御消息集 [A collection of Master Shinran's letters]. SSZ 2: 695–713 (T 83.722–728).

Shojin hongaishū 諸神本懐集 [A collection (of passages) on the fundamental purpose of the various kami]. SSS 1: 697–712.

Shōshinge 正信偈 [Hymns on true faith]; abbr. of *Shōshin nenbutsuge* 正信念仏偈 [Hymns on true faith and the nenbutsu]. SSZ 2: 43–46 (T 83.600).

Shōtoku Taishi kōshiki 聖徳太子講式 [A celebration of (the virtues of) Prince-regent Shōtoku] SSZ 5: 703–10.

Shōzōmatsu wasan 正像末和讃 [Hymns on the true, semblance, and last ages]. SSZ 2: 516–31 (T 83.664–669).

Shūjinki 捨塵記 [A miscellaneous record (of events in Rennyo's life)]. SSS 11: 599–610.

Shūjishō 執持鈔 [A tract on firmly-held (teachings)]. SSZ 3: 37–43 (T 83.735–738).

Songō shinzō meimon 尊号真像銘文 [Notes on the inscriptions on sacred scrolls]. SSZ 2: 560–603 (T 83.679–693).

Summer Letters. See *Natsu ofumi* (*Ge no gobunshō*).

Tandokumon 嘆徳文 [Passages in praise of (Shinran's) virtue]. SSZ 3: 661–64 (T 83.757).

Tannishō 歎異抄 [Notes lamenting departures (from the teaching)]. SSZ 2: 773–95 (T 83.728–735).

Yuishinshō mon'i 唯信鈔文意 [Notes on *Essentials of faith alone*]. SSZ 2: 621–38 (T 83.699–706).

Zonkaku hōgo 存覚法語 [Zonkaku's words on the dharma]. SSZ 3: 353–74.

SECONDARY SOURCES IN JAPANESE

Akamatsu Toshihide 赤松俊秀. *Kamakura bukkyō no kenkyū* 鎌倉仏教の研究 [Studies in Kamakura Buddhism]. Kyoto: Heirakuji Shoten, 1963.

_____. *Zoku Kamakura bukkyō no kenkyū* 続鎌倉仏教の研究 [Further studies in Kamakura Buddhism]. Kyoto: Heirakuji Shoten, 1968.

Akamatsu Toshihide and Kasahara Kazuo 笠原一男, eds. *Shinshūshi gaisetsu* 真宗史概説 [Outline of Shinshū history]. 1963; repr. Kyoto: Heirakuji Shoten, 1966.

Asaeda Zenshō 朝枝善照. *Heian shoki bukkyōshi kenkyū* 平安初期仏教史研究 [Studies in the history of early Heian Buddhism]. Kyoto: Nagata Bunshōdō, 1980.

_____. *Myōkōninden no shūhen* 妙好人伝の周辺 [On *Myōkōninden*]. Kyoto: Nagata Bunshōdō, 1984.

_____. *Myōkōninden kenkyū* 妙好人伝研究 [A study of *Myōkōninden*]. Kyoto: Nagata Bunshōdō, 1987.

_____. *Myōkōnin no kokoro* 妙好人のこころ [The heart and mind of the *myōkōnin*]. Kyoto: Nagata Bunshōdō, 1987.

_____. "Igi: Sangō wakuran 異議 — 三業惑乱 [Heresy: The Sangō Upheaval]." In *Shinshū denshō no ayumi* (1). Jōdo Shinshū Gendai Hōwa Taikei, 7: 343–61. Kyoto: Dōbōsha, 1987.

Bandō Shōjun 坂東性純. "Shinshū to hōon shisō 真宗と報恩思想 [Shinshū and the idea of gratitude]." *Shinshū kyōgaku kenkyū* 5 (1981): 16–25.

Chiba Jōryū 千葉乗隆. *Shinshū kyōdan no soshiki to seido* 真宗教団の組織と制度 [Formation and organization of the Shinshū order]. Kyoto: Dōbōsha, 1978.

_____. *Honganji monogatari* 本願寺ものがたり [The story of the Honganji]. Kyoto: Dōbōsha, 1984.

_____. "Bokie no omote to ura 慕帰絵の表と裏 [All about 'Bokie']." In *Bokie ekotoba*, Zoku Nihon Ekan Taisei 4, ed. Komatsu Shigemi, 102–14. Tokyo: Chūō Kōronsha, 1985.

_____. "Rennyo no honzon 蓮如の本尊 [Rennyo and the main image]." In *Rennyo*, ed. Minami Midō Shinbun, 201–20. Ōsaka: Nanba Betsuin, 1986.

_____. "Rennyo no ikonokurasumu 蓮如のイコノクラスム [Rennyo's iconoclasm]." In *Chiba Jōryū hakase koki kinen*, ed. Chiba Jōryū Hakase Koki Kinenkai, 1–54. Kyoto: Nagata Bunshōdō, 1990.

_____, ed. *Honpukuji kyūki* 本福寺旧記 [The old records of Honpuku-ji]. Kyoto: Dōbōsha, 1980.

_____, ed. *Honpukujishi* 本福寺史 [The history of Honpuku-ji]. Kyoto: Dōbōsha, 1980.

Daizōkyō Gakujutsu Yōgo Kenkyūkai 大蔵経学術用語研究会 , ed. *Taishō shinshū daizōkyō sakuin* 大正真宗大蔵経索引 [Index to the Taishō Tripiṭaka]. Vol. 43, *Zoku shoshūbu* 6. Tokyo: Taishō Shinshū Daizōkyō Kankōkai, 1987.

Dōbōsha Shuppan 同朋社出版 , ed. *Shinran ni deatta hitobito* 親鸞に出遇った人びと [People who encountered Shinran]. 5 vols. Kyoto: Dōbōsha, 1989.

Fudeuchi Yukiko 筆内幸子 . *Rennyo Shōnin to sono gonin no tsumatachi* 蓮如上人とその五人の妻たち [Master Rennyo and his five wives]. 2 vols. Kanazawa: Hokkoku Shuppansha, 1985.

Fugen Kōju 普賢晃寿 . "Anjin ketsujōshō to Shinshū resso no kyōgaku: Anjin ketsujōshō to Kakunyo/Zonkaku no kyōgaku 安心決定鈔と真宗列祖の教学 — 安心決定鈔と覚如 – 存覚の教学 [*Anjin ketsujōshō* in Shinshū thought: Kakunyo and Zonkaku]." *Ryūkoku Daigaku ronshū* 415 (1979): 81–107.

_____. "Anjin ketsujōshō to Rennyo kyōgaku 安心決定鈔と蓮如教学 [*Anjin ketsujōshō* in Rennyo's thought]." *Shinshūgaku* 62 (1980): 1–29.

_____, ed. *Anjin ketsujōshō* 安心決定鈔 . Kyoto: Dōbōsha, 1983.

Fujihara Toshie 藤原利枝 . *Asahara Saiichi no uta* 浅原才市の歌 [The poems of Saiichi Asahara]. Kyoto: Hōzōkan, 1989.

Fujii Otoo 藤井乙男 , ed. *Shasekishū* 沙石集 [Sand and pebbles]. Tokyo: Bunken Shoin, 1928.

Fujikawa Yū 富士川游 . *Shinsen myōkōninden* 新選妙好人伝 [A new selection of *myōkōnin* biographies]. Tokyo: Daizō Shuppan, 1971.

Fukuma Kōchō 福間光超 . "Kinsei hōken shakai ni okeru bukkyō: Toku ni Rennyo no shisō to jissen o chūshin ni 近世封建社会における仏教 ― とくに蓮如の思想と実践を中心に [Buddhism in early modern feudal society: Rennyo's thought and practice]." *Ryūkoku daigaku ronshū* 395 (1971): 93–118.

Futaba Kenkō 二葉憲香 . *Kodai bukkyō shisōshi kenkyū: Nihon kodai ni okeru ritsuryō bukkyō oyobi han-ritsuryō bukkyō no kenkyū* 古代仏教思想史研究 ― 日本古代における律令仏教及び反律令仏教の研究 [Studies in the intellectual history of ancient Buddhism: *Ritsuryō* and anti-*ritsuryō* Buddhism in ancient Japan]. Kyoto: Nagata Bunshōdō, 1962.

_____. *Shinran no kenkyū: Shinran ni okeru shin to rekishi* 親鸞の研究 ― 親鸞における信と歴史 [Shinran studies: (The meaning of) faith and history for Shinran]. 1962; repr. Kyoto: Hyakkaen, 1989.

_____. *Shinran no hiraita chihei* 親鸞のひらいた地平 [Horizons opened by Shinran]. Kyoto: Hyakkaen, 1975.

_____. "Shinshū ni okeru ōjō shinkō to rekishi to no kankei ni tsuite no kasetsu 真宗における往生信仰と歴史との関係についての仮説 [A hypothesis on the relationship of Pure Land piety and history in the Shinshū]." In *Shinshūshi no kenkyū*, ed. Miyazaki Enjun Hakase Kanreki Kinenkai, 507–29. Kyoto: Nagata Bunshōdō, 1966. Also in *Shinshūgaku kenkyū*, ed. Dendōin Kenkyūbu, 1: 45–68. 1971; repr. Kyoto: Nagata Bunshōdō, 1980.

_____. "Shinshū kindai dendō no mondaiten 真宗近代伝道の問題点 [Issues in modern Shinshū missionary work]." In *Shinshū kyōgaku kenkyū*, ed. Futaba Kenkō and Satō Michio, 3: 15–45. Kyoto: Nagata Bunshōdō, 1980.

_____, ed. *Shiryō: Nihon bukkyōshi* 史料 ― 日本仏教史 [Documents: Japanese Buddhist history]. Kyoto: Yamazaki Hōbundō, 1971.

_____, ed. *Kokka to bukkyō* 国家と仏教 [The state and Buddhism]. Nihon Bukkyōshi Kenkyū, vol. 1. Kyoto: Nagata Bunshōdō, 1979.

_____, ed. *Shinran no subete* 親鸞のすべて [All about Shinran]. Tokyo: Shinjinbutsu Juraisha, 1984.

Hābādo daigaku shinpojiumu to Beikoku tōbu kenshū ryokōdan ハーバード大学シンポジウムと米国東部研修旅行団 , ed. *Amerika no shūkyō o tazunete* アメリカの宗教をたずねて /*Shin Buddhism Meets American Religions*. Kyoto: Nishi Honganji Naijibunai "Amerika no shūkyō o tazunete" Henshūgakari, 1986.

Hanayama Shinshō (Nobukatsu) 花山信勝 . *Nihon bukkyō* 日本仏教 [Japanese Buddhism]. Tokyo: Sanseidō, 1944.

_____. *Heiwa no hakken: Sugamo no sei to shi no kiroku* 平和の発見 ―

巣鴨の生と死の記録 [Discovery of peace: An account of life and death in Sugamo (prison)]. Tokyo: Asahi Shinbunsha, 1949.

Hattori Shisō 服部之総. *Shinran nōto* 親鸞ノート [Notes on Shinran]. 1948; repr. Tokyo: Fukumura Shuppan, 1967.

_____. *Rennyo* 蓮如. 1948; repr. Tokyo: Fukumura Shuppan, 1970.

Hirai Shōryū 平井清隆. *Rennyo to sono haha* 蓮如とその母 [Rennyo and his mother]. Kyoto: Nagata Bunshōdō, 1983.

Honganji Shiryō Kenkyūjo 本願寺史料研究所, ed. *Honganjishi* 本願寺史 [A history of the Honganji]. 3 vols. Kyoto: Jōdo Shinshū Honganjiha, 1961–69.

_____, ed. *Honganji nenpyō* 本願寺年表 [A chronology of the Honganji]. Kyoto: Jōdo Shinshū Honganjiha, 1981.

Hoshino Genpō 星野元豊, Ishida Mitsuyuki, and Ienaga Saburō, eds. *Shinran* 親鸞. Nihon Shisō Taikei, vol. 11. Tokyo: Iwanami Shoten, 1971.

Hosokawa Gyōshin 細川行信. "Shinshū chūkō no shigan: Toku ni Rennyo no Honganji saikō ni tsuite 真宗中興の志願 — とくに蓮如の本願寺再興について [The aspiration of Shinshū's restorer: Rennyo's restoration of the Honganji]." *Ōtani gakuhō* 48/3 (1969):1–11.

_____. "'Hakkotsu no ofumi' sakugenkō 「白骨ノ御文」遡源考 [A consideration of the sources for (Rennyo's) 'Letter on white bones']." In Hiramatsu Reizō Sensei Koki Kinenkai, ed., *Nihon no shūkyō to bunka*, 409–23. Kyoto: Dōbōsha, 1989.

_____ et al., eds. *Kōza: Shinran no shisō* 講座—親鸞の思想 [Lectures: Shinran's thought]. Vol. 9, *Shinran shisō no bunken kaisetsu* 親鸞思想の文献解説. Tokyo: Kyōiku Shinchōsha, 1979.

Ibuse Masuji 井伏鱒二. *Kuroi ame* 黒い雨 [Black rain]. Shinchō Bunko, no. 400. Tokyo: Shinchōsha, 1989.

Ienaga Saburō 家永三郎. *Chūsei bukkyō shisōshi kenkyū* 中世仏教思想史研究 [Studies in the intellectual history of medieval Buddhism]. 1947; repr. Kyoto: Hōzōkan, 1966.

_____. "Nihon no kindaika to bukkyō" 日本の近代化と仏教 [Japan's modernization and Buddhism]. In *Kōza: Kindai bukkyō* 2: 7–35. Kyoto: Hōzōkan, 1961.

_____, Akamatsu Toshihide, and Tamamuro Taijō 玉室諦成, eds. *Nihon bukkyōshi* 日本仏教史 [The history of Japanese Buddhism]. 3 vols. Kyoto: Hōzōkan, 1967.

Inaba Masamaru 稲葉昌丸, ed. *Rennyo Shōnin gyōjitsu* 蓮如上人行実 [A record of Master Rennyo's deeds]. 1928; repr. Kyoto: Hōzōkan, 1948.

_____, ed. *Rennyo Shōnin ibun* 蓮如上人遺文 [The letters of Master Rennyo]. 1937; repr. Kyoto: Hōzōkan, 1983.

Inaba Shūken 稲葉秀賢 . *Rennyo Shōnin no kyōgaku* 蓮如上人の教学 [Master Rennyo's teaching]. Kyoto: Bun'eidō Shoten, 1972.

Inagi Sen'e 稲城選恵 . *Gobunshō gaiyō: Rennyo kyōgaku no chūshin mondai* 御文章概要 — 蓮如教学の中心問題 [An outline of *The Letters*: Major issues in Rennyo's teaching]. Kyoto: Hyakkaen, 1983.

_____. *Fukuzawa Yukichi to Jōdo Shinshū* 福沢諭吉と浄土真宗 [Fukuzawa Yukichi and Jōdo Shinshū]. Tokyo: Kyōiku Shinchōsha, 1984.

_____. *Rennyo Shōnin no kotoba* 蓮如上人のことば [Master Rennyo's words]. Kyoto: Hōzōkan, 1987.

Inoue Toshio 井上鋭夫 . *Honganji* 本願寺 . 1962; repr. Tokyo: Shibundō, 1968.

_____. *Ikkō ikki no kenkyū* 一向一揆の研究 [Studies of the Ikkō uprisings]. Tokyo: Yoshikawa Kōbunkan, 1968.

Ishida Mitsuyuki 石田充之 . *Rennyo*. Kyoto: Jinrinsha, 1949.

_____. "Rennyo Shōnin jidai no igi shisō to sono hihan 蓮如上人時代の異義思想とその批判 [Heretical thought in Master Rennyo's times and his critique]." In *Rennyo Shōnin kenkyū*, ed. Ryūkoku Daigaku, 160–94.

Ishida Yoshihito 石田善人 . "Rennyo to sono chichi Zonnyo 蓮如とその父存如 ." In *Rennyo*, ed. Minami Midō Shinbun, 147–59. Osaka, Nanba Betsuin, 1986.

Ishikawa Kenritsu Rekishi Hakubutsukan 石川県立歴史博物館 , ed. *Ikkō ikki* [The Ikkō uprisings]. Kanazawa: Hashimoto Kenbundō, 1988.

Iwami Mamoru 岩見 護 . *Akao no Dōshū* 赤尾の道宗 [Dōshū of Akao]. 1956; repr. Kyoto: Nagata Bunshōdō, 1983.

Izumoji Osamu 出雲路修 , ed. *Ofumi* 御ふみ [The letters (of Rennyo)]. Tōyō Bunko, no. 345. Tokyo: Heibonsha, 1978.

Jōdo Shinshū Shinrankai 浄土真宗親鸞会 , ed. *Shinrankai kaku kotaeru/Honganji naze kotaenu* 親鸞会かく答える — 本願寺なぜ答えぬ [The Shinrankai answers in this way—why does the Honganji not answer?]. Takaoka: Shinrankai, 1985.

_____, ed. *Shōshin seiten* 正信聖典 [Scriptures of true faith]. Takaoka: Shinrankai, 1988.

Jōdoshū Kaishū Happyakunen Kinen Kyōsan Junbi Kyoku 浄土宗開宗八百年記念慶讃準備局 , ed. *Jōdoshū zensho* 浄土宗全書 . Vol. 3. Kyoto: Sankibō Busshorin, 1970.

Kaneko Daiei 金子大榮 , ed. *Shinshū seiten* 真宗聖典 [Shinshū scriptures]. Kyoto: Hōzōkan, 1979.

Kaneko Daiei, Ōhara Shōjitsu 大原性実 , and Hoshino Genpō, eds. *Shinshū shinjiten* 真宗新辞典 [The new Shinshū dictionary]. Kyoto: Hōzōkan, 1983.

Kasahara Kazuo 笠原一男 . *Shinran to tōgoku nōmin* 親鸞と東国農民 [Shinran and the farmers of eastern Japan]. 1957; repr. Tokyo: Yamakawa Shuppansha, 1975.

_____. *Ikkō ikki no kenkyū* 一向一揆の研究 [Studies of the Ikkō uprisings]. Tokyo: Yamakawa Shuppansha, 1962.

_____. *Shinshū ni okeru itan no keifu* 真宗における異端の系譜 [The lineage of heresy in the Shinshū]. Tokyo: Tōkyō Daigaku Shuppankai, 1962.

_____. *Rennyo*. Jinbutsu Sōsho, no. 109. 1963; repr. Tokyo: Yoshikawa Kōbunkan, 1969.

_____. *Shinran kenkyū nōto* 親鸞研究ノート [Notes on studies of Shinran]. Tokyo: Tosho Shinbunsha, 1965.

_____. *Ikkō ikki: Sono kōdō to shisō* 一向一揆 — その行動と思想 [The Ikkō uprisings: Thought and action], Nihonjin no Kōdō to Shisō, no. 5. Tokyo: Hyōronsha, 1970.

_____. *Shinran to Rennyo: Sono kōdō to shisō* 親鸞と蓮如 — その行動と思想 [Shinran and Rennyo: Their thought and activity]. Nihonjin no Kōdō to Shisō, no. 40. Tokyo: Hyōronsha, 1978.

_____. *Ransei o ikiru: Rennyo no shōgai* 乱世を生きる — 蓮如の生涯 . [Living through turbulent times: A life of Rennyo]. Tokyo: Kyōikusha, 1981.

_____. "Jibun no ashi de ayume 自分の足で歩め [(The Christian church must) stand on its own]." *Fukyō: The Japan Missionary Bulletin* 21/1 (1967): 42–44.

_____. "Ima koso Rennyo ni manabu toki 今こそ蓮如に学ぶとき [Rennyo's lessons for today]." In *Rennyo*, ed. Minami Midō Shinbun, 1–7. Ōsaka: Nanba Betsuin, 1986.

_____. "Rennyo ni manabu koto 蓮如に学ぶこと [Learning from Rennyo]." In *Rennyo to Ōsaka*, eds. Nanba Betsuin/*Asahi Shinbun* Ōsaka Honsha Kikakubu, 9–11. Osaka: *Asahi Shinbun* Ōsaka Honsha Kikakubu, 1986.

_____. "Rennyo no genkō 蓮如の言行 [Rennyo's words and deeds]." In *Rennyo ni deau*, eds. Niwa Fumio et al., 49–92. Tokyo: Ōbunsha, 1986.

Kasahara Kazuo and Inoue Toshio, eds. *Rennyo/Ikkō ikki* [Rennyo and the Ikkō uprisings]. Nihon Shisō Taikei, no. 17. Tokyo: Iwanami Shoten, 1972.

Kashiwabara Yūsen 柏原祐泉 , ed. *Shinshū seiten* 真宗聖典 [Shinshū scriptures]. 1935; repr. Kyoto: Hōzōkan, 1969.

Kashiwabara Yūsen, Chiba Jōryū, Hiramatsu Reizō 平松令三 , and Mori Ryūkichi 森 龍吉 , gen. eds. *Shinshū shiryō shūsei* 真宗史料集成 [A collection of Shinshū historical materials]. 13 vols. Kyoto: Dōbōsha, 1974–83.

Kikumura Norihiko 菊村紀彦 . *Rennyo: Ransei ni ikita oruganaizā* 蓮如— 乱世に生きたオルガナイザー [Rennyo: His life as "organizer" in turbulant times]. Tokyo: Suzuki Shuppan, 1988.

Kimura Takeo 木村武夫 . *Rennyo Shōnin no kyōgaku to rekishi* 蓮如上人 の教学と歴史 [Master Rennyo's teaching and history]. Osaka: Tōhō Shuppan, 1984.

————, ed. *Rennyo Shōnin ron: Mō hitotsu no Ōsaka sengokuki* 蓮如 上人論 — もう一つの大阪戦国記 [A view of Master Rennyo: One more account of Osaka in the Sengoku period]. Tokyo: PHP Kenkyūjo, 1983.

Kitanishi Hiromu 北西 弘 . *Ikkō ikki no kenkyū* 一向一揆の研究 [Studies of the Ikkō uprisings]. Tokyo: Shunjūsha, 1981.

————. "Dangibon kenkyū josetsu 談義本研究序説 [Introductory study of sermon handbooks]." *Bukkyō shigaku* 11/3–4 (1964): 30–48.

————. "Shinshū kyōdan ni okeru 'chishiki' to dendō: Jūroku seiki no henbōki o chūshin to shite 真宗教団における知識と伝道 — 十六世紀の 変貌期を中心として [Teachers and missionary work in the Shinshū order: A sixteenth-century transformation]." In *Nihon shūkyōshi kenkyū*, ed. Nihon Shūkyōshi Kenkyūkai. Vol. 1, *Soshiki to dendō* 139–58. Kyoto: Hōzōkan, 1967.

————. "Honganji kyōdan no seiritsu to sono tenkai: Shūkyōsei sōshitsu no ichidan'men 本願寺教団の成立とその展開 — 宗教性喪失の 一断面 [Formation of the Honganji order and its development: On the loss of its religious quality]." In *Honganji kyōdan: Shinran wa gendai ni yomigaeru ka*, ed. Uehara Senroku and Matsugi Nobuhiko, 78–110. Tokyo: Gakugei Shorin, 1971.

————. "Watakushi no kenkyū 私の研究 [My studies]." In *Rennyo: Gendai to kyōdan*, ed. Kitanishi Hiromu Hakase Kanreki Kinen Kankōkai, 23–25. Kanazawa: Hokuriku Shuppansha, 1985.

————. "Motooka Saburōke zō Rennyo shojō: Yoshizaki gobō o meguru shomondai 本岡三郎家蔵蓮如書状 — 吉崎御坊をめぐる諸問題 [Writings of Rennyo in the possession of Motooka Saburō: Issues concerning the Yoshizaki temple." *Kanō shiryō kenkyū* 4 (1989): 4–21.

_____. "Rennyo hakkyū bunsho no kenkyū: Kaō no henka o chūshin to shite 蓮如発給文書の研究 — 花押の変化を中心として [A study of Rennyo's writings: With a focus on changes in his written seal]." In *Nihon no shūkyō to bunka*, ed. Hiramatsu Reizō Sensei Koki Kinenkai, 425–44. Kyoto: Dōbōsha, 1989.

_____. "Rennyo Shōnin kenkyū no kaname 蓮如上人研究のかなめ [Main points in Rennyo studies]." *Rennyo Shōnin kenkyūkai kaishi* 1 (1989), 1–2.

_____. "Rennyo Shōnin to Honganji kyōdan 蓮如上人と本願寺教団 [Master Rennyo and the Honganji order]." *Shūkyō* 329/7 (1989): 6–11.

Kōno Hōun 河野法雲 and Kumoyama Ryūju 雲山龍珠. *Shinshū jiten* 真宗辞典 [Shinshū dictionary]. Kyoto: Hōzōkan, 1968.

Kuroda Toshio 黒田俊雄. *Nihon chūsei no kokka to shūkyō* 日本中世の国家と宗教 [Religion and state in medieval Japan]. Tokyo: Iwanami Shoten, 1975.

_____. *Ōbō to buppō: Chūseishi no kōzu* 王法と仏法 — 中世史の構図 [Imperial law and Buddha-dharma: The design of medieval history]. Kyoto: Hōzōkan, 1983.

_____. "Tenkanki no shidōsha 転換期の指導者 (1) [A leader in transitional times (1)]." In *Rennyo*, ed. Minami Midō Shinbun, 128–34. Osaka: Nanba Betsuin, 1986.

Matsugi Nobuhiko 真継伸彦. *Watakushi no Rennyo* 私の蓮如 [My Rennyo]. Tokyo: Risōsha, 1982.

Minami Midō Shinbun 南御堂新聞, ed. *Rennyo*. Osaka: Nanba Betsuin, 1986.

Miyazaki Enjun 宮崎圓遵. *Shoki Shinshū no kenkyū* 初期真宗の研究 [Studies in early Shinshū]. Kyoto: Nagata Bunshōdō, 1971.

_____. "Honzon to shite no rokuji songō 本尊としての六字尊号 [The six-character Name as the main image]." In *Nihon Jōdokyōshi no kenkyū*, ed. Fujishima Tatsurō and Miyazaki Enjun, 323–32. Kyoto: Heirakuji Shoten, 1969.

Miyazaki Enjun et al. *Nishi Honganji: Sono bijutsu to rekishi* 西本願寺 — その美術と歴史 [Nishi Honganji: Its art and history]. Kyoto: Tankō Shinsha, 1961.

Mochizuki Shinkō 望月信享, ed. *Bukkyō daijiten* 仏教大辞典 [Larger Buddhist dictionary]. 10 vols. Kyoto: Sekai Seiten Kankō Kyōkai, 1954–1963.

Momose Meiji 百瀬明治 . *Daijitsugyōka: Rennyo* 大実業家 ― 蓮如 [Rennyo as industrialist]. Tokyo: Shōdensha, 1988

Mori Ryūkichi 森 龍吉 . *Honganji*. Tokyo: San'ichi Shobō, 1973.

_____. *Rennyo*. Kōdansha Gendai Shinsho, no. 550. Tokyo: Kōdansha, 1979.

_____. "Rennyo." In *Nihon bukkyō shisō no tenkai: Hito to sono shisō* 日本仏教思想の展開 ― 人とその思想 , ed. Ienaga Saburō. Kyoto: Heirakuji Shoten, 1956.

Murakami Sokusui 村上速水 , et al., eds. *Kōza: Shinran no shisō* 講座 ― 親鸞の思想 [Lectures on Shinran's thought]. Vol. 8, *Shinran shisō no shūyaku to tenkai*. Tokyo: Kyōiku Shinchōsha, 1978.

Nabata Ōjun 名畑応順 et al., eds. *Shinranshū/Nichirenshū* 親鸞集 ― 日蓮集 [A collection of the writings of Shinran and Nichiren]. Nihon Koten Bungaku Taikei, vol. 82. Tokyo: Iwanami Shoten, 1964.

Nagata Bunshōdō Henshūbu 永田文昌堂編集部 , ed. *Myōkōninden* 妙好人伝 [Biographies of saintly people]. Kyoto: Nagata Bunshōdō, 1958.

Nakamura Hajime 中村 元 . *Bukkyōgo daijiten: Shukusatsuban* 仏教語大辞典 ― 縮刷版 [Larger dictionary of Buddhist terms: Small print edition]. Tokyo: Tōkyō Shoseki, 1987.

Nakano Kyōtoku 中濃教篤 , ed. *Senjika no bukkyō* 戦時下の仏教 [Wartime Buddhism]. *Kōza: Nihon kindai to bukkyō*, no. 6. Tokyo: Kokusho Kankōkai, 1977.

Nanba Betsuin/*Asahi Shinbun* Ōsaka Honsha Kikakubu 難波別院 ― 朝日新聞大阪本社企画部 , eds. *Rennyo to Ōsaka* 蓮如と大阪 [Rennyo and Ōsaka]. Osaka: *Asahi Shinbun* Ōsaka Honsha Kikakubu, 1986.

Nishimoto Ryūgen 西元龍挙 . *Shinshū hyakuwa* 真宗百話 [One hundred items in the Shinshū]. Tokyo: Morie Shoten, 1909.

Nishimura Shinsen 西村真詮 , ed. *Okaru dōgyō* おかる同行 [Our companion, Okaru]. Shimonoseki: Rokkōkai, 1988.

Nishio Kōichi 西尾光一 , ed. *Senjūshō* 撰集抄 [Selected stories]. Iwanami Bunko, no. 6746–6749. Tokyo: Iwanami Shoten, 1970.

Niwa Fumio 丹羽文雄 . *Shinran*. 5 vols. Tokyo: Shinchōsha, 1969.

_____. *Hotoke ni hikarete: Waga kokoro no keiseishi* 仏にひかれて ― わが心の形成史 [Drawn to the Buddha: The shaping of my heart and mind]. Tokyo: Yomiuri Shinbunsha, 1971.

_____. *Rennyo*. 8 vols. Tokyo: Chūō Kōronsha, 1983.

Niwa Fumio et al., eds. *Rennyo ni deau* 蓮如に出会う . Tokyo: Ōbunsha, 1986.

Ōe Junjō 大江淳誠 and Ōhara Shōjitsu 大原性実 , eds. *Shinshū seiten* 真宗聖典 [Shinshū scriptures]. 1956; repr. Kyoto: Nagata Bunshōdō, 1969.

Ōhara Shōjitsu. *Rennyo goroku ni kiku* 蓮如語録に聞く [Listening to Rennyo's sayings]. Tokyo: Kyōiku Shinchōsha, 1964.

Okamura Shūsatsu 岡村周薩 , ed. *Shinshū daijiten* 真宗大辞典 [Larger Shinshū dictionary]. 3 vols. 1936; repr. Kyoto: Nagata Bunshōdō, 1972.

Okumura Gen'yū 奥村玄祐 . *Anjin ketsujōshō: Jōdo e no michi* 安心決定鈔 — 浄土への道 [*Anjin ketsujōshō*: Way to the Pure Land]. Tokyo: Suzuki Gakujutsu Zaidan, 1964.

Ōtani Chōjun 大谷暢順 , ed. *Rennyo Shōnin zenshū: Genkōben* 蓮如上人全集 — 言行篇 [The collected works of Master Rennyo: His words and deeds]. Tokyo: Kawade Shobō Shinsha, 1989.

Ōtani Kōshin, "Opening Address." In Hābādo daigaku shinpojiumu to Beikoku tōbu kenshū ryokōdan, ed. *Amerika no shūkyō o tazunete/Shin Buddhism Meets American Religions*. Kyoto: Nishi Honganji Naijibunai "Amerika no shūkyō o tazunete" Henshūgakari, 1986.

Rogers, Minor L. " 'Shinjin' to 'anjin': Jōdo Shinshū shisōshi ni okeru Faith ni tsuite no ichi kōsatsu 「信心」と「安心」— 浄土真宗思想史における Faith についての一考察 [*Shinjin* and *anjin*: A consideration of 'faith' in the intellectual history of the Jōdo Shinshū]." *Shinshūgaku* 63 (1981): 26–43.

Ryūkoku Daigaku 龍谷大学 , ed. *Rennyo Shōnin kenkyū* [Studies of Master Rennyo]. Kyoto: Onki Hōyō Jimusho, 1948.

———, ed. *Shinshū yōron* 真宗要論 [Essentials of the Shinshū]. 1953; repr. Kyoto: Hyakkaen, 1978.

Ryūkoku Daigaku Shinshū Gakkai 龍谷大学真宗学会 , ed. *Shinran Shōnin chosaku yōgo sakuin: Kyōgyōshinshō no bu* 親鸞上人著作用語索引 — 教行信証の部 [A concordance for Master Shinran's works: *Kyōgyōshinshō*]. Kyoto: Ryūkoku Daigaku Shinshū Gakkai, 1977.

———, ed. *Shinran Shōnin chosaku yōgo sakuin: Wakan senjutsu no bu* 親鸞上人著作用語索引 — 和漢撰述の部 [A concordance for Master Shinran's works: Chinese and Japanese writings]. Kyoto: Ryūkoku Daigaku Shinshū Gakkai, 1978.

Ryūkoku Daigaku Shinshū Kenkyūkai, ed. *Jōdo sanbukyō sakuin* 浄土三部経索引 [A concordance for the three Pure Land Buddhist sūtras]. Kyoto: Ryūkoku Daigaku Shinshū Kenkyūkai, 1979.

_____, ed. *Senjakushū sakuin* 撰択集索引 [A concordance for *Senjakushū*]. Kyoto: Nagata Bunshōdō, 1981.

Sakurai Tokutarō 桜井徳太郎 . *Nihon minkan shinkōron* 日本民間信仰論 [A theory of popular beliefs in Japan]. Tokyo: Kōbundō, 1970.

Sakurai Yoshirō 桜井好朗 and Fukuma Kōchō. *Ikkyū/Rennyo* 一休–蓮如. Nihon Meisō Ronshū, no. 10. Tokyo: Yoshikawa Kōbunkan, 1983.

Sasaki Hōyū 佐々木芳雄 . *Rennyo Shōnin den no kenkyū* 蓮如上人伝の研究 [A study of Master Rennyo's life]. Kyoto: Dōbōsha, 1926.

Sasaki Kentoku 佐々木憲徳 . *On ichigenron: Kōdō bukkyō no shinzui* 恩一元論 — 皇道仏教の心髄 [A theory of the oneness of benevolence: The essence of imperial-way Buddhism]. Kyoto: Kōkyō Shoin, 1942.

Sasaki Motoki 佐々木求巳 . "Ofumi kaihankō 御文開版考 [On printings of *The Letters*]." *Shinshū kenkyū* 9 (Oct. 1964): 62–75.

Satake Chiō 佐竹智応 , comp. *Chūkō Rennyo Shōnin goden'e shō* 中興蓮如上人御伝絵鈔 [An illustrated biography of Master Rennyo, the restorer]. 1898; repr. Kyoto: Kōkyō Shoin, 1940.

"Senji Kyōgaku" Kenkyūkai 「戦時教学」研究会 , ed. *Senji kyōgaku to Shinshū* 戦時教学と真宗 [Wartime studies and the Shinshū]. Vol. 1. Kyoto: Nagata Bunshōdō, 1988.

Shigaraki Takamaro 信楽峻麿 . *Gendai Shinshū kyōgaku* 現代真宗教学 [Shinshū doctrine in modern times]. 1973; repr. Kyoto: Nagata Bunshōdō, 1979.

_____. *Anjin ketsujōshō kōwa* 安心決定鈔講話 [Lectures on *Anjin ketsujōshō*]. Kyoto: Yobigoesha, 1983.

_____. "Shinshū ni okeru seiten sakujo mondai 真宗における聖典削除問題 [The issue of scriptural deletions in the Shinshū]." In *Senjika no bukkyō*, ed. Nakano Kyōtoku. *Kōza: Nihon kindai to bukkyō*, no. 6, 217–48. Tokyo: Kokusho Kankōkai, 1977.

_____. "Shinshū ni okeru shinzoku nitairon no kenkyū: Sono ichi" 真宗における真俗二諦論の研究 — その一 [A study of the theory of *shinzoku nitai* in the Shinshū: Part 1]. *Ryūkoku daigaku ronshū* 418 (1981): 44–67.

_____. "Shinshū ni okeru shinzoku nitairon no kenkyū: Sono ni [A study of the theory of *shinzoku nitai* in the Shinshū: Part 2]." *Shinshūgaku* 65 (1982): 1–34.

_____, ed. *Kindai Shinshū kyōdanshi kenkyū* 近代真宗教団史研究 [Studies in the history of the Shinshū order in modern times]. Kyoto: Hōzōkan, 1987.

Shigematsu Akihisa 重松明久 . *Kakunyo* 覚如 . Jinbutsu Sōsho, no. 123. Tokyo: Yoshikawa Kōbunkan, 1966.

_____. "Rennyo no Yoshizaki shinshutsu no keii 蓮如の吉崎進出の経緯 [The circumstances of Rennyo's move to Yoshizaki]." In *Shinshūshi no kenkyū,* ed. Miyazaki Enjun Hakase Kanreki Kinenkai, 287–315. Kyoto: Nagata Bunshōdō, 1966.

_____. "Hokuriku ni okeru Rennyo no katsudō 北陸における蓮如の活動 [Rennyo's activities in the Hokuriku]." In *Chūsei Shinshū shisō no kenkyū,* 383–425. Tokyo: Yoshikawa Kōbunkan, 1986.

Shinkō no Zōkeiteki Hyōgen Kenkyū Iinkai 信仰の造形的表現研究委員会 , ed. *Shinshū jūhō shūei* 真宗重宝聚英 [A collection of major Shinshū treasures]. Vol. 9. Kyoto: Dōbōsha, 1988.

Shinshū Seiten Hensan Iinkai 真宗聖典編纂委員会 , ed. *Jōdo Shinshū seiten: Gentenban* 浄土真宗聖典 — 原典版 [Jōdo Shinshū scriptures: Standard texts]. Kyoto: Honganji Shuppanbu, 1985.

_____, ed. *Jōdo Shinshū seiten: Chūshakuban* 浄土真宗聖典 — 註釈版 [Jōdo Shinshū scriptures: Annotated edition]. Kyoto: Honganji Shuppanbu, 1988.

Shinshū Shinjiten Hensankai 真宗新辞典編纂会 , ed. *Shinshū shinjiten* 真宗新辞典 [The new Shinshū dictionary]. Kyoto: Hōzōkan, 1984.

Shinshū Shōgyō Zensho Hensanjo 真宗聖教全書編纂所 , ed. *Shinshū shōgyō zensho* 真宗聖教全書 [A complete collection of Shinshū scriptures]. 5 vols. Kyoto: Ōyagi Kōbundō, 1969–70.

Shiroyama Saburō 城山三郎 . *Rakujitsu moyu* 落日燃ゆ [Burning sunset]. Tokyo: Shinchōsha, 1986.

Sugi Shirō 杉 紫朗 . *Gobunshō kōwa* 御文章講話 [Lectures on *The Letters*]. 1933; repr. Kyoto: Nagata Bunshōdō, 1979.

Suzuki Daisetsu 鈴木大拙 . *Nihonteki reisei* 日本的霊性 [Japanese spirituality]. Tokyo: Daitō Shuppansha, 1944.

_____. *Suzuki Daisetsu zenshū* 鈴木大拙全集 [Collected works of Suzuki Daisetsu]. Edited by Hisamatsu Shin'ichi et al. Vol. 8, *Nihonteki reisei/Nihon no reiseika.* Tokyo: Iwanami Shoten, 1968.

_____, ed. *Myōkōnin Asahara Saiichi shū* 妙好人浅原才市集 [A collection (of poems) by the *myōkōnin* Asahara Saiichi]. Tokyo: Shunjūsha, 1967.

Takakusu Junjirō 高楠順次郎 and Watanabe Kaikyoku 渡邊海旭 , eds. *Taishō shinshū daizōkyō* 大正新修大蔵経 . 85 vols. Tokyo: Taishō Issaikyō Kankōkai, 1924–32.

Tamura Yoshirō 田村芳朗 . *Kamakura shinbukkyō shisō no kenkyū* 鎌倉

新仏教思想の研究 [Studies in the thought of the new Buddhism of the Kamakura period]. Kyoto: Heirakuji Shoten, 1965.

Tokushi Yūshō 禿氏祐祥. *Rennyo*. Kyoto: Hōzōkan, 1948.

Tsubouchi Susumu 坪内 晋. "Renshi no michi: Rennyo Shōnin goei gekō/jōraku no zuikōki 蓮師の道 — 蓮如上人御影下向 — 上洛の随行記 [Master Rennyo's pathway: A diary of a trip from Kyoto (to Yoshizaki) and back with Master Rennyo's image]." *Shinshū kenkyū* 26 (1982), 151–63.

Tsuji Zennosuke 辻善之助. *Nihon bukkyōshi* 日本仏教史 [A history of Japanese Buddhism]. 10 vols. Tokyo: Iwanami Shoten, 1960–61.

Tsujikawa Tatsuo 辻川達雄. *Rennyo: Yoshizaki fukyō* 蓮如 — 吉崎布教 [Rennyo's Yoshizaki mission]. Tokyo: Seibundō Shinkōsha, 1984.

_____. *Honganji to Ikkō ikki* [Honganji and the Ikkō uprisings]. Tokyo: Seibundō Shinkōsha, 1988.

Uehara Senroku and Matsugi Nobuhiko 上原専禄 — 真継伸彦, eds. *Honganji kyōdan: Shinran wa gendai ni yomigaeru ka* 本願寺教団 — 親鸞は現代によみがえるか [The Honganji order: Is Shinran to live again today?]. Tokyo: Gakugei Shorin, 1971.

Uesugi Egaku 上杉慧岳. *Anjin ketsujōshō no kenkyū* 安心決定鈔の研究 [Studies of *Anjin ketsujōshō*]. Kyoto: Hōzōkan, 1964.

Umehara Ryūshō 梅原隆章. "Jōdo Shinshū ni okeru shinkō kokuhakumon no seiritsu 浄土真宗における信仰告白文の成立 [The rise of confessional literature in the Jōdo Shinshū]." In *Shinshūshi no kenkyū*, ed. Miyazaki Enjun Hakase Kanreki Kinenkai, 83–116. Kyoto: Nagata Bunshōdō, 1966.

Umehara Shinryū 梅原真隆. *Rennyo Shōnin kikigaki shinshaku* 蓮如上人聞書新釈 [A new commentary on *(A record of) Master Rennyo's life, according to oral tradition*]. Kyoto: Nishi Honganji Shuppansha, 1982.

Uryuzu Ryūyū 瓜生津隆雄. "Anjin ketsujōshō to Shinshū kyōgaku 安心決定鈔と真宗教学 [*Anjin ketsujōshō* and Shinshū teaching]." *Indogaku bukkyōgaku kenkyū* 10/1 (1962): 198–203.

_____. "Rennyo kyōgaku no 'tasuke tamae' ni tsuite 蓮如教学の「タスケタマエ」について [On 'tasuke tamae' in Rennyo's teaching]." *Indogaku bukkyōgaku kenkyū* 11/1–2 (1963): 302–5.

_____. "Rennyo Shōnin yōgojō no mondai: 'Tasuke tamae' o chūshin to shite 蓮如上人用語上の問題 — タスケタマエを中心として [Issues involving Master Rennyo's terms, focussing on 'tasuke tamae']." In *Shinshū kenkyū* 10 (1965): 35–44.

Wakaki Yoshihiko 嬰木義彦. "Shinran Shōnin no jingikan 親鸞上人

の神祇観 [Master Shinran's view of the kami]." *Shinshū kenkyū* 17 (1972): 111–27.

Yamaori Tetsuo 山折哲雄 . *Ningen Rennyo* 人間蓮如 [Rennyo the man]. Tokyo: Shunjūsha, 1970.

_____. "Honganji kyōdan to sono chi no yodomi: Kechimyaku sōshōron 本願寺教団とその血のよどみ — 血脈相承論 [The Honganji order and its stagnation: The theory of hereditary lineage]." In *Honganji kyōdan: Shinran wa gendai ni yomigaeru ka*, ed. Uehara Senroku and Matsugi Nobuhiko, 247–65. Tokyo: Gakugei Shorin, 1971.

_____. "Chosho 'Ningen Rennyo' o megutte 著書『人間蓮如』をめぐって [On my work, *Rennyo the man*]." In *Rennyo*, ed. Minami Midō Shinbun, 67–73. Osaka: Nanba Betsuin, 1986.

_____. "Shinran shisō no taishūka ni nirosen 親鸞思想の大衆化に二路線 [Two lines in the popularization of Shinran's thought]." In *Rennyo*, ed. Minami Midō Shinbun, 74–80. Osaka: Nanba Betsuin, 1986.

_____. "Rennyo ni miru 'yuigon' to 'ketsuen' 蓮如にみる「遺言」と「血縁」 ['Last words' and 'blood kinship' as seen in Rennyo]." In *Rennyo*, ed. Minami Midō Shinbun, 81–83. Osaka: Nanba Betsuin, 1986.

SECONDARY SOURCES IN ENGLISH

Anesaki, Masaharu. *History of Japanese Religion, With Special Reference to the Social and Moral Life of the Nation*. 1930; repr. Rutland, Vt., and Tokyo: Charles E. Tuttle, 1963.

Barth, Karl. *Evangelical Theology: An Introduction*. Grand Rapids: Eerdmans, 1980.

Bellah, Robert N. *Tokugawa Religion: The Values of Pre-Industrial Japan*. Glencoe: The Free Press, 1957.

_____. "Ienaga Saburō and the Search for Meaning in Modern Japan." In *Changing Japanese Attitudes Toward Modernization*, ed. Marius B. Jansen, 369–423. Princeton: Princeton University Press, 1965.

_____. "Values and Social Change in Modern Japan." In *Beyond Belief: Essays on Religion in a Post-Traditional World*, 114–45. New York: Harper and Row, 1970.

Bloom, Alfred. *Shinran's Gospel of Pure Grace*. Tucson: University of Arizona Press, 1965.

_____. "The Life of Shinran Shōnin: The Journey to Self-Acceptance." *Numen* 15 (1968): 1–62.

Coates, Harper H. and Ryūgaku Ishizuka, trans. *Honen the Buddhist Saint: His Life and Teaching*. Kyoto: Chion-in, 1925.

Collcutt, Martin. *Five Mountains: The Rinzai Zen Monastic Institution in Medieval Japan*. Cambridge: Harvard University Press, 1981.

Davis, David L. "*Ikki* in Late Medieval Japan." In *Medieval Japan: Essays in Institutional History*, ed. John W. Hall and Jeffrey P. Mass, 221–47. New Haven and London: Yale University Press, 1974.

Dobbins, James Carter. *Jōdo Shinshū: Shin Buddhism in Medieval Japan*. Bloomington and Indianapolis: Indiana University Press, 1989.

_____. "The Concept of Heresy in the Jōdo Shinshū." *Transactions of the International Conference of Orientalists in Japan* 25 (1980): 33–46.

_____. "The Emergence of Orthodoxy: A Historical Study of Heresy in the Early Jōdo Shinshu." Ph.D. dissertation, Yale University, 1984.

_____. "From Inspiration to Institution: The Rise of Sectarian Identity in Jōdo Shinshū." *Monumenta Nipponica* 41/3 (1986): 331–43.

Doi, Takeo. *The Anatomy of Self: The Individual Versus Society*. Translated by Mark A. Harbison. Tokyo, New York, and San Francisco: Kodansha International Ltd., 1986.

Eidmann, Phillip K. "Nyoshin and the Kudensho." *The Pacific World: Journal of the Institute of Buddhist Studies* 1/1 (1982): 15–17.

Eliade, Mircea, gen. ed. *The Encyclopedia of Religion*. 16 vols. New York: Macmillan and Free Press, 1987.

Eliot, Charles. *Japanese Buddhism*. 1935; repr. New York: Barnes and Noble, 1969.

Elison, George and Bardwell L. Smith, eds. *Warlords, Artists, and Commoners: Japan in the Sixteenth Century*. Honolulu: University of Hawaii Press, 1981.

Foard, James H. "Ippen Shōnin and Popular Buddhism in Kamakura Japan." Ph.D. dissertation, Stanford University, 1977.

French, R. M., trans. *The Way of a Pilgrim and The Pilgrim Continues His Way*. 2d ed. New York: Harper and Brothers, 1952.

Fujitani, Masami. "Problems of Calendar in Translation—Year of Shinran Shonin's Demise." *The Pacific World: Journal of the Institute of Buddhist Studies* 1 (1982): 13–14.

Futaba, Kenkō. "Future Challenge for Shinshū Followers in America."

Translated by Shojo Oi. *The Pacific World: Journal of the Institute of Buddhist Studies*, n.s., 1 (1985): 7–10.

_____. "Shinran and Human Dignity: Opening An Historic Horizon." Translated by Kenryu T. Tsuji. *The Pacific World: Journal of the Institute of Buddhist Studies*, n.s., 4 (1988): 51–59.

Gómez, Luis O. "Shinran's Faith and the Sacred Name of Amida." *Monumenta Nipponica* 38 (1983): 73–84. Reply by Ueda Yoshifumi and Dennis Hirota and response by Gómez in "Correspondence," *Monumenta Nipponica* 38 (1983): 413–17, 418–27.

Graham, William A. *Beyond the Written Word: Oral Aspects of Scripture in the History of Religion.* Cambridge: Cambridge University Press, 1987.

Groner, Paul. *Saichō: The Establishment of the Japanese Tendai School.* Berkeley: Berkeley Buddhist Studies Series, 1984.

Hall, John W. and Toyoda Takeshi, eds. *Japan in the Muromachi Age.* Berkeley: University of California Press, 1977.

Hanayama, Shinshō. *The Way of Deliverance: Three Years With the Condemned Japanese War Criminals.* Translated by Hideo Suzuki et al. New York: Charles Scribner's, 1950.

Hirota, Dennis, trans. *Tannishō: A Primer.* Kyoto: Ryūkoku University, 1982.

_____, trans. *No Abode: The Record of Ippen.* Kyoto: Ryūkoku University, 1986.

_____, trans. *Plain Words on the Pure Land Way: Sayings of the Wandering Monks of Medieval Japan.* Kyoto: Ryūkoku University, 1989.

_____. "Religious Transformation in Shinran and Shōku." *The Pure Land: Journal of Pure Land Buddhism*, n.s., 4 (1987): 57–69.

Honpa Hongwanji Mission of Hawaii, comp. *The Shinshu Seiten: The Holy Scripture of Shinshu.* 1955; repr. Honolulu: Honpa Hongwanji Mission of Hawaii, 1961.

Ibuse, Masuji. *Black Rain.* Translated by John Bester. 1979; repr. Tokyo and New York: Kodansha International, 1988.

Ienaga, Saburō. "Japan's Modernization and Buddhism." *Contemporary Religions in Japan*, 6/1 (1965): 1–41.

Inagaki, Hisao. *A Dictionary of Japanese Buddhist Terms.* Kyoto: Nagata Bunshōdō, 1984.

Ishida, Hōyū. "O-karu: Poems of Deep Sorrow and Joy." In *Shinran to Jōdokyō*, ed. Shigaraki Takamaro Kyōju Kanreki Kinen Ronshū Kankōkai, 25–78. Kyoto: Nagata Bunshōdō, 1986.

Itasaka, Gen, ed. in chief. *Kodansha Encyclopedia of Japan.* 9 vols. Tokyo and New York: Kodansha, 1983.

Kasulis, Thomas P. *Zen Action/Zen Person.* Honolulu: University of Hawaii Press, 1981.

_____. Review of "Letters of Shinran: A Translation of Mattōshō." In *Philosophy: East and West* 3 (1981): 246–48.

Kawamura, Leslie S. "The Myōkōnin: Japan's Representation of the Bodhisattva." In *Myōkōninden kenkyū,* ed. Asaeda Zenshō, 40–55. Kyoto: Nagata Bunshōdō, 1987.

King, Winston L. "An Interpretation of the *Anjin Ketsujōshō.*" *Japanese Journal of Religious Studies* 13/4 (1986): 277–98.

Kishimoto Hideo, ed. *Japanese Culture in the Meiji Era: Religion.* Translated by John F. Howes. Centenary Cultural Council Series, vol. 2. Tokyo: The Toyo Bunko, 1969.

Kitagawa, Joseph M. *Religion in Japanese History.* New York: Columbia University Press, 1966.

_____. "Reality and Illusion: Some Characteristics of the Early Japanese 'World of Meaning.'" *Oriental Society of Australia Journal* 11 (1976).

_____. "*Matsuri* and *Matsuri-goto*: Religion and State in Early Japan." In *On Understanding Japanese Religion,* 117–26. Princeton: Princeton University Press, 1987.

_____. "Some Remarks on Shintō." *History of Religions* 27/3 (1988): 227–45.

LaFleur, William R. *The Karma of Words: Buddhism and the Literary Arts in Medieval Japan.* Berkeley: University of California Press, 1983.

Levering, Miriam, ed. *Rethinking Scripture: Essays from a Comparative Perspective.* Albany: State University of New York Press, 1989.

Maruyama, Masao. *Thought and Behavior in Modern Japanese Politics.* Edited by Ivan Morris. London: Oxford University Press, 1963.

McMullin, Neil. *Buddhism and the State in Sixteenth-Century Japan.* Princeton: Princeton University Press, 1984.

_____. "Historical and Historiographical Issues in the Study of Pre-Modern Japanese Religions." *Japanese Journal of Religious Studies* 16/1 (1989): 3–40.

Miner, Earl, Hiroko Odagiri, and Robert E. Morrell. *The Princeton Companion to Classical Japanese Literature.* Princeton: Princeton University Press, 1985.

Morrell, Robert E. *Sand and Pebbles (Shasekishū): The Tales of Mujū*

Ichien, A Voice for Pluralism in Kamakura Buddhism. Albany: State University of New York Press, 1985.

_____. *Early Kamakura Buddhism: A Minority Report.* Berkeley: Asian Humanities Press, 1987.

Murakami, Shigeyoshi. *Japanese Religion in the Modern Century.* Translated by H. Byron Earhart. Tokyo: University of Tokyo Press, 1980.

Muraoka, Tsunetsugu. *Studies in Shinto Thought.* Translated by Delmer M. Brown and James T. Araki. Tokyo: Ministry of Education, 1964.

Nagao, Gadjin. *The Foundational Standpoint of Mādhyamika Philosophy.* Translated by John P. Keenan. Albany: State University of New York Press, 1989.

_____. "Ascent and Descent: Two-Directional Activity in Buddhist Thought." *The Journal of the International Association of Buddhist Studies* 7/1 (1984): 176–84.

Nakamura, Kyōko Motomochi, trans. and ed., *Miraculous Stories from the Japanese Buddhist Tradition: The Nihon Ryōiki of the Monk Kyōkai.* Cambridge, Mass.: Harvard University Press, 1973.

Nishitani, Keiji. "The Problem of Time in Shinran." Translated by Dennis Hirota. *The Eastern Buddhist,* n.s., 11/1 (1978): 13–26.

O'Dea, Thomas F. "Sociological Dilemmas: Five Paradoxes of Institutionalization." In *Sociological Theory, Values and Sociocultural Change: Essays in Honor of Pitirim A. Sorokin,* ed. Edmund A. Tiryakian, 71–89. New York: Harper and Row, 1967.

Ōtani, Kōshō. "In Memory of D. T. Suzuki." *The Eastern Buddhist,* n.s., 2/1 (1967): 160–65.

Reischauer, A. K. "A Catechism of the Shin Sect (Buddhism)." *Transactions of the Asiatic Society of Japan* 38/5 (1912): 331–95.

Rhodes, Robert F., trans. and intro. "Saichō's *Mappō Tōmyōki*: The Candle of the Latter Dharma." *The Eastern Buddhist,* n.s., 13/1 (1980): 79–103.

Rogers, Ann T. and Minor L. Rogers, trans. "Letters of Rennyo: (*Ofumi,* Fascicle One)." *The Pure Land: Journal of Pure Land Buddhism,* n.s., 5 (1988): 74–112.

_____, trans. and intro. "Rennyo's Letters (*Rennyo Shōnin Ofumi*): Fascicle Five." *The Eastern Buddhist,* n.s., 21/2 (1988): 95–123.

Rogers, Minor L. "Rennyo Shōnin 1415–1499: A Transformation in Shin Buddhist Piety." Ph.D. dissertation, Harvard University, 1972.

_____. "Rennyo and Jōdo Shinshū Piety: The Yoshizaki Years." *Monumenta Nipponica* 36 (1981): 21–35.

_____. "The Shin Faith of Rennyo." *The Eastern Buddhist*, n.s., 15/1 (1982): 56–73.

_____. "A View of Rennyo's Early and Middle Years." In *Jōdokyō no kenkyū: Ishida Mitsuyuki hakase koki kinen ronbun*, ed. Ishida Mitsuyuki Hakase Koki Kinen Ronbunshū Kankōkai, 101–24. Kyoto: Nagata Bunshōdō, 1982.

_____. "Textual Translation and Contextual Renewal: Reflections on the Shin Buddhism and Christianity Symposium." *Bulletin*, Center for the Study of World Religions, Harvard University (1984): 2–23.

_____. "Shin Buddhist Piety as Gratitude." In *Spoken and Unspoken Thanks: Some Comparative Soundings*, ed. John B. Carman and Frederick J. Streng, 93–111. Cambridge: Center for the Study of World Religions, Harvard University, 1989.

Ryūkoku Translation Center, trans. *The Shōshin Ge: The Gāthā of True Faith in the Nembutsu*. 4th ed. Ryūkoku Translation Series, vol. 1. Kyoto: Ryūkoku University, 1966.

_____, trans. *The Tanni Shō: Notes Lamenting Differences*. 4th ed. Ryūkoku Translation Series, vol. 2. Kyoto: Ryūkoku University, 1980.

_____, trans. *The Jōdo Wasan: The Hymns on the Pure Land*. Ryūkoku Translation Series, vol. 4. Kyoto: Ryūkoku University, 1965.

_____, trans. *The Kyō Gyō Shin Shō (Ken Jōdo Shinjitsu Kyōgyōshō Monrui): The Teaching, Practice, Faith, and Enlightenment* (abridged). Ryūkoku Translation Series, vol. 5. Kyoto: Ryūkoku University, 1966.

_____, trans. *The Kōsō Wasan: The Hymns on the Patriarchs*. Ryūkoku Translation Series, vol. 6. Kyoto: Ryūkoku University, 1974.

_____, trans. *Shōzōmatsu Wasan: Shinran's Hymns on the Last Age*. Ryūkoku Translation Series, vol. 7. Kyoto: Ryūkoku University, 1980.

_____, trans. *The Sūtra of Contemplation on the Buddha of Immeasurable Life as Expounded by Śākyamuni Buddha*. Kyoto: Ryūkoku University, 1984.

Sasaki, Shōten. "Shinshū and Folk Religion: Toward a Post-Modern Shinshū Theology." Translated by Jan Van Bragt. *Bulletin of the Nanzan Institute for Religion and Culture* 12 (1988): 13–35.

Satō, Taira. "The Awakening of Faith in the Myokonin Asahara

Saichi." Translated by Thomas L. Kirchner. *The Eastern Buddhist*, n.s., 18/1 (1985): 71–89.

Shiroyama, Saburō. *War Criminal: The Life and Death of Hirota Koki.* Translated by John Bester. Tokyo, New York and San Francisco: Kodansha International, 1977.

Smith, Wilfred Cantwell. *The Meaning and End of Religion.* New York: Macmillan, 1962.

_____. *The Faith of Other Men.* New York: Harper and Row, 1972.

_____. *Towards a World Theology: Faith and the Comparative History of Religion.* Philadelphia: Westminster Press, 1981.

_____. "Introduction to Part Eight: Religion as Symbolism." In *Encyclopaedia Britannica*, 15th ed., "Introduction to Propaedia," 1: 498–500. Chicago: Encyclopaedia Britannica, 1974.

Solomon, Ira Michael. "Rennyo and the Rise of Honganji in Muromachi Japan." Ph.D. dissertation, Columbia University, 1972.

_____. "Kinship and the Transmission of Religious Charisma: The Case of Honganji." *The Journal of Asian Studies* 33 (1974): 403–13.

_____. "Honganji under Rennyo: The Development of Shinshū in Medieval Japan." Unpublished paper presented at the annual meeting of the American Academy of Religion, St. Louis, October, 1976.

_____. "The Dilemma of Religious Power: Honganji and Hosokawa Masamoto." *Monumenta Nipponica* 33 (1978): 51–65.

Spae, Joseph J. "Twelve Scholars Comment on Christianity." *Fukyō: The Japan Missionary Bulletin* 22/2 (1968): 130–45.

Sugihira, Shizutoshi. "Rennyo Shōnin, the Great Teacher of Shin Buddhism." *The Eastern Buddhist* 8/1 (1949): 5–35.

Suzuki, Daisetz T. *Mysticism: Christian and Buddhist.* World Perspectives, vol. 12. New York: Harper and Brothers, 1957; repr. Westport, Conn.: Greenwood Press, 1975.

_____. *Japanese Spirituality.* Compiled by Japanese National Commission for Unesco. Translated by Norman Waddell. Tokyo: Japan Society for the Promotion of Science, 1972.

_____. *Collected Writings on Shin Buddhism.* Kyoto: Shinshū Ōtaniha, 1973.

_____, trans. *The Kyōgyōshinshō: The Collection of Passages Expounding the True Teaching, Living, Faith, and Realizing of the Pure Land*, ed. The Eastern Buddhist Society. Kyoto: Shinshū Ōtaniha, 1973.

Swanson, Paul L. *Foundations of T'ien-T'ai Philosophy: The Flowering of the Two Truths Theory in Chinese Buddhism.* Berkeley: Asian Humanities Press, 1989.

Takahatake, Takamichi. *Young Man Shinran: A Reappraisal of Shinran's Life.* SR Supplements, vol. 18. Waterloo, Ontario: Wilfrid Laurier University Press, 1987.

Takeda, Kiyoko. *The Dual-Image of the Japanese Emperor.* New York: Macmillan, 1988.

_____. "Emperor Hirohito and the Turbulent Shōwa Era." *The Japan Foundation Newsletter* 16/5–6 (1989): 1–5, 8.

Takeda, Ryūsei. "Shinran's View of Faith: A Translation Issue of 'Shinjin' and 'Faith'." In *Ryūkoku daigaku sanbyaku gojūshūnen: Kinen ronbunshū,* ed. Ryūkoku Gakkai, 2–30. Kyoto: Nagata Bunshōdō, 1989.

Tanaka, Eizo, trans. "Anjin Ketsujo Sho: On the Attainment of True Faith." *The Pure Land: Journal of European Shin Buddhism* 2/2 (1980): 26–33, 3/1 (1981): 21–25, 3/2 (1981): 24–27, 4/1 (1982): 17–21, 4/2 (1982): 34–36, 5/1 (1983): 35–39, 5/2 (1983): 40–44.

Thelle, Notto R. *Buddhism and Christianity in Japan: From Conflict to Dialogue, 1854–1899.* Honolulu: University of Hawaii Press, 1987.

Tri-State Buddhist Temples, comp. *Shinshū Seiten: Jōdo Shin Buddhist Teaching.* San Francisco: Buddhist Churches of America, 1978.

Troup, James. "The Gobunsho, or Ofumi, of Rennyo Shōnin." *Transactions of the Asiatic Society of Japan* 17 (1889): 101–43.

Tsuji, Kenryu Takashi. "Hoto Keisho Shiki — Transmission of the Light of Dharma." *Wheel of Dharma* 4/5 (1977): 1.

_____. "Brief Introduction to Jodo Shinshu." Pamphlet. San Francisco: Buddhist Churches of America, n.d.

Ueda, Yoshifumi. "Response to Thomas P. Kasulis' review of *Letters of Shinran.*" In *Philosophy: East and West* 31 (1981): 507–11.

_____. "The Mahayana Structure of Shinran's Thought." Translated by Dennis Hirota. *The Eastern Buddhist,* n.s., 17/1 (1984): 57–78, and 17/2 (1984): 30–54.

_____. "How is *Shinjin* to be Realized?" Translated by Dennis Hirota. *The Pacific World: Journal of the Institute of Buddhist Studies,* n.s., 1 (1985): 17–24.

_____. "Reflections on the Study of Buddhism." Translated by Dennis Hirota. *The Eastern Buddhist,* n.s., 18/2 (1985): 114–30.

_____. "Freedom and Necessity in Shinran's Concept of Karma."

Translated by Dennis Hirota. *The Eastern Buddhist*, n.s., 19/1 (1986): 76–100.

———. "On the Emergence of Mahāyāna Buddhism." Translated by Dennis Hirota. *The Pacific World: Journal of the Institute of Buddhist Studies*, n.s., 2 (1986): 3–10.

———, ed. *Letters of Shinran: A Translation of Mattōshō*. Shin Buddhism Translation Series. Kyoto: Hongwanji International Center, 1978.

———, gen. ed. *Notes on 'Essentials of Faith Alone': A Translation of Shinran's Yuishinshō-mon'i*. Shin Buddhism Translation Series. Kyoto: Hongwanji International Center, 1979.

———, gen. ed. *Notes on Once-calling and Many-calling: A Translation of Shinran's Ichinen-tanen mon'i*. Shin Buddhism Translation Series. Kyoto: Hongwanji International Center, 1980.

———, gen. ed. *Notes on the Inscriptions on Sacred Scrolls: A Translation of Shinran's Songō shinzō meimon*. Shin Buddhism Translation Series. Kyoto: Hongwanji International Center, 1981.

———, gen. ed. *Passages on the Pure Land Way: A Translation of Shinran's Jōdo monrui jushō*. Shin Buddhism Translation Series. Kyoto: Hongwanji International Center, 1982.

———, gen. ed. *The True Teaching, Practice and Realization of the Pure Land Way: A Translation of Shinran's Kyōgyōshinshō*. 4 vols. Shin Buddhism Translation Series. Kyoto: Hongwanji International Center, 1983–90.

Ueda, Yoshifumi and Dennis Hirota, *Shinran: An Introduction to His Thought*. Kyoto: Hongwanji International Center, 1989.

Unno, Taitetsu. "The Nature of Religious Experience in Shin Buddhism." In *The Other Side of God*, ed. Peter L. Berger, 252–71. New York: Anchor Press, 1981.

Varley, H. Paul. *The Ōnin War*. New York: Columbia University Press, 1977.

Weinstein, Stanley. "Rennyo and the Shinshū Revival." In *Japan in the Muromachi Age*, eds. John Whitney Hall and Toyoda Takeshi, 331–58. Berkeley: University of California Press, 1977.

Yamamoto, Kosho. *An Introduction to Shin Buddhism*. Ube: Karinbunko, 1963.

———, trans. "The Gobunsho." In *The Shinshu Seiten: The Holy Scripture of Shinshu*, 287–98. Honolulu: The Honpa Hongwanji Mission of Hawaii, 1955.

———, trans. *The Words of St. Rennyo*. Tokyo: Karinbunko, 1968.

Yanagi, Soetsu. "Genza, the Myokonin" (3). Translated by Dennis

Hirota. *The Pure Land: Journal of European Pure Land Buddhism* 5/1 (1983): 12–24.

Yokogawa, Kensho. "Shin Buddhism as the Religion of Hearing." *The Eastern Buddhist* 7 (1939): 336–39.

Index